Introduction to the Foundations of American Education

Tenth Edition

James A. Johnson

NORTHERN ILLINOIS UNIVERSITY

Victor L. Dupuis

PENNSYLVANIA STATE UNIVERSITY

Diann Musial

NORTHERN ILLINOIS UNIVERSITY

Gene E. Hall

UNIVERSITY of NORTHERN COLORADO

Donna M. Gollnick

NATIONAL COUNCIL for ACCREDITATION of TEACHER EDUCATION

Introduction to the Foundations of American Education

Allyn and Bacon

BOSTON   LONDON   TORONTO   SYDNEY   TOKYO   SINGAPORE

Editor-in-Chief, Education: Nancy Forsyth
Senior Editor: Virginia Lanigan
Series Editorial Assistant: Nihad Farooq
Developmental Editor: Alicia Reilly
Marketing Manager: Kathleen Hunter
Production Administrator: Susan McIntyre
Editorial-Production Service: Kathy Smith
Text Designer: Deborah Schneck
Photo Researcher: Susan Duane
Cover Administrator: Linda Knowles
Composition Buyer: Linda Cox
Manufacturing Buyer: Megan Cochran

Copyright © 1996, 1994, 1991, 1988, 1985, 1982, 1979, 1976, 1973, 1969
by Allyn and Bacon
A Simon & Schuster Company
Needham Heights, Mass. 02194

Library of Congress Cataloging-in-Publication Data
Introduction to the foundations of American education / James A.
   Johnson . . . [et al.]. -- 10th ed.
      p.   cm.
   Includes bibliographical references and indexes.
   ISBN 0-205-16141-3
   1. Education--United States.   2. Educational sociology--United
States.   I. Johnson, James Allen.
LB17.I59   1996
370'.973--dc20   95-24082
                                                          CIP

Printed in the United States of America
10 9 8 7 6 5 4 3 2 1   00 99 98 97 96 95

Cover and chapter opener art:
James B. Thompson, Ch. 1, "The TA Series: TA 1," 1985; Ch. 2, "The TA Series: TA VII," 1984-1985; Ch. 3, "The TA Series: TA 2," 1985; Ch. 4, "The Marriage Series: Live and Learn," 1986; Ch. 5, "The Marriage Series: The Cover Up," 1985-1986; Ch. 6, "The Marriage Series: Having Fun," 1985-1986; Ch. 7, "The Marriage Series: Hidden Secrets," 1985-1986; Ch. 8, "Razor's Edge," 1991; Ch. 9, "The TA Series: TA IX," 1984-1985; Ch. 10, "The TA Series: TA III," 1984-1985; Ch. 11, "The TA Series: TA VI," 1984-1985; Ch. 12, "The TA Series: TA V," 1984-1985; Ch. 13, "The Marriage Series: The Breakthrough," 1985-1986; Ch. 14, "The TA Series: TA 8," 1985; Ch. 15, "The TA Series: TA X," 1985; Ch. 16, "The TA Series: TA IV," 1984-1985; Ch. 17, "The Marriage Series: All That Love," 1985-1986; Ch. 18, "The Marriage Series: Communique," 1985-1986; Ch. 19, "The Marriage Series: Friend or Foe," 1985-1986.

Photo Credits
Joe McNally/Sygma: p. 5; Jim Pickerell: p. 6; Dom Dughi/UPI/Bettmann: p. 57; Courtesy of Carolyn Salisbury/NEA: p. 59; Stacy Rosenstock/Impact Visuals: p. 66; Bob Daemmrich: p. 67; Courtesy of Education International: p. 70; J.B. Diederich /Woodfin Camp & Associates: p. 114; Mike Maple/Woodfin Camp & Associates: p. 133; Sylvia Johnson/Woodfin Camp & Associates: p. 143; Mike Yamashita/Woodfin

Credits continue on page 544, which should be considered an extension of the copyright page.

Contents

Chapter 2

Employment Opportunities for Teachers   29

Part 2 **School and Society**   **76**

Chapter 4 **School and Society**   **79**

Chapter 7

Social Issues Affecting the School   153

Part 3 Governance and Support of American Education   182

Chapter 8 Structure and Finance of American Education   185

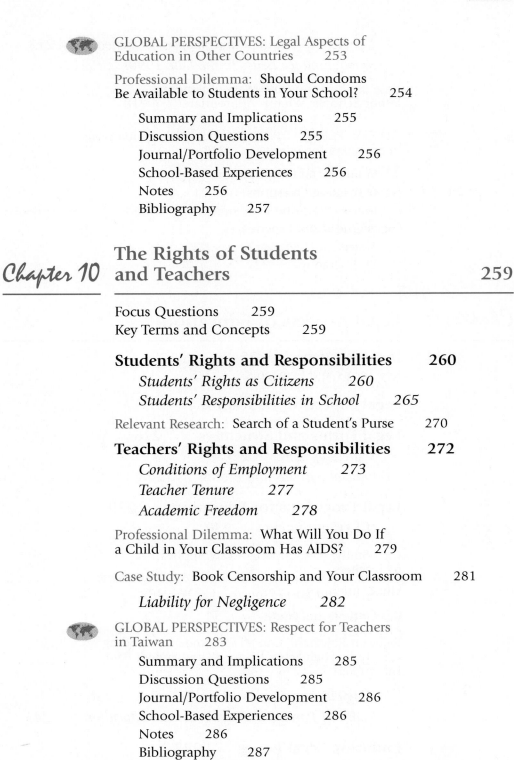

Part 4 **Historical Foundations of Education**   **290**

Chapter 12 **Early American Education   313**

Part 5 Philosophical Concepts, Educational Views, and Teaching Styles   366

Part 6   **School Programs
and Practices**   **428**

Chapter 17   **School Programs**   **431**

Chapter 18 **School Practices**   **455**

Preface

Writing the tenth edition of this text has prompted us to reflect on all that has gone on in education since the first edition was published. Thirty years ago, teacher education was in a mass production mold, as teacher educators struggled to train teachers fast enough to meet the demands of a rapidly growing school population that was the result of the World War II baby boom. The student body of our schools was mainly white, middle class, and still full of the 1950s mentality of "have fun, be conventional, and prepare for the good life" during the last part of the twentieth century. Educators were largely unaware of the criticisms and pressures they would face or the changes schools would undergo during the next thirty years.

Changes included a rapid decrease in enrollment, international struggles that were to tax the very heart and soul of the United States democracy, a technological explosion that was to challenge the brightest minds associated with teaching and learning, and—most significantly—a rapidly changing demographic make-up of the United States population. The Vietnam era did away with the protective environment of the 1950s, as young people of all races in the United States took to the streets to protest war, call their educational programs into question, and ask for more meaningful school preparation for life in the twenty-first century.

Demographic changes in the United States have brought about perhaps the single most significant change to education in the last thirty years and will continue to affect education as we enter the next century. While the nonwhite school population is increasing exponentially, few teachers-in-training are part of that minority population growth. Thus, the pertinent challenge to teacher education over the next decade or so is twofold. First, how do we get more minority young people to enter the education profession? Second, how can we help nonminority teachers educate a growing minority population? The text has changed considerably over ten editions. It has remained responsive to societal changes, yet true to its mission to uphold the profession of teaching. We have also continued to recognize the importance of the learner, and the role the teacher must play in meeting the needs of students and of society.

The Contents of This Book

We have attempted to cover those areas that every teacher must know in order to be an informed, thoughtful educator: the history of education, its philosophical underpinnings; the role of education in contemporary society; the legal and financial issues that affect teachers, students, and schools; and the future of education as we look forward to the next century.

Learning Aids in This Text

We have provided several features in this text designed to enhance your understanding and provoke your interest.

The Dreamcatchers. Each major section of the text profiles master teachers from around the country who offer inspiration and advice as it relates to the dreamcatcher legend. In accordance with this Ojibwa tradition, the dreamcatcher was hung over the cradles of infants or inside the lodges of Native American people. The dreamcatcher allowed good dreams through its spiderweb-like mesh center to become part of the lives of the Ojibwa. Bad dreams were caught and perished in the web with the first light of morning.

Focus Questions. Each chapter begins with a short set of questions intended to help you find the main concepts in the chapter and orient yourself to a critical reading of the material.

Key Terms and Concepts. There is a professional language in education. At the beginning of each chapter we have identified and defined important words that will be introduced in the chapter. These terms are also boldfaced and defined in the text.

Several of our features are **new** to this edition.

Professional Dilemmas. One of the challenges of education is that there are many questions and debates for which there are no clear-cut answers. In each chapter we select one of these for your consideration. Don't expect to find the perfect answer. Instead, be prepared to understand the consequences and implications of your response to the issue, and the impact they may have on students in your classroom.

Relevant Research. Each chapter profiles an interesting example of contemporary research in education with specific relevance to chapter material.

Case Studies. Each chapter presents one or more case studies involving students and teachers in real situations, demonstrating the complexity of life within America's classrooms.

Global Perspectives. Each chapter contains one or more sections that specifically address international viewpoints related to chapter content. In addition to recognizing diversity within our own domestic borders, educators are now much more willing to look to other societies and how they approach the challenges of education.

Journal/Portfolio Development. Journals and portfolios have become valuable tools for both teachers in their own career management and for students as benchmarks of their learning accomplishments. These exercises at the end of each chapter will help you learn to use these tools to their best advantage for both yourself and your students.

School-Based Experiences. At the end of each chapter, these field activities are designed to reinforce the connection between material covered in the chapter and its classroom applications.

Sharing Ideas

We hope that as a team of authors we have been successful in pooling our ideas and presenting them to you in a useful and thought-provoking way. If you have any suggestions for us, or questions about what we have written, please send in the reader response sheet at the back of the book.

As one of the first generation of teachers for American schools in the twenty-first century, you have a special responsibility and opportunity. You and the children that you teach will be setting the direction for the future. And, as with those who have gone before you, you will be building on the work of many other educators. It is their knowledge that we pass on to you here. Best of luck in your quest to become an outstanding teacher.

Acknowledgments

We are grateful to the many people who have helped make this textbook the bestseller that it is. We thank Allyn and Bacon for supporting us as authors over the years and allowing us to deliver the message as we wished. We are also grateful to the many people who have used previous editions and who provided suggestions and materials for this edition. In particular, we are grateful to the following persons:

Morris L. Anderson, *Wayne State College*
Alan Dean, *University of Rio Grande*
Dorothy Engan-Barker, *Mankato State University*
Geneva Gay, *University of Washington*
Tyll van Geel, *University of Rochester*
John Georgeoff, *Purdue University*
Michael James, *Connecticut College*
Jane A. Newburger, *Cazenovia College*
Rosalyn Ruffner, *Kentucky Christian College*
Paul Wagner, *University of Houston—Clear Lake*
John R. Zelazek, *Central Missouri State University*

Introduction to the Foundations of American Education

Part 1

Professional Aspects of Teaching

Dreamcatcher

ANGELA is completing her student teaching and will soon graduate from her teacher education program. According to her supervisors, she has been an outstanding student teacher. And like the Native American dreamcatcher that separates good dreams from bad ones, Angela has the ability to separate good educational ideas from bad ones. We believe she has earned the title of "Dreamcatcher Student Teacher," and we have asked her to share her thoughts on student teaching with you.

When I first entered what was to become my classroom for the next five months, I saw twenty-seven eager faces staring up at me. The children were all from different backgrounds, and each one had unique ideas and goals. At that moment, dozens of questions rushed through my mind. How will I reach each child? How will I know if they understand? What will I do if a student does not comprehend? At that point, I realized my students would become my number one priority, and sleep would be my last.

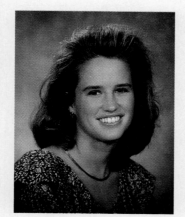

As a student teacher, you are faced with three different constituents: cooperating teacher, students, and university supervisor. Engage everyone with an open mind, get involved, and be willing to try everything. Be flexible, honest, and patient, and most of all be a good listener.

Fortunately, my cooperating teacher was an experienced and knowledgeable professional with attitudes similar to mine. Both of us enjoy change and believe in doing whatever is necessary to benefit the students. She was straightforward and honest about my performance from day one.

With respect to your students, never underestimate a child's potential. Get to know each student individually. Learn how to be fair to every child. Consequences and rewards must count for everyone. If you let one child slide, all the children will think it is okay to slack off. Always acknowledge good performance, for this will help each child to succeed. Your attitude and feelings play a big part in the overall class atmosphere. Great things will happen because you believe they will happen! A positive and enthusiastic personality will go far in creating a good learning environment.

The university supervisor can be a source of encouragement and information. Keep close ties with your supervisor, and try to converse once a week about progress and problems within the classroom.

Teaching is not a 9–3 job. You will find yourself always thinking of new ways to teach even the most basic concepts, not to mention grading papers, preparing lessons, gathering materials, and maintaining an open line of communication with parents.

Student teaching seemed overwhelming at first. There was so much to do that I often wondered how I would get it all accomplished. My advice is to stay focused, be organized, and accept the support of family and friends. A personal computer can be a big help in preparing the necessary classroom materials.

You will know you have succeeded if after five months you can honestly say you are able to accept failure. Learn from it and move on. Not every approach will succeed and not every lesson will make sense, but you will know all the time and energy has been well spent when you hear a student exclaim, "I *can* do this!"

While I will never forget Mrs. Greive and her third-grade class for giving me the opportunity to grow and learn, it was only the beginning!

Angela M. Raiff

Teachers and Teaching as a Career

Focus Questions

1 What makes teachers so important in a democratic society?
2 What are the characteristics of the best teachers you ever had?
3 Why do you want to be a teacher?
4 What can you do to effectively document what you see in schools and classrooms?
5 If you were asked to prepare a portfolio about your potential to be an outstanding teacher, what would you include?

Key Terms and Concepts

Classroom analysis systems: Clearly defined sets of procedures and written materials that can be used to analyze the interaction between teachers and students.

Educated citizenry: A goal according to which all members of our society are capable of participating intelligently in its direction and development.

Hypothesis: A proposed relationship between two or more events or qualities.

Information age: A dynamic view of society that emphasizes the problems of dealing with vast amounts of changing information.

Portfolio: A compilation for a specific purpose of the works, records, and accomplishments that a student prepares about his/her learnings, performances, and contributions.

Public confidence: The underlying trust that people have in their institutions.

Structured observations: Those judgments or impressions that are conducted according to a predetermined plan.

Teacher self-concept: How teachers view their participation in the profession of education.

Teacher stress: A condition that results from the many forces and pressures experienced through work as an educator.

Welcome to teacher education and the world of teaching. As you can see from the number of chapters and topics covered in this text, there is much to learn about becoming a teacher. In this first chapter you will begin the exploration of what you need to know to become an outstanding teacher; we will discuss the social condition of schools, list some of the positive and negative aspects of teaching, and provide a number of specific suggestions for tasks and activities that you can do to further clarify your aspirations and plans.

Teachers in America

Teachers play an extremely important role in our society. In this chapter, we will briefly explore why this is so, and we will also look at a variety of other interesting information about how the public views teachers, what teachers actually do, and how teachers view their profession.

The Importance of Teachers in Our Society

Teaching is one of the most important careers in any democratic society. In fact, a democracy is totally dependent on an **educated citizenry** that is well informed about the many political issues that must be resolved by the society. Furthermore, people in a democracy must feel that voting and participating in other ways in the democratic process are important—an attitude that must somehow be learned. Our nation looks to our teachers to provide the education essential to sustaining our democratic society.

To Our Children. It has often been said that our nation's most important natural resource is our children. Parents, legislators, and our society in general feel

Teachers play a crucial role in the lives of individuals and in the world at large.

that education is essential for our nation's children. Children must learn the basics, but they also must be cultured, nurtured, and inspired. Each child must be allowed to learn at her or his own pace, but all must be challenged—and accomplishing both tasks is extremely difficult because no two children are alike. In fact, our children—coming from multicultural backgrounds—are wonderfully diverse.

In the Information Age. Each year our society becomes more complex. In fact, we now live in what is often called an **information age**, in which knowledge has been expanded so much that managing the huge amount of available information is one of our largest problems. This rapid expansion of knowledge has required that citizens become information managers. Whom does our society expect to provide the education needed by our youth to help them function well in this capacity? If your answer is teachers, you are absolutely correct.

To Our Nation's Economy. Teachers play an extremely important role in our national economy in at least two major ways. It is well established that better educated people earn more money during their lifetimes. Teachers also contribute to the economy by providing the educated workers for our nation's businesses. Needless to say, the U.S. industrial complex simply could not function without a constant supply of workers who possess good basic skills. Interestingly, some states have recently increased their financial support of schools as catalysts for the development of high-tech industry.

In a Global Society. No longer can the role of teachers and schools be thought of only in terms of the national interest. Developing global awareness is crucial to our economic and political well-being. Teachers must understand and help their students learn about the complexities of the international system. Development of knowledge about world cultures, international events, and appreciation of the

American students today must be prepared to compete and coexist with students from all other societies in the world.

PROFESSIONAL DILEMMA

Should There Be a National Index to Rate Schools?

Should you be able to turn to your local newspaper, weekly news magazine or CNN and find a ranking of schools? We rank baseball teams and tennis players, and *U.S. News and World Report* annually offers rankings of colleges, hospitals, and mutual funds. We have the Dow Jones Index for stocks, and the odds makers in Las Vegas rank the chances of horses, football teams, and politicians being victorious. Should there also be an index for rating schools? The "Johnson-Hall" Index for schools has the high school you graduated from rated at a score of 235. The school where you will be student teaching has an index of 157.

Would having an index help you decide on the school where you want to teach? As a parent, would having an index help you choose the school where you will send your children? We don't have such a system for schools as of now, but what if we did? What kinds of factors should be built into such an index? The Dow Jones Index for the stock market is a sampling of traditional industrial stocks. There are other stock indices that look at growth stocks, computer stocks, and international markets. What would be the items you would use to construct a state or national Quality School Index?

James Gutherie[1] (1993) has proposed that a "national education index" be created. This would be a report card of how well public education is doing. Gutherie suggested the following set of composite indicators that would make up this national education index:

> *Student Performance* is the obvious place to start. The aspects chosen for inclusion in the composite indicator of student performance would require some deliberation. Would it be grades

diversities and commonalities of human values and interests are important content for the classrooms of today and essential aspects of the classrooms of the future. Developing a global perspective will mean major changes in how curriculum and courses are organized; there will be increasing emphasis on comparative and multinational perspectives, rather than on primarily American ones. The students of today will be employed in a global economy, and of necessity, they will need to have a wider knowledge base and global perspective.

How the Public Views Our Schools

Perhaps the most famous educational survey in the United States is that conducted each year by the Gallup Poll to determine the public's attitude toward our public school system. The twenty-sixth such poll has revealed a number of facts that should be of interest to people planning a teaching career.

One question that is always of interest to educators is: "Students are often given the grade A, B, C, D, and Fail to denote the quality of their work. Suppose the public schools in this community were graded in the same way? What grade would you give the public schools here—A, B, C, D, or Fail?" Table 1.1 shows the responses to this question over the past decade. The good news is that in recent years, the public has given our public schools pretty good grades. The bad news is that many Americans do not feel our public schools are doing a good job.

Another interesting question relates to what the public perceives to be the biggest problems faced by their local public schools. Table 1.2 on page 8 shows

Today's educators rely on the cooperation and support of parents.

only, or would it include a national exam? What subjects would be included? And what about using the results of individual versus group work?

Public support for education is important too. Logically, there is a link between students' doing better and the amount of community support for the schools. How would this composite indicator be measured? Would you use public opinion polls, the amount of expenditure on schools, and/or the amount of voter turnout for school board elections?

The living conditions of children are strongly related to how well they will do in school. To what extent are children seen as a resource and a critical part of the nation's long-term success? Extent of poverty, crime, family stability, attitudes, and confidence all could be included in this composite indicator.

Quality of educational service is another obvious indicator. Measurement could be made of the quality and adequacy of school buildings; the extent of professional preparation of school personnel; the kinds of science laboratories; the condition of the library; and the availability of early childhood, after-school, and extracurricular programs.

- What would be some of the advantages to having such a national index? What would be some of the disadvantages?
- What factors would you want to see included in such an index? What factors should not be included?
- Who should pay for this national index of schools? Taxpayers, the media, parents, teachers, state legislatures, or someone else?
- What difference would it make if there were a national index? More specifically, what difference would it make to you?

the responses to this question. As you can see, fighting/violence/gangs and lack of discipline are viewed as the biggest problems. These are followed by lack of proper financial support, and drug abuse and standards/quality of education. These problems are discussed in greater detail elsewhere in the book. For now, this table serves as a summary of what the public perceives to be the biggest public school problems at this time.

TABLE 1.1 **Ratings Given the Local Public Schools**

	1994	1993	1992	1991	1990	1989	1988	1987	1986	1985	1984	1983
A&B	44%	47%	40%	42%	41%	43%	40%	43%	41%	43%	42%	31%
A	9	10	9	10	8	8	9	12	11	9	10	6
B	35	37	31	32	33	35	31	31	30	34	32	25
C	30	31	33	33	34	33	34	30	28	30	35	32
D	14	11	12	10	12	11	10	9	11	10	11	13
FAIL	7	4	5	5	5	4	4	4	5	4	4	7
Don't Know	5	7	10	10	8	9	12	14	15	13	8	17

Source: Stanley M. Elan, Lowell C. Rose, and Alec M. Gallup, "The 26th Annual Gallup Poll of the Public's Attitude Toward the Public Schools." *Phi Delta Kappan,* September 1994, p. 45.

TABLE 1.2   **What do you think are the biggest problems with which the public schools of this community must deal?**

Problems	National Totals	No Children in School	Public School Parents	Nonpublic School Parents
Fighting/violence/gangs	18%	19%	16%	17%
Lack of discipline	18	18	17	22
Lack of proper financial support	13	12	16	9
Drug abuse	11	11	13	7
Standards/quality of education	8	8	5	11
Overcrowded schools	7	5	11	10
Lack of family structure/ problems of home life*	5	5	3	4
Crime/vandalism	4	5	4	3
Pupils' lack of interest/ truancy/poor attitudes	3	3	3	5
Parents' lack of support/ interest	3	4	2	3
Difficulty in getting good teachers	3	4	2	2
Poor curriculum/low curriculum standards	3	2	3	2
Lack of respect	3	2	3	1
Integration/segregation, racial discrimination	3	3	2	2
There are no problems	1	1	2	2
Miscellaneous**	9	9	8	13
Don't know	11	12	9	11

*New category
**A total of 33 different kinds of problems were mentioned by 2% or fewer respondents.
(Figures add to more than 100 percent because of multiple answers.)
Source: Stanley M. Elan, Lowell C. Rose, and Alec M. Gallup, "The 26th Annual Phi Delta Kappa/Gallup Poll of the Public's Attitudes Toward the Public Schools." *Phi Delta Kappan,* September 1994, p. 43.

A Look at American Teachers

Teachers are individuals and therefore differ from one another a great deal. In fact, it is very difficult to generalize about teachers in the United States. However, in an effort to help you better understand the nature of American teachers, let's look at some of their similarities and differences.

Profile of the Public School Teacher

There are 2.4 million public school teachers in the United States. Slightly over one-half of them teach at the elementary school level. Besides our large number of public school teachers, there are an additional 350,000 private school teachers and about 750,000 college and university teachers in the United States. Added to this total are over 800,000 other administrative and professional staff. It is also estimated that there are over a million education-related jobs in the United States, including such positions as education specialists in industry, instructional technologists in the military, museum educators, and training consultants in the business world.

Altogether, we have roughly five million educators in the country, ranking education as one of the largest professions in the United States. It is estimated, however, that about 6 percent of our teachers leave the classroom each year for various reasons (retirement, resignations, poor health, etc.). So roughly 300,000 new educators are needed just to replace those leaving the profession each year.

Interest in Teaching Careers.   Some experts feel that rising salaries and new respect for teachers are slowly helping to make teaching a more attractive profession. The Higher Education Research Institute at UCLA annually conducts a survey of college freshmen that, among other things, asks what career the student is planning to pursue. Figure 1.1 shows the results of this survey for the last twenty-seven years. In 1966, nearly 25 percent of freshmen were interested in becoming secondary school teachers compared to fewer than 5 percent today. Likewise, in 1966 about 9 percent of college freshmen expressed an interest in elementary teaching compared to about 5.3 percent today. Of course, this can be partly explained by the fact that our country experienced an oversupply of teachers and hence a poor job market during this period. The apparent downturn in 1993 in

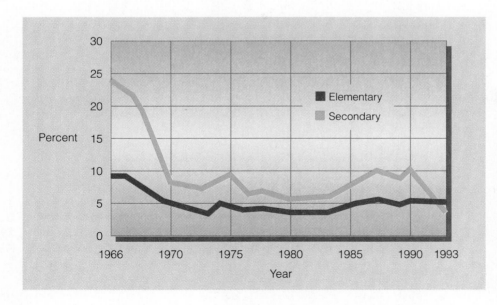

FIGURE 1.1

Freshmen Interested in Teaching Careers (percentages by level, 1966–1993)

(*Source: The American Freshman: National Norms for Fall 1993.* Higher Education Research Institute, UCLA Graduate School of Education, Los Angeles, CA 90024-1521. Reproduced with permission of the Higher Education Research Institute, Graduate School of Education, University of California, Los Angeles, CA.)

freshman interest in secondary teaching as a career could be either a short-term anomaly in the survey or an indicator that there will be fewer graduates in teacher education in the near future. If the latter is the case, then in the next several years there will once again be a shortage of teachers. Teacher demand will increase because the number of school-age children is increasing as the 1990s unfold. In fact, there are shortages already in some states and in most urban areas. This bodes well for today's teacher education students. They will likely find a strong job market, a choice of teaching positions available, and good teacher salaries upon graduation.

Reasons for Becoming a Teacher. There are many reasons why people wish to become teachers. In one recent survey teachers were asked to compare their original reasons for becoming a teacher with their reasons for continuing to teach. The primary reason for deciding to teach was the desire to work with young people (70 percent), which is probably one of your reasons too. The most impressive finding from this survey is that the primary reason teachers continue to teach is the desire to work with young people (78 percent). Teaching seems to be one of the few professions where the expectations of those who wish to join are matched with what the job is really like.

Teacher Demographics in the United States. In the United States, public school teachers are older and more likely to have advanced degrees than are private elementary school teachers. A recent survey by the National Center for Educational Statistics points out many interesting differences between public and private school teachers in this country, some of which are shown in Figure 1.2. This report, entitled *Background Experience Characteristics of Public and Private School Teachers,* shows that private schools have fewer minority teachers than public schools.

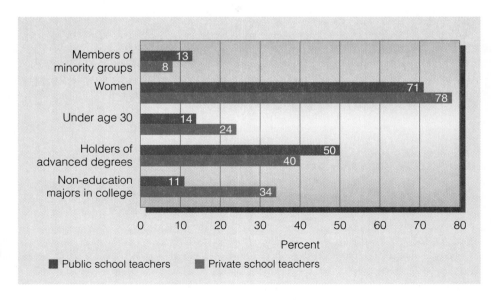

FIGURE 1.2

Differences between Public and Private School Teachers

(*Source:* The National Center for Education Statistics.)

Global Perspectives: Teaching in the United States versus in Other Countries.

American schools and student achievement are often compared with those in other countries. One recent study examined the differences in the preparation of teachers and the conditions of teaching in the United States and other economically advanced nations. Among the findings were that American teachers work longer hours and teach more classes. Elementary teachers in the United States spend more time with their students than teachers in the eighteen other countries studied. At the secondary level, teachers in the United States, Britain, and The Netherlands had the largest teaching loads—five classes, five days a week. Thus, teachers in Japan and the European nations have more time for class preparation during the school day. Interestingly, American high school teachers have less training than teachers in other countries. While U.S. high school teachers need a four-year college degree, in many European countries teachers in the upper secondary grades are required to spend five or six years in preparation at the college level. Teachers in the United States work an average of 185 days, while the international averages ranged from 190 to 195 days. However, U.S. teachers work more hours per week.[2]

Factors That Drive Teachers from the Classroom.

Historically, a high percentage of teachers who begin working in a classroom decide that teaching is not the profession they wish to pursue. Figure 1.3 shows that the main reasons why teachers leave the classroom are "students' social problems make teaching too difficult" and "need or want to earn more money." Other factors that contribute to teachers' leaving the classroom are "lack of administrative support" and a feeling that "teaching has become boring and less satisfying." This information reveals some of the more negative aspects of a teaching career—information you should consider seriously as you decide if you want to enter this profession.

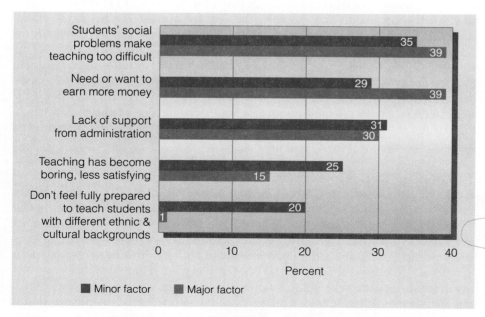

FIGURE 1.3

Factors That Drive Out Teachers

(*Source: The Metropolitan Life Survey of the American Teacher, 1991: Coming to Terms—Teachers' Views on Current Issues in Education.* New York: Louis Harris and Associates.)

Responsibilities outside the classroom such as grading papers can often be an unexpected burden for new teachers.

More Respect for Teachers. A number of surveys have shown that teachers are respected more today than they were over the past few decades. This is probably due to the fact that teachers are better prepared and have more skills. The Carnegie Foundation recently polled 13,000 teachers to determine whether the last five years of educational reform have had any effects on the respect that teachers receive from the general public. The results of this poll indicate that, while teachers have many problems and feel a need for improvement in many aspects of their working conditions, the recent educational reform movement has brought about at least minor improvements in the working conditions of the teacher, and in the respect they command from the public.

Teachers and Teaching

It is important for you, as someone planning to be a teacher, to explore what teachers must be able to do and to find out first hand what it is like to be a beginning teacher. This information will help you decide if you have the attributes needed to be an effective teacher and what skills you will need to develop.

What a Teacher Must Be Able to Do. Whereas teaching has historically been thought of as an art, in recent years it has moved increasingly in the direction of becoming a science, thanks to the advances of research. The effective schools research, discussed further in later sections of this book, suggests that there are a number of discernible things that a teacher needs to know and be able to do to be successful. For example, the North Carolina Teacher Performance Appraisal System requires that teachers be evaluated on the following eight functions: (1) Management of instructional time, (2) Management of student behavior, (3) Instructional presentation, (4) Instructional monitoring of student performance, (5) Instructional feedback, (6) Facilitating instruction, (7) Communicating within the educational environment, and (8) Performing noninstructional duties. These categories will give you a rough idea of the major sets of knowledge and skills that you will need to learn about, practice, and perfect if you are going to be a successful teacher.

Teachers as Decision Makers. A recent study by the Carnegie Foundation for the Advancement of Teaching, based on a survey of 22,000 American teachers, helps to shed light on the type of decisions that teachers help to make in our schools. A part of this survey is shown in Table 1.3, which shows that teachers are fairly heavily involved in choosing textbooks and instructional materials, helping to shape the curriculum, setting behavior standards, and making student tracking decisions. However, this survey also shows that teachers are generally not very involved in selecting new administrators, helping to select new teachers, evaluating teacher performance, making the school budget decisions, helping to decide promotion/retention policies, or designing in-service programs. These are inter-

| TABLE 1.3 | Teachers and Decision Making | | | |

Activity	Involved	Not Very Involved	Most Involved	Least Involved
Choosing textbooks and instructional materials	79%	21%	93% (VT)	61% (MD)
Shaping the curriculum	63	37	85 (VT)	40 (LA)
Setting behavior standards	47	53	68 (OR)	37 (FL, NJ, RI)
Making tracking decisions	45	55	63 (MN)	36 (LA)
Designing inservice programs	43	57	82 (OK)	30 (RI)
Setting promotion/retention policies	34	66	50 (VT)	21 (FL)
Deciding school budgets	20	80	57 (HI)	8 (ND)
Evaluating teacher performance	10	90	20 (GA, UT)	6 (FL, NV, NJ, RI)
Selecting new teachers	7	93	20 (CO, NH, OR)	1 (LA)
Selecting new administrators	7	93	20 (VT)	1 (NV)

Source: The Carnegie Foundation for the Advancement of Teaching, 1987 National Survey of Public School Teachers.

esting findings, since one of the outcomes of current educational reform initiatives deals with the goal of empowering teachers in many of these areas.

Teachers as Artists. While there are many technical skills a teacher must have, our very best teachers possess more elusive qualities that set them apart from the average educator. These qualities include a passion to help students learn, a genuine love of learning, and an overall enthusiasm for teaching that is reflected in their everyday work with students. Theorists speculate that these more ambiguous qualities of outstanding teachers cannot be taught in the same sense as technical teaching skills, but rather, are innately found in some individuals, probably partly inherited and partly gradually developed as a result of total life experiences. These qualities also give rise to the statement you have undoubtedly heard that "good teachers are born and not made." The truth is that you can learn and continue to refine technical teaching skills, as well as improve the more elusive attitudes and values that will enable you to become an outstanding educator.

Career Patterns for Educators. People who become teachers bring a surprising variety of background experiences and interests with them to the profes-

Relevant Research

Teacher Expectations and Student Achievement

Researchers have studied teacher expectations for the last twenty-five years. Early studies of teacher expectations and student achievement have led educators to emphasize the importance of having high expectations for all students.

A recent study of teacher expectations by Goldenberg (1992) revealed that teacher expectations can be a mitigating factor. Goldenberg studied two first-grade Hispanic girls in the same classroom. The teacher held low expectations for one girl and high expectations for the other. Contrary to the theme of the earlier expectations studies, the student that had lower teacher expectations did well in reading achievement, while the student with high teacher expectations did not do well! Goldenberg observed the students and the teacher carefully for long periods of time and was able to explain why these unexpected findings occurred, as well as point out a very important lesson about the way more effective teachers teach.

Goldenberg observed that although the teacher held different expectations for the two students, the teacher's behaviors were not influenced in the same way. The teacher worked very hard to help the low-expectation student engage with and complete assignments. The teacher understood that this student would need extra attention. At the same time, although the high-expectation student was not completing assignments, the teacher "assumed" that she would succeed and so did not monitor and push the student. The result was that the low-expectation student succeeded and the high-expectation student did not.

Goldenberg concluded: "My principal contention is that the teacher's behavior is what matters—what a teacher expects matters less than what a teacher does" (p. 522). A teacher may rightly expect some students to do less well than others, but the teacher must make every effort to see that *all* students achieve.

Sources: R. Rosenthal and L. Jacobson. *Pygmalion in the Classroom.* New York: Holt, Rinehart & Winston, 1968.

Ray Rist, "Student Social Class and Teacher Expectations: The Self-Fulfilling Prophecy in Ghetto Education," *Harvard Educational Review 40* (1970): 411–451.

Claude Goldenberg, "The Limits of Expectations: A Case for Case Knowledge about Teacher Expectancy Effects." *American Educational Research Journal 29* (3) (1992): 517–544.

sion. Some knew from an early age that they wanted to become teachers and concentrated on achieving that goal. Others come to teaching after having worked in business, the military, or government. Currently, a large proportion of teacher education students are *nontraditional*, that is, persons who are over the age of twenty-five. Many have had some sort of teaching-related experience before beginning their initial teacher education program. For example, many have had the opportunity to be peer tutors while in elementary or secondary school. Others have taught as a part of their work in industry, or through their church or synagogue, and some have served as classroom aides. The richer your background of teaching-related experience, the better prepared you will be to take advantage of your teacher education program.

Teacher Stress. A common condition among educators that results from the pressure-filled work they do is called **teacher stress**. Most teachers deal with large numbers of vastly different students, a shortage of time, unhappy parents, numerous colleagues, and the impossible task of teaching every student all that he or she can possibly learn regarding each subject. It is only in recent times that the education profession has come to recognize and admit that most teachers suffer from being overstressed from time to time. Most experts claim that the first step to reducing stress is to acknowledge its presence and begin to search for its source. Some larger schools are even hiring professionals to help teachers and administrators to cope with their stressful assignments. Typically, these counselors advise teachers to become more realistic about what they can accomplish. Other suggestions include the following:

- **Give yourself a break.** Take time off for trips to the bathroom, lunch breaks, and/or nutritious snacks. Before or after lunch, walk around the block or out to the football stadium to get some fresh air and a change of scenery.
- **Prepare for discipline problems.** "If you have difficult kids, work out a strategy with the guidance counselor or principal before behavior problems begin,"

Ashton urges. "That way, you'll know exactly what you're going to do ahead of time."

- Make a schedule of meetings, and then adhere to it. "Teachers have to schedule their phone calls and conferences," Ashton recommends. "They should set the meeting time, set the tone, set the agenda, and stick to it. I think that helps to diminish the sense that they're always at someone's beck and call."
- Talk to colleagues. Teachers need to find a network inside or outside of school for support and professional companionship.
- Limit the time you spend working at home. "Give yourself permission to take time off," Ashton says. Respect your limits, even if it means letting things go undone.
- Exercise. Regular exercise or activity will help release some of the tension that builds up during the day.
- Ask for help. When stress at school or home becomes overwhelming, consider talking to a professional counselor.[3]

New Teacher Expectations and Ideals. Surveys of American teachers conducted by the Metropolitan Life Insurance Company indicate that teachers generally love to teach—in spite of all the problems and frustrations in our schools. In 1991 this series of teacher surveys was directed toward teachers who had just completed their first year of teaching. Since you may be in that situation in the near future, we will discuss some of the reactions new teachers had to their first year in the classroom.

This survey asked teachers who had completed their first year "what things might have been more helpful in your teacher preparation program in preparing you to be successful in the classroom?" Figure 1.4 shows the results of that question, and indicates that they could have used more help from a skilled, experienced teacher, more practical training such as a year's internship before having their own class, and better training in working with students and families from a variety of ethnic backgrounds.

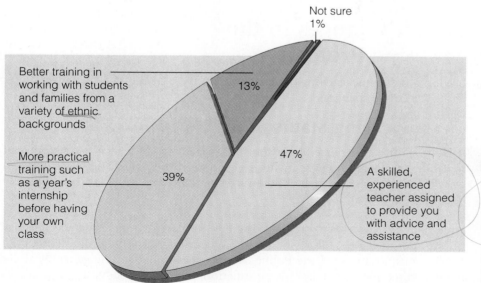

Not sure
1%

Better training in working with students and families from a variety of ethnic backgrounds

13%

More practical training such as a year's internship before having your own class

39%

47%

A skilled, experienced teacher assigned to provide you with advice and assistance

FIGURE 1.4

What Would Have Been Most Helpful in Preparing You to Be a More Effective Teacher?

(*Source: The Metropolitan Life Survey of the American Teacher, 1991: Coming to Terms—Teachers' Views on Current Issues in Education,* p. 15.)

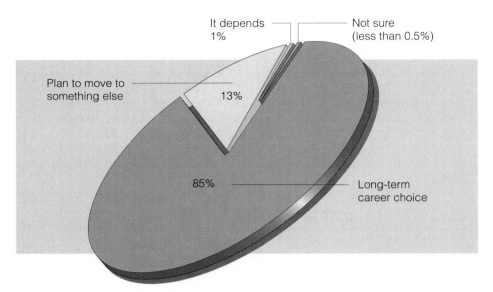

It depends 1%

Not sure (less than 0.5%)

Plan to move to something else

13%

85%

Long-term career choice

FIGURE 1.5

Career Plans of First-Year Teachers

(*Source: The Metropolitan Life Survey of the American Teacher, 1991: The First Year: New Teachers' Expectations and Ideals*, p. 19.)

This study also found out that virtually all first-year teachers believe that all children can learn, and it determined that teachers of low-income and minority students more often believe that family and other outside agencies present significant barriers to student learning. Another interesting finding was that, even among the best teachers, there is a general belief that it is difficult to do an excellent job of teaching with more than two-thirds of the students that a typical teacher encounters.

Last, these first-year teachers were asked about their long-term plans for a teaching career. Figure 1.5 shows the response to that question and indicates that the vast majority were not discouraged by their first year in the classroom and did plan long-term careers as teachers.

Recent Changes in the Teaching Profession

Like all professions, teaching has changed considerably in recent years. Let's look at some of these changes.

The Improving Status of American Teachers

If is difficult to generalize about the status of American teachers. Everyone can remember teachers who were ineffective, and nearly all parents have been unhappy with certain teachers their children have had. Even so, teachers have generally been respected in our society.

Increased Public Confidence. There is evidence that there is a good deal of **public confidence** in public schools and in teachers. The 1994 Gallup Poll of the Public's Attitudes toward the Public Schools shows that people generally think highly of their local schools. This information, presented in Table 1.1, also shows that people generally grade our nation's schools lower than they do their own local schools. This may be the result of a tendency of the media to dwell on the problems of schools more than the successes. It is also worth noting that the public's attitude toward our schools has been improving steadily over the past ten years. These facts should be encouraging to anyone contemplating a teaching career.

Improving Job Opportunities. An entire chapter is devoted to teacher supply and demand and salaries later in this part of the book; however, some information on these topics will be presented at this time to support a contention—that job opportunities and salaries for teachers have improved significantly in recent years. These changes have been sufficiently dramatic to improve the status of American teachers.

Better Working Conditions for Teachers

The working conditions for many teachers have not always been good. Fortunately, they have improved measurably in recent years, and the following sections will show you some of the ways in which these improvements are coming about. This information represents "good news" to those who are preparing for careers in the education field.

Better Salaries. Among the good news for new graduates of teacher education programs, teachers' salaries are improving and will likely continue to do so for some time into the future. For example, teacher salaries nationwide have risen 25 percent in recent years, according to a survey conducted by the American Federation of Teachers. Even when corrected for inflation, this figure amounts to a significant increase. We do not mean to say that teachers are currently overpaid—or for that matter, even adequately paid. Salary and its adequacy will very likely be debated as long as schools exist. The point is, however, that teachers' salaries have risen substantially. Furthermore, given the growing shortage of teachers, the laws of supply and demand will very likely continue to improve teachers' salaries for some time into the future—a phenomenon that will help to improve the status of American teachers.

Student Respect for Teachers. The extent to which students respect teachers is very difficult to determine and to generalize. Obviously, most students respect some teachers. Also, it is clear that some teachers are more respected by students than others. Likewise, the degree to which a given teacher is respected by students depends on many variables such as the given school, the nature of the students in each class, the personality and skills of the other teachers, and even the nature of the subject being taught.

A recent survey by the *Weekly Reader* of 90,000 students in grades 2 through 9 found that 55 percent of the students liked their teachers, but only 35 percent liked their school "a lot." The survey also found that younger students are generally more positive than older students.

Insight into what students like about teachers can be gleaned from a survey conducted by *Learning* magazine, which asked eighth graders in Michigan for tips for teachers. Students gave the following advice: Don't assign extra work to students who finish their work early; don't be mean; don't be overconfident; be patient; don't give up on students; let students go to the bathroom; be supportive and reassuring; have a sense of humor; don't leave the classroom; check on students while they work; correct papers with appropriate comments; be versatile; don't yell; be

TABLE 1.4 Teacher Satisfaction	
Area of Satisfaction	**Percent Satisfied**
Contribution to society	85
Job security	84
Level of responsibility	82
Challenge	81
Appreciation by parents	68
Respect from students	67
Relaxed environment	59
Recognition from administrators	55
Prestige	38

Source: Survey of NEA K-12 Teacher Members 1985. (Washington, DC: National Education Association, p. 11.) Used by permission.

qualified in your subject area; don't be too intelligent; use textbooks; don't have class favorites; don't complain; dress neatly; and stay young.

In summary, there is considerable evidence to suggest that most students like and respect the majority of their teachers. This compliment should be good news to teacher education students in colleges and universities throughout America.

Improving Teacher Self-Concept. The way teachers view their participation in their profession is commonly called **teacher self-concept.** In spite of the fact that teaching is a very demanding profession, and even though educators are not paid as much as they should be, teachers generally feel good about themselves and their profession. This contention is supported by a recent study conducted by the National Education Association, in which teachers were asked about their level of satisfaction concerning a number of job variables. As Table 1.4 shows, teachers were most satisfied with their contribution to society and least satisfied with the prestige of their profession.

Teachers Taking Charge. A recent survey conducted by *Instructor Magazine* tallied the responses of nearly 32,000 teachers across the country regarding the degree of freedom they have as professionals.[4] One of the interesting findings of this survey concerned the freedom teachers have in selecting the instructional materials they use in the classroom. Figure 1.6 shows that 47 percent of the respondents indicated they select instructional materials in consultation with their colleagues, 41 percent indicated they have total freedom in such selection, while only 12 percent indicated they must follow a mandate when selecting instructional materials. In other words, teachers generally have considerable freedom to select the materials that they will use in their classrooms.

Confidence, energy, and facility with a variety of teaching tools are some of the characteristics of excellent teachers.

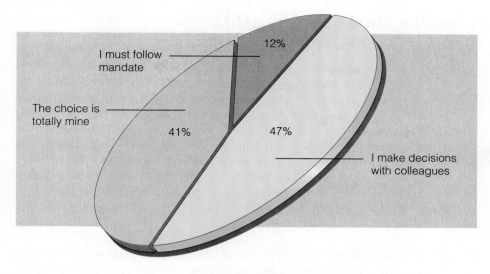

FIGURE 1.6

**How Much Freedom Do
You Have in Selecting
Instructional Materials?**

(*Source:* Instructor Survey
Results, *Instructor Magazine.* ©
1990 by Scholastic Inc. Used by
permission.)

Other findings from this survey include the following:

- 55 percent indicated that their schools had undergone a major shift in subject matter or instructional emphasis during the past three years.
- 73 percent indicated that the current move toward school/business partnerships is improving the educational program.
- 60 percent indicated that they did not believe that student achievement should play a role in determining the teacher's salary.
- 84 percent felt that higher teacher salaries would do more to raise the status of the teaching profession than anything else.
- 82 percent felt that the quality of teaching will improve when teachers become more involved in making curriculum decisions.

This survey, like many other typical teacher surveys, points out that teachers are slowly becoming more empowered as professional educators. This should be additional good news to college students who are preparing for careers in the teaching profession.

Developing Your Portfolio as You Learn about Teaching

A new educational and assessment strategy is to have students develop a **portfolio** of their accomplishments. Portfolios are compilations for a specific purpose of the works, records, and accomplishments that students prepare about what they have learned, performed, and contributed.

Portfolios are being used more frequently in teacher education too. Preservice teachers in their professional preparation programs are increasingly being asked to keep portfolios related to their development as teachers. School district employers are interested in reviewing portfolios of applicants for teaching positions, and states are requiring that teachers develop portfolios for submission when they request renewal of their teaching licenses. There are three key components to developing a professional portfolio: (1) observation and note taking, (2) reflecting on what you have done and learned, and (3) compiling the folio.

Learning about Teaching through Systematic Observation

As you proceed through your teacher education program, you should seize every opportunity to observe a wide variety of activities related to the world of education. For instance, in addition to the observation and participation assignments that you will have as part of the formal teacher education program, you should seek out opportunities to visit and observe a wide variety of classrooms. You should also attempt to find summer employment that allows you to work with youth and/or teachers. If you participate in church or synagogue activities, perhaps you could volunteer to teach young people. We encourage you to think creatively of other ways to provide yourself with opportunities to learn more about your chosen profession by participating with teachers and by working with youth every chance you get.

Informal Note Taking.   One of the most common ways to collect information is by writing down your observations—in other words, taking notes. This can be done in a variety of ways. For instance, when you go into your classroom, you could start by writing a brief description of the setting, such as the physical appearance of the room, number of students, teaching devices, and so on. You can then systematically describe each of the things you observe. The more detail you can record, the more you will learn from the observations.

Create a list of questions before you begin any given observation. If you are interested in how a teacher motivates students during a particular lesson, write down the question: What techniques does the teacher use to help motivate students? You would subsequently record your observations under that question.

Observation of actual teachers in real teaching situations is a key element in good teacher training.

| CASE STUDY | TEACHING IS COMPLEX WORK |

*C*ritics of teachers and schools often state that "anyone can teach." They point out how short the school year is, saying, "Teachers get two months of vacation." They exclaim about the short work day, "You are out of school as quick as the kids." And they harp about how simple the job of teaching is, "All you have to do is sit at a desk and tell them what you know." As much as we may wish, these simplistic stereotypes will not go away until teachers are able to explain in articulate ways what the job of teaching really entails.

A very interesting place to begin a presentation on the complexity of the work of teachers would be to look at a publication of the U.S. Department of Labor, the *Directory of Occupational Titles (DOT)*. This publication is a listing of different kinds of jobs. For each occupation, the DOT includes ratings of different aspects of the work and the needed qualifications of people who do the job. An education researcher, Brian Rowan, recently used this document to develop an analysis of how the work of teachers compared to work in other occupations.

In the DOT, three scales are used to define and analyze different occupations: (1) *worker functions*, which address the complexity of an occupation in relation to data, people, and things; (2) *general educational development*, a rating of the amount of knowledge that is required to perform the work, which includes reasoning development, mathematical development, and language development; and (3) *specific vocational preparation*, which addresses the amount of formal education and training that is required to do that occupation.

For the first Worker Functions subscale, "work with data," the highest scale options are: (0) synthesizing data, (1) coordinating, (2) compiling, (3) computing, and (4) copying. Teachers are rated a "2." On the second subscale, "work with people," the highest ranking are (0) mentoring, (1) negotiating, (2) instructing, and (3) supervising. On this subscale teachers are rated a "2." The third subscale of Worker Functions is "work with things," for which the scale rankings include (0) setting up, (2) precision working, (3) operating-controlling, (4) manipulating, (5) tending, (6) feeding-offbearing, and (7) handling. Teaching is rated a "7."

On the Knowledge and Preparation scales, again the work of teachers is seen as complex. They must be able to apply principles of logical or scientific thinking to define problems, collect data, and draw valid conclusions. Teachers must also be able to function at the highest range of skills in reading, writing, and speaking. And there is between two and four years of higher-level preparation to become a teacher.

In the concluding analysis, Rowan compared teaching with 591 occupations. When all of the occupations were rank-ordered, school teaching, both elementary and secondary, was placed just below the seventy-fifth percentile. Another way to view this analysis is that nearly 75 percent of the occupations studied were *less* complex than that of elementary and secondary school teaching.

This is a more objective analysis of how the occupation of teaching compares to many others. There are other ways that the challenges and complexities of the work of the teachers can be described and illustrated. How will you make the case when you are questioned? What aspects of teaching have you discovered already that illustrate the complexity of the work? One important dimension to consider is the number of people whose lives you will affect directly—your students and their parents. Later, these people will influence many others with what they have learned from you.

Source: Brian Rowan, "Comparing Teachers' Work with Work in Other Occupations; Notes on the Professional Status of Teaching." *Educational Researcher 23* (6) (1994): 4–17.

Structured Observations. Observations that are conducted according to a predetermined plan are often referred to as **structured observations.** As your college or university sends you out into the schools for various laboratory experiences, you will probably be provided with guidelines that will help structure your observations. In fact, some colleges have developed written structured observations forms that will guide you when participating in clinical experiences. We recommend that you create your own structured observations forms around the questions that particularly intrigue you. In other words, if you are especially interested in classroom diversity, devise your own structured observations form that will remind you to look for details concerning that particular topic the next time you are in a classroom. In fact, it might be fun for you to create some structured observations forms that you can use with the professors in your college classes. The more aware you are of what you are looking for as you observe a classroom, the more you are likely to learn about that particular topic.

Observation Instruments. You might find it difficult to believe, but literally hundreds of structured observations instruments have been devised to help educators collect more valid data about classrooms. These observation instruments range from quite simple devices to extremely complex systems that require computers for analysis. Generally, however, they fall into two basic categories—structured interviews and classroom analysis systems.

Structured Interviews. Structured interviews consist of a series of specific questions that are asked of a respondent as well as some provision for recording the respondent's answer. You could prepare a series of important questions that you would like to ask a principal, teacher, student, parent, or anyone else connected with the educational enterprise. You must make sure that these questions are not ambiguous and that the respondent will clearly understand what you are asking. You would then seek out a number of respondents and interview them with the same structured interview technique. Obviously, the more people you surveyed through such a technique, the more representative your data would be for the population in general. If you asked only one teacher the question, "What is the single best discipline technique that you utilize in your classroom?" you would have only one idea, whereas if you asked one hundred teachers that same question, you would obtain much more representative data about effective discipline techniques used by teachers.

When doing a structured interview, you must be very careful to record your respondent's answers accurately. It is best to utilize a tape recorder, which you simply let run during your interview. In this way you obtain a complete record of the answers and can go back and listen to it many times later on. You can also write down your respondent's answers; however, unless you are adept at shorthand, it might be difficult for you to record answers accurately and completely.

Classroom Analysis Systems. Over the last fifty years, as researchers have attempted to more objectively understand what takes place in our schools, they have created many systems to study classroom activity. In general, **classroom analysis systems** come in two types: quantitative and qualitative. Quantitative systems use well-defined categories and coding procedures to count the occurrence of different teacher and student behaviors. Qualitative systems are more open ended, or descriptive.

Learning about Teaching through Observation, Analysis, and Reflection

Once you have collected observations of teaching, children, classrooms, and schools, it is very important to take time to think about what you have seen. There are several techniques for systematically analyzing your observations, but equally important is taking time to reflect on the analyses. In our rush to get everything done, we frequently fail to take time to thoughtfully examine our experiences and impressions. However, being serious about finding time to reflect is an important part of becoming an excellent teacher, and there are some processes that can be helpful.

Reflective Journals. It is very important to keep a diary or journal in which you reflect, raise questions, and propose ideas related to your development as a teacher. You may be asked to keep a journal in some of your courses, but we encourage you to keep a professional journal regardless of course requirements. A journal is interesting to review from time to time to see how your thoughts, insights, and ideas have evolved. Do not be concerned about changes in your thoughts and opinions; the reflective journals of all outstanding teachers document a continuing evolution of questions, assumptions, and priorities.

Summarizing Educational Information. Regardless of the technique you use to record your educational observations, it is imperative that you take the time to study them. This is best done by rereading your recorded data many times. Once you have become thoroughly familiar with the content of your recorded data, you are ready to begin summarizing your findings. This requires an open mind. You should strive to disregard any previous prejudices you might have had on the topic. Remember that your goal is to understand objectively the accurately recorded data from your observations. It is sometimes helpful to talk with fellow students about your findings. This type of peer brainstorming will frequently allow you to see data from a slightly different and perhaps more objective viewpoint. In fact, you might want to team up with classmates who are making the same observations using the same data collection technique so that you all have the same frame of reference. The goal that you should keep in mind in summarizing your information is to draw accurate conclusions from the data you have collected.

Forming Hypotheses. Once you have condensed and summarized your data, you are ready to draw conclusions and form **hypotheses** based on your observations. If one of your original questions was "What techniques do teachers use to motivate their students?" you would obviously develop hypotheses to answer that particular question. The hypotheses that you form at this stage in your development as an educator make worthwhile all the effort you put into observing, collecting, and analyzing data. They allow you to verify for yourself some of what you have probably been reading and hearing in your college classes. In addition, they are the basis on which you will eventually pattern your own teaching style.

Testing Your Conclusions. Every belief, conclusion, or hypothesis that you develop as an educator should be considered tentative. In other words, it is important to formulate such beliefs at this point in your career, but you need to keep an open mind about them and continually revalidate them. The teacher who is constantly attempting to improve is also constantly forming new or modified beliefs, hypotheses, and conclusions about teaching. That is why it is critically important for you and all educators to continually observe and analyze classroom activity so that you can constantly seek to better understand this very complex field.

Developing Folios and Portfolios

As you move through your teacher education program and on into your career as a teacher, you will find that you have been collecting stacks, boxes, and files of information and "stuff" related to you, your teaching, and the accomplishments of the children you have taught. If you are like most teachers you will not know for sure what to do with all of it, yet you will be reluctant to throw any of it away. Our advice is, be very careful about discarding material until you have organized a folio and anticipated the needs of various portfolios that you might have to prepare. A *folio* is the organized compilation of all the products, records, accomplishments, and testimonies of a teacher and his or her students. Imagine the folio as being a large file drawer with different compartments and file folders. Some of the material that is included is related directly to you and your background. Other items or artifacts are things that others have said about you. And some are examples of projects that your students have completed. A portfolio is assembled from the folio when there is a specific occasion or purpose, such as a job interview or application for an outstanding teacher award. The folio can be organized around three major categories of items: background and experience, attestations, and products and outcomes (see Table 1.5).

Background and Experience. There are many pieces of information about you that are factual. Demographic information, where you attended school, the states where you are licensed to teach, and the record of your work experience are examples of items that you should maintain in your folio. When organizing your folio you will identify a number of areas where you should aim to add information. Now is the time to anticipate some of the material that you might need in preparing a particular portfolio in the future. For example, when you apply for most teaching positions, a prospective employer will want to know the kinds of experiences you have had in schools and classrooms with diverse students. If you currently do not have any examples in your folio, plan to add some related experiences as your teacher education program unfolds.

Attestations. The occasions on which other people recognize your contributions and achievements are called *attestations*. Awards, letters of commendation, newspaper articles, and elected positions on committees are examples of a second category of items to keep in your folio.

Products and Outcomes. Through your efforts as a teacher, students complete assignments, produce plays, achieve on examinations, and receive awards. In this part of the folio the works and successes of those you have worked with can be compiled, along with photographs and video records of your classroom and student projects. Also include copies of committee reports, grant proposals, and other products that have resulted from your leading the efforts of other adults.

TABLE 1.5	Types of Information and Artifacts to Include in Professional Folio

Background and Experience (Facts)	Attestations (Recognition by others)	Products and Outcomes (Works of others based on your teaching)
Demographics • age • birthdate • marital status Education • degrees • institutions Education Platform—philosophy Professional Credentials Work Experience Current Role and Responsibilities Multicultural Experiences Special Skills • languages • art/music Community Service • Red Cross volunteer Products • lesson plans • authored curriculum • media productions • written reflections	Awards Honorary Society Memberships Letters from • students • parents • professors • employers • colleagues Newspaper Articles about You TV Segments about You Committee Assignments Elected Offices	Examples of Student Work Photographs of Your Classroom Student Test Scores Video/audiotape of Lessons Grant Proposals Funded Student Awards Effects of Leadership • committee reports • school/class awards • curriculum developed • projects completed Subordinates Who Have Been Recognized or Promoted

Preparing a Portfolio. When the need arises to prepare a portfolio you will be delighted that you did the advance work with your folio. The time line always seems too short when a special portfolio needs to be developed. When you do the folio work along the way, you will find it relatively easy to pull specific examples and documents to fit a particular job interview, or to make final application for a teaching award. Also, when you develop the folio with the broader array of items suggested in Table 1.5, you will be able to prepare a higher quality presentation of your accomplishments.

Folio Tasks. To help you in beginning your folio we have included at the end of each chapter two "Journal/Portfolio Development" suggestions. In making the suggestions, we have anticipated some of the items that you may need to include in future portfolio presentations, and we have selected topics and tasks that are important to you at this early point in your teacher education program. In our discussions as authors we identified four components that were important to our task selections:

> *Content:* The content of the performances will be centered on the major concepts or big ideas of education.
> *Thinking:* The portfolio tasks will aim to assess a variety of thinking skills rather than focusing on just one skill within each task.

Thoughtful Engaging Approaches: As much as possible, the portfolio tasks should require serious thinking and encourage more cognitive complexity.

Rich Opportunities: The performances should allow learners to solve problems in a variety of creative ways.

Summary and Implications

This chapter has briefly introduced you to the world of the teacher. We hope that it has convinced you that teaching is an extremely important profession—important to the future success of our democracy, to the happiness and welfare of our children, and to our nation's economy. It has also reminded you that teaching is one of the largest professions in America and that despite some understandable frustrations and a considerable amount of stress, teachers generally feel that their careers are fulfilling and satisfactory. Another contention of this chapter is that society, parents, and students as a rule value and respect teachers.

The last section of this chapter stressed the importance of all teachers being reflective through gathering, analyzing, and using data. We suggest that our best teachers have a natural curiosity about their work and are continually searching for better answers to the problems they face. One important recommendation is to begin developing your professional folio *now*. It is very likely that you will need to develop a portfolio before completing your teacher education program. Most certainly, you will need items from your folio as you search for your first/next teaching position.

One final implication of this chapter for those who are contemplating a career in teaching is the following: You will be entering a time-honored profession that serves an extremely important function in our society and in which most of your colleagues find fulfillment at a time when jobs are available and salaries are improving.

Discussion Questions

1. Name three to five reasons why you want to become a teacher.
2. What are "typical" students' impressions of teachers?
3. What differences do you think teachers can make in your community, your state, the nation, and the world at large?
4. What are key characteristics of teachers you have known that you would like to emulate? What is one thing that you would not want to do?
5. What can teachers do that will make a positive difference in the public's perceptions of teachers?

Journal/Portfolio Development

1. Visit with a retired teacher. Ask what school was like when he or she began teaching. What were the pay and work conditions like then? How has school and the profession of teaching changed from then to now? What kinds of changes does this teacher see for the future? After the interview, review your notes (or did you get permission and tape record?) and write a two- to three-page narrative of your thoughts, impressions, and reflections. What did you learn? What surprised you? What was new or different in the perspective of this teacher? What questions do you have now? (Don't forget to send the teacher a follow-up thank you note.)
2. Your very first folio development task is to find and organize the many materials, artifacts, and records that you currently have. If you are like most of us, the bits and pieces are stored in a number of locations. Examples of term papers, transcripts, awards, letters of recognition, and journals from trips are scattered. Take some time now to find and begin organizing these materials. Organize them by categories such as those illustrated in Table 1.5. Keep in mind the ultimate purpose for developing this folio: At various points in the future you will be drawing items out of the folio to develop a portfolio for use when you apply for a teaching position or as part of the application process to receive national certification as a master teacher.

School-Based Experiences

1. The material contained in this chapter is designed to help you decide whether you want to be a teacher. The next time you have an opportunity to be in a classroom, analyze what you observe, keeping the following three very important basic questions in mind: Do I have the talent necessary to be a good teacher? Am I willing to develop the skills I will need as a teacher? Do I really want to be teacher?

   Talk to teachers about the rewards and frustrations associated with a teaching career. Talk to students about the characteristics of their favorite teachers. Talk to parents about their educational expectations. Talk to students about their educational goals.

2. Ask ERIC. No, that is not the name of a teacher education professor. ERIC is the national database for education, which is funded through the U.S. Department of Education. ERIC consists of a number of centers and an impressive array of information retrieval systems. ERIC staff compile nearly all of the papers, research reports, and curriculum materials that are developed each year. These materials are then made available through on-line computer retrieval systems, which should be available through your college library. There are some special services for teachers in training, including two-page research synthesis publications, a 48-hour turn-around electronic question-answering service, and hundreds of lesson plans that you can access through your computer. To find out more, call 1-800-LET-ERIC. If you have an Internet ID, you can use it too. For details on locating ERIC on Internet, send an e-mail message to: askeric@ericir.syr.edu

Notes

1. James W. Gutherie, "Do America's Schools Need a 'Dow Jones Index'?" *Phi Delta Kappan 74* (7): 523–528.
2. "How U.S. Teachers Measure Up Internationally: A Comparative Study of Teacher Pay, Training, and Conditions of Service." American Federation of Teachers, Research Department, 555 New Jersey Ave. N.W., Washington, D.C. 20001.
3. D. Ladestro, "Stressed Out," *Teacher Magazine* (January 1991): 58–59.
4. "Instructor Survey Results," *Instructor Magazine* (May 1990): 23–25.

Bibliography

Clark, David L., and Astuto, Terry A. "Redirecting Reform Challenges to Popular Assumptions about Teachers and Students." *Phi Delta Kappan* (March 1994): 513–520.

Bullough, Robert V., Jr. *First-Year Teacher: A Case Study.* New York: Teachers College Press, 1989.

Edelfelt, Ray A. *Careers in Education.* Lincolnwood, IL: VGM Career Horizons, 1988.

Gutek, Gerald L. *Education and Schooling in America.* Boston: Allyn and Bacon, 1992.

Hansen, Peter. *The Joy of Stress.* New York: Andrews, McMeel and Parker, 1986.

Johansen, John; Johnson, James; and Henniger, Michael. *American Education: An Introduction to Teaching.* 7th ed. Dubuque: Wm. C. Brown, 1993.

Kaplan, Leonard, ed. *Classrooms at the Crossroads: The Washinton Post Education Companion.* Boston: Allyn and Bacon, 1993.

Kozol, Johnathan. *Savage Inequalities: Children in America's Schools.* New York: Crown Publishers, 1991.

Myers, Charles B., and Myers, Lynn K. *An Introduction to Teaching and Schools.* Fort Worth: Holt, Rinehart and Winston, 1990.

Parkey, Forrest W., and Stanford, Beverly Hardcastle. *Becoming a Teacher.* 3rd ed. Boston: Allyn and Bacon, 1995.

Posner, George J. *Field Experience: A Guide to Reflective Thinking.* New York: Longman, 1985.

Ryan, Kevin, and Cooper, James M. *Those Who Can, Teach.* 6th ed. Boston: Houghton Mifflin Co., 1992.

Smith, Tom E. C. *Introduction to Education.* 2nd ed. St. Paul: West Publishing Co., 1990.

Wragg, E. C. *An Introduction to Classroom Observation.* New York: Routledge, 1994.

Wynn, Richard, and Wynn, Joanne Lindsay. *American Education.* 9th ed. New York: Harper & Row, 1988.

2 Employment Opportunities for Teachers

Focus Questions

1 What factors influence the supply and demand for teachers?
2 Illustrate the ways in which lower pupil-teacher ratios would aid classroom teachers. What classes would function just as well with larger numbers of students?
3 Why are teachers reluctant to follow the general population shifts in the country? Shouldn't teachers move to areas where they are most needed?
4 How do you account for teacher shortages in some fields and oversupply in others? Why is it that the beginning salary for teachers often is lower than the salary paid the beginner in business and industry?

Key Terms and Concepts

Annual increments: Standard salary increases based on the number of years of teaching experience.

Differential pay: Extra pay or incentives (added to standard increments) awarded to teachers on the basis of merit.

Fringe benefits: Job rewards in addition to salary that may include life, professional liability, health, and dental insurance; retirement programs; and tax-free investment opportunities.

Moonlighting: Holding a second job in addition to one's primary employment; it implies working in the evening, or "under the light of the moon."

Salary schedule: Salary chart organized by teaching experience and formal education.

Teacher certification: The process whereby each state determines the requirements for obtaining a license to teach, processes applications, and issues such licenses.

Teacher supply and demand: A comparison of the projected number of school-age students with the projected number of available teachers.

*T*his chapter will explore two questions that are near and dear to the hearts of all those preparing for a teaching career: (1) Will I find a teaching job when I graduate? and (2) How much money will I make as a teacher? We will look at the factors that influence the answers to these questions and attempt to help you develop the ability to analyze the variables that will assist you in eventually finding the teaching position you want.

Factors Affecting Teacher Supply and Demand

Many factors influence **supply and demand** for teachers in the United States. Of course, these factors change from time to time as conditions in our society change. Let's briefly look at some of the main variables that determine how easy or difficult it is for teachers to find a job.

Teacher Supply

The new teacher supply in a given year consists basically of two groups—new-teacher graduates and former-teacher graduates who were not employed as teachers in the previous year. New-teacher graduates have just graduated from institutions of higher education and are prepared to teach for the first time. Former-teacher graduates are prepared to teach, but do not currently hold teaching positions. Some of these former-teacher graduates taught previously; the remainder have never been employed as teachers.

New College Graduates. American colleges and universities produced a record number of new teachers about two decades ago when they graduated over one-third of a million teachers each year. That number declined rather dramatically up until a decade ago. Over the past ten years, teacher production has modestly increased each year; now 200,000 new teachers graduate each year. Obviously, the number of newly graduated teachers is one factor in the complicated subject of teacher supply in the United States. Ironically, each year, about one-third of the new-teacher graduates do not take teaching jobs. Another third of new-teacher graduates only devote a few years to teaching before moving out of the classroom. Thus, only about one-third of all new-teacher graduates make teaching a lifetime career.

Teachers Returning to the Classroom. Another interesting phenomenon in the question of teacher supply is that many teachers drop out of the profession for one reason or another for a period of time and then accept teaching positions later in life. An obvious example would be female teachers who begin teaching right out of college, drop out of the profession while raising young children, and return when their children become older. Many male teachers leave the teaching profession, at least temporarily, to try other occupations that typically pay larger salaries. Thus, teachers returning to the classroom also play a considerable role in the teacher supply picture in the United States. Estimates vary considerably, but it is probably a good estimate that between one-third to one-half of all newly hired teachers in each school district are experienced teachers, either returning to the classroom or moving from other school districts.

Thus, when you graduate from your teacher education program, you will be competing for teaching positions not only with other new graduates, but also with experienced teachers who are returning to the classroom or changing school districts. Teacher supply and demand is in many ways fickle, difficult to understand, and nearly impossible to predict on a long-range basis, so don't worry too much about it, because it will likely change many times during your career as an educator.

Teacher Demand

The demand for teachers in the United States varies considerably from time to time, from place to place, from subject to subject, and from grade level to grade level. Next, we will explore some of the factors that influence the demand for teachers.

The School-Age Population in the United States. One of the major factors related to the demand for teachers is the number of school-age children in the United States. This in turn is related to birth rates and school retention rates. Other factors influencing both teacher supply and demand include the amount of funds available to hire teachers, the pupil-teacher ratio, and any new programs that receive special funding. The following section will help you to better understand the variables that affect the supply and demand for teachers in the United States.

The Coming Baby Boomlet. School enrollment is predicted to rise rather dramatically over the next decade. The U.S. Bureau of the Census prediction is

Large increases in the population of school-aged children will have far-reaching effects on the education system in general, and on teacher demand specifically.

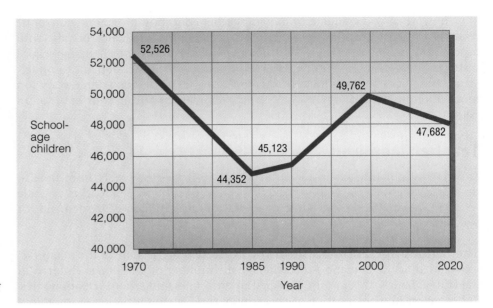

FIGURE 2.1

Number of School-Age (K-12) Children in Thousands

(*Source:* National Center for Education Statistics and U.S. Bureau of the Census.)

reflected in Figure 2.1, which shows the number of school-age children from 1970 projected into the future. As you can see, the number of school-age children in the United States bottomed out in 1985, is now at approximately 47 million plus, and is projected to reach nearly 50 million in the year 2000. This increasing number of school-age children is one of the reasons that many authorities are predicting a shortage of teachers in the United States over the next decade.

U.S. Population. According to recent information presented by *Education Week,* it is projected that the population of the United States will peak at slightly over 302 million people sometime during the next fifty years. Forecasters then predict that the population will shrink to approximately 292 million people by the year 2080. The U.S. Bureau of the Census also has made the following projections for school-age populations:

> For the next fifty years, the elementary school population will remain above its 1987 level of 30.8 million.
> By 1995, that population (ages 5 to 13) will have grown by about 3 million, reaching 33.9 million. It will shrink again, by 2 million, between 1995 and 2005, but will not dip below the 1987 level until the year 2038. Over the subsequent four decades, it will decline to 28.3 million.
> Only in the bureau's "highest" series of projections would the elementary population again reach, around the year 2010, its 1970 record level of 36.7 million. In that series, the numbers would then continue to rise, to 58.2 million in 2080.
> The population of children will shrink to 16.8 million by the year 2000. It will hover between 16 and 17 million until the year 2050, and then drop slowly to 15 million by 2080, according to the mean projections.
> The high school population (ages 14 to 17) declined from 14.5 million in 1987 to 13.2 million by 1990, but will rebound to the 1987 level by 1995. It will remain at or slightly above that level, according to the projections, until at least the year 2010. It will then drop slowly to 13.1 million in 2080.

The highest series projects growth in the high school population after the year 2000, up to 25.6 million in 2080; the lowest series envisions declines from the 1987 level after the year 2005—to 7.2 million in 2080.

In the Census Bureau's middle projections, the college-age population (ages 18 to 24) will never again achieve its 1987 level of 27.3 million.[1] While the overall population is on the decline, however, the population of minority children is on the increase. This demands that teachers be more sensitive to cultural differences among students and that more minority students become teachers.

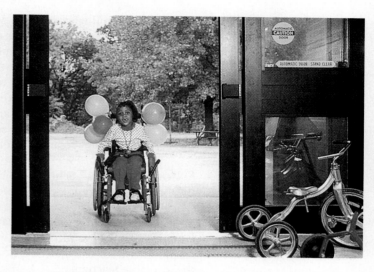

One trend in education today is the increased effort to include children with disabilities in the regular education system.

Trends in Special Education Enrollments. Our schools serve many types of handicapped students. The number of learning-disabled students has increased considerably over the last decade and now totals over four million. As a percent of the total public school enrollment, the number of special education students has risen to nearly 11 percent. This increase in the number of handicapped children served in our schools was due in large part to the Education of the Handicapped Act passed by Congress in 1975, which demands that all handicapped children be provided with a free and appropriate education.

Pupil-Teacher Ratios. The number of students taught by each teacher varies considerably from school to school and from state to state. Figure 2.2 shows pupil-teacher ratios in public and private schools for the entire United States. As

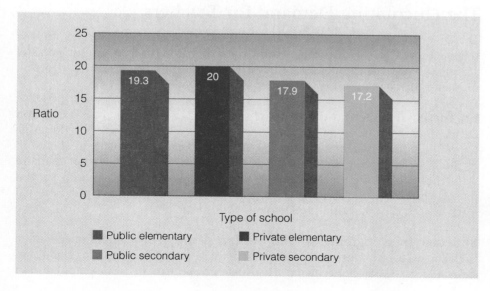

Ratio / Type of school

- Public elementary — 19.3
- Public secondary — 20
- Private elementary — 17.9
- Private secondary — 17.2

FIGURE 2.2

Pupil-Teacher Ratios in Public and Private Schools

(*Source:* National Center for Education Statistics.)

you can see, pupil-teacher ratios are highest in elementary schools. It is interesting to note that the pupil-teacher ratio in public schools is very similar to that in private schools and that it is somewhat lower in secondary schools than in elementary schools. Obviously, one measure of a teacher's work load is the number of students taught. Pupil-teacher ratios reflect the relationship between the number of students enrolled and the number of full-time equivalent instructional personnel available to teach them, and pupil-teacher ratios help to determine how many teachers get hired. In large school districts, lowering the pupil-teacher ratio by even one student creates a demand for many more teachers.

School Budgets.   Schools never have enough money to hire all the teachers they could use. When school budgets are higher, more teachers are employed, which creates an increased demand for teachers. Unfortunately, when school budgets are limited, few teachers are hired. It has been suggested that, due to inadequate financial resources, we never have an oversupply, but rather, "underemployment" of teachers; if schools had enough money, they would hire all of the available teachers.

 Global Perspectives: International Comparisons of Educational Staffing.   A recent study[2] revealed interesting differences among countries regarding the amount of money devoted to hiring nonteaching school staff members. The United States hires considerably more nonteaching school staff members than any other country. In fact, more than half of the employees of U.S. schools are not teachers; they are administrators, counselors, librarians, janitors, secretaries, cooks, maintenance workers, bus drivers, and so on. This study shows that 5.6 percent of the total American labor force works in education, but teachers make up only 2.6 percent of all U.S. workers. Japan and The Netherlands have the lowest percentage of nonteaching education employees. Some of these differences can be explained by the fact that many American school children must be bused to schools, thereby requiring bus drivers and maintenance people. How else might some of these differences be explained?

The Fluctuating Demand for Teachers

The demand for new teachers is increasing rapidly in the United States. In fact, there is a severe teacher shortage in some states, particularly in certain subjects and at certain levels and in our larger cities. Let's look more closely at the factors that influence the demand for teachers in the United States.

An Increasing Demand for Teachers.   The U.S. Department of Education publishes many educational statistics that are of interest to professional educators. One such statistic is related to the demand for classroom teachers, as shown in Figure 2.3. This figure shows a steady increase in classroom teacher demand throughout the United States through the year 1997. These projections suggest that it will be essential for our country to recruit a large number of additional teachers into the education profession over this time period.

Shortage by Geographical and Subject Areas.   As was mentioned earlier, the demand for new teachers varies from place to place, from grade to grade, and from subject to subject. Even within a given metropolitan area, one school district

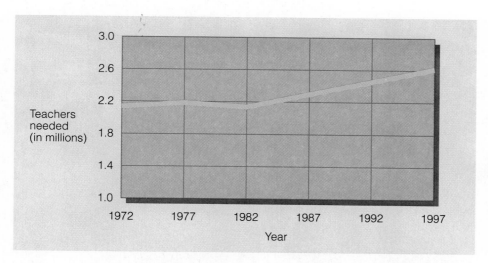

FIGURE 2.3

The Demand for Classroom Teachers Increases

(*Source:* U.S. Department of Education and National Center for Education Statistics.)

may be growing rapidly, building new schools, and hiring new teachers because of new housing developments, while the neighboring school district may be closing schools and reducing its number of teachers. Therefore, it is difficult to generalize about the nature of teacher shortages.

Generally, however, the greatest shortage of teachers exists in our larger cities—New York, Chicago, and Los Angeles, for instance—and in the southern and southwestern parts of the country.

Unfortunately, many teachers do not want to teach in large metropolitan schools, presumably because of heavy city traffic on the freeways, longer commuting time to and from work, more difficult student problems, and higher costs of living. High teacher turnover also contributes to the staffing problems of large-city schools. On the other hand, many teachers feel that teaching in a large city is challenging and fulfilling, with many advantages.

The general teacher shortage that exists in the southern and southwestern parts of the United States has come about as a result of the population shift that has occurred over the past twenty years. Many Americans have moved to the sun belt states largely because industrial development has made jobs available there. This migration has increased school enrollment, which, in turn, has created a considerable demand for teachers.

College and university placement directors suggest that students planning to become teachers should be apprised of the fact that opportunity exists in any field for the top-quality graduate. While it is true that, in times of a good supply of teachers, far more graduates are employed in elementary education, English, and social studies than in subject areas that need relatively few teachers (such as Russian language), at the same time, high-quality candidates in some teaching areas having less demand are still likely to find teaching positions, especially if they are willing to move to where vacancies exist.

Bilingual Teacher Shortage.   There is a critical shortage of bilingual teachers throughout the United States. This is particularly true in our large cities and in the southern and western states where large numbers of immigrant children have no or very limited English language skills. It is estimated that 5 percent of our stu-

One of the nation's most serious teacher shortages is in bilingual education.

dents have limited English proficiency and need the services of a bilingual teacher. It is also estimated that this problem will increase in the near future.

Global Perspectives: Overseas Teaching Opportunities. The U.S. Department of Defense operates a school system for the children of American men and women in the armed services abroad. This school system, the United States Dependents School, is one of our nation's largest school systems, enrolling about 130,000 students in over 260 schools in twenty-three countries. The approximately 7,500 teachers in this system come from every state in the union. Although not officially organized as an international education program, these U.S. Dependents Schools widen the chance for citizens of the United States and other nations to exchange cultural experiences. Opportunities for Americans to teach abroad are increasing. Demands for teachers in other nations, especially for English teachers, have heightened foreign employment. Recruiters from foreign countries have visited many college and university campuses, hoping to hire teachers from the United States.

A concise summary of opportunities for studying or teaching abroad can be found in *Educational and Cultural Exchange Opportunities,* a booklet published by the U.S. Department of State.[3]

Our Largest School Districts. New York City has the largest school district in the United States, enrolling nearly 10,000,000 students and employing about 52,000 full-time equivalent teachers. Other extremely large school districts in the United States are Puerto Rico, Los Angeles, Chicago, Dade County in Florida, Houston, Philadelphia, and Detroit. Needless to say, these large school districts

| TABLE 2.1 | Relative Demand by Teaching Area |

Teaching Fields with Considerable Shortage (5.00–4.25)	
Speech Pathology	4.48
Bilingual Education	4.45
Special Education—Multiple Handicap	4.34
Special Education—Visually Impaired	4.30
Special Educaion—Behavioral Disorders	4.28
Teaching Fields with Some Shortage (4.24–3.45)	
Special Education—Hearing Impaired	4.23
Special Education—Physically Impaired	4.23
Special Education—Mentally Handicapped	4.20
Special Education—Learning Disability	4.17
Audiology	4.13
Science—Physics	3.99
Languages—Japanese	3.89
English as a Second Language	3.88
Science—Chemistry	3.82
Languages—Spanish	3.73
Psychologist (School)	3.71
Mathematics	3.62
Science—Earth/Physical	3.62
Computer Science Education	3.56
Library Science	3.50
Teaching Fields with Balanced Supply and Demand (3.44–2.65)	
Science—General	3.43
Technology/Industrial Arts	3.43
Science—Biology	3.39

Social Worker (School)	3.34
Gifted/Talented Education	3.33
Counselor Education	3.23
Agriculture	3.20
Languages—French	3.15
Reading	3.15
Home Economics	3.14
Languages—German	3.12
Languages—Classics	3.05
Music—Instrumental	2.95
Music—Vocal	2.88
Teaching Fields with Some Surplus (2.64–1.85)	
Journalism	2.64
Speech/Drama/Theatre	2.56
English/Language Arts	2.51
Business Education	2.49
Driver Education	2.43
Elementary—Pre-Kindergarten	2.43
Dance Education	2.38
Art/Visual	2.36
Elementary—Intermediate	2.27
Elementary—Kindergarten	2.24
Elementary–Primary	2.05
Health Education	2.02
Physical Education	1.89
Teaching Fields with Considerable Surplus (1.84–1.00)	
Social Sciences/Studies	1.78

Source: The Job Search Handbook for Educators, 1995. Evanston, IL: Association for School, College and University Staffing, Inc. 1995, 11.

hire a great many new teachers each year. Furthermore, many of the best teachers' salaries are found in these school districts. Students looking forward to teaching careers should seriously consider large urban schools. Table 2.1 summarizes the current relative demand in the United States for teachers by teaching areas.

Teacher Salaries and Fringe Benefits

Just as many factors affect the supply of and demand for teachers, so do various factors determine educators' salary packages. Teachers' salaries, for instance, vary a great deal from one school district to another. This section discusses the variables affecting teacher salaries and fringe benefits.

Improving Salaries and Fringe Benefits

There is good news and bad news about salaries and fringe benefits for educators. The good news is that salaries have improved considerably in recent years and are projected to improve even more in the near future. The bad news is that teachers are still not paid as well as they should be.

Average Teachers' Salaries. Teachers' salaries vary considerably from state to state and from school district to school district. Table 2.2 shows the average teachers' salaries in each region of the United States.

Salary Schedules and Annual Increments. Each board of education is an agent of the state and therefore empowered to set salary levels for employees of the school district it governs. Each school system usually has a **salary schedule** that outlines the minimum and maximum salary for several levels of study

TABLE 2.2   Average Teachers' Salaries

		Elementary/Secondary		Special Education	
		Bachelors	Masters	Bachelors	Masters
Northwest	1991–1992	20,187	23,480	20,912	24,290
	1992–1993	20,196	23,266	20,048	23,671
	1993–1994	20,387	23,857	*	*
West	1991–1992	24,261	25,700	23,878	26,812
	1992–1993	24,447	26,484	24,679	27,137
	1993–1994	24,801	27,495	*	*
Rocky Mountains	1991–1992	18,528	24,087	20,017	23,775
	1992–1993	19,604	23,192	19,785	23,192
	1993–1994	20,624	22,640	*	*
Great Plains and Midwest	1991–1992	19,297	22,235	19,575	22,309
	1992–1993	20,068	23,073	20,630	23,333
	1993–1994	19,898	22,679	*	*
South Central	1991–1992	20,005	20,686	19,511	21,632
	1992–1993	20,401	21,890	20,871	22,525
	1993–1994	20,525	22,849	*	*
Southeast	1991–1992	20,083	22,361	20,483	22,785
	1992–1993	20,220	22,991	21,142	23,804
	1993–1994	21,310	24,116	*	*
Great Lakes	1991–1992	20,077	23,791	20,583	23,889
	1992–1993	21,093	24,630	21,811	25,296
	1993–1994	21,903	26,267	*	*
Middle Atlantic	1991–1992	22,235	25,426	23,228	25,972
	1992–1993	23,751	27,199	25,483	28,712
	1993–1994	24,157	27,335	*	*
Northeast	1991–1992	21,416	23,772	22,350	24,444
	1992–1993	21,022	24,718	21,067	24,632
	1993–1994	22,677	26,724	*	*
Alaska	1991–1992	30,000	34,000	30,000	34,000
	1992–1993	30,000	40,000	30,000	40,000
	1993–1994	30,540	36,486	*	*
Hawaii	1991–1992	25,100	26,990	25,100	26,990
	1992–1993	25,100	26,990	25,100	26,990
	1993–1994	25,033	27,663	*	*

*Data unavailable.
From data supplied by survey respondents. In some instances, the averages are based on limited input, and total reliability is not assured.

Source: The Job Search Handbook for Educators, 1995. Evanston, IL: Association for School, College and Univesity Staffing, Inc. 1995, 11.

beyond the bachelor's degree and for each year of teaching experience. For example, a beginning teacher with a bachelor's degree may be paid $20,000, one with a master's degree may be paid $25,000, and a beginning teacher with a master's degree and 30 additional semester hours of graduate study may be paid $30,000.

Teachers with less than a master's degree may be granted year-to-year increases for ten years; teachers with preparation beyond a master's degree may be granted **annual increments** for up to seventeen years. Therefore, teachers are rewarded both for a maximum number of years of experience and for additional education beyond the bachelor's degree. Teachers who have reached the maximum experience level for their particular education do not receive additional raises except when all the salaries listed in the salary schedule are revised upward.

Teachers' Salaries and Inflation.   The overall average teacher's salary is now approximately $36,000 per year. While this figure may sound good to a beginning teacher, experienced educators feel that their purchasing power has remained relatively unchanged over the years. Figure 2.4 shows the average salary paid teachers for the past twenty years—both in current dollars and in constant (1983) dollars. As you can see, while the average teacher salary has increased from $10,000 to about $35,000, inflation has caused the constant dollar average teacher salary to remain relatively unchanged during the past twenty years. Of course, one must remember that teacher salaries vary greatly from place to place; in some school districts, teacher salaries have in fact risen considerably over the past two decades—even when corrected for inflation.

Private School Salaries.   The need for private school teachers, preprimary through grade 12, will soon reach 400,000 in the United States. Thus, approximately one out of every seven teachers in the United States at the preprimary through twelfth-grade level is teaching in a private school. Many new teachers are

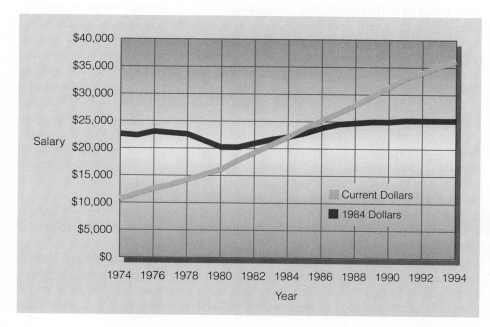

FIGURE 2.4

Average Salary Paid Teachers

(*Source:* National Education Association, 1994. 1993–94 Estimates of School Statistics, Washington, DC: NEA. Used with permission.)

PROFESSIONAL DILEMMA

Will You Be Able to Pay Your Bills on a Teacher's Salary?

A common professional dilemma among teachers is wanting to teach, but not being able to pay the bills. The issue of whether our teachers are adequately paid is prominent in school referenda and debates over various educational bills in state legislatures throughout the nation. Obviously, people who are unemployed, or qualify for welfare programs, find it difficult to believe that teachers are underpaid. Like-wise, many retired people who are living on fixed incomes, or those who have no direct, vested interest (i.e., children), typically feel that teachers, who on the average throughout the United States make over $30,000 per year, are adequately paid. Others point out that teachers typically work only ten months a year, which makes their annual salary somewhat misleading. Add to this the feeling among many that good teachers should be better paid and poor teachers are overpaid—even though there is no conclusive evidence that better pay necessarily means better teaching.

Those who argue that teachers are not adequately paid point out that our children's and nation's future is dependent on the success of our schools. They go on to point out that you tend to "get what you pay for,"

hired each year to teach in private schools throughout the country. While private schools are not usually required by law to hire fully certified teachers, increasingly they are attempting to do so, and most private school teachers are fully certified.

Teachers' salaries in private schools are generally somewhat lower than those in public schools. This lower salary level is due largely to the fact that a high percentage of private schools are religious and, of course, are not tax-supported.

Students who are now enrolled in teacher education programs should keep in mind that private schools represent another career option and should become familiar with these important educational institutions.

Merit Pay–Differential Pay. School systems in a number of states are considering various forms of **differential pay** as the means to reward the best teachers for teaching excellence and to address shortages in certain disciplines. The teacher unions have historically opposed incentive plans, claiming that they are often subject to the opinions of administrators, include questionable criteria for judging teaching excellence, and cause morale problems among teachers. However, many of the best teachers realize that the typical salary schedule rewards all teachers equally regardless of their effectiveness in the classroom, and these teachers may support the merit concept as a possible way to provide a differential for exceptional teaching above the provisions of the salary schedule. Previous limited attempts to utilize merit pay plans have not proven worthwhile, but basing teachers' salaries on some form of evaluation seems plausible. It is likely that more merit plans will be developed and implemented in the future.

In any case, the need for schools to provide additional incentive pay to attract top-notch teachers to the critical shortage areas seems without question. In private industry, additional pay is always used as a mechanism for attracting employees to fill critical needs. For example, though the computer science field is relatively new, the demand is relatively strong. Consequently, beginning salaries for graduates with a bachelor's degree in computer science have been high. If the need for computer science graduates declines, so will the amounts paid to attract those employees.

and that higher teacher salaries would attract our most talented young people into the teaching profession. These proponents of higher teacher salaries believe that a typical teacher's work load is very heavy and stressful—much more so than their counterparts in most other professions—and therefore justifies a higher salary. Many feel that it is more cost-effective to spend money educating children in our schools than it is to fight crime, pay for welfare, and support correctional systems and other adult programs that purportedly result from unsuccessful or ineffectual schooling.

As you prepare for your educational career, you should think realistically about this professional dilemma. Some teachers find it difficult to remain dedi-

cated in the face of inadequate salaries. You may face this dilemma during your career.

- Should teacher pay be based on individual ability?
- What is your image of teaching as a profession? Do you place teaching in the same professional category as medicine and law? Why or why not?
- How might teachers overcome the dilemma of inadequate pay?
- How do teachers justify working hard for low pay? Or do they?
- To what degree are you determined to teach in spite of the possibility of low or inadequate pay?

Fringe Benefits, Extra Pay, and Moonlighting

While a teacher's salary is extremely important, so are the fringe benefits and any opportunities to make additional income. This section of the book will help you better understand the more common fringe benefits, extra pay, and moonlighting opportunities available to teachers.

Fringe Benefits for Teachers. Almost all full-time teachers receive fringe benefits that, when added to their basic salary, constitute their total compensation package. When you pursue your first teaching position, you will want to inquire about the fringe benefits as well as the basic salary. While the salary is usually of first concern to a teacher, the fringe benefits are equally important over the long term. These **fringe benefits** vary from school to school but frequently include some type of insurance benefits—fairly complete hospitalization insurance, medical/surgical coverage, and major medical insurance. Somewhat less frequently, a teacher's medical insurance also includes dental care and prescription drugs; least frequently, it includes coverage of eyeglasses and other types of less common medical services. It is not unusual for a teacher's insurance benefits to include some type of group life insurance, although the amount can vary tremendously from school to school.

Many school districts also provide some type of professional liability insurance for their teachers. In fact, some states require by law that all school districts do so, presumably because parents could conceivably bring a liability lawsuit against the state, which is ultimately responsible for public education.

It is probably safe to say that all full-time public school teachers who are employed under regular continuing contracts also receive some type of retirement benefits as part of their total compensation package. As evidence of the variation in these retirement benefits, in some states, teachers receive a combination of state teacher retirement and social security retirement. In other states, a teacher's retirement may depend totally on a state program and be divorced entirely from our federal social security retirement system. It is usually possible for teachers who

Relevant Research

Teachers Welcome Constructive Suggestions about Their Work, But Rarely Receive Them

Research shows that when supervisors provide constructive feedback to teachers on specific skills, they help teachers become more effective and improve teacher morale. Unfortunately, a typical supervisor visit to a teacher's classroom takes place only once or twice a year and provides only general comments about the teacher's performance. This relative lack of specific supervision contributes to low morale, teacher absenteeism, and high faculty turnover. Supervision that strengthens instruction and improves teacher morale has these elements:

- agreement between supervisor and teacher on the specific skills and practices that characterize effective teaching
- frequent observation by the supervisor to see if the teacher is using these skills and practices
- a meeting between supervisor and teacher to discuss the supervisor's impressions
- agreement by the supervisor and teacher on areas for improvement
- a specific plan for improvement, jointly constructed by teacher and supervisor

We strongly encourage you to seek supervision as a beginning teacher. It will help you improve as a teacher, and may even eventually help lead to tenure and a higher salary.

Bird, T., and Little, J. S. "Instructional Leadership in Eight Secondary Schools," Final Report to the National Institute of Education. Boulder, CO: Center for Action Research, 1985, ERIC Document No. ED 263694.

Felding, G. S., and Schalock, H. S. *Promoting the Professional Development of Teachers and Administrators.* Eugene, OR: ERIC Clearinghouse on Educational Management, 1985.

Natriello, G. "Teacher's Perceptions of the Frequency of Evaluation and Assessments of Their Effort and Effectiveness," *American Educational Research Journal 21* (3) (1984): 579–595.

Source: What Works: Research About Teaching and Learning. Washington, DC: U.S. Department of Education, 1987, 68.

move from state to state to transfer their retirement benefits to the state in which they ultimately retire. In any event, a teacher's retirement program is an extremely important part of the total compensation package and needs to be well understood by everyone entering the profession.

Some schools also provide special leave provisions for their teachers, perhaps the most common being related to personal illness. Other types of leave provisions deal with family illness, emergency, and death. Another common type of leave provision deals with professional development, and, again, the conditions under which professional development leaves are granted vary considerably from school to school. Because of the high cost, relatively few public school systems allow teachers sabbatical leaves with pay in order to improve themselves professionally. This feature is much more common in colleges and universities than at the public elementary and secondary school level.

Moonlighting. A relatively large number of public school teachers **moonlight,** or hold a second job, according to a recent study by the National Center for Educational Statistics. Figure 2.5 shows some interesting data on this subject. As you can see, male teachers are more likely to moonlight than female teachers, and white, non-Hispanic teachers are more likely to moonlight than minority teachers.

Unfortunately, many moonlighting teachers indicate that they are forced to hold a second job because of relatively low salaries in the teaching profession. This is yet another factor that should be taken into account when considering a teaching career.

Getting Certified and Employed

It is never too early to start thinking about becoming certified and finding a job. There are issues about teacher certification and employment that you should know and start thinking about no matter where you are in your teacher education program. We will very briefly explore some of these topics in this section.

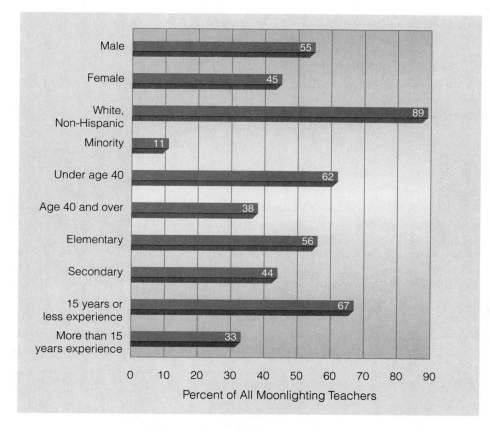

FIGURE 2.5

Moonlighting Teachers

(*Source:* Education Information Branch, Office of Educational Research and Improvement. Washington, DC: Room 300, 555 New Jersey Avenue NW, Washington, DC 20208.

Certification Requirements

All teachers must obtain an official teaching certificate before they can legally teach in our public schools. These certificates must then be periodically registered and renewed in most states.

A State Function. Each state determines the requirements for **teacher certification** and, understandably, they vary considerably from state to state. You undoubtedly will hear a good deal about the certification requirement in the state in which you are now going to school. However, you may wish to ask more specific questions regarding the certification options available to you. You may also wish to contact the certification offices in other states in which you may be interested in working sometime in the future. Appendix 2.1 on page 49 provides the addresses and phone numbers of all the state teacher certification offices throughout the United States. You should also be aware that states change their teacher certification requirements and even create new teaching certificates from time to time. Furthermore, certification requirements are not easy to understand, since they are filled with technicalities. You should very carefully explore and understand the requirements for any certificates that you will need to teach what you want to teach, where you want to teach it.

Alternative Certification for School Teachers.   A recent move in some states urges the development of alternative certification opportunities for people who would like to become school teachers. These alternative routes to certification have come under considerable criticism from the teacher education establishment. In some states a rather radical approach to alternative certification has been taken in which anyone with a bachelor's degree in just about any major may begin teaching with some type of provisional certificate. In other states, the alternative certification opportunity is aimed more at facilitating mid-career changes from other professions, such as business or the military, into the teaching profession. Often, such alternative certification grants career experience credits for work done in other professions.

Teacher Certification Examinations.   Most states now require some type of initial examination as a part of the teacher certification process. Many states require the National Teacher Examination (NTE), which consists of a series of separate tests aimed at measuring general knowledge, communication skills, and professional knowledge. The NTE has recently undergone major revision, and now consists of the following three stages:

Stage 1:   Consists of a basic skills examination designed to assess the reading, writing, and mathematical skills needed by beginning teachers. These tests will be accompanied by computer diagnostic and practice instructional modules to help prospective teachers discover and remediate any basic skills weaknesses they may have.

Stage 2:   Is designed to measure professional education and subject matter knowledge. These examinations may vary somewhat from state to state to allow some flexibility. Newer testing techniques such as computer simulations and interactive video disks may be used in these examinations.

Stage 3:   This stage consists of performance-based assessment devices aimed at assessing teaching skills such as planning for instruction, teaching lessons, classroom management, instructional effectiveness, and assessing student learning. These assessment sessions include observations of the teacher at work in the classroom.

National Implications.   While teacher certification has historically been regulated by each state, there is increasing discussion about moving to a national teaching certificate that would presumably be recognized in all states. While a number of states now have certification reciprocity agreements whereby teachers can move without too much trouble from one state to another, a national certificate has always been appealing to teachers since it would increase their mobility. Chapter 19 will provide you with more information about some of the possible future developments concerning teacher certification.

   As a future teacher, once you have determined the required certification, you should then systematically begin preparing to pass the required tests. This textbook and its ancillary materials will be helpful to you in passing any certification test that you may be required to take.

Searching for a Teaching Job

Teacher education students should start thinking about seeking employment very early in their college career. We highly recommend that if you have not already

CASE STUDY **MAXIMIZING JOB PROSPECTS**

John Anderson will graduate from his teacher education program soon, and he is searching for a teaching position, preferably in a large urban school. He is a Caucasian from a small-town, middle-class family, and has heard that urban schools prefer to hire experienced minority teachers. Even so, he is determined to teach culturally diverse students in a large city school, so he is doing his best to prepare for such a position. He studied urban educational problems, and has decided he would like to accept the challenge of teaching in a large city school system, even though he did not do his student teaching in such a setting.

John read a list of ten characteristics that schools look for when hiring new teachers,[*] and has attempted to measure his own abilities against this list. These characteristics include:

1. The ability to make a difference in a student's life
2. A variety of life experiences
3. Classroom management experience
4. Student teaching experiences
5. Academic preparation
6. Personal appearance
7. A sense of humor
8. Adaptability
9. Maturity
10. Involvement

John honestly believes he stacks up fairly well against this list, but doesn't know how to demonstrate all his abilities to hiring officials, or what the criteria for measuring them might be. For instance, how does one demonstrate "the ability to make a difference in a student's life," or "adaptability"? He thought about editing a videotape of his best student teaching lessons, and perhaps developing a portfolio of some of his best college work for submission along with his credentials, but he isn't sure what they should contain; anyway, he has heard that many hiring officials do not take the time to really look at such material. He wishes he could think of a really good way to get the attention of the hiring officials.

1. If you were a hiring official, how would you select the best teachers?
2. Are schools justified in giving preference to minority teachers? Why or why not?
3. How and in what ways might reviewing videotapes and portfolios help hiring officials select the best teachers?
4. What advice do you have for John?
5. How might one demonstrate the ten characteristics that schools look for when hiring new teachers?
6. How will you attempt to maximize your job prospects?

[*]Gene Parker, "Characteristics Which School Systems Value." *1994 ASCUS Annual.* Evanston, IL: Association for School, College and University Staffing, Inc., 1994, 4.

---

done so, you obtain a copy of the most recent Association for School, College and University Staffing (ASCUS) annual *Job Search Handbook for Educators* from your job placement office or by writing to ASCUS, 1600 Dodge Avenue S-330, Evanston, IL 60201-3451. This handbook makes many good suggestions for college students who will eventually be seeking jobs as teachers. It points out the importance of having good grades and an excellent variety of courses that will help to make you more employable upon graduation. It also contains hints for preparing your résumé, cover letters, and letters of inquiry, and provides excellent practical suggestions for improving your interviewing techniques. This handbook also provides up-to-date information on teacher supply and demand for the various fields within the teaching profession.

Maximizing Your Job Prospects. The most important job-hunting hint for any teacher education student is to study hard throughout college and get the best possible grades in all college classes. Also, select majors and minors that offer the most employment options. By careful planning, college students can graduate qualified to teach in a variety of fields and with more than one certificate.

All teacher education students should also seize every opportunity to gain on-the-job experience by working with children. Many volunteer programs are available in most geographical areas through schools, churches, synagogues, and various agencies that involve working with children. There are also many paid job opportunities such as summer recreation programs, youth camps, and teacher aide programs that provide opportunities to work with youths. The more experience teacher education students have in working with young people, the more they will learn about them.

The Mechanics of a Job Search. As teacher education students approach graduation, they also need to receive job-hunting hints about developing job placement files, writing letters of application, and developing good interview techniques. Fortunately, most teacher education programs and college job placement offices automatically provide such job-hunting hints. Appendix 2.2 on page 52 provides you with a job search timetable checklist that should help you get started on your search for a teaching position.

Summary and Implications

Total school enrollment is projected to increase in the 1990s, which could result in a boom that surpasses the peak levels of the early 1970s. Consequently, a teacher shortage is a distinct possibility in the late 1990s unless more college students enroll in teacher preparation programs.

The total number of elementary and secondary teachers in the United States increased from 1970 through 1980. During this period, additional teachers were readily available, and many were hired in order to decrease the pupil-teacher ratios in previously overcrowded classrooms. Consequently, the number of elementary school teachers is now on the rise. However, the number of secondary school teachers will continue to decrease in the 1990s as previous elementary school enrollment declines affect the secondary student population. At the same time, shortages in selected discipline areas will become more pronounced in response to the emphasis on given areas of the secondary curriculum.

Opportunities for Americans to teach abroad are increasing. The U.S. Department of Defense operates a school system for the children of American men and women in the services abroad. Teacher shortages in other nations also enhance opportunities for foreign employment.

Some school districts are attempting to devise salary incentive plans that reward the best teachers with additional merit pay. Another incentive would provide higher salaries for teachers in areas of short supply, such as special education. Although teachers' unions generally oppose such incentive plans, teachers realize that their salary schedules reward everyone equally regardless of effectiveness in the classroom. The general public and school boards tend to favor merit pay for the best teachers and extra stipends to attract well-qualified teachers in critical shortage areas. The 1990s may see more use of salary incentive plans than ever before.

More teachers will be needed in the 1990s than during the previous decade. To satisfy the clamor for improving the quality of education, these teachers will also need to be better prepared than ever before. Furthermore, teachers' salaries will be reviewed to determine ways to upgrade financial rewards for those prepared to teach in the critical shortage disciplines and for those determined to be most effective in the classroom. Teacher organizations and teacher preparation schools are challenged to upgrade the competency levels of certified teachers now on the job and of students entering teacher preparation programs.

This chapter concluded with a number of suggestions for obtaining a teaching position, including advice on this topic from the Association for School, College and University Staffing (ASCUS), an organization that publishes an annual job-search handbook for educators.

Discussion Questions

1. Teacher shortages are reported in the areas of special education, chemistry, mathematics, and physics. Why do shortages exist in some subjects?

2. Discuss the pros and cons of the early-retirement incentive plans offered by some school districts. In your response, explain your beliefs about the value of young teachers and older teachers in a school.

3. Many young teachers work at a second job to increase their yearly income. How do you feel about teachers holding additional jobs?

4. How can colleges and departments of education better prepare beginning teachers so that their chances of employment in a tight job market will be enhanced?

5. What should be done to meet demands for teachers in areas where there are shortages?

Journal/Portfolio Development

1. Develop a portfolio (any good system for safely and neatly keeping samples of your work) and fill it with examples of your best work in all your teacher education courses. This portfolio may eventually help you get the job you want.

2. Find a way to videotape your work in the schools. Edit these videotapes into short segments that demonstrate your skills as a teacher. Many hiring officials will be interested in seeing your tapes. Be prepared to answer questions about your performance on the videotapes.

School-Based Experiences

1. The material contained in this chapter should be very practical for you. It provides you with up-to-date information on employment opportunities available to you in the field of education when you graduate. As you have an opportunity to work in the schools, talk with the educators there about job opportunities, fringe benefits, salary schedules, merit pay, retirement benefits, and any other topics related to employment opportunities for teachers that interest you.

2. Talk to educators about moonlighting they have done in the past or are doing now. Ask why they moonlight (you may be surprised by some of the responses). Ask if their schools ever suggested that teachers should not moonlight—particularly at certain times and/or in certain jobs. Think about moonlighting you may want or have to do some day.

Notes

1. *Education Week*, 8 February 1989, 6.
2. *Education at a Glance.* Organization for Economic Cooperation and Development, 2001 L Street NW, Washington, DC 20036.

3. *Education and Cultural Exchange Opportunities.* Washington, DC: U.S. Department of State, Bureau of Cultural Affairs, 1986.

Bibliography

The American Federation of Teachers collects and distributes data on salaries and demand for educators throughout each year.

A Job Search Handbook for Educators. Published annually by the Association for School, College and University Staffing (ASCUS), 1600 Dodge Avenue S-330, Evanston, IL 60201-3451.

Gutek, Gerald L. *American Education in a Global Society.* New York: Longman, 1993.

Johansen, John J., Johnson, James A., and Henniger, Michael. *American Education: An Introduction to Teaching.* Dubuque, IA: Wm. C. Brown, 1993.

Sarason, Seymour B. *Are You Thinking of Teaching?* San Francisco: Jossey-Bass, 1993.

The National Education Association periodically publishes and reports on teacher supply, demand, and salaries.

Teacher Supply/Demand. Annual reports of the Association of School, College and University Staffing (ASCUS), 1600 Dodge Avenue S-330, Evanston, IL 60201-3451.

Appendix 2.1

U.S. Teacher Certification Offices

A teaching certificate is valid only in the state for which it is issued, and certification and testing requirements are never static. Even the very best book or chart may be out of date as soon as it is published. If you are planning to move to another state, you should contact that state's certification office, as listed below. The number code following each entry indicates the types of testing which the state required at the time of publication. . . . The key to the codes may be found at the end of the state listings.

When you write or call the state certification office, indicate the type of certificate you are receiving from your current state, which national tests you have taken, and ask for application materials and procedures for obtaining certification in the new state. Another source of information about certification requirements will be the actual districts to which you apply.

ASCUS members—career service professionals and school personnel administrators are commited to helping each other's graduates move around the country, and even around the world. For instance, each year ASCUS publishes the *National Directory of Job and Career Fairs for Educators,* listing recruiting fairs in every state. Many of these fairs are open to all interested candidates. Check your career services office for this publication. . . .

The *ASCUS Directory of Public School Systems in the United States* lists every school district in the nation by state and city. Look for it in your career planning office. . . .

Alabama
Department of Education
Division of Professional Service
5108 Gordon Persons Bldg.
50 North Ripley Street
Montgomery 36130–3901,
   205–242–9960

Alaska
Department of Education
Teacher Education and
   Certification
801 W. 10th Street, Suite 200
Juneau 99801–1894, 907–465–2031
   or 2065

Arizona (1)
Teacher Certification Unit
Department of Education
1535 W. Jefferson, Room 126
P.O. Box 85002
Phoenix 85007, 602–542–4368

Arkansas (3)
Teacher Education and Certification
Department of Education
#4 Capitol Mall, Rooms 106B/107B
Little Rock 72201, 501–682–4342

California (2)
Commission on Teacher
   Credentialing
1812 9th Street
Sacramento 94244–7000,
   916–445–7254

Colorado (1)
Teacher Education
Department of Education
201 East Colfax Ave
Denver 80203, 303–866–6628

Connecticut (2)
Bureau of Certification and
   Accreditation
State Department of Education
P.O. Box 2219
Hartford 06145, 203–566–5201

Delaware (3)
Department of Public
   Instruction
Office of Certification
Townsend Building, P.O.
   Box 1402
Dover 19903, 302–736–4686

District of Columbia (3)
Division of Teacher Services
District of Columbia Public Schools
415 12th Street, N.W., Room 1013
Washington 20004–1994,
   202–724–4250

Florida (1)
Department of Teacher Certification
325 W. Gaines Street, Room 203
Tallahassee 32399–0400, 904–488–5724

Georgia (1)
Professional Standards Commission
1452 Twin Towers East
Atlanta 30334, 404–656–2406

Hawaii (3)
State Department of Education
Office of Personnel Services
P.O. Box 2360
Honolulu 96804, 808–586–3240

Idaho (3)
State Department of Education
Teacher Education and Certification
Len B. Jordan Office Building
Boise 83720, 208–334–3475

Illinois (1)
State Teacher Certification Board
100 North First Street
Springfield 62777, 217–782–2805

Indiana (3)
Professional Standards Board
Center for Professional Development
Room 229, State House
Indianapolis 46204–2798,
    317–232–9010

Iowa
Board of Educational Examiners
Practitional Preparation and Licensure
    Bureau
Grimes State Office Building
Des Moines 50319–0416,
    515–281–3245

Kansas (3)
State Department of Education
Certification Office
120 East 10th Avenue
Topeka 66612, 913–296–2288

Kentucky (3)
State Department of Education
Division of Certification
18th Floor, Capital Plaza Tower
500 Mero Street
Frankfort 40601, 502–564–4606

Louisiana (3)
State Department of Education
Bureau of Higher Education and Teacher
    Certification
P.O Box 94064
Baton Rouge 70804–9064,
    504–342–3490

Maine (3)
Department of Education
Division of Certification and Placement
State House Station 23
Augusta 04333, 207–289–5944

Maryland (3)
State Department of Education
Division of Certification and
    Accreditation
200 West Baltimore Street, 2595
Baltimore 21201–2595, 301–333–2142

Massachusetts
State Department of Education
Division of Educational Personnel
Teacher Certification
350 Malden Street
Quincy 02168, 617–388–3300

Michigan (1)
Teacher/Administrator Preparation and
    Certification Services
Bureau of Postsecondary Education
Michigan Department of Education
P.O. Box 30008
Lansing 48909, 517–373–3310

Minnesota (3)
State Department of Education
Personnel Licensing
Capitol Square Building
550 Cedar Street
St. Paul 55101, 612–296–2046

Mississippi (3)
State Department of Education
Division of Teacher Certification
P.O. Box 771
Jackson 39205, 601–359–3483

Missouri (3)
Teacher Certification Office
Department of Elementary & Secondary
    Education
P.O. Box 480
Jefferson City 65102, 314–751–3486

Montana (3)
Office of Public Instruction
Teacher Education and Certification
Capital Building
Helena 59620, 406–444–3150

Nebraska (3)
Department of Education
Teacher Education and Certification
301 Centennial Mall South, Box 94987
Lincoln 68509, 402–471–2496

Nevada (3)
Department of Education
State Mail Room
1850 E. Sahara
Las Vegas 89158, 702–486–6455

New Hampshire
State Department of Education
Bureau of Teacher Education and
    Professional Standards
State Office Park South
101 Pleasant Street
Concord 03301–3860, 603–271–2407

New Jersey (3)
Department of Education
Division of Teacher Preparation &
    Certification
225 West State Street, CN 500
Trenton 08625–0500, 609–984–1216

New Mexico (3)
State Department of Education
Professional Licensure Unit
Education Building
Santa Fe 87501–2786, 505–827–6587

New York (1)
State Department of Education
Teacher Education and Certification
Cultural Education Center, Room 5A11
Nelson A. Rockefeller Empire State Plaza
Albany 12230, 518–474–6440

North Carolina (3)
Department of Public Instruction
Certification Section
301 N. Wilmington Street
Raleigh 27601–2825, 919–733–3077

North Dakota
Department of Public Instruction
Teacher Certification
600 East Boulevard Avenue
Bismarck 58505, 701–224–2264

Ohio (3)
Department of Education
Division of Teacher Education &
    Certification
65 S. Front Street, Room 1012
Columbus 43266–0308, 614–466–3593

Oklahoma (1)
Department of Education
Hodge Education Building
2500 North Lincoln Boulevard, Room
    211
Oklahoma City 73105–4599,
    405–521–3337

Oregon (2)
Teacher Standards and Practices
    Commission
580 State Street, Room 203
Salem 97310, 503–378–3586

Pennsylvania (3)
State Department of Education
Bureau of Teacher Preparation and
    Certification
333 Market Street, 3rd Floor
Harrisburg 17126–0333, 717–787–2967

Puerto Rico (3)
Department of Education
Certification Office
Box 759
Hato Rey 00910, 011–809–758–4949

Rhode Island (3)
Department of Education
School and Teacher Accreditation
Roger Williams Building
22 Hayes Street
Providence 02908, 401-277-2675

South Carolina (3)
State Department of Education
The Office of Education Professions
Room 1015, Rutledge Building
Columbia 29201, 803-734-8466

South Dakota
Division of Education & Cultural
    Affairs
Office of Certification
Kneip Building
700 Governor's Drive
Pierre 57501-2291, 605-773-2553

Tennessee (3)
State Department of Education
Teacher Licensing & Career Ladder
    Certification
6th Floor, North Wing
Cordell Hull Building
Nashville 37243-0377, 615-741-1644

Texas (1)
State Education Agency
Educational Personnel Records
1701 North Congress Avenue
Austin 78701-1494, 512-463-8976

Utah
State Office of Education
Certification and Personnel
    Development
250 East 500 South
Salt Lake City 84111, 801-538-7741

Vermont
State Department of Education
Educational Licensing Service
120 State Street
Montpelier 05620, 802-828-2444

Virginia (1)
Department of Education
Office of Professional Licensure
P. O. Box 6Q
Richmond 23216-2060,
    804-225-2022

Washington
Professional Education and
    Certification Office
Superintendent of Public Instruction
P. O. Box 47200
Olympia 98504-7200,
    206-753-6773

West Virginia (1)
Department of Education
Office of Professional Education
Capitol Complex, Room B-337,
    Bldg. 6
Charleston 25305, 304-558-2703

Wisconsin (3)
Department of Public Instruction
Bureau of Teacher Education, Licensing
    and Placement
Teacher Certification
125 S. Webster Street, P.O. Box 7841
Madison 53707-7841, 608-266-1879

Wyoming
State Department of Education
Certification and Licensing Unit
Hathaway Building, 2300 Capital Drive
Cheyenne 82002-0050, 307-777-6261

St. Croix District (3)
Department of Education
Educational Personnel Services
2133 Hospital Street
St. Croix, Virgin Islands 00820,
    809-773-5844

St. Thomas/St. John District (3)
Personnel Services
Department of Education
44-46 Kongens Gade
St. Thomas, Virgin Islands 00802,
    809-774-0100, ext.216

**United States Department of Defense
Overseas Dependent Section** (3)
Certification Unit
4040 N. Fairfax Drive
Arlington, Virginia 22203-1634
703-696-3081

Key to State Codes for Testing Requirements

No Code No testing is required.
1   State requires successful completion of its own examination.
2   State requires successful completion of its own examination *plus* completion of
    one or more national tests.
3   State requires successful completion of one or more national tests. States set
    their own minimum scores.

A Note on National Testing: For many years, the Educational Testing Service (ETS) has
made available two widely used national tests. The National Teacher Examinations (NTE)
encompass testing in three general areas: general knowledge, communication skills and professional knowledge, as well as testing in more than 100 specific subject areas. The Pre-Pro-
fessional Skills Test (PPST) is used to measure competency in reading, writing and
mathematics.

Beginning in 1993, ETS began implementation of an entirely new teacher testing program: The Praxis Series: Professional Assessments for Beginning Teachers. The three parts of
the Praxis Series include assessment of skills, subjects and classroom performance. Many
states are currently making transitions to the Praxis Series, and we encourage all teacher candidates to contact individual state certification offices to determine exact testing requirements.

Source: The Job Search Handbook for Educators, 1995. Evanston, IL: Association for School, College
and University Staffing, Inc., 1995, 32-34.

Job Search Timetable Checklist

This checklist is designed to help graduating students who are seeking teaching positions make the best use of their time as they conduct job searches. We encourage you to use this checklist in conjunction with the services and resources available from your college or university placement office.

August/September *(12 months prior to employment)*	_____	Attend any applicable orientations/workshops offered by your college placement office.
	_____	Register with your college placement office and inquire about career services.
	_____	Begin to define career goals by determining the types, sizes, and geographic locations of school systems in which you have an interest.
October *(11 months prior to employment)*	_____	Begin to identify references and ask them to prepare letters of recommendation for your credential or placement files.
	_____	See a counselor at your college placement office to discuss your job-search plan.
November *(10 months prior to employment)*	_____	Check to see that you are properly registered at your college placement office.
	_____	Begin developing a résumé and a basic cover letter.
	_____	Begin networking by contacting friends, faculty members, etc., to inform them of your career plans. If possible, give them a copy of your résumé.
December/January *(8–9 months prior to employment)*	_____	Finalize your résumé and make arrangements for it to be reproduced. You may want to get some tips on résumé reproduction from your college placement office.
	_____	Attend any career planning and placement workshops designed for education majors.
	_____	Use the directories available at your college placement office to develop a list of school systems in which you have an interest.

	Contact school systems to request application materials.
_____	
_____	If applying to out-of-state school systems, contact the appropriate State Departments of Education to determine testing requirements. Addresses are listed in Appendix 2.1.

February
(7 months prior to employment)

_____ Check the status of your credential or placement file at your college placement office.

_____ Send completed applications to school systems, with a résumé and cover letter.

_____ Inquire about school systems which will be recruiting at your college placement office, and about the procedures for interviewing with them.

March/April
(5–6 months prior to employment)

_____ Research school systems with which you will be interviewing.

_____ Interview on campus and follow up with thank you letters.

_____ Continue to follow up by phone with school systems of interest.

_____ Begin monitoring the job vacancy listings available at your college placement office.

May/August
(1–4 months prior to employment)

_____ Just before graduation, check to be sure you are completely registered with your college placement office, and that your credential or placement file is in good order.

_____ Maintain communication with your network of contacts.

_____ Subscribe to your college placement office's job vacancy bulletin.

_____ Revise your résumé and cover letter if necessary.

_____ Interview off campus and follow up with thank you letters.

_____ If relocating away from campus, contact a college placement office in the area to which you are moving and inquire about available services.

_____ Continue to monitor job vacancy listings and apply when qualified and interested.

_____ Begin considering job offers. Ask for more time to consider offers, if necessary.

_____ Accept the best job offer. Inform those associated with your search of your acceptance.

Adapted from material originally prepared at Miami University of Ohio.

Source: The Job Search Handbook for Educators, 1995. Evanston, IL: Association for School, College and University Staffing, Inc., 1995, 18.

Chapter 2

3 Professional Organizations for Educators

Focus Questions

1 Do you think principals and other school workers should belong to the teachers' union? Why?

2 What do you know about labor unions? How are teacher unions similar? How are they different?

3 To what extent do you think teacher organizations should have political clout?

4 Do you know the name of the specialty studies and job-related associations that are available to teachers?

5 As an aspiring teacher, which professional associations are you joining now?

Key Terms and Concepts

American Federation of Teachers: A national teachers' organization that is primarily concerned with improving educational conditions and protecting teachers' rights.

National Education Association: The largest organization of educators; the NEA is concerned with the overall improvement of education and of the condition of educators.

Political action committees in teacher education: Various organizations that engage in political activities in support of the organizations' purposes or causes.

Professionalism and Unionism: A distinction that the NEA used in 1960 to claim that only an organization that stressed the professional aspects could represent teachers; hence a union would not be adequate, since it stressed organized labor.

Teacher power: A term that stresses organized teacher groups that lobby for improvements in education; the group embodiment of individual teacher empowerment.

World Confederation of Organizations of the Teaching Profession (WCOTP): An organization that aims to foster international understanding and goodwill, stressing peace, freedom, and respect for human dignity. Members are from approximately one hundred nations and include the AFT and the NEA.

One of the special aspects of becoming a teacher is the opportunity to join with and work along with many other well-educated and highly dedicated professionals. There are many types of professional organizations and associations that teachers can join. In most school districts, teachers are represented by their organization or union when it comes to setting the specifications for contracts and working conditions. Teachers can also join specialty associations that are dedicated to improving teaching and learning in relation to specific curricula and teaching processes. These associations include national, regional, and local-level chapters. They provide teachers with the opportunity to work with other teachers who have like concerns and interests and also enable teachers to participate in various professional leadership activities. Before the 1960s, most of these organizations and associations were small in terms of membership size and were not particularly influential. Since that time, however, organizations and associations have become major influences in terms of the development of national education policy; the determination of state policies, laws, and rules and regulations as they relate to schooling; and (at the local level) studying curriculum and negotiating labor contracts. At all of these levels, teachers are actively involved and are responsible participants as well as part of the membership that works with the resultant policy decisions and the curriculum products.

In the past thirty years, most teachers have been represented in their contract negotiations by one of the two major professional associations: the National Education Association (NEA) or the American Federation of Teachers (AFT). In either case, the typical arrangement is that the professional organization leadership works as a union and negotiates the contract and working conditions with the district. These negotiations normally take place through a dialog with the central school administration, especially the superintendent, and in the end are agreed to by the school board. Teachers usually consider the advice provided at the national level by the professional association in regard to teachers' rights, legislation favoring education, and the development of ethical codes for teacher conduct. Similarly, political involvement, promotion of education, and lobbying the legislature at the state level is normally led by the professional organizations. However, the strongest reason for an individual teacher to join a teachers' union/organization is the support for efforts at the local level. Local teachers' organizations provide representation to the school board on matters related to working conditions such as class size, salaries, and fringe benefits. Assistance to each teacher on grievance procedures and provisional legal services with due process rights gives teachers warranties against reprisals. All of these resources come with membership in the professional organization.

Teachers have plenty of opportunities to become involved in professional/specialty associations as well. These associations deal directly with design of curriculum, innovation in teaching, improving the instructional processes, and so forth. There are a number of specialty organizations that deal with targeted areas such as science teaching, mathematics teaching, English teaching, reading, middle school, and early childhood. These associations also have national, state, and local chapters. Unlike their professional organization counterparts, these associations do not deal directly with work conditions and contracts. Instead, they focus on the design of curriculum, the optimal conditions for the delivery of effective instruction, staff development and training experiences for teachers, and efforts to influence the shape of state and national policy as it relates to the particular specialty area. Interestingly, today, teacher unionism and professionalism are not mutually exclusive. As will be described later in this chapter, both of the major professional organizations, NEA and AFT, have full-time professional staffs and a number of major initiatives that are targeted toward restructuring of schools, examining alternative assessment, empowering teachers as leaders, and other commitments that do not deal with contract and work conditions per se, but instead deal with the design of the teaching and learning processes and how to create more effective teachers in the schooling context. Clearly, teachers profit from membership and participation in both professional organizations and professional/specialty associations. In this chapter, each of these types of professional organizations will be described briefly and a sampling of their activities will be presented.

Teacher Unions

In the past thirty years, teachers have joined local, regional, and national organizations as a bargaining force. In the early years of this effort, the organizations behaved very much as any other type of labor union, which caused a great deal of concern among many educators who thought of themselves as professionals. However, in order to improve the working conditions for teachers, many felt that the only recourse was to become formally organized and to engage in collective bargaining.

Like labor unions, teachers have often used collective bargaining to improve working conditions.

National Education Association (NEA)

The **National Education Association (NEA)** is by far the largest teachers' organization, with over two million members, including teachers, administrators, clerical and custodial employees, and other school personnel. The NEA has its national headquarters in Washington, DC. The basic documents for the governance of the NEA are the Constitution of the National Education Association of the United States and the Bylaws of the National Education Association of the United States.

The NEA Representative Assembly: A Legislative and Policymaking Body. The Representative Assembly is the primary legislative and policymaking body of the NEA. The executive officers are the president, vice-president, and secretary-treasurer, who are elected by the Representative Assembly and are subject to the policies established by the Representative Assembly, board of directors, and executive committee. An executive director has the primary responsibility for implementing the policies of the association and is responsible to the executive committee. Standing committees may be established and discontinued by the Representative Assembly, the board of directors, or the executive committee for the purpose of accomplishing a specific task within a limited period of time.[1]

NEA: Basic Purpose and Chronology. The basic purposes of the NEA, as stated in its charter, are to elevate the character and advance the interests of the profession of teaching and to promote education in the United States. Figure 3.1

1857

The National Teachers' Association

Organized August 26, 1857, in Philadelphia, Pennsylvania.

Purpose　*To elevate the character and advance the interests of the profession of teaching and to promote the cause of popular education in the United States.* (The word *popular* was dropped in the 1907 Act of Incorporation.)

The name of the Association was changed at Cleveland, Ohio, on August 15, 1870, to the National Educational Association.

1870–1907

National Educational Association

Incorporated under the laws of the District of Columbia, February 24, 1886, under the name National Education Association, which was changed to National Educational Association, by certificate filed November 6, 1886.

1907–Present

National Education Association of the United States

Incorporated under a special Act of Congress, approved June 30, 1906, to succeed the National Educational Association. The Charter was accepted and Bylaws were adopted at the Fiftieth Anniversary Convention held July 10, 1907, at Los Angeles, California.

FIGURE 3.1

National Education Association 1857–Present

(*Source: NEA Handbook, 1988–89* (Washington DC: National Education Association, 1988), p. 149. Reprinted by permission.)

traces the organizational chronology of the NEA from its founding in 1857 as the National Teachers' Association (NTA). In 1870 the NTA united with the National Association of School Superintendents, organized in 1865, and the American Normal School Association, organized in 1858, to form the National Education Association. The organization was incorporated in 1886 in the District of Columbia as the National Education Association and was chartered in 1906 by act of Congress. The charter was officially adopted at the association's annual meeting of 1907, with the name "National Educational Association of the United States." The original statement of purpose of the NTA remains unchanged in the present NEA charter. NEA membership reached an all-time high of almost 1.9 million in 1976, stabilized at over 1.6 million in the early 1980s, and has now grown to over two million.

NEA Professional Initiatives

Given its long history of advocacy of teaching as a profession, it should not be surprising to learn that the National Education Association also has a wide portfolio of professional initiatives that are designed to introduce teachers to best practices, to facilitate teacher leadership, and to empower the restructuring of schools. The

NEA has organized a division of Educational Policy and Professional Practice, which consists of a number of areas: student assessment and accountability; professional preparation, state licensure, and certification; and governance and member activities. Each of these programs has an array of activities and initiatives to further advance teacher professionalism. In addition there is the NEA National Center for Innovation, which has a series of programs that are aimed toward the preparation of teachers and include experimental efforts in exemplary programs for schools and restructuring efforts. A sampling of the NEA professional initiatives includes the following.

Teacher TV. In a joint effort with the Learning Channel, a visionary television program is offered each Sunday for and about teachers. It is a magazine-style show that is shot on location at schools across the country and features teachers, schools, and communities that are challenging the educational status quo. Segments of the program include new education trends, teacher resources, practical tips and teaching strategies, and exploration of controversial issues.

Doubts and Certainties. *Doubts and Certainties* is a newsletter that is published bimonthly by the NEA for those who are interested in transforming schools. The newsletter continually presents descriptions of schools that engage in experimental activities. It runs feature articles that raise questions challenging conventional ways of thinking. The newsletter also includes paragraph reports from various sites around the country that are engaged in major transforming efforts. *Doubts and Certainties* also serves as a communication mechanism with the NEA School Renewal Network, which is a set of schools engaged in major experimental efforts to renew schooling.

NEA National Center for Innovation. The NEA National Center for Innovation is organized to advance the reform of public schools. It focuses on developing leadership through establishing learning communities and engaging, designing, and establishing the support of the experimental school renewal projects. The National Center includes exemplary programs in schools (Excellence in Action programs), school-based restructuring (The Mastery Learning Consortium), district-based restructuring (The Learning Laboratories Initiative), teacher preparation reform (The Teacher Education Initiative), and the use of technology and networking. There are four themes that unify all of these projects: (1) Teacher educational leaders: provisions for leadership activities; (2) National Vision: Local educational experimentation to meet national goals; (3) Restructuring: turning a fashionable idea into substantive change; and (4) Research-based risk-taking yields additional research.

The National Education Association is one of the major organizations overseeing and promoting the profession of teaching in the United States.

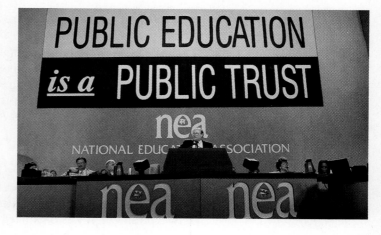

Topical Publications and Reports. The NEA provides to its membership an array of reports on critical issues and topics of interest to its members. Samples of recent reports

PREAMBLE

The educator, believing in the worth and dignity of each human being, recognizes the supreme importance of the pursuit of truth, devotion to excellence, and the nurture of democratic principles. Essential to these goals is the protection of freedom to learn and to teach and the guarantee of equal educational opportunity for all. The educator accepts the responsibility to adhere to the highest ethical standards.

The educator recognizes the magnitude of the responsibility inherent in the teaching process. The desire for the respect and confidence of one's colleagues, of students, of parents, and of the members of the community provides the incentive to attain and maintain the highest possible degree of ethical conduct. *The Code of Ethics of the Education Profession* indicates the aspiration of all educators and provides standards by which to judge conduct.

The remedies specified by the NEA and/or its affiliates for the violation of any provision of this Code shall be exclusive and no such provision shall be enforceable in any form other than one specifically designated by the NEA or its affiliates.

PRINCIPLE I

Commitment to the Student

The educator strives to help each student realize his or her potential as a worthy and effective member of society. The educator therefore works to stimulate the spirit of inquiry, the acquisition of knowledge and understanding, and the thoughtful formulation of worthy goals.

In fulfillment of the obligation to the student, the educator:

1. Shall not unreasonably restrain the student from independent action in the pursuit of learning.

2. Shall not unreasonably deny the student access to varying points of view.

3. Shall not deliberately suppress or distort subject matter relevant to the student's progress.

4. Shall make reasonable effort to protect the students from conditions harmful to learning or to health and safety.

5. Shall not intentionally expose the student to embarrassment or disparagement.

6. Shall not on the basis of race, color, creed, sex, national origin, marital status, political or religious beliefs, family, social or cultural background, or sexual orientation unfairly:
   a) Exclude any student from participation in any program.
   b) Deny benefits to any student.
   c) Grant any advantage to any student.

7. Shall not use professional relationships with students for private advantage.

8. Shall not disclose information about students obtained in the course of professional service, unless disclosure serves a compelling professional purpose or is required by law.

(Continued)

Code of Ethics of the Education Profession

(*Source:* The National Education Association, Washington, DC.)

include: Early Childhood Education in the Public Schools, Academic Tracking, and Student Testing. Each of these reports is available to members and can be of great help to school and district committees as they consider how to address current issues and concerns. Figure 3.2 presents the NEA's *Code of Ethics of the Education Profession.*

American Federation of Teachers (AFT)

The second largest teachers' union is called the **American Federation of Teachers (AFT).** The AFT, with national headquarters located in Washington, DC, is headed by a president. It was organized on April 15, 1916, and became affiliated with

PRINCIPLE II

Commitment to the Profession

The education profession is vested by the public with a trust and responsibility requiring the highest ideals of professional service.

In the belief that the quality of the services of the education profession directly influences the nation and its citizens, the educator shall exert every effort to raise professional standards, to promote a climate that encourages the exercise of professional judgment, to achieve conditions which attract persons worthy of the trust to careers in education, and to assist in preventing the practice of the profession by unqualified persons. In fulfillment of the obligation to the profession, the educator:

1. Shall not in an application for a professional position deliberately make a false statement or fail to disclose a material fact related to competency and qualifications.

2. Shall not misrepresent his/her professional qualifications.

3. Shall not assist any entry into the profession of a person known to be unqualified in respect to character, education, or other relevant attribute.

4. Shall not knowingly make a false statement concerning the qualifications of a candidate for a professional position.

5. Shall not assist a noneducator in the unauthorized practice of teaching.

6. Shall not disclose information about colleagues obtained in the course of professional service unless disclosure serves a compelling professional purpose or is required by law.

7. Shall not knowingly make false or malicious statements about a colleague.

8. Shall not accept any gratuity, gift, or favor that might impair or appear to influence professional decisions or actions.

Adopted by 1975 Representative Assembly

FIGURE 3.2   *(Continued)*

the American Federation of Labor in May 1916. John Dewey held the first membership card in the AFT. (Teachers' unions had existed earlier than 1916; for example, the Chicago Teachers' Federation was formed in 1897 and became affiliated with the American Federation of Labor in 1902.) AFT membership grew steadily from 110,522 members in 1965 to 205,323 members in 1970—almost doubling.

Membership. Membership exceeded 415,854 by 1974, reached 624,406 in May 1986, and by 1993 exceeded 806,000. The AFT has local unions in the United States, the Canal Zone, Guam, and the armed forces overseas schools for the dependents of military personnel. Besides the national federations, there are federations of teachers in most states.

Governance. The organization of the AFT includes a president, thirty-eight vice-presidents, a secretary-treasurer, an administrative staff, and eleven departments. It also includes standing committees and council committees. The Committee of Political Education (COPE) is becoming more active as the AFT participates increasingly in political discussions related to education.

Affiliation with the AFL-CIO. Since its inception the AFT has boasted of its affiliation with the AFL-CIO. The AFT has stressed that organized labor was an important force in establishing our system of free public schools and has actively supported school improvement programs at local, state, and national levels. Affiliation with organized labor gives the AFT the support of more than fifteen million members of the AFL-CIO. The support by local labor unions has often

CODE OF ETHICS
AMERICAN FEDERATION OF TEACHERS, AFL-CIO

I. **Teacher-Student Commitment**
   1. The Teacher works to develop each student's potential as a worthy and effective citizen.
   2. The Teacher works objectively to stimulate the spirit of inquiry, the acquisition of knowledge and understanding, and the thoughtful formulation of worthy goals in each of his/her students for their advancement.
   3. The Teacher works to develop and provide sound and progressively better educational opportunities for all students.

II. **Teacher-Public Commitment**
   1. The Teacher believes that patriotism in its highest form requires dedication to the principles of our democratic heritage.
   2. The Teacher shares with all other citizens the responsibility for the development of sound public policy and assumes full political and citizenship responsibilities.
   3. The Teacher has the privilege and the responsibility to enhance the public image of his/her school in order to create a positive community atmosphere which will be beneficial to education.

III. **Teacher-Profession Commitment**
   1. The Teacher believes that the quality of his/her service in the education profession directly influences the nation and its citizens.
   2. The Teacher exerts every effort to raise professional standards, to improve a climate in which the exercise of professional judgment is encouraged, and to achieve conditions which attract persons worthy of the trust to careers in education.
   3. The Teacher urges active participation and support in professional organizations and their programs.

IV. **Teacher-District Commitment**
   1. The Teacher strives to do the job for which he/she was hired with honesty and to the best of his/her ability.
   2. The Teacher pledges to communicate this code, along with a positive attitude toward it, to all teachers.
   3. The Teacher discourages the breaching of this code and requests that all charges be presented in writing to the Union Executive Board for their deliberation and judgment.

FIGURE 3.3

Code of Ethics of the American Federation of Teachers

(*Source:* American Federation of Teachers, AFL-CIO. Used by permission.)

worked to the advantage of local AFT unions in gaining better salaries and improved fringe benefits from local boards of education. Figure 3.3 presents the AFT's code of ethics.

AFT Programs for Professional Growth

The AFT has a rich and diverse portfolio of resources available to its members. In addition to lobbying and political action activities, there are resources in the form of staff services, publications (e.g., the AFT journal, *American Educator*), and workshops related to an array of professional topics. A few of the current initiatives are described on the following page.

Education for Democracy. This project was launched at the time of the bicentennial celebration to address perceived lack of attention to the education of Americans about their democratic heritage. Since that time, Education for Democracy has taken into account the increasing diversity of our people in terms of racial, national, linguistic, and religious origins. The current thrust of the project is not only to make history relevant at the high school level, but also to emphasize history in the elementary grades. Through a series of invited papers and related materials, this project is providing teachers with information about important aspects of history that should be included in the curriculum as well as suggestions for how to make history interesting. Along the way, the theme that has developed is appreciating and understanding the importance of democracy.

The AFT Critical Thinking Project. This project addresses issues in the area of critical thinking. Definitions of thinking skills and dispositions are offered along with what, as research indicated, would be useful for teachers to consider. In addition, an emphasis is placed on how to develop, enhance, and assess thinking skills in children. In this program, the "turn key" model of training is used, whereby some teachers are trained at the national level and then return to the local level to train others. A thirty-five-hour program of training is available for those at the local level who wish to learn more. In one of the reports that is available out of this project, an emphasis is made on distinguishing between "knowledge" and "knowing."

> It is important to stress here that in questioning the traditional reliance of the schools on a one-right-answer model of learning, the critical thinking movement is not denigrating the importance of knowledge in learning. Knowledge is essential and intrinsic to learning of all kinds. One cannot think critically without knowledge. When we think, we must always think about something. The development of critical thinking, says Cornbleth (1985), is highly knowledge dependent: We cannot think critically about the ideas we encounter unless we know something about the area in question. There is a difference, however, between memorization and understanding, as well as between "knowledge" and "knowing."

Relevant Research

Teacher Job Satisfaction Is Important for Successful Teacher Performance

A recent research project by Heller, Clay, and Perkins reported that in a national survey a majority of teachers claimed low job satisfaction.[2] Much of the dissatisfaction was associated with little academic and social support from administration, a self-perceived inability to meet student needs, and inadequate salaries. Too often, higher performance expectations and demands are not followed by supportive behaviors from administration that are geared to help teachers do a better job in meeting the needs of their diverse students. Job satisfaction is directly related to:

- the extent to which you can meet student needs,
- the degree of trust you have in your principal,
- the amount of work required of you,
- the way you interact with your students, and
- your satisfaction with your salary.

We suggest that you address these job satisfaction issues as a beginning teacher and continually during your career if you wish to be successful in meeting the needs of your students.

Source: William H. Heller; Rex J. Clay; and Cline M. Perkins, "Factors Related to Teacher Job Satisfaction and Dissatisfaction," *ERS Spectrum 10* (1) (Winter, 1992): 20–24.

The AFT Educational Research and Dissemination Program. Through this program, selected findings from recent research on classroom management and effective teaching have been made available to teachers. The research findings have been tested in classrooms and found to be most useful and relevant to teachers for improving student progress. Based on the research, a set of staff development programs for teachers has been made available. The programs can be offered as a part of a statewide network, a national network, or at the local level. The program also offers various types of resources such as one-page summary sheets of exemplary programs, profiles of teachers who are making a difference through extensive use of some of the concepts, a visiting practitioner program, a glossary of expressions and terms, and a sampling of interesting information about teachers and teaching drawn from the key studies. One of the unique features of this program is the interactive and collaborative dynamic that is possible with other teachers locally, regionally, and nationally who are engaged in similar explorations and trials of the research findings.

Leadership for Reform Program.   The Leadership for Reform Program is designed to address the emerging plans and trends to transform schools. In this effort, participants consist of teams from the local level who respond by writing a proposal to serve as a pilot site for a special project. Out of the meetings of these teams, a set of guiding principles has been developed that addresses the range of issues that should be considered when reforming a school or a school system. This is an effort to respond to national movements such as Education 2000 and the continuing criticism of schools.

One of AFT's proposals is an answer to the emerging interest in developing a transition from the traditional preservice teacher education program on the college campus to being a full-time in-service teacher. There is an in-between phase commonly referred to as *induction*, which typically covers the first one to three years of in-service teaching experience. The AFT is proposing professional practice schools at elementary, middle, and secondary levels that are "structured, staffed, and supported to achieve three goals: student achievement, teacher induction, and supportive research directed at the continuous improvement of practice." One of the key premises in this effort is the emphasis on making student teaching more useful and relevant to the beginning teacher. The second is the continuing agenda to make teaching a self-governing profession, and the professional practice schools are seen as another lever in achieving this aspiration. The third premise of the professional practice school model is the development of more productive collaborative relationships between universities and schools with the goal of establishing professional practice schools developed as a joint effort, with roles and responsibilities shared between the university and school district personnel. These professional practice schools would be like a medical teaching hospital—the teaching location for the clinical faculty and a place where university researchers could study this practice. Yet another goal for the professional practice schools is that they would demonstrate the best in teaching practice. They would provide a knowledge base to what is going on in classrooms, and there would be a heavy focus on student learning.

The American Federation of Teachers sponsors, among other things, the continuing education of teachers.

CASE STUDY TEACHER ORGANIZATION SUPPORT

*T*eachers' organizations such as the AFT and NEA attempt to defend the rights, materials, and interests of educators. This aid usually comes from the local organization to which the teacher belongs, but also can be obtained from the national organization if it is necessary. A very important right that organizations protect for teachers is the "right of due process" in hiring and dismissal. If a teacher believes this right has been violated in practice with employment, he or she can begin with the local association in seeking redress.

As a new teacher in your first year of employment, you are experiencing difficulty in getting information about whether your teaching contract will be continued for the second year. You are aware that the school board has indicated to the superintendent that because of enrollment decreases and shrinking tax dollars, the district administrators are to decide which teachers will be retained for the next school year. It is now the early part of the second semester and you still have not been formally visited in your classroom by the building administrator. Since there are other new, nontenured teachers in your building, you believe that the administrator will be choosing the people she wishes to retain for the next school year.

You feel that you need to begin taking steps to protect your employment.

1. How will you approach your local association to see what help they intend to give you?
2. How do you maintain your professional relationships with your other first-year teaching colleagues, knowing that some of you may be terminated?
3. Do you have "due process" rights that need to be addressed with this issue?

Discuss a course of action that you may begin planning to satisfy your professional concerns.

NEA and AFT Compared

In the early 1960s the NEA appealed to teachers by drawing a distinction between **professionalism and unionism.** As a *professional association*, it claimed, only the NEA could truly represent teachers. A union like the AFT, on the other hand, was seen as being beneath professionalism by the NEA leadership because of its alliance with other workers within the American Federation of Labor and Congress of Industrial Organizations (AFL-CIO). The NEA has since identified itself as a union and no longer distinguishes between professionalism and unionism.

AFT: Professionalism Not Possible without Unionism. To the AFT, professionalism is not possible without unionism. A degree of self-control, the ability to help set professional standards, mastery of a specific body of knowledge, and the authority to define conditions of work are essential elements in the AFT's definition of professionalism. Since none of these can be gained without the kind of collective assertion of power that unionism makes possible, the AFT maintains that without unionism teaching can never become truly professional.

AFT Strikes, NEA Sanctions. During the 1960s the AFT was generally viewed as a collection of teachers' unions that would willingly, though illegally in most

Teachers have exercised their right to strike with mixed emotions, realizing that the resulting disruption will affect their students directly.

states, close the schools by striking to gain their demands. Many educators, NEA members especially, looked on striking as a labor union technique that should not be used by "professional" teachers. At that time the NEA used a procedure termed *sanctions.* When sanctions were imposed against a school, the professional association advertised the school district as being an unacceptable place to work and discouraged association members from taking employment in the district. Teachers completed existing contractual agreements without closing the schools. Generally, several months' notice was given before sanctions were invoked, and they were applied by the NEA to local districts as well as to entire states (Oklahoma and Utah). Technically, the NEA did not have a no-strike policy at that time, but it was strongly implied. Both the AFT and NEA worked to increase **teacher power,** which stressed organizing teachers in order to enhance their ability to exert pressure for the improvement of education and teacher welfare.

Competition: AFT versus NEA. The strong competition between the AFT and NEA for memberships and bargaining rights during the late 1960s was vocally volatile and highly intense. Teacher militancy among members of both the NEA and AFT grew considerably. The strike tactic used by the AFT seemed to be more immediately effective than NEA sanctions, and as a consequence, the NEA came to embrace the strike rather than sanctions as a last resort. The NEA also came to embrace collective bargaining, which the AFT had initiated. Thus the influences of the AFT and the NEA on each other have produced a growing convergence of philosophy and purpose. Today, most teachers, administrators, and board members consider both organizations to be teachers' unions that use the tactics found most successful by the trade unions of organized labor.

However, in recent years, the NEA's emphasis on professionalism has been paralleled by the AFT's emphasis on teacher leadership. Both organizations have

---

PROFESSIONAL DILEMMA

Are Teachers Professional If They Strike?

Your school district association has been in negotiations with the local school board for almost one year now. Currently, you are working without a contract. It appears that the association and the board are at an impasse over salary and fringe benefits. The leader of the association has called a meeting in which she intends to discuss the potential issue of a work stoppage (strike) at the school district level. Your fall semester school term has only been in session for one and one-half months and the students are beginning to settle into a pleasant learning routine.

The community has learned of a possible strike vote and is openly against this action. Up until this time the community has always been supportive of teacher efforts and programs. However, they do not want to see their children's educational environment being totally disrupted. Local newspaper and radio releases in support of the community are now bringing out age-old arguments supporting the notion that teachers are public servants and should not resort to work stoppages. It is apparent that the public trust between school and community is being eroded. Your association has countered that strikes, in the long run, bring about better pay for teachers, which leads to higher professional morale and greater benefits for the children.

Questions you are facing include:

- Do you think that striking is more of a legal rights or a moral rights issue?
- Is a teachers' strike any different from the strikes of other professionals such as nurses, pilots, or auto workers?
- If the association votes on a strike, how will you vote? What will you do if the strike is called?

---

increased their emphases on school improvement, the restructuring process, and the empowerment of teachers. Thus, in the 1990s both organizations maintain a balance between unionism and professionalism.

An interesting breakthrough in the competition between the AFT and the NEA occurred in California, in the fall of 1989, when the two local unions merged. The resulting organization is known as the United Educators of San Francisco, and members belong to the state and national organizations of both the AFT and the NEA. At the national level, there is open discussion about the possibility of a formal merger at some point in the future. In 1993 formal discussion of merger began between the leadership of both organizations. Such a merger would bring 3,000,000 professionals under one leadership and significantly increase their political clout on the national scene.

Political Action

An area of rapid development within teachers' organizations is that of **political action committees.** The AFT has an active Committee on Political Education (COPE). A similar NEA committee is called the Political Action Committee (NEA-PAC).

Reason for Political Action. This development was motivated by the success other unions and organizations have had through systematic political action. In the past, many organizations used moral persuasion, in which delegates presented themselves to legislators or legislative committees to ask for legislation to meet organizational needs. The lessons of history show that this procedure does not work very well. Other organizations, including teachers' organizations, have found a much more effective method—helping to elect political candidates who are sympathetic to their particular needs. The political action committees monitor elected officials' voting records on education bills and analyze the platforms of new candidates. Teachers' organizations plan to support actively those candidates who will perform according to the organizations' views.

The Common Aim of National Political Committees. The state and national political action committees of the NEA and AFT have a common aim—to promote education by encouraging teachers to participate in the political life of their local, state, and national communities. These committees throughout the states are responsible for recommending political endorsements to their respective boards of directors. Interestingly, the NEA and AFT political action committees usually agree on which candidates to endorse during national elections. Both organizations have strongly endorsed Democratic party candidates, feeling that they would be more supportive of education at the national level. A significant sign of organizational professional growth, however, is the fact that national political party emphasis no longer directs COPE and PAC endorsements. Candidates of both parties are endorsed based on their support for the educational policies of both the NEA and AFT.

National teachers' union leaders continue to suggest that their political clout pays off for education. In terms of support of future political candidates, teachers' unions remain consistent in their claims that they will support those who seem to favor public education. Teachers' unions monitor the federal administration's actions that affect public education, and they have been vehement in their opposition to funding cuts in public education programs.

State and Local Teacher Organizations

While state and local units that are affiliated with a national organization operate under the umbrella of the parent national offices, these units are the power base of the organizations. The local association of teachers has the highest priority in the whole organization; however, the strength of any single local union lies in the solidarity in numbers, in resource personnel, and in services that the state organi-

---

Relevant Research

Teachers Need to Become Active Researchers

There is little doubt that teachers can become competent classroom researchers. A recent study concluded that if teacher-researchers are to contribute to educational change, they need to have school and district support for accomplishing this goal. Although most teachers in the survey indicated that a researcher role for the teacher is at best a difficult task for them because of the everyday realities of their job, their attitudes toward research would change if they developed confidence and understanding of research methods. Specifically, teachers need to:

- redefine their role to include responsibilities for doing classroom research;
- be given administrative and school district support;
- be encouraged to test new research findings in their classrooms; and
- have staff development practices that include conference attendance, formal research training, and available research resources.

We encourage you, as a beginning teacher, to actively prepare yourself to do classroom reasearch. Work through your teacher association to achieve some of your goals for becoming a successful researcher.

Source: Christene K. Bennett, "Teacher-Researchers: All Dressed Up and No Place to Go?" *Educational Leadership 51* (2) (October, 1993): 69–70.

zation provides. In the early 1960s, teachers generally became more militant regarding salary and working conditions. Classroom teachers' associations at the local level became more active in seeking assistance from state and national associations. As competition between the larger national associations grew in intensity, elections at the local level became the procedure for gaining the bargaining representation for each district. Local elections for the role of bargaining agent among competitive teacher groups remain the most important steps in the process for organizing teachers in any district, whether or not the local classroom teacher association is affiliated with a state or national organization.

Teacher Participation: Local Organization. For the most part, teachers participate directly in the affairs of local organizations. Solutions to the problems at hand are primarily the concerns of local teachers' groups. The influence of these groups would obviously be weakened without the support and resources of strong state and national parent organizations. At the same time, local organizations sometimes become indifferent about their national and state affiliation.

Local Relationships with State and National Organizations. Leadership at the national level views the problems and differences in beliefs among the local organizations as a viable part of the democratic process rather than as divisive. From the many geographic locations, grass roots views of local teacher organizations may surface through the state associations to the national level or from the local organizations directly to the national level. Decisions related to national policy are then made by majority vote with attention paid to input from all levels—local, state, and national. In some instances, local organizations have severed relations with their state and national affiliates when the members felt that their particular needs were not well met. Since the power of the state and national organizations is reduced somewhat each time a local organization withdraws state and national affiliation, state organizations especially are compelled to pay careful attention to the particular needs of local teachers' association affiliates.

Specialty Associations

There are many other associations that teachers may join, participate in, and provide leadership for that deal with their chosen profession. These specialty associations are organized around specific job assignments that teachers have (science teaching, mathematics teaching, etc.). They also relate to broad-based curriculum and school restructuring movements (effective schools, writing across the curriculum, and cooperative learning). There are a large number of these specialty associations that teachers can be a part of. An excellent listing of about 6,000 national trade associations; labor unions; professional, scientific, and technical societies; and other national organizations composed of groups united for a common purpose is given in the annual edition of *National Trade and Professional Associations of the United States* (published by Columbia Books, Inc., 1350 New York Avenue, NW, Suite 207, Washington, DC 20005). A recent edition listed 540 organizations under the "Education" heading, including those identified with specific academic disciplines, religions, and other education-related categories. Prospective teachers are encouraged to locate the most recent annual edition of this publication in their college or university library and peruse it to gain a broader perspective of the organizations that exist to serve their individual needs and purposes.

Assignment-Related Organizations

As one would think, teacher organizations have been formed for each of the academic disciplines, as well as for each of the other curriculum areas such as vocational-technical, business, health, home economics, physical education, and driver education. We cannot attempt to list all of these organizations here. For purposes of illustration only, a few of the teaching assignment–related organizations are presented in Appendix 3.1 on page 74. These organizations typically publish professional journals, sponsor conferences, establish standards, and generally work to advance the field they represent.

Religious Education Associations

There are many religious education associations of various denominations. These national and regional religious education associations are under denominational or interdenominational control and do one or more of the following: operate sectarian schools attended by students who prefer them to public or secular private schools, supplement the public or private school program by offering educational activities for youth and adults, operate adult educational programs open to the public, and formally promote scholarships among their members. A partial listing of religious education associations is as follows:

  Association of Seventh-Day Adventists Educators
  Catholic Biblical Association of America
  Council for Jewish Education
  National Association of Episcopal Schools
  Association of Christian Schools International
  Religious Education Association

**Educators United:
Ready for Change**

EI's First World Congress
Harare, Zimbabwe
19-23 July 1995

Global organizations such as Education International, which exists to promote the profession of teaching worldwide, indicate American educators' growing recognition of other societies.

World Confederation of Organizations of the Teaching Profession

The aims of the **World Confederation of Organizations of the Teaching Profession (WCOTP)** foster a conception of education directed toward the promotion of international understanding and goodwill, with a view to safeguarding peace, freedom, and respect for human dignity. The WCOTP supports efforts to improve teaching methods, educational organizations, and the academic and professional training of teachers so as to equip them better to serve the interests of youth; to defend the rights, materials, and moral interests of the teaching profession; and to promote closer relationships among teachers in the different countries.

Member institutions of the WCOTP come from approximately a hundred nations. The NEA and AFT are members. In a study based on questionnaire data gathered by the WCOTP, many educational problems common to all nations were identified, including lack of funds, shortage of excellent teachers, the need for school buildings, and the need for compulsory and free education. The WCOTP, facing these problems with determination, holds an assembly of delegates once each year. Resolutions of the assembly have ranged widely, from intensive literary programs to free education at all levels, from increased availability and status of technical education to special and adequate provision for the educational and medical needs of the physically and mentally handicapped. The WCOTP also sponsors regional conferences. In the past these conferences have dealt with such topics as the status of the teaching profession in Niamey, Niger; teaching science in elementary schools in Asia; and the teacher's part in nation building. The WCOTP's bulletin, *Echo*, designed to promote international understanding, is published in thirteen languages. *Educational Panorama*, another WCOTP publication, is published in English, French, Spanish, Japanese, and Arabic.

Global Perspectives: Education International (EI). In January 1993, Education International (EI) officially replaced the WCOPT. EI has united more than 240 national educator unions and professional associations from around the world. This new organization brings together over 20 million elementary, secondary, and college and university staffs. In the United States, this merger brings the NEA and AFT together under a world umbrella with former NEA president Mary Hatwood Futrell as EI President and the International Federation of Free Teachers' Union (IFFTU) General Secretary, Fred Van Leeuwen, as general secretary of EI. Since the United States AFT has been an affiliate of IFFTU, this should encourage the potential merger of the NEA and AFT in the United States.

Education International's First Action Agenda. Moving now on a total global perspective, EI is focusing its efforts on:

- Improving the quality of education,
- Upgrading education employee working conditions and compensation,
- Fighting for adequate educational funding,
- Sharing curriculum,
- Safeguarding human rights,
- Fighting for gender equality, and
- Building stronger educational organizations.

Summary and Implications

This chapter presented the concept of teacher power as a viable force in the formulation of education-related decisions. Discussion of teacher power was followed by information about teacher organizations (local, state, and national), which are the vehicles through which teacher power is expressed. The National Education Association (NEA) with over two million members and the American Federation of Teachers (AFT) with approximately 806,000 members are the largest teacher organizations (unions). Detailed attention was given to the organizational structures of these agencies and to comparisons of the two. Perhaps the ultimate manifestation of teacher power comes from the rapidly increasing development of the respective NEA and AFT political action committees, NEA-PAC and COPE.

Attention was also given to assignment-related and specialty study, religious education, and worldwide organizations. A list of teaching assignment-related specialty study associations was presented. Similarly, several associations related to religious education were listed. Finally, a brief description of the aims and memberships of the World Confederation of Organizations of the Teaching Profession (WCOTP) was presented.

The implications are straightforward. Prospective teachers will experience concerted pressure to affiliate with the recognized teacher organizations. Each teacher must decide the advantages and disadvantages of such paid memberships. In some school districts the climate of the working environment of teachers is very similar to that of trade unions. In other districts, teachers try to keep a more scholarly, professional climate analogous to that of traditional professions like law, dentistry, and medicine. How each teacher will contribute to the organizational climate associated with a particular membership must be a personal decision.

Similarly, teachers have an opportunity as well as a professional responsibility to join one or more of the specialty study associations. Through these associations it is possible to be continually updated regarding initiatives and procedures that are being tried, as well as to develop an extended array of contacts of people within the profession who think and care about the subject as much as you do. Most of the professional associations will issue monthly or bimonthly journals or newsletters and have an annual national meeting. In addition, in most cases, there will be regional and perhaps state meetings. In all of these situations it is possible to learn more about your profession as well as to become involved as a participant, contributor, and leader.

Discussion Questions

1. Teachers' organizations defend the rights, materials, and moral interests of the teaching profession. To what extent should the organization defend a teacher's choice of reading material for classroom use? To what extent should the organization defend the rights of gay teachers?
2. During a teachers' strike, members of a factory union from a neighboring city joined the teachers' picket line to support the teachers' demands. Do you agree or disagree with the factory union action? Explain your answer.
3. Should teacher organizations be involved in political action—for example, in helping to elect political candidates who are sympathetic to their cause? Why or why not?
4. Why are the local units of teacher organizations extremely important to the national organization? Discuss.
5. A major distinction between the professional initiatives of the NEA and AFT and those of the assignment-related/specialty studies associations is their scope. NEA and AFT activities tend to focus on school-wide and district-wide initiatives while specialty studies focus on classroom and curriculum-specific topics. How do you think teachers should go about taking advantage of and integrating both of these perspectives and sets of initiatives?
6. Most public school teachers know little about religious education associations and/or the World Confederation of Organizations of the Teaching Profession. What should public schools do (if anything) to provide their teachers with knowledge about these organizations? Discuss your rationale.

Journal/Portfolio Development

1. Gather information about your state and national organizations for your teaching field (math, science, elementary). From your perspective as a new teacher, evaluate their publications, activities, and espoused agendas and how they can benefit you.
2. Create a collection of five professional journals that will be helpful to you as a beginning teacher. Indicate how they can be useful from a content and/or instructional perspective.

School-Based Experiences

This chapter provides you with information about the two major teacher organizations, the National Educational Association (NEA) and the American Federation of Teachers (AFT). When you accept a teaching position, you will most likely be asked to become a member of the NEA or the AFT. You should try to become knowledgeable about teacher organizations. When you have the opportunity to visit schools and classrooms, ask teachers and administrators their opinions about teacher organizations.

Write to a few organizations to which you might wish to belong as an educator. Ask for materials and an application form. Seriously consider joining some of these organizations as a student member (which is typically at a very reduced membership fee).

Note

1. *NEA Handbook, 1991–92.* (Washington, DC: National Education Association), 13, 159, 175.

Bibliography

American Federation of Teachers. *The AFT v. the NEA.* Washington, DC: American Federation of Teachers, 1989.

National Education Association. *Doubts and Certainties 7* (4). (January/February, 1993) Washington, DC: The Association.

American Federation of Teachers. *American Teacher 77* (7). (April, 1993) Washington, DC: The Federation.

Constitution of the AFT. Washington, DC: American Federation of Teachers, AFL-CIO, 1988.

NEA Handbook, 1991–92. Washington, DC: National Education Association, 1991, 12.

American Federation of Teachers. *PSRP Reporter.* (Summer, 1993) Washington, DC: The Federation.

Nielsen, Robert M., and Polishook, Irwin H. *Academic Unions, Values and Democracy.* Pamphlet Series. Washington, DC: American Federation of Teachers, 1989.

Appendix 3.1

Professional Education Associations

American Alliance for Health, Physical Education, Recreation & Dance (AALR)
1900 Association Drive
Reston, VA 22091
(703) 476–3472

American Alliance for Theatre and Education (AATE)
Theatre Arts Department
Virginia Tech.
Blacksburg, VA 24061
(703) 231–7624

American Association of Physics Teachers (AAPT)
5112 Berwyn Road
College Park, MD 20740
(301) 345–4200

American Comparative Literature Association (ACLA)
c/o Larry H. Peer, Comparative Literature Department
Brigham Young University
Provo, UT 84602
(801) 378–5529

American Council on the Teaching of Foreign Languages (ACTFL)
(Classical and Modern)
Six Executive Blvd., Upper-Level
Yonkers, NY 10701
(914) 963–8830

Association for Educational Communications and Technology (AECT)
1025 Vermont Avenue,
SW, Suite 820
Washington, DC 20005
(202) 347–7834

American Federation of Teachers AFL-CIO (AFT)
555 New Jersey Avenue, NW
Washington, DC 20001
(202) 879–4400

American Home Economics Association (AHEA)
1555 King Street
Alexandria, VA 22314
(703) 655–4380 (703) 704–4600

American Speech-Language-Hearing Association (ASLHA)
10801 Rockville Place
Rockville, MD 20852
(301) 897–5700

American Vocation Association (AVA)
1410 King Street
Alexandria, VA 22314
(703) 683–3111

Association for Childhood Education International (ACEI)
11141 Georgia Avenue, Suite 200
Wheaton, MD 20902
(301) 942–2433

Association for Education in Journalism & Mass Communication (AEJMC)
1621 College Street
University of South Carolina
Columbia, SC 29208
(803) 777–2005

Association for Supervision and Curriculum Development (ASCD)
1250 N. Pitt Street
Alexandria, VA 22314
(703) 549–9110

Council for Exceptional Children (CEC)
1920 Association Drive
Reston, VA 22091
(703) 620–3660

International Reading Association (IRA)
800 Barksdale Road
P. O. Box 8139
Newark, DE 19714–8139
(302) 731–1600

International Technology Education Association (ITEA)
1914 Association Drive
Reston, VA 22091
(703) 860–2100

Modern Language Association of America (MLA)
10 Astor Place, 5th Floor
New York, NY 10003
(212) 475–9500

Music Teachers National Association (MTNA)
617 Vine Street, Suite 1432
Cincinnati, OH 45202
(513) 421–1420

National Art Education Association (NAEA)
1916 Association Drive
Reston, VA 22091
(703) 860–8000

National Association of Biology Teachers (NABT)
11250 Roger Bacon Drive, #19
Reston, VA 22090
(703) 471–1134

National Association for the Education of Young Children (NAEYC)
1834 Connecticut Avenue, NW
Washington, DC 20009
(202) 232–8777

National Association for Gifted Children (NAGC)
1155 15th Street, NW
Suite 1002
Washington, DC 20005
(202) 785–4268

National Business Education Association (NBEA)
1914 Association Drive
Reston, VA 22091
(703) 860–8300

National Council for the Social Studies (NCSS)
3501 Newark Street, NW
Washington, DC 20016
(202) 966–7840

National Council of Teachers of English (NCTE)
1111 Kenyon Road
Urbana, IL 61801
(217) 328–3870

National Council of Teachers of Mathematics (NCTM)
1906 Association Drive
Reston, VA 22091
(703) 620–9840

National Education Association (NEA)
1201 16th Street, NW
Washington, DC 20036
(202) 833–4000

National Middle Schools Association (NMSA)
4807 Evanswood Drive
Columbus, OH 43229
(614) 848–8211

National Science Teachers Association (NSTA)
1742 Connecticut Avenue
Washington, DC 20009–1171
(202) 328–5800

Dreamcatcher

JIM KUBIK *has been a senior government teacher at Norfolk Senior High School in Norfolk, Nebraska since 1977. He was the 1991 Nebraska Teacher of the Year and has won numerous awards for classroom teaching. He was awarded the 1994 H. Councill Trenholm Memorial Award for Promoting Racial Understanding from the National Education Association. Kubik wrote the Nebraska Multicultural Education Act, which the Nebraska Unicameral passed in 1992; the law requires all Nebraska public schools to infuse cultural awareness into the total curriculum K-12. Several of his students helped lobby the law into reality. He took a one-year leave from teaching to work for the Nebraska Department of Education during the 1992–1993 school year to help organize the statewide implementation of the law.*

When nonwhite students began appearing in my classroom as a result of a meat packing plant locating in Norfolk, I began to understand the need for more cultural awareness, not only in students, but in the whole community. I began to hear more racial jokes and stereotyping. These words were coming out of the mouths of good white students, who simply repeated what they heard at home. These students were graduating with scholarships, and yet some of them believed that all Hispanics are lazy and only blacks are on welfare. I began to wonder if we were really preparing our students for a world where they will be working with people from many different racial backgrounds. I concluded that we were not.

My nonpartisan political science club held a public forum on the issue of "Racism in Nebraska" in September of 1990. Over 1,000 people attended the forum and heard a racially diverse panel give their perspectives on race relations in Nebraska. Many of our students were so motivated by this forum that it caused them to start asking questions about multicultural education, and why they were not getting any cultural awareness education in school.

Several of these students and I approached our local school administration with the idea of infusing multicultural education into our local school district. During the next year, we tried in vain to get something started. Most of our school administrators dragged their feet and literally stalled. They felt it was just too controversial. Frustrated, my students and I approached State Senator Ernie Chambers of Omaha, the only African American state senator in the Nebraska Unicameral. We asked him to sponsor a law that would require the teaching of cultural awareness to be infused in all curriculum areas in all public schools in Nebraska. With Senator Chambers' leadership, the law passed. My students were instrumental in the lobbying efforts. This law has resulted in schools and communities thinking about the importance of cultural awareness and how it can begin to curb racial misunderstandings. Our schools will finally begin to recognize the contributions that all cultures of America have made to our great nation.

Speaking in support of multicultural education in Nebraska, at first, was not a popular thing to do, *but it was the right thing to do!* As teachers, it is our responsibility to speak out for what is right and to do what is needed to make sure *all* of our students get the best education possible.

As teachers, we have an obligation to prepare our students to appreciate the diversity that this nation has always had. This is as important as mathematics and science education.

4 School and Society

Focus Questions

1 What is the relationship between power and discrimination?
2 How do schools contribute to the socialization of children and youth?
3 How do schools assist in the reproduction of society?
4 Whose values are taught in schools?
5 What factors influence the subculture of a school?

Key Terms and Concepts

Discrimination: Individual or institutional practices that exclude all members of a group from certain rights, opportunities, or benefits.

Dominant group: The cultural group that has the greatest power in society; in the United States it is composed primarily of persons from a European background who are Protestant, middle class, not disabled, heterosexual, and male. This term is sometimes used synonymously with mainstream culture or group.

Equal educational opportunity: A policy to ensure that all students, regardless of their cultural background or family circumstances, are provided access to a similar education.

Equality: The state of being neither inferior nor superior.

Informal curriculum: The norms and values that define expectations for student behavior and attitudes, and that undergird the curriculum and operations of schools.

Meritocracy: A system that is based on the belief that those who achieve at the highest levels deserve the greatest rewards.

Prejudice: Preconceived negative attitudes toward the members of a group of people.

Racism: The conscious or unconscious belief that racial differences make one group superior to another, leading to discriminatory actions that limit the opportunities for members of the perceived inferior group to share in the same benefits of society.

Sexism: The conscious or unconscious belief that men are superior to women, and subsequent behavior and action that maintain the superior, powerful position of males.

Socialization: Process of learning the social norms of one's culture.

Values: Principles, standards, or qualities considered worthwhile or desirable.

*T*he United States prides itself on being the premier model of a democratic society. Most of us would probably agree with the dictionary that defines it as "a government in which the supreme power is vested in the people and exercised by them directly or indirectly through a system of representation usually involving periodically held free elections."[1] The definition further describes democracy as including the rule of the majority and practices that favor social **equality.**

Democracy has undergirded our political rhetoric for over two hundred years. The principles of democracy teach us that we can be equal and full participants in this democratic society. At the same time, we observe that Congress is not composed equally of men and women, nor is it representative of the ethnic, racial, religious, language, economic, or age diversity that actually exists in the nation. There are significant differences in the education levels, types of jobs, and family incomes across racial groups and between men and women. Children in low-income families suffer disproportionately from limited access to the best teachers, best instruction in our schools, good nutrition, safe environments, and community support and caring.

What is the nature of groups in a democratic society? How do our interactions with members of groups different than our own influence our ability to achieve a democratic state supportive of egalitarian ideals? Finally, how do schools contribute to the maintenance of society and help students engage in and promote the ideals of a democracy? We will address these issues in this chapter.

Groups in Society

A democratic society struggles with how to support individuality and yet develop a consciousness of shared concerns and actions that promote equality. This challenge is paramount in a society like the United States that includes many groups that impact and are impacted by political, social, and economic systems.

Some individuals are members of a group because of ascribed characteristics at birth such as race or gender. Others belong to groups where the members share the same national origin, native language, economic circumstances, religious affiliation, and/or residence in a specific geographic region. Of course, we each belong to all of these groups or microcultures. At the same time, we often interact with members of different groups in school, work, or social settings. We also may interact with others around common interests such as environmental concerns, school funding, moving drug dealers from the block, or day care support.

Members of society view the importance of group membership differently. Many European Americans, especially the Protestant middle class, do not identify themselves by their racial, ethnic, gender, religious, or socioeconomic group. They do not distinguish themselves from the larger society and often do not acknowledge the advantage that membership in these groups has provided them. On the other hand, persons whose ancestral roots are outside of Europe, or who are recent immigrants are more likely to identify themselves by their ethnicity, race, or religion. They or other members of their group have experienced **discrimination** in housing, jobs, educational opportunities, or treatment by store clerks or police officers. Their common history and experiences reinforce a group identity[2] that is distinct from mainstream society.

Having experienced discrimination, members of excluded groups can describe differential power relations among groups. However, members of groups who do not normally experience discrimination have a more difficult time acknowledging that differences in power and advantage exist. As a result, the rights of group membership versus those of individuals are debated on college campuses, in board meetings of corporations, by politicians, and in many formal and informal neighborhood meetings. These discussions focus on programs that are perceived to favor a group other than our own—affirmative action, bilingual education, and equality in funding for male and female athletes. An examination of power relationships and experiences with differences should highlight the struggles inherent in a democratic society.

Power and Domination

In 1916 John Dewey described a democratic society as one in which all of its members are able to share its benefits on equal terms.[3] Eighty years later, many persons of color, limited English speakers, women, persons with disabilities, gays and lesbians, persons with low incomes, and persons affiliated with religions other than Protestanism have still not experienced equality with members of the **dominant group.** Why have we not yet been able to achieve the egalitarian ideal that should characterize democracy? The primary factor is the inequitable power relationships that exist across groups as described by Seth Kreisberg:

> Across a broad spectrum of institutions that shape our lives, people have power over other people; that is, people have the ability to control, manipulate, and coerce other people for their own ends. These relationships of domination are not haphazardly and randomly developed. Rather, the very structures of our social institutions and the predominant norms, **values,** and beliefs of our society sanction, indeed define and reinforce, them. The ability to control and manipulate others also derives from privileged access to and control of valued resources such as education, personal wealth, housing, food, health care and weapons of war.[4]

Schools provide an example of an institution in which power relationships have been developed and maintained. Students' work and class rules are determined by teachers. Teachers are evaluated and disciplined when necessary by principals who report to a superintendent of schools. The rules and procedures for managing schools traditionally have been established by authorities who are not directly involved with the school and who may not even live in the community served by the school. Parents, especially in economically oppressed areas, often feel powerless in the education of their children.

Not only do power and domination characterize our political and economic systems, they influence relations within the family, between the sexes, among racial groups, and among members of many religious traditions. The father figure traditionally has been all powerful. Instead of there being shared relations between males and females, husbands and wives, and parents and children, one sometimes dominates the other. In these power relationships, someone or some group is viewed as inferior to another. It is no accident

The teacher-student relationship, as with many others in American society, is defined by one person having power over others

that politics, religions, and businesses have been controlled primarily by men. Until recently, they were the group more likely to be socialized to be in charge. Although this pattern is beginning to disintegrate in some families and groups, it remains so prevalent that it is often not questioned; it has been accepted as the natural way of behaving. As a result, when women are harassed, wives or children are beaten, and disproportionate numbers of African American young men are jailed, many members of the society do not react.

Many people with power in U.S. society believe that they have this status because of their individual abilities and accomplishments. They usually give no credit to their membership in the dominant group. The 1994 National Conference Survey on Inter-Group Relations[5] found that most whites do not think they have an advantage over members of other racial and ethnic groups. On the other hand, the majority of people of color in the survey characterized whites as "bigoted, bossy, and unwilling to share power."[6] There appears to be a large gap in the perceptions of power between the dominant and oppressed groups in this society.

Power not only allows domination over the powerless, it also allows access to societal benefits like good housing, tax deductions, the best schools, and social services. It is not an asset that the powerful are willing to give up or readily share with those whom they see as less deserving. A more equitable sharing of resources for schools would guarantee that all students, regardless of income or ethnic background, would have qualified teachers, sufficient books and other instructional resources, well-maintained buildings and playgrounds, and access to high-level academic knowledge. Such equality does not exist across schools that students attend today. The great disparities between schools for advantaged and underserved students have been described graphically in Jonathan Kozol's book, *Savage Inequalities: Children in America's Schools:*

> New Trier's physical setting might well make the students of Du Sable High School envious. The *Washington Post* describes a neighborhood of "circular driveways, chirping birds and white-columned homes." It is, says a student, "a maple land of beauty and civility." While Du Sable is sited on one crowded city block, New Trier students have the use of 27 acres. While Du Sable's science students have to settle for makeshift equipment, New Trier's students have superior labs and up-to-date technology. One wing of the school, a physical education center that includes three separate gyms, also contains a fencing room, a wrestling room and studios for dance instruction. In all, the school has seven gyms as well as an Olympic pool.
>
> The youngsters, according to a profile of the school in *Town and Country* magazine, "make good use of the huge, well-equipped building, which is immaculately maintained by a custodial staff of 48."
>
> It is impossible to read this without thinking of a school like Goudy, where there are no science labs, no music or art classes and no playground—and where the two bathrooms, lacking toilet paper, fill the building with their stench.[7]

Difference and Otherness

Power relationships between groups appear to influence young people's perceptions of themselves and the members of other groups. One of the struggles of youth is the construction of self, including identification and affiliation with one's gender and a racial or ethnic group. This process appears to be integrally tied to identifying "otherness," which involves assigning characteristics and behavior to members of other groups to distinguish them from oneself. The construction of others places them either in a dominating or submissive role relative to the individual. It is often dependent on stereotypes that are promoted among peers and reinforced by society.

Prejudice and Discrimination

Not only do our perceptions of others affect how we see ourselves in relationship to them, but they also have an influence on the treatment of members of the groups by society. **Prejudice** is a preconceived negative attitude against members of an ethnic, racial, religious, or socioeconomic group that is different from one's own. This prejudice sometimes extends to persons with disabilities or of a different sexual orientation. Such negative attitudes are based on a number of factors, including information about members of a specific group that is stereotypical and many times not true. The prejudiced individual often has had little or no direct social contact with members of the other group.

An individual's prejudice may have limited negative impact on members of the other group. However, these attitudes are passed on to children through the **socialization** process. They can be transferred into discriminatory behavior that prevents members of a group from being interviewed for a job, joining a social club, or being treated like other professionals. Prejudices are too often reinforced by schools in which a disproportionate number of students in low achieving tracks are from low-income families[8] and in special education have limited English proficiency.[9] Through this process, many students from low-income families and ethnic minority groups are prevented from gaining the skills and knowledge necessary to enter college or an apprentice trade.

Relevant Research

Development of Racial and Gender Identity

The construction of identities of white males and females was the focus of a mid-1980s ethnographic study in a high school located in a city where the major factory had recently closed. The researcher collected data from students, teachers, and other school personnel in classrooms, study halls, the cafeteria, and extracurricular activities.

The vast majority of the white working class males in the study believed that they would have wives and families in the future. Their descriptions of females exhibited an assumed male superiority in which females were both "other" and inferior. Their male identity was "dependent upon the construction of women as unable to take care of themselves monetarily and as having full responsibility for the day-to-day activities of children." The school appeared to offer no "sustained challenge to the vision of male dominance."

The identities of these young white men not only depended on their construction of gender; they were also based on their construction of race. The goodness of white was always contrasted with the badness of black. Black men were constructed as overly sexualized individuals from whom white women must be protected. The white men in this study elaborated "their own sexuality in relation to Blacks. Black men and women [were] the foil against which they set up their own heterosexuality." On the other hand, white females did not develop their identities in relationship to blacks.

Source: Lois Weiss, "At the Intersection of Silencing and Voice: Discursive Constructions in School," *Educational Studies* 24 (1): 1–23.

Institutional Discrimination

In addition to individual prejudice and discrimination, society has historically discriminated against members of powerless groups. The individuals who control and oversee our institutions are primarily members of the dominant culture. They tend to be ethnocentric in the view that their culture is superior to others, even though they have rarely experienced other cultures and have little knowledge about them. Laws and systems have been designed to promote and support the dominant culture to help maintain its superiority and the power of its members. "English only" laws that prevent official documents and communications from being printed or spoken in any language other than English is but one example of these efforts. Such practices have often become institutionalized in state and federal laws, the judicial system, schools, and other societal institutions. They have become so ingrained in the system that it is difficult to recognize them unless one is directly affected by the discriminatory policies.

Racism

Superiority is at the center of **racism,** in which members of a racial group believe that they are innately better than members of other groups. It is not a topic easily discussed in most classrooms. It is intertwined with the lived experiences of many and evokes emotions of anger, guilt, shame, and despair. Most of us learned that the United States is a just and democratic society. Therefore, it is difficult for us to confront the contradictions that support racism. Nevertheless, it is important to acknowledge the advantages or disadvantages that racism has wrought in one's life in order to overcome its negative impact on society.

Students and adults go through stages of racial identity as they address issues of discrimination and racial identification.[10] As teachers, we should be able to recognize these stages and help students in their struggle to know themselves. Cross identified five stages in black racial identity.[11] In the *preencounter stage,* an African American has assimilated into the mainstream culture, accepting many of the beliefs and values of the dominant society, including negative stereotypes about blacks. The *encounter stage* is usually entered when an individual is confronted directly by a racist act such as rejection by white peers or being the victim of racial

---

CASE STUDY   **INTERRACIAL DATING**

Revonda Bowen is president of the junior class at Randolph County High School in the small town of Wedowee, Alabama. She is also chairperson of the junior-senior prom committee and helped raise over $7,000 for the event. Revonda's mother is black and her father is white.

In February the school principal assembled the junior and senior classes and announced that he would cancel the prom if anyone came with a date of another race. Revonda asked whom she should bring since she was a mixed-race student. In front of the entire assembly, the principal told her that her parents had made a "mistake," meaning that she should not have been born. He then said that he was trying to prevent similar "mistakes" by banning interracial dates for the prom. Revonda was crushed and burst into tears.

1. What sociohistorical conditions contributed to this incident?
2. How would you have responded to interracial dating at the prom if you had been the principal?
3. As a teacher, how would you help black and white students in your class deal with this incident?

Source: Morris Dees, Memorandum from the Southern Poverty Law Center, Montgomery, AL, April 8, 1994.

slurs or attacks. In the *immersion/emersion stage,* identification as an African American becomes paramount. At first, this identification is manifested in anger against whites, but it evolves into building a knowledge base about African American history and culture. "The result of this exploration is an emerging security in a newly defined and affirmed sense of self."[12] Individuals in the fourth stage of *internalization* begin to build coalitions with members of other oppressed groups and relationships with whites who respect and acknowledge them. Those at the fifth stage of *internalization-commitment* are able to both maintain and move beyond their personal racial identity to be concerned with African Americans as a group.

The researchers who have investigated the stages of racial identity have found that it is not as linear as was described above. Individuals may move back and forth across stages as they encounter new experiences.[13] One of the first steps in this process is for us to begin to confront our own racial identity. How close are any of us to reaching an internalization stage? If we have not struggled with issues of racism, how it impacts on our lives, and how we may contribute to its perpetuation, it will be impossible for us to develop antiracist classrooms.

Sexism and Other Isms

Women, persons with disabilities, homosexuals, persons with low incomes, the elderly, and the young also suffer from discrimination and their lack of power in society. A number of individuals are members of many of these powerless groups. They may suffer double and triple indemnity as a result of racism, **sexism,** and classism. Their chances of reaching a standard of living to be comfortable in this nation are severely limited by their circumstances and group membership, as is shown in Table 4.1 on page 86.

Sexism has contributed to limited participation of young women in advanced mathematics and sciences[14]—areas that could improve their chances for attending and being successful in college. Our system, which has not viewed women's work as equal to men's work,[15] has kept women's wages lower than men's and contributed to poverty in over one-third of the households headed by women in this country.[16] Gays and lesbians continue to face legal discrimination in many areas of the nation. The young and elderly disproportionately face poverty. Policies related to child care, subsidized housing, and access to nutritious food sometimes have prevented husbands and wives of low-income families from maintaining a household together. Equality has not been achieved when great disparity in jobs, incomes, and access to quality education continues to exist among groups.

Democracy and Schooling

Children learn to function in society through a process called socialization. Parents and families are usually the primary socialization agents, especially in the early years of a child's life. Appropriate behaviors are also reinforced in religious training, the community, and even television. Upon entrance in school, whether as an infant or at age six, teachers and other school personnel take on these roles during a large portion of the student's waking hours. At this point, the family shares the teaching function with professionals in schools.

Since the beginning of the twentieth century, policies of the United States have promoted universal education for all students. Children are required to stay in school until they are sixteen years old. Approximately 87 percent of high school

| TABLE 4.1 | What Economists Say You Are Worth |

Age (Years)	Men			Women		
	Total	White	Nonwhite	Total	White	Nonwhite
Under 1	$ 89,645	$ 93,860	$ 57,467	$ 56,996	$ 58,065	$ 49,807
1–4	101,997	106,650	65,813	64,672	65,808	56,838
5–9	136,929	143,143	88,471	86,739	88,246	76,285
10–14	183,525	191,844	118,603	116,236	118,251	102,254
15–19	238,085	248,661	154,477	148,282	150,909	130,073
20–24	288,217	300,783	185,851	167,650	170,815	145,586
25–29	314,618	328,409	198,394	166,408	169,716	143,152
30–34	314,250	328,475	191,689	155,504	158,936	131,076
35–39	296,372	310,241	173,865	142,624	146,177	116,295
40–44	265,345	277,663	152,278	127,356	130,888	99,651
45–49	224,215	234,140	128,038	108,904	112,376	80,184
50–54	176,931	184,060	102,981	86,692	89,926	58,690
55–59	124,684	129,036	76,884	62,238	64,983	37,442
60–64	71,000	73,287	45,934	39,387	41,281	21,532
65–69	33,317	34,281	23,287	21,878	22,882	11,899
70–74	18,190	18,729	12,716	12,140	12,624	6,780
75–79	9,999	10,442	5,829	6,249	6,488	3,599
80–84	5,905	6,171	3,384	2,773	2,874	1,678
85 and over	955	999	535	357	368	236

These figures show the worth of an individual based on race and gender. They are based on a 1976 Social Security Administration paper, but have been updated to 1981.

Source: M. Sinclair, "How Does Society Put a Price Tag on Human Life?" *The Washington Post,* March 22, 1981. © 1981 *The Washington Post.* Reprinted with permission.

students complete high school,[17] but we believe that even more young people should finish school. The GOALS 2000 legislation passed by Congress in 1994 calls for 90 percent of all students to graduate by the end of this century. The goal to educate nearly all of the population is an undertaking few countries attempt.

Roles of Schools

Schools serve a number of roles for society. Not only do they prepare students to be contributors to society, they also reflect good practice (universal education) and bad practice (differential achievement based on race). One's philosophical perspective determines how the roles of schools are viewed.

Reproduction. Traditionally, schools are expected to reproduce the cultural, political, social, and economic order of society. However, theorists differ in their views of how schools operate in this reproduction role. Functionalism, conflict theory, and resistance theory provide contradictory descriptions of the goals of schools as they carry out their reproductive role for society.

Functionalists view schools as important in supporting technological development, material well-being, and democracy. Since the release of the federal report *Nation at Risk* in 1983, most reports calling for the reform of schools have referred to the need for an educated workforce. A less explicit message of those reports is that schools should socialize students for their roles as workers. Schools should provide **equal educational opportunity** for all students and be a primary step for improving their social and economic status.

Conflict theorists also view schools as reproductive of society, but for purposes less noble than those granted by functionalists. Their analysis concludes that schools have been structured to maintain the power and dominance of the individuals and groups that benefit most from the current system. Rather than being benevolent institutions that provide all students an equal chance to succeed, schools legitimize existing inequities. Advantages depend greatly on ascribed characteristics. Students whose parents graduated from college are much more likely to graduate from college. Students whose parents never finished high school are themselves more likely not to finish high school. The academic tracking systems in many schools reinforce this unequal distribution. The number of middle-class students in college preparatory and advanced placement courses is disproportionately high when compared to the total school population. The number of males and students of color in special education classes is disproportionately high; students of color and those from low-income families are underrepresented in gifted and talented programs. It appears to these critics that one group is being groomed for management positions in the labor market while the second group is being prepared to labor under the direction of the first group. Thus, schools provide neither equal educational opportunity nor a chance to improve one's status to any appreciable degree (except for rare individual achievements).

Over the past decade some researchers have investigated the interactions of students and teachers as schools carry out their reproduction function. It is not an automatic process that is implemented with systematic precision. Students sometimes resist domination by school authorities. They do not readily accept their inferiority status. Kreisberg describes student resistance:

> Students resist doing homework and delay the beginning of classes. They develop intricate systems of cheating and psyching out teachers. They smoke cigarettes and marijuana in school bathrooms and sell drugs in school stairwells. They are opinionated with teachers and wear clothes that offend adults. They refuse to participate in some classes and organize to change unfair rules. (p. 17)

The resistance theory suggests much more interaction in the reproduction process than has been described in the previous two theories. It also allows for possibilities to change the system of reproduction by encouraging the development of schools that are not based on domination and submission and that actually model democracy. Students become active participants who help define and redefine schools in the process of resistance.

Reconstructionism. Some educators believe schools are able to do more than just reproduce society. They believe that schools do not need merely to reflect the inequities that prevail in the broader society; rather, schools can reconstruct or transform society. They believe that all students can learn at a high level regardless of their race, ethnicity, gender, or socioeconomic status. Education can make more of a difference in the lives of students than it currently does.

To implement a reconstructionist approach, classrooms and schools become democratic settings in which both students and teachers are active learners and participants. Students study problems confronting society and learn the skills that allow them to attack practices that are inequitable to some students. Teachers and other school personnel actively work with the community to overcome inequities and injustices to students and their families. Social justice, human rights, human dignity, and equity are critical values that guide the work of reconstructionism. In the process the school itself should become a model of democracy that leads, rather than follows, societal practices.

Purposes of Schools

Sometimes the purpose of schools reflects a perceived shortcoming in the current education system. The plethora of reports calling for the reform of education that have been written over the past two centuries have identified different purposes for schools. The five purposes described below are only a sampling of those most often mentioned by educators and the public. Most schools address each of these issues, but one may receive more prominence than others because it is a trend at a particular time.

Citizenship. Educators, parents, and policymakers agree that schools should help students become *good citizens*. There is less agreement about how schools should do this. In some schools, especially elementary schools, students receive a grade or rating on their citizenship within the classroom. Historically, students have taken a civics or government course, or they study these issues in another social studies course. The focus of citizenship education or civics and government courses is usually on the structure of the United States political system and treasured documents such as the Constitution and Bill of Rights. Patriotism and loyalty to the United States are implicit values that often undergird these courses and

Civic education usually emphasizes patriotism and national loyalty.

the hidden curriculum. A limitation of this approach is that students are seldom provided the opportunity to grapple with the problems and issues that are inherent to our democratic society. Students may learn the civic values, but never be pushed to discuss why inequities remain in society.

In a discussion of reconceptualizing civic education, Pratte[18] suggests that preparation for citizenship cannot be limited to a course. The school should promote democratic citizens who respect others; believe in human dignity; are concerned about and care for others; and fight for justice, fairness, and tolerance. Dewey also believed that good citizenship involves participating in the making of laws as well as obeying them. Through education, students should be guided to develop habits of mind that will bring about social changes without introducing disorder.[19] Students will learn through practice how to be active, involved citizens. What better place to model democratic practice and equitable participation than in our schools?

Participation in the Work Force. One of the eight national education goals that President Clinton signed into law in 1994 stated that by the year 2000, "every American will be literate and will possess the knowledge and skills necessary to compete in a global economy." This statement parallels many of the education reform documents. A major concern expressed in these reports has been the quality of the workforce, which includes growing numbers of women and persons of color at all levels. Schools are blamed for not providing students with the skills and behaviors necessary to participate in today's economy. Some employers report that many young people do not read, write, and compute at the level needed for the jobs available. In response, these employers have sometimes established their own training to teach basic literacy.

There is a lack of agreement about the nature of these necessary skills, especially in an economy in which the greatest growth in jobs will be in the service areas, where persons of color and women have disproportionately high representation. Most high schools prepare students either to attend college or to get a job soon after graduation. Many areas of the country have vocational high schools to teach occupational skills. A number of school districts have established magnet schools with single purposes, including career preparation in the arts, health fields, computing, and service areas like foods, hotels, and tourism. A more serious dilemma is that low-income students, students of color, and females are disproportionately represented in nonacademic tracks.

Educators, policymakers, and the business community debate the "real" purpose of schools. Is the primary purpose to help students learn a trade, or learn how to learn, or learn how to take orders and follow the rules? This question is particularly important when conditions change as rapidly as they do in today's society. The vocation for which one was prepared may become obsolete. Perhaps

Many students begin to prepare for a job after graduation by taking vocational courses in high school or at the postsecondary level in vocational schools designed for that purpose.

John Dewey was on target in 1916 when he wrote that "a society which is mobile, which is full of channels for the distribution of changes occurring anywhere, must see to it that members are educated to personal initiative and adaptability."[20] Perhaps we should prepare students to think, adjust to change, and be active participants in their life's work.

Academic Competence. Periodically, the public becomes very concerned about the academic competence of students. This concern is reinforced by well-publicized reports of scores on achievement tests. Some school districts base their reputations on how well their students perform. Countries and their education systems are compared using performance on international tests. When the scores of U.S. students fall below those of students in other countries, policymakers become concerned. In the 1980s, concern about performance in reading, writing, and mathematics led to a back-to-basics movement in which the traditional academic subjects were emphasized. "Frills" such as the development of self-esteem, hobbies, and any other areas that took time away from academic study were condemned as a misuse of public funds. In response, a number of states and school districts increased the length of the school day so that students could have more time to learn what was expected. This emphasis reappears in two of the eight goals in GOALS 2000.

Social Development. One of the reasons that parents send their children to school is to give them the opportunity to develop interpersonal skills by interacting with other students. In this process students should learn to respect others; they also learn a set of rules for working appropriately with peers and others. Although there is usually not a course to teach skills in social development, appropriate behavior is constantly reinforced by teachers and other school personnel in the classroom and on the playground.

In our teaching we can give students opportunities to work with students from diverse cultural backgrounds and learn about those differences in the process. Interactions across groups can be encouraged through cooperative learning activities in which students from different groups are placed together. Other team projects allow us to place together students who might not seek each other out otherwise. A part of our teaching will be helping students to learn to work together positively.

Today's technology also opens many possibilities for interacting with students and adults in cultures beyond our own school boundaries. Internet and two-way video connections allow students in rural New Mexico to talk directly with students in inner city Chicago or Toyko, Japan. Many teachers have developed these linkages themselves with the assistance of other knowledgeable teachers they have met in college classes and at professional meetings. Your professor may know of easily accessible software to help you begin to make these connections across cultures.

Cultural Transmission. Schools around the world are expected to transmit the culture of their nation to young people so that they can both maintain it and pass it on to the next generation. This task often has been approached by teaching history with an emphasis on important events and heroes. As part of this process, children learn the importance of patriotism and loyalty. The formal and informal curricula have been designed to reflect and reinforce the values of the national culture.

These national values and rules are so embedded in most aspects of schooling that most participants—teachers and students alike—do not realize they exist. The only exceptions may be students who do not belong to the dominant culture or whose families have recently immigrated. In these cases, students and families quickly learn that schools do not reflect, nor do they usually support, aspects of their culture that differ from the mainstream. This dissonance between schools and families is most noticeable when students are from non-European backgrounds. Students from religious backgrounds that have not evolved from a Judeo-Christian heritage are also likely to question the culture that is being transmitted at school. The challenge for educators is to transmit the national culture while including the richness and contributions of many who do not yet see themselves as an integral part of that culture. In this way, we also begin to change and expand the national culture.

Whose Schools?

Although schools are expected to transmit the culture of the nation to the younger generation, we do not agree on *whose* culture. Is there really a national or common culture that the diverse racial, ethnic, language, and religious groups in the country accept? Dialects, behaviors, and values vary within the same cultural group as well as across groups whose members live in different regions of the country. Cultural differences are even experienced by people who move from rural areas to the city or vice versa.

How can schools begin to accommodate all of these differences? A number of conservative politicians and talk show hosts argue that schools should ignore diversity. They believe that all students should learn our common heritage and adopt the national culture as their own. In this approach, students who are not members of the dominant group are expected to leave their native language or dialect and other cultural characteristics at the doorstep of the school.

Multicultural theorists and educators argue that the diversity of students enriches the school community. They believe that cultural differences should be valued and integrated throughout the curriculum and all activities of the school. In this approach, the cultural background and experiences of students are used to teach academic and other skills at high levels.

Alternative Schools. The public schools in some districts offer options in which parents can choose the schools they deem appropriate for their children. (Similar to private schools, parents may not receive their first choice if more students have applied than there are spaces available.) In a number of large school districts, magnet schools offer specialized curriculum in the arts, languages, mathematics and science, and technical fields. Some schools have been established to place the students' ethnicity at the center of the curriculum. In an Afrocentric curriculum, for instance, African American history and experiences are the core from which the world is viewed, rather than the traditional center of Western Europe.

Some private schools were established to provide an alternative for whites who did not want their children to attend schools that were being desegregated.[21] Other private schools limit their enrollment to either males or females or to students of the same faith. The more elite boarding schools usually offer scholarships to some students who cannot afford the tuition, but are attended predominantly by children of the rich. A few public schools today have been designed for females only, with the goal of improving their academic achievement, especially in science and mathematics, and building their self-esteem. A few large cities like Detroit, Baltimore, and Minneapolis have established schools for African American and/or Native American students to provide positive gender and cultural identity models and teach skills that will empower them to overcome many of the obstacles they face. Thus, in some schools, students continue to be segregated for the purpose of avoiding integration. In other cases, the segregation has the goal of overcoming obstacles to success for members of selected powerless groups.

A growing number of parents do not enroll their children in either private or public schools. Instead, they receive permission from the state to teach their children at home. In some cases, they believe that they are more effective teachers. More often, they believe that schools teach values that they cannot support; home teaching allows them to instill the values that they think are important.

Whose Values? The selection of a private school or home schooling and support for segregated schools has been based, in part, on the values that parents believe schooling can impart. Although schools usually do not offer a course in which values are explicitly presented and discussed, values implicitly influence the formal and **informal curriculum.** They usually support the current ideological, political, and economic order of society in which individualism is much more highly regarded than the rights of the group. The Protestant work ethic is upheld in the expectation of hard work and the belief that one will be successful in life as a result. Although these may seem uncontroversial, they can be the cause of extensive debate and emotional pleas at meetings with groups of parents, school board meetings, community forums, and magazines.

Some parents are concerned that the curriculum does not reflect their religious values; often, they think that their religion is purposefully denigrated in schools. These concerns are expressed most frequently by members of some fundamentalist Christian communities, but also by Amish and Hutterite communities, and some Jewish, Muslim, and other non-Christian families and communities. On the other hand, atheists believe that religious values, especially Christian ones, pervade the school curriculum.

The emphasis on individualism and competition that is prevalent in many schools is not compatible with the cooperative patterns practiced by Native American tribes and many Latino and African American communities. These differences can lead to conflict between parents and schools and between groups within a community. The courts have often been asked to sort through these value issues since the plaintiffs believe that schools have acted inappropriately. They may also believe that either the schools do not have a democratic process in which they can be heard or the majority of the community will not support their petitions. Therefore, they turn to the justice system to help clarify the issues. School prayer, teaching creationism, banning books, sex education, and segregation are among the areas that have been tested in the courts.

Because parents and other groups in a community may vehemently disagree with the values to be reinforced in schools, we should be aware of our own values. Knowing our values as well as those of the families represented in the school should help us prepare for potential conflicts. Expectations can vary greatly from one community or school to another.

CASE STUDY | VALUES IN EDUCATION

*B*eginning in 1989, the Pennsylvania State Board of Education began revising its state code from Carnegie Units of coursework to student learning outcomes (sometimes called outcomes based education or OBE). Outcome #6, which was presented to the public in hearings in 1991, focused on appreciating and understanding others:

> (i) All students explore and articulate the similarities and differences among various cultures and the history and contributions of diverse cultural groups, including groups to which they belong. (ii) All students relate, in writing, speech or other media, the history and nature of prejudice to current issues facing communities, the United States, and other nations. (iii) All students develop skills of communicating, negotiating, and cooperating with others to solve interpersonal and intergroup problems and conflicts. (iv) All students work effectively with others, demonstrating respect for the dignity, worth, contributions, and equal rights of each person.

Reactions to the proposed fifty-seven core outcomes were diverse and intense. Outcome #6 was attacked by a well-organized special-interest group, Citizens for Excellence in Education. The opponents read the outcome as promoting a value system different than the student's own. "Other" was defined as alternative lifestyles, particularly homosexual. "Tolerance" was a value that they could not support.

The debate in Pennsylvania over values and OBE drew the media, and the controversy was expanded. The education reform package was defeated in January 1993. Outcome #6 and all references to attitudes and behavior were removed from the package. The revision was accepted in June 1993.

1. Why did the Citizens for Excellence in Education develop such an active interest in the Pennsylvania reform package?
2. How could a small, special-interest group take advantage of the public's lack of information on this issue?
3. How could state officials have prevented such an attack on the reform package? What impact do these debates have on local classrooms and schools?

Source: Judith McQuaide and Ann-Maureen Pliska, "The Challenge to Pennsylvania's Educational Reform," *Educational Leadership 51* (4) (December 1993/January 1994): 16–21.

Equality and Education

Although equality is an espoused goal of democracy, its meaning differs based on the speaker. Many believe that each individual has an equal chance to succeed, which is measured by the dominant group in terms of wealth and accumulated material goods. This system of **meritocracy** is built on the importance of the individual. With hard work, diligence, and persistence, an individual should be able to finish school, attend college, and obtain a well-paying job. Poverty and discrimination are obstacles to be overcome by individuals.

A problem with meritocracy is that not all individuals begin the game of life from the same starting line. Whites from the middle class and above start with advantages such as the dominant culture being their own, sufficient family income to support a college education, decent housing, adequate health care, and good schools with qualified teachers. The advantages of the parents are passed on to the children, allowing them a head start in the race. In reality, the children of the

As a result of family income, some students may have a head start over others in school.

wealthy have a much greater chance of being wealthy in their adulthood than the children of low-income families. The powerful are able to ensure that their advantages are inherited by their children. Therefore, equality could only begin to be realized in this system if the children from powerless groups were provided the same or similar advantages.

Critics of the public rhetoric on equality charge that our institutions and political and economic systems are rigged to support the privileged few rather than the pluralistic majority. Both the shrinking middle class and the widening gap between wealth and poverty contribute to this critique. Nevertheless, some people still think that a more equitable society is not only desirable, but possible to achieve. Resources could begin to be more fairly distributed if all workers received a decent wage (today's minimum wage leaves families at the official poverty level). The application of civil rights laws and a drastic reduction of discriminatory practices would contribute greatly to the provision of fairness and justice in the distribution of societal benefits. In the same spirit, schools should ensure that their policies and practices are equitable. They could begin this investigation by examining whether gifted and talented programs and honors programs are accessible to students from diverse cultural groups.

If a society accepts equality as one of its primary goals, its members must be active participants in achieving the goal. One step is the refusal to accept needless human suffering and exploitation that is reflected in homelessness; inadequate minimum wage; and schools that are dangerous, unsafe, and inadequately staffed. Another step is the confrontation and elimination of racism, sexism, and other forms of discrimination.[22]

Equal Educational Opportunity

One of the policies for addressing equality in the educational system is equal educational opportunity. All students, regardless of their backgrounds, are to be provided similar opportunities to learn and benefit from schooling. The dilemma in this approach is what comprises an equal educational opportunity. On the surface, it would seem that all students should have access to quality teachers, small classes, technology, college preparatory courses, a building that supports learning, and a safe environment. In reality, most equal educational opportunity programs have struggled with overcoming educational deficiencies of underserved students by providing compensatory or remedial programs to reduce the educational gaps that have given the advantaged students a head start. The other factors that would provide equal opportunity have not been addressed by most policymakers and educators.

Even when the school has the latest technology, is clean and well-maintained, and is staffed by qualified professionals, equal opportunity is not automatically guaranteed. A number of factors need to be considered. What percentage of female and minority students are found in advanced mathematics and science classes? Who comprises the college preparatory and advanced placement classes? Who is assigned or chooses a general or vocational track? Who is referred to special education classes? Who has access to the best teachers? Who participates in which extracurricular activities? If the percentage of students from diverse groups in these classes is somewhat proportional to their representation in school, equal educational opportunity may be approaching the goal of its supporters.

Opportunity to Learn Standards

According to the *Goals 2000: Education American Act*, schools must provide all students the opportunity to learn the skills outlined in the national standards being developed for mathematics, science, English, the arts, foreign languages, history, geography, civics, and economics. The provision of remediation for the underserved is no longer the focus. The expectation is that all students can learn. Because Goals 2000 also expects U.S. students to achieve better on international tests than students in any other part of the world, we may wonder if opportunity to learn actually means the ability to perform well on some tests. More optimistically, the standards could help prevent students from being tracked into courses and programs that limit their access to higher level knowledge. They could even encourage critical thinking and viewing the world and academic subjects from multiple perspectives.

Equality of Results

Some theorists and educators would argue that we must not stop at just providing the opportunity to learn. This approach again places the burden on individuals in that they choose whether to take advantage of the opportunity. If the goal is to ensure an equality of results, we would be expected to develop strategies for helping all students learn at a high level. We would start our careers with the disposition or belief that all children, regardless of their group memberships and environmental circumstances, are capable of learning. Students who are not performing well academically or otherwise would become the intellectual challenges for the teacher, or even better, a team of teachers and other support personnel. The goal would become the development of strategies to ensure learning rather than simply to move students to a different class to accommodate their limitations (and limit their chances for success in school).

PROFESSIONAL DILEMMA

What If There Are Only a Few Girls in the Calculus Class?

Many argue that the reason few females take advanced mathematics and science classes is simply that they are not interested in these fields. Few suggest that they don't participate because they are not as smart as the male students. Why are most young women not interested in these subjects?

In some cases, they may believe that there is no payoff in taking these courses, which are usually perceived to be very difficult. They may be planning to work only a short time before they marry and stay at home to raise children. Perhaps no one has encouraged them to attend college—the only reason that one would take these courses anyway. Learning the skills that will translate into a job immediately after graduation may be viewed as a more practical route to follow.

One reason that few females participate in advanced mathematics and science courses is that they do not view themselves as potential mathematicians or scientists. There are few female role models to help them develop such an identity. Teachers and other school personnel can play an important part in socializing girls to see themselves in roles other than the traditional ones of mother, wife, teacher, nurse, secre-

Culture of the School

The school itself is a cultural system that differs from the family and broader community in which we participate. Despite individual differences in ability, rate of learning, and personal interest, most students are subjected to the same type of instruction. The school's rules regulate classroom behavior as well as determine acceptable dress and speech. Common rituals are found in athletics, extracurricular clubs, graduation exercises, and school social events. The signs and emblems of the school's culture are displayed in school songs, colors, and cheers.

Formal Practices

The school operation embraces varied formal practices that are common across most schools in the nation. Students are generally assigned to grade levels on the basis of age rather than readiness, ability, or interest. Almost all children start the first grade at age six; most attend kindergarten if it is available.

The length of a high school class is relatively standard, at around 50 minutes no matter what needs to be learned and how much time it may take. The Carnegie Unit is still used to award one high school credit for 200 minutes per week for 36 weeks of class time; a student must have completed a specified number of Carnegie Units to graduate from high school. Authority is adult-centered. Students are allowed little input into the content to be taught or the way in which it is taught. Reporting of educational achievements is also formalized. Letter grades are traditionally awarded on the basis of a competitive system that compares the achievements of students.

Some schools have attempted to reduce the formal structured experiences of schools by creating learning centers, nongraded programs, and individualized learning packages based on readiness and interest. Assessments of student achievement are beginning to move beyond pencil and paper tests. Educators and test makers are designing systems that include multiple assessments that show

tary, or librarian. Too many parents, counselors, and teachers strongly encourage males to take these classes, but do not aggressively push the females to enroll in them.

Schooling contributes to this problem in other ways as well. Researchers who observe teachers' interactions with their male and female students find differences in the way teachers respond to the two groups. Teachers interacted more with males than females during lessons in mathematics. Teachers were more likely to work individually with males on classroom management, directions, and procedures. When teachers consciously changed their interactions to be more equitable, the females performed well. In fact, "the more that teachers asked high-level mathematics questions

and interacted about mathematics at a high cognitive level with girls, the more girls learned about a higher cognitive level of mathematics."

- Do you believe that males and females have different aptitudes for mathematics and science? Why?
- How would you encourage females in your classroom to both learn and like mathematics?
- What characteristics would you expect to find in a good, nonsexist classroom?

Source: Elizabeth Fennema and Penelope L. Peterson, "Effective Teaching for Girls and Boys: The Same or Different," in David C. Berliner and Barak V. Rosenshine, eds. *Talks to Teachers.* New York: Random House, 1987, 111–125.

much more than factual pieces of information that students can recall. They also indicate the ability to think critically and to perform effectively. They are becoming more authentic in that students are expected to perform in real life, rather than contrived, settings.

Traditions

Variations in the school culture are associated with regional influences, the social structure of a community, and location in a rural, urban, or suburban area. Some schools are influenced greatly by the religion of the children's families; others by the presence of a large military base.

Regional interests may influence the sports activities that are fueled through school spirit. In the Midwest, for example, basketball is the favored sport. In other parts of the country fierce athletic competition may be associated with football, swimming, wrestling, or gymnastics. Rural schools often emphasize Future Farmers of America clubs, agricultural programs, and 4-H clubs—activities that you are not likely to find in urban schools.

Schools with long histories have developed lasting traditions that are transferred from generation to generation. Sometimes graduates retain feelings of pride about their schools. For others, the memories are of mediocrity and of never being challenged.

Informal Curriculum

All schools offer a formal curriculum that includes coursework in numerous academic areas. In addition, there is an informal curriculum that is seldom discussed and sometimes not acknowledged by educators. It is composed of the rules that guide the work of the school. This curriculum defines the behaviors and attitudes expected of both students and teachers, and it signifies which students are privileged by promoting their cultural values and patterns. The teacher is acknowledged

A region's special interests are often demonstrated through a school's extracurricular activities.

as the expert and is granted authority for ruling over students.[23] Critical theorists argue that these practices help maintain the status quo and current inequities in society.

For most students from the dominant culture the informal curriculum generally reinforces behaviors expected by their parents. These students fit fairly easily into the school culture. On the other hand, students from different cultural backgrounds may find school practices foreign and even contradictory to what they learn at home. The emphasis on competition between students in the classroom provides an example of one learning style being valued over another.

The informal curriculum could become more equitable and supportive of democratic principles if educators acknowledged that many school policies and practices are discriminatory because they promote and reinforce only the dominant culture. Teachers must recognize their own prejudices and discriminatory practices in teaching and management of the classroom and work to develop strategies for eliminating them.

Global Perspectives: Studying in Japan

The Japanese are among the most highly educated people in the world. All young people finish junior high school, 94 percent attend high school, and nearly a third enroll in college.[24] Students in Japan spend more time in school than U.S. students. "The school day is longer, the school week is five and a half days, and the school year is broken only by a short summer vacation of a little over a month in late July and August, a New Year's holiday, and a break before the start of the school year at the beginning of April."[25] In addition, students are assigned daily homework, beginning in the first grade, and a large percentage of them spend their summer vacation studying. Of the 600 elementary school students surveyed in Tokyo, 75 percent went to *juku* (cram school).[26] Discrepancies in the quality of education across rural, urban, and suburban schools are limited as measured by the achievements of students in higher education.

Summary and Implications

Theories of functionalism, conflict, and resistance provide different descriptions of the role of schools in reproducing culture and society. The theory of reconstructionism suggests that schools can transform society into democratic and equitable institutions. Schools serve many purposes in society. Among these purposes are the development of citizenship, preparation for work, the development of academic and social competence, and the transmission of the culture to another generation. Although most parents would agree with these purposes, they may disagree about the values that undergird the curriculum and teaching practice. It is parents' perception of the values being taught that leads to conflict in some communities.

Group membership becomes important in schooling because many students come from families and communities that do not share the culture that is reinforced in school policies, practices, and expectations. U.S. society is based primarily on the cultural traditions of western Europe. Through historical and political developments, whites have been socialized to view themselves as superior to the members of other racial groups. This power differential is also found in relations between males and females and between individuals who are relatively wealthy and those in poverty. Individual achievement is highly valued within the dominant culture. In the meritocratic system that undergirds the U.S. economic and political system, successful individuals are the ones that deserve the greatest rewards from society. Individuals who are not

successful are blamed for their lack of ability or desire. Proponents of this view believe that discrimination no longer exists and they resent policies and practices that grant rights to members of a group rather than to individuals. Critics of meritocracy believe that greater equality could be achieved in society through a more equal distribution of resources, the serious application of civil rights laws, and a drastic reduction in discriminatory practices against the members of powerless groups. Educators debate the value of equal educational opportunity, opportunity to learn standards, and monitoring the equality of results in promoting greater equality in schools. As of the mid-1990s, schools are still far from providing equality for all students.

Discussion Questions

1. Why is it so difficult for middle-class whites to acknowledge that their group membership historically and currently places them in a privileged position?

2. Provide examples of discriminatory practices against females, African Americans, non-native English speakers, Native Americans, the disabled, the elderly, and/or homosexuals that have become institutionalized in the educational system.

3. How do functionalists and reconstructionists expect schools to implement the purposes outlined in this chapter?

4. How can teachers bridge the value differences between various groups in the community? What curriculum content could spark debates in the community?

5. Contrast meritocracy and equality. What characteristics in society would be indicators that equality exists across groups in this country?

Journal/Portfolio Development

1. Define democracy and write a paper that (a) describes a classroom that operates on democratic principles and (b) contrasts it with traditional classrooms. The description should include the set-up of the room, the interaction between the teacher and students, and the interactions of students, among other characteristics.

2. Select a school or community in which there has been debate regarding the values to be reflected in

the curriculum. (Widely publicized examples can be found in New York City, Pennsylvania, Ohio, and Kentucky.) Analyze the fundamental differences between the groups in a paper, chart, or pictorial format. Identify strategies that could have prevented the conflict.

School-Based Experiences

1. In one of your next observations of a class in a school, identify and record the written and unwritten rules that guide the interactions of students with each other and the teacher. What values are being reinforced with these rules that make up part of the informal curriculum?

2. During one of your next visits to a school, observe how students interact with individuals from cultural backgrounds different than their own. These observations could occur in the classroom, but also in the halls, at the principal's office, and during extracurricular activities. Are students interacting

across ethnic, racial, gender, and socioeconomic groups? What is the nature of the interactions? How has the school encouraged positive, productive interactions? Students, teachers, and parents could be helpful informants in your data gathering; ask them for their perceptions.

Notes

1. *Webster's Ninth New Collegiate Dictionary.* Springfield, MA: Merriam-Webster, 1991, 338.

2. James A. Banks, *Teaching Strategies for Ethnic Studies.* 5th ed. Boston: Allyn and Bacon, 1991.

3. John Dewey, *Democracy and Education: An Introduction to the Philosophy of Education.* New York: The Free Press, 1916, 99.

4. Seth Kreisberg, *Transforming Power: Domination, Empowerment, and Education.* Albany, NY: State University of New York Press, 11.

5. The National Conference of Christians and Jews. *Taking America's Pulse: A Summary Report of the National Conference Survey on Inter-group Relations.* New York: Author, 1994.

6. Ibid, 2.

7. Jonathan Kozol, *Savage Inequalities: Children in America's Schools.* New York: Crown, 1991, 65.

8. Jennie Oakes, *Keeping Track: How Schools Structure Inequality.* New Haven, CT: Yale University Press, 1985.

9. Richard A. Figueroa and Eugene Garcia, "Issues in Testing Students from Culturally and Linguistically Diverse Backgrounds," *Multicultural Education* (Fall 1994): 10–23.

10. J. E. Helms, Ed., *Black and White Racial Identity: Theory, Research and Practice.* Westport, CT: Greenwood Press, 1990.

11. William E. Cross, Jr., *Shades of Black: Diversity in African-American Identity.* Philadelphia: Temple University Press, 1991.

12. Beverly Daniel Tatum, "Talking about Race, Learning about Racism: The Application of Racial Identity Development Theory in the Classroom," *Harvard Educational Review* 62(1) (Spring 1992): 1–24.

13. T. A. Parham, "Cycles of Psychological Negrescence," *The Counseling Psychologist* 17(2) (1989): 187–226.

14. Oakes, 1985.

15. Harriet Bradley, *Men's Work, Women's Work: A Sociological History of the Sexual Division of Labour in Employment.* Minneapolis: University of Minnesota Press, 1989.

16. United States Bureau of the Census, *Statistical Abstract of the United States: 1992.* Washington, DC: U.S. Government Printing Office, 1992.

17. Ibid.

18. Richard Pratte, *The Civic Imperative: Examining the Need for Civic Education.* New York: Teachers College Press, 1988.

19. Dewey, 1916.

20. Ibid, 88.

21. Meyer Weinberg, *A Chance to Learn: A History of Race and Education in the United States.* New York: Cambridge University Press, 1977.

22. Henry A. Giroux, "Postmodernism as Border Pedagogy: Redefining the Boundaries of Race and Ethnicity," in Henry A. Giroux, Ed., *Postmodernism, Feminism, and Cultural Politics: Redrawing Educational Boundaries.* Albany, NY: State University of New York Press, 1991, 217–256.

23. John I. Goodlad, *A Place Called School: Prospects for the Future.* New York: McGraw-Hill, 1984.

24. Edwin O. Reischauer and Marius B. Jansen, *The Japanese Today: Change and Continuing* (enlarged edition). Cambridge, MA: Harvard University Press, 1995.

25. Ibid, 190.

26. Alexander Besher, *The Pacific Rim Almanac.* New York: HarperCollins, 1991.

Bibliography

Cookson, Peter W., and Persell, Caroline Hodges. *Preparing for Power: America's Elite Boarding Schools.* New York: Basic Books, 1985.

Edelman, Marian Wright. "Winson and Dovie Hudson's Dream." *Harvard Educational Review* 63(4) (Winter 1993): 463–491.

Estrada, Kelly, and McLaren, Peter. "A Dialogue on Multiculturalism and Democratic Culture." *Educational Researcher 22*(3) (April 1993): 27–33.

Giroux, Henry A. "Postmodernism as Border Pedagogy: Redefining the Boundaries of Race and Ethnicity," in Henry A. Giroux, Ed. *Postmodernism, Feminism, and Cultural Politics: Redrawing Educational Boundaries.* Albany, NY: State University of New York Press, 1991, 217–256.

———— *Teachers as Intellectuals: Toward a Critical Pedagogy of Learning.* Granby, MA: Bergin & Garvey, 1988.

Goodlad, John I. *A Place Called School: Prospects for the Future.* New York: McGraw-Hill, 1984.

———— *Teachers for Our Nation's Schools.* San Francisco: Jossey-Bass, 1990.

Gutmann, Amy. *Democratic Education.* Princeton, NJ: Princeton University Press, 1987.

———— "Democratic Education in Difficult Times." *Teachers College Record 92*(1) (Fall 1990): 7–20.

Hodge, John L. "Equality: Beyond Dualism and Oppression," in David Theo Goldberg, Ed. *Anatomy of Racism.* Minneapolis: University of Minnesota Press, 1990, 89–107.

Kozol, Jonathan. *Savage Inequalities: Children in America's Schools.* New York: Crown, 1991.

Kreisberg, Seth. *Transforming Power: Domination, Empowerment, and Education.* Albany, NY: State University of New York Press, 1992.

The National Conference of Christians and Jews. *Taking America's Pulse: A Report of the National Conference Survey on Inter-group Relations.* New York: Author, 1994.

Plank, David N., and Boyd, William Lowe. "Antipolitics, Education, and Institutional Choice: The Flight from Democracy. *American Educational Research Journal 31*(2) (Summer 1994): 263–281.

Pratte, Richard. *The Civic Imperative: Examining the Need for Civic Education.* New York: Teachers College Press, 1988.

Scheurich, James Joseph. "Toward a White Discourse on White Racism." *Educational Researcher 22*(8), (November 1993): 5–10.

Sleeter, Christine. "White Racism." *Multicultural Education* (Spring 1994): 5–8.

Weinberg, Meyer. "Diversity without Equality Equals Oppression." *Multicultural Education* (Spring 1994): 13–16.

Welch, Sharon. "An Ethic of Solidarity and Difference," in Henry A. Giroux, Ed., *Postmodernism, Feminism, and Cultural Politics: Redrawing Educational Boundaries.* Albany, NY: State University of New York Press, 1991, 83–89.

5 A Multicultural Society

Focus Questions

1 Why is culture so important in describing a group of people?
2 How do race, ethnicity, gender, and socioeconomic status interact in society to result in discrimination and inequity?
3 What impact do society and culture have on the education process?
4 What is the role of group memberships in determining one's own cultural identity?
5 What are the dangers in responding to students based only on what appears to be their ethnic group identity?

Key Terms and Concepts

Acculturation: The process of learning the cultural patterns of a second culture.

Assimilation: The process by which an immigrant group or culturally distinct group is incorporated into the dominant culture.

Cultural pluralism: A state that exists when different groups maintain their culture parallel and equal to the dominant one in a society.

Culture: The totality of socially transmitted ways of thinking, believing, feeling, and acting within a group of people that is passed from one generation to the next.

Diversity: The wide range of ways in which human groups and populations have observable and demonstrable physical and behavioral differences.[1]

Enculturation: The process of learning the characteristics of the culture of the group to which one belongs.

Ethnic group: Identification of membership in a group based on the national origin (that is, a specific country or area of the world) of one's ancestors, a shared culture, and sense of common destiny.

Ethnocentrism: The belief that members of one's group are superior to the members of other groups.

Social stratification: Levels of social class ranking based on one's income, education, occupation, wealth, and power in society.

Socioeconomic status: Criteria to describe the economic condition of individuals based on their income, occupation, and educational attainment.

Our actions, values, thoughts, and patterns of learning are controlled by our **culture.** Most of the time, we are not aware of the power of our cultural upbringing. This phenomenon often leads to **ethnocentrism,** in which members of a group view their culture as superior to all others. Persons from other cultural groups are perceived as odd, amusing, inferior, or immoral.[2] Ethnocentrism is sometimes promoted in emotional calls for patriotism, especially at times when a country is involved in a political conflict with another country. The other country is often denigrated by name calling based on negative stereotypes of its citizens; this occurred in the 1990 war between Iraq and the United States and its allies.

Ethnocentrism is not limited to relations with other nations; it occurs often between groups within the United States. Homosexuals are victims of abuse by radio talk show hosts and some religious groups. The religious right appears to believe that its cultural values and lifestyles are the only correct ones; alternatives are not tolerated. Historically, many members of the dominant culture have believed that their culture is superior to those with non-European roots. Ethnocentrism extends beyond individuals' views of their culture, and has led to discriminatory policies and practices that favor members of the dominant group.

One of the manifestations of ethnocentrism is the inability to accept differences among groups as natural and appropriate. Educational philosopher, Young Pai, describes this reaction to others:

> When the dominant group in a society adopts the posture that its own set of values constitutes the only idealized norm in that society, the ethnic practices or traits of minority cultures are likely to be seen as deficient patterns that must be corrected either through education or coercion. In other words, the dominant culture tends to treat the differences as *deficits.* This attitude makes it difficult for us to see that other cultures also provide effective means of dealing with the needs and problems of the respective societies.[3]

When differences are translated into a deficit model, groups that are not accepted as part of the dominant culture are expected to give up their culture in order to be accepted. Schools and other institutions marginalize members of these groups because their differences are not valued. These attitudes are translated into compensatory education for children of poverty, transitional bilingual education for students with limited English proficiency, and special education for students with disabilities.

If teachers believe that all students can learn and that teachers can ensure that learning occurs, they must confront their own ethnocentrism. Often we do not recognize that we subtly, and sometimes overtly, transmit our feelings of superiority over students and their cultural groups in our interactions in the classroom and in the curriculum content that we teach. To be effective teachers, we need to think about differences as part of our rich cultural history.

Culture and Society

Society is composed of individuals and groups that share a common history, traditions, and experiences with other members of the same group. Culture provides the blueprint for how we think, feel, and behave in society. It imposes rules and order on its members by providing the patterns that help them know the meaning of their behavior. Members of the same cultural group understand the subtleties of their shared language, nonverbal communications, and ways of thinking and knowing. They often misread the cultural cues of other groups, leading to miscommunications and misunderstandings between the members of the two groups.

People around the world have the same biological and psychological needs, but the way that they meet these needs is culturally determined. The location of the group, available resources, and traditions have a great influence on the foods eaten, grooming and clothing patterns, teaching and learning styles, and interactions of men and women and parents and children. The meaning and celebration of birth, marriage, old age, and death depend on one's culture. Culture impacts on all aspects of our lives, from the simplest patterns of eating and bathing to the more complex patterns of teaching, learning, and caring for those who are less fortunate.

Characteristics of Culture

Culture is learned, shared, adapted, and dynamic. We learn our own culture through **enculturation** that parallels the socialization process. Our parents and other caretakers teach us the culture and the acceptable norms of behavior within it. We internalize our cultural patterns so well and so early that it is difficult for us to accept that there are different, but just as appropriate, ways of behaving and thinking. When we live and actively participate in a second culture, we begin to more clearly see our own unique cultural patterns. Understanding cultural differences and learning to recognize when students do not share our own cultural patterns are critical steps in the provision of an equitable learning environment. Therefore, it is important to learn much more about cultures other than our own.

Culture is not static. It is dynamic and continually adapted to serve the needs of the group. Individuals and families adapt their culture as they move from a rural to an urban area. The conditions of a geographic region may require a number of adjustments. Technological changes in the world and society can also lead to changes in our cultural patterns.

Dominant or Mainstream Culture

The dominant culture in this country is that of white, middle-class Protestants whose ancestors immigrated from western Europe. It is primarily "an urban professional and business population, college educated, and increasingly characterized in the younger age groups by double incomes."[4]

The legal system, democratic elections, and middle class values have their underpinnings in institutions and traditions of western Europe. English is a polyglot of the languages of the invaders and rulers of Great Britain throughout history. This culture has had a major impact on society's institutions because it has been the male members of the group who have dominated the political system and related government positions of authority. Historically, other cultures have not been as highly valued. Thus, through centuries of control of these systems, policies and practices have been instilled within the system to both maintain the advantages of the dominant culture and limit the influence of other cultural groups.

What are some of the characteristics of the dominant culture today? Universal education and literacy for all citizens are valued. Mass communications, which have been enhanced by the media and computer networks, influence our view of ourselves and the world. A job or career must be pursued in order for a person to be recognized as successful. Fun is usually sought as a relief from work. Achievement and success are highly valued and portrayed to others by the accumulation of material goods like a house, car, boat, clothes, and vacations.

Individualism and freedom are core values that undergird the dominant culture. Members believe that individuals are totally in charge of their own destiny or success.[5] They define freedom as "being left alone by others, not having other people's values, ideas, or styles of life forced upon one, being free of arbitrary authority in work, family, and political life."[6] Members of this group rely on associations of common interest rather than strong kinship ties. They believe in absolute values of right and wrong rather than in degrees of rightness and wrongness.

Most members of this group identify themselves as American. They do not see themselves as white, Christian, English speaking, middle class, male, or heterosexual. Many middle-class Catholics and Jews share similar values and behaviors. Although many middle-class persons of color display similar behaviors, hold the same values, and view themselves as members of this dominant group, they simultaneously maintain a strong affiliation with their own **ethnic group.** Many low-income families also hold the same values, but do not have the income to support a similar lifestyle.

Microcultures

Our cultural identities are not determined by ethnicity and race alone. Figure 5.1 illustrates the interaction of microcultural memberships in determining our cultural identity. We are members of multiple microcultural groups, each with its own traditions and rules. We are female or male, and members of a specific socio-

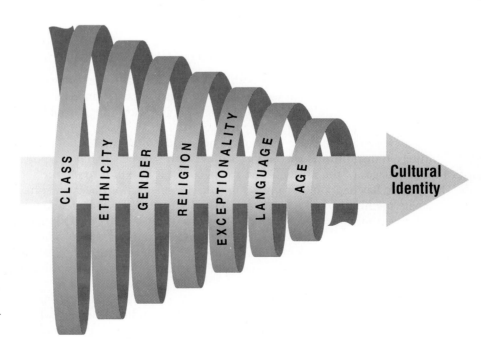

FIGURE 5.1

Cultural Identity Is Based on Membership in a Number of Microcultural Groups That Interact with Each Other

(*Source:* Donna M. Gollnick and Philip C. Chinn. *Multicultural Education in a Pluralistic Society,* 4th ed. Columbus, OH: Merrill, 1994, 14. © 1994 by Merrill.)

economic, religious, language, geographic, and age group. In addition, we may have a disability that interacts with membership in one or more of the other microcultural groups to determine our cultural identity.

The relationship of an individual's group memberships to the dominant culture may have a great influence on how he perceives himself. Because of the importance of power relationships between groups in discussions of **diversity** and equality, educators should understand how they themselves are centered in this dialogue. Educators need to know which groups they belong to and what influence those memberships have on their own identity. A critical self-examination may be helpful in our identification of otherness and difference that pervades a culturally diverse society. This chapter is designed to explore this diversity.

Diversity and Education

As an educator, you are likely to encounter students from diverse ethnic, racial, religious, age, disability, and economic groups during your career. Over time, the relationship of groups to society has been described differently by sociologists, politicians, philosophers, and educators. These differing ideologies and theories have led to the development of policies and practices that range along a continuum from promotion to condemnation of group differences. **Assimilation, cultural pluralism,** and cultural choice are three of the prevalent theories and ideologies.

The translation of these theories into educational practice leads to very different strategies and outcomes. Ethnographic studies are providing valuable information about how teachers and schools interact with students in the learning process. Researchers are discovering that schools often use teaching strategies that differ from those that are effective at home, particularly as they relate to language and cognitive style.

Assimilation

Assimilation is the process by which an immigrant group or culturally distinct group is incorporated into the mainstream **culture.** The group either adopts the culture of the dominant group as its own or interacts with it in a way that forges a new or different culture that is shared by both groups. Members of a group experience a number of stages in this process.

The first step involves learning the cultural patterns of the dominant group. The speed at which group members become acculturated is usually enhanced by interactions with members of this group in settings like work, school, and church. In many cases, the cultural patterns are shed—either enthusiastically or begrudgingly—and those of the dominant group are adopted. Native languages

Today's American classroom reflects the diversity present in society.

and traditions can be lost within a few generations. These steps are usually required by society for an individual to attain some modicum of financial success or achievement of the good life in the United States.

The final stage of assimilation is structural assimilation.[7] At this stage members of the immigrant or culturally distinct group interact with the mainstream group at all levels, including marriage. They no longer encounter prejudice or discrimination and share equally in the benefits of society.

At the beginning of the twentieth century, the melting pot theory emerged as a description of how immigrants contributed to the evolution of a new American culture. This theory described an egalitarian state that is central to the national rhetoric. Many immigrants believed that prejudices and inequities that they had experienced in their native countries would not exist in the United States, and that they would become valued members of the mainstream society. Although many European immigrants did melt into the mainstream, persons of color were prevented from melting—or becoming structurally assimilated—by the racist ideology that had prevented Native, African, Latino, and Asian Americans from becoming structurally assimilated for generations.

Assimilation remains the guiding principle in most schools. Immersion in the dominant culture is the **acculturation** strategy. School success depends on how well students are able to adjust to this culture. Their own cultural experiences and patterns are neither valued nor used in the teaching and learning process.

The poor academic performance of many students of color and from low-income families is sometimes explained by a cultural deficit theory in which students and their families are blamed for their failures. The problem may be that these students have not been socialized to think and act like children of the dominant culture. Proponents of this theory blame the educational deficiencies on the home environment and such factors as single parents, teenage mothers, lack of books, and poor child-rearing practices. The provision of equal educational opportunity is the policy response to this theory. Compensatory programs are offered to help the students overcome both their educational and cultural deficiencies by making them more like students from the dominant culture.

Cultural Pluralism

Cultural pluralism describes societies in which the maintenance of distinct cultural patterns, including languages, is valued and promoted. Groups may be segregated, but they have approximately equal political, economic, and educational opportunity.[8] In some cases, groups have been able to establish and maintain their own political, economic, and educational systems.

The concept of cultural pluralism does not describe the United States. Although diversity does exist, parity and equality between groups does not. Some Native American nations do have their own political and educational systems, but they do not share power and resources equally with the dominant group. Some immigrant groups choose to maintain their native culture and language. This goal is more likely to be attained if families live in communities where there is a fairly large concentration of others from a similar cultural background; Little Italy, Chinatown, Harlem, East Los Angeles, and Amish and Hutterite communities provide these settings. More often, culturally distinct groups have been forced into segregated communities because of discriminatory housing patterns.

The implementation of cultural pluralism requires the recognition of the multiple cultures that comprise society. Rather than dominant culture permeating the classroom and school, the culture of the particular group or groups served by the school are the predominant focus of the curriculum. Examples include the Afrocentric and Native-centric programs that exist today in some urban areas and tribal-controlled schools. A number of ethnic and religious groups have maintained their culture and history in private schools. The Amish and Hutterites, for example, operate their own schools to limit the destruction of their cultures by the dominant group.

In this approach, a cultural difference theory is used to explain the differential achievement of students of diverse backgrounds. Disjunctures in cultural patterns between the home and school prevent academic success. Language and cognitive styles are the areas most often studied by researchers. In a review of the literature on this theory, Ana Maria Villegas found that:

> Although students and teachers in a given classroom may speak the same language, they sometimes have different ways of using it. Children whose language use at home and in their immediate community corresponds more closely to the way in which it is used in the classroom have an advantage in the learning process. For these students, prior experience transfers to the classroom and facilitates their academic performance. This seems to be the case for White, middle-class, Anglo-American students. In contrast, minority children frequently experience discontinuity in the use of language at home and in school. They are often misunderstood when applying familiar patterns of language use to classroom tasks. Of what use is prior experience to these children if their established ways of using language and making sense of the world are deemed unacceptable or prohibited in the classroom?[9]

Schools in a culturally pluralistic society should be staffed by a diverse teaching force that at a minimum represents the cultures of students. Teachers from the same cultural backgrounds as students should be able to use language patterns similar to those of the students' families. Teachers from different cultural backgrounds also should be aware of multiple cultural patterns of communication and learning.

Relevant Research

The Interaction of Language and Culture

As a North American special education teacher for preschoolers, Cynthia Ballenger began to wonder why so many Haitian students were being referred to as "wild" and having no language, especially since she found that they were responsive and intelligent. As a teacher and "fledgling" sociolinguist, she embarked on her own research as a participant-observer. She learned Creole, studied Haitian culture, and began teaching in a bilingual Haitian Creole and English preschool. She still had difficulty in controlling her class.

Ms. Ballenger learned that the Haitian teachers "emphasize[d] the group in their control talk, articulating the values and responsibilities of group membership." (p. 204) The Haitian teachers had orderly classrooms of children who, in an equally affectionate and cheerful manner, *did* follow directions and kept the confusion to a [tolerable] level (pp. 200–201).

While North American teachers differentiated between misbehaviors and connected them to their consequences (for example, "pinching hurts Ana"), Haitian teachers referred to misbehaviors as bad. The focus of North American teachers was on the individual child or family rather than on the group and what is right or wrong. With this information, the teacher-researcher began to develop different styles for handling discipline in her class. Although her style did not always match the verbal intonation and accompanying nonverbal behavior of a native Haitian, her control of the classroom improved significantly.

Source: Cynthia Ballenger, "Teaching and Practice," *Harvard Educational Review* 62(2) (Summer 1992): 199–208.

Cultural Choice

As the twentieth century draws to a close, diversity in the United States is increasing. Some immigrants plan to assimilate into the dominant culture as soon as possible. They choose to adopt the new culture and shed the old. Others do not want to shed their unique cultural identity and patterns to be successful members of society. Many learn to be bicultural and bilingual, bridging the two cultures and learning when it is appropriate to use the patterns of each. Others do not have a choice. Ideally, we could choose to assimilate, maintain our native culture, or become bi- or multicultural in our ability to function effectively in more than one cultural group. Society would support these cultural choices and not value one choice over another or discriminate based on group membership.

Unfortunately, this description does not match reality for large segments of the population. Most persons of color, such as African Americans, are acculturated, but discrimination has prevented them from becoming structurally assimilated even if they choose that route. Strong identity and affiliation with their cultural group has been necessary for solidarity purposes to fight against existing inequities and to obtain adequate housing and education. Although some members may be able to live almost solely within their distinct cultural milieu, most are forced to work within the dominant culture. Those who choose to assimilate may not be accepted by the dominant group and sometimes are rejected by the group into which they were born.

Equality across groups does not yet exist, but it continues to be a value espoused by the society. As long as discrimination against groups is tolerated by society, cultural choice will be limited primarily to male, middle-class, heterosexual whites. As the barriers to equality are reduced, there is likely to be greater individual choice and mobility across groups. "We will move toward an open society in which cultural background may influence who an individual is, but become irrelevant in public interactions, especially as the reason for institutional discrimination. In this case, cultural differences will be valued, respected, and encouraged to flourish."[10]

Schools that value cultural choice promote diversity and consciously avoid the dominance of a single culture. The contributions and histories of diverse groups—particularly those represented in the school, but not limited to them—are integrated throughout the curriculum. Bilingualism and bidialectalism prevail in classrooms as well as halls. Students are the center of instruction and their cultural patterns are utilized to promote learning. Students learn to operate comfortably in both their own and other cultures, including the dominant culture. Equality is achieved as illustrated in the equal participation of all groups in courses and extracurricular activities, as well as in comparable achievement on academic assessments.

Microcultural Groups

Students in U.S. schools are among the most diverse in the world. By the year 2000, one-third of our students will be young people of color.[11] They are already the majority in schools in California, Texas, and the twenty-five largest cities. The native language of schools is no longer limited to English. Some school districts can identify nearly one hundred different languages that are used in the homes of their students. Religious diversity has also increased beyond the traditional Judeo-Christian heritage as immigrants from Asia, Africa, and the Middle East join our ranks. In addition, a greater number of students with disabilities are now active participants in schools and society.

Socioeconomic Status

Most people want the "good life," which allows a comfortable living. The image to many is a two-parent family who owns a home, has a stay-at-home mother and one or more children in school. In reality, only 4 percent of U.S. families fit this middle-class myth today.[12] **Socioeconomic status** is the primary determinant of the standard of living we are able to maintain. It also has a great impact on our chances of attending college and attaining a job that ensures material comfort throughout our lives.

Socioeconomic status (SES) is a criterion used by the U.S. Bureau of Census to measure the economic condition of individuals. It is determined by one's occupation, income, and educational attainment. Wealth and power are other important factors that affect the way one is able to live, but these data are difficult to measure through census data. We often can guess families' socioeconomic status if we know where they live, the type of car they drive, the schools attended by their children, and the types of vacations they take.

Social Stratification. Most societies are characterized by **social stratification** in which individuals occupy different levels of the social structure. Wealth, income, occupation, and education help define these social positions. However, high or low rankings are not based only on the SES criteria. Race, age, gender, religion, and disability can contribute to lower rankings as well. Although members of most ethnic groups can be found at all levels of the socioeconomic status scale, those from western European backgrounds have a disproportionately high representation at the highest levels. This difference was validated in a UNESCO study that compared the standard of living in different countries. Of the nations compared, the United States ranked sixth overall. However, when the population was divided into racial groups, great differences in stratification were obvious. The living standard of U.S. whites outranked that of all other nations. On the other hand, African Americans ranked thirty-first—at the same level as an underdeveloped country.[13]

Social mobility remains one of the core values of the dominant culture. We are taught to believe "that anyone can improve social status because the social structure is open and hard work will get you there."[14] We read the Horatio Alger stories of how individuals were born in poverty, but through hard work became wealthy as a corporate president, prestigious publisher, or successful writer, athlete, or entertainer. Such dramatic upward mobility continues to occur, but the chances of moving from poverty to riches, no matter how hard one works, are rare.

Class Structure. Traditionally, sociologists divide the population into distinct classes to study inequities in society as well as the characteristics of individuals and families at these different levels. One of the early categorization systems identified the population as lower, middle, and upper class, with finer distinctions in each of the three groups. The "underclass" is the label sometimes given to the portion of the population that lacks a stable income and is persistently poor. Individuals who do manual work for a living are sometimes described as the "working class." When this group includes farm laborers and service workers, it represents 43 percent of the employed population.[15]

The middle class includes professionals, managers, administrators, and white-collar workers who perform nonmanual labor. Annual incomes for this class usually fall between $20,000 and $50,000 and represent about 35 percent of the individuals submitting income tax returns.[16] This level of income is often possible only because both spouses work. Families in this class live very different lifestyles at the opposite ends of the income continuum. Professionals, managers, and administrators receive the higher incomes. They are the more affluent middle class, but view their condition as universal rather than unique. They often think that most of the U.S. population shares the same affluence, advantages, and comforts.[17]

The upper class is composed of wealthy and socially prominent families. There is great disparity in the income and wealth of members of this class as compared to the others, and the gap between them is growing. For example, in 1979 corporate chief executive officers earned twenty-nine times as much as their manufacturing employees; by 1985, they earned forty times as much; and by 1988 *Business Week* reported that the multiple had grown to ninety three.[18] These great differences contribute to limited interactions with members of other classes. Children in this class rarely attend public schools, which isolates them from other social classes. Probably the greatest assimilation of lifestyles and values occurs within this class.

Poverty. The U.S. government has established a poverty index that sets a conservative ceiling on poverty. Using this threshold, there are over 33 million persons in poverty—13.5 percent of the population. There are many myths about persons who are poor. One is that they do not work, but in reality, many work in full-time jobs that pay so poorly they cannot pull their families out of poverty. "Some two million people work year round but live in poverty and another seven million poor individuals work full time for part of the year or in part-time jobs."[19]

Children, the elderly, women, and minorities suffer disproportionately from poverty. A recent study by the United Nations found that "the percentage of children living in poverty in the United States is more than double that of other major industrialized nations . . . Other major industrialized nations have succeeded in reducing child poverty levels to below 5 percent."[20] (The comparison with other countries is shown in Figure 5.2.) This tragedy is reflected in an increase in the number of homeless families and students over the past decade. The number of homeless people is estimated at between 250,000 to three million. The estimate of the number of homeless children on any given night ranges from 68,000 to 500,000. In addition, there are nearly 14 million children living temporarily with friends or relatives.[21]

Although there are more European Americans who are below the poverty level than any other group, they represent only 11 percent of all European Americans in the country. The percentage of other racial groups in poverty is much higher. The median income of European Americans remains greater than other racial groups. African American families earn 58 percent as much as whites; Latino families earn 63 percent as much as whites.[22] The disparity in incomes between groups decreases when comparisons are made using two-income families with the same level of education, but they still are not equitable. Women also fight discriminatory practices that keep their incomes at 71 percent that of men.

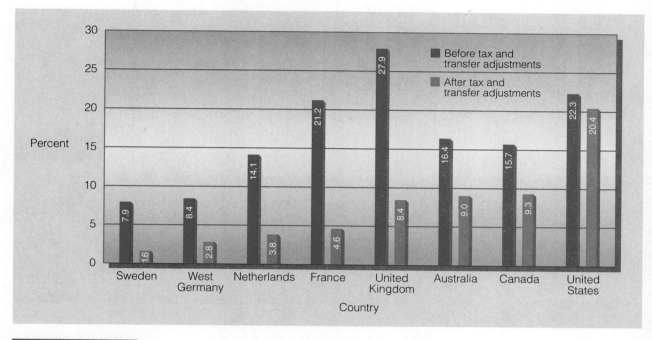

FIGURE 5.2

Percentage of Children Living in Poverty in Industrialized Nations
(*Source:* United Nations Children's Fund.)

Ethnicity and Race

National origin remains an important part of identity for many individuals. Because Native Americans are the only indigenous groups, over 99 percent of the population came from somewhere else or their ancestors did at some time during the past 500 years. Many people can identify a country of origin, although the geographical boundaries may have been moved since their ancestors immigrated. A growing number of people have mixed heritage, with ancestors from different parts of the world.

It is our national origin that determines our ethnicity. We often use continents as the broadest identification in classifications like European American, African American, South American, and Asian American. Many families can trace their heritage to specific countries (for example, Poland or Korea) and/or tribes (for example, Pueblo or Ibo). Although Latino Americans share a common language heritage of Spanish, families have come from Spain, Mexico, Central America, South America, Cuba, and Puerto Rico.

Ethnic Diversity. Within each of these broad continent classifications exist numerous ethnic groups with identities and often loyalties to a specific country. Many Americans whose ancestors immigrated either voluntarily or involuntarily identify themselves as German, Vietnamese, Hmong, Croatian, Russian, Punjabi, Argentinean, Mexican, Lebanese, or Ethiopian American. The U.S. Census Bureau asked the population to identify themselves by their ethnic origin for the first time

Native American children, and other minority students, are often caught between their traditional culture and new educational efforts.

in the 1990 census. Generally, these data are reported by the government in the following five broad categories that combine racial, language, and ethnic distinctions: White, not Hispanic; Black, not Hispanic; Hispanic; Asian American or Pacific Islander; and Native American or Alaskan Aleuts. One of the problems with these classifications is that a growing number of people can identify themselves in more than one of these groups. Their parents or grandparents or other ancestors have married across ethnic and/or racial and/or language groups; thus, they do not fit neatly into one single group. (See Figure 5.3.)

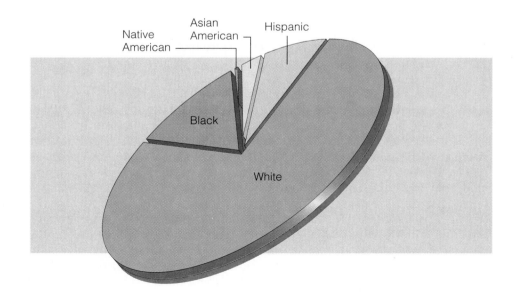

FIGURE 5.3

Membership in the Five Racial or Ethnic Groups, 1990 Census

(*Source:* "Children in Poverty," *Education Week* (September 29, 1993): 3.)

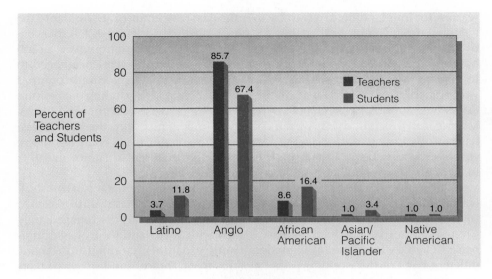

FIGURE 5.4

Distribution of Teachers and Students in U.S. K–12 Public Schools by Ethnicity, Fall 1991

(*Source:* U.S. Bureau of Labor Statistics, 1992 and U.S. Department of Education, 1993, as presented in The Tomas Rivera Center, *Resolving a Crisis in Education: Latino Teachers for Tomorrow's Classrooms.* Claremont, CA: author, 1993, 7.)

CASE STUDY   DIVERSITY IN THE TEACHING FORCE

The teaching force today is predominantly European American female, as shown in Figure 5.4. When compared with the diversity of the student population, teachers of color are currently underrepresented in teaching. These comparisons become even more disconcerting in states with large minority populations. "In California, for example, where Latinos are most heavily concentrated, Latinos comprised 33 percent of all students while Latino teachers represented only 7 percent of the state's teachers." The need for bilingual teachers in states like California, Texas, Florida, and New York is great, and shortages exist across the country.

Why is diversity in the teaching force important? Some argue that students of color would be better served by role models from their own cultural groups. Many believe that intergroup relations would be improved with the opportunities for all students to interact with teachers from both their own and other cultural groups. Even more importantly, teachers with intimate understandings of and regard for children's cultures, communities, and ways of learning and interacting appear to be more effective in helping students learn.

1. What strategies would you use to encourage more students of color to enter the teaching profession?
2. Why might it be in the best interest of the nation to attract more males and persons of color into the teaching force?
3. What should European American teachers know about cultural differences to help them be effective teachers of students of color?

Source: The Tomas Rivera Center, *Resolving a Crisis in Education: Latino Teachers for Tomorrow's Classrooms.* Claremont, CA: author, 7.

Global Perspectives: Diversity European Style. The reasons for immigration and the treatment of immigrants varies around the world. As an example, let's look at the different patterns of immigration in European countries. The reasons for immigration to a country over the past few centuries are similar to the voluntary immigration in the United States. Individuals or families left their native country because of debilitating economic or political conditions, war, or job opportunities. Often migrant workers from other countries were encouraged to immigrate to meet labor shortages. Citizens from formerly colonized countries were sometimes allowed to settle in the "mother country," expanding the nation's diversity to families from India, Pakistan, Hong Kong, Indonesia, the West Indies, Morocco, Algeria, and West African countries. Immigrants from the Middle East have greatly increased the religious diversity of many European countries. There were seven mosques in Britain in 1962 and fewer than ten in France in 1972; today there are over 600 and 1,000 respectively.[23]

European countries have responded differently to the immigrants. Historically, Italy has not encouraged immigration; in fact, it was illegal until recently. Immigration by families and reunification have been especially discouraged; only Chinese, Eritreans, and Iranians have settled with their families in large numbers.[24] Greece's immigration is predominantly expatriots returning from many different parts of the world; gypsies, Muslims from Thrace, and foreign workers also populate the country.[25] France is very diverse, but does not keep records of indigenous minorities and does not encourage the maintenance of allegiance to a second homeland.[26] Switzerland does not describe itself as an immigrant country, but over 16 percent of the population is non-Swiss from 169 countries.[27] Some eastern European countries like Croatia, Serbia, and Bosnia are undergoing a process of "ethnic cleansing," which has become an extended war, to rid their countries of persons from different ethnic or religious groups.

Although the initial intent of opening borders to guest or migrant workers was that they would eventually return to their original homeland, many subsequently settled in segregated areas, continued to use their native languages and religions, and began to raise families. Schools had to respond to students from diverse cultural backgrounds. Xenophobia and ethnocentrism abounded in policies and practices related to most of these students and their families; sometimes they face scapegoating and expulsion threats and are verbally and physically attacked.

Ethnic Identity.   Identification with an ethnic group helps sustain and enhance the culture of the group. Members share similar lifestyles, values, history, and common social and economic interests. There is often an identifiable dialectal and nonverbal communication system. Ethnicity is strongest when members have a high degree of interpersonal associations with other members and share common residential areas.[28]

Ethnic cohesiveness and solidarity are strengthened as members organize to fight discrimination and influence political and economic decisions that impact the group as a whole. In the 1960s these struggles with the dominant culture led to the calls for changes in institutions like schools, colleges, and government programs to support equality across ethnic groups. During this period, African, Latino, Asian, and Native Americans called for recognition of their ethnic roots in the school curriculum. By the 1970s European ethnic groups, especially those of southern and eastern origins, had also joined this movement. Ethnic studies programs were established in colleges and universities to study the history, contributions, and experiences of U.S. ethnic groups that had traditionally been excluded.

Gender

Males and females are culturally different even when they are members of the same socioeconomic, ethnic, and religious group. The ways they think and act are defined by their gender identity. The two groups are often segregated at social gatherings, located in different jobs, and expected to behave in a stereotypical fashion. "At school, at church, at work, at play, boys and girls and men and women are governed by different norms, rules of behavior and expectations; they are subject to different eligibility rules for rewards and different vulnerability to punishments."[29]

Differences between Females and Males. Learning the gender of a baby is one of the important rites of parenthood. However, the major difference between boys and girls is the way adults respond to them. There are few actual physical differences, particularly before puberty. It is the socialization process in child rearing and schools that determines gender identity and the related distinctive behaviors.

Some researchers attribute differences in mathematical, verbal, and spatial skills to different hormones that affect specific hemispheres of the brain. However, recent studies show that females and males are performing more alike, suggesting that the previously observed gender differences are not biologically determined. For example, there are no differences in quantitative abilities until the age of ten and then only slight differences that sometimes favor girls and sometimes favor boys in the middle school years. Males do perform better in high school, but the differences are declining as female students become more interested in mathematics. Gender differences in spatial abilities are declining and one's abilities in this area can be improved with training. There no longer appear to be differences in verbal abilities.[30]

By age two, children realize that they are a girl or boy; by five or six, they have learned their gender and stereotypical behavior.[31] Boys are generally socialized toward achievement and self-reliance, girls toward nurturance and responsibility. However, anthropologists have documented variations in the behaviors of males and females from culture to culture. In this country, there are differences in the expectations and behaviors of the two sexes that are rooted in their ethnicity, religion, and socioeconomic level.

A major difference between the two groups is how they are treated in society. Women tend to be equated with a natural world and men with controlling that world.[32] These power relations place men in a position of superiority, as evidenced by their disproportionate holding of the highest status and highest paying jobs. Many times this relationship extends into the home where the father and husband may both protect the family and rule over it. Sometimes this relationship leads to physical and mental abuse of women and children.

Although 90 percent of all women today will work outside the home at some time, society's view of them as inferior has contributed greatly to the current patterns of discrimination that keep many women in low prestige and low paying jobs. The jobs in which women are concentrated are those that naturally extend their role as nurturers and helpers: nursing, teaching, and secretarial work. Job and wage discrimination is a critical issue for women, especially today when a large number of families are headed by women without the advantage of a second income. These families are more likely to be in poverty than any other group; over 32 percent of the persons in these families fall below the official poverty level.[33]

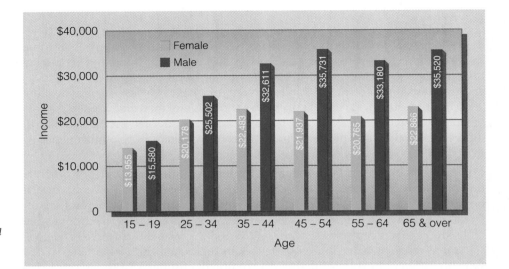

FIGURE 5.5

Differences between Male and Female Income

(*Source:* Donna M. Gollnick and Philip C. Chinn. *Multicultural Education in a Pluralistic Society,* 4th ed. Columbus, OH: Merrill, 1994, 130. © 1994 by Merrill.)

As barriers to professional education and employment are broken, the number of women in traditionally male occupations has increased. The number of female physicians increased from 6.5 percent in 1950 to 20 percent in 1991; female attorneys and judges increased from 4 to 19 percent; and female principals increased from 20 percent in 1982 to 38 percent in 1990.[34] (See Figure 5.5.)

Many males are also not well served by the current socialization patterns. Some do not fit neatly in the dominant culture's stereotypical vision of maleness. Society has not been very tolerant of deviation from the traditional masculine roles. Although much progress has been made over the past two decades, men still may be ridiculed for having "female characteristics" such as a high voice or non-agressive behavior. Some men would feel more comfortable working as preschool teachers, nurses, or librarians—traditionally female careers—but may have learned that those jobs are inappropriate for "real men."

Young women sometimes appear ambivalent, especially as it relates to education and family relations. Some undervalue themselves and become passive and self-sacrificing. This pattern may lead them into unwanted pregnancies and unfulfilling relationships. "Young women with poor basic skills are three times more likely to become teenage parents than women with average or above-average basic skills."[35] As a result, a disproportionately large number of these women drop out of school, limiting their ability to earn a decent income. Thus, they and their children are likely to be forced into poverty at least temporarily.

Schools also reinforce behavior that is stereotypically gender specific. Female students are expected to be quiet, follow the rules, and help the teacher. Boys and young men are expected to be more rowdy and less attentive. Many working class males develop patterns of resistance to school and its authority figures because schooling is feminine and emphasizes mental rather than manual work.[36]

Sexual Orientation. Many cultural groups place high value on heterosexuality and denigrate or outlaw homosexuality. However, sexual orientation is established by age five or six;[37] it is not learned in adolescence or young adulthood, nor is it forced on others by immoral adults. It has been estimated that 5 to 10 percent of the population is homosexual.

Like other powerless groups, gays and lesbians continue to face discrimination in housing, employment, and many social institutions as evidenced when universities prohibit the establishment of gay student clubs. Some states still have laws on the books that make it illegal to engage in homosexual relations. Homophobia, as expressed in harassment and violence against gays and lesbians, is tolerated in many areas of the country. As a result of these prejudices and discriminatory practices, many gays and lesbians hide their homosexuality and have established their own social clubs, networks, and communication systems to support each other.

Isolation and loneliness are the experiences of many gay and lesbian youth. If they openly acknowledge their sexual orientation, they are likely to be harassed and face reprisals from peers and school officials. Structures within the schools do not provide homosexuals the same kind of support that is available to other students. Educators often know little about this group and have had few or no contacts with homosexuals. Students in the classroom also may be the children of gay and lesbian parents since there are 8 to 10 million children in 3 million families.[38] Without a better understanding of homosexuality, we will not be able to effectively work with gay and lesbian students or the children of homosexual parents.

Language

Language interacts with our ethnic and socioeconomic background to socialize us into linguistic and cultural communities. Children learn their native language by imitating adults and their peers. By age five, they have learned the syntax of language and know the meaning of thousands of words.

When there are cultural similarities between the speaker and listener, the messages are decoded accurately. When the speaker and listener differ in ethnicity and/or class, miscommunication may occur. Even within English, a word or phrase or nonverbal gesture takes on different meanings in different cultural groups and settings. Educators need to recognize that miscommunications between them and students may be due to inaccurate decoding rather than lack of ability.

Language Differences. English is not the native language for approximately 32 million Americans.[38] Spanish, Italian, and sign language are the most common languages other than English. As immigrants assimilate into the dominant culture of the United States, the native language is often replaced with English within a few generations. The native language is more likely to be retained when schools and the community value bilingualism. As commerce and trade have become more global, professionals and administrators have realized the advantages of knowing the competitor's culture and language. They are encouraging their children to learn a second language at the same time that many of our educational policies are discouraging native speakers from using both languages. Ethnocentrism flourishes in the conservative call for "English only" usage in schools, in daily commerce, on street signs, and on official government documents. The implementation of bilingual education programs also implicitly reflects different views of the importance of a second language. Transitional bilingual programs use

PROFESSIONAL DILEMMA

How Much Can We Expect of Limited English Speaking Students?

The image of the United States as the land of boundless opportunity may seem a bit tarnished to many of its recession-weary citizens, but it is alive and well in many of the world's war-torn, poverty-ridden, politically oppressive countries. Indeed, immigrants from such countries are flocking to the United States in record numbers. Estimates are that some areas of the country will range from a one-third to over one-half minority, non-English-speaking population within the next few years.

A peculiar challenge arises for educators when students enter high school with little or no formal education from their native country, and with no proficiency in English. The situation may be further complicated because students come from many different countries, including Vietnam, Chile, Honduras, Ethiopia, Afghanistan, Korea, and Sierra Leone.

Immigrating late in their youth, these students are faced with a nearly impossible challenge to graduate with other students of their own age. Some educators think that the hurdle should be lowered for these students and opportunities created for them so that they may succeed and graduate with their peers. These educators see the alternative as increased frustration and dropout rates.

Others maintain that proficiency as measured by standardized tests should be retained as a requirement for all students, and that to relax these standards selectively would be patronizing and ultimately harmful to minority populations.

- How should educators' goals for limited English speakers be different than for English speakers?

- If there are several students with different native languages in your classroom, how will you ensure that they learn the concepts being taught?

- Where could you go for help in working with language diverse students?

the native language, especially in the early school years, to teach academic content while students concurrently learn English. As soon as possible, students move into English-only programs. There are a few schools and programs that offer bilingual maintenance programs in which English and a second language are equally valued and used for instruction.

American Sign Language (ASL) is officially recognized as a language with complex grammar and well-regulated syntax. It is the natural language developed and used for communication among deaf individuals. Like oral languages, it is learned very early by imitation of others using the language. To communicate with the hearing, many individuals who are deaf use signed English in which the oral or written word is translated into a sign. ASL is a critical factor in identification as a member of this group. The language can be more important to their cultural identity than their membership in a particular ethnic, socioeconomic, or religious group.

Dialectal Differences. Standard English is the dialect used by the majority of dominant group members for official or formal communications. However, there are numerous regional, local, ethnic, and class (or SES) dialects identifiable across this country. Each has its own set of grammatical rules that are known to its users. None is any better than another, but users of standard English are often viewed as more credible in schools and the work world. Television news anchors, reporters, and talk show hosts use standard English. Although they may be bidialectal, most teachers use standard English as the example that should be emulated by students.

Many Americans are bidialectal or multidialectal in that they use standard English at work, but use their native or local dialect at home or when they are socializing with friends. Social factors have an influence on which dialect to use in a specific situation. At one time, students were not allowed to use a dialect other than standard English in the classroom. Today, students are usually allowed to use their dialects, but are encouraged to learn standard English to provide them with an advantage in seeking employment in the dominant culture.

Exceptionalities

Twenty-five million or more Americans have been classified as having a disability or being gifted.[40] Individuals with a disability are usually identified as mentally retarded, learning disabled, speech impaired, visually impaired, hearing impaired, emotionally disturbed, behaviorally disturbed, or physically impaired. Those with physical disabilities can be readily recognized by their use of a cane, braces, wheelchair, or sign language. Some individuals are labeled very early in their school careers as mentally retarded or emotionally disturbed. Nondisabled persons often react with disdain to individuals with disabilities and view them as inferior. Critics of labeling declare the system to be demeaning and stigmatizing.

Like all other individuals, persons with disabilities want to be recognized as persons in their own right. They have the same needs for love and the same desire to be successful as the nondisabled. Instead, society has historically not accepted them as equals. Some individuals with severe disabilities are placed in institutions out of the sight of the public. Others are segregated in separate schools or classes. Too often, they are rejected and made to feel inept and limited in their abilities. Schools have contributed to this problem when they should be part of the solution.

Cultural Differences. Individuals with similar disabilities often find comfort and security with each other. Those who are hearing impaired share a language that is used by only a few of the hearing; the language provides them with a strong sense of community. In some cities like Louisville, Kentucky, many visually impaired individuals continue to live in the community near the School for the Blind where they can be close to potential work settings and provide support to each other. Individuals with mental retardation sometimes share group homes in which they can support each other and learn to be self-reliant. In these settings they establish patterns of communication and behavior that are natural to them, but may seem odd to nonmembers.

Disproportionate Placements. Some disabilities are linked to membership in one or more other microcultural groups. Individuals labeled as mentally retarded or emotionally disabled disproportionately are from low-income families. Low-income children are also overrepresented in seriously emotionally disturbed classes. Middle-class students are more likely to be classified as learning disabled. This pattern is also found in the placement of minority group members and males in special education and gifted classes. African and Native American students are overrepresented in many of the special education classes for mentally and emotionally disturbed students, as are males in general. On the other hand, Latino,

African, and Native American students are underrepresented in gifted and talented programs. Educators need to learn to monitor the reasons for their referrals of students to be tested for placement in these classes.

Religion

Religion can have a great influence on the values and lifestyles of families and can play an important role in the socialization of children and young people. Religious doctrines and practices often guide our beliefs about the roles of males and females. They also provide guidance regarding birth rates, birth control, child rearing, friendships, and political attitudes.

By age five, children are able to generally identify their families' religious affiliation. Although 90 percent of the population regards their religious beliefs as very or fairly important,[41] less than half attend a religious service on a weekly basis. However, strong religious perspectives are reflected in the daily lives of many families.[42]

The First Amendment.   The First Amendment of the U.S. Constitution, which requires the separation of church and state, is a cornerstone of American democracy. When it comes to schools, there is disagreement about the meaning of the amendment. Families appear satisfied with schools when they reflect the values that are important in their religion. However, schools may be attacked when the curriculum, assigned readings, holidays, and graduation exercises are perceived to be in conflict with religious values. Many court cases over the past century have helped sort out these issues.

The trend in recent years has been to recognize and learn more about differences, rather than cover them up and smooth them out.

Religious Pluralism.   Religious pluralism flourishes in this country. Members of religions other than those with a Judeo-Christian heritage are increasing as more immigrants arrive from Asia and the Middle East. Other families declare themselves atheists or simply do not participate in an organized religion. Still others live in cults that are established to promote and maintain a religious "calling." Some religious groups believe that their religion is the only correct and legitimate view of the world. Other groups recognize that the differences have grown out of different historical experiences and accept the validity of diverse groups.

Although they are not as dominant as earlier in our history, Protestants are still in the majority with 56 percent of the population. Two and one half percent of the population are Jewish and 26 percent are Catholic. Eleven percent do not indicate a preference. Within each of the major religious groups, there are distinct denominations and sects that have the same general history, but can differ greatly in their beliefs and perspectives on the correct and appropriate way to live. These western religions are compatible with the values of the dominant culture; they usually promote patriotism and emphasize individual control of life.

With the influx of immigrants from Asia, Africa, and the Middle East over the past few decades, religious diversity among the population has increased further with the introduction of non-Western religions like Islam and Buddhism. The interaction with Western religions and impact on mainstream society have yet to be determined. In the meantime, students from diverse religious backgrounds will appear in classrooms. Teachers will need to learn to respect these differences if they are going to serve the students and community well.

Some religious groups, such as the Amish and Hutterites, are very closed in that they establish their own communities and schools to help maintain the religion, support each other, and develop group cohesiveness. Members of some groups like Mormons promote primary relationships and interactions with other members of the same faith. Most social activities are linked to religion, and institutions have been developed to reflect and support the religious beliefs. In many rural areas the church is the center of most social and community activities. Fundamentalist churches in many urban areas expect members to spend much of their nonworking hours in church activities. For many people, religion is the essential element that determines their cultural identity.

Geography

Communities and their schools differ from one region of the country to another. We are likely to suffer culture shock in moving from one region to another. People behave differently, dress differently, and like different things even if they are from the same religious and ethnic backgrounds. An examination of differences in rural, suburban, and urban communities captures some of the cultural variation. However, differences in those communities will be found as one crosses from Northwest, Southwest, Midwest, South, and Northeast. Within these regions, an observer will find states that are culturally unique. The geography of a state like Colorado aids in the development of different cultural patterns of the population in the flat farmlands, urban centers, and mountains.

Rural Communities. Rural schools are often the center of rural life. Values tend to be conservative, and the immediate rural family tends to remain a cohesive unit. The extended family, however, has begun to disappear. School children may travel long distances to school, and social interactions at school are vital. By urban and suburban standards, rural families live long distances from one another. To the rural family, however, the distances are not great, and there is a feeling of neighborliness. The social structure is less stratified than in most populous geographical areas, and everyone tends to know everyone else.

Although employment in these areas is scarce, increasing numbers of urban and suburban dwellers are choosing to live in the country and commute to their employment in the more populous metropolitan areas. Those who have settled in the rural areas are generally young and well educated. They are fleeing the complexities of city life to acquire self-reliance and self-confidence, to return to a physically healthier environment, or simply to be able to own an affordable home. In some instances this exodus to the country has caused problems for rural schools because the newcomers' values have clashed with those of the rural community. Family living habits and expectations for school programs differ, and some newcomers demand increased social services. In many rural communities, it takes a considerable length of time for newcomers to be accepted into the social structure.

Suburban Communities. The suburban school is not a community school like the rural school, and recreation and social activities emanate from a variety of sources. Young people depend on the car and the telephone. Most suburban families have two cars and either an extension phone or a private phone for the children. Teenagers like to be on the move, and a car is considered a necessity.

Suburbs continue to grow in number and size, but the pattern for schooling has changed. The suburban areas close to the city are now experiencing a shift to an older population with fewer children and new middle-class minorities migrating from the cities. The schools in these areas continue to experience declining enrollments despite the baby boomlet that is affecting other schools. The boomlet is felt farther out in the newer suburbs, where property values are not as high and young parents with families can afford housing. In recent years many suburban areas have become settlement areas for southeast Asian refugee groups, who have introduced a whole new set of diversity issues for the schools to address.

Urban Communities.   Urban areas provide rich cultural experiences through museums, theaters, and the arts. Although some residential areas remain segregated, many areas are ethnically and racially diverse. With the exception of segregated oppressed areas, the city provides opportunities to interact with people from diverse backgrounds in community settings and at work. Usually there are several colleges and universities in the city with libraries, lectures, sporting events, and cultural events.

Although there are many single-family homes in a city, many children live in multifamily units such as apartments or condominiums. Children who live in oppressed sections of the city are often restricted by it, having few contacts outside the area. Although affluent areas of the city may have adequate, if not beautiful, parks, libraries, and schools, some areas suffer from too few and poorly kept parks, inadequate police protection, and old, poorly maintained schools.

Cultural Identity

You, the reader, and your future students are members of at least the seven microcultures described above. The interaction of one's membership in multiple microcultures determines one's cultural identity. However, each microcultural membership is weighted differently in determining one's own cultural identity. Membership in a particular microculture can greatly influence the membership in another group. For example, some religions have strictly defined expectations for women and men that will control how they behave as adolescents, newlyweds, and a married couple. Membership in some of the microcultural groups may have little impact on how we see ourselves, while others are very important. Cultural identity is dynamic and may change over time. For example, the behavior and values of a married female with two young children may be based on her ethnic, religious, and class background. If she divorces, her identification as a woman at a different class level may become more important determinants of her own identity than they previously were.

Intragroup Differences

There are many differences within the same microcultural group. For example, all women belong to the same gender microculture, but not to the same ethnic, religious, or socioeconomic group—all of which could have a great impact on how they see themselves as females and how they are treated by society. Socioeconomic status has a great impact on how families are able to live. As a result, individuals from the same ethnic group may have very different language and behavioral patterns as well as lifestyles. Educators must be careful not to stereotype students based on a single microcultural membership.

Biculturalism

Individuals who have competencies in and can operate successfully in two or more different cultures are bicultural or multicultural, and are often multilingual as well. Having proficiencies in multiple cultures does not lead to rejection of the primary cultural identification. It does allow a broad range of abilities on which one can draw as needed.

Many individuals who are not members of the dominant culture become bicultural to work or attend school and to participate effectively in their own ethnic community. Different behaviors are expected in the two settings. To be successful on the job usually requires proficiency in the ways of the dominant group. Because most schools reflect the dominant society, students are forced to adjust if they are going to be academically successful. On the other hand, many European Americans find almost total congruence between the culture of their family, schooling, and work. Most remain monocultural throughout their lives, and do not comprehend the value of becoming competent in a different culture. Thus, being multicultural and multilingual is not promoted in most communities and schools.

Summary and Implications

The way individuals behave and think is determined by their culture. Culture is so pervasive in our lives that we often are not aware that our actions and thoughts are culturally determined. Culture is learned, shared, adapted, and dynamic. Although characteristics and contributions of diverse cultural groups are reflected in society, the dominant cultural group (white, Protestant, middle-class, European Americans) has the greatest impact on societal values and behavioral expectations. Ethnocentrism takes group membership to an extreme when members believe that they are superior to members of other groups. The interaction of culture and society are critical elements in studying students, families, communities, and schools.

A number of theories have evolved to describe the nature of diversity in the United States. Assimilation has been the predominant theory during the twentieth century. To be successful in society, newcomers and other visibly distinct groups were expected to shed their cultural identities and adopt those of the dominant group. In a culturally plural society, the maintenance of distinct cultural patterns is valued, promoted, and treated as equal to the dominant culture. Cultural choice allows individuals, families, and groups to maintain their own cultures, assimilate into the dominant society, or be bicultural or multicultural. Each of these theories has been translated into educational strategies that guide a school's curriculum and the interactions of students and teachers.

Individuals belong to numerous microcultural groups, which determine their unique cultural identity. The groups that appear to be the most important in our identity are race, gender, and class or socioeconomic status. To many, religious affiliation is most critical in determining cultural patterns. One's language, disability, or sexual orientation may also be essential in the determination of cultural identity. Membership in one of these microcultural groups may be so important that it influences membership in all of the others.

Discussion Questions

1. How do culture and society interact to produce inequities between diverse groups?
2. Why do we often not recognize our own cultural patterns?
3. Why might it be important to help students learn more about their own cultural background and heritage?
4. How have theories describing diversity impacted on the educational process in the past decade?
5. What impact does poverty have on a family's or student's cultural identity?

Journal/Portfolio Development

1. Contrast educational practices that have evolved to support the different theories of diversity. Develop an argument for incorporating those practices into your own teaching.
2. Prepare an autobiographical description of the importance of your membership in the microcul-

tural groups described in this chapter to your own cultural identity. The description should indicate why membership in one or more groups is especially important in the identification of who you are.

School-Based Experiences

1. In a school with students from diverse language backgrounds, interview a teacher about the strategies that are used to ensure that students do not fall academically behind because their native language is not English.

2. Ask a sample of students of color in a school in which they are the numerical minority how their ethnic background is reflected in the curriculum and activities of the school.

Notes

1. National Council for Accreditation of Teacher Education. NCATE *Refined Standards.* Washington, DC: Author, 1994.
2. Norman R. Yetman, *Majority and Minority: The Dynamics of Race and Ethnicity in American Life.* 4th ed. Boston: Allyn and Bacon, 1985.
3. Young Pai, *Cultural Foundation of Education.* Columbus, OH: Merrill, 1990.
4. George Spindler and Louise Spindler, *The American Cultural Dialogue and Its Transmission.* New York: Falmer Press, 1990, 38.
5. R. N. Bellah, R. Madsen, W. M. Sullivan, A. Swidler, and S. M. Tipton, *Habits of the Heart: Individualism and Commitment in American Life.* New York: Harper & Row, 1985, 23.
6. Ibid., 23.
7. Milton M. Gordon, *Assimilation in American Life: The Role of Race, Religion, and National Origins.* New York: Oxford University Press, 1964.
8. Richard Pratte, *Pluralism in Education: Conflict, Clarity, and Commitment.* Springfield, IL: Charles C. Thomas, 1979.
9. Ana Maria Villegas, *Culturally Responsive Pedagogy for the 1990s and Beyond (Trends and Issues Paper No. 6).* Washington, DC: ERIC Clearinghouse on Teacher Education, 1991.
10. Donna M. Gollnick and Philip C. Chinn, *Multicultural Education in a Pluralistic Society.* Columbus, OH: Merrill, 1994, 20.
11. American Council on Education and Education Commission of the States, *One-third of a Nation.*

Washington, DC: American Council on Education, 1988.
12. Harold Hodgkinson, "The Schools We Need for the Kids We've Got" (Paper presented at the 1987 annual meeting of the American Association of Colleges for Teacher Education, February 1986).
13. R. Spencer, "U.S. Ranks 6th in Quality of Life; Japan Is 1st," *The Washington Post,* (May 18, 1993), A7.
14. Spindler and Spindler, 23.
15. Bureau of the Census, *Statistical Abstract of the United States, 1992,* 108th ed. Washington, DC: Government Printing Office, 1992.
16. Donald L. Barlett and James B. Steele, *America: What Went Wrong?* Kansas City, MO: Andrews and McMeel, 1992.
17. Stephen J. Rose, *Social Stratification in the United States: The American Profile Poster Revised and Expanded.* New York: The New Press, 1992.
18. K. P. Phillips, *The Politics of Rich and Poor.* New York: Random House, 1990 , 179–180.
19. Sar A. Levitan and Isaac Shapiro, *Working but Poor: America's Contradiction.* Baltimore, MD: The Johns Hopkins University Press, 1987, vii.
20. "Children in Poverty," *Education Week* (September 29, 1993): 3.
21. M. F. Linehan, "Children Who Are Homeless: Educational Strategies for School Personnel," *Phi Delta Kappan* 74 (1) (1992): 61–66.
22. Bureau of the Census, *Statistical Abstract of the United States, 1992.*

23. Jorgen S. Nielsen, "Muslims, Pluralism and the European Nation State," *European Journal of Intercultural Studies* 5(1) (1994): 18–22.

24. Giovanna Campani, "Intercultural Education in Italy," *European Journal of Intercultural Studies* 4(3) (1994): 44–53.

25. George Markou, "Intercultural Education in Multicultural Greece," *European Journal of Intercultural Studies* 4(3) (1994): 32–43.

26. Claude Liauza, "Interculturalism: New Lands to Discover in France," *European Journal of Intercultural Studies* 4(3) (1994): 25–31.

27. Christopher Szaday, "Schooling in Multicultural Switzerland," *European Journal of Intercultural Studies* 5(1) (1994): 38–50.

28. William L. Yancey, Eugene P. Ericksen, and Richard N. Juliani, "Emergent Ethnicity: A Review and Reformulation," in Norma R. Yetman, ed., *Majority and Minority: The Dynamics of Racial and Ethnic Relations.* Boston: Allyn and Bacon, 1985.

29. Jessie Bernard, *The Female World.* New York: Free Press, 1981, 4.

30. Myra Sadker, David Sadker, and Susan Klein, "The Issue of Gender in Elementary and Secondary Education," in Gerald Grant, ed., *Review of Research in Education,* vol. 17. Washington, DC: American Educational Research Association, 1991.

31. Bernard, 1981.

32. Pai, 1990.

33. Bureau of the Census, 1992.

34. Ibid.

35. Michelle Fine, "Sexuality, Schooling, and Adolescent Females: The Missing Discourse of Desire," *Harvard Educational Review* 58(1) (February 1988): 48.

36. P. E. Willis, *Learning to Labour: How Working Class Kids Get Working Class Jobs.* Farnborough, England: Saxon House, 1977.

37. *Joseph Acanfora* v. *Board of Education of Montgomery County, et al.* 359 F. Supp. 843 (1973); aff'd 491 F. 2nd 498 (4th Cir. 1974); cert. denied, 419 U.S. 836 (1974).

38. American Bar Association, ABA Annual Meeting Provides Forum for Family Law Experts, 13 Fam. L. Rep. (BNA), 1542, 1543, 1987. As quoted in Elaine Wickens, "Penny's Question: 'I Will Have a Child in my Class with Two Moms—What Do You Know about This?'" *Young Children* 48(3) (March 1993): 25–28.

39. Bureau of the Census, *Statistical Abstract of the United States, 1992.*

40. Gollnick and Chinn, 1994.

41. "Church Attendance Constant," *Emerging Trends* 14(3) (1992).

42. R. Bezilla, *Religion in America.* Princeton, HJ: Princeton Religion Research Center, 1993.

Bibliography

Bellah, R. N., Madsen, R., Sullivan, W. M., Swidler, A. and Tipton, S. M. *Habits of the Heart: Individualism and Commitment in American Life.* New York: Harper & Row, 1985.

Connell, R. W. "Poverty and Education." *Harvard Educational Review* 64(2) (Summer 1994): 125–149.

Corbett, Susan. "A Complicated Bias." *Young Children* 48(3) (March 1993): 29–31.

Gollnick, Donna M., and Chinn, Philip C. *Multicultural Education in a Pluralistic Society.* Columbus, OH: Merrill, 1994.

Sleeter, Christine E., ed. *Empowerment through Multicultural Education.* Albany, NY: State University of New York Press, 1991.

Spindler, George, and Spindler, Louise. *The American Cultural Dialogue and Its Transmission.* New York: Falmer Press, 1990.

Wickens, Elaine. "Penny's Question: 'I Will Have a Child in My Class with Two Moms—What Do You Know about This?'" *Young Children* 48(3) (March 1993): 25–28.

6

Education That Is Multicultural

Focus Questions

1 What philosophical beliefs support education that is multicultural?
2 What role does cultural diversity play in education that is multicultural?
3 How do teachers deliver education that is multicultural?
4 What differences could schools make in the lives of children?
5 How is education that is multicultural different from what is delivered by most good schools today?

Key Terms and Concepts

Bias: A preference or inclination that inhibits impartial judgment, leading to prejudice or discrimination.

Censorship: The condemnation of books, instructional materials, teaching content, or teaching methods because they are perceived as unsupportive of or in opposition to the values of an individual or group.

Multicultural education: An educational strategy that incorporates the teaching of exceptional and culturally diverse students, human relations, and the study of ethnic and other cultural groups in a school environment that supports diversity and equal opportunity.

Social justice: The desire for all individuals and families to share equally society's benefits.

Stereotyping: The application of common traits, characteristics, and behavior to a group of people without acknowledging individual differences within the group.

Voice: The right and opportunity to speak and be heard as an equal.

Diversity and equality are the perspectives through which education that is multicultural should be developed. All teaching and school activities should be designed and evaluated with these characteristics in mind. All aspects of education—including the hidden curriculum, staffing patterns, discipline, and extracurricular activities—should be viewed through these perspectives to ensure that the needs of all students are an integral part of the education process. Education must do more than reflect only dominant society; it must begin to reflect diversity and support all students. The challenge for you as an educator will be to deliver an education that is multicultural. Constant vigilance of the content and delivery of the subject matter will be required.

Many educators have mistakenly thought that **multicultural education**[1] or education that is multicultural is only for students who are not members of the dominant group in society. Rather, it is for all students regardless of their microcultural memberships. It is as important for students and teachers of European, Protestant backgrounds as it is for those from ethnic and cultural groups that have traditionally faced discrimination in society. All content should be multicultural and presented through the viewpoints of many different groups to help students understand that there is more than one perspective on the interpretation of events and facts.

Too many educators have thought they were "doing" multicultural education simply by including information about groups other than their own in a lesson. This additive approach is evident in black history and women's history months or a highlighted section in a textbook that discusses Japanese Americans. In some schools attention to multiculturalism begins and ends with tasting ethnic foods and participating in ethnic festivals. While these activities can contribute to the development of education that is multicultural, they are side attractions and do not represent an integrated curriculum and school environment.

In education that is multicultural all teaching is multicultural and classrooms and schools are models of democracy and equity. This effort requires educators to

1. place the student at the center of the teaching and learning process;

2. promote human rights and respect for cultural differences;

3. believe that all students can learn;

4. acknowledge and build on the life histories and experiences of students' microcultural memberships;

5. critically analyze oppression and power relationships to understand racism, sexism, classism, and discrimination against the disabled, young, and aged;

6. critique society in the interest of social justice and equality; and

7. participate in collective social action to ensure a democratic society.[2]

Education that is multicultural is much more than tasting ethnic foods or participating in an ethnic festival.

Although you should begin to struggle with these issues now, the process of learning about others and reflecting on one's attitudes and actions in these areas will be a lifelong activity.

Undergirding Tenets

For centuries women, persons with low incomes, and members of oppressed ethnic and religious groups have fought for an education equal to that available to members of the dominant group. In the nineteenth century courageous educators established schools to serve some of these students, often encountering opposition from the community at the time. Nearly eighty years ago educators at the Intercultural Service Bureau in New York City were fighting for the incorporation of intercultural education into the curriculum to increase knowledge about new immigrants and to reduce the prejudice against them. In 1954 the Supreme Court declared illegal separate-but-equal education for black and white students in the *Brown* vs *Board of Education* case. The civil rights struggles in the 1960s laid the groundwork for adding content to the curriculum about African Americans, Latinos, Native Americans, and Asian Americans. Attention to equity for women, individuals with disabilities, or limited-English speakers soon followed.

These events became the foundation for education that is multicultural. A number of related beliefs about schooling and society guide the development of education that supports democracy for all. One is the belief that cultural diversity is a national strength that should be valued and promoted. Another is that **social justice** and equality remain viable goals for society and should be modeled in classrooms and schools. In this section, we will examine two of the major tenets on which multicultural education is built.

Diversity

There has been a great amount of public and academic discussion of multiculturalism in the past few years. Editorials, national news programs, radio talk shows, and debates among college students and faculty periodically focus on the importance of diversity in society and the curriculum. Simply put, the argument on one side is that the recognition and promotion of cultural and ethnic diversity will strengthen the nation. The other side argues that the promotion of diversity will divide the nation and lead to even greater conflict among groups. This second group also argues that the Western tradition is denigrated as diversity is highlighted.

The claim that multicultural education will divide the nation suggests that the nation is already united.[3] Campaigns for members of Congress, governors, and mayors in 1994 included debates about immigration, provision of services to undocumented workers and their children, the use of only English, and gay rights. Multiculturalists argue that "multicultural education is designed to help unify a deeply divided nation rather than to divide a highly cohesive one."[4] In addition, as we have the opportunity to learn more about each other and to interact on an equal basis in schools and society, members of diverse groups can maintain their ethnic and cultural diversity while developing together a common civic culture. An outgrowth of these debates has been the establishment of general education requirements in colleges and universities for ethnic, women's, and/or global studies. At least thirty-three states also expect teacher education candidates to study diversity and to be able to incorporate it into their teaching.[5] The national accrediting agency for teacher education programs in colleges and universities, NCATE, has required the inclusion of multicultural content in teacher education curriculum since 1978. Most of the developing state and national standards for preschool through high school curriculum include references to diversity.

What does the public think of incorporating diversity into the curriculum of our schools? The National Conference Survey found that

> On the whole, the data suggest that cultural diversity is hardly a foreign or unfamiliar concept in contemporary American society. Asked "How important do you think it is that people from different groups learn to understand and appreciate the lifestyles, tastes, and contributions of each other's groups?" 67% of those surveyed nationwide said such understanding and appreciation is "very important," while another 25% feel it is "important." Across the board, roughly nine in ten people in all diverse groups surveyed endorse this concept, including 91% of whites.
>
> As a counterpart question, survey participants were also asked about the desirability of "teaching all students about the racial, ethnic, and cultural groups that make up America today." A substantial 57% say they find it "very desirable" and another 31% "somewhat desirable," while only 9% deem such education "undesirable," adding up to an 88% mandate from the adult public. Again, roughly 9 in 10 respondents endorse the teaching of cultural diversity in the nation's schools.
>
> These results indicate that whatever negative perceptions groups have about each other, many of the prerequisites of tolerance and inter-group cooperation are present in today's America: respect for the differences among us and a commitment to increased understanding of those differences.[6]

According to the National Conference survey, most Americans believe that diversity should be taught in schools. In another study of public perceptions of the *good society,* researchers concluded that "Pluralism does not contradict the idea of a good society, for the latter would be one that would allow a wide scope for diversity and would draw on resources from its pluralistic communities in discerning those things that are necessarily matters of the good of all."[7]

Social Justice and Equality

Peace, prosperity, freedom, and justice traditionally have defined the good society for Americans.[8] What is meant by *justice* in a society that places so much emphasis on individualism and the freedom to be left alone? Justice itself is related to fairness, moral rightness, and equity. Our judicial system is designed to guarantee legal justice for individuals and groups. **Social justice,** on the other hand, focuses on how we help others in the community who are not as advantaged as we are. In fact, most religions measure the quality of society by the justice and care given to the downtrodden—the homeless, the sick, the powerless, the uneducated.[9]

The ethic of social justice, especially as it relates to the teacher-student relationship, is essential in the profession of teaching along with moral commitments to inquiry (that is, the nurturing of thinking), knowledge, competence, and caring.[10] It requires "that schools provide equal access to and equal receipt of a quality education for *all* students. Any structures or practices that interfere with the simultaneous goals of equity and excellence, that perpetuate preexisting social and economic inequities, are subject to critique and elimination."[11] The acceptance of

Social justice is measured by the care provided to individuals in society who are not as advantaged as most.

social justice as a moral and ethical responsibility of educators and schooling is critical in the provision of education that is multicultural.

As discussed in previous chapters, schools are currently full of social injustices that need to be addressed and eliminated to provide educational equality for all students. As you reflect on the inequitable conditions in most of our schools, ask yourself the following questions:

- How fair is it for some students to attend school in dilapidated, foul-smelling, crowded buildings while others attend classes in beautiful buildings with future-oriented technology and well-groomed grounds?
- How fair is it for wealthier students to have the most experienced and best qualified teachers who earn the highest salaries of all teachers?
- How fair is it that wealthier students are exposed to intellectually challenging curriculum and experiences while many low-income students do not even have an advanced placement class offered in their school?
- How fair is it that students of color, especially males, and students with disabilities or limited English proficiency are pulled out of regular classes and isolated in segregated classes during much of the school day?
- How accurate is a curriculum and pedagogy that does not reflect the rich plurality of the people, histories, experiences, and perspectives of the groups that comprise the United States and world?

These are among the numerous questions that educators should be asking themselves if they are serious about providing social justice in schools. The promise of a democratic society has been that all students have a fair chance to learn and succeed. Instead, the current system supports the same inequities that exist in society. The already advantaged student normally continues to be advantaged over students in low-income areas from the day they enter school. A theory of social justice suggests that those students with the least advantage should receive the greatest advantage in their education and schooling to begin to ensure an equal and fair playing field. The goal might be to use the best funded and successful schools as the norm for all schools, with the least advantaged receiving the greatest resources for their education.

Global Perspectives: For What Purpose? The Debate in the United Kingdom

Even the advocates for changing schools to reflect democracy and equality sometimes disagree about what to call the educational strategy. In the United Kingdom the debate between antiracists and multiculturalists began to flourish in the 1970s after the release of a number of national reports on immigrants and race relations. The differences between the two went beyond the label for what is called *multicultural education* or *education that is multicultural* in the United States. The supporters of antiracist education focused on the structure of the education system and power relationships between the dominant Anglo society and the powerless immigrant groups. The primary emphasis of the advocates for multicultural education was on the content of the curriculum. Finally, in the 1990s a synthesis of the two is evolving in which the strategy for social justice is an education that is antiracist *and* multicultural.[12]

Educational Challenges

The challenges for delivering education that is multicultural are many. The diversity of the student population is growing differently than in the past. By the time you start teaching, approximately one-third of the students in schools across the nation will be from ethnic groups other than European. By 2020 over 45 percent of the school-age population will be students of color.[13] Because many teacher candidates have either no or limited experience with the ethnic groups that will be in their classrooms, they will face the unknown. The tenets of diversity and social justice will require continuous learning about and with these communities to be effective teachers.

In some schools teachers may still face fairly homogeneous student populations with little exposure to diversity and the multicultural nature of the country. Even with limited ethnic diversity, most schools will have males and females from different religious and economic backgrounds. The ethic of social justice is just as important in these settings as in those with great ethnic and language diversity. To provide a well-rounded and balanced curriculum for these students, teachers will need to work harder at bringing different perspectives to presentations and discussions. Innovative strategies for providing direct exposure to diversity and issues of equality will need to be developed.

Diverse Approaches to Teaching and Learning

We all have preferred learning and teaching styles that are embedded in our cultural background and experiences. Unfortunately, most of us think that everyone else shares our learning style. Until a teacher learns to recognize these differences and develops a repertoire of different ways to teach the subject matter, some students will be deprived of appropriate assistance in the learning process.

CASE STUDY	SCIENCE SUCCESS FOR LEP STUDENTS

The city of Yakima, located in south central Washington, serves a large, rather isolated agricultural region with a culturally diverse population. One of the city's two high schools, Davis High School, enrolls Anglo (42 percent), Latino (33 percent), African American (15 percent), and Asian American (10 percent) students. Eighty-five percent of the students are eligible for free or reduced lunches.

Although the school had a fairly successful retention rate, migrant and immigrant students were not being prepared well for college, as was evidenced in their lack of success in science courses. Science faculty decided to adapt a regular chemistry course for students with limited English proficiency. The chemistry teacher participated in an intensive workshop on English as a Second Language (ESL) and then integrated ESL strategies into the curriculum. Bilingual materials were developed, and a bilingual aide was hired to work with the teacher and students. Information in class was presented visually as well as verbally, and videodiscs with English and Spanish soundtracks were used.

Students in the first class included Mexican Americans, a Peruvian, a Japanese exchange student, and an Ethiopian. They performed as well as the students in the traditional chemistry course, and some are now college students. Their self-confidence improved, as did their grades, attendance, and motivation. In addition, faculty outside the science department began to see that students with limited English proficiency could perform academically at a level equal to the other students—a fact that they had doubted in the past.

1. What components of multicultural education were integrated into the chemistry course at Davis High School?
2. What may have occurred in this course that ensured that the limited English proficient students were able to perform at a level comparable to classmates in the traditional course?
3. Why did the successful experiences of these students in science cause some teachers to rethink their expectations for them?

Source: "Davis High School: Helping Bilingual Science Students Succeed." *Rural Adult Education Forum* 5 (2) (December 1992/January 1993): 7.

Valuing Differences. Understanding the cultures of students and drawing on them to teach the subject matter is a critical component in helping students learn. Students usually can determine rather quickly whether the teacher values them and their cultures. To demonstrate a respect for the students' background and experiences, teachers should be able to help students see the relationship between the subject matter and the world in which they live. Students should be able to see themselves in the representations (that is, books, examples, word problems, and films) used by teachers. If the teaching style and representations are based totally on the culture of the teacher, it will be difficult to convince students that their cultures are also valued.

Use of students' prior knowledge and experiences with the subject matter is also critical in providing meaningful learning experiences in the classroom. Students make sense of new information in different ways. Therefore, the teacher must be able to teach the same concept by explaining it in different ways, relating it to something meaningful in the student's life and demonstrating it with multiple

Teachers must be able to transcend their own cultural background in the development of learning experiences that build on the cultural background of their students.

representations. For most beginning teachers, repertoires are rather limited; with experience, good teachers are able to draw on many different strategies to take advantage of a student's unique learning style and cultural patterns.

It is important to know what kind of knowledge, skills, and commitments are valued in the students' cultures. Researchers have found that some students rebel against academic study and school authority as a form of resistance against the values of dominant society and its institutions.[14] For example, some white working-class families value common sense and working with one's hands. They place less value on "book learning" than most middle-class families. Understanding these differences should help the teacher develop different strategies for presenting and discussing the subject matter.

Avoidance of Stereotyping. After studying a program for training teachers to teach culturally different students in Los Angeles, G. Williamson McDiarmid raised a number of issues, including the fact that generalizations about culturally diverse learners are often very dangerous. Teachers need to be thoughtful about the role that culture—values, behaviors, language—may play in learning and, at the same time, avoid characterizing all students as the same because they appear to share the same ethnicity or class.[15]

At first glance, it may seem that handling diversity in a classroom would be much easier if we could just pick up a recipe book that clearly states what instruction will be effective for students from a specific group. The problem with this approach is that not only are there differences across ethnic and cultural groups, there are many differences among members within the same group. Therefore, the descriptions and recommendations of a group usually do not apply to all members of that group. The intragroup differences may be based on socioeconomic level, religion, language, and degree of assimilation. The generalizations in the recipe book would lead to **stereotyping** and prejudging students in a way that concerned McDiarmid in his Los Angeles observations.

Just like teaching itself, multicultural teaching is complex. A teacher cannot determine the learning styles, prior knowledge, or cultural experiences of students by simply knowing that they are from a specific ethnic group or socioeconomic level. The teacher will need to observe and listen to students and their parents as well as assess student performance to develop the most effective teaching strategy.

Use of Competition and Cooperation. Traditionally classrooms have been organized with the teacher as the authority figure who lectures and controls all aspects of the learning process. In this system students compete for recognition by the teacher to answer a question and receive positive or negative reinforcement. Tests and grades are also competitive in that students compete against each other and are ranked accordingly. Competition in the classroom generally supports the learning styles of members of the dominant culture.

Cooperative learning, on the other hand, provides greater opportunities for learning by many students of color because it reflects their preferred learning style, which is group-oriented. Cooperative learning supports a more democratic climate than the traditional classroom. Students work together in small, preferably heterogeneous groups and take responsibility for themselves and other members of the group. They help each other learn and, in the process, develop skills in interpersonal relations.[16]

Inclusion in Regular Classrooms

Inclusion is a term that evolved from the work of persons with disabilities, the parents of students with disabilities, and special educators to ensure that physically and mentally challenged young people could be educated in the same classrooms as students without disabilities. In the broader society, inclusion has confronted discrimination policies and practices that have made it very difficult for some individuals to be mobile, receive a college education, and be offered jobs. As a result of the activism of these individuals, persons with disabilities have become more integrated into society. It is no longer unusual to be in meetings with professionals who are in wheelchairs or who are using sign language.

Today, inclusion is used more broadly to promote the involvement of all underrepresented groups in regular classrooms and society's institutions. In applying the ethic of social justice, one should be concerned to find white middle-class students overly represented in advanced placement classes. One should wonder why the advanced classes are intellectually stimulating and interesting while the remedial classes are usually practice oriented and dull. Why are young women and students of color underrepresented in the high-level mathematics and science courses?

Inclusion is expected in a school that provides education that is multicultural. However, it is not a common practice in many schools today. Educators have begun to accept students with mild disabilities in classrooms, but many others are transported to special schools or sent to a pull-out program within the school for much or all of the day. Although schools have been working to desegregate for forty years, the population of many urban schools is predominantly students of color while many suburban schools are predominantly white. Within desegregated schools, students are often segregated to an ever greater degree by race or language in classes. Such practices should trigger an investigation about the lack of social justice and provision of equality for all students.

High Expectations.   A key element in multicultural education is the belief that all students, regardless of their cultural backgrounds, can learn at high levels. Most persons who select teaching as their career probably want to help all students learn and believe that they can. Somewhat surprisingly, a 1994 survey of teachers in Kentucky did not support that assumption. Only about one-third of the teachers believed that all students could learn at a high level.[17]

In most cases, we also have not acknowledged our **biases** about some groups; this can have a great impact on our expectations for their ability to learn. Research on self-fulfilling prophecies has found that students perform better when the teacher has high expectations of their abilities.[18] Conversely, it is very difficult for students to overcome the teacher's low expectation. They often begin to accept that they cannot achieve, they lose interest in trying, and they take on the stereotypical role of the nonacademic student. Thus, both teachers and students interact to fulfill the prophecy, even when the expectations are based on inaccurate information.

It is important that teachers develop a classroom climate that values students and makes them feel capable of academic success.[19] To be successful, this expectation interacts with teacher behaviors to communicate that the teacher cares about students as individuals and believes that they can learn. "The teacher ceases seeing his or her students as 'the other' and addresses students' psychological and social development along with their academic development."[20]

Ability Grouping.   Ability grouping and tracking of students go against an ethic of social justice and equality. These practices provide the most advantaged students with the best possible school experiences while ensuring that the least advantaged students receive separate, and often ineffective, instruction. There are at least three serious repercussions of ability grouping. It "separates students along socioeconomic lines, separating rich from poor, whites from non-whites. The end result is that poor and minority children are found far more often than others in the bottom tracks. And once there, they are likely to suffer far more negative consequences of schooling than are their more fortunate peers."[21]

Tracking also "retard[s] the academic progress of many students—those in average and low groups. Tracking seems to foster low self-esteem among these same students and promotes school misbehavior and dropping out. Tracking also appears to lower the aspirations of students who are not in the top groups."[22] Finally, many students are placed in a track very early in their schooling—a track in which they remain throughout their school career. These unfortunate students have little opportunity to achieve academically, or even to move out of the lowest track.

Tracking has no place in education that is multicultural. Social justice can only exist if all students are provided equal access to educational opportunities that are high level, stimulating, and effective. Educators must begin to examine why students are not learning and take on the challenge to make changes in the classroom climate and nature of instruction to promote learning by all students.

Student Voices

In a democratic classroom all participants must have a **voice**—the right and opportunity to speak and be heard as an equal. The dialogue cannot be dominated by teachers. They are viewed by students, especially low-income students and students of color, as representing the dominant cultural group and not being open to hearing other perspectives represented by their cultures.

Education that is multicultural encourages and validates the diverse voices of students in helping them construct their own learning.

Including student voices in the classroom dialogue is not always an easy pursuit. Students usually have limited experience in active participation in their own learning. When the classroom climate begins to include student voices, they may express anger and be confrontive; they may even test the limits of the type of language that can be used and the subjects that can be broached. Allowing student voices to be an integral part of classroom discourse often tests the patience of teachers as they and their students figure out how to listen and contribute to the learning process. At the same time, tolerance, patience with each other, and the willingness to listen will develop as student voices contribute to the exploration of the subject matter.

Affirmation of Student Voices. Respect for differences is key in affirming student voices. For many educators it requires relinquishing the power that they have traditionally had as the voice of authority with the *right* answers. Class time can no longer be monopolized with teacher talk. The meaningful incorporation of student voices requires the development of listening skills and the validation of multiple perspectives, languages, and dialects. It should allow students to participate in the dialogue through speaking, writing, and artistic expression. It should allow them to use the modes of communicating with which they feel the most comfortable while teaching them other modes as well.

Student voices are also affirmed by encouraging students to relate the subject matter to their own realities or lived experiences. Because most of us have very limited experiences in other cultures, we must expand our knowledge about them. Students can become active participants in helping others learn about their cultures and everyday experiences. Teachers can facilitate learning activities to guide students in teaching each other. If we are not able to help students see the relationship of the subject matter to their own lives, we may not be able to help them learn. Listening to them and being able to adjust our teaching strategies appropriately will help make us effective teachers.

The affirmation of student voices requires that educators listen to the voices of *all* students. It is particularly important to hear the voices of students of color, low-income students, girls and young women, limited English speakers, and students with disabilities. The formal and hidden curriculum has validated the voices of the dominant groups throughout their lives. One of the goals of education that is multicultural is to also validate the voices and stories of others. Teachers must ensure that these voices are not drowned out again in their classrooms. The stories or narratives of others will increase the knowledge and tolerance of differences. Many students will learn to value both their own culture and that of others. In the process we will also learn that we have much in common.[23]

Cross-Cultural Communications. Some of the conflict in student-teacher interactions is the lack of information and understanding about cultural differences in oral and nonverbal communications. "Just as cultures differ in the structure of their language, they also differ in the structure of oral discourse. Moves made in teaching-learning discourse, who is to make them, and the sequence they should take vary from culture to culture."[24] Communicating is like other aspects of culture. We usually think that the way that we communicate with other members of the culture is "normal." We don't realize that there are many other ways to communicate that make as much sense as our own, but we have just not had the opportunity to experience them. As long as we interact only with members of the same culture, we use the same cultural cues for whose turn it is to speak, the meaning of a raised eyebrow, or the seriousness of a statement.

Often teachers do not realize that they and their students are reading the cultural cues differently. In many cases, students are punished for responding inappropriately when they may have read the teacher's intent differently based on their own cultural experiences. Recognizing that miscommunications may be based on cultural differences is the first step in improving cross-cultural communications. A next step is to be able to admit that we may be part of the problem. Next, we should be able to develop alternate means for communicating and understanding the messages from other cultures.

One approach is to systematically teach the communication patterns of the dominant culture to students who are not members of that culture. In this strategy the students' communication patterns are still valued, but they learn when it is to their advantage to use the communication patterns of the dominant group. In other words, they begin to become bicultural. However, teachers who also learn to function effectively in more than one culture will most often gain respect from students, and begin to genuinely model a multicultural pedagogy.

Multicultural Curriculum

A major dimension of education that is multicultural is the integration of diversity and equality throughout the curriculum. The curriculum for all academic areas should reflect these concepts. Adding a course on ethnic studies or women's studies to the curriculum is an easy way to introduce students to the culture, history, and experiences of others, but it is not enough. Education that is multicultural calls for the inclusion of others throughout the curriculum.

The additive approach of including a unit on one of these groups sporadically during the year suggests that they are not an integral part of society. They are somewhat interesting to study, but they are not really a part of the whole picture. As a result, the curriculum places the culture, values, history, and experiences of the dominant group at the center. The implicit message is that the dominant culture is the most important in society, and that other cultures do not count or are certainly not as important. Learning will be increased for many students if their cultures become the center of the curriculum. As they learn within their own cultural context, they see themselves and their cultures valued by the teacher and school authorities.

One-third of the students in our nation's schools do not see themselves, their families, or their communities in the curriculum. It is not only students of color who seldom find themselves at the center of the curriculum; the curriculum does not normally include information on or the stories of women, the disabled, limited English speakers, families in poverty, the elderly, or members of religions that are not Judeo-Christian. The curriculum must become more inclusive; in the process, it will begin to reflect the reality of our multicultural world rather than just the piece of it that belongs to the dominant group.

No matter how great or limited the ethnic diversity is in a school, the curriculum should be multicultural. Rural white students should have the same opportunities to view the world and subject matter from multicultural and global perspectives as students in diverse settings. Because they do not have the opportunities to interact directly with members of diverse groups, the curriculum often becomes the primary source for their exploration of diversity, social justice, and related issues.

Multiple Perspectives.   The perspective of the dominant group in society has become almost universal in most textbooks, instructional materials, and teacher-student dialogue. As a result, the voice of the dominant group is centered in curriculum and instruction. Because it is the voice most prevalent, it takes on an air of superiority over all other voices and perspectives. Education that is multicultural requires an approach that validates and gives more equitable treatment to perspectives that may differ somewhat or dramatically from that of the dominant group.

The introduction and exploration of multiple perspectives are very important in the curriculum. Every historical period, as well as current events, can be viewed through the eyes of others as well as those of the dominant group. When social studies emphasizes wars, women are seldom included. Discussions of power struggles, political leaders, and business usually ignore the working class, persons of color, and women. Attention to multiple perspectives draws in the voices of the individuals and groups without power; it begins to provide them an equal voice in the interpretation of events. A study of the struggles between Native American tribes and the federal government should always include a view from the perspective of the tribes as well as the powerful influence of the government.

In the humanities multiple perspectives are available in the literature, music, and art of individuals from diverse cultural and ethnic backgrounds. The works of authors and performers can be critiqued from different perspectives as well. Reading the works of authors from diverse backgrounds, observing performances, and listening to music provides teachers and their students a more well-rounded education than possible when the voices and perspectives of those who are like them are the only ones to which they are exposed. These activities also allow students to begin to understand the experiences and feelings of others as viewed from their perspectives on the world.

Although not as readily as the social sciences and humanities, science and mathematics also lend themselves to examination from multiple experiences. For example, Native Americans' approach to science has begun to have an impact on our treatment of the earth that is very different than the industrialized Western model. As we learn to appreciate and value multiple perspectives in academic areas, we realize that there are multiple answers to many questions. As a result, our knowledge expands beyond that of the limited perspective of our family and cultural group.

Another strength of the inclusion of multiple perspectives is that it allows many voices to participate in defining a common curriculum.[25] In the process the curriculum will change from a representation predominantly of middle and upper class whites to a balanced representation of others alongside the dominant group. Diversity and equality will be valued and promoted as an inclusive curriculum and practices evolve.

Controversial Issues.   Multicultural teaching helps students struggle with social problems and issues that many students face daily. Racism, sexism, classism, prejudice, and discrimination are felt differently by students of color than by members

PROFESSIONAL DILEMMA

What If He Has Two Mommies?

In the 1950s most students came from families with both a mother and father. In the subsequent forty years more and more students were being raised by single mothers, and now a growing number of single fathers. Even during this period, some students were not living with either parent, but stayed instead with relatives or in a foster home. As society becomes more tolerant of a variety of family structures and as adults become more open about their sexual orientation, teachers also will be introduced to lesbian and gay parents who may be living with a partner or separated from a partner.

The curriculum in most schools, especially at the primary and elementary levels, is often developed around the family—a nuclear family with a mother, father, and siblings. For decades now, schools have been populated with students whose families do not fit that model. The curriculum and instructional materials seldom mirror the diversity of families that may include parents with special needs, interracial parents, single parents, gay and lesbian parents, and foster parents.

The dilemma for teachers extends beyond the curriculum. They must figure out how to value and respect the diversity of families. Otherwise, both students and parents will feel ignored and isolated from the school setting. Teachers may have to help other students develop an understanding of the diversity. Sometime students respond to such differences in negative and hurtful ways. Teachers will need to develop strategies for confronting homophobic behavior from the onset.

- How could a primary teacher introduce gay and lesbian parents into a reading lesson?

- What are different ways that teachers are likely to learn that some of their students have gay or lesbian parents?

- How should a teacher with strong views against homosexual relationships approach the reality of having the children of gays and lesbians in the classroom?

- How can a school develop a climate of acceptance of all students regardless of the structure and nature of the families in which they live?

---

of the dominant group. The ensuing anger, denial, guilt, and affirmation of identity are critical parts of learning about and struggling with the pernicious practices that permeate most of our institutions. Although it is sometimes difficult to discuss these issues in classrooms, they must be confronted in a system based on diversity and equality or changes will be impossible.

Most students of color, females, low-income students, students with disabilities, and gay students have probably already experienced discrimination in some aspect of their lives. They may have not acknowledged it or they may be very angry or frustrated by it. On the other hand, many students from the dominant group have never experienced discrimination and often do not believe that it exists. In most cases, they do not see themselves as advantaged; they do not think that they receive any more benefits from society than anyone else. These students will have a difficult time fighting social injustices if they have neither experienced them nor become aware of their existence. Are they receiving a good education if they are never exposed to the injustices that do exist or helped to confront their own biases?

Instructional Resources

Because the textbook remains a major resource in most classrooms, teachers need to know how to use it and other instructional materials effectively in delivering education that is multicultural. Almost no textbook fully integrates diversity and equality throughout the text. Therefore, the teacher often will draw on supplementary materials and discussion to provide the full, more accurate representation of an inclusive society.

As a new teacher, you may have to make a conscious effort to examine textbooks and other readings for biases, stereotyping, and the lack of coverage of diverse groups. With experience and expanding knowledge about differences, some educators quickly recognize the lack of information and intuitively counteract with appropriate adjustments to ensure a balanced exposure to multiple perspectives. It is impossible for a text or a teacher to present all perspectives on the topic or concepts presented in a lesson. However, teachers can incorporate the voices of their own students or discuss the perspectives of groups that may

Many students have faced discrimination in some aspects of their lives. They and other students should be provided an opportunity to struggle with the reality of discrimination and how to confront it in their own lives.

be in the current news. Good teachers never limit themselves and their students to the single textbook that was assigned to the course. Not only do they draw on other readings, but they often use other resources in the popular culture with which students are familiar, including movies, music, and cultural events.

Stereotyping and Unreality. Over the past two decades, many publishers and authors have committed themselves to eliminating the **biases** and stereotypes that existed in the 1960s and before. Researchers who analyze textbooks report that there has been great improvement in many areas. Nevertheless, many instructional materials still provide superficial coverage of ethnic and cultural groups, including white ethnic groups,[26] and of issues related to diversity and equality. Real issues of poverty, AIDS, teenage pregnancy, sex education, homophobia, the great gap between the poor and the rich, homelessness, and violence against children and women are often ignored. The events of which we are most proud are highlighted, while the injustices that remain are slighted. In education that is multicultural, a balance must be provided.

When a group is stereotyped in the materials being used by students, the teacher has the responsibility for providing another representation of the group. Native Americans are most often portrayed historically.[27] The teacher should also introduce students to contemporary Native Americans who live in urban areas and on reservations, and who are scientists, lawyers, and members of Congress. Their contributions to ecology, the arts, and the dominant culture should be interwoven into the study of those topics. The intent is to present a more accurate representation of the group, to prevent one image of the group from being generalized to all members of the group, and to teach that there are many intertribal and intragroup differences. Teachers cannot undertake this task unless they first recognize that the materials are stereotyping a group.

Censorship. Not all people believe that the curriculum and textbooks should be changed to reflect multiple perspectives of diversity. In fact, schools and teachers are sometimes attacked by parents and conservative groups who believe that these changes are anti-Christian and anti-American.[28] *Education Week* reported that The People for the American Way, a liberal constitutional-rights watchdog group, found **censorship** and other challenges to school materials and practices in 395 incidents in 44 states during the 1992–1993 school year. This represented the greatest number of incidents in its eleven-year history of conducting the study.[29]

Until the late 1970s, censorship attacks were usually on a specific book that the censors wanted removed from the curriculum or public and school libraries. Today the attacks have expanded to include literature series, curriculum for sex education, and programs that encourage students to take control of their own decisions related to drugs and alcohol. In addition, "many course offerings (e.g., sociology, psychology, health, and biology) as well as instruction pertaining to values clarification, self-esteem, multicultural education, evolution, AIDS education, and global education are being contested."[30] It no longer is an individual parent who is upset about the content of a book or curriculum not supporting the family's values. A number of conservative groups have undertaken well-orchestrated efforts to warn parents of the danger of certain books and teachings. To counteract the perceived denigration of their values, cases have been reviewed by the courts with limited success by the plaintiffs. The more popular approach today is to ensure that members of the group are elected to local school boards, where they can influence the adoption of curriculum.

As educators begin to implement education that is multicultural, they may face similar challenges. The most effective way of deterring such attacks is to involve parents very early in the decisions being made.[31]

Equitable Practices

Caring and fairness are two qualities that students use to describe successful teachers.[32] Students know whether teachers view them as very special or incompetent or worthless. Teacher perceptions may be based on personal characteristics of the student; sometimes, they are based on group membership. Homeless children who smell and arrive in dirty clothes may be given little chance of success. Children from one-parent homes may be pitied and their lack of academic achievement blamed on their not having two parents. Limited English speaking students are ignored until they learn English and can communicate with the teacher. Are these fair practices?

A school that provides an education that is multicultural would not tolerate such unjust practices by a teacher. Both the classroom and school would be models of democracy in which all students are treated equitably and fairly. In such a school, teachers and instructional leaders confront their own biases and develop strategies for overcoming them in their own interactions with students and colleagues. They learn to depend on each other for assistance in both developing a multicultural curriculum and ensuring that students are not subject to discrimination. In the process the classroom and school will reflect both diversity and equality. As a result, students learn to respect differences and to interact within and across ethnic and cultural groups as they struggle for social justice in the school and community.

Instruction. Researchers have found that many teachers unknowingly discriminate between males and females and between members of their own and other ethnic groups.[33] More help is given to some students than to others. Some students are praised, while others are more likely to be corrected and disciplined. Expectations for academic success differ depending on family income or ethnic biases. However, most teachers do not deliberately set out to discriminate against certain students, especially in any harmful way. The problem is that we have been raised in a racist, sexist, and classist society in which the biases are so embedded in society that it is difficult to recognize anything other than the very overt signs. Teachers often need others to point out their discriminatory practices.

A good pattern to begin to develop even now, early in your teacher education program, is to reflect on your practice and the practice of teachers who you observe. Among the questions that might be asked are:

- Are students from different gender, economic, and ethnic groups treated differently? What are the differences?

- Are there fewer discipline and learning problems among the students who are from the same background as the teacher? What is contributing to the differences?

- Do the least advantaged students receive the most assistance from the teacher? What are the differences in instruction between the groups?

- How are the students' cultures being incorporated into the curriculum and instruction?

A key to ensuring that interactions with students are equitable is the ability to recognize one's own biases and make appropriate adjustments. Educators must be able to admit that they sometimes make mistakes. Being able to reflect on the mistakes and why they occurred should lead to the improvement of teaching.

Assessment of Students. The assessment of children begins before they are born. Physical signs of health are normally assessed while the child is in the womb; treatment is provided if necessary and available to correct serious "abnormalities" that may adversely affect the child's health for a lifetime. Even at this early stage of life, a family's income is a primary determinant of the amount and nature of assessment and care provided.

Even before many students enter a preschool or kindergarten, assessment has moved beyond monitoring the physical signs of health to also determining their

Relevant Research

The Role of Schools in Students' Construction of Ethnic Identity

An in-depth study of the role of ethnicity for ten students in two urban high schools included students from middle- and working-class families and represented Mexican, Vietnamese, African, Italian, and Anglo heritages.

In one school setting, most of the immigrant students reported verbal or physical assaults against them. They seldom saw students of their ethnic group in advanced classes and believed that those that were at that level had abandoned their ethnic identity. They felt ignored and discounted by most of their teachers.

None of the students in the second school had experienced abuse from Anglo students. Their ethnic peers encouraged them to both maintain their ethnic identity and be academically successful.

Ethnicity was found to be important in the students' definitions of themselves and their academic achievement, but it was dynamic, and varied with the social setting. Some students used their ethnicity as a fortress that both protected and entrapped them. Others functioned biculturally or situationally, using different patterns of interaction at home than in school. The third set of students experienced their ethnicity as a resource that helped them succeed in what they perceived to be a racist society. School practices were found to support the role of ethnicity in a student's life, encourage academic achievement for all students, and to either reduce intergroup conflict or do just the opposite.

Source: Ann Locke Dividson, Hanh Cao Yu, and Patricia Phelan, "The Ebb and Flow of Ethnicity: Constructing Identity in Varied School Settings," *Educational Foundations* 7 (1) (Winter 1993): 65–87.

intellectual capabilities for productivity in society. At this time some parents begin to prepare their children to attend elite universities by enrolling them in the "right" preschool, which is likely to ensure admission to the appropriate elementary school. Testing of students' potential for success in these schools begins in some settings prior to admission into a preschool or kindergarten. (The practice of testing young children for admission is not supported by the major organization of early childhood educators, the National Association for the Education of Young Children.)

Assessment in educational settings has developed into a mechanism for sorting students, rather than serving as a system to monitor progress and determine instructional strategies needed to ensure that learning occurs. Instead, assessments indicate grades, placement in special education or gifted classes, placement in college preparatory or vocational tracks, and admission into postsecondary education. Beginning as early as kindergarten, these assessments may lead to the establishment of a school life in an exciting, stimulating environment or one in dull, boring classes in which it is clear that the student is not valued.

The students who perform well on current national standardized assessments mirror the most privileged in society. For example, white middle-class male students are overrepresented in the most demanding mathematics and science courses in high schools.[34] With the exception of Asian Americans, students of color are underrepresented in the ranks of college attenders. Thus, the sorting of students appears to be based more on gender, ethnic or racial background, language, and income than on ability to perform. This conclusion is supported by research that shows that norm-referenced tests are culturally biased. The norm is the dominant society and test questions reflect the knowledge and experiences that are common to members of that group. The problem is that not all test takers, especially if they are not members of that group, have had equal or similar exposure to the content of the tests.[35]

Some political ideologues and even some researchers believe that such sorting of the population is not only appropriate, but also that it reflects the genetic differences between groups of people.[36] Others believe that current assessments only sort the privileged from other members of society. "Assessments tell people how they should value themselves and others. They open doors for some and close them for others."[37] The lower academic classes have disproportionately high representation of students of color, limited-English speakers, low-income families, and males. Is this disproportionate representation due to genetic differences, as one group suggests, or to an assessment system that is not fair to students from diverse backgrounds? If educators believe in social justice and that all students can learn regardless of their cultural backgrounds, they will develop strategies that ensure that those students who have been treated most inequitably in the system are able to compete academically with students from more privileged backgrounds. If educators believe that nonprivileged students perform poorly on tests because they are genetically inferior, the current system of sorting students will continue.

Norm-referenced, pencil-and-paper tests are rather inexpensive and easy to conduct, but they are not the only assessments available to educators. Authentic, performance-based assessments are promising. Portfolios are one example in which students and teachers compile examples of their work that can be evaluated for growth over time (see Chapter 1 for additional information). These types of assessments should encourage diversity if educators are sensitive to differences in ethnicity, language, gender, and class. "In classrooms that are taught without regard

Tests are as common in schools as the textbook, but are they used to help improve student learning or to sort the powerful from the powerless?

for the use of the primary language, the portfolios of limited English-speakers will provide a portrait of many futile struggles at making meaning. In classrooms that are optimal learning environments (where constructivism, biliteracy, literature, and authentic writing projects occur) the portfolio will track development and academic achievement in-context."[38]

As a teacher, you will need to decide how you will effectively use assessments in your classroom. Will you let your expectations for a student's academic success be driven by his or her performance on a national standardized test? Will you assess performance primarily to help you identify prior knowledge and experience for use in developing the most effective instructional strategies to help students learn? Will your goal be to help students learn to understand the subject matter and to think critically about it or to will it be to help them perform well on the next national test by systematically teaching the content of the test? Assessments of students and their use in the classroom provide a number of dilemmas that are influenced by a teacher's philosophical and political beliefs.

The Role of the Teacher

Education that is multicultural requires educators to be active participants in the educational process. Social justice, democracy, power, and equity become more than concepts to be discussed in class; they become guides for actions in the classroom, school, and community. Educators become advocates not only for their own empowerment, but for that of students and other powerless groups.

Thinking Critically

Educators who think critically ask questions about why inequities are occurring in their classroom and school. They wonder why girls are responding differently to the science lesson than boys. But they don't stop with wondering; they explore and try alternatives to engage the girls in the subject matter. They realize that teaching equitably does not mean teaching everyone the same way. Nor does it mean that there are thirty different lesson plans to build on the uniqueness of the learning style and cultural background of each student. It may mean that teachers help students function effectively in multiple cultural settings used by the students in the classroom. These teachers are able to draw on their vast repertoire of strategies that build on the diverse cultural backgrounds and experiences of the students, acknowledge the value of that diversity, and help them all learn.

Critical thinkers are able to challenge the philosophy and practices of the dominant society that are not supportive of equity, democracy, and social justice. They are open to alternative views, and they are not limited by the narrow parochialism that is based on absolutes and the one, right way. They question the content for accuracy and biases and value multiple perspectives. They seek explanations and attributions for the educational meanings and consequences of race, class, and gender.[39]

"When they have opportunities to raise questions about knowledge and difference, both preservice and inservice teachers report that they become increasingly committed to school and pedagogial reform, increasingly conscious of their own efficacy as individual teachers, and increasingly involved in concrete efforts to alter the educational prospects of culturally diverse populations of students."[40]

The best teachers are those who are committed to continuing to learn about their academic areas, their students, and the world. They stay current with their field and they realize when they need to seek out additional information and resources.

Involvement with Communities and Parents

In the delivery of multicultural education, parents and the community are the essential resources on which an educator must draw to understand the cultural context in which students live. It will be impossible to develop meaningful learning experiences for students if the teacher cannot relate to the real-life experiences of students who come from different ethnic, racial, and income backgrounds than the teacher. Students usually sense very quickly when teachers view their own background as superior to that of their students.

Few beginning teachers will have had direct involvement in multiple cultural communities. Therefore, they must be open to continuing to learn about cultural differences and must depend on parents, students, and other community members to assist them. Many parents, especially those from powerless groups, are not comfortable in the school setting. Rather than waiting for them to come to a parent-teacher meeting or conference on their own, it is often necessary for the teacher to approach the parent in a nonthreatening setting. Development of a trusting relationship in which both teachers and parents work together for the benefit of the child is key in establishing positive relationships. A growing number of schools have parent advocates or liaisons who can assist the teacher in working with parents and communities. These individuals can be valuable resources in helping educators work effectively in communities with which they have little background or experience.

Learning to function effectively in several cultural communities requires participants to be comfortable with their own background. They also should understand the possible privilege they have had in society because of their race, gender, sexual orientation, or socioeconomic status. Teachers who are most successful in helping students from diverse cultural backgrounds learn are those who "struggle to confront their own histories, hear the dissonance in their own profession, and begin to construct working alliances with colleagues, parents, and communities to meet the needs of all students."[41] Teachers who provide education that is multicultural may begin to face these challenges in college, as beginning teachers, or after a number of years in the classroom.

Summary and Implications

Education that is multicultural is based on the principles of democracy and social justice to ensure that all students participate equally in the education system. It values the cultural diversity of students as reflected in their gender and ethnic, racial, language, religious, and socioeconomic backgrounds. Educators strive for the provision of educational equality in which all students are provided challenging and stimulating learning experiences. Inequalities in instruction, school environment, quality of teachers, facilities, and resources are confronted in an effort to overcome current injustices based on privilege and power.

Educators face many challenges in delivering education that is multicultural. The teaching style of the teacher may be very effective for some students, but not for others from cultural backgrounds different from that of the teacher. To help all students learn at higher levels, the teacher must develop a wide array of strategies to build on the prior experiences and cultural backgrounds of students. The curriculum and instructional materials must continuously be critiqued and expanded to integrate diversity throughout the study of an academic area. Interactions with students must be monitored to ensure that students are not being discriminated against because of their race, gender, sexual orientation, or socioeconomic status.

The four or five years that students spend in college to prepare for teaching only begin to prepare them to work with students who are culturally diverse or to be able to deliver education that is multicultural. Beginning and experienced teachers will continue to learn about diversity and its implications for teaching and learning. Students, parents, and communities will be valuable resources in this learning process. Most educators will find it a life-long and worthwhile endeavor.

Discussion Questions

1. What conditions and practices exist in schools to suggest that social justice is not a principle that undergirds the educational system?
2. What are the potential benefits and perceived dangers of allowing student voices to be an integral part of instruction?
3. Why is multicultural education just as important for students who are members of the dominant group in society as for those who are members of powerless groups?
4. How are student assessments used by teachers and schools?
5. How can a teacher take advantage of the knowledge and experiences of parents to develop effective instructional strategies?

Journal/Portfolio Development

1. Investigate the debates related to the adoption of a multicultural curriculum in a state or local school district (New York State Department of Education's *One Nation, Many Peoples: A Declaration of Cultural Interdependence* or New York City's *Children of the Rainbow*). Prepare a paper that describes the issues involved in the debates and summarizes your recommendation for the adoption of the curriculum.
2. For the subject and level that you plan to teach, design a lesson that incorporates multiple voices.

School-Based Experiences

1. As part of an early field experience activity in your teacher education program, gather a minimum of five observational sets of data on a student of color in a classroom. In particular, look for the nature of the interaction between the student and the teacher, the communication patterns with one or two other students, the oral classroom participation patterns, and the student's engagement with the subject matter.
2. Visit an inner city school and a rural or suburban school and observe how student voices are incorporated in classes. Record the nature of the dialogue between students and teachers and among students; be able to describe the degree of equality across the voices and whether any significant patterns of differences emerged.

Notes

1. Carl A. Grant and Christine E. Sleeter, *Turning On Learning: Five Approaches for Multicultural Teaching Plans for Race, Class, Gender, and Disability*. Columbus, OH: Merrill, 1989.
2. Donna M. Gollnick and Philip C. Chinn, *Multicultural Education in a Pluralistic Society*. 4th ed. New York: Macmillan, 297.

3. James A. Banks, "Multicultural Education: Development, Dimensions, and Challenges," *Phi Delta Kappan 75* (1) (September 1993): 55–60.

4. Ibid. 23.

5. Donna M. Gollnick, "National and State Initiatives for Multicultural Education," in James A. Banks and Cherry A. McGee Banks, eds., *Handbook of Research on Multicultural Education.* New York: Macmillan, 1995, 44–64.

6. National Conference of Christians and Jews, *Taking America's Pulse: A Summary Report of the National Conference Survey on Inter-Group Relations.* New York City: Author, 1994, 9.

7. Robert N. Bellah, Richard Madsen, William M. Sullivan, Ann Swidler, and Steven M. Tipton, *The Good Society.* New York: Vintage Books, 1991.

8. Ibid.

9. Ibid.

10. Kenneth A. Sirotnik, "Society, Schooling, Teaching, and Preparing to Teach," in John I. Goodlad, Roger Soder, and Kenneth A. Sirotnik, eds., *The Moral Dimensions of Teaching.* San Francisco: Jossey-Bass, 1990, 296–327.

11. Ibid, 310.

12. Peter Figueroa, "Multicultural Education in the United Kingdom: Historical Development and Current Status," in James A. Banks and Cherry A. McGee Banks, eds., *Handbook of Research on Multicultural Education.* New York: Macmillan, 1995, 778–800.

13. Aaron M. Pallas, "The Changing Nature of the Disadvantaged Population: Current Dimensions and Future Trends," *Educational Researcher* (June/July 1989): 16–22.

14. Signithia Fordham, "Racelessness as a Factor in Black Students' School Success: Pragmatic Strategy or Pyrrhic Victory," *Harvard Educational Review* 58(1) (1988): 54–84.

15. G. Williamson McDiarmid, *What to Do About Differences? A Study of Multicultural Education for Teacher Trainees in the Los Angeles Unified School District* (Research Report 90-11). East Lansing, MI: National Center for Research on Teacher Learning, 1990.

16. Robert E. Slavin, "Cooperative Learning and Intergroup Relations," in James A. Banks and Cherry A. McGee Banks, eds., *Handbook of Research on Multicultural Education.* New York: Macmillan, 1995, 628–634.

17. "Kentuckians Show Strong Support for School Reform But Want Adjustments to Improve Program Operations." Frankfort, KY: The Kentucky Institute for Education Research, October 3, 1994.

18. Jerry E. Brophy and Thomas L. Good, *Teacher-Student Relationships: Causes and Consequences.* New York: Holt, Rinehart & Winston, 1974.

19. J. Cummins, "Empowering Minority Students: A Framework for Intervention." *Harvard Educational Review 56*: 18–36.

20. Kenneth M. Zeichner, *Educating Teachers for Cultural Diversity.* East Lansing, MI: National Center for Research on Teacher Learning, February 1993, 7.

21. Jeannie Oakes, *Keeping Track: How Schools Structure Inequality.* New Haven, CT: Yale University Press, 1985, 40.

22. Ibid.

23. Maxine Greene, "Diversity and Inclusion: Toward a Curriculum for Human Rights," *Teachers College Record 95* (2) (Winter 1993): 211–221.

24. Gollnick and Chinn, 314.

25. Michael W. Apple, "The Politics of Official Knowledge: Does a National Curriculum Make Sense?" *Teachers College Record 95* (2) (Winter 1993): 222–240.

26. Jesus Garcia, "The Changing Image of Ethnic Groups in Textbooks." *Phi Delta Kappan 75* (1) (September 1993): 29–35.

27. Christine E. Sleeter and Carl A. Grant, "Race, Class, Gender, and Disability in Current Textbooks." in Michael W. Apple, and L. K. Christian-Smith, eds., *The Politics of the Textbook.* New York: Routledge, 78–110.

28. Martha M. McCarthy, "Challenges to the Public School Curriculum: New Targets and Strategies." *Phi Delta Kappan 75* (1) (September 1993): 55–60.

29. Millicent Lawton, "Differing on Diversity." *Education Week* (December 1, 1993): 23–25.

30. McCarthy, 56.

31. Ibid.

32. Institute for Education in Transformation, *Voices from the Inside: A Report on Schooling from Inside the Classroom.* Claremont, CA: Author, 1992.

33. Myra P. Sadker and David M. Sadker, "Between Teacher and Student: Overcoming Sex Bias in Classroom Interaction," in Myra P. Sadker and David M. Sadker, eds., *Sex Equity Handbook for Schools.* New York: Longman, 1982, 96–132.

34. Oakes, 1985.

35. Richard A. Figueroa and Eugene Garcia, "Issues in Testing Students from Culturally and Linguistically Diverse Backgrounds." *Multicultural Education* (Fall 1994): 10–19.

36. Richard J. Herrnstein and Charles Murray, *The Bell Curve: Intelligence and Class Structure in American Life.* New York: Free Press, 1994.

37. Georgia Earnest Garcia and P. David Pearson, "Assessment and Diversity," *Review of Research in Education 20.* Washington, DC: American Educational Research Association, 1994, 337–391.

38. Ibid, 19.

39. Marilyn Cochran-Smith and Susan L. Lytle, "Interrogating Cultural Diversity: Inquiry and Action."

Journal of Teacher Education 43 (2) (March-April 1992): 104–115.

40. Ibid, 111.

41. Ibid, 113.

Bibliography

Apple, Michael W., and Christian-Smith, Linda K., eds. *The Politics of the Textbook.* New York: Routledge, 1991.

Garcia, Georgia Earnest, and Pearson, P. David. "Assessment and Diversity." *Review of Research in Education 20.* Washington, DC: American Educational Research Association, 1994, 337–391.

Gollnick, Donna M., and Chinn, Philip C. *Multicultural Education in a Pluralistic Society.* 4th ed. New York: Macmillan, 1994.

Goodlad, John I., Soder, Roger, and Sirotnik, Kenneth A., eds. *The Moral Dimensions of Teaching.* San Francisco: Jossey-Bass, 1990.

Grant, Carl A., and Sleeter, Christine E. *Turning on Learning: Five Approaches for Multicultural Teaching Plans for Race, Class, Gender, and Disability.* Columbus, OH: Merrill, 1989.

Lacelle-Peterson, Mark W., and Rivera, Charlene. "Is It Real for All Kids? A Framework for Equitable Assessment Policies for English Language Learners." *Harvard Educational Review 64* (1) (Spring 1994): 55–75.

Multicultural Education: The Magazine of the National Association for Multicultural Education.

"Multicultural Issues." *Phi Delta Kappan 74* (3) (November 1992): 208–227.

National Conference of Christians and Jews. *Taking America's Pulse: A Summary Report of the National Conference Survey on Inter-Group Relations.* New York City: Author, 1994.

Oakes, Jeannie. *Keeping Track: How Schools Structure Inequality.* New Haven, CT: Yale University Press, 1985.

"Race-Ethnicity-Family-Community-Student Success." *Equity and Choice* (2) (Winter 1994).

Robenstine, Clark. "The Illusion of Education Reform: The Educational System and At-Risk Students." *Educational Foundations 6* (1) (Winter 1992): 49–65.

Sobol, Thomas. "Revising the New York State Social Studies Curriculum." *Teachers College Record 95* (2) (Winter 1993): 258–272.

Social Issues Affecting the School

Focus Questions

1 Why, despite increased expenditures for schools, does the dropout rate continue to be so high in the United States?
2 What is the relationship between poverty and school completion?
3 How can the school begin to combat some of the major social problems facing students?
4 What is the relationship between the social problems of youth and performance in school?
5 Should our schools help to solve social problems? Why?

Key Terms and Concepts

Chemical dependency: The habitual use, either for psychological or physical needs, of a substance such as drugs, alcohol, or tobacco.

Delinquency: A term generally ascribed to the youth culture that denotes violation of rules and regulations of the society.

Dropouts: Students who fail to complete a high school education.

Exceptional learners: A classification identification used to describe handicapped and gifted learners.

Inclusion: The federally mandated practice of placing all handicapped learners, except for profoundly handicapped, in regular classrooms where itinerant special education teachers assist the regular teacher.

Magnet schools: Specialized schools that are open to all students in a district, sometimes on a lottery basis or special needs basis.

Poverty: A relative standard of living defined by a number of complex and changing factors that may include hunger or lack of luxuries.

Poverty level: A level of family income judged by the United States Labor Department to be below the basic needs requirements of a family.

School-based clinics: Medical and advisory clinics in schools that are offered to provide personal help for students experiencing problems of sexuality.

*T*here is a considerable amount of debate over how far the schools can and should go to help solve our country's social problems. Some people believe that the schools should be concerned only with the academic development of students. Others believe that the schools are in a unique position to help solve many of the nation's pressing social problems—and should do so. While this debate continues, social problems persist and noticeably affect students and schools. In this chapter we identify a wide variety of social problems that have a direct effect on students. Note that the severity of the problem causes varying amounts of stress for learners as they move through the school program.

Problems of the Youth Culture

Young people today face numerous problems as they mature to adulthood. Changing family structures, alteration of what was once considered to be a societal set of expected values, and increased pressures to grow up quickly and be adult all have contributed to the social problems of youth. Reacting to the pressures of the time, young people have found their own ways of countering what appear to them to be circumstances with which they cannot cope. As learners in the schools, they need special attention.

Effects of the Changing Family

The American family has changed rather dramatically during the past four decades. The traditional description of a family with a working father, a mother at home with the children, and two or more school-age children exists for a very small part of the population. Recent reports from the U.S. Bureau of Statistics following the 1990 census suggest that about 5 percent of American families fit this description. The lifestyle of married couples with children, once the norm, is now the exception. Family descriptions are as varied as our cultural diversity. Families include a mother working with a father tending children, mothers working away from home, increasing numbers of single-parent families, increasing numbers of second marriages with unrelated children, large numbers of childless marriages (especially among the dominant white groups), unmarried couples with and without children, gay and lesbian parents, and the combinations go on. These family differences, with varying intensities of family instability, all have had their effects on the youth culture. It is little wonder that the children of these families struggle immensely in their search for their own identities and a place in life.

The latest United States census data point to the following profile for families:

- There are over 80 million households in the United States.
- Twenty-eight million married couples have no children.
- Seven out of ten women with children are in the work force.
- The divorce rate has quadrupled in the past twenty years, and the number of single-parent families is estimated at 25 percent. There are 18.2 million children being raised in single-parent families. The figure for single-parent families is estimated to grow to 30 percent by 2020.
- Sixteen percent of single-parent children have mothers under the age of 25, and 6 percent of these children have young teenage mothers.

- Sixty-eight percent of all births to teenagers (those under age 20) occur out of wedlock.
- Sixty percent of all teenage families live in poverty as compared to 13.5 percent of the total population.
- The percentage of teenage pregnancies, with children born out of wedlock, is higher among some minority groups, but the percentage and numbers for white teenagers is increasing.
- Families without children have the highest socioeconomic status, but 50 percent of that group is 55 years and over.

Parents. In the past, parents could be described as a couple with children living in a home with room for grandparents; the couple's relationship was male-dominated, and they expected to live out their years together. There has been a rapid decline in the number of such families. As suggested in the profile above, this type of family is best described as the nuclear family. The number of nuclear families is decreasing in America.

Families are small today; average size, as projected from census reports for 1990 by the Bureau of the Census, is 3.16 members. Average household size is 2.62. However, the average figures can be deceiving because family membership size is considerably greater among the minority population. That is why the change in school population statistics for the 1990s and beyond is so significant. In 1990 *Time* magazine reported that one American in four defined himself or herself as Hispanic or nonwhite. If current birth rates continue for minority groups, the Hispanic population will increase approximately 21 percent, Asians about 22 percent, African Americans about 12 percent, Native Americans about 50 percent, and Anglo-Americans about 2 percent by the turn of the century.

Extended families are not common, except among some minority groups. The frequencies of other types of families are increasing; for example, although the divorce rate continues to escalate, four out of five divorced people remarry. The divorce rate for remarried people is higher still. There is an increase in communal living, and more single parents.

Children. All of these family changes have affected children. The family now has considerably less influence on family members' religious practices, education, and values as well as on the general socialization of the child. Although the school has assumed many of these responsibilities, other institutions also contribute to the child's socialization. These institutions include peer groups from the schools and the streets; organized groups such as scouts, 4-H, and Little League groups; and TV, radio, newspapers, and movies. The influence of the formal and informal peer groups cannot be overestimated. Because of increased female influence in the family, the family is no longer patriarchal but rather has become increasingly matriarchial and in more cases egalitarian.

The Persistence of Poverty

Poverty has existed since the human race appeared on the earth and probably will be around as long as humans are. **Poverty** in the United States is complex, and determining what factors contribute to it is difficult, if not impossible. Notions about what constitutes poverty are continually changing. One person might define poverty as physical hunger or even starvation; another might define it as a lack

TABLE 7.1	Percentage of Families below the Poverty Level
White	9.1%
Black	29.7
Hispanic	30.6
Native American	62.5
Total U.S.	14.7

Source: Educational Research Service, 1992.

of luxuries. In other words, poverty is relative. The poor in the United States include people who are literally starving to death as well as people who have relatively little compared to those who have very much.

Since the majority of people in the United States are not in poverty, they tend to believe that there is less poverty today than there was in the past. Not only is this not true, but in fact the number of poverty-level families is on the increase, and the increase is predominantly among minority populations. One of the difficulties in determining poverty is that its definition, based upon economic conditions, changes yearly. The government's definition of poverty is based on changing economic conditions, further adjusted by such factors as family size, sex of family head, number of children, and farm or nonfarm residence. Table 7.1 presents information about the percent of families below the poverty level in the United States. This table illustrates that the **poverty level** is greater for minority families. Table 7.2 shows the percentage of children, by race, that live in poverty.

Slightly over 14 percent of U.S. families live in poverty. African Americans suffer three times the rate of poverty of whites, and Hispanic Americans have greater than three times the poverty rate of the white population. Although there is a higher percentage of nonwhite families living in poverty, numerically there are many more impoverished white families. For instance, the per capita income of many Appalachian white families is far less than that of the rest of the country. Many Appalachian adults are unemployed, and many have very little formal schooling. The Appalachian subculture has created a way of life that keeps these mountain people impoverished. Farming and mining have traditionally furnished their livelihood; however, the mountain farms are no longer productive enough

TABLE 7.2	Percentage of Children by Race and Ethnicity That Live in Poverty		
Age	White	Black	Hispanic and Others
Total (all ages)	13.0	33.0	34.3
Under 15	17.3	46.4	40.0
15–17	14.9	44.7	35.1
18–21	15.3	40.3	30.0

Source: U.S. Bureau of the Census, 1990.

to provide a good living, and automation has largely replaced humans in the coal mines. Those who have left the mountains to go to the cities have found that their education and skills do not qualify them for desirable jobs. Many people believe that education alone cannot solve the problem. Immediate needs such as employment, housing, medical care, and legal advice must also be met. Although prompt assistance in these areas is essential to solving the problems of poverty, it cannot solve the long-range problem in the way that better education can.

Welfare. Fortunately for people in poverty, our nation is concerned about this social dilemma. Moreover, tax money spent to eradicate poverty is a profitable investment. It costs less in the long run to help people lift themselves out of poverty than to pay the consequences of allowing them to remain impoverished. One need only check the cost of welfare programs and crime fighting to be convinced of this statement.

One of the persistent problems with the welfare programs is the lack of renewal performances in many of the families on welfare. Because of circumstances many times beyond their control, large numbers of families are second and third generation welfare families. The economic development programs associated with the many welfare programs have not been successful in providing meaningful avenues out of poverty. Thus, many young people in poverty today have known nothing but welfare during their lives and the lives of their parents. The expected development of a work ethic and the availability of jobs to promote that ethic have not taken place. The feeling of hopelessness that many young people experience today makes the job of convincing them about the importance of education very difficult.

We must realize that if we are to eradicate poverty and reduce welfare existence we must treat the disease itself, not just the symptoms. Indeed, we must try to prevent the disease in the first place, and the most effective "vaccine" at our disposal is education. It is incongruous that a nation that has amassed far more material wealth than any other in history can still contain pockets of severe poverty. Poverty prevents people from being productive citizens, from pursuing excellence, and from developing a sense of dignity. Total dependence on welfare becomes a generational "catch-all" way of life. If we are committed to the importance of democratic ideals, we must continue to work toward eliminating poverty in the United States. Fortunately, we have begun to realize the democratic, human, and economic necessity of reducing poverty, and we have initiated many immediate and long-range programs—some of which involve education—aimed at eradicating the problem.

Unemployment. Unemployment rates in the United States are directly affected by the general economic condition of the country. However, many other factors also influence the unemployment picture. The additional women entering the labor force, the continuing high level of dropouts among minority youth, the decreasing number of young people in military service, and changing trends in college enrollments all contribute to the country's unemployment rates.

Certain groups within our society are more affected by unemployment than others. Although actual employment rates change from year to year, the relative unemployment picture for the various groups has remained essentially the same in recent history. During 1985–1989, national unemployment varied between 5 and 6 percent. Unemployment rates in late 1994 were averaging almost 6.5 percent. Generally, nonwhites and teenagers have had the highest unemployment

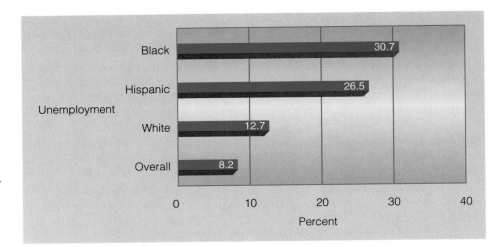

FIGURE 7.1

Teenage Unemployment by Race/Ethnicity Compared with Overall Unemployment 1994

Source: U.S. Department of Labor.

rates. Recently, unemployment rates have increased among middle-aged workers whose industries have experienced "down-sizing" because of economic conditions. As Figure 7.1 points out, teenage unemployment rates are about three times greater than general unemployment rates. Minority teens suffer unemployment at three times the rate of white teens.

However, there is a correlation between teenage unemployment and high school completion. Inner-city teens have the highest unemployment rates, are from a variety of minority groups, and have the highest dropout rate in the nation. The job market is changing, and the changes have serious implications for the schools if poverty is to be reduced. As can be seen in Table 7.3, the majority of new jobs are in the service occupations and technology. If the schools are to contribute to the efforts to correct poverty, computer training must receive increased emphasis. As the majority population in the country becomes nonwhite, and if the school has given greater attention to meaningful job preparation, the minority unemployment figures of the 1990s should decrease significantly by the turn of the century.

Chemical Abuse

One of the most tragic social problems in America today is the misuse of drugs by young people. As reported by many recent surveys, the number one problem facing the school, in the eyes of the public, is the overuse of drugs. Alarmingly, the U.S. Public Health Service reports that about two-thirds of all high school seniors have used illicit drugs, and over 90 percent of high school seniors have used alcohol. A 1991 Gallup Poll of young people concluded that the number one problem, and the one that they were most concerned about, was the use of drugs and alcohol by themselves and the general population. It is important to note, however, that the 1993 Gallup Poll on the public attitude toward school shows that drugs in schools is no longer the number one problem. The number one problem in that poll was clearly a lack of financial support for schools. **Chemical dependency,** whether on drugs, alcohol, or tobacco, is one of the leading causes of other social and academic problems of youth. People are judged to be dependent when they find that their need for chemicals is constant and they can no longer control

TABLE 7.3	Growth of New Jobs and Occupations through 1995
Occupations	Number of New Jobs by 1995
Services	4,490,000
Janitors	
Nurses Aides	
Sales Clerks	
Waitresses	
Clerks	
Nurses	
Secretaries	
Food Preparers	
Computer Technology	903,000
Data Processing	
Systems Analysts	
Computer Operators	
Computer Programmers	
Software Developers	
Computer Technicians	

Source: U.S. Department of Labor.

their use. Figure 7.2 on page 160 provides information on the extent of this chemical problem in our society.

Drugs. To counter the drug problem, schools have embarked on a variety of programs, many of which have been funded by state and federal governments and are intended to be preventive. The problem is acute and affects all age groups. In 1989 the White House launched a nationwide effort to educate the public in an attempt to curb the use of drugs. Additionally, stronger enforcement efforts were employed against the use of chemicals and their importation into the United States. Unfortunately, the rhetoric of the federal government, in the absence of adequate funding, has not put a substantial dent in the sale and use of drugs.

Many state and national programs provide students with information about drugs so that they will realize the dangers of drug abuse. The major objective of these programs is that students, as informed persons, will decide that they are better off not using illicit drugs. Generally, the most successful drug education programs are those that have been adequately funded, involve parents and students, are taught by well-trained teachers, and avoid preaching and moralizing.

Alcohol. Student use of alcohol has risen sharply in recent years. A survey by the National Institute on Drug Abuse asked high school seniors to estimate the percentage of their friends who used various drugs and the degree of use. The survey found that alcohol was the most commonly used drug and that sizable percentages of students get drunk at least once a week. In many schools, students consume alcohol in school buildings during the day. Furthermore, medical authorities report a rapid rise in "polydrug" use—combining drugs and alcohol—

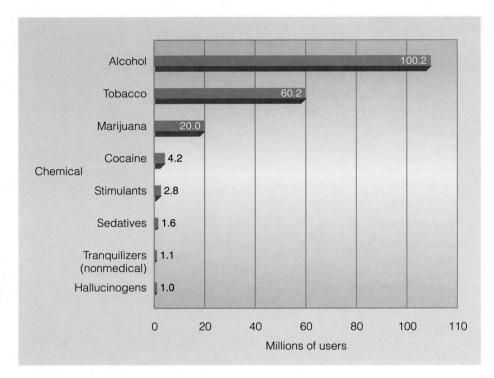

Chemical Use in the United States

(*Source:* Data for the graph compiled from various U.S. government Bureaus.)

among students. Polydrug use is extremely dangerous because alcohol used with barbiturates, sedatives, or tranquilizers heightens the effect of each substance and can cause death. Clearly, alcohol and drugs have become the foremost chemical problem for young people in America.

Tobacco. Millions of American students regularly smoke cigarettes. The evidence that smoking is a serious health hazard has prompted educators to search for ways to combat this problem. National and state educational efforts directed toward the physical hazards of smoking have been successful in reducing the total number of Americans who smoke. However, young people, particularly young women, continue to smoke. This increased use of tobacco by young women has led to increased rates of female lung cancer, making the rates among the female and the male populations about equal.

Most people believe that the school is the only agency that has a chance to reduce teenage smoking significantly, and more and more schools are accepting the challenge. Some schools include a systematic study of the effects of smoking as part of their curriculum. The most promising approach to smoking education is one in which the students themselves run their own antismoking campaigns. Some schools have joined parent groups, the American Cancer Society, the American Heart Association, and the National Tuberculosis and Respiratory Diseases Association to fight teenage smoking.

Prevention. The Department of Education has created the school team approach, which was developed under the Alcohol and Drug Abuse Education

Program. Designed to help local schools prevent and reduce drug and alcohol abuse, this program has established five regional centers that provide training and technical assistance to local schools. Some other representative national efforts are being provided by the following agencies:

1. The American Council on Drug Education: This council organizes conferences and develops national media campaigns for drug education. It also provides films, books, and education kits for libraries and schools.

2. Narcotics Education, Inc.: This organization provides pamphlets, books, teaching aids, posters, audiovisual aids, and prevention magazines that can be used with preteens and teens.

3. National Federation of Parents for Drug-Free Youth: This national organization helps parent groups to get started, and provides current literature on drug legislation and resource lists for schools and libraries.

4. Target: This national federation of state high school associations, an arm of the organization of interscholastic activities associations, offers workshops, seminars, and current information on chemical abuse and prevention.

5. Toughlove: This national self-help group is for parents, children, and communities; it stresses cooperation, personal initiative, avoidance of blame, and suggested action for abusers.

These organizations and others have been assisting communities and schools in their efforts at combating the chemical problem. One such effort is Project DARE, in Los Angeles, which is operated by the school district in cooperation with the local police department. The program uses specially trained police officers to teach students how to say "no" to drugs. Other parts of the program include building self-esteem, managing stress, and developing personal skills to help resist drugs. The police work in the schools with students and also conduct parent seminars in the evening. Because of the success of this program, it has spread to other California communities and other states.

Drug and alcohol abuse awareness and prevention programs have become fairly common in schools, especially at junior and senior high school levels.

Suicide

Suicide rates among young people are on the rise. In fact, the rate of teen suicide has tripled during the past thirty years. By 1992, as reported by the National Institute of Mental Health, the leading cause of death for fifteen- to twenty-four-year-olds was suicide. At the same time, suicide rates for the rest of the U.S. population have remained relatively stable. Although the suicide rate is thought to be highest among lower-socioeconomic groups and many minorities, it is not. The highest-risk group for *teen suicide* is white, Protestant, and above-average in school performance. Most of these students appear to be performing normally, and many hold part-time jobs. Although many more teenage girls than teenage boys attempt suicide, the boys tend to be more successful in their attempts.

Adolescent Perceptions.   The usual cause of adolescent suicide is extreme depression. It usually appears during early adolescence, when normal physical and social development directs teenagers away from family ties. During this period, teens begin to look beyond the home for friendship and assistance in making value decisions. Chief causes that become specific contributors to attempted teen suicide are conflict with one or both parents, the breakup of boyfriend-girlfriend relationships, parental divorce, moving to a new school or area, and trouble with a teacher.

Effects of Stress.   There is little doubt that young people are less able to cope with stress than older people are. Young people have not yet had enough independent life experiences to balance the stressful periods that all people endure. School relations and family relations are extremely stressful at an age when physical and psychological maturation are taking place. Effects of stress are seen in school attendance, academic performance, peer relationships, and adult encounters. Many times, students under stress seek other students who have similar types of problems, and these relationships often do not lead to good mental health. In fact, such relationships have led to a significant increase in *suicide clusters*. This type of suicide behavior is most common among teenagers. The National Institute of Mental Health has offered a list of suggestions for schools and communities to follow when there are suspicions of potential cluster suicides among young people. These are offered for study in Figure 7.3. Teachers should be especially aware of how they can be part of a preventive program against teenage suicide.

Warning Signs.   There is a high coincidence rate between adolescent suicide and some forms of chemical dependency. Alcohol and/or drugs are used to counter depression, and when these drugs fail to deliver the desired effects, the teen is ripe for a suicide attempt. Teachers need to be especially sensitive to the early signs of depression among students. Student withdrawal behaviors, irritability, and sudden changes in work, sleep, or eating habits are all early signs of a teen going through some stage of depression and in need of professional help. The best aid that a teacher can give is to encourage the student to talk about the problem and to seek medical help. Although teen suicide is growing at an alarming rate, it can be prevented if sensitive parents and professionals seek help for an adolescent when the early signs of depression are observed.

1. Have a community plan to deal with events that could lead to cluster suicide.

2. Establish a community and school committee to coordinate the handling of suicide problems among youth.

3. Identify community people and groups who can respond quickly to problems.

4. Avoid any signs that could be interpreted as glorifying suicide, and minimize any sensationalism of any attempts.

5. Be watchful for potentially suicidal students and get them to counselors.

6. Identify elements in the environment—school, home, community—that could increase the likelihood of suicide and seek to eliminate them.

FIGURE 7.3

Suggestions for Combating Potential Cluster Suicides

(*Source:* National Institute of Mental Health.)

Dropouts: Students at Risk

Although high school and college students drop out of school for different reasons, both represent a substantial loss to our society. In most states, students must attend school until they are sixteen. They cannot drop out of school during the early years of high school. However, once they are past the compulsory attendance age, a disturbing number of them become **dropouts.** Approximately 25 percent of the eighteen-year-olds in the United States have not completed high school. This rate has not decreased in more than two decades, and it is considerably higher among minority groups. Current estimates from the Bureau of the Census data for 1990 are that 40 percent of Hispanic Americans and 25 percent of African Americans, ages eighteen to twenty-one, are dropouts. Other minority groups have even greater rates. Urban Native Americans and Puerto Ricans have dropout rates of 70–80 percent. The rate of school dropouts is particularly disturbing because most of these students cannot get jobs, many get into trouble with the law, and many do not qualify for military service. Most of them are not yet prepared to be productive citizens, and a large number are destined to become social liabilities. Figure 7.4 on page 164 shows the breakdown of various dropout groups.

Characteristics of Dropouts. Dropouts come primarily from low-income backgrounds. As Figure 7.4 shows, most come from minority groups, the exceptions being Asian Americans and Pacific Islanders. Dropouts tend to be deficient in basic reading, language arts, and mathematics skills, and often they are children of high school dropouts. Single-parent families account for a significant number of dropout students. Males tend to drop out more than females. Males often drop out to get a job, but, as was shown earlier, the highest rates of unemployment are among teenagers who have not completed high school. The major reason for females dropping out of school is early pregnancy. Most dropout students suffer

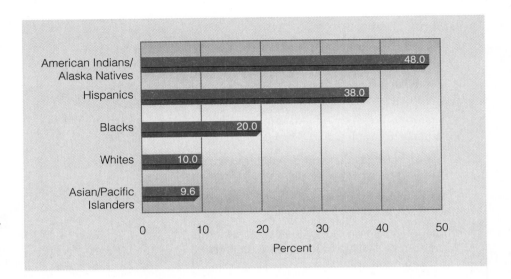

FIGURE 7.4

National Dropout Rates by Racial or Ethnic Group

(*Source:* National Center for Educational Statistics, 1992.)

from extremely low self-esteem and have judged themselves failures long before they drop out.

Some of the early signs of potential dropouts are seen in students who:

1. have poor school attendance,
2. lack observable interest in learning,
3. experience continuing failing grades,
4. experience continuous classroom discipline problems, and
5. have failed one or more grades in the elementary and secondary school.

Teachers need to watch for these early warning signs and seek help for a student who exhibits them before he or she becomes another dropout statistic. Schools with high dropout rates need to establish prevention programs that address the special needs of their students so that positive self-esteem and a desire to learn become part of the learner's personality.

Economic and Social Effects. The national data on dropouts point to the desperate need for the school and society to find ways to keep children in school and to teach them at least basic life skills—not only for their own good but also for the good of society. The economic cost of ignoring the problem is staggering. In 1992 the U.S. House Ways and Means Committee reported that the cost of welfare benefits and lost tax dollars is estimated to be 75 billion dollars; 60 percent of prison inmates are dropouts; and some 87 percent of pregnant teenagers are dropouts. In other words, the money spent to keep our children in school is not really an expense but an excellent long-term investment that returns handsome dividends to our society.

The gifted high school graduate who does not go to college represents still another kind of school dropout. Furthermore, half of the students who enter college never graduate. Although some of these students leave college for academic reasons, many of them have exceptional academic ability. The underdeveloped talent of these students represents a substantial loss to society. Needless to say, our society and our schools have a long way to go before they solve the school dropout problem.

Delinquency and Crime

There is a definite relationship between juvenile **delinquency** and dropping out of school. Delinquency is defined for youth as a regular behavior that violates rules and regulations of the society. Various studies of delinquency have also shown that many delinquents did failing work while in school and often were less academically able than were nondelinquents. The alarming point is that many of today's dropouts will be tomorrow's criminals, and statistics on crime in the United States are staggering. Figure 7.5 shows the dramatic increase in serious crime in recent years. To make matters worse, fewer than one in four serious crimes leads to arrest; in other words, three-fourths of the people who commit serious crimes do not get caught.

Crime Statistics.   During 1985–1989, total arrests for all areas of crime were up 10 percent, according to the U.S. Government sources. Adult arrests still constituted the majority of the arrests, but those for people under the age of eighteen increased by 6 percent. Drug abuse violations grew by 14 percent during 1988–1989 alone. Five percent of all the people arrested in the United States were under the age of fifteen, 16 percent were under the age of eighteen, and 30 percent were under the age of twenty-one. As the data indicate, a significant number of young people get involved in crime. Over 80 percent of all arrests are of males. For 1988–1989, 69 percent of all arrestees were white, 30 percent were African American, and the rest were from other races. Arrest rates for children fifteen years and younger increased by 3 percent during 1988–1990. Within that increase the majority of offenses were in the areas of assault, carrying weapons, drug abuse, and vagrancy. The vast majority of these offenders were from low-socioeconomic groups and were, or were about to become, dropouts.

Cost and Effects.   The President's Commission on Law Enforcement and the Administration of Justice recently reported that organized crime has become so widespread and sophisticated that it now involves narcotics, prostitution, murder, gambling, protection rackets, real estate, confidence games, politics, and the stock market. Organized crime touches every American and costs our society an

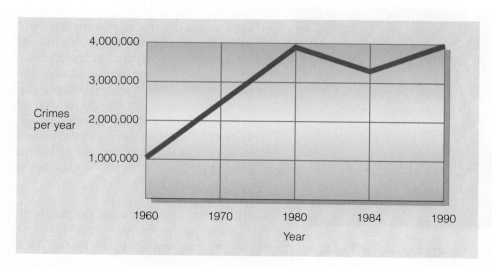

FIGURE 7.5

Growth of Serious Crime (Murder, Rape, Robbery, and Burglary) in the United States

(*Source:* U.S. Bureau of Justice Statistics.)

TABLE 7.4	Cost of Law Enforcement, 1960–1992

Year	Cost
1960	$3,349,000,000
1970	$8,571,000,000
1975	$17,249,000,000
1980	$27,026,000,000
1985	$32,801,000,000
1988	$38,000,000,000
1990	$40,000,000,000
1992	$43,000,000,000*

*Estimated from U.S. Bureau of Justice Statistics.

Source: U.S. Bureau of the Census, 1992.

unbelievable amount of money. Table 7.4 shows the escalating cost of law enforcement. Law enforcement alone now costs every American man, woman, and child over $100 a year. Included in these figures are associated incidents of crime in the schools.

Violent Crime and Vandalism. As the world has witnessed increasing violence, so have the schools, where violence and vandalism have become very serious problems. The U.S. Senate Committee on Delinquency has estimated that school vandalism costs our nation over $600 million each year. The National Association of School Security Directors estimates that each year there are 12,000 armed robberies, 270,000 burglaries, 204,000 aggravated assaults, and 9,000 rapes in our schools. Furthermore, an estimated 70,000 serious physical assaults are made on teachers each year.

These statistics suggest the size of the problems of vandalism and violence faced by the schools. Some schools have hired police officers, adopted strict rules, expelled troublesome students, and taken a determined stance. Others have solicited the help of students and parents; have tried to change the curriculum to make it more appealing to students; have gone to great lengths to keep all students in school; and have generally adopted a democratic, humanistic, and sympathetic attitude. Unfortunately, very few solutions to these problems have been found. (See the Case Study on page 168.)

Gangs. There are now more gangs that involve more students in our schools than ever before. In addition to the problems that these people bring to the school, they have become

Educators have found it necessary to establish routines that address the threat of violence on school grounds.

violent in their neighborhood communities. Gang warfare is all too common in the urban areas. It is not confined to the ghetto areas of the city but has spread to include the larger area of ethnic neighborhoods. The violence of these teen activities has led to increasing numbers of murders among the members of the gangs. The gang's quest for social control over its environment carries into the school and threatens the safety of educational staff and students who do not belong. Unfortunately, most of the gang activities are found in welfare-type areas of the community where the amenities of the culture are scarce or nonexistent and the schools are not adequately responding to the special needs of these students.

Few schools have been successful in combating violence. There are two reasons for this. First, schools lack the financial resources to make a serious, concerted attack on the problem. Second, violence has become so prevalent in American society that some social scientists believe there is simply no way to keep it out of the schools. Violence, crime, and a general disregard for the rights and welfare of others have become commonplace. The size and diversity of the violence problem can be understood only by considering a list of related problems: child abuse and neglect, spouse abuse, juvenile delinquency, television and movie violence, teen pregnancy, divorce rates, tax fraud, governmental corruption, welfare cheating, price fixing, stock manipulation, organized crime, business crime, and employee theft. Crime and violence indeed pervade both American life and the schools.

Sexuality

Sexual differences and societal expectations regarding those differences cause considerable concern for young people. The traditional roles associated with biological sexual differences no longer hold true as national norms. However, these types of cultural changes have caused difficulties for young people growing up, and these difficulties have been brought to the doors of the school. The whole issue of male and female sex roles has had a pronounced effect on self-esteem, self-concept, vocational choice, and social behavior. This has led to increased problems related to *sexuality* among young people.

Teenage Pregnancy. The youth culture of American society is experiencing a sexual revolution. *Teenage pregnancy,* venereal disease, and sex-related psychological problems are on the increase. The National Center for Health Statistics reports that teenage pregnancy is at an epidemic rate. For fifteen- to nineteen-year-olds the rate

---

Relevant Research

How School Boards Are Responding to Violence in the Schools

A recent survey by the National School Boards Association examined how school districts were working to prevent violence in the schools. More than 2000 school districts responded to the survey. General findings asserted that there is an epidemic of school violence nationally and unless schools take corrective action immediately, the violent behaviors will continue to increase. A significant finding of this study was that 82 percent of the respondents indicated that violence is worse today than it was five years ago. Additional findings suggested that school efforts to curb violence did not focus on a single approach. Some twenty-two different strategies were being used by the participant schools, with the top three being suspension (78 percent), student conduct/discipline code (76 percent), and collaboration with other agencies (73 percent). Thirteen percent of the schools (near the bottom of the list) reported using volunteer parent patrols.

Reducing violence in the schools requires a team effort. Required consistency in student behavior must be enforced by the total professional staff. As a beginning teacher you need to be concerned about the safety of your workplace and involved with the school's efforts in promoting and enforcing a positive learning and working environment.

Source: National School Boards Association, "Violence in the Schools: How America's School Boards Are Safeguarding Our Children." Alexandria, VA: The Association, 1993.

CASE STUDY ACCEPTING OR NOT ACCEPTING STUDENT TRANSFERS WHO HAVE A HISTORY OF SCHOOL VIOLENCE

Schools constantly receive student transfers throughout the school year. These transfers primarily come as a result of family moves associated with job changes or social displacement. There are, however, some students who are transferred out of volatile school situations where they have been part of that volatility. It is generally thought that if the student is put into a new environment, he or she may change behavior practices and be recovered for societal inclusion. Many times, these transfers involve inner-city students being moved to suburban settings that are not experiencing problems of violence in the school.

There is little doubt that a school should accept these kinds of transfers if they are legal, but the receiving schools need to have policy in place before engaging or being forced to engage in receiving these learners. As a new teacher in a suburban school that abuts a large metropolitan area, it is highly possible that you will experience some of these types of school transfers in your classroom. You could be asked to participate in the development of a school policy to address these types of school issues. If asked to serve in this capacity, how would you respond to the following questions pertaining to such a policy?

1. What guidelines and/or rules should be established for students of this nature? Should the regular school policies (the school handbook) be the same for all students, or should there be a distinct set of policies for these students since their volatile past is a known fact?
2. What kinds of special academic and counseling help should be provided for these types of students? It is intended that these students be provided an equal opportunity to learn and achieve.
3. Should there be any special program provided for the parents and/or guardians of these students?
4. Should you as a teacher not be concerned about this type of social problem and let the school administration and school board deal with it?

You cannot run away from this problem because it will have an impact on your classroom if this type of transfer student is assigned to you. Also, you need to keep in mind the safety and benefit of the remainder of your students who will also be encountering the potential antisocial behavior of this student. What will you do?

---

has risen almost 100 percent in the past fifteen years. Despite national efforts by right-to-life groups opposing abortion, teenage girls, like their older counterparts, often resort to abortion to terminate unwanted pregnancies. Although illegitimate birth rates among nonwhite teenagers are very high, white illegitimate birth rates have increased during the same period. This social phenomenon is a response to the changing sexual values of the teen culture, and it is important to note that this change in values is little different from the change in values of the general society.

Annual reports issued jointly by the American Public Health Association, the American Social Health Association, and the Venereal Disease Association continue to show increases in venereal diseases among teenagers. Gonorrhea and syphilis head the list of venereal infections. Syphilis is a medically serious venereal disease that, if left untreated, can cause serious health problems such as sterility, paralysis, blindness, heart disease, insanity, and death. Often, babies of infected mothers are born with mental and physical defects.

Motivated by the emergence of the AIDS epidemic, many schools now have programs that promote awareness about sexually transmitted diseases.

Acquired Immune Deficiency Syndrome (AIDS).   Increased sexual activity among teens and adults has led to the spread of AIDS, a major, rapidly growing national health problem. At first this disease was commonly thought to be associated only with homosexuality, but the Surgeon General of the United States has reported the spread of this virus among all ages and classes of people. Figure 7.6 shows the 1979 through 1992 estimates of the expected growth of this disease. The 1993 data show these early estimates to be extremely accurate.

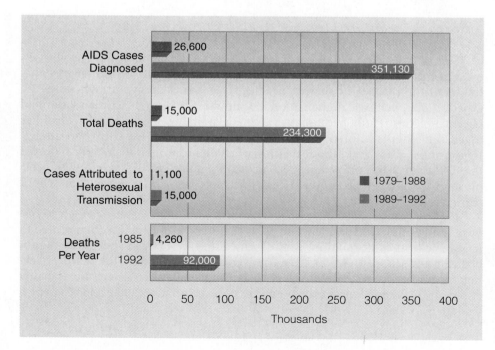

FIGURE 7.6

The Status of the AIDS Virus and Its Projected Growth

(*Source:* The Surgeon General's Report on AIDS)

PROFESSIONAL DILEMMA

Can You Be a Personal Counselor for Your Students?

In your first year of teaching you have been assigned to a middle school. All of the forewarnings of the problems and joys of working with young adolescents have proved to be accurate. As you are coming back from your lunch break one day, one of your students, a thirteen-year-old female, asks if she can have a confidential conference with you. You agree, and tell her that you will call her from class during your planning period.

You have the student called from class at the designated time, and the two of you meet in one of the guidance offices. The young girl is visibly disturbed and in tears when she comes to meet with you and it takes some time to calm her down. She is a very attractive young lady and appears to be physically and mentally more mature than other girls her age. At first, she is hesitant to say anything substantive and seems to be waiting for you to question her about her need for a private conference. With some prodding from you, she finally bursts into tears again and blurts out, "I'm pregnant and don't know what to do!"

The student tells you that her family is "highly moral" and will probably do something drastic when they find out about her problem. You move away from the family action discussion and attempt to get some additional information from her such as: How does she know she's pregnant? How far into the pregnancy does she think she is? Has she seen a doctor? Who is the male involved? She cooperates fully in telling you all you think you need to know. Thus far, you have only pursued information and served as a supportive listener.

The student, sensing your apprehension in giving advice concerning her problem, finally says, "What should I do? My life is ruined. I'll have to quit school and get a job. I'm too young to be married. I haven't told the boy and I don't know how. Should I have an abortion? Will you please help me?"

- You don't remember this type of situation being "covered" in your education courses.

- What should you do?

- What course of action should you take, and where can you turn for help in assisting this young learner?

- As a professional, what moral and ethical principles should you espouse when faced with this type of dilemma?

Some 70 percent of AIDS cases are attributed to sexual transmission—by heterosexual as well as homosexual intercourse. Some 25 percent of AIDS cases are linked to the practice of sharing needles when using drugs intravenously. The expected sharp increase in the national death rate is due to the current lack of an effective vaccine. Partly because no vaccine is available, the Surgeon General has urged the schools to offer educational programs, for which efforts are underway in most cities and school districts of the nation. *Education Week* reported that forty-one states offered at least curriculum guides for the teaching of AIDS prevention. Nine states required that this topic be part of the regular school curriculum.

Problems associated with sexual values will continue to challenge the schools. Even though mounting evidence suggests that these problems are often related to ignorance or misinformation, well-designed and well-taught sex education programs in the schools have not been universally supported by the public. Lacking program efforts, teachers need to be knowledgeable about the sexuality issues of youth and to recognize symptoms of behavior that can be referred to professionals for help.

Child Abuse

Largely hidden until recent years, child abuse has become a major problem for the schools. The latest national reports estimate that almost two million school-age children suffer some form of physical or mental abuse each year, including child molestation and abduction. Over one-half of the abused children are female, and the majority of abusers are parents.

Myths and Facts. The U.S. Department of Justice reports that a child is abused every two minutes in the United States. Over 2,000 children die each year from some form of child abuse. The child abuser is most often not a dangerous stranger but a trusted friend or relative of the child. Sexual abuse is an especially insidious form of child abuse. At least one girl in four and one boy in ten will be sexually abused before they are eighteen years old, and the principal abuser will likely be a parent. Table 7.5 identifies the myths associated with sexual abuse of children. Although it is reported by the National Center of Child Abuse and Neglect that abusers are not mentally ill, the fact that they abuse children questions their mental health.

Teachers need to be watchful for possible victims of child abuse in their classrooms. The telltale signs of child abuse are the following behaviors:

- A sudden change of behavior in school learning
- No visible sign of medical attention to a child's physical or medical problems after the parents have been alerted
- Overly watchful behavior, as though the child thought something dangerous was about to happen
- Overly compliant behavior, in which the child tries to please everyone
- Behavior indicating a lack of adult supervision

TABLE 7.5   Myths and Facts about Sexual Abuse of Children

Myths	Facts
Children are sexually abused by strangers.	About 80% of children are sexually abused by family members or someone known to the child.
Sexual abuse of children is a violent act.	Only 5% of cases are acts of violence.
Persons who abuse children are mentally ill.	Not all persons who abuse children are mentally ill, but many have difficulty with appropriate child-adult relationships.
Sexual abuse of children happens only in poor families, certain ethnic groups, or uneducated families.	Child abuse takes place at all economic and educational levels of society and in all ethnic groups.
Sexual abuse does not occur in foster care.	About 25% of abuse complaints in foster care are sex-related.
Only men sexually abuse children, and the victims are always female.	Both sexes abuse children, and both male and female children are victims.

Source: The National Center of Child Abuse and Neglect.

- Exhibition of learning problems that are foreign to expected normal behavior
- Continual early arrival at school, desire to stay late, and little desire to go home

Effects on Learning. Children who come from homes where child abuse is prevalent have extreme difficulty in the classroom. Their attention spans are seriously reduced, and they tend to look for things to do that will take them away from a task. Generally, they become very distrustful of adults, which is carried over into the classroom with the teacher. Such distrust may be manifested by extra demands on the teacher for attention, in an attempt to be sure that the teacher's learning expectations are being met, or it may be exhibited as total isolation from the teacher and the learning expectations. The child's psychological and social needs dominate his or her behavior in the classroom, and the child experiences difficulty in learning.

Teachers should not be reluctant to report these types of abnormal behaviors to the proper authorities. The national statistics on child abuse suggest that it is important for the teacher and school to become involved in suspected cases of abused children. Teachers and schools are protected from civil and criminal liability if the report of child abuse is rendered honestly from suspicion, based on behaviors listed above, and is considered valid.

A Collage of Special Issues for the School

In addition to the collage of social problems facing the teacher and the school, there is a growing list of pressing issues that the school must address as it responds to the everyday needs of its students. Although schools might not consider these issues quite as difficult to handle, they do have an effect on the learning environment. Formerly, many of these problems were not considered issues for the public schools to address because some other societal agency was responding or the issue had not yet surfaced. However, as we know more about learning and how it can be affected by physical, mental, and emotional development and the social environment, the school has had to face new, pressing issues.

Special-Needs Children

There is little doubt that the school has always encountered learners with special needs. However, schools often didn't recognize these special needs or couldn't cope with them if they were recognized. As teachers, specialists, and administrators became better trained, some of these special problems were identified. Once problems or needs could be identified, the schools could mount efforts to attend to them. It should be pointed out, however, that the degree of effort that the school employs to take care of special needs depends on the wishes of the community, state, and nation. Taking care of these needs can be controversial, and a teacher should remember that the community determines the direction of the school.

Exceptional/Handicapped Learners. With the passage in 1975 of Public Law 94-142, the special education law provided millions of **exceptional learners** with mandated public education. At the other end of the ability continuum, however, there have been only sporadic institutionalized attempts to provide special programs for gifted and talented learners. Some states, in carrying out the federal mandates of Public Law 94-142, have included special programs for talented and gifted students. Most accelerated programs, advanced placement programs, and the like, whether they be "pull out of class" programs or enrichment programs, do little more than deliver new learning information faster and at an earlier age.

The criteria used to identify gifted and talented children are usually based on some academic norm such as I.Q. scores, achievement battery test scores, or teacher grades. The true notions of giftedness and special talents seem to get lost in the rush to provide special programs for these types of exceptional children. There is little doubt that some of the Individualized Education Program (IEP) requirements mandated for special education children by Public Law 94-142 are appropriate for gifted and talented learners, but also needed are broader criteria by which the schools identify these special learners. Exceptional learners in special education are defined as those evaluated as mentally retarded, hard of hearing, deaf, speech-impaired, visually handicapped, seriously emotionally disturbed, orthopedically impaired, other health impaired, deaf-blind, multihandicapped, or having specific learning disabilities.

Major legislation passed in recent years has given individuals with disabilities equal rights to free public education.

The main features of Public Law 94-142 are as follows:

1. All handicapped learners between the ages of three and twenty-one are to be provided with a free public education.
2. Each handicapped child is to have an Individualized Education Program (IEP), developed jointly by a school official, a teacher, the parents or guardian, and, if possible, the learner.
3. Handicapped children are not to be grouped separately unless they are severely handicapped, in which case separate facilities and programs would be deemed more appropriate. (The stress is on creation of the least restrictive environment.)
4. Tests for identification and placement are to be free of racial and cultural bias.
5. School districts are to maintain continuous efforts at identifying handicapped children.
6. School districts are to establish priorities for providing educational programs in compliance with the law.
7. Placement of the handicapped must require parental approval. Private schools are to comply with the Act.
8. Retraining or in-service training of all workers with the handicapped is required.
9. Special federal grants are available for modifying school buildings.
10. State departments of education are to be designated as the responsible state agencies for all programs for the handicapped.

Least Restrictive Environment.   In addition, the law clearly explains least restrictive environment placement, Individualized Education Programs, due process protection, and teacher education. The least restrictive environment placement ensures that handicapped children are educated with nonhandicapped children to the maximum extent possible, and that the placement of a handicapped child outside the regular classroom occurs only when the nature or severity of the handicap is such that education in regular classes with the use of supplementary aids and services cannot be achieved satisfactorily. An Individualized Education Program must comprise written statements developed by the public agency, the child's teacher, one or both of the child's parents, and the child when appropriate. Other specialists may be involved if the parents or public agency so desires. Each written IEP must include the following:

1. The child's present level of educational performance.
2. Annual goals, including short-term instructional objectives.
3. Specific special education and related services to be provided to the child and the extent to which the child will be able to participate in regular educational programs.
4. Projected dates for initiation and anticipated duration of special services.
5. Objective criteria, evaluation procedures, and schedules for determining on at least an annual basis whether or not the short-term instructional objectives are being met.

Mainstreaming/Inclusion. Public Law 94-142 does not specify any requirement for mainstreaming. The law speaks strictly of the need to provide for a least restrictive environment for learning, and many times the least restrictive environment is found in the regular classroom with regular students. These classrooms, considered to be the mainstream of school learning environments, have led to the popular use of the term **mainstreaming** in placing special education students in the regular classroom for part of their instruction. Since the 1960s the Council for Exceptional Children (CEC) has directed its efforts for special education toward the provision of mainstreaming services.

Many special education services are dictated by the type of physical environment provided for the learner. Typically, regular classrooms and schools are not physically designed to accommodate many special education students. For example, few regular classrooms are built to handle the physically handicapped learner. Chalkboards are too high for learners using wheelchairs, wheelchairs don't easily fit at desks, light and sound equipment don't address special physical needs, and special ramps and elevators are often nonexistent. As new schools are built they will probably be required, as a result of Public Law 94-142, to address these kinds of physical needs in school buildings. The "new perspective," as CEC calls it, makes regular learning areas more powerful and diverse.

The regular classroom environment in this plan is a model of individualized instruction for all learners. Physically, learning spaces are treated better acoustically and include amplification devices and alternative treatments of illumination. Greater use of learning centers with a multiplicity of equipment and materials is provided for special needs and preferences. Collaborative teaching is expected, in which special educators, other professionals, and aides work with regular teachers. Instruction is individualized for all learners. Special education students are moved out of the regular environment for minimal periods and only for complex individual needs.

The new stress on **inclusion** has raised serious issues for the school. Although not covered specifically by Public Law 94-142, the push nationally and statewide comes from a broader interpretation of the law. This interpretation involves putting the exceptional child in the regular classroom and bringing the special services to the classroom rather than sending the child out of the classroom for special services. This added diversity to the regular classroom has created the need for additional special education skills for the regular classroom teacher in schools moving to inclusion programs.

Homeless Students

The National Coalition for the Homeless reported in 1993 that over one million children in the United States can be classified as homeless. Like their older counterparts, the adult homeless, these young people live in shelters, abandoned buildings, welfare centers, and on the street. Half of them do not attend school regularly, and even when they do, their school performance is far from what it should be if they are to have any chance of breaking the cycle of homelessness and withstanding the social pressures on self-esteem that homeless students must surely face.

If homeless students are no longer to be the most "at-risk" students, they need to find in the school the shelter they lack at home. Unfortunately, many of these students are not allowed to attend school because they lack permanent addresses and personal records such as birth certificates and health charts and therefore cannot prove residency. The recently passed Homeless Assistance Act established a national policy, with modest funds available to the large urban areas that apply for them, that eliminates the residency requirement for homeless children and directs the schools to secure the needed documentation to get these children into the classroom.

Latchkey Children

The continuing change in family structure and living has heightened national awareness of children's problems in families in which

Relevant Research

Homeless Students Can Be Productive and Succeed

A case study report of research on the homeless points to the potential limitless strategies that can be used by the schools to accommodate homeless learners in their attempts to be successful and overcome their dire social situations. This case study reports on a young man and woman, who when given the proper chance, support, and school program were able to graduate and point their lives in a positive direction.

Living in a homeless shelter found for them by the school, the two homeless married students completed high school, including going to the prom. The school provided partial credit courses for them as they worked toward graduation. Homeless students need flexible admission criteria, course offerings, and class assignments, as well as special services and emotional support. As a professional educator you need to be flexible to accommodate all types of learners. The numbers of homeless students continue to rise, and you need to be ready to meet the needs of these special learners.

Source: Yvonne M. Vissing; Dorothy Schroepfer; and Fred Bloise, "Homeless Students, Heroic Students." *Phi Delta Kappan* 75 (7) (March, 1994): 535–539.

both parents work or single-parent families in which the parent works. Almost 50 percent of working parents acknowledge that their children are home alone from after school until five-thirty in the evening (or later) when parents come home from work. Such children are referred to as latchkey (because they wear the housekey around their neck) children, and they now number six million school children, ages five to twelve. Because their parents work, latchkey children are left to care for themselves after school.

This practice has led to the development of school programs for children who have no other after-school care. The programs work with them on such issues as first aid, nutrition and health, baby-sitting, and being on their own at home. Nationally, however, the public does not seem to be willing to fund programs for

Disadvantaged and homeless students are among the large number of students at risk of not receiving the education to which they are entitled.

these children. Since the number of latchkey kids is growing, teachers must be sensitive to the fact that they may become frightened and bored and suffer from being denied normal social interaction with their peers after school.

Increasing numbers of school districts are beginning to offer after-school programs in cooperation with local churches and community groups such as the YMCA. These programs help young children to deal with such problems as how to get home from school safely, how to use the telephone and be familiar with emergency telephone numbers, what to do in case of fire, how to deal with strangers, and how to use their time wisely instead of wasting it watching soap operas and other, sometimes violent, television programs. Many latchkey children, lacking strong family influences, experience problems in school, suffer from low self-esteem, and are failing to reach their full potential. The alarming aspect of this school issue is that the nation is witnessing a growing number of such "at-risk" young learners.

Multicultural Reform

As discussed in Chapter 5, the United States is not the melting pot that we believed it was for so many decades. In fact, our differences, and multiculturalism, are growing rapidly. This change in the population makeup, which is especially pronounced among the school-age population, has created two major issues for the school and society. These are debates about, first, monolingual versus multilingual school programs and instruction and, second, English as a Second Language (ESL) for the growing numbers of non-English speakers who are gaining entrance into the United States.

Monolingual/Bilingual.   One current debate in the halls of increasing numbers of state legislatures (now estimated at over twenty-five) centers on the use of English as the national language. Passage of legislation in some states to mandate the use of English has already produced significant problems. In Florida, Spanish-speaking maintenance workers have been dismissed because they were speaking Spanish on the job, violating the English-only law in that state. (Currently, that law is being challenged in the court system.) A similar law in California whereby non-English-speaking citizens must learn the English language for everyday use if they wish to receive welfare benefits has placed considerable stress on the Los Angeles school system. The California law also mandates that the local schools must provide programs for non-English-speaking adults. This has led to a need for some 25,000 evening classes to be offered by the Los Angeles school district. Beyond the financial burden on the schools, the major problem is finding the necessary teachers to conduct these adult classes.

The U.S. English Speaking Union now seeks, at the national level, to have English declared the official language of the United States. This group wants to have bilingual ballots removed from voting and bilingual education in schools to be used only as a short-term approach to teach all citizens to use English. This move is in direct conflict with the multilingual movement supported in the schools by diverse minority and ethnic groups.

The Bilingual Education Act—Title VII of the Elementary and Secondary Education Act—was enacted into law in 1968. This Act and its various amendments were enacted to address the special needs of growing numbers of American children whose first language is not English. Originally, the Act was intended to focus on low-income learners, early childhood education, adult education, dropouts, and vocational students. Funds were also provided for preservice and in-service training of teachers for these programs.

Bilingual-bicultural education is formal instruction for learners, using their native language for learning all subjects until second-language (English) skills have been developed. This approach increases equal educational opportunities for minority children. Census reports of the 1980s indicated that the size of the non-English-language background population in the United States was 30 million people. This number is expected to increase to 39.5 million by the year 2000. People of Spanish, German, and Italian descent make up the majority of this group, the Spanish-speaking people who have migrated from Latin America and Puerto Rico comprising by far the largest portion. The Spanish-speaking portion will continue to grow. As we discussed in Chapter 5, minority populations are soon to be the majority in an increasing number of border and coastal states. The recently passed California law declaring English to be the primary language of California will face serious legal challenge as the minority numbers continue to grow there.

Bilingual programs currently in use include the following:

1. Maintenance programs are designed to teach skills needed for English that emphasize instruction in the learner's native tongue. The culture of the ethnic group receiving instruction is stressed through teaching about the group's history, literature, and art. The native language of the learner is considered an asset to society; retention of that language is a significant goal of this program.

2. Transitional programs are designed to provide intensive instruction in English, yet retain support for instruction in the native language. Learners are integrated into the regular classroom as soon as they acquire sufficient skills in English. It is critical in these programs that the learner not be disadvantaged in expected achievement areas of the curriculum.

The need for bilingual-bicultural programs will continue to grow, but how that need will be addressed by the federal and state governments in the future remains a question. As social legislation continues to suffer from financial cutbacks and the efforts to establish English as the national language are extended, attempts to provide education for non-English-speaking people may unfortunately diminish.

English as a Second Language. English As a Second Language groups have traditionally not been supported financially in their educational pursuits, as have groups advocating bilingual programs. Because rising numbers of non-English-speaking immigrants from all over the world are sending their children to American schools, ESL programs are requiring more time during the school day if the children are to succeed in learning while using the English language.

The school finds itself in the middle of this national debate, but without clear direction from the states or national government, it cannot provide the needed leadership in program development and implementation.

School Clinics

Societal trends that have influenced the establishment of **school-based clinics** include the increasing use and misuse of illicit drugs, alcohol, and tobacco by youth; increasing suicide rates; and the sexual revolution, which has resulted in increased rates of teenage pregnancy, abortion, sexually transmitted diseases, and sex-related psychological problems. There is little doubt that these trends have had an undermining effect on the social behavior and academic success of students.

School-based clinics have emerged as a means of combating these trends. These clinics are controversial because, in addition to the regular services provided—physicals, immunizations, and first aid—they now provide birth control counseling and, in some cases, contraceptives. The clinics also provide prenatal care for pregnant teenagers and drug and alcohol abuse counseling. People who oppose these clinics do so on the basis that such services should be handled by the family, religious institutions, and community social service agencies. In fact, many people believe that because they provide birth control counseling and contraceptives, these clinics are actually promoting sexual promiscuity. Additionally, since many clinics are located in urban centers that have high proportions of low-socioeconomic students who also happen to be members of minorities, the critics argue that the clinics are using students for social engineering. Data supporting the use of such clinics in public schools suggest that, where they are in use, there are fewer teenage pregnancies and fewer instances of venereal disease. The National Academy of Science and the American Medical Association support the distribution of contraceptives to teenage youth to combat the serious problem of unwanted pregnancies. Now, with the spread of AIDS, the use of school-based clinics is even more important.

Magnet Schools

During the late 1980s, Buffalo, New York, established **magnet schools** to meet federal court requirements for desegregation that had been ordered for the city. One of the particular aims of the desegregation order in Buffalo was to provide for the growing Native American population. It had been determined that the regular school program was not providing for the special needs of Native American and African American students.

Magnet schools, as the name implies, attract particular types of students who have special educational needs. In the case of the Native American students in Buffalo, it was determined that their special needs for cultural preservation could best be handled by concentrating them in impact programs. Even though they live in concentrated neighborhoods, the regular schools do not attend to their cultural needs, because instruction is geared to the mainstream. Magnet schools attend to diversity through their programs.

Currently, there are magnet schools for African American, Native American, Greek American, and Hispanic American students in Buffalo. No one school is exclusively all Native American or all Hispanic American. The Buffalo plan calls for a maximum of 50 percent of a school's students to be members of any one minority. If the minority students do not live in the area of the designated magnet school, they are given free bus transportation. The remainder of the student body comes from the regular attendance unit of the school.

Minneapolis and St. Paul, Minnesota, have established magnet elementary schools to satisfy the special needs of the city school population. Patterned after the program for the schools in Buffalo, students are bused, in stated proportions, to the schools selected for special purposes. The magnet idea is not new. Many urban areas have had magnet-type schools at the secondary level for many years. Two such schools in New York City have been in operation for quite some time; one was highlighted in the movie *Fame*. Chicago has provided special high schools for technical, pre-engineering, and vocational training for many years. However, these schools have not been sensitive to minority differences and sometimes have become ghetto centers of education or centers of elite programs serving mostly white students. The magnet school concept, as it is currently being used, addresses social and academic needs for special programs for all kinds of students. Magnet schools are now found across the country.

Adult Literacy

Adult education includes any course or activity taken regularly or part time by adults seventeen years of age or older. This definition is used by the federal government to identify the increasing numbers of adults taking part in programs since the early 1980s. The total number of adult participants approached thirty million in 1990. The U.S. Department of Education estimates that about 11 percent of these adult students are attempting to complete elementary requirements or high school graduation requirements. Some 17 percent are completing requirements for a vocational certificate, and the remaining adults are pursuing two-year, four-year, or postgraduate degree programs. Although these figures seem impressive, they do not fully address the literacy problems of the adult population. Eighty percent of the participants are from the white majority population and have at least a high school education. Most are already gainfully employed and have annual family incomes of $13,000 or more.

Despite what appears to be a healthy situation among adults, the Department of Education has estimated that almost 13 percent of all American adults—between eighteen million and twenty-two million people—are illiterate. Most of these people belong to minorities. These data have spurred national efforts to establish and improve adult literacy programs administered by state agencies, pub-

National efforts are aimed at improving adult literacy, which is seen as directly affecting children's literacy.

lic schools, and institutions of higher education. In addition, the national media have joined the effort to reduce adult illiteracy.

Global Perspectives: Problems and Progress

Reporting in the *NEA Today*, UNESCO provides data on literacy gains and losses in countries around the world. While developing countries are gaining ground on literacy development, the underdeveloped countries are losing the literacy battle. Illiteracy rates are the highest in sub-saharan Africa, South Asia, and the Arab states. To a large part, this illiteracy problem is due to the fact that people spend so few years in formal education in underdeveloped countries. This lack of school time, coupled with a dire shortage of textbooks, provides about 60 to 80 days of effective schooling during the lifetime of people in the underdeveloped countries. This compares very unfavorably with sixteen years of formal education in North America.

Generally, around the world, the work with illiteracy is showing positive results. The UNESCO estimates suggest that adult illiteracy in the world has fallen from 946 million in 1980 to 905 million in 1990. The forecast is that this number will fall to 869 million in the year 2000.

While the data on worldwide illiteracy are not overly positive, the overall progress in children's welfare shows considerable gains over the past ten years. Infant mortality has almost been cut in half per thousand live births, falling from 137 to 70. Life expectancy has increased during this same period from forty-six years of age to sixty-one years of age. Dropout rates in many of the developing areas (the Middle East, North Africa, East Asia/Pacific, and Central America) have improved significantly. However, the underdeveloped areas still suffer from extremely high dropout rates.

While the problems of youth in this nation appear to be insurmountable at times, this society and its educational system still provide a broader and more secure learning environment for its youth than any other country. Comparisons with other nations of the world support this assertion, despite the growing negative problems facing United States youth as they enter into and engage in their educational programs.

Summary and Implications

There are many serious social problems in the United States that have important effects on our schools. Schools cannot adequately meet the educational needs of their students without considering the society in which the young people live. Our schools and our society are so intimately related that any problem affecting one affects the other; therefore the schools alone cannot solve many of the problems confronting young people.

The implication here is clear. If we are serious about solving the problems facing young people, both society at large and our schools must work together purposefully—probably in a way not yet envisioned by planners. This effort will undoubtedly require that more money be spent on education than is currently the case. It will require that parents work much more closely with educators than they do now. And it will ask American society to make a much deeper and broader commitment to education than it has up to now.

Discussion Questions

1. How can the school help in combating the chemical problems of youth?
2. How can the school develop special programs in an attempt to curb juvenile crime?
3. To what degree should schools be involved in AIDS education?

4. How is learning performance affected when the learner is an abused child?
5. There is little doubt that the use of school-based clinics will remain controversial. What role should teachers assume in defending or not defending these clinics?

Journal/Portfolio Development

1. Develop a working file that contains brochure-type materials that address problems of chemical abuse, suicide, sexuality, and child abuse. Prepare a written evaluation of each of these collection topics, and assess how the brochure information can be used in your teaching.

2. Prepare a due-process-type IEP format that you can use in your student teaching to diagnose a regular classroom learner's needs and prescribe a learning module for him or her.

School-Based Experiences

1. When you visit a school as part of your field experience program, gather information about the numbers of children in that school who are classified as welfare children. Additionally, gather numbers on school dropouts, alcohol and drug abuse, delinquency, and child abuse. Compare your findings with national figures for these types of school problems. If your findings are lower or higher than national averages, attempt to determine what that particular school and community have or have not done to affect the statistics you have gathered. After

preparing a short report on your fieldwork, share it with a teacher from the school and a few of the students. Record in writing their reactions to your findings and analyses.
2. Secure permission to examine a select set of student performance data from some school files. Examine these data in light of social activities and performances of the learners. How is school performance affected by the out-of-school activities and/or problems encountered by students?

Bibliography

Dryfoos, Joy G. *Adolescents at Risk: Prevalence and Prevention.* New York: Oxford University Press, 1990.

Gutek, Gerald L. *Education and Schooling in America.* 3rd ed. Boston: Allyn and Bacon, 1992.

Havighurst, Robert J., and Levine, Daniel U. *Society and Education.* 8th ed. Boston: Allyn and Bacon, 1992.

Hodgkinson, Harold L. *A Demographic Look At Tomorrow.* Washington, DC: Institute for Educational Leadership, 1992.

Kozol, Jonathan. *Savage Inequalities.* New York: Crown Publishers, 1991.

National Center for Educational Statistics. *Projections of Educational Statistics to 1997–99.* Washington, DC: U.S. Government Printing Office, 1991.

Rich, John Martin. *Foundations of Education: Perspectives on American Education.* New York: Macmillan Publishing Company, 1992.

Stewart, Donald. *Immigration and Education, The Crisis and Opportunities.* New York: Lexington Books, 1993.

Weatherford, James M. *Native Roots: How the Indians Enriched America.* New York: Fawcett Columbine, 1991.

Webb, L. Dean; Metha, Arlene; and Jordan, K. Forbus. *Foundations of American Education.* New York: Macmillan Publishing Company, 1991.

Part

3

Governance and Support of American Education

CHAPTER 8

Structure and Finance of American Education

CHAPTER 9

Legal Aspects of Education

CHAPTER 10

The Rights of Students and Teachers

Dreamcatcher

*Schools are the front line of the American educational system, and one of the most important educators in each school is the principal. Therefore, our Dreamcatcher for Part 3 is a very exciting and dedicated school principal, **DR. TIM WESTERBERG**. He is principal of Littleton High School in Littleton, Colorado. Prior to becoming a principal some fifteen years earlier, he was a social studies teacher and football and track coach.*

As a principal he is a visionary leader and role model for teachers. He offers his staff ideas, a quick wit, and a participatory style of management. During the summer months he frequently works with teachers serving on teams or committees. Their frequent laughter symbolizes the collegial rather than hierarchical nature of the relationships he maintains. When a decision affecting the whole school is made, the entire staff votes. He serves on the decision-making body for the school, but does not chair it. He visits every classroom in the building on a regular basis and chats with teachers informally in their offices during planning time. He believes in a consistent, clearly articulated, and honest approach to communicating with teachers, and, as a result, they trust him.

One of Dr. Westerberg's primary values concerns his belief that students should be able to demonstrate the intellectual skills and knowledge necessary to thrive in a changing world. Consequently, he led the staff in its development of an innovative educational program where students earned graduation by demonstrating their mastery of stated school goals through such methods as exhibitions, demonstrations, and portfolios. Each student's education is an individual one based on identified personal needs, interests, and learning styles. Faculty, parents, and students work together in groups and on committees to determine through shared decision making the kinds of learning projects and activities appropriate for students in their community. Every staff person, including the principal, meets with students weekly to track their progress. To support the program, Dr. Westerberg established a school foundation that applied for and received grant monies and corporate donations that go primarily to pay teachers for their work on the project.

Dr. Westerberg believes in knowing the law fully, so that he can allow for individual differences. He feels the system should work to support people rather than people work to support systems. "Because of the guiding values in our school," Dr. Westerberg said, "I have certain expectations about how we treat people. We trust kids here, and we treat each other with trust, dignity, and respect." Instead of establishing rules, he encourages individual initiative and creativity by staff members, and he values dealing with student issues individually rather than by strict procedures. "When students leave the office, they should feel that any decision affecting them was based on their individual circumstances rather than on the school's need to comply with a predetermined set of rules." Being open to change, being a positive and enthusiastic leader for students and staff, and working to provide a climate of educational excellence characterize Dr. Westerberg's leadership at Littleton High School.

Structure and Finance of American Education

Focus Questions

1. Who is in charge of the school? How much say do teachers have?
2. What is the relationship of the school district to teachers and principals in a school?
3. What do district superintendents do? And, what is the authority relationship of the superintendent to the school board?
4. Do schools and school districts have to do what the state government says? What is the role of federal government in education?
5. How are schools paid for?
6. Property taxes have been the major source of revenue for schools. What is wrong with this?
7. In recent years there have been a large number of court cases dealing with school finance. What is the common theme in all of them?
8. How well does the spending for public schools in the United States compare with what other developed countries spend?

Key Terms and Concepts

Accountability: Holding schools responsible for what students learn.

Block grants: Federal monies that are consolidated into a broader-purpose fund from categorical funds that had more focused purposes. Block grants give more discretion to the state and local agencies that receive them.

Current expenses: Expenditures necessary for daily operation and maintenance.

Independent school: A nonpublic school that is unaffiliated with any religious institution or agency.

Intermediate unit: A level of school organization between the state and the local district; a subdivision of the elementary school including grades 4, 5 and 6.

Line: An organizational arrangement in which a subordinate is directly responsible to a supervisor.

Progressive tax: A tax scaled to the ability of the taxpayer to pay.

Property tax: A tax based on the value of property, both real estate and personal.

Regressive tax: A tax that affects low-income groups disproportionately.

Staff: An organizational arrangement in which one party is not under the direct control or authority of another.

*T*he purpose of this chapter is to explain how the pieces making up the American education system are organized and fit together. We shall begin with the school. Our assumption is that you are familiar with schools; however, we should be able to add some important insights to your current understanding. From schools, we will move to descriptions of the structure of school districts, the organization of states, and the current role of the federal government. As you might have guessed, there are some parts of the system that don't fit nicely into this "bottom-up" story, and we will describe those parts after we have developed a picture of the whole. After the structure and organization of the American education system is presented, we will address how it is financed.

The Structure of the American Education System

Describing how the American education system is organized is generally done by starting at the "top" of the organization chart, with the U.S. Department of Education, moving "down" through the state structures, and ultimately arriving at the school district and school levels. This "top-down" approach reflects, in an organizational sense, that it is easier to understand the pieces when you first have a view of the whole. Also, the top-down approach indicates that there is more authority and responsibility the further up one is in the structure. In many ways this is true.

However, in education, unlike many businesses, the "bottom" is composed of professionals (teachers and principals) who know as much or more about their "business" as those who are more removed from the day-to-day life in classrooms. Thus, teachers and principals correctly advocate that they should have a great deal of say in determining what happens with their students on a day-to-day basis. Our decision to start this chapter with a description of schools, rather than at the federal level, is in some ways offering a symbolic statement that teachers can be viewed as being at the "top."

In order to avoid many of the problems implied in a vertical (top-down) picture of the American education system, a horizontal perspective, as is represented in Table 8.1, has been advocated by some theorists. One important emphasis of this horizontal Policy-to-Practice Continuum is that in order for education to

TABLE 8.1 The Policy-to-Practice Continuum in the American Education System

Federal	State	Intermediate	District	School	Classroom
President	Governor		Superintendent	Principal	Teacher
Congress	Legislature	Board	Board	Site Council	
Secretary	Chief State School Officer	Director	District Office Staff	Teachers	Students
U.S. Department of Education	State Department of Education				

improve, the agencies and people at each point along the continuum have to do their job well. A second critical feature is that all have to trust people and agencies at other points along the continuum. This means, for example, that teachers have to develop an understanding of the functions and purposes of other parts of the system. Teachers cannot stay isolated in their classrooms, unaware of the issues and expectations of the school, school district, and the state. At the other end of the continuum, it is important that policymakers learn more about the work of teachers and what goes on in schools.

Another important organizational concept to keep in mind is the difference between **line** and **staff** relationships. In any organization, some people will have the job of being supervisors, bosses, honchos, managers, or directors. Other people will "report" to these persons. The supervisor typically has the authority, at least to some degree, to direct, monitor, and evaluate the work of the subordinate. When one person has this type of authority over another there is a "line" relationship. If there is no formal organizational authority of one person over the other then they have a "staff" relationship. This distinction becomes important in education, since, in many instances, it is not clear or absolute who has the authority/responsibility to direct the work of others. For example, teachers, as professionals, legitimately can claim more independence than can employees of other organizations. But teachers are not completely free to do whatever they want. If they were, the *system* of education would break down, at least as it is experienced by students who must move through it.

The Organization of Schools

The basic building block of the American education system is the school. To an amazing extent schools are organized in the same way in each state. In fact, schools are organized pretty much the same in other countries too.

Each school consists of a set of classrooms, with corridors for the movement of students, and a central office. There will be one or more large spaces for a cafeteria and gymnasium/auditorium. This building will have outside spaces for a playground, staff parking, and a driveway for dropping off and picking up students. Wherever you go you will find this basic architecture.

The design of schools is frequently criticized for being like an "egg crate." If you viewed a school building with the roof off, you would see that it resembles an egg carton from the grocery store. There are a series of cells or pockets with routes running between them. Some educational critics see this architecture as interfering with the need to introduce new educational practices. For example, the walls restrict communication between teachers and channel the flow of student traffic.

Even when a school is built with modest attempts to change the interior space, teachers and students are able to preserve the egg crate concept. For example, you may have seen an elementary school that was "open space" in design. Instead of having "self-contained" classrooms, there is an open floor plan equivalent in size to three or four classrooms. However, if you observed the arrangement of furniture, book shelves, and screens you probably noted that teachers and students had constructed zones and areas that were equivalent to having three or four self-contained classrooms.

We are not criticizing teachers for being unadaptive to new school architectures; rather, we are pointing out how the organization of the space parallels the activity of the people who use it. There are many good reasons for organizing schools around self-contained classrooms. And in the case of open-concept space, the noise from three or four teachers and 90 to 120 children can be so disruptive that little learning can occur. One key to successful use of open-space plans then, is to be sure the structure is designed in ways to control and dampen noise.

The Roles and Responsibilities of Principals. The principal is in charge of the school. In law the principal is the final authority at the school. The principal is typically responsible for instructional leadership, community relationships, staff (including teachers, secretaries, and custodians), teacher selection and evaluation, pupil personnel, building and grounds, budgets, administration of personnel, provisions of contracts, administration of the attendance center office, and business management. The principal is in a line position with the school district superintendent. In larger school districts, the principal may have an intermediate supervisor such as an assistant superintendent or director of elementary or secondary education.

Every year, principals are being assigned more tasks and responsibilities. For example, there are a number of movements to increase teacher participation in the making of school decisions. And there is a movement to increase parent and community involvement in making school decisions. Both of these movements have led to the creation of a team or committee of teachers and parents to work with the principal. Working with these committees places new demands on the principal's time and new expectations for the types of leadership skills a principal needs to possess or develop.

The principal is responsible for the actions of all school personnel.

When teachers have an idea about the school, or want to try something different, it is important for them to talk with their principal. If there are department heads or team leaders, then the first discussions should be with them. In any organization, including schools, it is normal protocol to first talk with the person at the next level above. When there is a concern or problem, it is important to use the official administrative system. Contact the principal. If this method fails and there is a serious problem, then a teacher may continue up the line, by contacting the principal's supervisor—the assistant superintendent or the superintendent. If there is a serious disagreement, then a teacher may file a grievance through procedures outlined in the negotiated contract. In any instance it is wise for a beginning teacher, or one new to the system, to seek advice from experienced colleagues before taking action. In addition to knowing the system, one must know how the system works; colleagues and principals can be helpful in this regard.

Assistant Principals. In larger elementary schools and in most junior high schools, middle schools, and high schools, there will be one or more additional administrators. Normally they are called assistant principals, although sometimes in high schools they are titled vice principals. Large high schools will have several assistant or vice principals and some other administrators that have "director" titles, such as director of athletics and director of counseling. These administrators share in the tasks of the principal and provide additional sources of communication between teachers, students, staff, parents, community, and the district office. In elementary schools the job differentiation between the assistant principal and the principal will be less clear, and each will be a part of most operations. In the high school setting, frequently specific roles and tasks will be assigned to the different assistant principals. For example, one assistant principal will handle discipline. Another example would be the evaluation of teachers. In most districts, each teacher must be observed formally. This activity takes more time than the principal will have available, so the assistant principal(s) will observe some teachers. Normally, in the case of teacher observations, the principal will concentrate on observing the new teachers. This is especially important since the principal will be the one who makes the recommendation on rehiring beginning teachers.

Department Heads and Team Leaders. In elementary schools there will normally be another less formal level of leadership: grade level or team leaders. These persons are full-time teachers who assume a communication and coordination role for their grade level(s) or team. In junior high schools and high schools there will be department chairs. Normally the departments will be organized around the major subject areas (mathematics, science, English, and social studies), and the co-curricula (athletics and music). Teachers will be members of one of the departments, and there will be regular meetings to plan curriculum and to facilitate communication. In middle schools the leaders of the interdisciplinary teams will likely serve in the same way. In each case these department heads or team leaders will meet with the principal from time to time and meet regularly with their teachers.

Teachers. The single largest group of adults in the school are the teachers. A typical elementary school will have from fifteen to thirty-five teachers, and there will be more than one hundred in a large high school. Teachers are busy in their class-rooms working with their students, and this is where the egg crate architecture of schools can be a problem. Unless special mechanisms are used, such as team leaders or department chairs, it is very easy for individual teachers to become isolated from the school as a whole. The self-contained classroom architecture and the busy work of attending to twenty to forty students in the classroom gives each teacher little time or opportunity to communicate with other adults. As a consequence, each teacher and the principal need to work hard with the other members of the school staff to facilitate communication, and all must make an effort to work together to continually improve the school.

School Support Staff. There are personnel in a school in addition to administrators and teachers, and one of the most important of these role groups is the school secretary. Every teacher and principal will advise you to be sure to support and get along with the school secretary, who is at the nerve center of the running of the school. When a student has a problem, when a teacher needs some materials, when the principal wants a piece of information from the files, or when a student-teacher wants to know about parking a car, the first person to contact is the school secretary. Another important resource to the school are the custodians. How clean your classroom and school are will depend on the efforts of the custodians, and they also can be helpful to teachers in locating supplies and moving furniture. Keep in mind that they observe and talk with students. Frequently custodians and other support staff will know before the teachers about something that is going on. Cafeteria workers are another group of adult workers in the school who can make a positive difference in how the school feels and functions.

The School Organization Chart. All of the personnel described above are located in the school building. The principal is the single line authority for all of these adults *and* all of the students! Most experts on organizations will advocate that no more than five to seven people should be directly supervised by one administrator. Yet, in nearly all schools the principal will be responsible for a minimum of thirty adults and several hundred students. In very large schools the principal may have two hundred adults to supervise. As you can see, the simple picture of top-down direction for education breaks apart when one considers the wide array of tasks and the sheer number of people at work in each school. There have to be a number of structures for arranging the relationships between the varied role groups and facilitating coordination and communication. A typical school organization chart is presented in Figure 8.1.

Organization of the School District

Public schools in the United States are organized into school districts, which have similar purposes but widely different characteristics. Some districts provide only elementary education; others provide only high school education; still others provide both elementary and secondary education. Approximately 26 percent of the districts have fewer than 300 pupils, and their total enrollments make up about 1.3 percent of the national enrollment. Only 1.1 percent of the districts have an enrollment in excess of 25,000 students, yet these districts enroll about 28 percent of the total student population. Thousands of school districts have only one school campus; in comparison a few urban districts have as many as 500 schools.

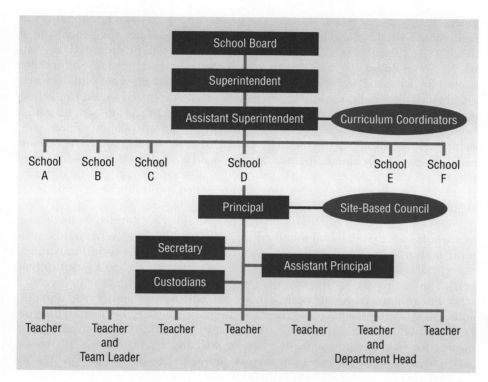

FIGURE 8.1

A School Organization Chart

The school district is governed by a school board, and its day-to-day operations are led by a superintendent. Each district will have its own district office that houses an array of administrative, instructional support, financial, and clerical support staff. As the state and federal levels of government have become active in setting educational agendas, there has been a concomitant response at the district level through an ever-increasing list of tasks that must be accomplished. These additional tasks have brought more functions and personnel to the district office.

Local Board of Education. Legal authority for operating local school systems is given to local boards of education through state statutes. The statutes prescribe specifically how school board members are to be chosen and what duties and responsibilities they have in office. The statutes also specify the terms of board members, procedures for selecting officers of the board, duties of the officers, and procedures for filling any vacancies. Local citizens serving as school board members are official agents of the state.

About 92 percent of the school boards in the United States are elected by popular vote; most members are elected in special, nonpartisan elections. About 7 percent are appointed. The percentage of appointed school boards is higher in school districts enrolling over 25,000 pupils; yet even in three-fourths of these larger districts, the board members are elected.

Normally teachers may not be board members in the districts where they teach; however, they may be board members in districts where they live if they teach in different districts. The trend by which more teachers are becoming board members most likely results from the goal of professional associations to secure seats on school boards.

Powers and Duties of School Boards. The powers and duties of school boards vary from state to state; the school codes of the respective states spell them out in detail. (The general powers and duties of local boards will be discussed in Chapter 9.) Some duties are mandatory, while others are discretionary. Some duties cannot be delegated. If, for example, boards are given the power to employ teachers, the boards must do this; the power may not be delegated—even to a school superintendent. Boards can delegate much of the hiring process to administrators, however, and then act officially on administrative recommendations for employment. An illustration of a discretionary power left to the local board is the decision of whether or not to participate in a nonrequired school program—for example, a program of competitive athletics. Another illustration of discretionary power is the decision to employ only teachers who exceed minimum state certification standards.

Powers and duties granted to boards of education are granted to the boards as a whole, not to individual members. An individual member of a board has no more authority in school matters than any other citizen of the community unless the school board legally delegates a task through official action to a specific member; in those instances, official board approval of final actions is necessary. A school board, as a corporate body, can act officially only in legally held and duly authorized board meetings, and these meetings usually must be open to the public. Executive or private sessions may be held, but ordinarily only for specified purposes such as evaluating staff members or selecting a school site. Usually, any action on matters discussed in private session must be taken officially in an open meeting.

Superintendent of Schools.

One of the primary duties of the local board is to select its chief executive officer, the local school superintendent. There is one notable exception to the general practice of selection of the superintendent by school boards. In a few states, especially in the Southeast, school district superintendents are selected by the voters. In these situations, school superintendent selection is a political process just like that used for the election of mayors, county commissioners, some judges and others. In either case, the superintendent is responsible for the day-to-day operations of the school district, responding to school board members' interests, planning the district's budget, and setting long-term aspirations for the district. The superintendent is expected to be visible in the community and to provide overall leadership for the district.

The Importance of Leadership by the Superintendent and Board Members Cannot Be Overemphasized. The quality of the educational program of a school district is influenced strongly by the leadership that the board of education and the superintendent provide. Without the communication and support of high expectations by boards and superintendents, high-quality education is not likely to be achieved. Curriculum programs over and above state-required minimums are discretionary. For a school district to excel, the local authorities, board members, and the superintendent must convince their communities that specified school programs are needed and desirable.

The Superintendent and Central Office Staff. The superintendent of schools works with a staff to carry on the program of education. The size of the staff varies with the school district; and of course, some kind of organization is necessary. Many school systems use a line and staff organization like that shown in Figure 8.2.

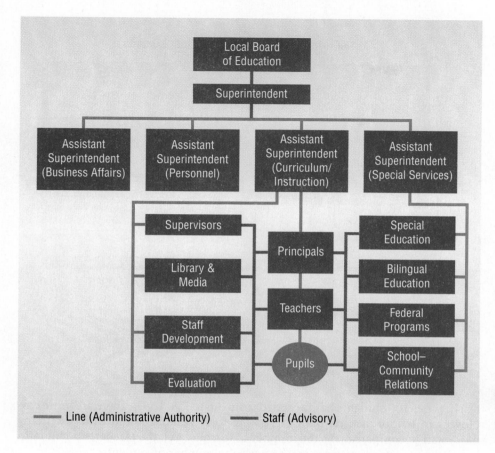

Typical School District Line and Staff Organization

In this pattern, line officers hold the administrative power as it flows in a line from the local board of education down to the pupils. Superintendents, assistant superintendents, and principals are line officers vested with authority over the people below them on the chart. Each person is directly responsible to the official above and must work through that person in dealing with a higher official. This arrangement is frequently referred to as the "chain of command."

Administrative staff members are shown in Figure 8.2 as branching out from the direct flow of authority. Staff includes librarians, instructional supervisors, guidance officers, transportation officers, and others. They are responsible to their respective superiors, generally in an advisory relationship. Staff members usually have no authority and issue no orders. They assist and advise others from their special knowledge and abilities. Teachers are generally referred to as staff persons even though they are in the direct flow of authority. Their authority in this arrangement prevails only over pupils.

There is continuing controversy about the increasing number of people in the district office as compared to the number of teachers in schools. As can be seen in Figure 8.3 on page 194 the total number of public school staff per 100 students almost doubled between 1950 and 1981. Since then the increases have been small. During the same forty-year period the percentage of school staffs that are classroom teachers has decreased from 70 to 53 percent. However, the number of

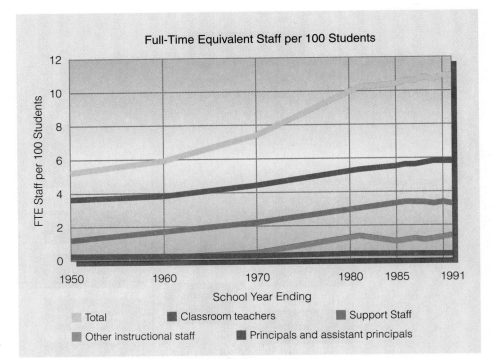

FIGURE 8.3

**Full-Time Equivalent Staff
per 100 Students**

Note: Plotted points in each chart
include school years ending: 1950,
1960, 1970, 1981, 1985–1991.

(*Source:* U.S. Department of Education, National Center for
Education Statistics, *Statistics of
State School Systems.* Common
Core of Data, and unpublished
estimates. *Digest of Educational Statistics, 1992,* tables 78 and 3.)

teachers per 100 students has increased from 3.6 to 5.8. Today, there are more employees in school districts than there were forty years ago, and there are many
more staff in comparison to the number of teachers. Yet, the teacher/student ratio
has changed in favor of more teachers per the number of students.

Organization of Education at the State Level

In certain countries, such as Taiwan, the national constitution specifies responsibility for education, but the U.S. Constitution does not specifically provide for
public education. However, the Tenth Amendment has been interpreted as granting this power to the states. As a consequence, the states are the governmental
units in the United States charged with the responsibility for education. Local
school districts then receive their empowerment through state law to administer
and operate the school system for the local communities. State legislatures, within the limits expressed by the federal constitution and by state constitutions, are
the chief policymakers for education. State legislatures grant powers to state
boards of education, state departments of education, chief state school officers,
and local boards of education. These groups have only the powers granted to them
by the legislature, implied powers from the specific grant of power, and the necessary powers to carry out the statutory purposes. The responsibilities and duties
of intermediate units are also prescribed by the state legislatures. Figure 8.4 shows
a typical state organization for education.

Stability, continuity, and leadership for education can come from the state
board. However, as identified in Figure 8.4, many others are increasingly likely to

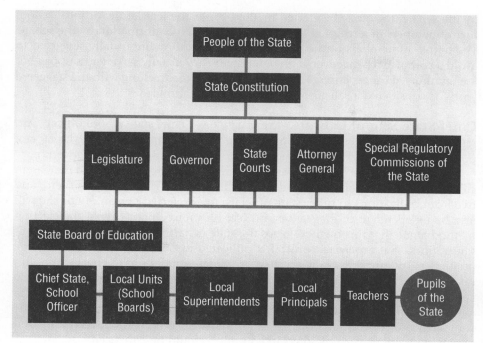

FIGURE 8.4

Typical Structure of a State School System

engage in education issues. For example, many legislators have established records of heavy influence on the direction of education. Through their initiatives new laws are established related to any and all parts of the education system. There are "education governors" as well. A number of our state leaders have been very involved in supporting and attempting to shape education in their states. Suffice it to say, there is a large number of participants, agencies, and ways to influence the shape and direction of the American education system.

State Boards of Education. State boards of education are both regulatory and advisory. Some regulatory functions are the establishment of standards for issuing and revoking teaching licenses, the establishment of standards for approving and accrediting schools, and the development and enforcement of a uniform system for gathering and reporting educational data. The advisory function includes considering the educational needs of the state, both long- and short-range, and recommending to the governor and the legislature ways of meeting these needs. State school boards, in studying school problems and in suggesting and analyzing proposals, can be invaluable to the legislature, especially since the legislature is under pressure to decide so many issues. A state board can provide a continuity in an educational program that ordinary legislative procedures don't allow for. A state board can also coordinate, supplement, and even replace study commissions appointed by a legislature for advising on educational matters. These commissions frequently include groups studying textbooks, finance, certification, school district reorganization, school building standards, and teachers' education.

State Board Membership. Members of state boards of education get their positions in various ways. Usually, they are appointed by the governor, with confirmation by the senate; they may be elected by the people, the legislature, or local school board members in a regional convention—also with confirmation by the senate. The terms of members of the state boards of education are usually staggered to avoid a complete changeover at any one time. They usually serve without pay but are reimbursed for expenses. The policy of nonpayment, along with the staggered terms, is considered a safeguard against political patronage.

Chief State School Officers.   Every state has a chief state school officer. Currently, nineteen of these officers are elected by the people, twenty-seven are appointed by state boards of education, and four are appointed by the governor.

Arguments advanced for electing the chief state school officer hold that, as an elected official, the person will be close to the people, responsible to them, and free from obligations to other state officials. As an elected person, he or she will also be independent of the state board of education. Opponents of the election method argue that this method keeps the state department of education in partisan politics, that an elected official is obligated to other members of the same political party, and that many excellent candidates prefer not to engage in political contests. Those who advocate that the chief state school officer should be appointed by a state board of education claim that policymaking should be separated from policy execution, that educational leadership should not rest on the competence of one elected official, and that, with this method, recruiting and retaining qualified career workers in education would be enhanced.

Opponents of appointment by a state board of education claim mainly that the chief school officer would then not be responsible to the people. The principal objection to gubernatorial appointment is the inherent danger of the appointee's involvement in partisan politics. Another perspective on this issue is that an elected state school officer is legally an "official" of the state, whereas an officer appointed by a state board of education is generally an "employee," not a legal official.

State Departments of Education.   The state government carries on its activities in education through the state department of education, which is directed by the chief state school officer. These activities have been classified in five categories: operational, regulatory, service, developmental, and public support and cooperation activities.[1] Operational activities are those in which the state department directly administers schools and services, such as schools for the blind. Regulatory activities include making sure that teacher license standards are met, that school buses are safe, and that curricular requirements are fulfilled. Service activities include advising and consulting, disseminating research, and preparing materials (on state financial aid, for example). Developmental activities are directed to improving the department itself and include planning, staffing, and research into better performance for the operational and regulatory, as well as service functions. Public support and cooperation activities involve public relations, political activities with the legislature and governor, and relations with various other governmental and nongovernmental agencies.

The Federal Government's Role in Education

Under the Tenth Amendment to the U.S. Constitution, education is a function of the states. In effect, states have the primary responsibility for education, although the schools are operated by local governmental units commonly called school districts. Although the states have the primary responsibility for education and the schools are operated at the local level, the federal government has an ever-increasing involvement in education. In the 1960s and 1970s the rationale for this interest and involvement was linked to national security and solving social problems. In the early 1990s the rationale was based on economic competitiveness. The result has been the establishment of federal agencies, programs, and laws that address various aspects of the American education system.

Leadership. The federal government has historically provided leadership in education in specific situations, usually in times of need or crises that could not be fully addressed by the leadership in states or local school districts. In the 1980s, the time was right for a more active leadership role for the federal government, such as establishing national priorities in education and raising issues such as those addressed in *A Nation at Risk*, the report prepared by the National Commission on Excellence in Education, published in 1983.

That report was not a mandate, nor was funding recommended, but it did provide recommendations to be considered by states and local school districts. The identifying of national educational issues and the encouraging of forums on these issues at the state and local levels, along with soliciting responses, are appropriate federal activities. Such activities could be made regular, rather than sporadic. Other activities include research on significant national educational issues and dissemination of exemplary practices.

The federal government also has included the Department of Education, which directly operated some education programs, funded special projects, and provided financial aid to states and local school districts.

The U.S. Department of Education.   In October 1979, then President Carter signed legislation creating a cabinet-level federal agency, the Department of Education. The Department of Education took on the functions of the U.S. Office of Education, which was created in 1953 as a unit within the Department of Health, Education, and Welfare. The first-ever unit of education in the federal government, established in 1867 through the diligent efforts of Henry Barnard, was also called the Department of Education. Later, it was called the Office of Education (1869); at another time it was the Bureau of Education within the Department of the Interior. In 1939 the Office of Education became a part of the Federal Security Agency, which in 1953 became the Department of Health, Education, and Welfare, wherein the U.S. Office of Education was assigned until the new department was created in 1979.

The latest version of the Department of Education, in contrast with the first Department of Education (1867), has the potential for becoming a powerful agency. The original 1867 Department had the following stated purpose:

> To collect such statistics and facts as shall show the condition and progress of education in the several States and Territories, and to diffuse such information respecting the organization and management of schools and school systems, and methods of teaching as shall aid the people of the United States in the establishment and maintenance of efficient school systems, and otherwise promote the cause of education throughout the country.

There is no question that offering aid and awarding grants are effective ways to influence the goals of education nationally. However, there is continuing debate

The federal government provides funding for many aspects of education, and houses organizations such as Very Special Arts, which provides programs in creative writing, and the visual and performing arts for individuals with physical and mental disabilities.

about whether the offices of the federal government should have a stronger or weaker influence on education. Some maintain that the socioeconomic forces of society are not contained within local school districts or state boundaries, and therefore direct federal intervention is needed. Others advocate dissolution of the Department.

It was within this political-educational context that the new Department of Education was created. Those who favored creating a new department felt that education was too important to be lost in the gigantic Department of Health, Education, and Welfare. Opponents took the position that a national Department of Education would result in more federal control and standardization.

In the short life of the U.S. Department of Education the influencing of education has continued to be primarily based on the use of grants and aid. However, the first several Secretaries of Education have been strong spokespersons for particular education agendas. For example, former Secretaries Bennett and Alexander were strong advocates for choice and voucher plans. The Secretaries of Education and their staffs also set funding priorities within the constraints laid down by Congress. As described next, there is a wide array of federal programs and involvement in education both within the Department of Education and within other federal agencies.

Educational Programs Operated by the Federal Government. The federal government directly operates some school programs. For example, the public school system of the District of Columbia depends on Congress for funds. The department of the Interior has the educational responsibility for children of National Park employees, for Samoa (classified as an outlying possession), and for the trust territories of the Pacific, such as the Caroline and Marshall Islands. Many of the schools on Native American reservations are financed and managed through the Bureau of Indian Affairs of the Department of the Interior. Twenty-five of these schools have become what are called contract schools, in which the tribe determines the program and staff, but the Bureau of Indian Affairs supports the schools financially. The Department of Defense is responsible for the Military Academy at West Point, the Naval Academy at Annapolis, the Coast Guard Academy at New London, and the Air Force Academy at Colorado Springs. The Department of Defense also operates a school system for the children of the military staff wherever members are stationed. The instruction supplied in the vocational and technical training programs of the military services has made a big contribution to the education of our nation as well.

Categorical Aid. Another strategy for federal involvement in education is categorical financial aid. These funds are granted to be used for a specific purpose, such as compensatory education for the disadvantaged, bilingual education, education for the handicapped, and vocational education. Categorical aid is accompanied by strict rules and regulations to ensure that the aid is used for the purposes intended by Congress. The intended uses of these funds evolve from year to year as Congress and society perceive new needs.

Other Types of Education Agencies

The description of the American education system laid out so far has been in a straight line. We have described how education is organized from "bottom to top," (or is it top to bottom?). Obviously the whole system is not this simple. There are a number of related agencies and organizations that are important as well. Some of them that will play a more direct role in your work as a teacher are highlighted here.

Intermediate Units.   The **intermediate unit** of school organization, which may consist of one or more counties, functions between the state department of education and the local school districts. These units have different names in different states. For example, in a number of states, such as New York and Colorado, they are called BOCES (Boards of Cooperative Educational Services); in Texas, they are called Regional Service Centers; and in California, County Education Offices.

A fundamental purpose of the intermediate unit of today is to provide two or more local districts with educational services that they cannot efficiently or economically provide individually; cooperative provisions for special education and vocational-technical education have been very successful. Other services that intermediate units can provide include audiovisual libraries, centralized purchasing, in-service training for teachers and principals, as well as other school workers, health services, instructional materials, laboratories, legal services, and special consultant services. The in-service dimension of the intermediate units has escalated in some states in the past few years, stimulated by educational reform.

Regional Educational Laboratories.   The Regional Labs are a federal creation. In 1965, as part of the Elementary Secondary Education Act, authorization and funding to establish a new type of educational agency was initiated. The nation was divided into geographic regions, with each region consisting of three to seven states, and a new type of education agency was established to serve each of these regions. The purpose of these Regional Educational Laboratories is to link education personnel in schools, school districts, and state agencies with the latest findings from research and development efforts. Each lab conducts its own education research and curriculum development efforts. It also consults with educators, conducts training sessions, and organizes regional conferences. A list of the names and locations of these regional laboratories is likely available through your instructor or at your library.

National R&D Centers.   Another important resource for educators has been the National Educational Research and Development (R&D) Centers. These, too, were established under President Johnson's "Great Society" program, more specifically the Elementary Secondary Education Act of 1965. For the first time in the history of the United States there was a national commitment to ongoing support for conducting research in education. To address this goal, a set of multidisciplinary research and development centers were established. Each of these R&D centers is based at a major university and receives multi-year funding. Names and locations of the current set of national R&D centers are also likely available through your instructor or your library.

Foundations. The preceding list of agencies and involvements in education is based on public funds (tax dollars). There are also private funds that support a large number of activities in our public schools, including an impressive array of foundations. Foundations are not hamstrung by government regulations, so they are more able to support experimentation and test novel educational activities. Some are large and widely known, such as the Kellogg Foundation. Others are smaller or target their funding to particular states or particular topics. For example, the Hogg Foundation in Texas invests mainly in that state and primarily supports issues related to mental health. A new and very promising foundation in the Midwest is the Ewing Marion Kauffman Foundation in Kansas City. One of their novel projects is called Project Choice, in which eighth graders and their parents sign a contract that the student will graduate from high school on time and drug free. If the student completes the contract, the Kauffman Foundation will support the student in going to college.

Alternatives to Regular Public Schools

Currently, in many localities, parents, teachers, administrators, and children can choose from a number of alternatives to the regular school arrangement. Many of these options are being installed within public school districts, while the alternative of private schools has existed all along. Some of these options bring the opportunity for increased parent and student involvement in school decision making. All represent, in some way, a break with the traditional public school and classroom structures. The following are examples of some of the alternatives that are increasingly available.

Site-Based Decision Making (SBDM). School-based management (SBM) or site-based decision making (SBDM) emerged in the School Restructuring movement of the 1980s. It permits individual schools within a district to be more involved in decisions related to the educational operations of that school—for example, budgeting, personnel, and curriculum. The increase in decision-making authority may be granted by the school board or the state. An example of the latter would be the Kentucky Reform Education Act, which includes a mandate for SBDM in all public schools in the state.

The concept came about in part through educational reform recommendations for greater participation of teachers in governance at the local school level. Parents' demands to have more say in the education of their children were also a factor in promoting school-based management. Two objectives of school-based management are to reduce school district regulatory control of individual schools and to empower teachers with the opportunity to participate in making decisions for their schools.

School-based management is based on two fundamental beliefs: Those who are most affected by decisions ought to play a significant role in making those decisions, and educational reform efforts will be most effective and long-lasting when carried out by people who feel a sense of ownership and responsibility

QUESTION: *Some people are concerned about the decision-making powers that reside at the federal, state, and local school boards as opposed to at the school level. In general, do you think the amount of decision-making power the local schools have is about right, too much, or too little?*

	SCHOOL LOCATION					
	Total	**Inner City**	**Urban**	**Suburban**	**Small Town**	**Rural**
Base	1000	123	105	258	308	205

	PERCENT					
About Right	38	30	24	39	40	45
Too Much	5	3	3	5	8	3
Too Little	57	66	71	55	52	51
Not Sure	*	*	*	*	*	*

*Less than 0.5%

FIGURE 8.5

Appropriateness of School-Based Decision-Making Authority

(*Source: The Metropolitan Life Survey of the American Teacher, 1993.* Teachers Respond to President Clinton's Education Proposals. New York: Louis Harris and Associates, Inc., 13.)

for the process. As you can see in the results of a national survey presented in Figure 8.5, these beliefs are consistent with what teachers think. More than half of all teachers surveyed and two-thirds of the inner city teachers believe that they have too little say in decision making.

What Are the Obstacles to SBDM? There are a number of obstacles in implementing school-based management. It is not a panacea for solving all of a school's or a school district's problems, and it might inspire excessively high expectations. There might be efforts by administrators and teachers to reduce administrative personnel, whereby the effectiveness of school-based management could be jeopardized. Changes in collective bargaining agreements might be necessary. Questions about educational equity might arise. Under school-based management, not all schools will have the same programs. Is that an inequity? State mandates may increase curriculum uniformity and, in so doing, stifle the educational programs developed through school-based committees. It is also possible under school-based management that teachers, principals, and other staff members might be skeptical or outright critical.[2]

Magnet Schools. Many school districts are being pressured by citizens and ordered by the courts to equalize the proportions of different racial groups in each school. One response, especially by large urban school districts such as Houston and Kansas City, has been to develop special academic programs and custom-designed facilities that will attract all students; hence, the name "magnet" schools. There are elementary, middle, and high school magnets. The program might emphasize the performing and visual arts, or math and science, or the liberal arts. Whatever the theme, the faculty, curriculum, and all students in that school are there because of their interest in the school's theme.

Charter Schools. A new approach to providing communities with alternative schools that are supported by public funds is charter schools. A number of states, including California, Colorado, and Minnesota, have authorized the establishment of charter schools. The specifics are different in each state, but the basic design is that a local group of teachers (in California and Minnesota) or community members (in Colorado) develop a plan for the school that includes curriculum, staffing, and instructional expectations. This "charter" then must be accepted by the local school board and the state board of education. Charter schools function as independent public schools that students choose to attend. One of the strengths of this approach is that it is a way to be freed from many state and district regulations.

Year-Round Schools. The normal school year of nine to ten months with the full summer off is often criticized. One concern is that students will forget too much over the summer. Critics point out that the current school year was put into place over a hundred years ago when most people lived on farms and the children were counted on to perform summer chores. One interesting solution is the year-round school. This is not an extended school year in that students attend school for more days. Rather, year-round schools spread the time in school across twelve months. One way this is done is to have multiple tracks of six to eight weeks. During any one cycle, one-fourth to one-third of the students will be on vacation and the others will be attending classes. This way, students have more frequent and shorter times away from school. An additional advantage is that the school site can handle more students on an annual basis. Year-round schools are on a steady increase. In the 1992–1993 school year, 301 public school districts in 26 states and 29 private schools had year-round programs.[3]

Private, Parochial, and Independent Schools. Alternative structures of schools exist outside the public school system too. These range from elite secondary schools, mainly in the Northeast, to dynamic alternative schools for high school dropouts, to church-supported schools, to schools that are operated for profit.

Independent Schools. Private education, which preceded public education in the United States, continues to be available as an alternative to the public schools. Private schools are increasingly being referred to as independent schools. One source of information is the Council for American Private Education (CAPE), which is a coalition of fourteen private-school organizations. Another is the National Association of Independent Schools (NAIS). The following quotations, which describe independent schools and compare them to public schools, are taken from an NAIS publication.[4]

An **independent school** is a nonprofit institution governed by a board of trustees that depends almost entirely on private funds—tuition, gifts, grants—for its financial support. Most independent schools are accredited by their regional accrediting group and state departments of education. All must meet state and local health and safety standards as well as the mandatory school attendance laws. Unlike public schools, independent schools are not involved in or part of large, formal systems. They do, however, share many informal contracts among themselves and with public schools. The vast majority offer programs that prepare students for college.

Independent schools vary greatly in purpose, organization, and size, and they serve students from all racial, religious, economic, and cultural backgrounds. Some are progressive and innovative, some are conservative and traditional. They are both large and small, day and boarding, single-sex and coeducational. Independent schools have been an integral part of our nation's educational resources since colonial times.

Since each school is free to determine and practice its own philosophy of education, spirit and environment vary from school to school, even though they may display similar organizational structures and educational programs. This diversity among schools is one of their most distinctive characteristics.

Governance of Independent Schools.   Each independent school is incorporated as a nonprofit, tax-exempt corporation and governed by a board of trustees that selects its own members, determines the school's philosophy, selects the chief administrative officer, and bears ultimate responsibility for the school's resources and finances. The chief administrator responsible for the day-to-day operation of the school may be called the headmaster, headmistress, president, or principal. The head's duties are comparable to those of a public school superintendent.

Issues Related to Organization and Structure

So far this description of how the American education system is organized and works has been free of discussion of issues, problems, conflicts, and ambiguities. Well, all you have to do is pick up a newspaper or watch the television news and you will be quickly confronted with one or more of the debates about what education *should* be doing or *should not* be doing. The following is a short list of topics and issues that we are grappling with in the 1990s.

Local Control.   An important and unique feature of American education is local control; however, its value has been challenged recently. Some critics argue that the mobility of our population and the interdependence of social elements have undermined the traditional concept that local people should have a strong role in determining the directions of education. Some also argue that our national survival requires policies and programs laid down under centralized control by states and the federal government.

Local Control Is Challenged Each Time a Decision by a Local Board or a Local School District Is Taken to the Courts.   As is discussed in Chapter 9 many court decisions dealing with the relationship between religion and the public school or with desegregation have been in response to local control. Currently, in most states, courts are ruling that local control, combined with the traditional system of financing education, has resulted in inequality of educational opportunity rather than equality.

Centralization Is the Alternative to Local Control.   We have come full circle; education in large cities is already centralized, and many of these large districts are trying to solve some of their problems by decentralization. Frequently, a centralized authority does not respond well to citizens' needs and demands. Ex officio boards and councils for local community or neighborhood schools, which advise officials on large city or county boards, represent efforts to keep some form of local control in the large centralized systems.

Local school board meetings are often the main opportunity community members have to express their opinions about their children's education.

The operational control of education today is still primarily local, carried out under the powers delegated by the states. However, federal and state involvement—both direct, through court decisions and mandates, and indirect, through federal and state aid—has been steadily increasing. How the local, state, and federal governments are related in their control is complicated and must be resolved. New and intricate relations keep forming.

Politics in Education. So far in this chapter we have provided information about the formal structures of public education at the local, state, and federal levels. Although these organizational structures illustrate the line and staff relationships, there is another set of relationships that is important to consider and understand. Each of these levels is involved in politics—the politics of education. For example, local school districts are likely to be interested in federal educational programs and grants, so they will contact members of Congress to express their opinions. The purpose is to influence their representatives' understanding of local needs and how they act on them. That is politics, partisan and nonpartisan. (Partisan politics is associated with political parties.) The same activities take place at the state level. Local school districts and professional associations follow closely what is happening in their state legislature. There is little hesitation to let members in the legislature know their opinions and urge action. It is not unusual for local school superintendents and board members to lobby their senators and representatives in person. These contacts with federal and state agencies are representative of political action. There are a number of other types of education politics that you need to be aware of as well.

Election Politics Are Becoming Increasingly Volatile. One common example of politics in elections is found in school board elections. The individuals who are on the school board can make a major difference in what you can and cannot do as a teacher. This is especially true with the concerted efforts of the Religious Right to increase their voice in school matters. They are very skilled at orchestrating campaigns to elect school board members who are favorably disposed to their interests, which include demanding curriculum changes, challenging sex education programs, pushing for prayer in the classroom, and purging reading lists in libraries. Their political strategies are good examples of what politics are about. They are well organized and use state-of-the-art combinations of fund raising, mass communication, and old-fashioned door-to-door campaigning. Since there tends not to be very much interest in school board elections, a relatively small number of people (say the membership of one or two churches) voting as a block can swing an election. The definition of what is fair in politics is not always clear. For example, the Religious Right has been criticized for running "stealth" candidates. In other words, the candidates do not

Community members may at times feel the need to air their feelings about education in a larger forum than a local school board meeting.

say explicitly what they believe and what they plan do to if elected. Still, they are using the democratic process to influence policy and practice.

Politics at the School District Level. The people who are likely to be involved in politics at the local level include board members, superintendents, and community members. Politics begins for prospective board members when they decide to run for the school board. As President John F. Kennedy said, "The first thing you need to be is elected."

A recent survey indicated that the top five motives for seeking board membership were:

- To exercise your civic duty (66 percent),
- To increase academic standards (53.4 percent),
- To improve your own child's education (40.3 percent),
- To make local schools more accountable (39.7 percent), and
- To make the schools more fiscally sound (31.7 percent).[5]

A sixth motive was to revise the curriculum. Only about 7 percent of those who sought board membership represented a special-interest group.

The motives expressed in the survey of those seeking board membership appear to be honorable. The encouragement to run for the school board by friends and neighbors, current school board members, and family members seems innocuous. In elections, however, depending on the circumstances and issues, bitterness and resentment in the school district can occur. The healing, when and if it happens, is likely to be resolved by political procedures.

School Board Politics. Board members are expected to be accountable to their public constituency. However, some board members feel that they should be accountable to the entire community, while others feel that they should be accountable only to a specific segment of the community. The two positions are not compatible and may bring about strife among board members and within the community. Political activity is the likely result.

Most school districts have at-large elections for board members. At-large elections allow the entire electorate to vote for each candidate or each board member who is running for reelection.

> When the entire electorate votes there is less chance that a minority candidate will win a seat than if voters from specific areas within the district choose their own board members. A recent survey found more minorities among appointed board members than among those who were elected.[6]

This is an issue that will continue to fester and will probably be resolved politically.

There are other political issues that board members and the public might view as more emotional and more difficult to deal with. Among them might be firing a superintendent, having a strike, closing schools, opening a school-based clinic that provides sexual advice and contraceptives to teenagers, raising taxes, reducing staff and educational opportunity, busing students, admitting a child with AIDS, desegregating schools, and having consistently losing athletic teams. Such issues are divisive and can result in political havoc until resolved.

The Superintendent and Board Politics. The superintendent is the chief executive officer of the school district. The superintendent's formal power comes from the

PROFESSIONAL DILEMMA

What Is the Appropriate Role for Teachers When the Politics Get Rough?

In the 1980s and 1990s teachers and school administrators have been asked to make serious efforts to change the way schools operate. In the 1980s policymakers, business leaders, and citizens at large demanded that schools "reform" and "restructure." In the late 1990s schools are engaging in "systemic reform." Yet, making major changes in the structure and operations of schools is difficult to accomplish. It is hard for teachers to give up or change what they have been doing. It takes a great deal of time to work through the process that is necessary to develop a consensus among teachers, administrators, and parents about how a school should be restructured and what it should become. It also takes several years to work out the bugs when trying something new.

As a teacher, what would you do if, after you had spent three years in discussions and then two years in implementing a major restructuring of your school, a newly elected majority on the school board demanded that you return to the old way?

This is not a hypothetical question. After more than three years of broad-based discussions involving teachers, administrators, students, parents, and community members, the Littleton, Colorado, School Board approved alternative graduation requirements for Littleton High School. The new requirements were based on student accomplishments, instead of seat-time. Students would have to demonstrate that they had achieved the required outcomes. Littleton High School became nationally recognized for its efforts.

In November of the second year of implementation, three conservative members were elected to the

board of education, but he or she also gains power through access to various sources of information. The control of information is power.

Generally, boards are considered to be policymakers, and superintendents implement the policies. Cooperative development of specific policies helps to establish the roles of both the board of education and the superintendent. However, specific education issues and others can bring about rigorous debate between the superintendent and the board and among board members. It is likely that the public will also wish to express its opinions.

The Superintendent and Staff Politics. In addition to dealing with boards, the superintendent also works with a staff to carry on the education programs. Figure 8.1 illustrates a typical organization. The superintendent interacts directly with assistant superintendents and principals. Depending upon the school district policy, the superintendent may interact directly with the teachers' union representatives in collective bargaining. The superintendent may also be the negotiator for the school district in bargaining with the representatives of the noncertified employees, including secretaries and custodians. The more contacts the superintendent has, particularly if those contacts are controversial, the greater the potential for political activity among the staff—commonly referred to as "office politics." The staff has power in that it can also control information. The staff can initiate and spread vicious rumors, which will in time spread to the community. Enter dirty politics, full of intrigue and maneuvering. A school district involved in such political activities will suffer until the issues are resolved, which may involve dismissing personnel.

The Positive Side of Politics. Note that politics and political activities need not be negative: They can be positive and have positive results. For example, effective politicians can bring about compromises that are better solutions to issues than

five-member school board. A major theme in their election campaign was attacking the new graduation requirements, which they promised to remove. In January the new majority on the school board proceeded to implement its campaign promise. Although students from the school, parents, and school staff asked that the board not do this, or that it would at least allow the new graduation requirements to be optional, the board voted three-to-two to return to the traditional requirements. Remember that there were now students in their second year of high school who had been told that they must meet the new graduation requirements.

The school board did not stop there. In the same month, January, the superintendent, who was viewed as a very able educator and was well known and respected nationally, was terminated. By the end of the school year a number of school principals and teachers had taken positions elsewhere, and the district was running advertisements nationally for principals and teachers who held "traditional" educational values.

This may be an extreme case in some ways, but it has happened in more than one school district. And it will happen in one form or another again. If you were a teacher in Littleton High School, what would you do? Of course, it would make a difference depending on which side of the issue you were on. Either way, what would you do? Your colleagues, the school, your students, and the innovative program have been challenged. It is clear that there is the potential for casualties, including your job.

- Would you speak out, or wait for others to do so?
- What would you tell your students?
- Would you help your principal, or leave him or her on his or her own?
- How do you think you will feel the next time you are asked to invest four or five years in designing and implementing a change in your school?

any of the many singular proposals put forward. Politics are a necessary ingredient for a democracy, and a necessary ingredient for public education as well.

School-Based Management: Local Councils and Political Actions. Two issues that are likely to generate political action are the roles of the local school councils and their relationship and interaction with principals. If the members of the council are honest and sincere and, after serious debate, are willing to compromise, positive political action will have taken place. However, if some members of the council come with a special interest—such as firing the principal—political infighting is likely to happen within the council, particularly if the members are deeply entrenched and are not open to modification in their positions. Such political infighting is bound to spread into the community and thus escalate the controversy. Again, the possible solution is likely to result from political action.

The Financing of Education

A basic goal of public education in the United States is to provide an adequate education that is equally available to everyone. To achieve that goal, government must design a system of taxation that is equitable for taxpayers. The United States has not yet met the goal for public education nor achieved equitable taxation, although progress has been made.

Money to support education comes from a variety of taxes paid to local, state, and federal governments. These governments in turn distribute tax money to local school districts to operate the schools. The three principal kinds of taxes that provide revenue for schools are property taxes, sales or use taxes, and income taxes. The property tax is generally a local tax, while the sales tax generally is a state and local mix, and the income tax is collected at the state and federal levels.

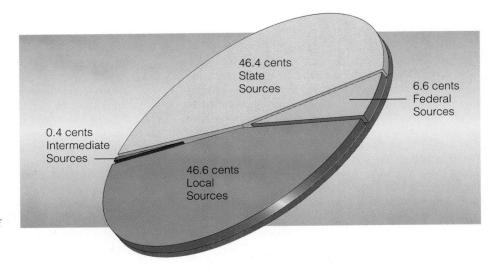

FIGURE 8.6

The Public Education Dollar: Revenues from Various Sources: School Year 1991–1992

(*Source:* National Center for Education Statistics, Common Core of Data, "National Public Education Financial Survey—Fiscal Year 1992")

Figure 8.6 portrays the percentages of education revenues received nationwide from federal, state, and local sources. As you can see, public education is primarily funded by local and state sources of revenue. Table 8.2 presents similar data for selected states. An emerging trend is indicated here: private sources of revenue. In response to budget limitations and cutbacks, schools are turning to citizens and local agencies for gifts to support special programs and services. Many school districts are establishing foundations to collect and manage these funds.

This chapter now turns to an analysis of the financing of public education through a closer look at the different sources of funding and related issues of equality of educational opportunity and taxpayer equity. It also addresses other issues related to funding for schools, including taxpayer revolts, reform in education financing, accountability, and international comparisons.

Property Taxes and Local Revenue

The **property tax** has been the primary source of local revenue for schools. It is based on the value of property, both real estate and personal. Real estate includes land holdings and buildings such as homes, commercial buildings, and factories. Personal property consists of automobiles, machinery, furniture, livestock, and intangibles, such as stocks and bonds. The property tax has both advantages and limitations.

Property Taxes: Advantages and Limitations. The main advantage of the property tax is its stability. Although it lags behind other changes in market values, it provides a steady, regular income for the taxing agency. Also, property is fixed; that is, it is not easily moved to escape taxation, as income might be.

Limitations of Property Tax. The property tax has numerous limitations. It bears heavily on housing: It tends to discourage rehabilitation and upkeep, since both of these would tend to raise the value of the property and therefore its taxes. It is often a deciding factor in locating a business or industry. And it is likely not to be applied equally on all properties.

TABLE 8.2   Receipts of Public Elementary and Secondary Schools by Source and by State for Selected States, Including the District of Columbia

State	Percent of Receipts			
	Local and Intermediate	State	Federal	Private
District of Columbia	91.2	—	8.6	0.3
New Hampshire	86.8	7.8	2.8	2.5
Oregon	65.6	25.4	6.1	2.9
Michigan	65.2	26.8	5.8	2.3
Nebraska	55.1	31.0	5.9	8.0
Wyoming	43.8	47.8	5.3	3.1
Illinois	59.0	31.7	6.6	2.6
U.S. Average	44.1	47.3	6.2	2.5
Florida	39.3	50.1	6.6	4.1
Minnesota	36.9	55.3	4.2	3.6
California	25.6	66.0	7.2	1.2
Mississippi	25.4	54.2	16.6	3.8
Alabama	20.6	60.1	11.1	8.2
Alaska	18.3	68.5	11.3	1.9
Washington	19.0	72.1	5.7	3.2
New Mexico	12.5	72.7	12.2	2.5
Hawaii	0.5	89.9	7.8	1.8

Source: Digest of Educational Statistics, 1993. Washington, DC: National Center for Educational Statistics, 152.

Determining the Value of Property. One difficulty with the property tax lies in determining the value of property. In some areas, assessors are local people, usually elected, with no special training in evaluating property. Their duty involves inspecting their neighbors' properties and placing values on them. In other areas, sophisticated techniques involving expertly trained personnel are used for property appraisal. In either circumstance, assessors are likely to be subject to political and informal pressures to keep values low in order to keep tax rates low.

The assessed value of property is usually only a percentage of its market value. This percentage varies from county to county and from state to state. Attempts are made within states to equalize assessments or to make certain that the same percentage of full cash value is used in assessing property throughout the state. In recent years, attempts have been made to institute full cash value for the assessed value. For the property tax to be a fair tax, equalized assessment is a necessity.

Assessed Valuations: Quality of Education. Limited tax rates for **current expenses** and limitations on indebtedness point out further the significance of assessed valuation as a factor in determining the quality of an educational program. A local school district can be making the maximum effort, taxing to the limit, and still not be able to offer a program comparable to what a wealthier neighboring district offers under a medium effort. The effort made by a local school district indicates the value that the citizens place on education; yet equal effort does not produce equal revenue, equal expenditures per pupil, or equal opportunity.

Expenditures per Pupil: A Wide Variance.   Expenditures per pupil vary widely, partly because districts are not equally wealthy. States also differ in wealth and correspondingly in expenditures per pupil. The current average annual expenditure per pupil in the United States is $5,029. Alaska, Connecticut, New Jersey, and New York, along with the District of Columbia, all spend over $7,000 per pupil; while Alabama, Mississippi, Idaho, Tennessee, and Utah all spend less than $3,500 per pupil.[7]

Property assessment practices and formulas differ from state to state; hence, one cannot use assessed valuation per pupil as a measure in comparing the wealth of states. More accurate indices are household income and poverty rates. Eight states have household incomes greater than $35,000—Alaska, California, Connecticut, Hawaii, Maryland, Massachusetts, New Hampshire, and New Jersey. Ten states have more than 16 percent of their population below the poverty level—Alabama, Arkansas, District of Columbia, Kentucky, Louisiana, Mississippi, Montana, Oklahoma, Texas, and West Virginia.[8] In general, higher household income results in higher expenditures per pupil.

Property Tax: Proportionate and Regressive.   Property tax is most generally thought of as a proportionate tax—that is, one that taxes according to ability to pay; the more wealth one has in property, the more one pays. Since assessments may be unequal and since frequently the greatest wealth is no longer related to real estate, the property tax can be regressive. **Regressive taxes,** like sales and use taxes, are those that affect low-income groups disproportionately. There is some evidence to support the contention that persons in the lowest-income groups pay a much higher proportion of their income in property taxes than persons in the highest-income groups.

Inequities of the Property Tax: What the Courts Have Said.   Significant support for schools across the nation has been provided by the property tax. However, as has been described in the last several pages, because of this heavy dependence on property taxes for financing, enormous discrepancies in resources and quality have built up between schools located in rich and poor communities.

To illustrate the school finance consequences of differences in local wealth, let's look at a simple example. A school district having an assessed valuation of $30 million and a responsibility for educating 1,000 pupils would have $30,000 of assessed valuation per pupil. Since property taxes are applied to assessed valuations, a district with a high assessed valuation per pupil is in a better position to provide quality education than is one with a low assessed valuation per pupil. If school district A has an assessed valuation of $90 million and 1,000 pupils, for example, and school district B has an assessed valuation of $30 million and 1,000 pupils, a tax rate of $2 per $100 of assessed valuation would produce $1.8 million for education in district A and only $600,000 in district B. School district A could therefore spend $1,800 per pupil, compared with $600 per pupil in school district B, with the same local tax effort.

Can the Property Tax Continue to Be the Primary Base for Financing Schools (the Federal Perspective)? This question was asked of the U.S. Supreme Court in *San Antonio (Texas) Independent School District* v. *Rodriguez* (1979). Keep in mind that the U.S. Constitution does not mention education, so any litigation has to be based on indirect connections. In *Rodriguez* the challenge was initiated under the equal protection clause of the Fourteenth Amendment. This clause prohibits state action that would deny citizens equal protection. The U.S. Supreme Court, in a five-to-four decision, reversed the lower court in *San Antonio Independent School District* v. *Rodriguez* and thus reaffirmed the local property tax as a basis for school financing. Justice Potter Stewart, voting with the majority, admitted that "the method of financing public schools . . . can be fairly described as chaotic and unjust." He did not, though, find it unconstitutional. The majority opinion, written by Justice Lewis F. Powell, Jr., stated: "We cannot say that such disparities are the product of a system that is so irrational as to be invidiously discriminatory." The opinion also noted that the poor are not necessarily concentrated in the poorest districts, that states must initiate fundamental reform in taxation and education, and that the extent to which quality of education varies with expenditures is inconclusive. Justice Thurgood Marshall, in the dissenting opinion, charged that the ruling "is a retreat from our historic commitment to equality of education opportunity."

Using the Property Tax to Finance Schools (the State Perspective). Equal protection challenges have been, or are currently being made at the state level. In some states the plaintiffs have emphasized a claim of equal protection; in others the focus has been on specific language in the education clause. In all cases the challenge is whether the state has fulfilled its constitutional obligation to provide for education. The answer by the state supreme courts in some states has been that education is not a fundamental right, and as long as there is provision for a minimally adequate education the equal protection clause is met. In *Serrano* v. *Priest* the California Supreme Court was called on to determine whether the California public school financing system, with its substantial dependence on local property taxes, violated the Fourteenth Amendment. In a six-to-one decision in 1971 the court held that heavy reliance on unequal local

Relevant Research

State Spending Is Related to Student Achievement

There is continuing discussion and debate about whether spending more money on schools results in greater outcomes with students. As with other topics, the answer one gets depends on the variables considered. The amount of money spent per student can be identified in reports from the National Center for Educational Statistics. However, does a dollar buy the same in New Jersey ($8,645 per pupil) as it does in Alabama ($3,627 per pupil)? Picking the student outcome variable is even more difficult. The measure must be standardized, the student sample must be representative, and the data must be available for all states.

One student outcome measure that has been used frequently is Scholastic Aptitude Test (SAT) scores. But as Wainer (1993) has pointed out, there are a number of problems in using SAT scores to compare across states. For example, the proportion of students in each state that take the SAT varies greatly. A more representative estimate of student performance would be results from the National Assessment of Educational Progress (NAEP). This measure is given to a representative sample of students in each state. When a comparison is made of the ranking of state per-pupil expenditure to student NAEP scores by state, the results indicate that increased spending is associated with higher student achievement. "We find that for every thousand dollars spent, a state's NAEP ranking improves by two places." (p. 24) In other words, using comparable measures, it has been shown that student achievement increases when the per-pupil expenditure increases.

Source: Howard Wainer, "Does Spending Money on Education Help? A Reaction to the Heritage Foundation and the *Wall Street Journal.*" *Educational Researcher* (December, 1993): 22–23.

property taxes "makes the quality of a child's education a function of the wealth of his parents and neighbors." Furthermore, the court declared: "Districts with small tax bases simply cannot levy taxes at a rate sufficient to produce the revenue that more affluent districts produce with a minimum effort." Officially, the California Supreme Court ruled that the system of school financing in California was unconstitutional but did not forbid the use of property taxes as long as the system of finance was neutral in the distribution of resources. Within a year of *Serrano* v. *Priest* (1971), five other courts—in Minnesota, Texas, New Jersey, Wyoming, and Arizona—ruled similarly.

Recent Challenges to School Finance within the States.   The number of court cases related to school finance has increased in recent years. Some states have had new suits initiated, while others are continuing to struggle to respond to earlier court decisions and directives. In 1989 and 1990 several significant state supreme court decisions about school finance were made. In a number of states the education finance systems were knocked down by the courts, and the state legislatures were directed to remedy the wrongs.

In Montana, in *Helena Elementary School District* v. *State* (1989), the Montana Supreme Court ruled that the state's school finance system violated the state constitution's guarantee of equal educational opportunity. The state's constitution article mandates that the state establish an educational system that will develop the full educational potential of each person. In 1990 the court delayed the effects of its decision in order that the legislature could enact a new finance system.[9]

The Kentucky Supreme Court ruled that the entire system of school governance and finance violated the state constitution's mandate for the provision of an efficient system of common schools throughout the state (*Rose* v. *The Council for Better Education Inc.*, 1989). An excerpt from the Kentucky Supreme Court's opinion stated that "The system of common schools must be adequately funded to achieve its goals. The system of common schools must be substantially uniform throughout the state. Each child, *every child*, in this commonwealth must be provided with an equal opportunity to have an adequate education. Equality is the key word here. The children of the poor and the children of the rich, the children who live in poor districts and the children who live in the rich districts must be given the same opportunity and access to an adequate education. This obligation cannot be shifted to local counties and local school districts." The court directed the state legislature to develop a new educational system, which was adopted as the Kentucky Education Reform Act (KERA) in 1990.

It is clear that throughout the 1990s, there will continue to be suits, court actions, and legislative initiatives regarding how to best address funding inequities for public schools. Further, earlier court decisions can be revisited. For example, in a turnaround of earlier decisions, in 1994 the State Supreme Court of Arizona ruled that the state's property-tax-based school financing system was unconstitutional because it creates wide disparities between rich and poor school districts. As has been true in other states, the court is leaving it up to the legislature to rectify the problem.

Undoubtedly, changes are occurring in the state provisions for financial support for education. Equal expenditures per pupil might not, because of other factors, assure equal opportunity, but equal expenditures per pupil do, in fact, enhance the likelihood of equal opportunity.

A System of Taxation and Support for Schools

We should look at each type of tax as a part of a system. Each individual kind of tax has advantages and disadvantages, yet it is unlikely that any one of these taxes used by itself for education will be the answer. In evaluating a system of taxes, one should consider the varying ability of citizens to pay, the economic effects of the taxes on the taxpayer, the benefits that various taxpayers receive, the total yield of the tax, the economy of collection, the degree of acceptance, the convenience of paying, the problems of tax evasion, the stability of the tax, and the general adaptability of the system. It is apparent that systems of taxation are complicated; each is an intricately interdependent network.

Taxation exists to produce revenue. The allocation of revenue is complex; however, the education theme applied to allocation is equality of educational opportunity. State equalization programs were designed to accomplish this objective, and they have had limited success. Many have suggested that the logical solution to the inequities that exist in the ability of states to support education is a massive shift to federal aid.

State Sources of Revenue and Aid.   On the average in the United States, the states provide about 50 percent of the fiscal resources for local schools. This money is referred to as state aid, and within most states all of the money or a portion of this money is used to help achieve equality of opportunity.

The main sources of tax revenue for states have been classified by the Department of Commerce in four groups: sales and gross receipts, income taxes, licenses, and miscellaneous. Sales and gross receipt taxes include taxes on general sales, motor fuels, alcohol, insurance, and amusements; income taxes include both individual and corporate; licenses include those on motor vehicles, corporations, occupations, vehicle operators, hunting, and fishing. The largest miscellaneous classification includes property taxes, severance or extraction of minerals taxes, and death and gift taxes. The two largest sources of state revenues are sales and income taxes.

Sales and Income Taxes.   Sales and income taxes are lucrative sources of state revenue, and it is relatively easy to administer both. The sales tax is collected bit by bit, in a relatively painless way, by the vendor, who is responsible for keeping records. The state income tax can be withheld from wages; hence, collection is eased. Income taxes are referred to as **progressive taxes,** since they frequently are scaled to the ability of the taxpayer to pay. Sales taxes are regressive, since they affect low-income groups disproportionately. All people pay the sales tax at the same rate, so people in low-income groups pay as much tax as people in high-income groups. Part of the regression of the sales taxes and income taxes is direct and certain; they fluctuate with the economy, and they can be regulated by the legislature that must raise the money.

Gaming: A New Source of Revenue.   In 1964 New Hampshire implemented a lottery. By 1994 thirty-one states were operating lotteries. Legalized gambling in its many forms, from casinos and riverboats to horse racing, has become the newest source of state and local revenues. Gambling is an indirect source of revenue in the sense that it is not seen as a direct tax on citizens; instead, the revenues come through taxes on the games. In 1993 gamblers bet a record $394.3 billion. In

The link between lottery proceeds and education is not always well known to the general public.

eleven states part or all of the net proceeds from the lottery is allocated to education. In some states, such as California, the original intent was that these funds would be used for educational enhancements. However, within three years of its implementation, in a tight budget year, the California legislature had incorporated the lottery funds into the base education budget.

A recent study of the Florida lottery found the same thing. In the 1989–1990 school year the level of state funding for education decreased and approximately 56.8 percent of the lottery proceeds were used as a substitute for existing resources. The findings from the study also indicated that there was equity in the distribution of the funds. Clearly lotteries and other games represent a new source of funds.[10] It also is clear that without careful wording in the original statutes and continuous monitoring, these funds will become another revenue stream for the ongoing budget, rather than being set aside for educational enhancements.

State Aid.   State aid for education exists largely for three reasons: The state has the primary responsibility for educating its citizens, the financial ability of local school districts to support education varies widely, and personal wealth is now less related to real property than it once was. State aid can be classified as having general or categorical use. *General aid* can be used by the recipient school district as it desires; *categorical aid* is earmarked for specific purposes. Categorical aid may include, for example, money for transportation, vocational education, driver education, and programs for handicapped children. Frequently, categorical aid is given to encourage specified education programs; in some states these aid programs are referred to as incentive programs. Categorical aid funds may be granted on a matching basis; thus for each dollar of local effort, the state contributes a specified amount. Categorical aid has undoubtedly encouraged development of needed educational programs.

General State Aid: Equality of Opportunity.   Historically, general aid was based on the idea that each child, regardless of place of residence or wealth of the local district, should be entitled to receive a basic education. General state aid was established on the principle of equality of opportunity and is usually administered through a foundation program. A *foundation program* involves determining the dollar value of the basic education opportunities desired in a state, referred to as the foundation level, and determining a minimum standard of local effort, considering local wealth. The foundation concept implies equity for taxpayers as well as equality of opportunity for students.

Foundation Programs: The Way They Work.   Figure 8.7 represents graphically how a foundation program operates. The total length of each bar represents the foundation level of education required per pupil, expressed in dollars. Each school dis-

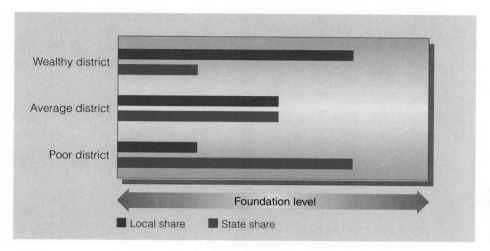

Foundation level

■ Local share   ■ State share

FIGURE 8.7

Equalization and the Foundation Principle

trict must put forth the same minimum local effort to finance its schools; this effort could be a qualifying tax rate that produces the local share of the foundation level. This tax rate will produce more revenue in a wealthy district than it will in a poor district; therefore the poor district will receive more state aid than the wealthy district. Local school districts do not receive general state aid beyond that amount established as the foundation but are permitted in most instances to exceed foundation levels at their own expense.

State Foundation Programs: Limited Effectiveness. The effectiveness of the use of various state foundation programs to achieve fiscal equalization has been limited. A major limitation is that the foundation established is frequently far below the actual expenditure or far below the level needed to provide adequate educational opportunity. For example, if a state established a per-pupil foundation level of $1,500 and the average per-pupil expenditure was $3,000, equalization would not have occurred.

A second limitation is that most general state aid programs do not provide for the different expenditure levels for different pupil needs. Special education and vocational education, for example, both require more money to operate than the usual per-pupil expenditure for the typical elementary or secondary school pupil.

It is possible to replace the property tax with combinations of other sources of revenue for schools. One closely watched initiative took place in Michigan beginning in the summer of 1993 when the legislature abolished the use of property taxes as the major source of school financing without naming an alternative. Educators, the public at large, the Governor, and legislators entered into intensive discussions about the pros and cons of financing education with a new combination of taxes. In March, 1994, a statewide election was called, with one question on the ballot. Nearly 70 percent of the voters approved increasing the sales tax from 4 percent to 6 percent to finance schools. Other sources of revenue will be used as well, but the role of property taxes is greatly diminished. The new Michigan plan also includes movement toward the gradual equalizing of per-pupil expenditures, and sets a minimum $4,200 per pupil.

In summary, the property tax is the largest local revenue source, and sales and income taxes are the largest state revenue sources. State taxes may be utilized to equalize opportunity resulting from unequal local tax bases. The need for local, state, and federal funds to support education through various kinds of taxation necessitates a tax system.

Federal Aid. The United States has a history of federal aid to education, but it has been categorical and not general aid; it has been related to the needs of the nation at the time. Federal aid actually started before the U.S. Constitution was adopted, with the Northwest Ordinance of 1785, which provided land for public schools in "western territories." Such federal aid has continued in a steady progression to the present. Almost two hundred federal aid-to-education laws have been passed since the Northwest Ordinance. The Elementary and Secondary Education Act of 1965 has been discussed elsewhere in this book. Nevertheless, we note here one significant part of the Act: It was categorical, yet it came as close to general aid to education as federal aid ever has, and it therefore established a precedent for ways that federal aid can be used.

Educational Improvement and Consolidation Act (EICA). Federal funding in recent years continued to be categorical until the passage of the Education Improvement and Consolidation Act (EICA) in 1981. The act consolidated twenty-eight separate federally sponsored educational programs into one **block grant.** Left out of the Act were education for the handicapped; vocational, bilingual, and adult education; impact aid; ESEA Title IV civil rights programs; and the Women's Education Equity program. ESEA Title I programs for the disadvantaged were kept as the first title of the new consolidation act, now called Chapter I. Title II of the Act consolidated the aforementioned twenty-eight programs, providing greater discretion for state and local educational agencies. The trend toward block grants is an early indication of possible transformation of the federal role in education.[11]

Federal Aid: The Controversy. Although it is seemingly historically established, federal aid is still controversial. Advocates of federal aid point out that it is a logical answer to the need for providing equality of educational opportunity for all children regardless of wealth or residence. They point out that federal aid to education helps the national defense and general welfare, ultimately, and that these national concerns cannot be adequately pursued at the local or state level. Proponents of federal aid to education hold also that this help does not necessarily mean federal controls, citing the land grant acts and the National Defense Education Act of 1958 as federal aid that was not accompanied by control. They feel that federal aid, through the income tax, is the most equitable way of paying for public education, and for providing equal educational opportunity.

Opponents of federal aid point out that education is a state and a local function. They argue that variations in fiscal ability to pay will always exist and that the distribution of federal funds will not guarantee that whatever differences now exist will be reduced appreciably. They point out that the nation is weakened by its dependency on the federal government for funds, that categorical aid is federal control, and that states can use the income tax as effectively as the federal government.

School Finance Issues in the Late 1990s

The basic issue in school financing is not likely to be different in the late 1990s from what it has been in the past. That issue is making an adequate education equally available to everyone, along with a system of taxation designed to be equitable—that is, a system in which taxpayers are all called on to support education in proportion to their ability to pay, a progressive tax plan. Both equal opportunity and equitable taxation are difficult to achieve, as was illustrated earlier in this chapter. Some trends of the early 1990s have continued into the late 1990s. These trends include increasing enrollments, taxpayer revolt, inflation, financing educational reform, and accountability, which are likely to affect the adequacy of school funding and therefore further complicate the basic issue in school finance—providing an adequate education with equality of opportunity through an equitable system of taxation.

Increasing Enrollments. Enrollment in elementary and secondary schools grew rapidly during the 1950s and 1960s and reached its peak in 1971. From 1971 to 1983, total enrollment decreased rapidly, reflecting the decline in the school-age population over that period. Enrollment reached a low of 39.3 million in 1984. By 2002, enrollment is projected to reach 54 million, an increase of 7 million over ten years.[12]

Increased enrollments have effects on the amount of money needed to support education adequately. While the new surge of students will be somewhat gradual, it will undoubtedly increase expenditures, and increased revenue is very likely to be needed to maintain the current level of expenditures per pupil. Furthermore, according to one educator, "the rising public school enrollments will include larger numbers and percentages of minority, limited-English-proficient, poor, and learning disabled students. All these special categories of students will require extra services to meet their needs."[13] Whether additional revenues will be available to provide educational services to the growing student population remains speculative.

Taxpayer Revolt. A most dramatic instance of taxpayer revolt occurred in California in June 1978 with the passage of Proposition 13, which limited by constitutional amendment the property tax as a source of revenue. Subsequent and similar propositions have been added in other states. The trend is toward tax limitation, which will reduce funds available for education. These efforts, along with a low success rate of local school bond referenda and the closing of school districts for periods of time because of insufficient funds to operate, indicate problems for the funding of public schools.

Funding Educational Reform: Questionable. With enrollments increasing and with inflation, though modest, continuing to be a factor—along with taxpayer revolt—significant increases in funding for educational reform in the 1990s appears to be unlikely.

Accountability. Accountability in education is holding schools responsible for what students learn. This is directly related to the financing of education. Schools

| CASE STUDY | INNOVATIVE WAYS OF FUNDING PUBLIC SCHOOLS: WHAT IS APPROPRIATE? |

*C*olorado Springs School District 11 has approved the placement of commercial advertising on its school buses. National fast food and soft drink company logos now appear on the sides of the buses. While the district has set guidelines for the advertising it will accept, questions abound about the appropriateness of public agencies becoming involved in commercial acts. Some advocate that these are symbols that businesses are interested in education. Clearly, these activities provide the schools with monies they would not have otherwise. On the other side one can ask about the potential for a conflict of interest between the business and the needs of schools as public education entities.

More radical strategies to solve the school funding problem are being tried as well. Districts are experimenting with having certain functions "privatized," which means that instead of the work being done by school district employees, it is contracted out to a private firm. Custodial work, security provision, and bus driving are three of the services that have been privatized in a number of school districts.

In a more extreme example, the day-to-day operations of several schools and school districts have been turned over to private corporations. These for-hire corporations have contracted to run schools for a profit! For example, in 1994 a business, Education Alternatives Inc., agreed to a five-year contract to oversee the running of thirty-two public schools and the education of 25,000 students in Hartford, Connecticut. The only profit for the company will be 50 percent of any money that it saves in running the schools, which is based on the district's regular $200 million budget.

A number of issues and questions about the organization and financing of schools emerge from these many different funding experiments. For example, if the school district cannot maintain its own buildings and sustain student success, what can a for-profit corporation do that will be different? The teaching staff will be the same, the buildings will be the same, and so will the students. If there are "profits" from the use of public dollars, should they be given to a private company? Can a private corporation be held accountable in the same way that we hold public schools accountable?

1. What are your views on these issues?
2. What changes do you believe should be made in school funding?

in the 1990s will continue to be called on to be accountable. Although there are many definitions of the term *accountability*, in education it means that schools must devise a way of relating the vast expenditure made for education to the educational results. For many years the quality of education was measured by the number of dollars spent or the processes of education used. In other words, a school system that had a relatively high cost per pupil or used educational techniques judged to be effective was considered an excellent system. Seldom was the effectiveness of school systems judged by student outcomes—the educational achievements of students. Now those outcomes and a clear record of the cost of them must be accounted for.

Roots of Accountability.   Accountability has its roots in two fundamental modern problems. One is the continuous escalation of educational costs, and closely related is the loss of faith in educational results. The failure of the American educational system, particularly in the cities and in some remote rural areas, has been accurately documented. The expectations of citizens for their children have not been met. Although American public schools historically have done the best job of any nation in the world in providing education for *all the children of all the people,* they still have failed for some of their constituents. Educational accountability is necessary.

When the Elementary and Secondary Education Act of 1965 went into effect, the federal government issued its first formal call for accountability; it asked to receive documented results of educational attainment.

Becoming Accountable.   How can school systems become accountable? First, they must specify goals. In other words, if one goal of an elementary school is "to have pupils learn to read," then this goal must be spelled out specifically for each grade or child, whichever makes better sense, and success in meeting the goal must be measured and reported. Only in this way can results be conveyed to the public. Some states are requiring a "school report card" to be submitted to the public annually. The report cards provide information about student achievement by subject, as measured by standardized tests, along with financial and other relevant data about the school district.

Expenses and Educational Results.   The second aspect of accountability, that dealing with accounting for expenses related to educational results, is easier to achieve because of modern technology. Financial accounting systems that are designed specifically to record expenditures on each educational program can effectively reveal the costs of educational results. When costs are known, one must measure them against what has been accomplished in performance. Advanced computer technology has increased the sophistication of accountability reporting systems; thus better informed educational decisions are possible, and the way is cleared for regaining the public's confidence in the educational establishment.

Teachers: Importance for Accountability.   Teachers play an important role in the quest for accountability. They are the primary contact with students, and they are responsible for instruction and student achievement. Thus they are expected to do their utmost to motivate students to learn and achieve. Accountability rests on data; therefore teachers need to keep accurate records with respect to achievement, particularly if standardized tests are not utilized.

Global Perspectives: International Comparisons in Spending for Schools.

There are continuing debates about the amount of investment the United States makes in public education and how well it compares with what other countries invest. International comparisons are difficult to make. Teacher salaries are different, the way budgets and educational functions are organized is different, and measuring student success is difficult. Yet the comparisons need to be made. As can be seen in Table 8.3 on page 220 the United States is much wealthier than other countries. The number of students per teacher is higher in

| TABLE 8.3 | Gross Domestic Product per Capita, Educational Expenditures, and Student-Teacher Ratios, Excluding Higher Education, 15 Industrial Countries |

	Gross Domestic Product per Capita		Education Expenditures per Capita		Expenditures per Pupil		Number of Students per Teacher	
	Dollars	Rank	Dollars	Rank	Dollars	Rank	Ratio	Rank
Australia	13,523	6	646	9	2,060	15	15.7	8
Austria	11,582	15	625	11	2,972	7	9.5	2
Belgium	11,755	14	613	12	2,492	9	10.5	4
Canada	17,355	2	1,153	1	4,054	21	6.2	10
Denmark	13,218	8	969	2	3,997	3	12.2	6
France	12,791	10	723	7	2,486	10	16.9	11
Italy	12,136	13	528	15	2,320	14	11.0	5
Japan	13,137	9	635	10	2,379	13	20.0	14
Netherlands	12,196	12	723	6	2,495	8	15.5	7
Norway	16,161	3	966	3	3,636	5	8.6	1
Sweden	14,052	5	911	4	4,279	1	10.3	3
Switzerland	15,570	4	715	8	3,733	4	NA	—
United Kingdom	12,529	11	604	13	2,474	11	15.7	8
United States	18,297	1	860	5	3,398	6	18.4	13
West Germany	13,296	7	536	14	2,450	12	18.3	12
Unweighted Avg.	13,840		747		3,015		14.15	

Note: Expenditure data are for preschool through high school but exclude capital outlay and debt service. NA = not available. Original data are from OECD and UNESCO reports for 1986 and 1987. Student-teacher ratios are adjusted for part-time vocational enrollment. Various other adjustments were made to enhance comparability of the original data.

Source: Adapted from Nelson (1991), pp. 32–34, Tables 4–6 by Levine, Daniel U. "Educational Spending: International Comparisons." *Theory Into Practice 33* (2), (Spring, 1994): 126–131.

the United States than for most other developed countries. How well is the United States doing in investing in education in comparison to other countries? Clearly we are at least average, and in many ways doing well. But your answer will depend on which data you use and how you interpret them.[14]

Summary and Implications

Teaching does not take place in a classroom that is an island, disconnected from the rest of the system. All parts are intertwined. What a teacher does in his or her classroom is affected by the rest of the school, the principal, the district, the state, and the federal government. Conversely, what you do in your classroom will affect the rest of the system. Contrary to the stereotype associated with the "self-contained" classroom, American education is a highly complex system.

You need to understand how schools and school districts are organized. To be effective, you will need to know the names of the key administrators and their areas of responsibility. In time you will need to know and be able to work with these key people. Also, keep in mind that very few decisions are made in isolation from district, state, and federal rules, regulations, and policies. Most aspects of schooling have been addressed at one time or another by the various levels in the organizational charts presented in this chapter.

Another point relates to the financing of education. The brief overview of issues related to taxation, aid programs, and developing a fair and equitable system for financing education should bring you to an appreciation of the highly complex and difficult challenge we have. There are no simple solutions that will be correct. Increasing sales taxes versus tax limitations, general aid versus categorical aid, and local versus state versus federal support are basic questions.

Discussion Questions

1. Some education experts are advocating a shift in thinking from "top-down" and "bottom-up" to a *horizontal* perspective. What are some possible implications of making this shift?
2. Do you think that school-based management will be effective in improving education at the elementary and secondary levels? Why or why not?
3. How has the local control of education eroded? Why has it eroded?
4. How can teachers affect the operations of the local school district?
5. What are the advantages of using the sales and income taxes to fund elementary and secondary education instead of relying on the property tax?
6. What are some of the likely implications of using lotteries and limited stakes gambling to fund schools?
7. What are three trends that could seriously affect the adequacy of school funding? Why?

Journal/Portfolio Development

1. In order to understand more about how site-based decision making systems work, interview a council member and, if possible, observe a site-council meeting. Questions to consider include: What are the areas where the council has decision-making authority? When is it advisory? Does it have budget-making authority? What role do teachers play on the council? What do you think are the strengths and issues in having site-based councils?
2. The Republican Contract with America advocated major cuts in federal support for education programs, including free and reduced lunches and student loans. Select one of the federal education programs that you are interested in. Collect information about the program, including the amount of money budgeted by Congress and how much money the typical school/classroom/child receives. Then compile notes about the debate for and against continuation of the program and its desired level of funding. Develop a summary and conclusion of where you stand on the need for the program and the size of its budget. A useful place to gain insight into the debate can be television programs such as the Sunday morning news interview shows, CNN, MacNeil/Lehrer, and CSPAN. Insert your notes in your folio under a topic heading such as "Federal government's role in education."

School-Based Experiences

1. Visit a school and develop an organization chart for the school. Place the names of people and their roles on the chart. For one or more persons in each role group (teacher, custodian, secretary) ask

them who their supervisor is. Also, ask them if there are other persons who monitor their work. The purpose here is to determine the line and staff relationships. It is quite likely that you will find that many people have a number of relationships.

2. Seek an opportunity to study a school budget. Determine the different sources of revenue (local, state, and grants). What are the biggest line items?

Which items does the principal have authority over? Are there some monies that are discretionary for teachers? Note that in most schools, especially high schools, there will be a surprising number of activities that generate cash. Inquire about the implications of having cash on hand, and ask how these amounts are secured and what the policies are in relation to their uses.

Notes

1. Roald F. Campbell, ed; Gerald E. Stroufe; and Donald H. Layton, *Strengthening State Departments of Education.* Chicago: University of Chicago Midwest Administration, 1967, 10.

2. American Association of School Administrators and the National Associations of Elementary and Secondary School Principals, *School-Based Management: A Strategy for Better Learning.* Arlington, VA: AASA, 15–17.

3. *Directory for the National Association for Year-Round Education.* P.O. Box 711386, San Diego, CA.

4. Bobette Reed and William L. Dandridge, *Minority Leaders for Independent Schools.* Boston: National Association of Independent Schools.

5. Beatrice H. Cameron; Kenneth E. Underwood; and Jim C. Fortune, "Politics and Power: How You're Selected and Elected to Lead This Nation's Schools." *The American School Board Journal* (January 1988).

6. Cameron, Underwood, and Fortune, "It's Ten Years Later, and You've Hardly Changed at All," 20.

7. *Statistic in Brief, April, 1994.* Washington, DC: National Center for Education Statistics, 7.

8. *Digest of Educational Statistics, 1993.* Washington, DC: National Center for Education Statistics, 28.

9. *Helena Elementary School District No.1* v. *State,* 769 P.2d 684 (Mont. 1989).

10. Steven Stark; Craig R. Wood; and David S. Honeyman, "The Florida Education Lottery: Its Use as a Substitute for Existing Funds and Its Effects on the Equity of School Funding." *Journal of Education Finance* 18 (Winter, 1993): 231–242.

11. Joel S. Berke and Mary T. Moore. "A Developmental View of the Current Federal Government Role in Elementary and Secondary Education," *Phi Delta Kappan* 63 (January 1982): 337.

12. William J. Hussar, *Projections of Education Statistics to 2003.* Washington, DC: National Center for Educational Statistics, 1.

13. Allan Odden, "Sources of Funding for Education Reform." *Phi Delta Kappan* 67 (January 1986): 340.

14. Daniel U. Levine, "Educational Spending: International Comparisons." *Theory Into Practice* 33 (2) (Spring, 1994): 126–131.

Bibliography

Bakalis, Michael J. "Power and Purpose in American Education." *Phi Delta Kappan* 65 (September 1983): 7–13.

Burns, Leonard T., and Howes, Jeanne. "Handing Control to Local Schools: Site-Based Management Sweeps the Country." *The School Administrator* 45 (7) (August 1988): 8–10.

Campbell, Roald F. et al. *The Organization and Control of American Schools.* 6th ed. Columbus, OH: Merrill Pub. Co. 1990.

Elmore, Richard F. and Associates. *Restructuring Schools: The Next Generation of Educational Reform.* San Francisco: Jossey-Bass. 1990.

Gordon, James, Anthony, Ward and Patricia, eds. *Who Pays for Student Diversity?: Population Change and Educational Policy.* Newbury Park, CA: Corwin Press, 1992.

Kirst, Michael. "Sustaining the Momentum of State Educational Reform: The Link Between Assessment and Financial Support." *Phi Delta Kappan 67* (January 1986): 341–345.

Odden, Allan R., ed. *Rethinking School Finance: An Agenda for the 1990's.* San Francisco: Jossey-Bass, 1992.

Slavin, Robert E. "After the Victory: Making Funding Equity Make a Difference." *Theory Into Practice 33* (2) (Spring 1994): 98–102.

Swanson, Austin D., and King, Richard A. *School Finance: Its Economics and Politics.* New York: Longman, 1991.

Legal Aspects of Education

Focus Questions

1   What are the different sources of law, and how does the judicial process work?
2   What rights are ensured under the First and Fourteenth Amendments of the U.S. Constitution?
3   Under what conditions can religious activities take place in public schools?
4   What is the difference between *de jure* and *de facto* segregation?
5   What is affirmative about Affirmative Action?
6   Does the law require that handicapped children be placed in regular classrooms?

Key Terms and Concepts

Affirmative action: A plan by which personnel policies and hiring practices do not discriminate against women and members of minority groups.

Child benefit theory: A criterion used by the U.S. Supreme Court to determine whether services provided to public and nonpublic school students benefit children and not the school or religion. If they benefit only the children, the courts have ruled that the services may be funded by public funds.

Compulsory education: School attendance that is required by law on the theory that it is for the benefit of the state or commonwealth to educate all the people.

***De facto* segregation:** The segregation of students resulting from circumstances such as housing patterns rather than from school policy or law.

***De jure* segregation:** The segregation of students on the basis of law, school policy, or a practice designed to accomplish such separation.

Desegregation: The process of correcting past practices of racial or any other form of illegal segregation.

Discrimination: The determination that an individual or a group of individuals has been denied constitutional rights.

Integration: The process of mixing students of different races in school to overcome segregation.

Resegregation: A situation following desegregation in which segregation returns.

Reverse discrimination: A situation in which a majority or an individual of a majority is denied certain rights because of preferential treatment provided to a minority or an individual of a minority.

This chapter deals with the legal basis for and control of education at the federal, state, and local levels. Attention is directed toward the different types and sources of law, and the organization of courts and the current interpretations of the Constitution, particularly as they relate to the separation of church and state, desegregation, affirmative action, and education for the handicapped. Each of these topics includes a discussion of relevant and important rulings of the U.S. Supreme Court.

Legal Aspects of Education

There is a caution that is important for you to keep in mind while reading this chapter and whenever you are thinking about legal issues. As was pointed out in the introduction to Part 3 of this text, there are different assumptions and different rules—different frameworks—for making decisions. In this chapter, as well as the next, the framework is a legal one. Do not try simply to apply some other framework to interpret the issues that are presented here and expect to necessarily come up with the same decision. For example, a "common sense" framework, or some form of "professional judgment" framework about what is best for students will not necessarily give you the same decisions that have come from legal reasoning. The legal framework really is based in the "letter and word" of the law. When the words are questioned the courts will decide on an interpretation. And that decision will be carefully and closely linked to decisions made in past cases. Educational philosophies and everyday "logic" are not the basis for the reasoning of courts, nor are abstract definitions of what is "right." The courts' legal logic is based on precedent, as well as the rules of procedure and evidence that have been handed down from court to court and decision to decision.

Legal Forms and Structures

There are several sources of laws at the federal and state levels, and there are several processes for addressing disputes. Some, but not all, laws are developed out of the legislative process. These are referred to as *enabling*; they provide opportunity, or make it possible for educators to do certain things. Also, laws may impose mandates or prohibitions. Once the legislation is enacted into law, if a question of interpretation is raised, then the judicial process is engaged. The judicial process can be used also when there is the appearance that a law has been violated.

   To help you understand the legal aspects of education we first briefly describe the different sources of laws and the basic structure of the judicial system. Then, when you read about an interpretation of the Tenth Amendment of the U.S. Constitution, or what a state supreme court decided in a certain case, you will hopefully have a background for understanding how the whole legal system works.

Sources of Law

There are several different forms of law in the United States. Some have authority over all citizens and parts of the country, while others only apply to a specific state, type of school, or type of student and program. Some have been constructed through the democratic process of legislation and others are simply announced by designated authorities. In all cases you as an educator need to be attentive to the implication of laws for determining what you can, cannot, and should do. Five different sources of law are presented here: (1) constitution, (2) legislation, (3) case law, (4) executive order and attorney general opinion, and (5) administrative agencies.

Constitution. The U.S. Constitution and each state's constitution provide the overarching framework within which all school operational decisions are made. All policies and practices must be within the boundaries and intents of the state and U.S. constitutions. The U.S. Constitution has authority over all state constitutions in those areas that it addresses either directly or indirectly. Constitutions can be added to or changed by con-

The United States Constitution laid the groundwork for the notion of equal access to education for all.

structing and having amendments approved. Interestingly, there is no mention of education in the U.S. Constitution. Since nothing is said, the interpretation has been that decisions about the provision of education are primarily a state responsibility. The key question then, is What does each state's constitution say about education?

Legislation. New laws or *statutes* are constructed through the legislative process. National laws are enacted by the U.S. Congress, and each state legislature enacts laws for that state. Other levels of government, such as county and city, enact laws that apply within their jurisdiction. In general, there is a nesting of authority with the higher level of state and ultimately the federal level being able to set the laws of the land.

In the case of education, since nothing was stated, there is no constitutional authority assigned directly to the U.S. government. In order to affect education from the federal level, statutes have to be written or court cases initiated. In recent decades the federal government has increasingly involved itself in education through authoring statutes that derive authority through the offering of money or the threat of taking it away. Congress also impacts education through its authority to regulate "interstate commerce." Through this power Congress can regulate even if the entity is not receiving federal funding. Lawsuits threatened and initiated at the federal level have been on the increase as well. A clear example of federal influence in this way can be seen in the efforts to desegregate/integrate schools.

Keep in mind that the legislative process in a democratic society entails committees, public comment, draft language, and compromise, so that the final wording of a statute may not be clear or necessarily consistent. The federal government is steadily increasing its rate of producing statutes that affect education.

Case Law. Court decisions offer another source of law. When a particular question is addressed by the judicial system and a decision is made, that decision becomes a part of the record, and some cases set precedents. Subsequently when similar situations arise, there is a tendency to refer back to the earlier decision and decide the current case in the same way; thus the name *case law*. Courts rely heavily on this form of the law in making decisions. As you will read later in this chapter, in the last several decades case law at the federal level has played a major role in shaping education. Keep in mind though that for many questions different "lower" courts can make different decisions; thus there may not be one decision that applies to the entire nation until the U.S. Supreme Court renders the final decision.

Executive Orders and Attorney General Opinions. The President of the United States and state governors can issue executive orders that apply to education. These orders can have the effect of law until such time that they are withdrawn or changed by legislative or judicial action. Often the U.S. Attorney General or a state attorney general will be asked to offer an opinion about the likely legality of a statute or educational practice. This is an advisory opinion only and may or may not be what ultimately would be decided by the judicial system. However, these opinions do save time and can help to advise and clarify points that would likely be supported in a court review.

Administrative Agencies. Another form of law is authored by the many federal and state agencies that receive their authority through constitutional and legislative law. These administrative agencies issue guidelines, rules, and regulations, which in most cases become the details for making statutes operational. All of these "rules and regs" must be consistent with the statute on which they are based. They also add up to many pages of fine print that educators need to understand. For example, when you sign your first teaching contract, that will be a legal agreement between the employing school district/agency and you. Read it carefully. There will be reference to the law and, more than likely, there will be references to the district employee handbook, or district personnel policies. As we will explain in Chapter 10, these administrative documents are legal statements too.

Judicial Systems and Process

When there are disputes about whether a particular educational practice or statute is legal, the courts are asked to make a determination of the facts, review related laws, and render a decision. The first role of the judicial system is *interpretive;* the courts review relevant parts of federal and state constitutions, statutes, and case law, and draw a conclusion about what was meant and what can or cannot be done. In some cases the court will respond by writing new law.

This judicial process usually begins with a suit and trial that is heard by a *trial court,* in other words, the court of original jurisdiction. The problem, practice, or point of dispute is presented along with related facts. Relevant parts of the constitution, statutes, and case law are presented to support each side of the case. Then the court renders, usually through a jury, a decision. This decision can be appealed to a "higher court." If one of the parties is dissatisfied, the decision can be appealed to an *appellate court,* where one or more judges will review the case. If it is appealed further, ultimately the Supreme Court makes the final ruling on the legality of the point being disputed.

In the United States there are two basic judicial systems: (1) the federal court system, and (2) the state court systems. In general there are clear differences in jurisdiction. However, sometimes there are overlaps and disagreements between the two systems.

Federal Court System. Article III, Section I of the U.S. Constitution authorizes the Supreme Court and gives authority to Congress to create other federal courts. There are federal courts with special jurisdictions such as the Tax Court, Claims Court, and the Court of International Trade. General jurisdiction is covered by three levels—district courts (which are the trial courts), circuit courts of appeal, and the Supreme Court. Each state has at least one district court, and large states such as California and New York have four district courts. Decisions at this level are usually made by one judge.

At the federal appeals level, there are twelve regional circuit courts of appeal, and one other that has national jurisdiction to handle specific claims for areas such as copyrights and international trade. These courts have from three to fifteen judges. A federal appeals court decision only applies to the state from which the appeal came; this can be a source of confusion since different appeals courts may make different decisions in regard to similar disputes.

The highest court is the U.S. Supreme Court. There is no appeal beyond this court. The Supreme Court's decisions apply across the nation and can only be changed through Congress's amending federal statutes or by subsequent decisions of the Court. One of the reasons that the U.S. Supreme Court has such an impact on education is that the Court only has jurisdiction is cases in which a state or a public official is a party to the dispute. Since education is delivered by public schools, the U.S. Constitution and the federal courts have become a vehicle for various interests to address their concerns.

State Court Systems. In structure the state court system parallels the federal system. The provisions in each state's constitution address the structure and authority for that state's judicial system. State courts can review whatever types of controversies that state's laws allow. In most states the highest court is the supreme court, although in a few states it is called the Court of Appeals. This court normally reviews the decisions of lower courts of appeal. At the next level down are appeals courts, and at the lowest level are the trial courts, usually referred to as district courts, circuit courts, or superior courts. There can be special jurisdiction courts too, such as juvenile, probate, and small claims courts. Normally, the state judicial system only addresses issues related to that state's constitution and that state's statutes, while the federal judicial system addresses issues of federal statute and the U.S. Constitution. Thus, a key decision at the beginning of a legal challenge is whether to use federal or state laws and courts.

Legal Provisions for Education

The educational systems of the United States, both public and nonpublic, are governed by law. The U.S. Constitution is the fundamental law for the nation, and state constitutions provide the basic law for each state. A state legislature has no right to change the Constitution. When state legislatures make laws that apply to education, these laws must be in accordance with both the U.S. Constitution and the applicable state constitutions. The enabling and legislative agents of education are illustrated in the top portion of Figure 9.1 on page 230. The lower portion of Figure 9.1 shows interpretive and administrative agents. Conflicts in this system of governance are not unusual. In such instances, state and federal court systems make legal interpretations that form a body of case, or common, law.

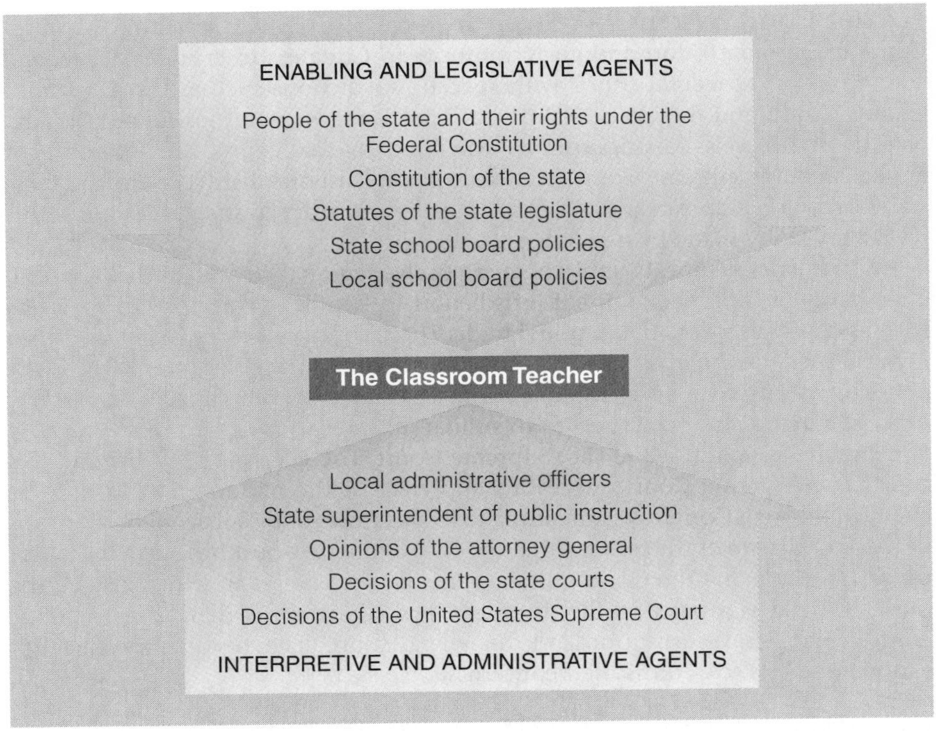

ENABLING AND LEGISLATIVE AGENTS

People of the state and their rights under the Federal Constitution

Constitution of the state

Statutes of the state legislature

State school board policies

Local school board policies

The Classroom Teacher

Local administrative officers

State superintendent of public instruction

Opinions of the attorney general

Decisions of the state courts

Decisions of the United States Supreme Court

INTERPRETIVE AND ADMINISTRATIVE AGENTS

FIGURE 9.1

Sources of Legal Control in American Education as They Affect the Classroom Teacher

U.S. Constitution

The rights assured to citizens of the United States by the U.S. Constitution are valid, practical, and enforceable in public schools as well. However, since much of the Bill of Rights only applies to public officials, the extent and conditions under which it applies to private schools has been a continuing source of debate and judicial interpretation. In general, when nonpublic schools accept public money, then they must abide by the requirements that accompany that acceptance. For example, they may not have discriminatory practices. However, accepting public monies does not necessarily mean that a nonpublic school has to comply with all aspects of the U.S. Constitution. The power of state government in educational matters was made quite clear by the U.S. Supreme Court as a part of its opinion in *Pierce* v. *Society of Sisters* (1925), discussed later in this chapter. The opinion stated:

> No question is raised concerning the power of the State reasonably to regulate all schools, to inspect, supervise, and examine them, their teachers, and pupils; to require that all children of proper age attend some school; that teachers shall be of good moral character and patriotic disposition; that certain studies plainly essential to good citizenship must be taught; and nothing be taught which is manifestly inimical to public welfare.

The following subsections explain how the Tenth, First, and Fourteenth Amendments of the U.S. Constitution relate to the governance of education, public and private, in the United States.

Tenth Amendment. The U.S. Constitution does not specifically provide for public education; however, the Tenth Amendment has been interpreted as granting this power to the states. The amendment specifies that "The powers not delegated to the United States by the Constitution, nor prohibited by it to the States, are reserved to the States respectively, or to the people." Therefore education is legally the responsibility and the function of each of the fifty states. Education in the United States is not nationalized as it is in many other nations of the world.

Each state, reflecting its responsibility for education in its state, has provided for education either in its constitution or its basic statutory law. For example, Section 1, Article X of the Illinois Constitution reads:

> A fundamental goal of the People of the State is the educational development of all persons to the limits of their capabilities.
>
> The State shall provide for an efficient system of high quality educational institutions and services. Education in public schools through the secondary level shall be free. There may be such other free education as the General Assembly provides by law.
>
> The State has the primary responsibility for financing the system of public education.

For example, the current Michigan Constitution states in Section 2, Article VIII:

> The Legislature shall maintain and support a system of free public elementary and secondary schools as defined by law. Each school district shall provide for the education of its pupils without discrimination as to religion, creed, race, color, or national origin.

The Utah Constitution, Section 1, Article X reads:

> The Legislature shall provide for the establishment and maintenance of a uniform system of public schools, which shall be open to all children of the State, and be free from sectarian control.

Through such statements the people of the various states commit themselves to a responsibility for education. The state legislatures are obliged to fulfill this commitment. While the interpretation of the Tenth Amendment places the responsibility for education on the states, the rights of citizens of the United States are protected by the Constitution and cannot be violated by any state.

First Amendment. The First Amendment ensures freedom of speech, of religion, and of the press, as well as the right to petition. It specifies:

> Congress shall make no law respecting an establishment of religion, or prohibiting the free exercise thereof; or abridging the freedom of speech, or of the press; or the right of the people peaceably to assemble, and to petition the Government for redress of grievances.

The application of the First Amendment to public education as considered in this chapter deals primarily with the establishment clause: "Congress shall make no law respecting an establishment of religion." In addition to ensuring other freedoms, the First Amendment ensures free practice of religion, which will be discussed in this chapter as well. The "free speech" clause of the First Amendment will be addressed more heavily in the next chapter, which focuses on teacher and student rights.

CASE STUDY   THE COPYRIGHT LAW APPLIES TO TEACHERS

Teachers constantly come across poems, charts, stories, photographs, and computer programs that they would like to use in their teaching. Most of the time, the material will have on it a copyright statement, or a circled Ⓣ indicating that there is a registered trademark. Is it legal for a teacher to make one or more copies of this material? Legal research related to copyrights provides the answer.

Two primary sources establish the foundation quickly: The Copyright Act of 1976 and a 1991 federal court decision involving Kinko's Graphic Corporation and eight textbook publishers. The Copyright Act grants owners of copyrighted material the sole right to reproduce all or part of the work, to distribute copies, to prepare new versions based on the original work, and to perform and display the work publically. For a corporation, copyright protection lasts for seventy-five years from the date of first publication. For an individual it is the length of the author's life plus fifty years.

The court case between Kinko's and the eight textbook publishers reconfirmed the law; that is, reproduction of copyrighted materials requires that proper permissions be obtained and, if required, fees paid. The court decision also increased sensitivity to the fact that copyrights apply to multimedia, computer disks, and video and compact disk technologies.

What about a teacher who wants to make a single copy? As with many other legal questions, there are some areas where the answer is clear cut, and others where there is need for interpretation. In the Copyright Act, Congress made a provision for educators through what is called the "fair use" guideline. First of all, purchasing something that is copyrighted does not bring with it the right to make many copies. Nor does saying that it is for "educational use." However, a teacher can make a single copy of a brief part of a copyrighted work for teaching or research purposes. Multiple copies (not to exceed one per pupil) may be made for one course only if the copying meets the tests of *brevity* and *spontaneity*.

Examples of brevity would be a poem that is fewer than 250 words or an excerpt of prose that is fewer than 1,000 words or 10 percent of the work. Spontaneity means that there was inspiration and decision to use the work at a teachable moment that made it unreasonable to expect a timely reply to request for permission to copy. Another requirement in the clause is that each copy includes a notice of the copyright. Keep in mind, however, that the fair use clause is not an excuse to circumvent the Copyright Law.

Secondary sources of information about this law can be very useful to teachers. A good place to begin is with the retail copying service you use regularly. They will have guidelines for photocopying, and most stores will have standardized forms that you can use to obtain permission to make multiple copies. The larger copying services will have personnel to help you with obtaining permission, and in some cases may already have such permission on file.

In summary, the Copyright Law does apply to teachers. Teachers can make a single copy for teaching or research purposes, but in general the operating rule is, "no copying of copyrighted material without permission." The right thing to do is plan ahead and use the various services available to obtain permission. After all, one of the valued traditions in America is the creativity of its people. Their efforts should be recognized, and they are protected by law. What are your thoughts on this subject?

For information about copyrights and permissions related to textbooks contact, Association of American Publishers, Inc., 220 East 23rd St., New York, NY 10010–4685.

Fourteenth Amendment.

The Fourteenth Amendment protects specified privileges of citizens. It reads in part:

> No state shall make or enforce any law which shall abridge the privileges or immunities of citizens of the United States; nor shall any State deprive any person of life, liberty, or property without due process of law; nor deny to any person within its jurisdiction the equal protection of the laws.

The application of the Fourteenth Amendment to public education as considered in this chapter deals primarily with the equal protection clause: "nor shall any State . . . deny to any person within its jurisdiction the equal protection of the laws." Equal educational opportunity is protected under the Fourteenth Amendment. In effect, the rights of citizens of the United States are ensured by the Constitution and cannot be violated by state laws or action.

State and Local Governance

State and local agencies play major roles in the governance of education. States have constitutions, with provisions for education as granted to them by the Tenth Amendment. State legislatures provide the laws that govern education within their respective states. Local school districts have boards of education whose major function is to develop policy for the local school district—policy that must be in harmony with both state and federal law.

State Legislatures.

State legislatures are generally responsible for creating, operating, managing, and maintaining state school systems. The legislators are the state policymakers for education. State departments of education are created by legislatures to serve as professional advisors and to execute state policy. State legislatures, though powerful agencies, also operate under controls. The governors of many states can veto school legislation as they can other legislation; and the attorney general and the state judiciary system, when called on, will rule on the constitutionality of educational legislation.

State legislatures make decisions about how education is organized in the state; the certification standards and tenure rights of teachers; programs of study; standards of building construction for health and safety; financing of schools, including tax structure and distribution; and compulsory attendance laws.

State legislatures, in their legislative deliberations about the schools, are continually importuned by special-interest groups. These groups, realizing that the legislature is the focus of legal control of education, can exert considerable influence on individual legislators. Some of the representative influential groups are illustrated in Figure 9.2 on page 234.

It is not uncommon for over a thousand bills to be introduced each year in a state legislative session. Many of these bills originate with special-interest groups. In the past few years, state legislatures have dealt with educational bills on a wide range of topics, including: accountability, state aid, textbooks, adult basic education, length of the school year, legal holidays, lotteries, teacher and student testing, "no-pass-no-play," and school standards of various sorts.

Local Boards of Education.

Local school boards are governmental units of the state, are created by the state, and are responsible to it for educating pupils

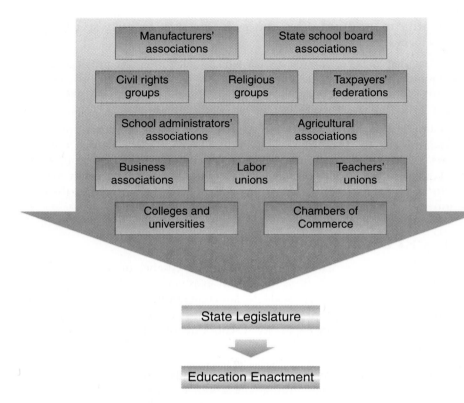

FIGURE 9.2

**Influences on Legislative
Decision Making**

within specified local school districts. Their major function is the development of policy for the local school district—policy that must be in harmony with both federal and state law. They have only those powers granted or implied by statute that are necessary to carry out their responsibilities. Powers usually granted or implied to local school boards include the power to act as follows:

- Obtain revenue
- Maintain schools
- Purchase sites and build buildings
- Purchase materials and supplies
- Organize and provide programs of studies
- Employ necessary workers and regulate their services
- Admit and assign pupils to schools and control their conduct

Church and State

Traditionally, the United States has strongly supported separation of church and state. Yet drawing clear lines of demarcation in terms of what can and cannot be done in schools has continued to be difficult. In part, the difficulty is due to what is and is not stated literally in the U.S. Constitution. For example, separation of church and state is not explicit in the First Amendment; instead, that is the way that Thomas Jefferson and most courts have interpreted the establishment clause. The principle was designed by our forefathers to ensure each citizen freedom to practice the religion of his or her choice. The argument then follows that education, a governmental function that is necessary if an effective democracy is to survive, must be carried on so as to preserve this basic right of religious freedom.

Our nation also has a strong religious heritage. In colonial times, education was primarily a religious matter; furthermore, much of this education was conducted in private religious schools. Many private schools today are still under religious sponsorship. Approximately 13 percent of the total school population is now enrolled in nonpublic parochial and secular schools.

Court cases concerned with separation of church and state most frequently involve both the First and Fourteenth Amendments of the U.S. Constitution. The First Amendment is interpreted as being applicable to the states by the Fourteenth Amendment. For example, a state law requiring a daily prayer to be read in classrooms throughout the state could be interpreted as "depriving persons of liberty" (see the Fourteenth Amendment due process clause) and as the state establishing a religion, or at least "prohibiting the free exercise thereof" (see the First Amendment establishment clause). States are not permitted to make laws that abridge the privileges of citizens, and the right to the free practice of religion must be insured.

Court cases related to the separation of church and state can be classified in three categories: (1) those dealing with the use of public funds to support religious education, (2) those dealing with the practice of religion in public schools, and (3) those dealing with the rights of parents to provide private education for their children. Key cases related to each of these categories are presented next.

Public Funds and Parochial Education. The use of public funds to support parochial schools has been questioned on many occasions. Typically, state constitutions deny public funds to sectarian institutions or schools. However, public funds have been used to provide transportation for students to church schools and to provide textbooks for students in parochial schools. From the 1960s on, there has been renewed attention given to the use of public funds for parochial education. Other topics directly related to the use of public funds for parochial education include tuition tax credits and child benefit theory. A sampling of these cases and issues are provided here to illustrate the reasoning and to assess trends in this difficult area. The use of funds for these purposes has been challenged in many instances.

Public Funds Provide Transportation for Students of Church Schools. The landmark case on the use of public funds to provide transportation for students to church schools was *Everson* v. *Board of Education,* ruled on by the U.S. Supreme Court in 1947. The Court held that in using tax-raised funds to reimburse parents for bus fares expended to transport their children to church schools, a New Jersey school district did not violate the establishment clause of the First Amendment. The majority of the members of the Court viewed the New Jersey statute permitting free bus transportation to parochial school children as "public welfare legislation" to help get the children to and from school safely and expeditiously. Since the *Everson* decision, the highest courts in a number of states, under provisions in their own constitutions, have struck down enactments authorizing public funds to bus children attending denominational schools; others have upheld such enactments.

For example, in 1975 the U.S. Supreme Court affirmed a federal district court decision in Missouri that although a state may provide free transportation to parochial school students (*Everson* v. *Board of Education*), principles of equal protection do not require a state to do so merely because such services are provided to public school pupils. Thus a law may be in harmony with the U.S. Constitution but not with the state constitution.

Public Funds Provide Textbooks for Private Schools. A similar question exists concerning the use of public funds to provide textbooks for private schools. The landmark case originated in Louisiana, where a statute provided for textbooks to be supplied to nonpublic school children free of charge. The statute had been upheld by a state court on the theory that the children, and not the nonpublic schools, were the beneficiaries.

In *Cochran* v. *Louisiana State Board of Education* (1930) the U.S. Supreme Court held the Louisiana textbook statute valid under the Fourteenth Amendment. The Court discounted the taxpayers' contention that tax-raised funds for furnishing textbooks to private school pupils constituted a tax for a private rather than a public purpose and a deprivation of taxpayers' money without due process of law.

In a later case (*Board of Education of Central School District No. 1, Town of Greenbush* v. *Allen*, 1968) the Court upheld the constitutionality of a New York textbook statute. The New York law required boards of education, on individual request, to lend textbooks free to children in grades 7 through 12 in private schools if these schools complied with the state compulsory attendance law.

The Supreme Court, in its decisions in the *Everson* and *Cochran* cases, made it clear that providing transportation or textbooks per se does not violate the First Amendment.

The *Lemon* Test: Excessive Entanglement.

The *Lemon* test, emanating from *Lemon* v. *Kurtzman* (1971) in Pennsylvania, asks for answers to three questions: (1) Does the act have a secular purpose? (2) Does the primary effect of the act either advance or inhibit religion? (3) Does the act excessively entangle government and religion? The Court envisioned excessive entanglement between government and religion in accomplishing the necessary state supervision to ensure that the state aid would support only secular education. The Court pointed out another defect of the Pennsylvania statute—it provided for the aid to be given directly to the school. In the *Everson* case the aid was provided to the student's parents, not to the church-related school.

Relevant Research

Can a Deaf Student Attending a Catholic High School Have a Government-Paid Interpreter?

Law research has a different design than other types of educational research. Instead of the researcher observing classrooms or developing and administering a student questionnaire, the legal researcher studies different sources of information related to the legal question at hand. The legal researcher works through these sources to develop an analysis of the likely legality of a particular issue.

In 1993, the question of whether it is legal to assign a government-paid interpreter to a deaf student attending a Catholic high school was tested in *Zobrest* v. *Catalina Foothills School District*. In a case brought by Jim Zobrest of Tucson, Arizona's Salpointe Catholic High School, the U.S. Supreme Court had to consider: (1) the Education of the Handicapped Act, a statute that requires special accommodation for the handicapped, (2) the 1971 "*Lemon* Test," which requires a court to look at a law's purpose (it should be secular), its effects on religion (it should be neutral) and whether the law results in excessive entanglement between church and state, and (3) several amendments of the U.S. Constitution (including the First and the Fourteenth). In *Zobrest* the tutor was available all day, including for religious instruction.

In a sharply divided five-to-four decision the Court has ruled that it is not unconstitutional for a public school district to send a sign language interpreter into a religious school to help a deaf student learn. This brief overview of one case illustrates the intricate array of elements that come together when you raise what seems to be a simple question about what is legal to do in your classroom.

In 1980, by a five-to-four vote, the U.S. Supreme Court finally settled a ten-year dispute over a New York law that provided for reimbursement to private and parochial schools for record keeping and standardized testing, both required by state law. The Court envisioned no excessive entanglement and voted that testing and record keeping have neither a religious purpose nor a religious effect, nor do they violate the intent of the First Amendment.

In a 1994 case, *Board of Education of Kiryas Joel Village School District* v. *Grumet*, the U.S. Supreme Court ruled that a New York state law that created a public school to serve disabled children in a village of Hasidic Jews is a form of "religious favoritism" that violates the First Amendment. Interestingly, in this case as with some others recently, the *Lemon* case was ignored by justices in making the decision. Instead, the focus was on the legislature creating a special school and that there was no guarantee that "the next similarly situated group seeking a school district of its own will receive one." Another implication of this decision was the indication that the court would be willing to revisit *Aquilar* v. *Felton* (1985) and *Grand Rapids* v. *Ball* (1985), which invalidated sending public school teachers to private religious schools to provide supplemental instruction.

The issue of public aid to church-related schools is still in the process of being settled. Although it is clear that aid for certain secular services (such as transportation, textbooks, and—under prescribed circumstances—testing, diagnostic, therapeutic, and remedial services) can be provided, it is not yet absolutely clear what further aid will be approved. In fact, the whole body of law in this area continues to be somewhat confused and contradictory. Some state legislatures are continuing to try to find new ways to provide aid to parochial schools without violating the First Amendment. (See Table 9.1 on page 238 for a summary of U.S. Supreme Court cases in this area.)

Child Benefit Theory. The use of public funds to provide secular services has led to a concept referred to as "child benefit theory." **Child benefit theory** can be defined as providing benefits to children in parochial schools with no benefits to the schools or to a religion. More recent decisions supporting the use of public funds for transportation and textbooks for students in private schools have generally been based on the child benefit theory; this theory emerged out of commentary about the *Everson* v. *Board of Education* case. The reasoning was that transportation and books provide benefits to the children and not to the school or to a religion. Those opposed to the child benefit theory argue that aid to children receiving sectarian education instruction is effectively aiding the institution providing instruction.

The child benefit theory, as supported by the U.S. Supreme Court, has penetrated federal legislation. The Elementary and Secondary Education Act of 1965 (ESEA), for example, and its subsequent amendments provide for assistance to both public and nonpublic school children. Title I of ESEA, which dealt with assistance for the education of children from low-income families, stated that children from families attending private schools must be provided services in proportion to their numbers. As a summary, Table 9.2 on page 239 presents brief statements about the relationship of religion and public education, particularly the use of public funds for parochial education.

Another issue related to separation of church and state focuses on religious activities in public schools, which will be treated in the next section.

TABLE 9.1   Selected U.S. Supreme Court Cases Related to the Use of Public Funds for Private Education

Case	Issue	Decision
Everson v. *Board of Education* (1947)	Use of tax-raised funds to reimburse parents for transportation of students to church schools	Court ruled that reimbursement did not violate the First Amendment
Cochran v. *Louisiana Board of Education* (1930)	Loan of public school textbooks to children in private schools	Court ruled that state loans of secular textbooks to nonpublic school children served public purposes and did not violate the federal constitutional ban on spending public funds for private purposes
Board of Education of Central School District No. 1, Town of Greenbush v. *Allen* (1968)	Loan of public school textbooks to children in private schools	Court ruled that the loan of books did not alone demonstrate an unconstitutional degree of support for a religious institution
Lemon v. *Kurtzman* (1971)	Legislation to provide direct aid for secular services to nonpublic schools, including teacher salaries, textbooks, and instructional materials	Court ruled the legislation unconstitutional because of the excessive entanglement between government and religion
Wolman v. *Walter* (1977)	Providing nonpublic school pupils with books, standardized testing and scoring, diagnostic services, and therapeutic and remedial services	Court ruled that providing such materials and services to nonpublic school pupils was constitutional
	Provision of instructional materials and field trips to nonpublic school pupils	Court ruled that providing such materials and service to nonpublic school pupils was unconstitutional
Grand Rapids School District v. *Ball* (1985), and *Aguilar* v. *Felton* (1985)	Having public school teachers instruct nonpublic school students in supplementary education	Court ruled that the action violated the Establishment Clause in that it promoted religion
Board of Education of Kiryas Joel Village School District v. *Grumet* (1994)	New York State creating and supporting a public school district for Hasidic Jews	Court ruled it violated the Establishment Clause in that it was a form of "religious favoritism"

Religious Activities in Public Schools

Four topics to be addressed with regard to religious activities in public schools are released time from regular classes for religious instruction, prayer and Bible reading in schools, the teaching of creationism or the biblical version of creation in public schools, and the use of school facilities for religious purposes.

Released Time. Providing released time for religious instruction in public schools has been challenged and was first acted on by the U.S. Supreme Court, in 1948. The Court held that the released-time program of the Champaign, Illinois,

TABLE 9.2	Summary Statements on Church and State Related to Public Funds and Parochial Education

Laws and policies that have the effect of establishing religion in the schools will not be upheld by the courts.

Public tax funds to pay for secular textbooks for loan to students and transportation of parochial school children have been upheld by the courts.

Public tax funds to pay for salaries of teachers in parochial schools have not been upheld by the courts.

Tuition payments for parents of parochial school children have not been upheld; in Minnesota, a tax deduction has been upheld for parents of children in public *and* private schools.

Special support services such as speech and hearing teachers may be provided to parochial schools.

Parochial schools may be reimbursed for administrative costs of standardized tests, test scoring, and record keeping required by the state.

Public tax funds may not be used in support of public school teachers offering remedial or enriched instruction in parochial schools.

schools violated the principle of separation of church and state (*People of the State of Illinois ex rel. McCollum* v. *Board of Education of School District No. 71, Champaign, Illinois,* 1948). Four years later, the court made what initially appears to be a contradictory decision.

The Concept of Released Time Does Not Violate the First Amendment. A released-time program in New York was challenged a few years after the *McCollum* case; in *Zorach* v. *Clauson* (1952) the Supreme Court upheld a New York statute that provided for released time. The chief difference between the Champaign and New York cases is that in New York, students were released from school to go to religious centers to receive religious instruction, whereas in Champaign the instruction was given in public school classrooms. The Court indicated that the precise type of released-time program is significant; programs differ in the extent of school cooperation and in the degree of sectarianism. We can conclude that the concept of released time in and of itself does not necessarily violate the First Amendment.

Prayer and Bible Reading. The courts have rendered a number of opinions on prayer and Bible reading in the public schools. In 1962 the U.S. Supreme Court (*Engle* v. *Vitale*) held that a prayer composed by the New York State Board of Regents and used as part of the opening exercises of school violated the U.S. Constitution. The prayer read as follows: "Almighty God, we acknowledge our dependence upon Thee, and we beg Thy blessings on us, our parents, our teachers, and our country." Pupils who objected to the prayer could be excused. The Court based its decision on the establishment clause of the First Amendment: "Congress shall make no law respecting an establishment of religion, or prohibiting the free exercise thereof." Justice Hugo Black, who wrote the decision, stated:

> The constitutional prohibition against laws respecting an establishment of religion must at least mean that . . . it is no part of the business of government to impose official prayers for any group of American people to recite as a part of a religious program carried on by the government.

The right to pray in school, or its appropriateness in the school day routine, have been debated often in recent decades.

Other U.S. Supreme Court decisions related to Bible reading and prayer include: outlawing the reading of the Bible and reciting the Lord's Prayer as religious exercises in public schools (*Schempp* v. *School District of Abington Township*, 1963, and *Murray* v. *Curlett*, 1963); and the overturning of Alabama legislation of 1982 which authorized teachers to lead willing students in a prescribed prayer (*Wallace* v. *Jaffree*, 1985).

The constitutionality of prayer at graduation ceremonies has been considered too. In *Lee* v. *Weisman* (1992), the U.S. Supreme Court ruled, in a five-to-four decision, that it was unconstitutional to include an invocation or benediction as an official part of the program. The Court's majority reasoned that this was in violation of the establishment clause. More specifically, the effects test of *Lemon* was violated whenever government action "creates an identification of the state with a religion, or with religion in general."

Lee v. *Weisman*, may settle, for the moment, the role of prayer and Bible reading as an official part of the graduation ceremony. But what about invited speakers including religious references in their remarks, or student-led prayer? A number of related cases are currently moving through lower courts. It appears that, under certain circumstances (yet to be clarified), an individual speaker may make unsolicited reference to religious views. But school officials cannot issue a vote or encourage any such action. For example, in a 1992 decision, a federal appeals court ruled on a case from Texas that graduation prayer is allowed if it is student-initiated, nonsectarian, and nonproselytizing. Since that time, legislatures in Texas, Louisiana, Mississippi, and a number of other southeastern states have passed laws with this intent. These statutes are now being challenged in the courts. Keep in mind that decisions in lower courts may well apply only in their jurisdiction; only time will tell whether any of these cases will reach the U.S. Supreme Court. There are sure to be continuing questions and court cases about the delicate balancing of the relationship between prayer and Bible reading and official school actions. For example, the current question of the legality of establishing in statutes a "moment of silence" in schools will surely be tested in the courts. For now, in these and other cases the opinions of the courts emphasize that government must remain neutral in matters of religion.

Teaching Creationism in the Public Schools. Another volatile church-state controversy pertains to teaching in public schools about the origin of humanity. The initial controversy involved the constitutionality of state prohibitions against instruction suggesting that human beings evolved through a process of natural selection from lower forms of animals. The Tennessee Supreme Court upheld such a state law in the famous 1927 Scopes "monkey trial," but the Supreme Court reached an opposite conclusion in 1968. In *Epperson* v. *Arkansas* (1968) the Court ruled that an Arkansas antievolution statute violated the First Amendment.

It declared that "the state has no legitimate interest in protecting any or all religions from views distasteful to them." It stated further that the amendment does not "permit the state to require that teaching and learning be tailor-made to the principles or prohibitions of any religious sect or dogma."

The more recent controversy has focused on the constitutionality of teaching the biblical version of creation in public schools. Creationists assert that this theory deserves equal treatment to that of the scientific theory of the evolution of life. In 1980–1981, "equal-time" provisions were introduced in the legislatures of fifteen states, with two states, (Arkansas and Louisiana) passing statutes. The intent of these initiatives was to require that each theory be given equal instructional time. The Arkansas statute was struck down by a federal district court in 1982. The judge reviewed the legislative history of the statute and concluded that it failed to satisfy the three-pronged *Lemon* test. The judge ruled that there was no evidence of secular purpose; rather it was an attempt to introduce the biblical version of creationism into the public schools. Reasoning that creation science is religious dogma, the court concluded that the only real effect of the statute was to advance religion. The court also held that the act created excessive governmental entanglement with religion because the Genesis account cannot be taught in a secular fashion.

The U.S. Supreme Court ruled in 1987 (*Edwards* v. *Aguilard*) that the Louisiana statute was in violation of the establishment clause. The act lacked a secular purpose, and it tended to show a preference for the teaching of the biblical version as opposed to the scientific version of creation. There was further evidence that the act's sponsors intended to promote religion, a violation of the *Lemon* test.

Religious Meetings in Public Schools.   In 1988, President Reagan signed the Equal Process Act, which gives students—under certain, very limited circumstances—the right to hold religious meetings in public schools. This law guarantees to students the right to meet for "religious, political, philosophical, or other" discussions in any high school that allows other extracurricular activities. The U.S. Supreme Court in 1990 and again in 1993 ruled that schools must allow student Bible clubs as well as political and ideological groups to meet on campus after hours if other outside activities are held in school facilities.

Another issue related to the separation of church and state deals with the rights of parents to provide education for their children. This issue, which is discussed in the next section, is closely related to compulsory education.

Rights of Parents to Provide Private Education

The United States has a strong religious heritage. That heritage fostered the development of private religious schools and school systems dedicated to teaching religion along with secular subjects including reading, writing, and arithmetic. Some private schools are not religious-sponsored and essentially offer secular subjects. As our nation grew, sectarian private schools also grew, frequently associated with established traditional religions, such as Catholicism and Lutheranism. In recent years, many fundamentalist religious schools have been established. The fundamentalist schools have had steadily increasing enrollments. The amount of instruction of students in their homes has also escalated. The increased enrollments in fundamentalist schools and the increased amount of home instruction are attributed in part to the perceived, if not real, lack of instruction of morality in the public schools.

TABLE 9.3   Selected U.S. Supreme Court Cases Related to the Practice of Religion in Public Schools and the Right to a Private Education

Case	Issue	Decision
Creationism		
Epperson v. *State of Arkansas* (1968)	Arkansas antievolution statute	Court held that to forbid the teaching of evolution as a theory violated the First Amendment.
Edwards v. *Aguilard* (1987)	Balanced treatment of biblical and scientific creation	A state cannot require that schools teach the biblical version of creation.
Practice of Religion		
Wallace v. *Jaffree* (1985)	Legislation authorizing prayer in public schools, led by teachers; and a period of silence for meditation or voluntary prayer	Court held that state legislation authorizing a minute of silence for prayer led by teachers was unconstitutional.
Mozert v. *Hawkins County Public Schools* (1987)	Request that fundamentalist children not be exposed to basal reading series in the public schools of Tennessee	Rejected by the Sixth Circuit Court of Appeals' reasoning that the readers did not burden the students' exercise of their religious beliefs.
Board of Education of the Westside Community Schools v. *Mergens* (1990)	Holding student religious club meetings at public school	Court ruled that based on Equal Access Act (EAA) of 1984, if only one noncurriculum-related student group meets, then the school may not deny other clubs.
Lee v. *Weisman* (1992)	Conducting a religious exercise at a graduation ceremony where young graduates who object are induced to conform	Prayers as an official part of graduation exercises are unconstitutional.

Private Education: An Alternative. The court cases having to do with the rights of parents to provide private education for their children are closely related to cases about **compulsory education.** Compulsory attendance laws generally require parents, or whoever has custody of a child between specific chronological ages, to cause the child to attend school. The constitutional objection raised regarding compulsory attendance laws is that they infringe on the individual liberty guaranteed by the Fourteenth Amendment. The constitutionality of compulsory education laws has been attacked in numerous cases, but the principle has been uniformly upheld. Courts have generally reasoned that education is so necessary to the welfare of our nation that compulsory school attendance laws are valid and desirable. Compulsory education does not mean compulsory public education, however.

Whether a state can compel children to attend a public school was settled in a case in Oregon. (See Table 9.3 for a summary of this case and other important Supreme Court cases related to the practice of religion in public schools and the right to a private education.) In 1922 the Oregon legislature passed a law requiring all children to attend public schools. The U.S. Supreme Court ruled that such a law was unconstitutional in that it infringed on the rights of parents to control the education of their children (*Pierce* v. *Society of Sisters*, 1925). This ruling established a precedent, permitting parents to have their children educated in private

schools. In this same case the Court also established beyond doubt that the state may
reasonably regulate all schools, public and
private, and require certain subjects to be
taught. It established that private schools
have a right to exist, that pupils may meet the
compulsory attendance laws by attending private schools, and that private schools are subject to state regulation.

Home Instruction. The courts have also
ruled that education in a child's home can
meet the requirements of compulsory education. In an early case in Indiana[3] the court
specified that a school is a place where education is imparted to the young; therefore a
home can be a school if a qualified teacher is

Parents may be granted permission to educate their children at home.

engaged in instruction as prescribed by the state. The state controls home instruction, and the instruction generally must be equivalent to what a school provides.
Home instruction must be carried out in good faith and not practiced as a sub-
terfuge to avoid sending children to school.

   As of 1989, every state permitted home instruction in some form, and two
states, Iowa and Michigan, required that all teachers in home schools be certified.
Nevertheless, there are wide differences among the states in the restrictions controlling home instruction and home schools. The trend is toward easing restrictions. Various restrictions on home instruction and home schools over the years
have included requiring certified teachers, following state curriculum mandates,
passing the state teachers' examinations, requiring students to take annual standardized achievement tests and competency tests, and setting a minimum length
for the instructional day and year.

Balancing the Rights of Individuals and the Rights of the State. The
interpretation of compulsory education laws indicates that a reasonable balance
is sought between the rights of the individual and the rights of the state. Parents
who want a religious education for their children may meet the requirement of
compulsory education by enrolling their children in private or parochial schools
or in approved home instruction programs. At the same time the state reserves the
right to reasonably regulate private education.

   Much of our discussion in this section dealt with issues associated with the
separation of church and state (see Table 9.4 on page 244 for a summary) and
judicial decisions made by the Supreme Court related to those issues (see Table
9.3). Frequently, the decisions made by the Court were based on the First Amendment. The next few pages address issues associated with segregation and desegregation directly related to the Fourteenth Amendment.

Enduring Legal Issues

There are a number of pressing issues where the needs of society, the laws of the
land, and the role of schools intersect. These enduring issues do not have easy, simple, quick, or final answers. Instead, each represents an area where difficult prob-

TABLE 9.4	Summary Statements on Church and State and the Practice of Religion in Public Schools

To teach the Bible as a religion course in the public schools is illegal, but to teach about the Bible as part of history of literature is legal.

To dismiss children from public schools for one hour once a week for religious instruction at religious centers is legal.

Reading of scripture and reciting prayers as religious exercises are in violation of the Establishment Clause.

Public schools may teach the scientific theory of evolution as a theory; a state may not require that the biblical version of evolution be taught.

lems must be addressed through gradual development of understanding of the underlying problem(s) and experimentation with different approaches to find what will work. The pressing needs being addressed require the legal, legislative, and educational systems to work together to develop and test workable solutions. Each of these enduring issues carries with it emotion, high cost, high risk, and uncertainty as to whether the desired ends can be achieved with the legal and educational mechanisms employed. At the same time the willingness to confront these types of difficult societal problems is a strength and testimony to the confidence Americans have in their educational system. Several of these enduring issues that have been addressed through legal actions are summarized in the remainder of this chapter.

Segregation and Desegregation

Segregation in the context of this chapter refers to the separation of people by race specifically in the public schools. A major concern in the United States has been the separation of African American students from white students, resulting in segregated schools—schools that have predominantly African American students and schools that have predominantly white students. Such segregation has occurred by state law or other official action *(de jure)* and through other causes such as housing patterns *(de facto)*.

Desegregation is an effort to abolish racial segregation. For example, African American students may be transferred to predominantly white schools, and white students may be transferred to predominantly African American schools. The intent is to achieve a numerical balance of African American and white students in each school. Such a school would be referred to as an integrated school. Closely related to segregation and desegregation are the issues of busing, white flight, and resegregation, which are also discussed here.

***De Jure* Segregation.** Before 1954, many states had laws either requiring or permitting racial segregation in public schools. Until 1954, lower courts had adhered to the doctrine of "separate but equal" as announced by the Supreme Court in 1896 (*Plessy v. Ferguson*). In *Plessy* v. *Ferguson* the Court upheld a Louisiana law that required railway companies to provide equal accommodations for the African American and white races. The Court indicated in its opinion that the Fourteenth Amendment implied political, not social, equality.

The Separate-But-Equal Doctrine Has No Place.   This separate-but-equal doctrine appeared to be the rule until May 17, ~~1954~~ when the Supreme Court repudiated it in *Brown v. Board of Education of Topeka*. The Court said that in education the separate-but-equal doctrine has no place and that separate facilities are inherently unequal. In 1955 the Court rendered the second *Brown* v. *Board of Education of Topeka* decision, requiring that the principles of the first decision be carried out with all deliberate speed.

From 1954, the time of the *Brown* decision, to 1964, little progress was made in eliminating segregated schools. On May 25, 1964, referring to a situation in Prince Edward County, Virginia, the Supreme Court said: "There has been entirely too much deliberation and not enough speed in enforcing the constitutional rights which we held in *Brown* v. *Board of Education.* " The Civil Rights Act of 1964 added legislative power to the 1954 judicial pronouncement. The Act not only authorized the federal government to initiate court suits against school districts that were laggard in desegregating schools but also denied federal funds for programs that discriminated by race, color, or national origin.

Subsequently, many types of efforts have been made to meet the expectations of the Court decisions and legislation. The objective of these initiatives has been **integration,** that is, to achieve a representative mix of students of different races in schools. In the more than forty years since *Brown* there have been many efforts by school districts and communities, and many additional law suits.

***De Facto* Segregation.**   The U.S. Supreme Court has yet to rule on *de facto* discrimination—that is, discrimination based on causes *other than* state law or official state actions such as when the composition of neighborhood populations results in part from housing patterns.

A case heard by the U.S. Supreme Court that touched on *de facto* segregation was *Keyes* v. *School District No. 1, Denver, Colorado*. The Court, announcing its decision in 1973, sent the suit back to a district court; this court was to decide whether or not school authorities had intentionally segregated a substantial portion of the school system. If proof affirmed that the school district was operating a dual system (segregated) even though there had never been any *de jure* or legal provisions for school segregation, then the entire system would be required to desegregate. In 1974, Judge William E. Doyle of the Tenth U.S. Circuit Court of Appeals ordered integration of the city's 70,000 children. The Supreme Court, however, had not resolved the question of *de jure/de facto* segregation. In a separate opinion, Justice Powell stated: "We should abandon a distinction which long since has outlived its time, and formulate constitutional principles of national rather than merely regional applications." The Supreme Court did, however, change the concept of *de facto* segregation by turning over to federal and state trial courts the discretion to determine, as an issue of fact and not as a question of law, whether or not a local school board presides over a *de facto* or a *de jure* segregated school district. In a sense, the Supreme Court broadened the concept of *de jure* segregation.

Integration Forty Years Later.   Currently, there are more than 500 formerly segregated school districts under some federal court jurisdiction. Unfortunately, while *de jure* segregation has been removed, it has been replaced in many situations with a more virulent form of segregation. The demographics and economic conditions of the country have changed in ways that have not facilitated accomplishing integration in local schools. Many strategies have been tested and there

Attempts to integrate students of different races by transporting them to schools outside their own neighborhoods have proven to be a difficult and emotional issue for communities.

are some indicators of success, but the goal is still a dream in many ways. One of the enduring strategies to achieve integration has been busing. Unanticipated countering points during this period include the movement of the middle class away from urban areas and the lower birth rates of whites. Also, the economic conditions and extent of racial diversity in the country have changed dramatically. These dynamic factors, along with numerous others, have not made it easy for schools and communities to achieve the desired end of desegregation.

Busing Has Been Mandated by Federal District Courts as a Means to Bring about School Desegregation. Busing has also been used voluntarily to bring about desegregation. Many school districts—including those of Boston, Seattle, Tulsa, Oklahoma City, Louisville, Austin, Dallas, Dayton, San Francisco, Los Angeles, Pontiac, and Indianapolis—have been ordered to bus school children to end segregation. But the issue remains extremely controversial.

Proponents view busing as a necessary way, and sometimes the only way, to give children of all races a chance for equality of opportunity in education. They further argue that an integrated society is essential and that if people are going to live in an integrated society, preparation must begin in school. Opponents of busing claim that it does not improve the quality of education and that it requires large expenditures that ought to go toward compensatory education.

Resegregation *Generally Means a Situation in Which an Integrated School Population Becomes Almost Totally a Minority School Population.* Sometimes, resegregation occurs within a school when the neighborhood from which the school's population is drawn changes from an integrated to a predominantly minority neighborhood. If the population of a city becomes predominantly minority, the schools in the city will become the same. Often the growth of the minority populations proceeds from the inner part of the city toward the outer fringe areas. Resegregation can also occur after a governmental desegregation order. In such instances, white students may withdraw or simply not reenter when the next term begins. Furthermore, white families may move to another area that is not affected by the desegregation order.

One Serious Consequence in the 1990s Is a Growing Sense of Despair in Many Minority Children. This must be understood and actively addressed by teachers such as yourself. The above description of resegregation is based on demographic and economic factors. There is another set of dynamics to resegregation that includes educational, social, and psychological factors.

Quality of education is one significant factor. As the urban areas have lost their tax base, the condition of school buildings has deteriorated. Tracking is another educational strategy that is contributing to resegregation. In some schools many minority students are scheduled out of advanced classes and clustered in more remedial classes. Minority students are experiencing less success in schools, and they have higher dropout rates as well. There also is a sense of social isolation that occurs in many schools that is defeating the goal of integration. Additionally, there is a belief among many minorities that teachers, as well as white students, do not treat them as equals. Whether or not these conditions are true, as long as students perceive that they are, the tendency to resegregate will increase.

There Is a Success Side to the Desegregation Agenda That Should Be Appreciated. For example, African Americans who graduate from integrated schools have higher incomes than those who graduate from segregated schools. They are more likely to graduate from college and to hold good jobs. And there is an increasing number of middle-class black families. Still, there is a long way to go before the dream born over forty years ago is achieved. And schools will continue to be the primary vehicle from the points of view of the courts and teachers in classrooms.

Release from Court Orders. After forty plus years of court actions related to desegregation and school district responses, questions are now being raised about the conditions that must be in place for a school district to be released from federal court supervision. Four recent cases offer the first instances of the conditions under which the courts will back away. The *Board of Education of Oklahoma City* v. *Dowell* (1991) is important for at least three reasons. First, the U.S. Supreme Court made clear that "federal supervision of local school systems was intended as a temporary measure to remedy past discrimination." Second, the Court made clearer what was meant by unitary status: "the District Court should look not only at student assignments, but to every facet of school operations—faculty, staff, transportation, extracurricular activities and facilities." And third, for the first time, the Court ruled that a district had achieved this status:

> In the present case, a finding by the District Court that the Oklahoma City School District was being operated in compliance with the commands of the equal protection clause of the Fourteenth Amendment, and that it was unlikely that the school board would return to its former ways, would be finding that the purposes of the desegregation litigation had been fully achieved.

Two other cases add additional clarity to what the Court expects in order to release a school district from supervision. In *Freeman* v. *Pitts* (1992) the U.S. Supreme Court ruled that districts do not have to remedy racial imbalances caused by demographic changes, but the districts still have the burden of proving that their actions do not contribute to the imbalances. The third case is a return to *Brown*. The Court had ordered the 10th Circuit Court to re-examine its 1989 finding that the Topeka district remains segregated. In 1992 the Appellate Court refused to declare Topeka unitary. The court concluded that the district has done little to fulfill its duty to desegregate that was first imposed on it in 1954. The judges wrote that to expect the vestiges of segregation to "magically dissolve" with so little effort "is to expect too much."

These three cases in combination make clear that it is possible for school districts to be released from court order. The decisions also make clear that school districts have to make concerted efforts across time to address any and all remnants of *de jure* segregation. Further, it now appears that school districts are not expected to resolve those aspects of *de facto* segregation that are clearly beyond their control.

The fourth case related to achieving release from a court desegregation order has to do with the amount of effort that a school district must invest on desegre-

Changing demographics in the United States have made diverse classrooms commonplace.

gation programs and the criteria for judging success. This question was addressed in an appeal by the state of Missouri in the Kansas City case. In a 1995 landmark decision, with a 5–4 vote, the Court overturned a federal judge's order that Missouri pay for two costly aspects of Kansas City's massive desegregation program. In Kansas City, the state, as well as local tax payers, has been paying for a major set of desegregation initiatives, which included construction of new school buildings with magnet programs, across-the-board teacher salary increases, and a program to help minority children reach national norms in educational achievement. This case is reputed to be the most costly in the nation, with $1.3 billion spent between 1984 and 1995.

In returning the case to federal judge Russell Clark, the Court ruled that school desegregation programs may not spend unlimited amounts of money, go on indefinitely, uniformly insist on academic achievement, or seek to lure white students from blameless suburban districts. The court's insisting on minority students achieving at national norms was seen as outside the purview of the case. Judge Rehnquist stated for the majority, "Insistence upon academic goals unrelated to the effects of (past) legal segregation unwarrantably postpones the day when the (Kansas City District) will be able to operate on its own." In reversing the lower court, Judge Rehnquest criticized them for approving a desegregation goal that appeared unlimited in costs and duration.

This section has dealt with *de jure* and *de facto* segregation and with desegregation. Integration and resegregation were also discussed. (See Table 9.5 for a summary of these issues.) All of these issues have prejudice and discrimination at their core, as does the next major topic, affirmative action.

TABLE 9.5	**Summary Statements on Segregation and Desegregation**

The assignment of a child to a school on the basis of race is in violation of the equal protection clause of the Fourteenth Amendment.

Where school boards have indirectly contributed to segregated communities, the school district can be required to desegregate.

Desegregation plans that have the effect of delaying integration of the school have not been upheld by the courts.

Busing may be required for the operation of a unitary school system.

Once a school district has been fully desegregated, the school board does not need to draw up a new plan if resegregation occurs.

The merger of school districts may be required where the involved districts helped create the segregated school systems.

The neighborhood school concept is not in conflict with the equal protection clause.

Once the district has achieved unitary status, it can be released from court supervision.

Affirmative Action

Affirmative action has its basis in the protection clause of the Fourteenth Amendment, in Titles VI and VII of the Civil Rights Act of 1964, and in Title IX of the Education Amendments of 1972. Title VI of the Civil Rights Act states:

> No person in the United States shall, on the ground of race, color, or national origin, be excluded from participation in, be denied the benefits of, or be subjected to discrimination under any program or activity receiving federal financial assistance.

Title VII states:

> It shall be an unlawful employment practice for an employer (1) to fail or refuse to hire or to discharge any individual, or otherwise to discriminate against any individual with respect to his compensation, terms, conditions, or privileges of employment, because of such individual's race, color, religion, sex, or national origin; or (2) to limit, segregate, or classify his employees or applicants for employment in any way which would deprive or tend to deprive any individual of employment opportunities or otherwise adversely affect his status as an employee, because of such individual's race, color, religion, sex, or national origin.

Title IX of the Education Amendments of 1972 states:

> No person in the United States shall, on the basis of sex, be excluded from participation in, be denied the benefits of, or be subjected to discrimination under any education program or activity receiving federal financial assistance.

Discrimination and Reverse Discrimination. **Discrimination** can be defined as a determination that an individual or a group of individuals—for example, African Americans, women, or handicapped people—has been denied constitutional rights. In common usage the term applies to various minorities or individual members of a minority who lack rights typically accorded the majority. The term **reverse discrimination** implies that a majority or an individual of a majority has not been accorded certain rights because of different or preferential treatment provided to a minority or an individual of a minority.

Reverse discrimination has been cited with respect to admissions to law schools and medical schools. It has also been cited in connection with affirmative action— that is, positive efforts undertaken by society to integrate the races and to assure equal opportunities. An early test case concerned Allan Bakke, a white male, who claimed that he was discriminated against when denied admission to the University of California Medical School at Davis. In the medical school's class of one hundred students, sixteen spaces were set aside for minority applicants. The Supreme Court of California upheld Bakke's claim and ordered him admitted. Regents of the university appealed to the U.S. Supreme Court to overturn the state ruling.

In general, the arguments supporting the denial of Bakke's admission pointed out that (1) special admissions programs based on race are not quotas but goals; (2) color-sensitive admissions policies are necessary to bring minorities fully into the mainstream of American society; (3) benefits accrue to society at large from special admissions; (4) merit alone, determined by academic grades and test scores, has not been the single criterion of selection for schools; and (5) the denial did not violate the equal-protection clause of the U.S. Constitution. The arguments supporting Bakke's admission emphasized that (1) the special admissions program was a racial quota and (2) quotas are harmful to society and are unconstitutional.

Education for the Handicapped

Another area being given extensive legal and legislative attention is the rights of the handicapped. Before the 1970s handicapped children were not necessarily entitled to a public education. The extent to which schooling was available to them was dependent on the state and community in which they resided. The amount and type of schooling available was a local government decision. Then in the early 1970s a series of court decisions and congressional acts established that handicapped children had constitutional entitlement to an "appropriate" education. Since then there have been a series of judicial decisions and legislative initiatives to define what is appropriate.

Public Law, Rules and Regulations for the Handicapped.   Three statutory initiatives serve as the cornerstones for education of the handicapped: Section 504 of the Rehabilitation Act, the Education for All Handicapped Children Act (EAHCA), also known as Public Law 94-142, and the Individuals with Disabilities Education Act (IDEA). Each of these instruments addresses student eligibilities, definition of what comprises appropriate education, and elements of due process.

Section 504 of the Rehabilitation Act.   Under this Civil Rights Act established in 1973, recipients of federal funds are prohibited from discriminating against "otherwise qualified individuals." Note that this is a federal statute and regulations, not a court decision. Three important themes addressed in Section 504 are Equal Treatment, Appropriate Education, and Handicapped Persons. Equal Treatment, as in other civil rights contexts, must be addressed. However, this does not mean the same treatment. For example, giving the same assessment procedure to handicapped and regular students may not be equal treatment. There is a "heightened standard" when making educational judgments. The measures must fit the student's circumstances, and procedural safeguards must be employed. Appropriate Education means that the school system and related parties must address indi-

As in other professions, teachers cannot be denied employment due to physical disability.

vidual needs of handicapped students as adequately as do the education approaches for regular students. In Section 504, a handicapped person is:

> Any person who (i) has a physical or mental impairment which substantially limits one or more major life activities, (ii) has a record of such an impairment, or (iii) is regarded as having such an impairment. (34 CFR 104.3)

Public Law 94-142 (EAHCA). Passed by Congress in 1975, Public Law 94-142 has been amended several times since. This law assures "a free appropriate public education" to all handicapped children between the ages of three and twenty-one. Exceptional children cannot be excluded from education because of their differences. The law is very specific in describing the kind and quality of education and in stating that each handicapped child is to have an individually planned education. (The specifics of this law are presented in Part Four of this text.) Originally, substantial increases in funding were provided for; however, in subsequent years the funding authorizations have been lower than the original commitment. Two priorities for funding were identified: (1) the child who currently receives no education; and (2) the child who is not receiving all the services needed to succeed. This direction places the emphasis on need, rather than the specific disability.

The Individuals with Disabilities Education Act (IDEA). This Act (1992) develops tighter specifications for the delivery of education services to handicapped children. At the time, more than half of the children with disabilities were not receiving appropriate educational services. The purpose of IDEA is to make available to all children with disabilities a free appropriate public education. IDEA establishes at the federal level an Office of Special Education Programs headed by a Deputy Assistant Secretary. Further, the Act makes clear that states shall not be immune under the Eleventh Amendment of the Constitution from suit in federal court for a violation of the Act. The Act encourages the employment of individuals with disabilities by making grants to states and local education agencies for children aged three to five, requires the federal government to be responsive to the increasing ethnic diversity of society and those with limited English proficiency, and funds programs to provide education to all children with disabilities.

Handicapped Students and the Courts.
The judicial basis for the current approaches to education of the handicapped are closely linked to the statutory parameters of Section 504 and EAHCA, as well as the due process clause of the Fourteenth Amendment.

Mills *v.* Board of Education *(1972).* In this case, seven children enjoined the District of Columbia Public Schools from excluding them from publicly supported education.

> They allege that although they can profit from an education either in regular classrooms with supportive services or in special classes adapted to their needs, they have been labeled as behavioral problems, mentally retarded, emotionally disturbed, or hyperactive, and denied admission to the public schools or excluded therefrom after admission, with no provision for alternative educational placement or periodical review. . . .

Up to that time the District of Columbia School District had not documented the number of "exceptional" children that resided within the District. There were estimates of as many as 22,000 handicapped children, with as many as 18,000 not being provided specialized education. As typical in earlier times, the District was not systematically addressing the educational needs of this student population. For example, in a 1971 report, the D.C. Public Schools estimated that 12,340 handicapped children were not going to be served in the 1971–1972 school year.

The Circuit Judge based his decision on the due process clause of the Fifteenth Amendment since this only applies to states. He concluded that the doctrine of equal educational opportunity (the education application of the equal protection clause) did apply and that due process was a binding component for the District. The Court concluded that the District was required by the Constitution, District of Columbia Code, and the District's own regulations to provide a publicly supported education for these "exceptional" children. Further, if there were not sufficient funds, then whatever funds there were must be expended equitably so that no child is entirely excluded.

> 1. That no child eligible for a publicly supported education in the District of Columbia public schools shall be excluded from a regular public school assignment by a rule, policy, or practice of the Board of Education of the District of Columbia or its agents unless such child is provided (a) adequate alternative educational services suited to the child's needs, which may include special education or tuition grants, and (b) a constitutionally adequate prior hearing and periodic review of the child's status, progress, and the adequacy of any educational alternative. . . .

> 2. The District of Columbia shall provide to each child of school age a free and suitable publicly supported education regardless of the degree of the child's mental, physical, or emotional disability or impairment. Furthermore, defendants shall not exclude any child resident in the District of Columbia from such publicly supported education on the basis of a claim of insufficient resources. . . .

Pennsylvania Association for Retarded Children (PARC) *v.* Commonwealth *(1971)*. A consent order, issued prior to *Mills* v. *Board of Education*, required Pennsylvania to provide a free, public program of education and training appropriate to the child's capacity, within the context of a presumption that, among the alternative programs of education and training required by statute to be available, placement in a regular public school class is preferable to placement in a special public class (that is a class for "handicapped" children), and placement in a special public school class is preferable to placement in any other type of program of education and training.

Congress seems to have based much of the subsequent legislation, rules, and regulations on *Mills* and *PARC*. EAHCA and Section 504 outline procedures that must be addressed by schools, parents, and the state. For example, the most appropriate educational placement for the handicapped child must be determined using EAHCA procedures. And Section 504 is used to make judgments about whether the child is otherwise qualified to be educated in a particular setting.

The Individualized Educational Program (IEP), Which Is Mandated under EAHCA, Is the Key to Implementing Congressional Goals for Handicapped Children. Each district will have a protocol for these "staffings," during which representatives of the school district, the child's teacher, the parents or guardians, and, whenever appropriate, the disabled child meet to review the child's performance and progress. Annual goals and short-term objectives are identified and the needed instruction and services are planned. These meetings must occur at least once a year.

The intent of Congress throughout has been to build in heavy involvement of parents. There are procedural safeguards that include parents' meaningful input into all decisions affecting their child's education, the right to examine all relevant records, and prior written notice whenever a change in the child's placement is proposed, as well as a series of administrative review steps.

Throughout all of the IEP process there is a "stay put" provision, which requires that the child be continued in the current educational context. The only exception to this would be in those instances when the parent and the education agency agree that a change is desirable.

This brief summary of congressional actions and government decisions related to education of the handicapped documents the unique evolution in perspective that has occurred in the last thirty years. Education of handicapped students has moved from the option of the local district to a policy and law of the land. In an analysis of education spending the Sandia National Laboratories noted that most of the increase in educational expenditures in the last twenty years has been in special education. Altogether, these actions signify a major new commitment in American education to address individual needs.

AIDS as a Handicap. Under IDEA the courts have found that AIDS is a handicapping condition. Also, the 1990 Americans with Disabilities Act expanded the definition of "disability" in such a way as to include persons with AIDS. AIDS is an issue charged with emotion, as was desegregation. People do not always approach these difficult situations with calmness or equanimity. The courts, as well as school administrators and teachers, are constantly struggling to determine what is appropriate education for students handicapped with AIDS, and what are suitable educational environments for children with these handicaps. During this time there will be other exceptional and spiritually strong children, such as Ryan White, who challenged the educational system's capabilities. Ryan White was the Indiana adolescent with AIDS who, because of attitudes within the school, was forced to leave town. Others with handicaps will have the courage to challenge the limits of our systems. In those situations, educators, the courts, and our policymakers will be further tested but at the same time will have the opportunity to move our educational system ahead by developing creative approaches and innovative practices. Calm heads will be needed, as will wisdom from all the players in order for the education system to succeed for all its students.

The final issue in this chapter has been education for the handicapped. Prior to 1972, handicapped children received whatever level of public education was made available by their local school districts. Over the last twenty years, a series of legislative acts, rules, and regulations established that handicapped children, including those with AIDS, are entitled to an "adequate" education. The extent and meaning of "adequate" are still being worked out and will continue to be topics of discussion, contention, and legal actions in the remaining 1990s and beyond.

Global Perspectives: Legal Aspects of Education in Other Countries.

The legal aspects of school systems in other countries offer some interesting differences in comparison to the American system. For example, other democratic countries do not have the apparently never ending debates about the separation of church and state. As nearby as provinces of Canada and as far away as Belgium and The Netherlands, public dollars fund nondenominational and church-based

PROFESSIONAL DILEMMA

Should Condoms Be Available to Students in Your School?

Obviously, there are moral, philosophical, religious, and ethical questions related to students having easy access to condoms. Parents would like to believe that their children are not sexually active. Most church and religious groups are opposed to premarital sex. Others are concerned that it is important to educate students about "safe sex," especially with the ever-increasing threat of AIDS.

To help you put this issue into perspective, here are some statistics: A 1991 Centers for Disease Control national survey of teenagers found that 54 percent had had sexual intercourse and that 35 percent had had two or more sexual partners. Among older teenagers, 48 percent had used condoms, while among the fifteen-year-olds, 57 percent had used condoms—which might suggest attempts at early education regarding the dangers of AIDS are having limited effect on the safe-sex practices of students.

When these questions are raised in your classroom, will you limit the discussion and the curriculum that is available to teach young people preventive health behaviors in the face of such epidemics as AIDS, or will you teach specific treatment measures for preventing communicable diseases? For comparison purposes you might be interested in knowing that there was a time when inoculations against disease, such as polio and measles, were administered at school. What about the use of condoms today?

However pressing the realities of health concerns, you and the faculty in your school will have to grapple with this critical question: "Should students have access to condoms at school?" As you might imagine, emotions will have to be placed in juxtaposition to the diverse values and beliefs of various members of the school staff and the community, as well as what the law allows.

- As a teacher, how will you respond to the request to teach about life-threatening epidemics, such as AIDS, that will stir moral controversy?
- Do you see a difference between schools administering vaccinations against disease and schools dispensing condoms to prevent disease? Explain your position.

---

schools. In the Dutch system there are three separate school systems: public, Catholic, and Protestant. Each is supported with public funds, yet each is governed independently.

Germany incorporates instruction in religion in all schools. In fact, often there is one teacher who is hired specifically to teach religion in regularly scheduled classes. Students have to take instruction on religion, and are given a choice of Protestant or Catholic classes. In the higher grades, this instruction shifts toward more emphasis on human values.

Also in Germany there are no school boards, and there are no publicly elected state boards of education. The school system is run by government bureaucracies. The curriculum and exams are set by the state. However, parents are very actively involved in the education of their children at the school site. For example, when there is a "parent evening," *both* parents will attend. At these evenings much of the "talk" between parents will be about the homework assignments that their children have been doing. The reason is that parents are expected to help their children with homework. Yes, in Germany children have three to four hours of homework assignments *every day*. The school day ends at 1:00 P.M. Children return home and work on their homework during the afternoon.

There is a different approach to consideration of special needs children in Germany. These children either have tutors or are assigned to different schools. If a child cannot keep up with the others at a school, he or she is told "You do not belong here." The parents and the child will then either have to work harder at keeping up or move to a different school.

Another legal aspect of the education system in Germany is that teachers as government employees cannot be sued. One consequence is that teachers do not supervise children during nonteaching times. Also, as government employees, teachers are not evaluated after their first year of teaching. As this description of legal aspects of schooling in Germany illustrates, the major aspects of education and schools can be very different from country to country. Be careful to not assume that schools are the same everywhere.

Summary and Implications

The law is involved with American education, and each level of government has legal responsibilities. The U.S. Supreme Court has interpreted the Constitution in many cases related to education. Of special interest are the cases dealing with the First and Fourteenth Amendments. The First Amendment ensures freedom of speech, religion, and the press and the right to petition. Public financial support of nonpublic education and the practice of sectarian religion in public schools have persisted as issues in American education.

The Fourteenth Amendment protects specified privileges of citizens. Segregated schools existed in the United States for many years. Desegregation in the public schools began in 1954 with the U.S. Supreme court ruling on *Brown* v. *Board of Education of Topeka*. These social issues have a decided effect on how schools operate. Currently, you will observe that legal actions are increasing in attempts to be released from court desegregation orders.

The implication of court decisions based on the First and Fourteenth Amendments are many. Local boards of education must develop and adopt policies that harmonize with federal and state legislation and court decisions. The board policies guide administrators and teachers as they carry out their responsibilities. Deciding policy on sensitive subjects like religion and desegregation is often not easy. In classrooms throughout the United States, teachers will need to deal with the proper relationship between religion and public education and with the increasing diversity that is part of schools today.

As was indicated earlier in the chapter, public schools have tended to avoid some of these topics. One reason given by parents for withdrawing their children from public schools was that public schools were promulgating secular humanism and ignoring religion. Public schools cannot foster any particular religion or have religious ceremonies. They can, however, recognize the religious dimension of human existence and conduct appropriate study *about* religion. Public schools and their teachers must address rather than avoid this issue.

A third issue presented in this chapter is affirmative action. The legal basis of affirmative action is found in Titles VI and VII of the Civil Rights Act of 1964 and in Title IX of the Education Amendments of 1972. In essence, they deal with prohibiting discrimination in employment with respect to race, color, religion, sex, or national origin, particularly in educational programs or activities that receive federal financial assistance. Affirmative action also involves positive efforts to recruit and employ individuals and admit students who are underrepresented in the workplace or educational setting. Furthermore, affirmative action is involved in releasing employees. Recent court cases indicate that the courts are more lenient in issues involving hiring than in issues involving releasing employees. Members of minorities can be given preference in hiring to correct past discrimination, but they cannot be given preference over more senior employees in termination of employment.

The concluding section of this chapter described some aspects of law and schooling in Germany. In some way every country will have legal structures related to schools. You are reminded to not expect every country to view schooling, in a legal sense, in the same way.

Discussion Questions

1. The appropriate place, if any, for prayer in public schools continues to be a source of contention. What position should public school teachers take relative to this issue? What will you say if a parent wants you to have a moment of prayer in your classroom?

2. Your state legislators offer many bills related to operation of the public schools. Are there any examples of proposed bills that you think the courts would find unconstitutional?

3. Segregation is illegal, yet there are many schools and school districts in which there are disproportionate numbers of minority students. What do you see as the educational implications of the continuation of these situations?

4. What experiences have you had with Affirmative Action? What implications for teaching do you see in Affirmative Action and Equal Opportunity initiatives?

5. How would you define an "appropriate education" for handicapped children?

Journal/Portfolio Development

1. A number of enduring issues have been described in this chapter. Each has continuing legal challenges, and there is the possibility of new statutory initiatives that could have significant implications for schools. Select one of these issues that you would like to know more about and prepare an "issues brief." Search your college library for relevant material. Review related reports in news magazines and newspapers for the last two years. Develop an analysis of the issue, being sure to describe the different sides and perspectives, not just the side you prefer. In the concluding section of your brief, examine implications of different decision possibilities for you as a teacher and your classroom. Place your notes in your folio under a title such as "Legal Issues."

2. Prayer in public schools is the center for seemingly endless debates. As a teacher, you will probably be asked to offer an opinion, or asked to include a moment of silence in your classroom. Now is the time for you to prepare your position. Certainly, you have a personal position related to whether prayer should be permitted/encouraged/required in public schools. On one page make notes about the key points in your personal position. Then review the position of the courts as outlined in this chapter. Is your personal position consistent with legal precedent? Add to your page of notes where your position is supported and refuted by law. Place your notes in your folio under a title such as "Legal: Prayer in Schools."

School-Based Experiences

1. Interview a school district administrator about the effects of laws and court decisions on schools. How has the administrator had to adjust his or her workday based on the legal aspects of education? Write a report that relates what this person had to say to the legal concepts and issues that were developed in this chapter.

2. Interview a special education teacher about his or her knowledge of Section 504, PL 94–142, and

IDEA. How has the work of this teacher changed with the implementation of these laws? Is this teacher working more or less or about the same as regular classroom teachers? Write a report that contrasts what this teacher is doing with the legal expectations for providing an adequate education for the handicapped.

Notes

1. *Lemon* v. *Kurtzman* (1971).
2. *DiCenso* v. *Robinson* (1971).
3. *State* v. *Peterman* (1904).
4. *Pasadena City Board of Education* v. *Spangler* (1976).

Bibliography

Banks, James A., and Banks, Cherry A. McGree, eds. *Multicultural Education: Issues and Perspectives.* Boston: Allyn and Bacon, 1989.

Fisher, Louis; Schimmel, David; and Kelley, Cynthia. *Teacher and the Law.* New York: Longman, Inc., 1987.

LaMorte, Michael W. *School Law: Cases and Concepts.* Boston: Allyn and Bacon, 1982.

Salome, Rosemary C. *Equal Education Under Law.* New York: St. Martin's Press, 1986.

Sandia National Laboratories. "Sandia Study Helps Focus Educational Improvement Agenda." Albuquerque, NM: Sandia National Laboratories, 1991.

Zerkel, Perry. "Courtside." *Phi Delta Kappan.* (A regular feature in each issue of the *Phi Delta Kappan* providing timely and pertinent information about legal issues.)

10

The Rights of Students and Teachers

Focus Questions

1 Do students have the same rights as adult citizens?
2 What is the difference between procedural and substantive due process?
3 Do teachers and school administrators have to obtain a search warrant before they can search a student?
4 Is it legal for teachers to strike?
5 What is meant by the balance concept between the interest of teachers and the interest of the state?

Key Terms and Concepts

Academic freedom: The opportunity for a teacher to teach without certain coercion, censorship, or other restrictive interference.

Due process: The procedural requirements that must be followed to safeguard individuals from arbitrary, capricious, or unreasonable policies, practices, or actions.

Educational malpractice: Culpable neglect by a teacher in the performance of his or her duties as an educator.

In loco parentis: A term used to describe the implied power of schools to function in place of a parent.

Liability: The failure to use a reasonable amount of care when such conduct results in injury to another.

Teacher certification: The process whereby each state determines the requirements for obtaining a license to teach, processes applications, and issues such licenses.

Tenure: A system of school employment in which educators, after serving a probationary period, retain their positions indefinitely unless they are dismissed for legally specified reasons through clearly established procedures.

$\mathcal{T}$eachers and students have rights and responsibilities. The U.S. Constitution again becomes the primary document and the courts the final arbiters of the extent of these rights. There are some special conditions and constraints on teachers as public employees that are narrowing in comparison to one's rights as a U.S. citizen. Students' rights are constrained due to their age and the custodial and care responsibilities that schools assume. Teachers and students still have rights, and, along with these rights responsibilities. The extent and limits of these as currently defined and adjudicated are presented in this chapter.

Students' Rights and Responsibilities

The rights of students have been through some dramatic shifts during the last twenty-five years. Prior to 1969, school authorities clearly had the final say as long as what they decided was seen as reasonable. A key U.S. Supreme Court decision in 1969 changed the balance by concluding that students do not "shed their constitutional rights to freedom of speech or expression at the schoolhouse gate." Going further on behalf of student rights, in 1975 the Court decided that the principle of due process applied to students. These decisions led to several successful student challenges of school policies and procedures. In the late 1980s Court decisions moved back toward increasing the authority of public school officials. Along the way student life has become more complex, not only through such threats as the increased use of drugs and the presence of weapons and gangs, but also through a diverse multicultural and shifting political context that has made it more difficult to determine what is and what is not appropriate to be able to do and say within a school environment.

To illustrate some of the issues and decisions related to student rights and responsibilities, specific court cases are presented here. Note that the cases do not necessarily constitute the last word regarding student rights, but rather are used to provide an overview of some of the issues that have been decided by our courts. Table 10.1 is a summary of key cases; however, it is not intended to provide a complete understanding of the court decisions. You should read the following narrative and pursue references provided in the Notes and Bibliography to learn more about these and other student rights issues.

Students' Rights as Citizens

Remember, the U.S. Constitution does not mention education. However, through a series of court decisions, all children in the United States have been granted the opportunity for a public school education. Still, as has been pointed out above, this situation is open to change, as is reflected in the 1994 California referendum vote on Proposition 187. Further, although school officials have a great deal of authority, children as students maintain many of the constitutional rights that adult citizens enjoy all the time. As obvious as each of these points may seem, each has been the subject of debate and court decision.

Students' Right to an Education. American children have a right to an education; this right is ensured in many state constitutions. It has been further defined

TABLE 10.1	Selected U.S. Supreme Court Decisions Related to Students' Rights and Responsibilities	
Case	**Issue**	**Decision**
Plyler v. *Doe* (1982)	Rights to education of illegal aliens	Struck down Texas law that denied a free public education to these children.
Goss v. *Lopez* (1975)	Suspension of high school students without a hearing	Court ruled only in an emergency can a student be suspended without a hearing.
Wood v. *Strickland* (1975)	Can school board members be sued for depriving students of their constitutional rights? (suspension)?	Students can seek damages from individual school board members but not from the school district.
Tinker v. *Des Moines Independent Community School District* (1969)	Free speech rights of students to wear black armbands to protest war in Vietnam	Court ruled against school district—recognized to an extent constitutional rights of pupils.
Board of Education, Island Trees Union Free District No. 26 v. *Pico* (1982)	Challenged school board's decision to remove books from the school library	Court issued decision that, under certain circumstances, children may challenge board's decision to remove books.
Ingraham v. *Wright* (1977)	May states authorize corporal punishment without consent of the student's parent?	Yes, states may constitutionally authorize corporal punishment.
Bethel School District No. 403 v. *Fraser* (1986)	May school officials restrain student speech?	School officials may discipline a student for making lewd and indecent speech in a school assembly attended by other students.
Hazelwood School District v. *Kuhlmeier* (1988)	School district control of student expression in school newspapers, theatrical productions, and other forums	School administrators have broad authority to control student expression in the official student newspaper, which is not a public forum—considered as a part of the curriculum.
Honig v. *Doe* (1988)	Violation of the Education for All Handicapped Children Act P.L. 94–142; indefinitely suspended and attempted to expel two emotionally disturbed students	The Act authorizes officials to suspend dangerous and crippled children for a maximum of ten days. Justice Brennan said, "Congress very much meant to strip schools of unilateral authority to exclude disturbed students."
New Jersey v. *T.L.O.* (1985)	Search and seizure	School officials must have a reasonable cause when engaged in searches.

by court decisions and is now interpreted to mean that each child shall have an equal opportunity to pursue education.

The right to an education, however, is not without certain prerequisites. Citizenship alone does not guarantee a free education. Statutes that establish public school systems also generally establish how operating costs will be met. Real estate taxes are the usual source of funds, so the residence requirement is necessary for school attendance without tuition. *Residence* does not mean that the student, parent, or guardian must pay real estate taxes; it means that the student must live in the school district in which he or she wants to attend school. Residence then is a prerequisite to the right of a free public education within a specific school district.

The Children of Undocumented Illegal Aliens Have a Right to a Public Education.
In *Plyler* v. *Doe* (1982) the controversial five-to-four majority decision struck down a Texas law denying a free public education to these children. The majority opinion held that the Texas law "imposes a lifetime of hardship on a discrete class of children not accountable for their disabling status and promotes the creation and perpetuation of a subclass of illiterates within our boundaries, surely adding to the problems and costs of unemployment, welfare, and crime."

As part of the continuing taxpayer revolt, the rights of children of undocumented and illegal aliens were challenged in California in the 1994 election. A citizens' referendum, Proposition 187, was approved by the voters. One aspect of this initiative directs that public services (schools) cannot be made available to children whose parents are not U.S. citizens. Although this referendum only applies to California, it is being challenged in state and federal courts and would seem to directly violate *Plyler* v. *Doe.*

Homeless Children Have the Right to Go to School.   There are over 500,000 homeless children in the United States. Since access to public school usually requires a residence address and a parent or guardian, as well as transportation, in the past homeless children were squeezed out of the system. This growing problem was addressed by Congress in 1987 with passage of the Stewart B. McKinney Homeless Assistance Act, which requires that "each State educational agency shall assure that each child of a homeless individual and each homeless youth have access to a free, appropriate public education." The law was amended in 1990 to require each school district to provide services to the homeless that are comparable to the services offered other students in the schools. These services include allowing homeless children to finish the school year in the school they were in before they lost their housing, providing transportation to school, tutoring to help catch students up, and giving the opportunity to take part in school programs offered to other children.

Students' Right to Sue.   The U.S. Supreme Court has affirmed that students may sue school board members who are guilty of intentionally depriving students of their constitutional rights. In *Wood* v. *Strickland* (1975) the Supreme Court held that school officials who discipline students unfairly cannot defend themselves against civil rights suits by claiming ignorance of pupils' basic constitutional rights. As a result of this decision, Judge Paul Williams, a federal judge in Arkansas, ordered that the students who had been suspended could seek damages from individual school board members—though not from the school district as a corporate body. The judge also ruled that the school records of the pupils must be cleared of the suspension incident. From these decisions it is apparent that the U.S. Supreme Court is taking into account the rights of students.

Rights of Students to Collect Damages.   The Supreme Court extended and clarified its ruling in *Wood* three years later when it considered the right of students to collect damages for having been suspended without a hearing.[1] The case treated two issues: under what conditions damages may be awarded to students who have been deprived of their constitutional rights and the amount of damages they can receive. The Court held that a student must first clearly establish that an injury has occurred before damages can be collected. Since that condition had not been established, the Court ruled that the students were entitled only to symbolic damages of $1.00.

Students' Right to Due Process. Much of the recent involvement of the courts with student rights has concerned due process of law for pupils. Due process is guaranteed by the Fourteenth Amendment. The protection clause states that "nor shall any State . . . deny to any person within its jurisdiction the equal protection of the laws." **Due process** of law means following those rules and principles that have been established for enforcing and protecting the rights of the accused. Due process has two connotations—procedural and substantive. *Procedural* due process has to do with whether or not the procedures used in disciplinary cases are fair; *substantive* due process is concerned with whether or not the school authorities have deprived a student of basic substantive constitutional rights such as personal liberty, property, and privacy.[2]

The application of due process to issues in schools is a recent phenomenon. Historically, schools functioned under the doctrine of **in loco parentis** (in place of a parent). This doctrine meant that schools could exercise almost complete control over students because they were acting as parent substitutes. Under the doctrine of *in loco parentis* the courts have usually upheld the rules and regulations of local boards of education, particularly about pupil conduct. However, the courts have not supported rules that are unconstitutionally "vague" and/or "overboard." The following cases illustrate the difficult balance between protecting students' right to due process, and at the same time allowing schools to have sufficient authority to pursue their mission.

Procedural Due Process Is Frequently Scrutinized in Cases of Suspension and Expulsion. These cases most often result from disciplinary action taken by the school, which may or may not have violated a pupil's substantive constitutional rights. For example, in *Goss v. Lopez* (1975) the U.S. Supreme Court dealt with the suspension of high school students in Columbus, Ohio. In that case the named plaintiffs alleged that they had been suspended from public high school for up to ten days without a hearing. The action was brought up for deprivation of constitutional rights. Two students who were suspended for a semester brought suit charging that their due process rights were denied—because they were not present at the board meeting when the suspensions were handed out.

In ruling that students cannot be suspended without some kind of hearing, the Court said:

> The prospect of imposing elaborate hearing requirements in every suspension case is viewed with great concern, and many school authorities may well prefer the untrammeled power to act unilaterally, unhampered by rules about notice and hearing. But it would be a strange disciplinary system in an educational institution if no communication was sought by the disciplinarian with the student in an effort to inform him of his defalcation and to let him tell his side of the story in order to make sure than an injustice is not done. Fairness can rarely be obtained by secret, one-sided determination of the facts decisive of rights. . . . Secrecy is not congenial to truth-seeking and self-righteousness gives too slender an assurance of rightness. No better instrument has been devised for arriving at truth than to give a person in jeopardy of serious loss notice of the case against him and opportunity to meet it.

Students have frequently organized to strike for their rights.

Procedural due process cases usually involve alleged violations of the Fourteenth Amendment, which provides for the protection of specified privileges of citizens, including notice to the student, impartiality of the hearing process, and the right of representation. They may also involve alleged violations of state constitutions or statutory law that call for specific procedures. For example, many states have procedures for expulsion or suspension. Expulsion usually involves notifying parents or guardians in a specific way, perhaps by registered mail, and giving students the opportunity for a hearing before the board of education or a designated hearing officer. Suspension procedures are usually detailed as well, designating who has the authority to suspend and the length of time for suspension. Teachers and administrators should know due process regulations, including the specific regulations of the state where they are employed.

Substantive Due Process Frequently Addresses Questions of the Students' Constitutional Rights to Free Speech versus the Schools' Authority to Maintain Order in Support of Education. The *Tinker* case (*Tinker* v. *Des Moines Independent Community School District,* 1969) was significant. It involved a school board's attempt to keep students from wearing black armbands in a protest against hostilities in Vietnam. In 1969 the U.S. Supreme Court ruled against the Des Moines school board. The majority opinion of the Court was that

> the wearing of armbands in the circumstances of this case was entirely divorced from actually or potentially disruptive conduct by those participating in it. It was closely akin to "pure speech" which, we have repeatedly held, is entitled to comprehensive protection, under the First Amendment. . . .
>
> First Amendment rights, applied in the light of the special characteristics of the school environment, are available to teachers and students. It can hardly be argued that either students or teachers shed their constitutional rights to freedom at the schoolhouse gate.

In the *Tinker* opinion the Court clearly designated that the decision "does not concern aggressive, disruptive action or even group demonstrations." The decision did make it clear that whatever their age, students have constitutional rights; and the decision has had widespread effect on the operation of schools in the United States. Schools have had to pay attention to school law. Educators as well as lawyers have been guided by the principles set forth in the decision regarding the constitutional relationship between public school students and school officials.

A more recent U.S. Supreme Court decision appears to have at least narrowed the breadth of application of the *Tinker* ruling. The case involved Matthew Fraser, a high school senior in a school outside Tacoma, Washington. In the spring of 1983, Fraser was suspended from school for two days after he gave a short speech at a school assembly nominating a friend for a position in student government. School officials argued that Fraser's speech contained sexual innuendos that provoked other students to engage in disruptive behaviors unfavorable to the school setting. The U.S. District Court for the Western District of Washington held that Fraser's punishment violated his rights to free speech under the First Amendment and awarded him damages. The U.S. Court of Appeals for the Ninth Circuit affirmed the decision, holding that Fraser's speech was not disruptive under the standards of *Tinker*.[3] However, in the majority opinion in *Bethel School District No. 403* v. *Fraser* (1986), Chief Justice Warren Burger wrote: "The determination of what manner of speech in the classroom or in school assembly is inappropriate properly rests with the school board."

Attorney Thomas J. Flygare suggests that the major unanswered question appears to be whether *Fraser* will be interpreted to permit school officials to place an outright ban on political speech as "inappropriate" or whether it will be interpreted only to permit punishment for "indecent" and similar forms of speech.[4]

Efforts Have Been Made to Define Student Rights. One such effort, *A Bill of Rights for High School Students,* was developed by the American Civil Liberties Union of Maryland. It is based partly on court decisions and illustrates current thinking about student rights. It addresses, for example, freedom of expression, religion, and privacy and rights of equality of opportunity and due process. (The complete text is given in Appendix 10.1 on page 288.) Many school systems also have established their own bill of rights.

Students' Responsibilities in School

The right, or privilege, of children to attend school also depends on their compliance with the rules and regulations of the school. To ensure the day-to-day orderly operation of schools, boards of education have the right to establish reasonable rules and regulations controlling pupils and their conduct. In a number of instances the boards' actions have been challenged. Most challenges have concerned corporal punishment, rights of married students to an education, dress codes, freedom of expression, and involvement with drugs.

Dress Codes and Grooming. Lower-court cases dealing with grooming have been decided in some instances in favor of the board of education—in support of their rules and regulations—and in other instances in favor of the student. A general principle seems to be that if the dress and grooming do not incite or cause disruptive behavior or pose a health or safety problem, the court ruling is likely to support the student. Dress codes, once very much in vogue, are much less evident today. Although the U.S. Supreme Court has yet to consider a so-called long-hair case, federal courts in every circuit have issued rulings in such cases; half of them found such regulations unconstitutional, and half upheld them. In all, over a two-decade period, more than three hundred cases on this subject were decided by federal and state courts. If there is a trend, it is that students have won most of the cases that dealt with hairstyle.

The courts have usually refused to uphold dress and hair length regulations for athletic teams or extracurricular activities unless the school proves that the hair or dress interfered with a student's ability to play the sport or perform the activity.[5]

In the late 1970s and continuing through the 1980s, courts entertained fewer challenges to grooming regulations. The later decisions, however, continued to be consistent with earlier court rulings. Courts have supported school officials who attempted to regulate student appearance if the regulation could be based on disruption, health, or safety. Presumably, the controversy over the length of a student's hair or one's grooming in general is no longer critical because officials and students have a more common ground of agreement about what is acceptable. However, as the 1990s continue, new questions could be raised in relation to school efforts to control the clothing and other grooming symbols of gangs.

Corporal Punishment. In 1977 the U.S. Supreme Court ruled on and finally resolved many of the issues related to corporal punishment (*Ingraham* v. *Wright*, 1977). The opinion established that states may *constitutionally* authorize corporal punishment without prior hearing or notice and without consent by the student's parents, and may as a matter of policy elect to prohibit or limit the use of corporal punishment. It also held that corporal punishment is not in violation of the Eighth Amendment.

In response to the greater sensitivity to student rights, many school districts have adopted administrative rules and regulations to restrict the occasions, nature, and manner of administering corporal punishment. In some instances, school districts specify that corporal punishment may be administered only under the direction of the principal and in the presence of another adult.

For the most part, courts have been consistent over the years in upholding school personnel in administering *reasonable* corporal punishment. Reasonableness frequently reflects local attitudes; its definition will therefore vary from region to region. In determining whether or not to administer corporal punishment, school personnel should consider these factors: age, sex, and size of pupil; size and suitability of the instrument and force employed; and the degree of the punishment in respect to the nature of the infraction. It should be noted that the lower courts across the country vary in their judgments regarding the reasonableness of corporal punishment. Teachers are cautioned to be very careful in the use of corporal punishment. Failure to exercise force with limits imposed by common law can expose a teacher to a suit for excessive use of force (battery).

Sex Discrimination. Until relatively recently, educational institutions could discriminate against females—whether they were students, staff, or faculty. In 1972 the Ninety-Second Congress enacted Title IX of the Education Amendments Act to remove sex discrimination against students and employees in federally assisted programs. The key provision in Title IX states: "No person in the United States shall, on the basis of sex, be excluded from participation in, be denied the benefits of, or be subjected to discrimination under any education program or activity receiving federal financial assistance." Title IX is enforced by the Department of Education's Office of Civil Rights. An individual or organization can allege that any policy or practice is discriminatory by writing a letter of complaint to the Secretary of Education. An administrative hearing is the next step in the process. Further steps include suing for money damages under Title IX, which the U.S. Supreme Court affirms in *Franklin* v. *Guinneth County Schools* (1992).

Marriage and Pregnancy. In the past it was not unusual for school officials to expel students who married. Some educators reasoned that marriage brought on additional responsibilities such as the establishment of a household and thus they could not perform well in school. They believed that exclusion would be a deterrent to others. Courts tended to uphold school officials in these positions. Both courts and school officials acted consistently in not rigidly enforcing compulsory attendance statutes for underage students. However, school officials today cannot prohibit a student from attending school merely because he or she is married. This position is based on the notion that every child has a right to attend school and the above-mentioned Title IX.

Public policy today encourages students to acquire as much education as they can. Not only are married students encouraged to remain in school, but they are also entitled to the same rights and privileges as unmarried students. Thus they have the right to take any course the school offers and to participate in extracurricular activities open to other students. That is, participation in extracurricular activities cannot be denied a student solely on the basis of married status. However, a student's attendance and participation rights may be removed when his or her behavior is deleterious to other students.

Today's schools also enroll more pregnant students than ever before. Title IX prohibits their exclusion from school or from participation in extracurricular activities. A number of school systems have reorganized their school programs so that courses can be offered during after-school hours or in the evenings to accommodate married and pregnant students. This arrangement makes it easier for students to work during the day and complete their education at a time convenient to them. Included in such programs are courses and topics aimed at the specific audience and a counseling program to assist students with their adjustment to marriage and family life.

Child Abuse and Neglect. Our system of government has the right of exercising police power, which means that government is entrusted with the responsibility of looking after the health, safety, and welfare of all its citizens. In effect, a state acts as a guardian over all its people, exercising that role specifically over individuals not able to look after themselves. This guardianship extends to care for children who have been either abused or neglected by their parents. To date, all fifty states have statutes dealing with this issue. These statutes generally protect children under the age of eighteen, but the scope of protection and definitions of abuse and neglect vary considerably among the states. In 1974 Congress passed the Child Abuse Prevention and Treatment Act, which provides financial assistance to states that have developed and implemented programs for identifying, preventing, and treating instances of child abuse and neglect.

The severity of this problem has been highlighted by the requirement of mandatory reporting of suspected abuse and neglect. Formerly, this reporting was limited mainly to physicians, but today educators are also required to report instances of suspected abuse and neglect. Some teachers are reluctant to do so because they fear a breakdown in student-teacher-parent relationships and the possibility of a lawsuit based on an invasion of privacy, assault, or slander. Their fear should be diminished, however, by statutes that grant them immunity for acting in good faith.

School Records. Before November 19, 1974, the effective date of the Buckley Amendment, the law regarding the privacy of student records was extremely unclear. Many school administrators—and most parents—do not yet realize that parents now have the right to view their children's educational records. Students over the age of eighteen also have the right to see their school records for themselves. Many teachers are not yet aware that their written comments, which they submit as part of a student's record, must be shown at a parent's request, or at a student's request if the student is eighteen or older.

The new law (Public Law 93–380 as amended by Public Law 93–568) requires that schools receiving federal funds must comply with the privacy requirements or face loss of those funds. What must a school district do to comply? According to a 1976 clarification by HEW, the Buckley Amendment sets forth these main requirements that the school district must follow:

> Allow all parents, even those not having custody of their children, access to each educational record that a school district keeps on their child.
>   Establish a district policy on how parents can go about seeing specific records.
>   Inform all parents what rights they have under the Amendment, how they can act on these rights according to school policy, and where they can see a copy of the policy.
>   Seek parental permission in writing before disclosing any personally identifiable record on a child to individuals other than professional personnel employed in the district (and others who meet certain specific requirements).[6]

Since the loss of federal funds could present serious problems to some school districts, the responsibility for procedures to meet the requirements of the Buckley Amendment is self-evident. Many school districts have carefully formulated procedures; others are striving to clarify procedures in order to prevent conflicts.

Student Publications. A significant decision relative to "underground" student newspapers was made in Illinois in 1970.[7] Students were expelled for distributing a newspaper named *Grass High*, which criticized school officials and used vulgar language. The students were expelled under an Illinois statute that empowered boards of education to expel pupils guilty of gross disobedience or misconduct. The board of education was supported by a federal court in Illinois, but on appeal the Court of Appeals for the Seventh Circuit reversed the decision. The school board was not able to validate student disruption and interference as required by *Tinker*. The plaintiffs were entitled to collect damages. An implication is the rights of students regarding newspapers they print at home are stronger.

Early in 1988, in a landmark decision (*Hazelwood School District* v. *Kuhlmeier*), the U.S. Supreme Court ruled that administrators have broad authority to control student expression in official school newspapers, theatrical productions, and other forums that are a part of the curriculum. In reaching that decision the Court determined that the *Spectrum*, the school newspaper of the Hazelwood District, was not a public forum. A school policy of the Hazelwood District required that the principal review each proposed issue of the *Spectrum*. The principal objected to two articles scheduled to appear in one issue. One of the articles was about girls at the school who had become pregnant; the other discussed the effects on students of divorce. Neither article used real names. The principal deleted two pages of the *Spectrum* rather than delete only the offending articles or require that they be modified. He stated that there was no time to make any changes in the articles and that the newspaper had to be printed immediately or not at all.

Three student journalists sued, contending that their freedom of speech had been violated. The Supreme Court upheld the principal's action. Justice Byron White decided that the *Spectrum* was not a public forum, but rather a supervised learning experience for journalism students. In effect, the censorship of a student press was upheld by the Supreme Court.

In Justice White's words,

> schools must be able to set high standards for the student speech that is disseminated under [their] auspices—standards that may be higher than those demanded by some newspaper publishers and theatrical producers in the "real" world—and may refuse to disseminate student speech that does not meet those standards.
>
>   Accordingly, we hold that the standard articulated in *Tinker* for determining when a school may punish student expression need not also be the standard for determining when a school may refuse to lend its name and resources to the dissemination of student expression.

The issue of institutional control over publications has not yet been fully resolved. Student publications and their distribution have prompted school boards to write rules and regulations that will withstand judicial scrutiny. A prompt review and reasonably fast appeal procedures are vital. Students should also be advised of distribution rules and abide by them.

Student Rights for the Handicapped.   Before the early 1970s handicapped students' access to education was left to the discretion of different levels of government. In the early 1970s court decisions established the position that handicapped students were entitled to an "appropriate" education and to procedural protections against arbitrary treatment. Congress subsequently specified a broad set of substantive and procedural rights via Section 504 of the Rehabilitation Act and the Education for All Handicapped Children Act (EAHCA). (These acts were described in Chapter 9.) Since that time there has been a continuing series of legislative and legal refinements and extensions of the intents to see that handicapped students have appropriate educational opportunities. The problem has been to define what is meant by "appropriate." This examination and clarification process continues to unfold.

The Individuals with Disabilities Education Act guarantees all students with disabilities access to an equal education.

One recent case dealing with student rights dealt with a violation of the Education for All Handicapped Children Act, PL 94-142. That law requires public school officials to keep disruptive or violent handicapped students in their current classrooms pending hearings on their behavior. In the decision made in *Honig* v. *Doe* (1988) the U.S. Supreme Court upheld lower court rulings that San Francisco school district officials violated the act in 1980 when they indefinitely suspended and then attempted to expel two emotionally disturbed students whom the officials claimed were dangerous.

Relevant Research

Search of a Student's Purse

A New Jersey teacher discovered two girls smoking in a lavatory, a violation of school rules. While one of the girls admitted to smoking, the second, T.L.O. denied it. The assistant vice principal demanded to see T.L.O.'s purse., opened it, and found a pack of cigarettes. He accused her of lying and reached in to pull out the cigarette pack.

As he reached into the purse he noticed a package of cigarette rolling papers. A thorough search of the purse revealed a small amount of marijuana, a pipe, empty plastic bags, a substantial quantity of money, an index card that appeared to be a list of students who owed T.L.O. money, and two letters that implicated T.L.O. in marijuana dealing.

T.L.O. subsequently confessed to the police that she had sold marijuana at the high school, but later contended that the search of her purse had been unlawful under the Fourth Amendment.

The case was brought to the U.S. Supreme Court in *New Jersey* v. *T.L.O.* (1985). The court first held that the Fourth Amendment's prohibition of unreasonable searches and seizures does apply to public school officials. The Court then explored how to strike the balance between the student's right to privacy and the school's need to maintain a proper learning environment. The Court concluded that school officials need not obtain a warrant before searching a student and that the legality of a search should depend on the reasonableness of the search. The Court concluded that the school officials' actions were correct.

The act authorizes officials to suspend dangerous handicapped children for a maximum of ten days. Longer suspensions or expulsions are permissible only if the child's parents consent to the action taken or the officials can convince a federal district judge that the child poses a danger to himself or herself or to others. The rules under which school officials must operate also are more limiting if the misbehavior is a manifestation of the student's handicap.

It is clear that Congress meant to restrain the authority that schools had traditionally used to exclude disabled students, particularly emotionally disturbed students from school. PL 94–142 did not leave school administrators powerless to deal with dangerous students.

Student and Locker Searches.   Most courts have refused to subject public school searches to the strict Fourth Amendment standards. In general, the Fourth Amendment protects individuals from search without a warrant (court order). Many lower courts have decided in favor of a more lenient interpretation of the Fourth Amendment in school searches. The rationale is that school authorities are obligated to maintain discipline and a sound educational environment and that responsibility, along with their *in loco parentis* powers, gives them the right to conduct searches and seize contraband on reasonable suspicion without a warrant. First, however, school officials may only search for evidence that a student has violated a school rule or law. Then, there must be a valid rule or law in place.

School authorities do not need a warrant to search a student's locker or a student vehicle on campus. For searches of a student's person, however, courts apply a higher standard. Where reasonable suspicion exists, a school official will likely be upheld. Reasonable suspicion exists when one has information that a student is in possession of something harmful or dangerous, or there is evidence of illegal activities such as drug dealing (money, a list of customers, or selling papers). The second consideration is the way in which the search of a student's person is conducted. School officials are advised to have students remove contents from their clothing rather than have a teacher or administrator do it. A further caution is not to force students to remove all their clothing or undress to their underwear. To date, courts have not upheld school officials in strip searches. These cases evoke the greatest judicial sympathy toward student damages for illegal searches.[8]

The rights of students include their right to privacy. For example, should teachers be able to search a student's locker without a search warrant?

Peer Sexual Harassment   Title IX prohibits sex discrimination, and this includes students harassing other students. Teasing, snapping bra straps, requesting sexual favors, making lewd comments about one's appearance or body parts, telling sexual jokes, engaging in physical abuse, and touching inappropriately are examples of sexual harassment. It is important for teachers to make it clear that sexual harassment will not be tolerated. School districts are supposed to have in place a grievance procedure for sex discrimination complaints. Students and/or their parents can file a complaint with the Office of Civil Rights also. All allegations must be investigated promptly, and immediate action must be taken in those cases where harassment behaviors have been confirmed. Keep in mind that sexual harassment is not limited to high school students; middle school and in some cases elementary school children are also sexually harassed.

Educational Malpractice.   Culpable neglect by a teacher in the performance of his or her duties is called **educational malpractice**. The courts of California[9] and New York[10] dismissed suits by former students alleging indirect injury. The plaintiffs claimed that they did not achieve an adequate education and that this was the fault of the school district. In the California case the student, after graduating from high school, could barely read and write. The judge in his opinion stated:

> The science of pedagogy itself is fraught with different and conflicting theories . . . and any layman might—and commonly does—have his own emphatic viewpoints on the subject. . . . The achievement of literacy in the schools, or its failure, is influenced by a host of factors from outside the formal teaching process, and beyond the course of its ministries.

In essence, the judge stated that there is no way to assess the school's negligence. In the New York case the judge said, "The failure to learn does not bespeak a failure to teach." In the 1990s, with the push for accountability, there are likely to be more tests of the educational malpractice question.

As a summary of the discussion of this section, Table 10.2 on page 272 lists brief statements related to the rights and responsibilities of students.

TABLE 10.2   Summary Statements on Students' Rights and Responsibilities

State constitutions provide that a child has the right to an education; to date, students have been unsuccessful in suing school board members on the ground that they have not learned anything.

The due process clause provides that a child is entitled to notice of charges and the opportunity for a hearing prior to being suspended from school for misbehavior.

Students enjoy freedom of speech at school unless that speech is indecent or leads to disruption; courts are in agreement that school officials can regulate the content of student newspapers. Underground newspapers are not subject to this oversight.

Students may be awarded damages from school board members for a violation of their constitutional rights if they can establish that they were injured by the deprivation and that the school official deliberately violated those rights.

The use of corporal punishment is not prohibited by the U.S. Constitution, but excessive punishment may be by the Fourteenth Amendment.

Students may be restricted in their dress when there are problems of disruption, health, or safety.

Assignments of students to activities or classes in general on the basis of sex is not consistent with Title IX. These assignments may be made in such areas as sex education classes or when sports are available for both sexes.

Restricting a student's activities on the basis of marriage or pregnancy is inconsistent with the equal protection clause and Title IX.

Teachers are required to report to proper authorities suspected instances of child abuse and neglect.

Parents have the right to examine their children's educational records; students age eighteen and older have the right to examine their records; school officials may search students, lockers, and student property without a search warrant, but they must have reasonable grounds for believing that the student is in possession of evidence of a school rule or law violation.

Teachers' Rights and Responsibilities

Teachers have the same rights as other citizens. The Fourteenth Amendment provides for substantive due process (protection against the deprivation of constitutional rights such as freedom of expression) and procedural due process (procedural protection against unjustified deprivation of substantive rights). Most court cases related to teachers evolve from either liberty or property interests. Liberty interests are created by the Constitution itself; property interests are found in some form of legal entitlement such as tenure or certification.

Teachers also have the same responsibilities as other citizens. They must abide by federal, state, and local laws and by the provisions of contracts. As professionals, they must also assume the heavy responsibility of educating young people. Specific court cases are discussed briefly to illustrate some of the issues and decisions related to aspects of teacher rights and responsibilities. Note that the cases selected do not necessarily constitute the last word regarding teacher rights but rather are used to provide an overview of some of the issues that have been decided in our courts. Table 10.3 summarizes the issues and decisions in selected cases involving teacher rights and responsibilities. This summary table is not intended to provide a complete understanding of the court decisions cited. You should read

TABLE 10.3	Selected U.S. Supreme Court Decisions Related to Teachers' Rights and Responsibilities	
Case	**Issue**	**Decision**
North Haven Board of Education v. *Bell* (1982)	Former women faculty members alleged sex discrimination	Court ruled that school employees as well as students are protected under Title IX.
Cleveland Board of Education v. *LeFleur* (1974)	Rights of pregnant teachers	Court struck down the board policy forcing all pregnant teachers to take mandatory maternity leave.
Board of Regents of State Colleges v. *Roth* (1972)	Rights of nontenured teachers	Teacher had been hired under a one-year contract. Court concluded that he did not have a property interest that would entitle him to procedural rights under the Fourteenth Amendment.
Perry v. *Sindermann* (1972)	Rights of nontenured teachers	A state employee may acquire the property interest if officially fostered customs, rules, understandings, and practices imply a contract promise to grant continuing contract status and thus establish a *de facto* tenure system.
Pickering v. *Board of Education* (1968)	Illinois teacher dismissed for criticizing a school board and superintendent in a letter published by a local newspaper	Court upheld teacher's claim that his First and Fourteenth Amendment rights were denied.
Hortonville Joint School District No. 1 v. *Hortonville Education Association* (1976)	May boards of education dismiss teachers who are striking illegally?	Court said the law gave the board power to employ and dismiss teachers as a part of the municipal labor relations balance.

the textual narrative for better comprehension. Note also that most of the court cases were decided in the 1970s and 1980s; as is illustrated in the examples, more recently new federal statutes have been the defining force.

Conditions of Employment

There are a number of conditions that must be met in order for you to be hired as a teacher. These include successfully completing a professional preparation program, being credentialed or licensed by the state, and receiving a contract from the hiring school district. In each of these instances you have rights established in law and statute, as well as responsibilities.

Teacher Certification and Licensure. The primary purpose of **teacher certification** and licensure is to make sure there are qualified and competent teachers in the public schools. All states have established requirements for teacher certification and licensure. Carrying out the policies of certification is usually a function of a state professional standards board. The board first has to make certain that applicants meet legal requirements; it then issues the appropriate license/certifi-cates. Certifying agencies may not arbitrarily refuse to issue a certificate to a qualified candidate. The courts have ruled that local boards of education may pre-scribe additional or higher qualifications beyond the state requirements, provid-ed that such requirements are not irrelevant, unreasonable, or arbitrary. A teaching certificate or license is a privilege granted to practice a profession—it is not a right. Teacher certification is a property interest that cannot be revoked without consti-tutional due process. Certification laws usually require, in addition, that the can-didate show evidence of citizenship, good moral character, and good physical health. A minimum age is frequently specified.

Teacher Employment Contracts. Usually, boards of education have the statutory authority to employ teachers. This authority includes the power to enter into contracts and to fix terms of employment and compensation. In some states, only specific members of the school board may sign teacher contracts. When statutes confer the employing authority to boards of education, the authority can-not be delegated. It is usually the responsibility of the superintendent to screen and nominate candidates to the board. The board, meeting in official session, then acts officially as a group to enter into contractual agreement. Employment procedures vary from state to state, but the process is fundamentally prescribed by the legislature and must be strictly followed by local boards.

A contract usually contains the following elements: the identification of the teacher and the board of education, a statement of the legal capacity of each party to enter into contract, a definition of the assignment specified, a statement of the salary and how it is to be paid, and a provision for signature by the teacher and by the legally authorized agents of the board. In some states, contract forms are pro-vided by state departments of education, and these forms must be used; in others, forms are optional.

A teacher may not enter into legal contract without having a valid teaching certificate issued by the state. Funds may not be legally expended under a contract with a teacher who is not legally certified. Teachers are responsible for making cer-tain that they are legally qualified to enter into contractual agreements. Further-more, they are responsible for carrying out the terms of the contract and abiding by them. In turn, under the contract they can legally expect proper treatment from an employer.

Discrimination. School districts are prohibited from use of discriminatory practices in the hiring, dismissal, promotion, and demotion of school personnel. In addition to court decisions, federal statutes, such as the Civil Rights Acts of 1964 and 1991, have had a defining influence on the legal basis for discrimina-tion. For example, the 1991 law expanded protection beyond race to also include discrimination based on sex, disability, religion, and national origin. Further, employment practices must be "job-related for the position in question and con-sistent with business necessity." The 1991 law also places the burden on the defen-dant (schools) to show that a legitimate nondiscriminatory reason existed for the personnel decision.

Sex Discrimination. In *North Haven Board of Education* v. *Bell* (1982) the U.S. Supreme Court ruled that school employees as well as students are protected under Title IX. The North Haven decision involved former women faculty members who alleged sex discrimination in employment. In upholding Title IX regulations the decision not only allows the U.S. Department of Education to investigate complaints from school employees but also permits the department to cut off federal aid to institutions that discriminate.

Pay Equity.   *Burkey* v. *Marshall County Board of Education* (1981) was a decision regarding pay equity. It ruled that the Marshall County school board's policy of paying the female coach of the girls' basketball team half the salary of the male coach of the boys' basketball team violated the Equal Pay Act, Title VII of the Civil Rights Act of 1964, and the Constitution. The Court also ruled that the board's policy of hiring only male teachers as coaches of boys' sports constituted illegal sex discrimination.

Racial Discrimination.   Courts will not intervene when the school board can prove that its decision not to hire or promote a minority was based on legitimate criteria, such as academic qualifications, work experience, licensing, attitude, or job performance. In Missouri, an untenured African American school teacher was laid off because of declining enrollment. When she was not recalled to fill a subsequent teaching vacancy, she sued the school board. The U.S. Court of Appeals, Eighth Circuit, denied her claim of racial discrimination, saying that the board had based its decision on the fact that she lacked permanent state licensing.[11]

Handicap Discrimination.   In another instance a legally blind librarian in Arkansas brought suit against a local school board claiming that she was unlawfully discriminated against in not being hired for a librarian position. The librarian then brought suit in a U.S. district court in Arkansas that held that although she was an "otherwise qualified handicapped individual" under Section 504 of the Rehabilitation Act, the school board had articulated genuine nondiscriminatory reasons for the failure to hire her. The court therefore concluded that the librarian was not denied employment by the school board because of her handicap and that the board had a rational basis for hiring the other applicant. Thus there was no violation of the Rehabilitation Act, and the board's decision was upheld.[12]

Teacher Pregnancy.   In *Cleveland Board of Education* v. *LaFleur* (1974), a landmark decision, the U.S. Supreme Court struck down a school board policy that forced all pregnant teachers to take mandatory maternity leave at fixed periods before and following the pregnancy term, without regard to the ability of different women to continue to work through different stages of pregnancy or recovery. School boards may reasonably regulate pregnancy situations to ensure continuity of instructional services by requiring teachers to notify the school district early in their pregnancy so that school needs may be anticipated. Board policies may not, however, establish arbitrary leave and return dates. Those decisions are best made by the teacher and her physician.

In 1979 Congress passed the Pregnancy Discrimination Act as an amendment to Title VII. The act stipulates that discrimination "because of or on the basis of pregnancy, childbirth or related medical conditions" is prohibited. Women may not be fired, denied promotions, or refused employment as a consequence of their being pregnant or having an abortion. They cannot be forced to take sick leave or exhaust their vacation time. They are entitled to the same disability or sick leave and health insurance benefits as other employees. If other employees are entitled to resume their jobs after disability leave, so too are women who have been pregnant. However, they are not guaranteed the same grade, classroom, or school.

Right to Bargain Collectively. The rights of teachers to bargain collectively has been an active issue over the last three decades. In the past, teacher groups met informally with boards of education to discuss salaries and other teacher welfare provisions. Sometimes, the superintendent was even the spokesperson for such teacher groups. In recent years, formal collective procedures have evolved. These procedures have been labeled collective bargaining, professional negotiation, cooperative determination, and collective negotiation. Collective bargaining has been defined as a way of winning improved goals and not the goal itself. The right of employees to bargain collectively and the duties of the district to bargain are not constitutionally granted, but are a right typically guaranteed by statute.

A contract means that salaries, working conditions, and other matters within the scope of the collective bargaining agreement can no longer be decided unilaterally by the school administration and board of education. Instead, the contract outlines effective participation by the teachers' union and its members in formulating the school policies and programs under which they work.

The first teachers' group to bargain collectively with its local board of education was the Maywood, Illinois, Proviso Council of West Suburban Teachers, Union Local 571, in 1938. In 1957 a second local, the East St. Louis, Illinois, Federation of Teachers, was successful in negotiating a written contract. The breakthrough, however, came in December 1961, when the United Federation of Teachers, Local 2 of the American Federation of Teachers (AFT), won the right to bargain for New York City's teachers. Since then, collective bargaining agreements between boards of education and teacher groups have grown phenomenally. Both the AFT and the NEA have been active in promoting collective bargaining. Today, approximately 75 percent of the nation's teachers are covered by collective bargaining agreements.

Right to Strike. Judges have generally held that public employees do not have the right to strike. For example, the Supreme Court of Connecticut,[13] and the Supreme Court of New Hampshire[14] ruled that teachers may not strike. The court opinion in Connecticut stated:

> Under our system, the government is established by and run for all of the people, not for the benefit of any person or group. The profit motive, inherent in the principle of free enterprise, is absent. It should be the aim of every employee of the government to do his or her part to make it function as efficiently and economically as possible. The drastic remedy or the organized strike to enforce the demands of unions of government employees is in direct contravention of this principle.

At least eight states—Alaska, Hawaii, Illinois, Minnesota, Ohio, Oregon, Pennsylvania, and Wisconsin—permit strikes in their collective bargaining statutes. At least twenty states have statutes that prohibit strikes. Whether or not there are specific statutes prohibiting strikes, boards of education threatened by strikes can usually get a court injunction forestalling them. Both the NEA and the AFT view the strike as a last-resort technique, although justifiable in some circumstances.

Recently, by a six-to-three vote, the U.S. Supreme Court ruled that boards of education can discharge teachers who are striking illegally. Ramifications of this decision, involving a Wisconsin public school, are potentially far-reaching. The Court viewed discharge as a policy matter rather than an issue for adjudication: "What choice among the alternative responses to the teachers' strike will best serve the interests of the school system, the interests of the parents and children who depend on the system, and the interests of the citizens whose taxes support it?"

The Court said the state law in question gave the board the power to employ and dismiss teachers as a part of the balance it had struck in municipal labor relations (*Hortonville Joint School District No. 1* v. *Hortonville Education Association,* 1976).

One can argue that strikes are unlawful when a statute is violated, that the courts in their decisions have questioned the right of public employees to strike, and that some teachers and teacher organizations consider strikes unprofessional. The question before teachers seems to be whether the strike is a justifiable and responsible means—after all other ways have been exhausted—of declaring abominable educational and working conditions and trying to remedy them.

Teacher Tenure

Teacher tenure legislation exists in most states. In many states, tenure or fair dismissal laws are mandatory and apply to all school districts without exception. In other states they do not. The various tenure laws differ not only in extent of coverage but also in provision for coverage.

Tenure laws are intended to provide security for teachers in their positions and to prevent removal of capable teachers by capricious action or political motive. Tenure statutes generally include detailed specifications necessary for attaining tenure and for dismissing teachers who have tenure. These statutes have been upheld when attacked on constitutional grounds. The courts reason that since state legislatures create school districts, they have the right to limit their power.

Becoming Tenured and Tenure Rights.   A teacher becomes tenured by serving satisfactorily for a stated time. This period is referred to as the probationary period and varies in length from state to state. The actual process of acquiring tenure after serving the probationary period depends on the applicable statute. In some states the process is automatic at the satisfactory completion of the probationary period; in other states, official action by the school board is necessary. Teachers may be dismissed for a number of reasons, including: "nonperformance of duty, incompetency, insubordination, conviction of crimes involving moral turpitude, failure to comply with reasonable orders, violation of contract provisions or local rules or regulations, persistent failure or refusal to maintain orderly discipline of students, and revocation of the teaching certificate."[15]

A school board in Tennessee dismissed Jane Turk from her teaching position after she was arrested for driving under the influence of alcohol (DUI).[16] Turk's appeal was upheld by the lower-court judge, since there was no evidence of an adverse effect on her capacity and fitness as a teacher. The school board appealed to the Tennessee Supreme Court, which found that the school board "acted in flagrant disregard of the statutory requirement and fundamental fairness in considering matters that should have been specifically charged in writing." Tennessee law requires that before a tenured teacher can be dismissed, "the charges shall be made in writing specifically stating the offenses which are charged." Thus teacher tenure may be affected by teacher conduct outside school as well as inside. This issue, in a sense, deals with the personal freedom of teachers; freedom to behave as other citizens do, freedom to engage in political activities, and academic freedom in the classroom.

Tenure laws are frequently attacked by those who claim that they protect incompetent teachers. There is undoubtedly some truth in the assertion, but it must be stated clearly and unequivocally that they also protect the competent and most able teachers. Teachers who accept the challenge of their profession and dare to use new methods, who inspire curiosity in their students, and who discuss controversial issues in their classrooms need protection from dismissal through political or capricious methods. Incompetent teachers, whether tenured or not, can be dismissed under the law by capable administrators and careful school boards who allow due process while evaluating teacher performance.

Rights of Nontenured Teachers. Although due process has been applicable for years to tenured teachers, nontenured teachers do not, for the most part, enjoy the same rights. Tenured teachers enjoy two key rights—protection from dismissal except for cause as provided in state statutes and the right to prescribed procedures, also spelled out in the statutes. Nontenured teachers may also have due process rights if spelled out in state statutes, or they may be nonrenewed without any reasons being given in those states not providing for due process. If a nontenured teacher is dismissed (as distinguished from nonrenewed) before the expiration of the contract, the teacher is entitled to due process. In most states, however, provisions are only perfunctory, such as providing calendar dates for nonrenewal of contracts. Cases in Massachusetts[17] and Wisconsin[18] point to the necessity of following due process in dismissing nontenured teachers. In the Massachusetts case the court said: "The particular circumstances of a dismissal of a public school teacher provide compelling reasons for application of a doctrine of procedural due process."[19] In the Wisconsin case the court said:

> A teacher in a public elementary or secondary school is protected by the due process clause of the Fourteenth Amendment against a nonrenewal decision which is wholly without basis in fact and also against a decision which is wholly unreasoned, as well as a decision which is impermissibly based.

In 1972 the Supreme Court helped to clarify the difference in the rights of tenured and nontenured teachers. In one case (*Board of Regents* v. *Roth*, 1972) it held that nontenured teachers were assured of no rights that were not specified in state statutes. In this instance the only right that probationary teachers had was the one to be notified of nonrenewal by a specified date. In a second case the Court ruled that a nontenured teacher in the Texas system of community colleges was entitled to due process because the language of the institution's policy manual was such that an unofficial tenure system was in effect. Guidelines in the policy manual provided that a faculty member with seven years of employment in the system acquired tenure and could be dismissed only for cause (*Perry* v. *Sindermann*, 1972).

Whether a teacher is tenured or not, that person cannot be dismissed for exercise of a right guaranteed by the U.S. Constitution. A school board cannot dismiss a teacher, for example, for engaging in civil rights activities outside school, speaking on matters of public concern, belonging to a given church, or running for public office. These rights are guaranteed to all citizens, including teachers. However, if a teacher's behavior is disruptive or false, dismissal is possible without violating that teacher's right to freedom of speech.

Academic Freedom

A sensitive and vital concern to the educator is **academic freedom**—freedom to control what one will teach and to teach the truth as one discovers it, without fear of penalty. Academic freedom is thus essentially a pedagogical philosophy that has been applied to a variety of professional activities. A philosophical

PROFESSIONAL DILEMMA

What Will You Do If a Child in Your Classroom Has AIDS?

In the fall of 1993 the national media reported two stories of children who had become infected with the AIDS virus through contact with another child who was infected. These reports once again stimulated discussion and concern among parents and students about what to do when an AIDS-infected child attends the school where they teach or that their children attend.

There are several sides to this issue. First of all, as has been pointed out in this Chapter and Chapter 9, *all* children have a legal right to attend public school (see the U.S. Constitution and your state's constitution). And the school is responsible for providing an appropriate education to all children (see PL 94–142, IDEA, and Section 504).

It is important to learn the truth about the potential for other children, and you to become infected through contact with a child who has AIDS. Becoming infected through casual contact with someone who has AIDS is impossible. To contract the AIDS virus, one must be in contact with blood or other body fluids, such as bleeding from the nose, gums, and cuts,

or open sores. Transmission of AIDS through sex and the sharing of needles and razors is well documented. Even when there is contact with contaminated blood on the skin or mucus membranes in the nose or mouth, infection is rare. There are no known cases of the AIDS virus being transmitted through eating utensils or bathroom facilities. However, if an infected child is injured and starts to bleed, then preventive actions are necessary.

The Centers for Disease Control (CDC) recommends that spilled blood *always* be treated as though it contains disease. Latex gloves should be worn when wiping up blood. And, contaminated surfaces should be cleaned with a solution of 1 part bleach diluted with 10 parts water. If you want more information about AIDS, the CDC operates a 24-hour toll-free hot line seven days a week (800) 342–2437.

- What should you do to familiarize yourself with the steps and resources that your school has in place for responding to any accident that might happen?
- As a teacher, how will you respond to a child in your classroom who has been identified as HIV-positive?
- What will you do to insure that the other children in your classroom treat the infected child equitably?

position, however, is *not necessarily* a legal right.[20] Federal judges have generally recognized certain academic protections in the college classroom while exhibiting reluctance to recognize such rights for elementary and secondary school teachers.

The contract of a history teacher at the University of Arkansas–Little Rock was not renewed after he announced that he taught his classes from a Marxist point of view. The court ordered the teacher be reinstated in light of the university's failure to advance convincing reasons related to the academic freedom issue to warrant his nonrenewal.[21] In another case a university instructor claimed that he was denied tenure because he refused to change a student's grade. He argued that awarding a course grade was the instructor's right of academic freedom. Since the university had given several reasons for the nonrenewal of the instructor's contract, the court did not order a reinstatement.[22]

Academic Freedom for Elementary and Secondary Teachers. Although federal courts generally have not recognized academic freedom for elementary and secondary school teachers, the most supportive ruling was made in 1980[23] in a case that involved a high school history teacher who used a simulation game to introduce her students to the characteristics of rural life during the post–Civil War

Reconstruction era. While the role playing evoked controversy in the school and community, there was no evidence that the teacher's usefulness had been impaired. Therefore the school erred in not renewing the teacher's contract, and she was ordered reinstated.

In *Pickering* v. *Board of Education* (1968) the U.S. Supreme Court dealt with academic freedom at the public school level. Pickering was a teacher in Illinois who, in a letter published by a local newspaper, criticized the school board and the superintendent for the way they had handled past proposals to raise and use new revenues for the schools. After a full hearing, the board of education terminated Pickering's employment, whereupon he brought suit under the First and Fourteenth Amendments. The Illinois courts rejected his claim. The U.S. Supreme Court, however, upheld Pickering's claim and, in its opinion, stated:

> To the extent that the Illinois Supreme Court's opinion may be read to suggest that teachers may constitutionally be compelled to relinquish the First Amendment rights they would otherwise enjoy as citizens to comment on matters of public interest in connection with the operation of the public schools in which they work, it proceeds on a premise that has been unequivocally rejected in numerous prior decisions of this Court.

In general, teachers are not free to disregard a school board's decision about which textbook to use, but they are able to participate more when it comes to their choice of supplementary methods.

Balancing the Interest of Teachers and the Interest of the State. The Court then addressed the problem of dealing with cases involving academic freedom. It held that the problem was how to arrive at a balance between the interests of the teacher, who as citizen comments on matters of public concern, and the interests of the state, which as employer promotes the efficiency of its public services through its employees. It is difficult to define precisely the limits of academic freedom. In general, the courts strongly support it yet recognize that teachers must be professionally responsible when interacting with pupils.

Generally, teachers have been supported in their rights to criticize the policies of their local school boards, wear symbols representing stated causes, participate in unpopular movements, and live unconventional lifestyles. But where the exercise of these rights can be shown to have a direct bearing on the teacher's effectiveness, respect, or discipline, these rights may have to be curtailed. For example, a teacher may have the right to wear a "punk" outfit to class, but if the wearing of the outfit leads to disruption and an inability to manage students, the teacher may be ordered to wear more traditional clothes.

Debates rage over whether books deemed objectionable can be banned from schools without interfering with the principles of free speech.

Book Banning. Ever since we have had public schools, there have been people who have taken issue with what has been taught,

CASE STUDY   BOOK CENSORSHIP AND YOUR CLASSROOM

Since 1983, challenges to library books and school materials have increased by 168 percent. In the 1992–1993 school year, there were 347 attempts to censor books, plays, and other material. A number of organized groups, such as Colorado for Family Values and the Christian Action Network, are systematically targeting books and the policymaking process to have books banned that they find offensive. As a result, teachers, school boards, state boards of education, and legislatures are under intense pressure to ban various books. The established literary merit of a book makes no difference; for example, *Catcher in the Rye, Of Mice and Men, Romeo and Juliet,* and *I Know Why the Caged Bird Sings* have been challenged. Various reasons are offered as to why certain books should not be in schools, including: (1) they are frightening for children (*Scary Stories to Tell in the Dark.*); (2) they are racist (*Tom Sawyer, Little House on the Prairie,* and *Tarzan of the Apes*); and (3) they are "obscene and pornographic" (*The Bible*).

Pressure to ban and censor books comes from inside schools as well. Teachers may unwittingly withhold certain books out of fear of the possibility of controversy. In other instances, the actions of teachers are more direct. For example, teachers in Westlake Middle School in Erie, Pennsylvania (1993) used felt-tip pens to black out passages in *Gorillas in the Mist.*

Censorship and book banning is another aspect of the legal rights and responsibilities of students and teachers.

1. How will you decide if a certain book or game, such as *Where's Waldo?*, is "appropriate" for the students in your classroom?
2. What will you say when a parent pressures you to remove a book from your classroom?
3. And if fellow teachers raise questions about certain educational materials being used, how will you prepare yourself to respond?

Note: Each year a consortium of book publishers, library associations, author associations, and book seller associations publish a list of book titles that have been challenged (*Banned Books: 1994 Resource Guide*). They also make available materials for local observance of Banned Books Week in the early fall. For more association, contact the American Library Association, Office for Intellectual Freedom, 50 East Huron St., Chicago, IL 60611.

how it has been taught, and the materials used. The number of people challenging these issues and the intensity of their feeling have escalated over the past two decades. Well-organized and well-financed pressure groups have opposed the teaching of a number of topics, including political, economic, scientific, and religious theories; the teaching of values grounded in religion, morality, or ethnicity; and the portrayal of stereotypes based on gender, race, or ethnicity. Some complaints have involved differences of opinion over the central role of the school—whether it is to transmit traditional values, indoctrinate students, or teach students to do their own thinking.

A number of court cases in the last twenty years have involved the legality of removal of books from the school curriculum and school libraries. The courts have given some guidance but have not fully resolved the issue. In 1972 a court of appeals held that a book does not acquire tenure, so a school board was upheld in the removal of *Down These Mean Streets.* The seventh circuit court in 1980 upheld the removal of the book *Values Clarification,* ruling that local boards have considerable authority in selecting materials for schools. Removal of books on the basis of the vulgar language they contain has also been upheld.

The U.S. Supreme Court treated this issue in 1982.[24] The decision disappointed people who had hoped that the justices would issue a definitive ruling on banning of books. Instead, Justice Brennan ruled that students may sue school boards for a denial of their rights, including the right to receive information. The Court indicated that removal of a book because one disagrees with its content cannot be upheld. The net effect of this decision was that the school board decided to return the questionable books to the library.

Liability for Negligence

With about 42 million students enrolled in elementary and secondary schools, it is almost inevitable that some will be injured in educational activities. Each year, some injuries will occasion lawsuits in which plaintiffs seek damages. Such suits are often brought against both the school districts and their employees. Actions seeking monetary damages for injuries are referred to as *actions in tort.* Technically, a tort is a legal wrong—an act or the omission of an act that violates the private rights of an individual. Actions in tort are generally based on alleged negligence; the basis of tort liability or legal responsibility is negligence. Understanding the concept of negligence is essential to understanding liability.

Legally, *negligence* is the result of a failure to exercise or practice due care. It includes a factor of foreseeability of harm. Court cases on record involving negligence are numerous and varied. The negligence of teacher supervision of pupils is an important topic that includes supervision of the regular classroom, a teacher leaving a classroom, supervision of the playground, and supervision of extracurricular activities. **Liability** is the failure to use a reasonable amount of care when such conduct results in injury to another.

Negligent Chemistry Teacher. In a California high school chemistry class, pupils were injured while experimenting in the manufacture of gunpowder.[25] The teacher was in the room and had supplemented the laboratory manual instructions with his own directions. Nevertheless, an explosion occurred, allegedly caused by the failure of pupils to follow directions. A court held the teacher and the board of education liable. Negligence in this case meant the lack of supervision of laboratory work, a potentially dangerous activity requiring a high level of due care.

Field Trip Negligence. In Oregon a child was injured while on a field trip.[26] Children were playing on a large log in a relatively dry space on a beach. A large wave surged up onto the beach, dislodging the log, which began to roll. One of the children fell seaward off the log, and the receding wave pulled the log over the child, injuring him. In the subsequent court action the teacher was declared negligent for not foreseeing the possibility of such an occurrence. The court said:

> The first proposition asks this court to hold, as a matter of fact, that unusual wave action on the shore of the Pacific Ocean is a hazard so unforeseeable that there is no duty to guard against it. On the contrary, we agree with the trial judge, who observed that it is common knowledge that accidents substantially like the one that occurred in this case have occurred at beaches along the Oregon coast. Foreseeability of such harm is not so remote as to be ruled out as a matter of law.

Although negligence is a vague concept involving due care and foreseeability, it is defined more specifically each time a court decides such a case. In each instance, somewhat reflecting past decisions, courts decide what constitutes reasonable due care and adequate foresight.

Governmental Immunity from Liability.

Historically, school districts have not been held liable for torts resulting from the negligence of their officers, agents, or employees while the school districts are acting in their governmental capacity. That concept was based on the doctrine that the state is sovereign and cannot be sued without consent. A school district, as an arm of state government, would therefore be immune from tort liability. Unlike school districts, employees of school districts have not been protected by the

Schools must deal with the issue of responsibility for student safety on field trips outside the school premises.

immunity school districts enjoy; teachers may be held liable for their actions. Teachers must act as reasonable and prudent people, foreseeing dangerous situations. The degree of care that is required increases with the immaturity of the pupil. Lack of supervision and foresight forms the basis of negligence charges.

There has been a trend away from governmental immunity. As of 1986, over half of the states had abrogated governmental immunity either judicially, statutorily, or through some form of legal modification. There has also been an increase in the number of lawsuits.

Liability Insurance.

Many states authorize school districts to purchase insurance to protect teachers, school districts, administrators, and school board members against suits. It is important that school districts and their employees and board members be thus protected, through either school district insurance or their own personal policies. The costs of school district liability insurance have increased so dramatically in the past few years that many school districts are contemplating the elimination of extracurricular activities. Consequently, state legislatures are being pressured to fix liability insurance rates for school districts, as well as passing laws to limit maximum liability amounts for school-related cases. For teachers, membership in the state affiliates of the NEA and membership in the AFT permit them to participate in liability insurance programs sponsored by those organizations.

As a summary of the discussion of this section, Table 10.4 on page 284 lists brief statements related to the rights and responsibilities of teachers.

Global Perspectives: Respect for Teachers in Taiwan

In this chapter we have highlighted many of the legal rights of American teachers. You are protected by a negotiated contract, you have the right to due process as defined by the U.S. Constitution, and you have a great deal of academic freedom. In large measure what you can and cannot do as an American teacher is defined

TABLE 10.4	Summary Statements on Teachers' Rights and Responsibilities

Prospective teachers must fulfill the requirements of laws and policies regarding certification prior to being employed as teachers.

Boards of education have the authority to employ teachers, including the authority to enter into contracts and to fix terms of employment and compensation.

School districts are prohibited from use of discriminatory practices; discrimination in employment and salary of teachers on the basis of sex is in violation of Title IX of the Education Amendments Act.

Most states have tenure laws that provide protection for teachers against their arbitrary dismissal; rights of nontenured teachers are found in state laws.

Teachers may speak out on matters of public concern, even in criticism of their school board, as long as their speech is not disruptive or a lie.

Boards of education may remove books from library shelves under their authority to select materials for schools; however, the removal of a book merely because someone disagrees with its content was not upheld by the U.S. Supreme Court.

Many states provide for school boards and teacher unions to bargain collectively on wages, hours, and terms and conditions of employment.

Teacher strikes are unlawful when a statute is violated; in some states it is legal for teachers to strike.

Teachers are expected to exercise due care in foreseeing possible accidents and in working to prevent their occurrence; teachers may be sued for their negligence that led to pupil injury.

Teachers who administer corporal punishment must act in a way consistent with state laws, local board policies, and reasonable practices.

in statute, law, and case history. What would your professional life be like if you were a teacher in another country or at another time?

Since ancient times, the Chinese have been very respectful of their teachers. You may have noticed in the movie *The Last Emperor* that only the teachers of the Emperor could ride a horse all the way into the palace. Also, the Emperor bowed to his teachers, although he did not bow to anyone else.

A country where teachers are given great respect today is Taiwan. For example, September 28, the birthday of Confucius, is a national holiday on which teachers are recognized at special ceremonies at the national, county, and local levels. At these ceremonies politicians must sit in the audience, and only teachers are allowed to sit at the head table. Another symbol of the respect for teachers in Taiwan is that teachers of the compulsory grades (K-8) do not pay any income tax! Their salaries are the same as those of high school and college teachers, but they do not have to pay income taxes.

Teachers do not have contracts in Taiwan; instead, each year the principal writes a letter of invitation to each teacher, stating the following: "On behalf of the parents I invite you to be a member of the faculty to teach their children. I hope that you will teach their children as if they were your own. . . ." How is this for showing respect for teachers and also expressing high expectations for what teachers do? Although stated differently in the United States, most parents and school administrators wish the same for teachers in this country.

Summary and Implications

Although student rights and responsibilities are being more clearly defined by court decisions, many court decisions have gone against students whose nonconformism seems to exceed a reasonable norm. American children have a right to an education but not without certain prerequisites. Boards of education have the right to establish rules and regulations provided they are reasonable, rather than arbitrary, regarding student rights. Courts are faced with determining the reasonableness of the student behavior and/or the reasonableness of board rules and regulations. Most student challenges have been related to corporal punishment, rights of married students, dress codes, and freedom of expression. Particularly in cases of suspension and expulsion, corporal punishment, dress codes, and sex discrimination, actions of school administrators and teachers may be examined regarding the due process dimensions of fairness and constitutionality. Procedures for dealing with school records, student publications, student searches, child abuse, and locker searches are being studied more thoroughly to avoid conflicts, which often end up in the courts.

Teachers have the same rights and responsibilities as other citizens. With the assistance of support organizations such as the American Civil Liberties Union (ACLU) and the teacher unions, more and more teachers are airing their grievances in court. The courts have said that a teaching certificate is a license to practice a profession and that it cannot be revoked without constitutional due process. At the same time, the courts have ruled that boards of education may prescribe requirements beyond the state requirements for certification. Teachers are responsible for making certain that they are legally certified to enter into contracts. The grounds and procedures for dismissing teachers are usually spelled out as part of the tenure statute of the respective states. Teacher dismissals by capricious

actions of boards of education are often taken to court for consideration of due process. School districts are prohibited from use of discriminatory practices in the hiring, dismissal, promotion, and demotion of school personnel. The law regarding academic freedom is unsettled, especially for elementary and secondary teachers, since federal judges have been reluctant to recognize academic freedom rights at this level. Controversy over the curriculum continues. It is expected that school boards, administrators, and teachers will continue to receive complaints about what has been taught, how it has been taught, and the materials used. The courts have clarified teachers' rights to bargain collectively and to strike (where state law permits). Court cases brought against both the school districts and their employees involving negligence are numerous and varied. Teachers should be fully aware that negligence is the result of failure to exercise or practice due care.

The implications of the actions of the courts are highly significant to the teaching profession. From the many court decisions relating to education a framework has evolved for acceptable conduct of teachers within the school setting. Today's teacher no longer can assume that personal ignorance of acceptable standards of conduct will be overlooked by the courts in adjudicating a suit brought against the teacher. (Nor should the teacher be intimidated by the courts when reasonable rules of conduct are being evolved for the practice of teaching.) Courts do not start hearings on their own efforts; school boards, school employees, or teachers must be sued before a court case can develop. However, prospective teachers need to be deliberately sensitive to the legal boundaries in teaching. Although beginning teachers need not have the knowledge and expertise of a lawyer, knowing the law well as it relates to education can contribute more than incidentally to becoming a successful teacher.

Discussion Questions

1. Examine "A Bill of Rights for High School Students" presented in Appendix 10.1. What are the strengths of this bill? Are there some elements of it that will be problematic for teachers?

2. What are your thoughts about the balancing of student rights with the need of the school officials to maintain an environment that is conducive to learning? Should school officials have more authority? Or should the students have greater freedom?

3. Each fall there are teacher strikes somewhere in the country that delay the opening of school. Have you ever been involved in a strike? What do you think are the most critical consequences of teacher strikes? If your association leaders called for a strike, would you join the picket line or teach your classes?

4. The "Global Perspectives" section describes the respect given to teachers in Taiwan. How would

you feel about having that kind of respect? Would you teach any differently? Have you had contact with teachers from other countries? If so, what have they said about the respect for teachers there?

5. What precautions should teachers take to avoid charges of negligence?

Journal/Portfolio Development

1. From time to time there will be reports in the newspapers and weekly news magazines about disagreements between students and school officials. Collect these reports, paying special attention to the legal interpretations drawn by each side, and considering the implications for you. In all instances keep in mind that both teachers and students have legal rights, as well as responsibilities. These clippings and notes might be a useful resource for you someday, when as a teacher you are confronted with a question about student and teacher rights.

2. The rights of teachers will be an ever-present theme in the background of your teaching career.

Now is the time to begin compiling notes and a file folder of clippings related to this topic. Your file could include information about teachers' rights from your state's offices of the National Education Association and the American Federation of Teachers. You also could obtain copies of teacher contracts from the school district where you went to school or where you hope to be employed. Watch the newspapers and news magazines for articles about teachers who are being sued. In reading about these cases, note the legal principles being applied as well as the specific teacher rights that are at issue.

School-Based Experiences

1. Obtain a copy of the contract agreement between the teachers' union and a school district. Develop a description and analysis of the due process rights and procedures for teachers.

2. Beginning teachers do not have the same rights as tenured teachers. Compare and contrast the rights

of beginning teachers in two school districts. Some of the items to check are: length of the probationary period, basis for tenure decision, how the tenure decision-making process works, and the rights of probationary teachers.

Notes

1. *Carey* v. *Piphus* (1978).
2. Lee O. Garber and Reynolds C. Seitz, *The Yearbook of School Law, 1971.* Danville, IL: Interstate, 1971, 253.
3. Thomas J. Flygare, "De Jure," *Phi Delta Kappan 68* (October 1986): 165–166.
4. Ibid., 165.
5. *Long* v. *Zopp* (1973).
6. Lucy Knight, "Facts about Mr. Buckley's Amendment," *American Education 13* (June 1977): 7.
7. *Scoville* v. *Board of Education* (1970).
8. William D. Valente, *Law in the Schools.* Columbus, OH: Merrill, 1980, 282.
9. *Peter W.* v. *San Francisco Unified School District* (1976).
10. *Donahue* v. *Copiague Union Free School District* (1978).
11. *1986 Deskbook Encyclopedia of American School Law.* Rosemount, MN: Data Research, 55.
12. Ibid., 61.
13. *Norwalk Teachers Association* v. *Board of Education* (1951).
14. *City of Manchester* v. *Manchester Teachers' Guild* (1957).
15. Michael La Morte, *School Law Cases and Concepts.* 4th ed. Boston: Allyn and Bacon, 1993, 190.
16. *Turk* v. *Franklin Special School District* (1982).
17. *Lucia* v. *Duggan* (1969).
18. *Gouge* v. *Joint School District No. 1* (1970).

19. Haskell C. Freedman, "The Legal Rights of Untenured Teachers," *Nolpe School Law Journal 1* (Fall 1970): 100.

20. Frank W. Kemerer, "Classroom Academic Freedom: Is It a Right?" *Kappa Delta Pi Record 19* (Summer 1983): 101.

21. *Cooper v. Ross* (1979).

22. *Hillis v. Stephen F. Austin University* (1982).

23. *Kingsville Independent School District* v. *Cooper* (1980).

24. *Board of Education, Island Trees Union Free District No. 26* v. *Pico* (1982).

25. *Mastrangelo* v. *West Side Union High School District* (1935).

26. *Morris* v. *Douglas County School District* (1966).

Bibliography

Appenzeller, Herb. *The Right to Participate.* Charlottesville, VA: Michie, 1985.

Hudgins, H. C., Jr. "The Perspective of the Courts: Their Effect on Educational Policy." *Thresholds in Education 12* (May 1986): 912.

McCarthy, Martha M., and Cambron-McCabe, Nelda H. *Public School Law: Teachers' and Students' Rights.* 3rd ed. Boston: Allyn and Bacon, 1992.

Salome, Rosemary C. *Equal Education Under Law.* New York: St. Martin's Press, 1986.

Tuthill, Doug. "Exploring the Union Contract: One Teacher's Perspective." *Phi Delta Kappan 71* (10) (June 1990): 775–780.

Zerkel, Perry. "Courtside." *Phi Delta Kappan.* (A regular feature in each issue of the *Phi Delta Kappan* providing timely and pertinent information about legal issues.)

Zerkel, Perry, and Richardson, Sharon Nalbone. *A Digest of Supreme Court Decisions Affecting Education.* 2nd ed. Bloomington, IN: Phi Delta Kappa Educational Foundation, 1988.

A Bill of Rights for High School Students

Neither teacher nor students shed their constitutional right to freedom of speech or expression at the schoolhouse gate. That has been the unmistakable holding of the Supreme Court for almost fifty years. (*Tinker* v. *Des Moines*, 1969)

The following statement of students' rights is intended as a guide to students, parents, teachers, and administrators who are interested in developing proper safeguards for student liberties. IT IS NOT A SUMMARY OF THE LAW, BUT SETS FORTH IN A GENERAL WAY WHAT THE ACLU THINKS *SHOULD* BE ADOPTED. . . .

Article I.   Expression
A. Students shall be free to express themselves and disseminate their views without prior restraints through speech, essays, publications, pictures, armbands, badges, and all other media of communication. Student expression may be subject to disciplinary action only in the event that such expression creates a significant physical disruption of school activities.
B. No reporter for a student publication may be required to reveal a source of information.
C. Students shall have the right to hear speakers and presentations representing a wide range of views and subjects in classes, clubs, and assemblies. Outside speakers and presentations may be limited only by considerations of time, space, and expense.
D. Students shall be free to assemble, demonstrate, and picket peacefully, to petition and to organize on school grounds or in school buildings subject only to reasonable limitations on time, place, and manner designed to avoid significant physical obstruction of traffic or significant physical disruption of school activities.
E. Students shall be free to determine their dress and grooming as they see fit, subject only to reasonable limitations designed to protect student safety or prevent significant ongoing disruption of school activities.

F. No student shall be required to participate in any way in patriotic exercises or be penalized for refusing to participate.

Article II.   Religion
A. Students shall be free to practice their own religion or no religion.
B. There shall be no school-sanctioned religious exercises or events.
C. Religious history, ideas, institutions, and literature may be studied in the same fashion as any other academic subject.

Article III.   Privacy
A. Students should be free from undercover surveillance through the use of mechanical, electronic, or other secret methods, including undercover agents, without issuance of a warrant.
B. Students should be free from warrantless searches and seizures by school officials in their personal effects, lockers, or any other facilities assigned to their personal use. General housekeeping inspections of lockers and desks shall not occur without reasonable notice.
C. Student record files
   1. A student's permanent record file shall include only information about academic competence and notification of the fact of participation in school clubs, sports, and other such school extracurricular activities. This file shall not be disclosed to any person or agency outside the school, except to the student's parents or guardian, without the student's permission.

2. Any other records (e.g., medical or psychological evaluations) shall be available only to the student, the student's parents or guardian, and the school staff. Such other records shall be governed by strict safeguards for confidentiality and shall not be available to others in or outside of the school even upon consent of the student.

3. A record shall be kept, and shall be available to the student, of any consultation of the student's files, noting the date and purpose of the consultation and the name of the person who consulted the files.

4. All records shall be open to challenge and correction by the student.

5. A student's opinions shall not be disclosed to any outside person or agency.

Article IV.   Equality

A. No organization that officially represents the school in any capacity and no curricular or extracurricular activity organized by school authorities may deny or segregate participation or award or withhold privileges on the basis of race, color, national origin, sex, religion, creed, or opinions.

Article V.   Government

A. All students may hold office and may vote in student elections. These rights shall not be denied for any reason.

B. Student government organizations and their operation, scope, and amendment procedures shall be established in a written constitution formulated with full and effective student participation.

Article VI.   Due process

A. Regulations concerning student behavior shall be formulated with full and effective student participation. Such regulations shall be published and made available to all students. Regulations shall be fully, clearly, and precisely written.

B. No student shall be held accountable by school authorities for any behavior occurring outside the organized school day or off school property (except during school-sponsored events) unless such behavior presents a clear, present, and substantial ongoing danger to persons and property in the school.

C. There shall be no cruel, unusual, demeaning, or excessive punishments. There shall be no corporal punishment.

D. No student shall be compelled by school officials to undergo psychological therapy or use medication without that student's consent. No student may be required to participate in any psychological or personality testing, research project, or experiment without that student's written, informed, and willing consent. The nature, purposes, and possible adverse consequences of the testing, project, or experiment shall be fully explained to the student.

E. A student shall have the right to due process in disciplinary and investigative proceedings. In cases that may involve serious penalties, such as suspension for more than three days, expulsion, transfer to another school, a notation on the student's record, or long-term loss of privileges:

1. A student shall be guaranteed a formal hearing before an impartial board. That student shall have the right to appeal hearing results.

2. Rules for hearings and appeals shall be written and published, and there shall be full and effective student participation in their formulation.

3. The student shall be advised in writing of any charges brought against that student.

4. The student shall have the right to present evidence and witnesses and to cross-examine adverse witnesses. The student shall have the right to have an advisor of his or her own choosing present.

5. The hearing shall be open or private as the student chooses.

6. The student shall have a reasonable time to prepare a defense.

7. A student may not be compelled to incriminate himself or herself.

8. The burden of proof, beyond a reasonable doubt, shall be upon the school.

9. A written record of all hearings and appeals shall be made available to the student, at the school's expense.

10. A student shall be free from double jeopardy.

Source: American Civil Liberties Union of Maryland, Baltimore, Md. Reprinted by permission.

Part

4

Historical Foundations of Education

Dreamcatcher

Mary McLeod Bethune (1875–1955) was one of seventeen children born to African American parents in Mayesville, South Carolina, the first family member not born as a slave. Her first formal schooling took place at age nine in a free school for African American children. It is reported that she would come home from school and teach her brothers and sisters what she had learned each day. She believed education was the key to helping African American children move into the mainstream of American life, and she devoted her life to improving educational opportunities for African American young women. She started the Daytona Normal and Industrial School for Negro Young Women and later Bethune-Cookman College, which she served as president until 1942. She also believed that education helps everyone to respect the dignity of all people, regardless of color or creed— and is needed equally by Caucasian Americans, African Americans, and all other Americans. Mary McLeod Bethune went on to serve as founder and head of the National Council of Negro Women, Director of the Division of Negro Affairs of the National Youth Administration, President Franklin D. Roosevelt's special advisor on minority affairs, and special consultant for drafting the charter of the United Nations.

Insight into the optimistic outlook that allowed Mary McLeod Bethune to accomplish so much can be gleaned from her diary entry of 7 December 1937:

> Tuesday at five in the afternoon I attended a tea at the executive mansion. This was an annual occasion at which Mrs. Roosevelt entertained the women administrative workers in the government.
>
> One curious but affable woman inquired, "Who are you?"
>
> "My name is Mary McLeod Bethune."
>
> "What do you do?"
>
> "I am the Director of Negro Affairs in the N.Y.A."
>
> "Isn't it nice of Mrs. Roosevelt to have you here?"
>
> "Yes, isn't it nice of Mrs. Roosevelt to have us *all* here!"
>
> While I felt very much at home, I looked about me longingly for other dark faces. In all that great group I felt a sense of being quite alone.
>
> Then I thought how vitally important it was that I be here, to help those others get used to seeing us in high places. And so, while I sipped tea in the brilliance of the White House, my heart reached out to the delta land and bottom land.
>
> I know so well why I must be here and why I must go to tea at the White House—to remind them always that we belong here; we are a part of America.

Mary McLeod Bethune was an effective, energetic human rights activist throughout her life, and also a dedicated and professional career educator—an outstanding "dreamcatcher" indeed.

11

Antecedents of American Education

Focus Questions

1 Is it important for teachers to understand the history of education? Why or why not?

2 When and why do you think people first created schools?

3 Who were some of the most important educators through the ages?

4 What lessons, if any, can we learn from very early educators?

5 What has characterized the evolution of education through different periods of history?

6 How important has education been in the history of humankind? In what ways?

Key Terms and Concepts

Age of Pericles (455–431 B.C.): A period of Greek history in which sufficiently great strides were made in human advancement to generate an organized concern for formal education.

Age of Reason: The beginning of the modern period of educational thought that emphasizes the importance of reason. The writings of Voltaire strongly influenced this movement and formed the basis for rationalism.

Emergence of Common Man: Coincides with the Age of Reason and emphasizes the rights of the common people for a better life, politically, economically, socially, and educationally. Rousseau was a leader in this movement.

Herbartian teaching method: An organized teaching method based on the principles of Pestalozzi that stresses learning by association and consists of five steps (preparation, presentation, association, generalization, and application).

Historical interpretation: Different ways to study and understand history, such as celebrationist, liberal, revisionist, and postmodernist historians would tend to do.

Latin grammar school: An early type of school that emphasized the study of Latin, literature, history, mathematics, music, and dialectics.

Scholasticism: The logical and philosophical study of the beliefs of the church.

Seven liberal arts: A curriculum that consisted of the trivium (grammar, rhetoric, logic) and the quadrivium (arithmetic, geometry, music, astronomy).

Socratic method: A way of teaching that centers on the use of questions by the teacher to lead students to certain conclusions.

293

In this part of the book, we will explore the historical foundations of education, first by looking at the antecedents of American education, then the early development of American education, and finally, educational developments in the United States over the past fifty years. Remember as you read this part of the book that there are various methods of **historical interpretation** and that historians often disagree when attempting to understand history. For example, *celebrationist* historians tend to see the brighter side of historical events and praise schools of the past for their accomplishments. By way of contrast, *liberal* historians would tend to look for conflict, stress, and inconsistency when studying educational history. Yet another approach to understanding history is that used by *revisionist* historians, who see history as fundamentally flawed and would likely dwell on education's failures down through the ages. *Postmodernist* historians believe that one's understanding of history is greatly influenced by social class, race, ethnicity, gender, and even age. So, history is not an exact science by any means, but rather, is open to many interpretations. We challenge you to think creatively and critically about the history of education presented in the next three chapters. Strive to learn the historical facts and then create your own historical interpretations.

The Beginnings of Education (to A.D. 476)

It is generally believed that human beings have been on earth for several million years. During 99 percent of this time there was very little progress toward civilization. Not until about ten thousand years ago did people start to raise food, domesticate animals, build canoes, and live in some semblance of community life, and not until approximately six thousand years ago was a written language developed.

Once there was a written language, humans felt the need for formal education. As societies became more complex and the body of knowledge increased, people recognized a need for schools. What they had learned comprised the subject matter; the written language allowed them to record this knowledge and pass it from generation to generation.

Global Perspectives: Educational Ideas Borrowed from around the World

The educational ideas now used in the United States had their inception a long time ago. Our contemporary schools are a mixture of educational ideas, concepts, and practices borrowed from around the world. Much of whatever credit and accolades our current American educational system receives must be shared with those who long ago conceived of the idea of formal education and who then slowly developed and refined these educational concepts.

This chapter is devoted to a brief review of some of the early educational developments that occurred long before any formal education took place in the United States. These developments became the basis on which our schools were built and are the antecedents of American education.

Eastern Education

It is impossible to determine the date that schools first came into existence. However, the discovery of cuneiform mathematics textbooks that have been dated to 2000 B.C. suggests that some form of school probably existed in Sumeria at that time. There is also evidence to suggest that formal schools existed in China during the Hsia and Shang dynasties, perhaps as early as 2000 B.C. Let's briefly explore several examples of the origins of education.

Hindu Education.   The ancient Hindu societies were deeply rooted in the caste system, in which a person's family status determined his social and vocational position in life. The Hindu religion emphasized nonearthly values, which resulted in little interest in education for anyone but boys from the highest castes. Priests were in charge of what education existed. Clues from the writing of Buddha suggest that education consisted of a heavy emphasis on morals, writing with a stick in the sand, and frequent punishments with a rod. Further education was reserved for the priestly caste, which, over the ages, gradually cultivated such disciplines as logic, rhetoric, astronomy, and mathematics. Many of our contemporary educational values, including our European languages, are partially derived from the early Hindu societies.

Hebrew Education.   Perhaps no culture has valued education more than the Hebrew societies. Hebrew education was derived from their bible, which taught religious faithfulness and strict adherence to Old Testament laws. Discipline was harsh both at home and in school, justified by many Bible verses such as the proverb "He that spareth his rod, hateth his son." Early Hebrew schools taught boys to read and write, and girls to prepare food, spin, weave, sing, and dance. Teachers were greatly respected; the Talmud states "If your teacher and your father have need of your assistance, help your teacher before helping your father, for the latter has given you only the life of this world, while the former has secured for you the life of the world to come." From Hebrew society we have inherited the value we place on education.

Chinese Education.   It has been said that China has been civilized longer than any other society in the world. The Chinese invented printing, gun powder, and the mariner's compass, among other things. Chinese education has always been characterized by tradition, formality, and conformity—all designed to help students to function in a regular, mechanical, and predictable routine.

In the sixth century B.C., two philosophers/reformers exerted enormous influence on Chinese thinking and education through their writings. The first of these was Lâo-tsze, who wrote:

> Certain bad rulers would have us believe that the heart and the spirit of man should be left empty, but that instead his stomach should be filled; that his bones should be strengthened rather than the power of his will; that we should always desire to have people remain in a state of ignorance, for then their demands would be few. It is difficult, they say, to govern a people that are too wise.
>
> These doctrines are directly opposed to what is due to humanity. Those in authority should come to the aid of the people by means of oral and written

instruction; so far from oppressing them and treating them as slaves, they should do them good in every possible way.

The second Chinese reformer, Hkung-tsze (551–478 B.C.), who later became known as Confucius, is the most famous Asian philosopher. Since his time, all Chinese students have been taught Confucius's five cardinal virtues (universal charity, impartial justice, conformity, rectitude of heart and mind, and pure sincerity) as well as many of his famous sayings, such as "There are three thousand crimes . . . of these no one is greater than disobedience to parents." Interestingly, early Chinese education did not include geography, history, science, language, or mathematics—all subjects so highly valued by early Western societies. Also, unlike many of their Western counterparts, early Chinese educators placed little importance on the individual. From early Chinese educational traditions we have inherited our respect for others and for authority, patience, and advances in written language.

African Education.   In Egypt, civilization and intellectual advancement occurred at a very early time. There, as in most early societies, education was provided only for the privileged males. The fact that the pyramids were built several thousand years before Christ attests to the skills of this ancient civilization. In addition, several notable Greek philosophers, including Pythagoras, Plato, Lycurgus, and Solon completed their education in Egypt.

The Egyptian society was divided into castes, with priests holding the highest position and receiving instruction in philosophy, astronomy, geometry, medicine, history, and law. The priests also provided education for others who were worthy of that privilege.

All of the great early Eastern civilizations developed educational systems long before Western civilizations did. The Eastern civilizations contributed substantially to the development of knowledge, education, and schools in the world.

The influence of ancient civilizations is felt and preserved in modern times.

Greek Education

It was not until about 500 B.C. that a Western society sufficiently advanced to generate an organized concern for formal education. This happened in Greece during the **Age of Pericles.** Greece consisted of a number of city-states, one of which was Sparta—a militaristic state whose educational system was geared to support military ambitions. Infants were exposed to the elements for a stated period; if they survived the ordeal, they were judged sufficiently strong for soldiering if male or to bear healthy children if female. From the ages of eight to eighteen, boys were wards of the state. During this time they lived in barracks and received physical and moral training. Between the ages of eighteen and twenty, boys underwent rigorous war training, after which they served in the army. All men were required to marry by the age of thirty so that they might raise healthy children to serve the state. The aims of Spartan education centered on developing such ideals as courage, patriotism, obedience, cunning, and physical strength. Plutarch (A.D. 46–120), a writer of later times, said that the education of the Spartans "was calculated to make them subject to command, to endure labor, to fight, and to conquer." There was very little intellectual content in Spartan education.

In sharp contrast to Sparta was Athens, another Greek city-state, which developed an educational program that heavily stressed intellectual and aesthetic objectives. Between the ages of eight and sixteen, some Athenian boys attended a series of public schools. These schools included a grammatist school, which taught reading, writing, and counting; a gymnastics school, which taught sports and games; and a music school, which taught history, drama, poetry, speaking, and science as well as music. Because all city-states had to defend themselves against aggressors, Athenian boys received citizenship and military training between the ages of sixteen and twenty. Athenian girls were educated in the home. Athenian education stressed individual development, aesthetics, and culture.

Relevant Research

Fewer Requirements and Lower Enrollments Are Contributing to a Decline in Students' Knowledge of the Past

Earlier generations of American students commonly learned the history of American institutions, politics, and systems of government, as well as some of the history of Greece, Rome, Europe, and the rest of the world. Today, most states require the study of only American history and other course work in social studies. Indications are that students now know and understand less about history.

In most state requirements for high school graduation, a choice is offered between history on the one hand and courses in social science and contemporary social issues on the other. Most high school students, even those in the academic track, take only one history course. Students enroll in honors courses in history at less than half the rate they enroll for honors courses in English and science. Typically, requirements have also declined for writing essays, producing research-based papers, and reading original sources. Similar declines are reported in the requirements for such reasoning skills as evaluating sources of information, drawing conclusions, and constructing logical arguments.

Sources: What Works: Research About Teaching and Learning.
  Washington, DC: U.S. Department of Education. 1987, 77.
Fitzgerald, F. (1979). *America Revised: History School Books in the Twentieth Century.* Boston: Atlantic Little-Brown.
Owings, J. A. (1985). "History Credits Earned by 1980 High School Sophomores Who Graduated in 1982." *High School and Beyond Tabulation.* Washington, DC: National Center for Education Statistics.
Thernstrom, S. (1985). "The Humanities and Our Cultural Challenge." In C. E. Finn, D. Ravitch, and P. Roberts (eds.). *Challenges to the Humanities.* New York: Holmes and Meier.

The Western world's first great philosophers came from Athens. Of the many philosophers that Greece produced, three stand out—Socrates (470–399 B.C.), Plato (427–347 B.C.), and Aristotle (384–322 B.C.).

Of the many philosophers of ancient Greece whose teachings have lasted over time, Socrates, along with Aristotle and Plato, stands out the most.

Socrates. Socrates left no writings, but we know much about him from the writings of Xenophon and Plato. In the **Socratic method** of teaching, a teacher asks a series of questions that leads the student to a certain conclusion. This method is still commonly used by teachers today.

Socrates traveled around Athens teaching the students who gathered about him. He was dedicated to the search for truth and at times was very critical of the existing government. In fact, Socrates was eventually brought to trial for inciting the people against the government by his ceaseless questioning. He was found guilty and given a choice between ending his teaching or being put to death. Socrates chose death, thereby becoming a martyr for the cause of education. Socrates' fundamental principle, "Knowledge is virtue," has been adopted by countless educators and philosophers throughout the ages. Incidentally, some authorities speculate that Socrates may not really have existed, but rather was a mythical character created by other writers.

Plato. Plato was a student and disciple of Socrates. In his *Republic*, Plato set forth his recommendations for the ideal society. He suggested that society should contain three classes of people: artisans, to do the manual work; soldiers, to defend the society; and philosophers, to advance knowledge and to rule the society. Plato's educational aim was to discover and develop each individual's abilities. He believed that each man's abilities should be used to serve society. Plato wrote: "I call education the virtue which is shown by children when the feelings of joy or of sorrow, of love or of hate, which arise their souls, are made conformable to order." Concerning the goals of education, Plato wrote: "A good education is that which gives to the body and to the soul all the beauty and all the perfection of which they are capable."

Aristotle. Like Plato, Aristotle believed that a person's most important purpose was to serve and improve humankind. Aristotle's educational method, however, was scientific, practical, and objective, in contrast to the philosophical methods of Socrates and Plato. Aristotle believed that the quality of a society was determined by the quality of education found in that society. His writings, which include *Lyceum, Oraganon, Politics, Ethics,* and *Metaphysics,* were destined to exert greater influence on humankind throughout the Middle Ages than the writings of any other man.

Insight into some of Aristotle's views concerning education can be obtained from the following passage from *Politics:*

> There can be no doubt that children should be taught those useful things which are really necessary, but not all things; for occupations are divided into liberal and illiberal; and to young children should be imparted only such kinds of knowledge as will be useful to them without vulgarizing them. And any occupation, art, or science, which makes the body or soul or mind of the freeman less fit for the practice or exercise of virtue, is vulgar; wherefore we call those arts vulgar which tend to deform the body, and likewise all paid employments, for they absorb and degrade the mind.[1]

It was the early Greek philosophers, including Plato and Aristotle, who initiated the idea that females and slaves did not possess the intelligence to be leaders and therefore should not be educated. Unfortunately, our world's current struggle with racism and sexism is deeply rooted in Western civilization, and is traceable to the ancient world.

Roman Education

In 146 B.C. the Romans conquered Greece, and Greek teachers and their educational system were quickly absorbed into the Roman Empire. Many of the educational and philosophical advances made by the Roman Empire after that time were actually inspired by enslaved Greeks.

Roman Schools. Before 146 B.C., Roman children were educated primarily in the home, though some children attended schools known as *ludi,* where the rudiments of reading and writing were taught. The Greek influence on Roman education became pronounced between 50 B.C. and A.D. 200, during which time an entire system of schools developed. Some children, after learning to read and write, attended a grammaticus school to study Latin, literature, history, mathematics, music, and dialectics. These **Latin grammar schools** were somewhat like twentieth-century secondary schools in function. Students who were preparing for a career of political service received their training in schools of rhetoric, which offered courses in grammar, rhetoric, dialectics, music, arithmetic, geometry, and astronomy.

The Roman Empire contained numerous institutions of higher learning that were continuations of former Greek institutions. A library founded by Vespian about A.D. 70 later came to be known as the Athenaeum, and eventually offered studies in law, medicine, architecture, mathematics, and mechanics.

Quintilian. Quintilian (A.D. 35–95) was the most influential Roman educator. In a set of twelve books, *The Institutes of Oratory,* he described current educational practices, recommended the type of educational system needed in Rome, and listed the great books in existence at that time.

Quintilian had considerable insight into educational psychology; concerning the punishment of students, he wrote:

> I am by no means in favor of whipping boys, though I know it to be a general practice. In the first place, whipping is unseemly, and if you suppose the boys to be somewhat grown up, it is an affront to the highest degree. In the next place, if a boy's ability is so poor as to be proof against reproach he will, like a worthless slave, become insensible to blows. Lastly, if a teacher is assiduous and careful, there is no need to use force. I shall observe further that while a boy is under the rod he experiences pain and fear. The shame of this experience dejects and discourages many pupils, makes them shun being seen, and may even weary them of their lives.[2]

Regarding the motivation of students, Quintilian stated:

> Let study be made a child's diversion; let him be soothed and caressed into it, and let him sometimes test himself upon his proficiency. Sometimes enter a contest of wits with him, and let him imagine that he comes off the conqueror. Let him even be encouraged by giving him such rewards that are most appropriate to his age.[3]

These comments apply as well today as they did when Quintilian wrote them nearly two thousand years ago. Quintilian's writings were rediscovered in the 1400s and became influential in the humanistic movement in education.

The Romans had a genius for organization and for getting the job done. They made lasting contributions to architecture, and many of their roads, aqueducts, and buildings remain today. This genius for organization enabled Rome to unite much of the ancient world with a common language, a religion, and a political bond—a condition that favored the spread of education and knowledge throughout the ancient world.

Education in the Middle Ages (476–1300)

By A.D. 476 (the fall of the Roman Empire) the Roman Catholic Church was well on the way to becoming the greatest power in government and education. In fact, the rise of the church to a very powerful position is often cited as a main cause of the Western World's plunge into the Dark Ages. As the church stressed the importance of gaining entrance to heaven, life on earth became less important. Many people viewed earthly life as nothing more than a way to a life hereafter. We can see that a society in which this attitude prevailed would be unlikely to make intellectual advances, except perhaps in areas tangential to religion.

In this section we will briefly review the history of education in the Dark Ages and the Revival of Learning. We begin our study by examining the achievements of two educators who lived during the Dark Ages: Charlemagne and Alcuin.

The Dark Ages (400–1000)

As the name implies, the Dark Ages was a period when human learning and knowledge not only stood still, but actually regressed in the Western world. This was due to a variety of conditions, including political and religious oppression of the common people. However, there were some examples of human progress during this historical period.

Charlemagne. During the Dark Ages, one of the very few bright periods for education was the reign of Charlemagne (742–814). Charlemagne realized the value of education, and, as ruler of a large part of Europe, he was in a position to establish schools and encourage scholarly activity. In 768, when Charlemagne came into power, educational activity was at an extremely low ebb. The little educating that was carried on was conducted by the church, mainly to induct people into the faith and to train religious leaders. The schools in which this religious teaching took place included *catechumenal schools,* which taught church doctrine to new converts; *catechetical schools,* which at first taught the catechism but later became schools for training church leaders; and *cathedral (or monastic) schools,* which trained clergy.

Alcuin. Charlemagne sought far and wide for a talented educator who could improve education in the kingdom, finally selecting Alcuin (735–804), who had been a teacher in England. While Alcuin served as Charlemagne's chief educational advisor, he became the most famous educator of his day. His main educational writings include *On Grammar, On Orthography, On Rhetoric,* and *On Dialectics.* In addition to trying to improve education generally in the kingdom, Alcuin headed Charlemagne's Palace School in Frankland. Charlemagne himself often sat in the Palace School with the children, trying to further his own meager education.

Astronomy was one of the "seven liberal arts" taught during the time of Charlemagne and Alcuin.

Roughly during Alcuin's time, the phrase **seven liberal arts** came into common usage to describe the curriculum that was then taught in many schools. The seven liberal arts consisted of the trivium (grammar, rhetoric, and logic) and the quadrivium (arithmetic, geometry, music, and astronomy). Each of these seven subjects was defined broadly, so collectively they constituted a more comprehensive study than today's usage of the term suggests. The phrase *liberal arts* has survived time and is common now.

The Revival of Learning

Despite the efforts of men such as Charlemagne and Alcuin, very little educational progress was made during the Dark Ages. However, between 1000 and 1300—a period frequently referred to as the "Age of the Revival of Learning"—humankind slowly regained a thirst for education. This revival of interest in learning was helped by two events: first, the rediscovery of the writings of some of the ancient philosophers (mainly Aristotle) and renewed interest in them and, second, the reconciliation of religion and philosophy. Before this time the church had denounced the study of philosophy as contradictory to its teachings.

Thomas Aquinas, more than any other person, helped to change the church's views on learning. This change led to the creation of new learning institutions, such as the medieval universities.

Thomas Aquinas. The harmonization of the doctrines of the church with the doctrines of philosophy and education was rooted in the ideas of Aristotle and largely accomplished by Thomas Aquinas (1255–1274), himself a theologian. Aquinas formalized **scholasticism** (the logical and philosophical study of the beliefs of the church). His most important writing was *Summa Theologica,* which became the doctrinal authority of the Roman Catholic Church. The educational

Can You Provide Adequate Multicultural Education in Your Classroom?

When you become a teacher, you will be expected to provide multicultural education for your students—regardless of the age level or subjects you teach. Most teachers today face the dilemma of wanting to provide their students with a high-quality multicultural program, but being frustrated with the lack of time and support for doing so.

As indicated in chapters 11, 12, and 13, racial and ethnic prejudice and injustice have been present throughout our educational history. Unfortunately, there is still considerable racial and ethnic strife throughout the United States today, and much of this strife has filtered into the halls of education. Debates rage about how schools should meet the educational demands of a complex, multicultural society. As a teacher, you will be expected to join in this debate and help search for answers.

James Banks, a leading researcher in multicultural education at the University of Washington,

feels past efforts have been too superficial. He asserts that "additive approaches" treat multicultural material as "an appendage to the main story of the development of the nation and to the core curriculum." Instead, multicultural education should integrate multicultural perspectives throughout the curriculum, on an equal footing with white European perspectives.

Despite the lack of time and adequate school district encouragement and support, there are many things that a determined and creative teacher can do to integrate multicultural education throughout the curriculum. Teachers can also encourage the school district to develop and support comprehensive laws for multicultural education and then participate in developing these plans.

- What are the historical antecedents that have contributed to the lack of racial and ethnic understanding in our society?
- Should education programs seek to eliminate differences among individuals or to preserve and perhaps celebrate them?
- What can you do in your classroom to improve multicultural education?
- What additional information would you like about multicultural education, and where might you find such information?

and philosophical views of Thomas Aquinas were made formal in the philosophy Thomism—a philosophy that has remained important in Roman Catholic parochial education.

Medieval Universities. The revival of learning brought about a general increase in educational activity and a growth of educational institutions, including the establishment of universities. These medieval universities, the true forerunners of our modern universities, included the University of Bologna (1158), which specialized in law; the University of Paris (1180), which specialized in theology; Oxford University (1214); and the University of Salerno (1224). By 1500, approximately eighty universities had been established in Europe.

Although the Middle Ages produced a few educational advances in the Western world, we must remember that much of the Eastern world did not experience the Dark Ages. Mohammed (569–632) led a group of Arabs through northern Africa and into southern Spain. The Eastern learning that the Arabs brought to Spain spread slowly throughout Europe over the next few centuries through the writings of such scholars as Avicenna (980–1037) and Averroes (1126–1198).

These Eastern contributions to Western knowledge included significant advances in science and mathematics, particularly the Arabic numbering system.

Education in Transition (1300–1700)

Two very important movements took place during the transition period of 1300–1700—the Renaissance and the Reformation. The Renaissance represented the protest of individuals against the dogmatic authority the church exerted over their social and intellectual life. The Renaissance started in Italy (around 1130), when humans reacquired the spirit of free inquiry that had prevailed in ancient Greece. The Renaissance slowly spread through Europe, resulting in a general revival of classical learning, called *humanism*. Erasmus (1466–1536) was one of the most famous humanist educators, and two of his books, *The Right Method of Instruction* and *The Liberal Education of Boys*, formed a humanistic theory of education.

The second movement, the Reformation, represented a reaction against certain beliefs of the Roman Catholic Church, particularly those that discouraged learning and that, in consequence, kept lay people in ignorance. We will examine both the Renaissance and the Reformation in this section.

The Renaissance

The common people were generally oppressed by wealthy landowners and royalty during the eleventh and twelfth centuries. In fact, the common people were thought to be unworthy of education and to exist primarily to serve landed gentry and royalty. The Renaissance represented a rebellion on the part of the common people against the suppression they experienced from both the church and the wealthy who controlled their lives. At that time masses of common people developed a spirit of inquiry and demanded a better life.

Vittorino da Feltre. One of the educators from the Renaissance period was a man from the eastern Alps by the name of Vittorino da Feltre (ca. 1278–1446).[4] Vittorino studied at the University of Florence, where he developed an interest in teaching. He also developed a keen interest in classical literature and, along with a number of other educators of that time, began to believe that people could be educated and also be Christians at the same time—a belief that the church generally did not share.

Vittorino established several schools, taught in a variety of others, and generally helped to advance the development of education during his lifetime. He believed that education was an important end in itself and thereby helped to rekindle an interest in the value of human knowledge during the Renaissance.

Erasmus. Erasmus has a good deal of educational insight. concerning the aims of education, he wrote:

> The duty of instructing the young includes several elements, the first and also the chief of which is that the tender mind of the child should be instructed in piety; the second, that he love and learn the liberal arts; the third, that he

Erasmus (1466–1536)

be taught tact in the conduct of social life; and the fourth, that from his earliest age he accustom himself to good behavior, based on moral principles.[5]

The Reformation

It is difficult for people today to imagine the extent to which the Roman Catholic Church dominated the lives of the common people through most of what we think of as Europe during the fifteenth and sixteenth centuries. The Roman Catholic Church and the Pope had an enormous amount of influence over European royalty during this time. In fact, some historians suggest that the Pope and other officials of the Roman Catholic Church were in some ways more powerful than many individual kings and queens. After all, the Roman Catholic Church could and frequently did claim that unless members of royalty abided by its rules, they were destined to spend eternity in hell—an extremely frightening prospect for any human being. Consequently, it is understandable that the church came to be a powerful influence throughout most of Europe.

Luther and Melanchthon. The Protestant Reformation had its formal beginning in 1517, when Martin Luther (1483–1546) published his ninety-five theses, which stated his disagreement with the Roman Catholic Church. One of these disagreements held great implications for the importance of formal education. The church believed that it was not desirable for each person to read and interpret the Bible for himself or herself; rather, the church would pass on the "correct" interpretation to the laity. Luther felt not only that the church had itself misinterpreted the Bible, but also that people were intended to read and interpret the Bible for themselves. If one accepted the church's position on this matter, formal education remained unimportant. If one accepted Luther's position, however, education became necessary for all people so that they might individually read and interpret the Bible. In a sense, education became important as a way of obtaining salvation. It is understandable that Luther and his educational coworker, Melanchthon (1497–1560), soon came to stress universal elementary education. Melanchthon's most important educational writing was *Visitation Articles* (1528), in which he set forth his recommendations for schools. Luther and Melanchthon felt that education should be provided for all, regardless of class, and should be compulsory for both sexes. They also believed that it should be state-controlled, state-supported, and centered on classical languages, grammar, mathematics, science, history, music, and physical education. Luther's argument for increased governmental support for education has a familiar twentieth-century ring:

> Each city is subjected to great expense every year for the construction of roads, for fortifying its ramparts, and for buying arms and equipping soldiers. Why should it not spend an equal sum for the support of one or two schoolmasters? The prosperity of a city does not depend solely on its natural riches, on the solidity of its walls, on the elegance of its mansions, and on the abundance of arms in its arsenals; but the safety and strength of a city reside above all in a good education, which furnishes it with instructed, reasonable, honorable, and well-trained citizens.[6]

Martin Luther (1483–1546) was an early supporter of state-sponsored, state-controlled education.

Ignatius of Loyola. To combat the Reformation movement, Ignatius of Loyola (1491–1556) organized the Society of Jesus (Jesuits) in 1540. The Jesuits worked to establish schools in which to further the cause of the Roman Catholic Church, and they tried to stem the flow of converts to the Reformation cause.

Although the Jesuits' main interest was religious, they soon grew into a great teaching order and were very successful in training their own teachers. The rules by which the Jesuits conducted their schools were stated in the *Radio Studiorum;* a revised edition still guides the Jesuit schools today. The improvement of teacher training was the Jesuits' main contribution to education.

Another Catholic teaching order, the Brothers of the Christian Schools, was organized in 1684 by Jean Baptiste de la Salle (1651–1719). Unlike the Jesuits, who were primarily interested in secondary education, de la Salle and his order were interested in elementary schools and in preparing elementary school teachers. De la Salle was one of the first educators to use student teaching in the preparation of teachers.

Comenius (1592–1670)

Comenius. Among many other outstanding educators during the transition period was Johann Amos Comenius (1592–1670). Comenius is perhaps best remembered for his many textbooks, which were among the first to contain illustrations. The invention and improvement of printing during the 1400s made it possible to produce books, such as those of Comenius, more rapidly and economically—a development that was essential to the growth of education. Much of the writing of Comenius reflected the increasing interest that was then developing in science.

Locke. John Locke (1632–1704) was a very influential English educator during the late seventeenth century. He wrote many important educational works, including *Some Thoughts on Education* and *Essay Concerning Human Understanding*. He viewed a young child's mind as a blank slate (*tabula rasa*) on which an education could be imprinted. He believed that teachers needed to create a nonthreatening learning environment—a revolutionary idea at that time.

Modern Period (1700–Present)

As we have shown, educational progress in Europe was slow and took place in only a few places through the seventeenth century. In this section we will see why many of our current educational ideas can be traced to the early 1700s. We will look at two movements, commonly referred to as the Age of Reason and the Emergence of Common Man.

The Age of Reason

The first movement of the early modern period that influenced education was a revolt of the intellectuals against the superstition and ignorance that dominated people's lives at the time. This movement became known as the **Age of Reason,** and Francois Marie Arouet (1745–1827), A Frenchman who wrote under the name Voltaire, was one of its leaders. Those who joined this movement became known as *rationalists* because of the faith they placed in human rational power. The implication for education in the rationalist movement is obvious: If one places greater emphasis on human ability to reason, then education takes on new importance as the way by which humans develop this power.

Voltaire and Descartes. The work of Descartes (1596–1650) resulted in three axioms that gradually became well accepted by thinking men. These axioms were

Descarte
scientific
method   →

(1) that reason was supreme, (2) that the laws of nature were invariable, and (3) that truth was verified by exact methods of testing. These ideas became the basis for disputing some of the traditional teaching of the church and for resisting the bonds that royalty had traditionally placed on the common people. These axioms also formed the basis of rationalism, which influenced the thinking of Voltaire. Voltaire was a very articulate writer who was also brilliant, clever, witty, and vain—qualities that helped him to become extremely influential. In fact, many authorities give him considerable credit for both the American and French Revolutions, which took place during his lifetime.

While Voltaire was not technically an educator, his writings helped to bring about a renewed interest in learning and a conviction that knowledge, and therefore schools, was extremely powerful in shaping the lives of people. His views contributed to the development of educational philosophies such as rationalism and empiricism, which helped to elevate the importance of education in the Western world.

Frederick the Great.   One of the influential leaders during the Age of Reason was Frederick the Great (1712–1786). Frederick was a friend of Voltaire and became supportive of the notion that education was of value. He was a liberal thinker for his time and was one of the few leaders who did not attempt to force the common people into a particular form of religion. Frederick also permitted an unusual amount of freedom of speech for his era and generally allowed the common people a degree of liberty that most rulers considered dangerous.

As a consequence, education was given an opportunity to develop, if not flourish, during his reign as leader of Prussia. It was during Frederick's reign that laws were passed regarding education, and teachers were required to obtain special training as well as licenses to teach.

While the progress of education during Frederick's reign was meager in comparison to what we know today, nevertheless, for his time, Frederick must be given considerable credit for contributing to the development of schools during the Age of Reason. Concerning education for all children, Frederick stated, "In the open country it is sufficient if they learn to read and write a little; if they know too much they will go to towns and become secretaries and such like." It is likewise true that Frederick did not place much value on education for young children beyond learning to read and write. It is interesting to note, however, that he was particularly interested in better training for teachers.

The Emergence of Common Man

The second movement of the early modern period that affected education was the **Emergence of Common Man.** Whereas the Age of Reason was a revolt of the learned for intellectual freedom, the Emergence of Common Man was a revolt of common people for a better life—politically, economically, socially, and educationally.

Rousseau.   One of the leaders in this movement was Jean Jacques Rousseau (1712–1778), whose *Social Contract* (1762) became an influential book in the French Revolution. Scholars have suggested that *Social Contract* was also the basal doctrine of the American Declaration of Independence.[7] Rousseau was a philosopher, not an educator, but he wrote a good deal on the subject of education. His most important educational work was *Émile* (1762), in which he states his views concerning the ideal education for youth. Rousseau felt that the aim of education should be to return human beings to their "natural state." His view on the subject is well summed up by the opening sentence of *Émile*: "Everything is good as it comes from the hand of the author of nature: but everything degenerates in the hands of man." Rousseau's educational views came to be known as *naturalism*. Concerning the best method of teaching, Rousseau wrote:

> Do not treat the child to discourses which he cannot understand. No descriptions, no eloquence, no figures of speech. Be content to present to him appropriate objects. Let us transform our sensations into ideas. But let us not jump at once from sensible objects to intellectual objects. Let us always proceed slowly from one sensible notion to another. In general, let us never substitute the sign for the thing, except when it is impossible for us to show the thing. . . . I have no love whatever for explanations and talk. Things! Things! I shall never tire of saying that we ascribe too much importance to words. With our babbling education we make only babblers.[8]

Rousseau's most important contributions to education were his belief that it must be a natural process, not an artificial one, and his compassionate, positive view of the child. Rousseau believed that children were inherently good—a belief that was in opposition to the prevailing religiously inspired belief that children were born full of sin. The contrasting implications for teaching methods suggested by these two views are self-evident, as is the educational desirability of Rousseau's view over that which prevailed at the time. Although Rousseau never taught a day of school in his life, he likely did more to improve education through his writing than any of his contemporaries.

Pestalozzi. Johann Heinrich Pestalozzi (1746–1827) was a Swiss educator who put Rousseau's theory into practice. Pestalozzi established two schools for boys,

Jean Jacques Rousseau (1712–1778) felt that education should seek to return humans to their natural state.

Johann Heinrich Pestalozzi (1746–1827)

one at Burgdorf (1800–1804) and the other at Yverdun (1805–1825). Educators came from all over the world to view Pestalozzi's schools and to study his teaching methods. Pestalozzi enumerated his educational views in a book entitled *Leonard and Gertrude.* Unlike most educators of his time, Pestalozzi believed that a teacher should treat students with love and kindness:

> I was convinced that my heart would change the condition of my children just as promptly as the sun of spring would reanimate the earth benumbed by the winter. . . . It was necessary that my children should observe, from dawn to evening, at every moment of the day, upon my brow and on my lips, that my affections were fixed on them, that their happiness was my happiness, and that their pleasures were my pleasures . . . I was everything to my children. I was alone with them from morning till night. . . . Their hands were in my hands. Their eyes were fixed on my eyes.[9]

Key concepts in the Pestalozzian method included an expression of love, understanding, and patience for children; a compassion for the poor; and the use of objects and sense perception as the basis for acquiring knowledge.

Herbart.   One of the educators who studied under Pestalozzi and was influenced by him was Johann Friedrich Herbart (1776–1841). While Pestalozzi had successfully put into practice and further developed Rousseau's educational ideas, it remained for Herbart to organize these educational views into a formal psychology of education. Herbart stressed apperception (learning by association). The **Herbartian teaching method** developed into five formal steps:

1. *Preparation:* Preparing the student to receive a new idea
2. *Presentation:* Presenting the student with the new idea
3. *Association:* Assimilating the new idea with the old ideas
4. *Generalization:* The general idea deriving from the combination of the old and new ideas
5. *Application:* Applying the new knowledge

Herbart's educational ideas are contained in his *Science of Education* (1806) and *Outlines of Educational Doctrine* (1835).

Froebel.   Friedrich Froebel (1782–1852) was another European educator who was influenced by Rousseau and Pestalozzi and who made a significant contribution to education. Froebel's contributions included the establishment of the first kindergarten (or *Kleinkinderbeschaftigungsanstalt,* as he called it in 1837), an emphasis on social development, a concern for the cultivation of creativity, and the concept of learning by doing. He originated the idea that women are best suited to teach young children. Froebel wrote his main educational book, *Education of Man,* in 1826.

Two developments in the late 1800s were the last important European antecedents of American education: the maturing of the scientific movement, hastened by the publication of Charles Darwin's *On the Origin of Species* (1859), and the formulation of educational psychology near the end of the century.

The student of educational history must realize that even though many educational advances have been made by 1900, the average European received a pathetically small amount of formal education, even at that late date. Historically, education had been available only to the few who were fortunate enough to be born into the leisure class; the masses of people in the working class had received little or no education up to that time. What formal education the working person might have received was usually provided for religious purposes by the church.

CASE STUDY   A STUDENT TEACHER'S DILEMMA

Jean Angotti was in the middle of her student teaching assignment at the Jefferson School. As far as she knew, she was doing a good job. Both her classroom supervisor, Mrs. Serrano, and her college supervisor, Dr. Hoffman, had given her numerous compliments about her lessons, in spite of the fact that she was having some discipline problems. Mrs. Serrano had warned her at the beginning that the class was a "handful"—even for her. There were several students in the class who were difficult to motivate and, at times, disruptive.

Jean was surprised and somewhat shaken one day, when the principal, Mrs. Quanli, called her into the office to discuss a parent complaint about the lack of discipline in her classroom. This parent, who was a teacher in a nearby school district, felt that his son's learning was being inhibited by what he called "a permissive and unstructured" classroom. Mrs. Quanli told Jean that she had a policy of taking all parental complaints seriously, and of immediately sharing any parent concerns with the teachers involved. She also stated that she had visited with the classroom supervisor, Mrs. Serrano, who had told her that Jean was a very good, mature student teacher. Mrs. Serrano had recommended that Mrs. Quanli talk to Jean about the complaint before meeting with the parent again.

After visiting about the situation for a while, Mrs. Quanli asked Jean for her reaction to this parent's complaint about the lack of discipline in her classroom. Jean responded she had been impressed with the theories of Rousseau concerning children, especially his idea that children were born "good," and became "bad" only in the hands of people. This concept was revolutionary at the time and ran counter to the long-accepted religious "doctrine of original sin," which suggested that children were born "full of the devil," which sometimes had to be beaten out of them. This commonly held belief resulted in schools that were very strict, and in discipline that was very harsh. Jean felt that many of her own public school teachers had appeared to believe that students were inherently bad—as suggested by the doctrine of original sin—and therefore could not be trusted to behave or to learn on their own. In conclusion, Jean stated that she was attempting to use the Rousseauian philosophy in her student teaching—giving the students more freedom and more learning options.

1. What do you feel are Mrs. Quanli's options at this point? Of those options, which do you feel is best?
2. How do you feel about a teacher in one district complaining about a teacher in another district? In the same district?
3. How much freedom do you feel a student teacher should have to experiment with new ideas?
4. How would you feel and what would you do at this point if you were Jean's classroom supervisor, Mrs. Serrano?
5. If Jean were a close friend who asked for your advice, what suggestions would you give her? Would you recommend that Jean offer to meet with the parent?

Summary and Implications

This chapter has pointed out that many of the first educational efforts were made in China, India, and Africa, but the historical roots of our educational traditions can be traced back to Europe. People who have helped to mold Western education include Socrates, Plato, Aristotle, Qunitilian, Alcuin, Aquinas, Erasmus, Melanchthon, Rousseau, Pestalozzi, and Herbart. These and other educational pioneers labored against overwhelming odds to advance the cause of education, and many of the concepts and practices they developed are still in use today. However, perhaps their greatest contribution was in helping humankind to discover and appreciate the potential value of education. One important implication of this chapter for current ideas is that many of our contemporary educational beliefs are very old ideas. Today's teachers also have an obligation to study the history of education so that they will not repeat mistakes of the past but rather capitalize on past successes.

Discussion Questions

1. What were the major factors that first caused humans to create schools, especially in the Eastern world?
2. What were the major differences between the Spartan and Athenian school systems? Why did these differences exist?
3. Discuss the educational achievement of the Roman Empire.
4. What factors contributed to the decline of education during the Dark Ages?
5. What were the major educational advances made during the Reformation period?
6. What were the strengths and weaknesses of Jean Jacques Rousseau's ideas about children and education?

Journal/Portfolio Development

1. Write a paper summarizing and criticizing the work and writing of one of the early educators mentioned in this chapter.
2. Make a list of historical educational ideas mentioned in this chapter that are still valid and useful for educators today.

School-Based Experiences

1. Over two hundred years ago, Jean Jacques Rousseau advocated that children should be taught with love patience, understanding, and kindness. As you work in the school, experiment with this basic approach to students to see whether it is effective. You might also wish to observe experienced teachers to determine the extent to which they teach children with love, patience, understanding, and kindness. We suggest that you experiment with other ideas in this chapter as you observe and participate in the classroom.
2. As you work in schools, observe how they have changed in contrast to schools of the past. How are schools today similar to those of the past? How much and in what ways are students today similar to their historical counterparts? In what ways are they probably different?

Notes

1. Paul Monroe, *Source Book of the History of Education.* New York: Macmillan, 1901, 282.
2. Quintilian, *The Institutes of Oratory,* trans. W. Guthrie. London: Dewick and Clark, 1905, 27.
3. Ibid., 12.
4. Glenn Smith et al., *Lives in Education.* Ames, IA: Educational Studies Pres, 1984, 84–88.
5. Gabriel Compayre, *History of Pedagogy,* trans. W. H. Payne. Boston: Heath, 1888, 12–13; 88–89.
6. Ibid., 115.

7. Paul Monroe, *History of Education*. New York: Macmillan, 1905, 283.

8. Gabriel Compayre, 299.

9. Ibid., 425.

Bibliography

Armytage, W. H. G. "William Byngham: A Medieval Protagonist of the Training of Teachers." *History of Education Journal 2* (1951): 107–110.

Butts, R. Freeman. *A Cultural History of Western Education*. New York: McGraw-Hill, 1955.

Chambliss, J. J., ed. *Nobility, Tragedy and Naturalism: Education in Ancient Greece*. Minneapolis: Burgess, 1971.

Cole, Luella. *A History of Education: Socrates to Montessori*. New York: Holt, Rinehart and Winston, 1950.

Compayre, Gabriel. *History of Pedagogy*. Translated by W. H. Payne. Boston: Heath, 1888.

Hamilton, E. *The Greek Way*. New York: W. W. Norton, 1930.

Keating, M. W. *Comenius*. New York: McGraw-Hill, 1931.

Lucas, Christopher J. *Our Western Educational Heritage*. New York: Macmillan, 1972.

Meyer, Adolph E. *An Educational History of the Western World*. New York: McGraw-Hill, 1965.

Painter, A. M. *A History of Education*. New York: Appleton, 1987.

12

Early American Education

Focus Questions

1   If you had been one of the early American colonists, how important would education have been to you? Why?

2   How important has our federal government been in advancing education in the United States?

3   What do you suppose life was like for the colonial school teacher?

4   What has characterized the education provided for minorities and women throughout the development of our educational history?

5   How has education improved through the history of our country?

Key Terms and Concepts

Committee of Ten: An historic NEA committee that studied secondary education in 1893.

Common elementary schools: An early attempt to provide a basic elementary education for all children.

Compulsory education: School attendance that is required by law on the theory that it is to the benefit of the state or commonwealth to educate all the people.

Dame school: A low-level primary school in the colonial and other early periods, usually conducted by an untrained woman in her own home.

Hornbook: A single printed page containing the alphabet, syllables, a prayer, and other simple words, tacked to a wooden paddle and covered with a thin transparent layer of cow's horn, used in colonial times as the beginner's first book or preprimer.

Normal school: The first American institution that was devoted exclusively to teacher training.

Old Deluder Satan Act: The first colonial educational law (1647), which required colonial towns of at least 50 households to provide education for youth.

Parochial school: An educational institution operated and controlled by a religious denomination.

Religious-affiliated school: A private school over which, in most cases, a parent church group exercises some control or to which it provides some form of subsidy.

*T*he first permanent European settlements in what is now the United States included Jamestown (1607), Plymouth (1620), Massachusetts Bay (1630), Maryland (1632), Connecticut (1635), and Providence Plantations (1636). The motives that prompted most early settlers to move to America were religious, economic, and political. Generally, these people were not dissatisfied with education in their homelands; therefore nearly all educational practices and educational materials in early colonial America were simply transplanted from the Old World.

The religious motive was very strong in colonial America, and it permeated colonial education. Colonists generally felt that a child should learn to read so that he or she could read the Bible and thus gain salvation. Beyond this desire, there was no demand for mass education. Since the clergy possessed the ability to read and write, and since the ultimate utility of education was to read the Bible, it was logical for the clergy to do much of the teaching.

Providing Education in the New World

The early settlement of the East Coast was composed of groups of colonies: the Southern Colonies, centered in Virginia; the Middle Colonies, centered in New York; and the Northern Colonies, centered in New England.

Colonial Education

The earliest settlers from Europe brought with them a sincere interest in providing at least rudimentary education for their children. Naturally, they brought their European ideas about education with them and, soon after arrival, created educational programs throughout colonial America. Let us briefly examine these early colonial school programs.

Southern Colonies. The Southern Colonies soon came to be made up of large tobacco plantations. Because of the size of the plantations, people lived far apart, and few towns were established until later in the colonial period. There was an immediate need for cheap labor to work on the plantations, and in 1619, only twelve years after Jamestown was settled, the first boatload of slaves were imported from Africa. Other sources of cheap labor for the Southern Colonies included white Europeans from a variety of backgrounds, who purchased passage to the New World by agreeing to serve a lengthy period of indentured servitude on arrival in the colonies. There soon came to be two very distinct classes of people in the South—a few wealthy landowners and a large mass of laborers, most of whom were slaves. The educational provisions that evolved from this set of conditions were precisely what one would expect. No one was interested in providing education for the slaves, with the exception of a few missionary groups, such as the English Society for the Propagation of the Gospel in Foreign Parts. Such missionary groups tried to provide some education for slaves, primarily so that they could read the Bible. The wealthy landowners usually hired tutors to teach their children at home. Distances between homes and slow transportation precluded the establishment of centralized schools. When the upper-class children grew old enough to attend college, they were usually sent to well-established schools in Europe.

Middle Colonies.   The people who settled the Middle Colonies came from various national (Dutch, Swedish) and religious (Puritan, Mennonite, Catholic) backgrounds. This is why the Middle Colonies have often been called the "melting pot" of the nation. This diversity of backgrounds made it impossible for the inhabitants of the Middle Colonies to agree on a common public school system. Consequently, the respective groups established their own parochial schools. Many children received their education through an apprenticeship while learning a trade from a master already in that line of work. Some people even learned the art of teaching school through an apprenticeship.

Northern Colonies.   The Northern Colonies were settled mainly by the Puritans, a religious group from Europe. In 1630, approximately one thousand Puritans settled near Boston. Unlike people in the Southern Colonies, people in New England lived close to one another. Towns sprang up and soon became centers of political and social life. Shipping ports were established, and an industrial economy developed that demanded numerous skilled and semiskilled workers—a condition that created a large middle class.

Early School Laws.   These conditions of common religious views, town life, and a large middle class made it possible for the people to agree on common public schools. This agreement led to very early educational activity in the Northern Colonies. In 1642 the General Court of Massachusetts enacted a law that stated:

> This Co^t, [Court] taking into consideration the great neglect of many parents & masters in training up their children in learning . . . do hereupon order and decree, that in every towne y chosen men . . . take account from time to time of all parents and masters, and of their children, concerning their . . . ability to read & understand the principles of religion & the capitall lawes of this country. . . .

This law did nothing more than encourage citizens to look after the education of children. Five years later (1647), however, another law was enacted in Massachusetts that required towns to provide education for the youth. This law, which was often referred to as the **Old Deluder Satan Act,** because of its religious motive, stated:

> It being one chiefe proiect of y ould deluder, Satan, to keepe men from the knowledge of y Scriptures. . . . It is therefore orded [ordered], ye evy [every] towneship in this jurisdiction, aft y Lord hath increased y number to 50 household, shall then forthw appoint one w [with] in their towne to teach all such children as shall resort to him to write & reade . . . & it is furth ordered y where any towne shall increase to y numb [number] of 100 families or househould, they shall set up a grammar schoole, y m [aim] thereof being able to instruct youth so farr as they shall be fited for y university [Harvard]. . . .

⎱ High
⎰ school

These Massachusetts school laws of 1642 and 1647 served as models for similar laws that were soon created in other colonies.

Types of Colonial Schools.   Several different kinds of elementary schools sprang up in the colonies, such as the **dame school,** which was conducted by a housewife in her home; the writing school, which taught the child to write; a variety of parochial schools; and charity, or pauper, schools taught by missionary groups.

To go back a few years, in 1635 the Latin Grammar School was established in Boston—the first permanent school of this type in what is now the United States. This school was established when the people of Boston, which had been settled only five years before, voted "that our brother Philemon Pormont, shal be intreated to become scholemaster, for the teaching and nourtering of children with us." The grammar school was a secondary school, its function was college preparatory, and the idea spread quickly to other towns. Charlestown opened its first grammar school one year later, in 1636, by contracting William Witherell "to keep a school for a twelve month." Within sixteen years after the Massachusetts Bay Colony had been founded, seven or eight towns had Latin grammar schools in operation. These schools, transplanted from Europe where similar schools had existed for a long time, were traditional and designed to prepare children for college and "for the service of God, in church and commonwealth."

Harvard, the first colonial college, was established in 1636 for preparing ministers. Other early American colleges included William and Mary (1693), Yale (1701), Princeton (1746), King's College (1754), College of Philadelphia (1755), Brown (1764), Dartmouth (1769), and Queen's College (1770). The curriculum in these early colleges was traditional, with heavy emphasis on theology and the classics. An example of the extent to which the religious motive dominated colonial colleges can be found in one of the 1642 rules governing Harvard College, which stated: "Let every Student be plainly instructed, and earnestly pressed to consider well, the maine end of his life and studies is, to know God and Jesus Christ. . . ."

The Struggle for Universal Elementary Education

When the colonists arrived in this country, they simply established schools like those they had known in Europe. The objectives of colonial elementary schools were purely religious. It was commonly believed that everyone needed to be able to read the Bible to receive salvation; therefore parents were eager to have their children receive some type of reading instruction.

Christopher Dock.   A good idea of what a colonial elementary school was like, and the extent to which religion dominated its curriculum, can be gleaned from the following account of a school conducted in 1750 by Christopher Dock, a Mennonite school teacher in Pennsylvania:

> The children arrive as they do because some have a great distance to school, others a short distance, so that the children cannot assemble as punctually as they can in a city. Therefore, when a few children are present, those who can read their Testament sit together on one bench; but the boys and girls occupy separate benches. They are given a chapter which they read at sight consecutively. Meanwhile I write copies for them. Those who have read their passage of Scripture without error take their places at the table and write. Those who fail have to sit at the end of the bench, and each new arrival the same; as each one is thus released in order he takes up his slate. This process continues until they have all assembled. The last one left on the bench is a "lazy pupil."
>
> When all are together, and examined, whether they are washed and combed, they sing a psalm or morning hymn, and I sing and pray with

them. As much as they can understand of the Lord's Prayer and the Ten Commandments (according to the gift God has given them), I exhort and admonish them accordingly.[1]

Monitorial Schools. In 1805, New York City established the first monitorial school in the United States. The monitorial school, which originated in England, represented an attempt to provide mass elementary education for large numbers of children. Typically, the teacher would teach hundreds of pupils, using the better students as helpers. By 1840, nearly all monitorial schools had been closed; the children had not learned enough to justify continuance of this type of school.

Horace Mann (1796–1859)

Horace Mann. Between 1820 and 1860 an educational awakening took place in America. This movement was strongly influenced by Horace Mann (1796–1859). As secretary of the State Board of Education, Mann helped to establish **common elementary schools** in Massachusetts. These common schools were designed to provide a basic elementary education for all children. Among his many impressive educational achievements was the publication of one of the very early professional journals in this country, *The Common School Journal*. Through this journal, Mann kept educational issues before the public.

In 1852, Massachusetts passed a compulsory elementary school attendance law, the first of its kind in the country requiring all children to attend school. By 1900, thirty-two other states had passed similar **compulsory education** laws.

Global Perspectives: Educational Transplantation from Europe. As indicated in Chapter 11, Pestalozzianism and Herbartianism considerably affected elementary education when they were introduced into the United States in the late 1800s. Pestalozzianism emphasized teaching children with love, patience, and understanding. Furthermore, children should learn from objects and firsthand experiences, not from abstractions and words. Pestalozzian concepts soon spread throughout the country. Herbartianism was imported into the United States at the Bloomington Normal School in Illinois by three students who had learned about the ideas of Herbart while studying in Germany. Herbartianism represented an attempt to make a science out of teaching. The more formal system that Herbartianism brought to the often disorganized elementary teacher was badly needed at the time. Unfortunately, Herbartianism eventually contributed to an extreme formalism and rigidity that characterized many American elementary schools in the early 1900s. One school administrator bragged that at a given moment in the school day he knew exactly what was going on in all the classrooms. One can infer from this boast that teachers often had a very strict, rigid educational program imposed on them.

If we look back at the historical development of American elementary education, we can make the following generalizations:

- Until the late 1800s the motive, curriculum, and administration of elementary education were primarily religious. The point at which elementary education began to be more secular than religious was the point at which states began to pass compulsory school attendance laws.
- Discipline has traditionally been harsh and severe in elementary schools. The classical picture of a colonial schoolmaster equipped with a frown, dunce cap, stick, whip, and a variety of abusive phrases is a more accurate picture than one

might expect. It is no wonder that children have historically viewed school as an unpleasant place. Pestalozzi had much to do with bringing about a gradual change in discipline when he advocated that love, not harsh punishment, should be used to motivate students.

- Elementary education has traditionally been formal and impersonal. The ideas of Rousseau, Pestalozzi, Herbart, and Froebel helped to change this condition gradually and make elementary education more student-centered; this was becoming apparent about 1900.
- Elementary schools have traditionally been taught by poorly prepared teachers.
- Although the aims and methodology have varied considerably from time to time, the basic content of elementary education has historically been reading, writing, and arithmetic.

The Need for Secondary Schools

Our contemporary high schools have a long and proud tradition. They have evolved from a series of earlier forms of secondary schools that were created to serve the needs of society at various points in our history. Let us briefly review the historical need for secondary schools in the United States.

Latin Grammar School. The first form of secondary school in the colonies was the Latin grammar school mentioned previously, first established in Boston in 1635 only five years after colonists settled in the area. The Latin grammar school was concerned largely with teaching Latin and other classical subjects, such as Greek, and was strictly college preparatory.

Harvard was the only university in existence in the colonies at that time. The entrance requirements to Harvard stated:

> When any Scholar is able to understand Tully, or such like classicall Latine Author extempore, and make and speake true Latine in Verse and Prose, suo ut aiunt marte; and decline perfectly the Paradigms of Nounes and Verbes in the Greek tongue; let him then, and not before, be capable of admission into the college.

European colleges and later colonial colleges also demanded that students know Latin and Greek before they could be admitted. For instance, in the mid-eighteenth century, the requirements for admission to Yale stated:

> None may expect to be admitted into this College unless upon Examination of the President and Tutors, they shall be found able Extempore to Read, Construe, and Parce Tully, Vergil and the Greek Testament; and to write true Latin in Prose and to understand the Rules of Prosodia, and Common Arithmetic, and Shal bring Sufficient Testimony of his Blameless and inoffensive Life.

Since Latin grammar schools were designed to prepare students for college, it is little wonder that the curriculum in these schools was so classical and traditional. Needless to say, a very small percentage of children attended any Latin grammar school because very few could hope to attend college. Young women did not attend, because colleges at that time did not admit them. As late as 1785 there were only two Latin grammar schools in Boston, and the combined enrollment in these two schools was only sixty-four young men.

1751

American Academy. By the middle of the eighteenth century there was a need for more and better trained skilled workers. Benjamin Franklin, recognizing this need, proposed a new kind of secondary school in Pennsylvania. This proposal brought about the establishment, in Philadelphia in 1751, of the first truly American educational institution, the American Academy. Franklin established this school because he thought the existing Latin grammar schools were not providing the practical secondary education that youth needed. The philosophy, curriculum, and methodology of Franklin's academy were all geared to prepare young people for employment. Similar academies were established throughout America, and these institutions eventually replaced the Latin grammar school as the predominant secondary education institution. They were usually private schools, and many of them admitted girls as well as boys. Later on, some academies even tried to train elementary school teachers.

High School. In 1821 an English classical school (which three years later changed its name to English High School) was opened in Boston, and another distinctively American educational institution was launched. This first high school, under the direction of George B. Emerson, consisted of a three-year course in English, mathematics, science, and history. The school later added to its curriculum the philosophy of history, chemistry, intellectual philosophy, linear drawing, logic, trigonometry, French, and the U.S. Constitution. The school enrolled about one hundred boys during its first year.

The high school was established because of a belief that the existing grammar schools were inadequate for the day and because most people could not afford to send their children to the private academies. The American high school soon replaced both the Latin grammar school and the private academy, and has been with us ever since.

About 1910 the first junior high schools were established in the United States. A survey in 1916 showed fifty-four junior high schools existing in thirty-six states. One year later a survey indicated that the number had increased to about 270. More recently, some school systems have abandoned the junior high school in favor of what is called the *middle school*, which usually consists of grades 6, 7, and 8.

Relevant Research

Critiquing Curriculum

As you prepare for your teaching career, you should have an opportunity to read and think about original historical research sources.

The following letter, written in 1712 by Nathaniel Williams, briefly describes the curriculum of the first Latin grammar school established in the colonies—the Boston Latin Grammar School, which was created in 1635, soon after the first colonists settled in that area. From "Letter from Nathaniel Williams to Nehemia Hobart," in Robert F. Seybold, *The Public Schools of Colonial Boston* (Cambridge, MA, 1935), 69–71.

Curriculum of the Boston Latin Grammar School (1712). The three first years are spent first in Learning by heart & then acc: to their capacities understanding the Accidence and Nomenclator, in construing & parsing acc: to the English rules of Syntax Sententiae Pueriles Cato & Cordcrius & Aesops Fables.

The 4th year, or sooner if their capacities allow it, they are entered upon Erasmus to which they are allou'd no English . . . & upon translating English into Latin out of m^r Garreston's Exercises.

The fifth year they are entred upon Tullies Epistles . . . the Elegancies of which are remarked and improv'd in the afternoon of the day they learn it, by translating an English which contains the phrase somthing altered, and besides recited by heart on the repetition day. . . .

The sixth year they are entred upon Tullies Offices & Luc: Flor: for the forenoon, continuing the use of Ovid's Metam: in the afternoon, & at the end of the Year they read Virgil. . . . Every week these make a Latin Epistle, the last quarter of the Year, when also they begin to learn Greek, & Rhetorick.

The seventh Year they read Tullie's Orations & Justin for the Latin & Greek Testam^t Isocrates Orat: Homer & Hesiod for the Greek in the forenoons & Virgil Horace Juyenal & Persius afternoons . . . Every fortnight they compose a theme. . . .

What was the apparent purpose of the Boston Latin Grammar School? In what ways was the curriculum similar to that in our current comprehensive high schools? In what ways was it different?

Aims of Early American Public Education

The aims of American public education have gradually changed over the years. During colonial times the overriding aim of education at all levels was to enable students to read and understand the Bible, to gain salvation, and to spread the gospel.

After independence was won from England, educational objectives—such as providing Americans with a common language, attempting to instill a sense of patriotism, developing a national feeling of unity and common purpose, and providing the technical and agricultural training our developing nation needed—became important tasks for the schools.

Committee of Ten. In 1892 a committee was established by the National Education Association to study the function of the American high school. This committee, known as the **Committee of Ten**, made an effort to set down the purposes of the high school at that time, and made the following recommendations:

- High school should consist of grades 7 through 12.
- Courses should be arranged sequentially.
- Students should be given very few electives in high school.
- One unit, called a Carnegie unit, should be awarded for each separate course that a student takes each year, provided that the course meets four or five times each week all year long.

The Committee of Ten also recommended trying to graduate high school students earlier to permit them to attend college sooner. At that time the recommendation implied that high schools had a college preparatory function. These recommendations became powerful influences in the shaping of secondary education.

Seven Cardinal Principles. Before 1900, teachers had relatively little direction in their work, since most educational goals were not precisely stated. This problem was partly overcome in 1918 when the Commission on Reorganization of Secondary Education published the report *Cardinal Principles of Secondary Education*, usually referred to as the Seven Cardinal Principles. In reality, the Seven Cardinal Principles constitute only one section of the basic principles discussed in the original text, but it is the part that has become famous. These principles stated that the student should receive an education in the following fields:

1. Health
2. Command of fundamental processes
3. Worthy home membership
4. Vocation
5. Civic education
6. Worthy use of leisure
7. Ethical character

The Eight-Year Study. The following goals of education, or "needs of youth," were listed by the Progressive Education Association in 1938 and grew out of the Eight-Year Study:

1. Physical and mental health
2. Self-assurance
3. Assurance of growth toward adult status

4. Philosophy of life
5. Wide range of personal interests
6. Esthetic appreciations
7. Intelligent self-direction
8. Progress toward maturity in social relations with age-mates and adults
9. Wise use of goods and services
10. Vocational orientation
11. Vocational competence

"Purposes of Education in American Democracy." Also in 1938, the Educational Policies Commission of the National Education Association (NEA) set forth the "Purposes of Education in American Democracy." These objectives stated that students should receive an education in the four broad areas of self-realization, human relations, economic efficiency, and civic responsibility.

"Education for All American Youth." In 1944 this same commission of the NEA published another statement of educational objectives, entitled "Education for All American Youth":

> Schools should be dedicated to the proposition that every youth in these United States—regardless of sex, economic status, geographic location, or race—should experience a broad and balanced education which will
>
> 1. equip him to enter an occupation suited to his abilities and offering reasonable opportunity for personal growth and social usefulness;
> 2. prepare him to assume full responsibilities of American citizenship;
> 3. give him a fair chance to exercise his right to the pursuit of happiness through the attainment and preservation of mental and physical health;
> 4. stimulate intellectual curiosity, engender satisfaction in intellectual achievement, and cultivate the ability to think rationally; and
> 5. help to develop an appreciation of the ethical values which should undergird all life in a democratic society.

"Imperative Needs of Youth." In 1952 the Educational Policies Commission made yet another statement of educational objectives, entitled the "Imperative Needs of Youth":

> 1. All youth need to develop salable skills and those understandings and attitudes that make the worker an intelligent productive participant in economic life. To this end most youth need supervised work experience as well as education in the skills and knowledge of their occupations.
> 2. All youth need to develop and maintain good health and physical fitness.
> 3. All youth need to understand the rights and duties of the citizen of a democratic society, and to be diligent and competent in the performance of their obligations as members of the community and citizens of the state and nation.
> 4. All youth need to understand the significance of the family for the individual and society and the conditions conducive to successful family life.
> 5. All youth need to know how to purchase and use goods and services intelligently, understanding both the values received by the consumer and the economic consequences of their acts.
> 6. All youth need to understand the methods of science, the influence of science on human life, and the main scientific facts concerning the nature of the world and of man.

7. All youth need opportunities to develop their capacities to appreciate beauty in literature, art, music, and nature.
8. All youth need to be able to use their leisure time well and budget it wisely, balancing activities that wield satisfactions to the individual with those that are socially useful.
9. All youth need to develop respect for other persons, to grow in their insight into ethical values and principles, and to be able to live and work cooperatively with others.
10. All youth need to grow in their ability to think rationally, to express their thoughts clearly, and to read and listen with understanding.

These various statements concerning education objectives, made over the last century, sum up fairly well the history of the aims of American public education.

History of Federal Involvement

Our federal government has had a long and extensive involvement in educational affairs. In fact, it has historically supported education at all levels in a variety of ways and continues to do so today. The recent role of our federal government in educational affairs is discussed in detail elsewhere in this book. At this point we will briefly look at some of the early federal efforts to help provide education for U.S. citizens.

U.S. Constitution.　The U.S. Constitution does not mention education. Therefore, by virtue of the Tenth Amendment—which states, "The powers not delegated to the United States by the Constitution, nor prohibited by it to the states, are reserved to the states respectively, or to the people"—education is a function of each state. There is some question whether the makers of the Constitution thoughtfully intended to leave education up to each state or whether they merely forgot to mention it. Some historians believe that our founding fathers wisely realized that local control of education would build a better America. Other historians believe that the framers of the Constitution were so preoccupied with what they believed were more important issues that they never thought to make national provision for education.

Northwest Ordinance.　Even though the Constitution does not refer to education, the federal government has been active in educational affairs from the very beginning. In 1785 and 1787 the Continental Congress passed the Northwest Ordinance Acts. These Acts provided for disposing of the Northwest Territory and encouraged the establishment of schools in the territory by stating: "Religion, morality and knowledge being necessary to good government and the happiness of mankind, schools and the means of education shall forever be encouraged." As the various states formed the Northwest Territory, they were required to set aside the sixteenth section of each township to be used for educational purposes.

Morrill Land Grant.　In 1862, when it became apparent that existing colleges were not providing the **vocational education** needed, the federal government passed the Morrill Land Grant Act. The Hatch Act of 1887 established agricultural experimental stations across the country, and the Smith-Lever Agricultural Extension Act of 1914 carried the services of land grant colleges to the people through extension services. These early federal acts did much to improve agriculture and industry at a time when our rapidly developing nation badly needed such improvement.

Smith-Hughes Act. In 1917 the federal government passed the first act providing financial aid to public schools below the college level, the Smith-Hughes Act. This Act provided for high school vocational programs in agriculture, trades and industry, and homemaking. High schools were academically oriented then, and the Smith-Hughes Act stimulated the development of badly needed vocational programs.

The 1930s were depression days, and the government was trying to solve national economic difficulties. Legislation was enacted during these years to encourage economic development, and this legislation indirectly provided financial aid to education. Five relief agencies related to education during this time included the Civilian Conservation Corps, National Youth Administration, Federal Emergency Relief Administration, Public Works Administration, and Federal Surplus Commodities Corporation.[2]

The more recent involvements of the federal government, from 1940 to the present, are discussed in the next chapter. Appendix 13.1 on page 360 contains a chronology of the more important federal education acts.

Preparation of Teachers

Knowing that our present-day teachers have at least four—and often five to eight—years of college education, it is difficult to believe that teachers have historically had little or no training. One of the first forms of teacher training grew out of the medieval guild system, in which a young man who wished to enter a certain field of work served a lengthy period of apprenticeship with a master in the field. Some young men became teachers by serving as apprentices to master teachers, sometimes for as long as seven years.

Global Perspectives: European Beginnings of Teacher Training. The
first formal teacher-training school in the Western world of which we have any record was mentioned in a request to the king of England, written by William Byngham in 1438, requesting that "he may yeve withouten fyn or fee (the) mansion ycalled Goddeshous the which he hath made and edified in your towne of Cambridge for the free herbigage of poure scolers of Gramer. . . ."[3]

Byngham was granted his request, and established Goddeshous College as a teacher-training institution on June 13, 1439. Students at this college gave demonstration lectures to fellow students to gain practice teaching. Classes were even conducted during vacations so that country schoolmasters could also attend. Byngham's college still exists today as Christ's College of Cambridge University. At that early date of 1439, Byngham made provision for two features that are still considered very important in teacher education today: scheduling classes so that teachers in service may attend and providing some kind of student teaching experience. Many present-day educators would probably be surprised to learn that these ideas are at least 550 years old.

Colonial Teachers. Elementary school teachers in colonial America were very poorly prepared; more often than not, they had received no special training at all.

The single qualification of most of them was that they themselves had been students. Most colonial college teachers, private tutors, Latin grammar school teachers, and academy teachers had received some kind of college education, usually at one of the well-established colleges or universities in Europe. A few had received their education at a colonial American college.

Teachers in the various kinds of colonial elementary schools typically had only an elementary education, but a few had attended a Latin grammar school or a private academy. It was commonly believed that to be a teacher required only that the instructor know something about the subject matter to be taught; consequently, no teacher, regardless of the level taught, received training in the methodology of teaching.

Teaching was not considered a prestigious occupation, and the pay was poor. Consequently, many school teachers viewed their jobs as only temporary. For young women who taught elementary school, the "something better" was usually marriage. Men frequently left teaching for careers in the ministry or business. Not uncommonly, career teachers in the colonies were undesirable people. Records show that many teachers lost their jobs because they paid more attention to the tavern than to the school or because of stealing, swearing, or conduct unbecoming to a person in such a position.

Since many colonial schools were conducted in connection with a church, the teacher was often considered an assistant to the minister. Besides teaching, other duties of some early colonial teachers were "to act as court messenger, to serve summonses, to conduct certain ceremonial services of the church, to lead the Sunday choir, to ring the bell for public worship, to dig the graves, and to perform other occasional duties."

Teachers as Servants.   Sometimes the colonies used white indentured servants as teachers; many people who came to America bought passage by agreeing to work for some years as indentured servants. The ship's captain would then sell the indentured servant's services, more often than not by placing an ad in a newspaper. Such an ad appeared in a May 1786 edition of the *Maryland Gazette:*

Men and Women Servants

JUST ARRIVED

In the ship *Paca*, Robert Caulfield, Master, in five Weeks from Belfast and Cork, a number of healthy Men and Women SERVANTS.

Among them are several valuable tradesman, viz.

Carpenters, Shoemakers, Coopers, Blacksmiths, Staymakers, Bookbinders, Clothiers, Diers, Butchers, Schoolmasters, Millrights, and Labourers.

Their indentures are to be disposed of by the Subscribers,

Brown, and Maris
William Wilson

Teaching Apprenticeships.   Some colonial teachers learned their trade by serving as apprentices to schoolmasters. Court records reveal numerous such indentures of apprenticeship; the following was recorded in New York City in 1772:

> This Indenture witnesseth that John Campbel Son of Robert Campbel of the City of New York with the Consent of his father and mother hath put himself and by these presents doth Voluntarily put and bind himself Apprentice to George Brownell of the Same City Schoolmaster to learn the Art Trade or Mastery—for and during the term of ten years. . . . And the said George Brownell Doth hereby Covenant and Promise to teach and instruct or Cause the said Apprentice to be taught and instructed in the Art Trade or Calling of a Schoolmaster by the best way or means he or his wife may or can.

Teacher Training in Academies.   One of Benjamin Franklin's justifications for proposing an academy in Philadelphia was that some of the graduates would make good teachers. Speculating on the need for such graduates, Franklin wrote:

> A number of the poorer sort [of academy graduates] will be hereby qualified to act as Schoolmasters in the Country, to teach children Reading, Writing, Arithmetic, and the Grammar of their Mother Tongue, and being of good morals and known character, may be recommended from the Academy to Country Schools for that purpose; the Country suffering at present very much for want of good Schoolmasters, and obliged frequently to employ in their schools, vicious imported servants, or concealed Papists, who by their bad Examples and Instructions often deprave the Morals and corrupt the Principles of the children under their Care.

The fact that Franklin said some of the "poorer" graduates would make suitable teachers reflects the low regard for teachers typical of the time. The academy that Franklin proposed was established in 1751 in Philadelphia, and many graduates of academies after that time did indeed become teachers.

Normal Schools.   Many early educators recognized this country's need for better qualified teachers; however, it was not until 1823 that the first teacher-training institution was established in the United States. This private school, called a **normal school** after its European counterpart, which had existed since the late seventeenth century, was established by the Rev. Mr. Samuel Hall in Concord, Vermont. Hall's school did not produce many teachers, but it did signal the beginning of formal teacher training in the United States.

The early normal school program usually consisted of a two-year course. Students typically entered the normal school right after finishing elementary school. Most normal schools did not require high school graduation for entrance until about 1900. The curriculum was much like the curriculum of the high schools of that time. Students reviewed subjects studied in elementary school, studied high school subjects, had a course in teaching (or "pedagogy" as it was then called), and did some student teaching in a model school usually operated in conjunction with the normal school. The subjects offered by a normal school in Albany, New York, in 1845 included English grammar, English composition, history, geography, reading, writing, orthography, arithmetic, algebra, geometry, trigonometry, human physiology, surveying, natural philosophy, chemistry, intellectual philosophy, moral philosophy, government, rhetoric, theory and practice of teaching, drawing, music, astronomy, and practice teaching.

Horace Mann was instrumental in establishing the first state-supported normal school, which opened in 1839 in Lexington, Massachusetts. Other public normal schools, established shortly afterwards, typically offered a two-year teacher-training program. Some of the students came directly from elementary school; others had completed secondary school. Some states did not establish state-supported normal schools until the early 1900s.

State Teachers' Colleges.   During the early part of the twentieth century, several factors caused a significant change in normal schools. For one thing, as the population of the United States increased, so did the enrollment in elementary schools, thereby creating an ever-increasing demand for elementary school teachers. Likewise, as more people attended high school, more high school teachers were needed. To meet this demand, normal schools eventually expanded their curriculum to include secondary teacher education. The establishment of high schools also created a need for teachers who were highly specialized in particular academic subjects, so normal schools established subject matter departments and developed more diversified programs. The length of the teacher education program was expanded to two, three, and finally four years, which helped to develop and diversify the normal school curriculum. The demand for teachers increased from about twenty thousand in 1900 to more than two hundred thousand in 1930.

Another factor contributed to the growth of the normal schools: The United States had advanced technologically to the point where more college-educated citizens were needed. The normal schools assumed a responsibility to help meet this need by establishing many other academic programs in addition to teacher training. As normal schools extended their programs to four years and began granting baccalaureate degrees, they also began to call themselves **state teachers' colleges.** For most institutions the change in name took place during the 1930s.

Recent Teacher Education.   Universities entered the teacher preparation business on a large scale about 1900. Before then, some graduates of universities had become high school teachers or college teachers, but not until about 1900 did universities begin to establish departments of education and add teacher education to the curriculum.

Just as the normal schools expanded in size, scope, and function to the point where they became state teachers' colleges, so did the state teachers' colleges expand to become *state colleges.* This change in name and scope took place for most institutions about 1950. The elimination of the word *teacher* really explains the story behind this transition. The new state colleges gradually expanded their programs beyond teacher education and became multipurpose institutions. One of the main reasons for this transition was that a growing number of students coming to the colleges demanded a more varied education. The state teachers' colleges developed diversified programs to try to meet their demands.

Many of these state colleges became state universities, offering doctoral degrees in a wide range of fields. Some of our largest and most highly regarded universities evolved from normal schools. Figure 12.1 pictures the evolution of American teacher preparation institutions.

Obviously, establishing the teaching profession was a long and difficult task. Preparation of teachers has greatly improved since colonial times—when anyone

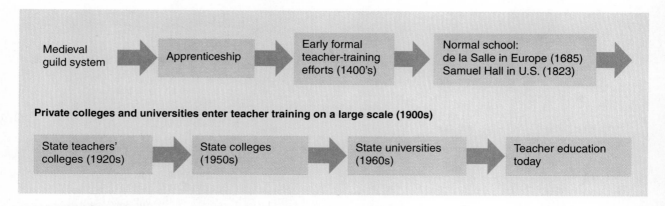

FIGURE 12.1

Evolution of Teacher Preparation Institutions

could be a teacher—until the present, when the rigorous requirements for permanent teacher certification cannot easily be met by everyone.

Evolution of Teaching Materials

As we have said, the first schools in colonial America were poorly equipped. In fact, the first elementary schools were usually conducted by housewives right in their homes. The only teaching materials likely to be found then were a Bible and perhaps one or two other religious books, a small amount of scarce paper, a few quill pens, and hornbooks.

The Hornbook. The **hornbook** was the most common teaching device in early colonial schools (see Figure 12.2 on page 328). Hornbooks differed widely but typically consisted of a sheet of paper, showing the alphabet, covered with a thin transparent sheet of cow's horn tacked to a paddle-shaped piece of wood. A leather cord was often looped through a hole in the paddle so that students could hang the hornbooks around their necks. Hornbooks provided students with their first reading instructions. Records indicate that hornbooks were used in Europe in the Middle Ages and were common there until the mid-1700s.

As paper became more available, the hornbook evolved into a several-page "book" called a *battledore*. The battledore, printed on heavy paper, often resembled an envelope. Like the hornbook, it typically contained the alphabet and various religious prayers and/or admonitions.

New England Primer. The first real textbook to be used in colonial elementary schools was the *New England Primer*. Records show that the first copies of this book were printed in England in the 1600s. Copies of the *New England Primer* were also printed as early as 1690 in the American colonies. The book was advertised in the *News From the Stars Almanac*, published in 1690 in Boston

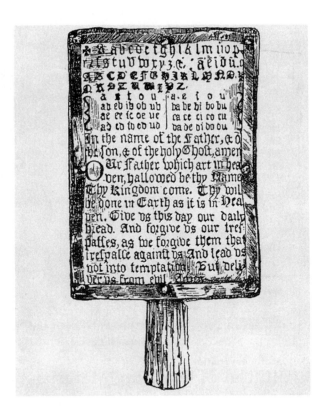

FIGURE 12.2

A Hornbook

(see Figure 12.3). The oldest extant copy of the *New England Primer* is a 1727 edition, now in the Lenox Collection of the New York Public Library.

The *New England Primer* was a small book, usually about 2 1/2 by 4 1/2 inches, with thin wooden covers covered by paper or leather. It contained 50 to 100 pages, depending on how many extra sections were added to each edition. The first pages contained the alphabet, vowels, and capital letters. Next came lists of words arranged from two to six syllables, followed by verses and tiny woodcut pictures for each letter in the alphabet. A reproduction of verses and pictures is presented in Figure 12.4. The contents of the *New England Primer* reflect the heavily religious motive in colonial education.

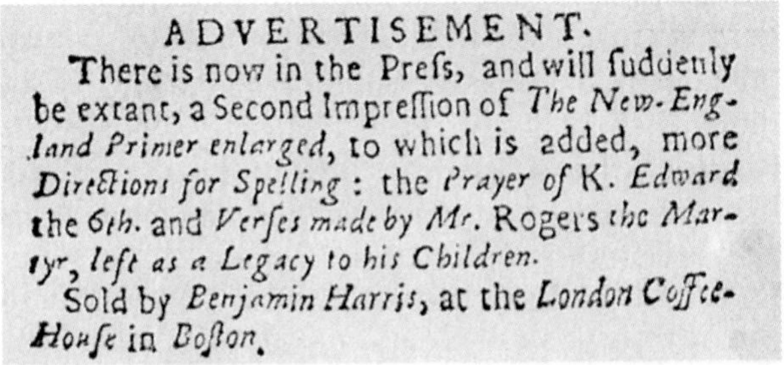

FIGURE 12.3

Advertisement (1690) for the *New England Primer*

ADVERTISEMENT.
There is now in the Prefs, and will fuddenly be extant, a Second Impreffion of *The New-England Primer enlarged*, to which is added, more *Directions for Spelling* : the *Prayer of* K. *Edward* the 6th. and *Verfes made by* Mr. Rogers *the Martyr, left as a Legacy to his Children.*
Sold by *Benjamin Harris*, at the *London Coffee-Houfe* in *Bofton*.

In Adam's Fall
We finned all.

Thy Life to mend,
This Book attend.

The Cat doth play,
And after flay.

A Dog will bite
A Thief at Night.

An Eagle' flight
Is out of fight.

The idle Fool
Is whipt at School

FIGURE 12.4

New England Primer

Blue-Backed Speller. The primer was virtually the only reading book used in colonial schools until about 1800, when Noah Webster published *The American Spelling Book*. This book eventually became known as the *Blue-Backed Speller* because of its blue cover. It eventually replaced the *New England Primer* as the most common elementary textbook. The speller reportedly sold over 24 million copies; its royalties supported Noah Webster and his family while he prepared his famous dictionary. The speller was approximately 4 by 6 1/2 inches; its cover was made of thin sheets of wood covered with light blue paper. The first part of the book contained rules and instructions for using the book; next came the alphabet, syllables, and consonants. The bulk of the book was taken up with lists of words arranged according to syllables and sounds. It also contained rules for reading and speaking, moral advice, and stories of various sorts. Figure 12.5 on page 330 shows a page from a *Blue-Backed Speller* printed about 1800.

Noah Webster (1758–1843)

Very few textbooks were available for use in colonial Latin grammar schools, academies, and colleges, though various religious books, including the Bible, were often used. A few books dealing with history, geography, arithmetic, Latin, Greek, and certain classics were available for use in colonial secondary schools and colleges during the eighteenth century. Harvard College had a large library for its day, since John Harvard, its benefactor, had bequeathed his entire library of four hundred volumes to the school.

An Early School. By 1800, nearly two hundred years after the colonies had been established, school buildings and teaching materials were still very crude and meager. You can understand something of the physical features and equipment of an 1810 New England school by reading the following description written by a teacher of that school:

FIGURE 12.5

The Blue-Backed Speller

The size of the building was 22 × 20 feet. From the floor to the ceiling it was 7 feet. The chimney and entry took up about four feet at one end, leaving the schoolroom itself 18 × 20 feet. Around these sides of the room were connected desks, arranged so that when the pupils were sitting at them their faces were towards the instructor and their backs toward the wall. Attached to the sides of the desks nearest to the instructor were benches for small pupils. The instructor's desk and chair occupied the center. On this desk were stationed a rod, or ferule; sometimes both. These, with books, writings, inkstands, rules, and plummets, with a fire shovel, and a pair of tongs (often broken), were the principal furniture. . . .

The room was warmed by a large and deep fireplace. So large was it, and so efficacious in warming the room otherwise, that I have seen about one-eighth of a cord of good wood burning in it at a time. In severe weather it was estimated that the amount usually consumed was not far from a cord a week. . . .

The school was not infrequently broken up for a day or two for want of wood. The instructor or pupils were sometimes compelled to cut or saw it to prevent the closing of the school. The wood was left in the road near the house, so that it often was buried in the snow, or wet with rain. At the best, it was usually burnt green. The fires were to be kindled about half an hour before the time of beginning the school. Often, the scholar, whose lot it was, neglected to build it. In consequence of this, the house was frequently cold and uncomfortable about half of the forenoon, when, the fire being very large, the excess of heat became equally distressing. Frequently, too, we were annoyed by smoke. The greatest amount of suffering, however, arose from excessive heat, particularly at the close of the day. The pupils being in a free perspiration when they left were very liable to take cold. . . .

Instructors have usually boarded in the families of the pupils. Their compensation has varied from seven to eleven dollars a month for males; and from sixty-two and a half cents to one dollar a week for females. Within the past ten years, however, the price of instruction has rarely been less than nine dollars in the former case, and seventy-five cents in the latter. In the few instances in which instructors have furnished their own board the compensation has been about the same, it being assumed that they could work at some employment of their own enough to pay their board, especially the females.[4]

Slates. About 1820 a new instructional device was introduced in American schools—the slate. These school slates were thin, flat pieces of slate stone framed with wood. The pencils used were also made of slate and produced a light but legible line. The wooden frames of some of the slates were covered with cloth so that noise would be minimized as students placed the slates on the desk. There were even double slates made by hinging two single slates together with cord or leather. Students wrote their assignments on the slates, just as today's students write on tablet paper. Later on, large pieces of slate made up the blackboards that were added to classrooms.

McGuffey's *Reader*. In the same way that Noah Webster's *Blue-Backed Speller* replaced the *New England Primer,* so did the McGuffey's *Reader* eventually replace the *Blue-Backed Speller.* These readers were carefully geared to each grade and were meant to instill in children a respect for hard work, thrift, self help, and honesty. McGuffey's *Reader* dominated the elementary school book market until approximately 1900, when it was gradually replaced by newer and improved readers written by David Tower, James Fassett, William Elson, and others.

During the twentieth century, teachers have gradually adapted a variety of tools to assist them in educating American youth. This variety has come about partly through the influence of Pestalozzi, John Dewey, and others, who demonstrated that children learn best by firsthand experiences. Likewise, school buildings have become larger, more elaborate, and better designed to encourage learning. Today, many schools are equipped with an impressive array of books, laboratory equipment, movie projectors, filmstrip projectors, tape recorders, television devices, single-concept films, teaching machines, computers, programmed materials, and learning devices of all kinds. Some of the modern school buildings are not only excellent from an educational standpoint but magnificent pieces of architecture as well. One cannot help but be awed by the contrast between American education today and its humble beginning years ago.

William Holmes McGuffey (1800–1873)

School boards have historically been given a good deal of legal authority and responsibility for running local school districts. Most school boards are elected and therefore vary a good deal in personality and opinions about schools. Each school board eventually takes on a personality of its own. Some boards decide that their main job is to hire an excellent school superintendent, and then leave the running of the schools up to the professional education staff. In such cases, however, citizens sometimes accuse the school board of shirking their duty by simply "rubber stamping" every decision the school staff makes. Most school boards strive to set broad school policy and concentrate on the financial problems of the district. On the other hand, occasionally a school board wants to become very involved in detailed decision making and engages in activities such as interviewing all new teachers and making specific curriculum decisions.

The River View school district has the reputation of being a very conservative school district. In fact, the school board is made up mainly of rather elderly folks who are known for their conservative Christian views on life in general and on education specifically. River View is a small community of about 5,000 people, where most folks know everyone in the community and where people take a good deal of interest and pride in their schools.

Recently the school board voted to require its teachers to use the McGuffey *Eclectic Readers*, which were written in the mid-1800s, in each elementary grade. The board, which has frequently been critical of "modern" teaching methods, believes that the McGuffey *Readers* will help children learn to be more honest, patriotic, kind, punctual, and conscientious. The board has also raised questions about other curriculum questions such as creation versus evolution science, objectionable literature, and sex education.

The superintendent, Mr. Modell, in his first year in the district, has appointed a committee of teachers to study and make recommendations to the school board on these issues. As a first-year teacher in the River View School District you have been asked to serve on this committee. The Superintendent, who is chairing this committee, has asked each committee member to prepare a position paper on three basic issues [(1) the use of the McGuffey *Readers*; (2) creation versus evolution science, and (3) sex education in the schools], prior to the first meeting, which is scheduled for one week from today. What will your position paper say? Include answers to the following questions in your paper.

1. How should school curriculum be determined?
2. To what degree do you feel a school board should be involved in curriculum questions?
3. Since you are a first-year teacher without tenure, are you concerned about expressing your totally honest views on these debatable topics? Why or why not?
4. What do you think the superintendent should do in this situation?
5. What, if anything, do you feel the faculty and/or the teachers' union should do in a situation such as this?

Education for Special Populations

In this section we will examine briefly the development of education of African Americans and females in the United States. We will also review the extremely important role of private education in America.

Education of African Americans

It is sad but true that, until very recently, few efforts were made in our country to provide an education for African Americans. In the following section we will briefly explore why this was the case and discuss some of the early African American educators who struggled to correct this injustice.

Slavery. In 1619, only a dozen years after Jamestown was established, the first boatload of slaves arrived in the colonies. In that year, John Rolfe wrote in his *Journal* that the captain of a Dutch ship "sold us twenty Negroes." These slaves were imported as a source of cheap labor for the new colonies.

The number of imported slaves steadily increased; between 1700 and 1750, thousands of blacks were brought to the American colonies each year. By the Revolutionary War there were approximately 700,000 blacks in the colonies; by 1860 there were about 4.5 million.

The Church's Efforts to Educate African Americans. Probably the first organized attempts to educate the African Americans in colonial America were by French and Spanish missionaries.[5] These early missionary efforts set an example that influenced the education of both African Americans and the numerous offspring who were the result of mixed breeding. Educating slaves posed an interesting moral problem for the church. The English colonists had to find a way to overcome the idea that converting a slave to Christianity might logically lead to his or her freedom. The problem they faced was how to eliminate an unwritten law that a Christian should not be a slave. The church's governing bodies and the Bishop of London settled the matter by decreeing that conversion to Christianity did not lead to formal emancipation.

The organized church nevertheless provided the setting in which African Americans were allowed to develop skills in reading, leadership, and educating their brethren. Often African Americans and whites attended church together. Eventually, some preachers—former slaves—demonstrated exceptional skill in "spreading the gospel." The Baptists in particular, by encouraging a form of self-government, allowed African Americans to become active in the church. This move fostered the growth of African American congregations, and because of it, enslaved as well as free African Americans were given an opportunity for education and development that was not provided by many other denominations.

The efforts of the English to educate slaves were carried out largely by the Society for the Propagation of the Gospel in Foreign Parts. The Society was created by the Established Church of London in 1701. In 1705 the Reverend Samuel Thomas of Goose Creek Parish in South Carolina established a school fostered by the society, enrolling sixty African American students. Nine years later the society opened a school in New York City where two hundred African American pupils were enrolled. Despite stringent opposition from many whites, who believed that educating slaves was a "dangerous business," the society went on to establish other schools for African Americans. The degree of success of these early efforts varied greatly. Initially, many people were not generally opposed to educating African Americans; however, education seemed to make the slaves aware of their plight. In the South, much of the unrest concerning slavery was attributed to the education of slaves. Insurrections, uprisings, and threats to overseers, masters, and their families produced fear among the whites. Consequently, some states even passed legislation that eliminated any form of education for slaves.

John Chavis. The African Americans' individual success in acquiring education, as well as their group efforts to establish schools, was greatly enhanced by sympathetic and humanitarian white friends. John Chavis, a free man born in 1763 in Oxford, North Carolina, was an African American who was helped by whites. Chavis became a successful teacher of aristocratic whites, and his white neighbors sent him to Princeton "to see if a Negro would take a college education." His rapid advancement under Dr. Witherspoon soon indicated that the adventure was a success. He returned to Virginia and later went to North Carolina, where he preached among his own people. The success of John Chavis, even under experimental conditions, represented a small step forward in the education of African Americans.

Benjamin Banneker. Benjamin Banneker, a distinguished African American, was born in Baltimore County, Maryland, in 1731. Baltimore maintained a liberal policy toward educating African Americans, which permitted Banneker to learn to read, write, and do arithmetic at a relatively early age. He became extremely well educated. One of his accomplishments was to manufacture the first clock made in the United States in 1770. He then turned his attention specifically to astronomy. Without any instruction but with the help of books borrowed from an encouraging white inventor, Banneker soon was able to calculate eclipses of the sun and moon. His accuracy far excelled that of any other American. The outstanding works of this inventor aroused the curiosity of Thomas Jefferson, who in 1803 invited Banneker to his home, Monticello. The acknowledgment of an African American's achievement by a noted American was still another milestone in the education of the African Americans.

Frederick Douglass. Frederick Douglass, born a slave in Maryland in 1817, ran away from slavery and began talking to abolitionist groups about his experiences as a slave. He attributed his fluent speech to listening to his master talk. Douglass firmly believed that if he devoted all his efforts to improving vocational education, he could greatly improve the African Americans' plight. He thought that previous attempts by educators to combine liberal and vocational education had failed, so he emphasized vocational education solely.

One of the first northern schools established for African Americans appears to have been that of Elias Neau in New York City in 1704. Neau was an agent of the Society for the Propagation of the Gospel in Foreign Parts.

In 1807, free African Americans, including George Bell, Nicholas Franklin, and Moses Liverpool, built the first schoolhouse for African Americans in the District of Columbia. Not until 1824, however, was there an African American teacher in that district—John Adams. In 1851, Washington citizens attempted to discourage Myrtilla Miner from establishing an academy for African American girls. However, after much turmoil and harassment the white schoolmistress from New York founded her academy, and it is still functioning today.

Prudence Crandall. Prudence Crandall, a young Quaker, established an early boarding school in Canterbury, Connecticut. The trouble she ran into dramatizes some of the northern animosity to educating African Americans. Trouble arose when Sarah Harris, a "colored girl," asked to be admitted to the institution. After much deliberation, Miss Crandall finally consented, but white parents objected to the African American girl's attending the school and withdrew their children. To keep the school open, Miss Crandall recruited African American children. The pupils were threatened with violence, local stores would not trade with her, and the school building was vandalized. The citizens of Canterbury petitioned the state legislator to enact a law that would make it illegal to educate African Americans from out of state. Miss Crandall was jailed and tried before the state supreme court in July 1834. The court never gave a final decision because defects were found in the information prepared by the attorney for the state, and the indictment was eventually dropped. Miss Crandall continued to work for the abolition of slavery, for women's rights, and for African American education. Prudence Crandall became well known, and deserves considerable credit for the advances made by minorities and women in the United States.

Finally, Boston, the seat of northern liberalism, established a separate school for African American children in 1798. Elisha Sylvester, a white man, was in charge. The school was founded in the home of Primus Hall, a "Negro in good standing." Two years later, sixty-six free African Americans petitioned the school committee for a separate school and were refused. Undaunted, the patrons of Hall's house employed two instructors from Harvard; thirty-five years later, the school was allowed to move to a separate building. The city of Boston opened its first primary school for the education of African American children in 1820—one more milestone in the history of African American education.

African American Colleges. Unfortunately, despite these efforts, African Americans received pathetically little formal education until the Emancipation Proclamation, issued by President Abraham Lincoln on January 1, 1863. At that time the literacy rate among African Americans was estimated at 5 percent. Sunday school represented about the only opportunity most African Americans had to learn to read. In the late 1700s and early 1800s, some communities did set up separate schools for African Americans; however, only a very small percentage ever attended the schools. A few colleges such as Oberlin, Bowdoin, Franklin, Rutland, and Harvard admitted African American students; but, again, very few attended college then. There were even a few African American colleges, such as Lincoln University in Pennsylvania (1854) and Wilberforce University in Ohio (1856); however, the efforts and opportunities for the education of African Americans were pathetically few relative to the size of the African American population.

Booker T. Washington. Booker T. Washington (1856–1915) was one of the early African American educators who contributed immensely to the development of education in the United States. He realized that African American children desperately needed an education to compete in society, and he founded Tuskegee Institute in 1880. This Alabama institution provided basic and industrial education in its early years and gradually expanded to provide a wider ranging college curriculum. It stands today as a proud monument to Booker T. Washington's vision and determination concerning the education of African American youth.

Although there was no great rush to educate African Americans, the abolishment of slavery in 1865 signaled the beginning of a slow but steady effort to improve their education. By 1890, African American literacy had risen to 40 percent; by 1910 it was estimated that 70 percent of African Americans had learned to read and write. These statistics showing the rapid increase in African American literacy are impressive; however, they are compromised by a report of the U.S. Commissioner of Education showing that, by 1900, fewer than 70 of 1,000 pub-

Booker T. Washington (1856–1915)

lic high schools in the South were provided for African Americans. Ironically, while educational opportunities for African Americans were very meager, for other minority groups such as Native Americans and Hispanic Americans they were nonexistant.

The most significant developments in the education of African Americans have been in the twentieth century, and mostly since 1950. They are discussed more fully in the next chapter.

Education of Women

Historically, women have not been afforded equal educational opportunities in the United States. Furthermore, many authorities claim that our schools have traditionally been sexist institutions. Although there is much evidence to support both these assertions, it is also true that an impressive list of women have made significant contributions to our educational progress.

Colonial schools did not provide education for girls in any significant way. In some instances, girls were taught to read, but they were not admitted to Latin grammar schools, academies, or colleges. Let us look briefly at a few of the many outstanding female educators who helped to develop our country's educational system, in spite of their own limited educational opportunity.

Emma Willard. Emma Willard (1778–1870) was a pioneer and champion of education for females during a time when there were relatively few educational opportunities for them. While well-to-do parents hired private tutors or sent their daughters away to a girl's seminary, girls from poor families were taught only to read and write at home (provided that someone in the family had these skills). Emma Willard opened one of the first female seminaries in 1821 in Troy, New York. Her school offered an educational program equal to that of a boy's school. In a speech designed to raise funds for her school, she proposed the following benefits of seminaries for girls:

1. Females, by having their understandings cultivated, their reasoning power developed and strengthened, may be expected to act more from the dictates of reason and less from those of fashion and caprice.
2. With minds thus strengthened, they would be taught systems of morality, enforced by the sanctions of religion; and they might be expected to acquire juster and more enlarged views of their duty, and stronger and higher motives to its performance.
3. This plan of education offers all that can be done to preserve female youth from a contempt of useful labor. The pupils would become accustomed to it, in conjunction with the high objects of literature and the elegant pursuits of the fine arts; and it is to be hoped that both from habit and association they might in future life regard it as respectable.
4. The pupils might be expected to acquire a taste for moral and intellectual pleasures which would buoy them above a passion for show and parade, and which would make them seek to gratify the natural love of superiority by endeavoring to excel others in intrinsic merit rather than in the extrinsic frivolities of dress, furniture, and equipage.
5. By being enlightened in moral philosophy, and in that which teaches the operations of the mind, females would be enabled to perceive the nature and extent of that influence which they possess over their children, and the oblig-

ation which this lays them under to watch the formation of their characters with unceasing vigilance, to become their instructors, to devise plans for their improvement, to weed out the vices of their minds, and to implant and foster the virtues. And surely there is that in the maternal bosom which, when its pleadings shall be aided by education, will overcome the seductions of wealth and fashion, and will lead the mother to seek her happiness in communing with her children, and promoting their welfare. . . .[6]

Many other female institutions were established and became prominent during the mid- and late 1800s, including Mary Lyon's Mount Holyoke Female Seminary; Jane Ingersoll's Seminary in Cortland, New York: and Julia and Elias Mark's Southern Carolina Collegiate Institute at Barhamville, to name just a few. Unfortunately, not until well into the twentieth century were women generally afforded access to higher education.

Even though women eventually could attend college, they were not given equal access to all fields of study. Considerable progress has been made in recent years, but remnants of this problem still exist today.

Global Perspectives: Maria Montessori. Maria Montessori (1870–1952), born in Italy, became first a successful physician and later a prominent educational philosopher. She developed her own theory and methods of educating young children. Her methods utilized child-size school furniture and specially designed learning materials. She emphasized independent work by children under the guidance of a trained directress. Private Montessori schools thrive in the United States today.

The fact that women have made significant contributions to our educational progress through the years has been well documented. In addition to the examples just mentioned and those discussed elsewhere in this book, we can add the following: Catherine Beecher (who founded the Hartford Female Seminary), Jane Addams (who proposed an expanded school as part of her new liberal social philosophy), Susan Anthony (who was a teacher in her early professional life), and Mrs. Carl Schurz (who founded the first kindergarten in this country).

The Nineteenth Amendment. The first great interest in advancing the cause of females came about in the mid-1800s in the United States. At that time the women's rights convention passed twelve resolutions that attempted to spur interest in feminism and provide for females more equal participation and rights in our society. The Civil War also furthered interest in the rights of women throughout the country, very likely as a spinoff of the abolition of slavery as a basic way of improving the lives of African Americans. It is interesting to note that not all of the people who were in favor of doing away with slavery supported improved rights for women. For instance, not until 1920 was the Nineteenth Amendment passed, giving voting rights to women for the first time.

Unfortunately, the right to vote did not necessarily do much to improve the status of women, and they continued to be denied equal educational and employment opportunities for a long time. The civil rights movement after World War II served as another impetus to the women's movement and gave rise to an additional round of improvements for females in American society. Some authorities would trace the emergence of the current feminist movement to the 1960s, when a variety of activist groups coalesced to work against discrimination of all kinds in our society.

Maria Montessori (1870–1952)

PROFESSIONAL DILEMMA

Can a Teacher Both Defend and Critique Schools?

When you become a teacher, you will undoubtedly be able to find both good and bad things about your school. You will also eventually face a parent who is critical of your school and who suggests that schools used to be better in the past. You will then be faced with the common professional dilemma of having to decide to what degree you are willing to defend your classroom and/or school.

Are our schools better or worse today than they were in the "good old days"? Those who argue that schools have deteriorated often point out that the one-room school practiced many of the educational "innovations" that one reads about today. For instance, students received a considerable amount of individual attention in the small, one-room schools. Cooperative learning, which is being touted as a promising educational practice today, was commonplace, with older students helping the younger ones. Those who remember the one-room school frequently point out that values and ethics were a part of the school curriculum, and students were taught love of country, respect for law and authority, and often religious values.

On the other side of this debate, those who defend our contemporary schools point out that our society has become much more complex and that students must now receive a very different and more elaborate educational experience if they are to be successful. The small, simpler schools of the past could not possibly offer the curricular variety and experiences that are afforded students today. Defenders of contemporary schools argue that American society could not have advanced to its present state if it had been hampered by the education typically provided in the past. They point to the advancements of society as proof that public schools have provided an excellent education.

This controversy concerning whether or not our schools have improved or degenerated though history will likely continue. One of the reasons it is important for educators to understand their profession's history is to enable them to capitalize on our historical successes and to avoid our past mistakes. As a future teacher, you should consider educational history and ponder the successes and failures of our ever-evolving school system.

- Should schools return to a focus on basic skills?
- How realistic, valid, and representative are memories of the "good old days"? Is it reasonable to consider returning to an earlier state of U.S. educational history? Why or why not?
- To what degree should teachers defend or criticize their school? How and when?

Private Education in America

Private education has been extremely important in the development of America, and private schools carried on most of the education in colonial times. The first colonial colleges—Harvard, William and Mary, Yale, and Princeton—were private. Many of the other early colonial schools—which can be thought of as **religious-affiliated schools**—were operated by churches, missionary societies, and private individuals.

The Right of Private Schools to Exist. In 1816 the state of New Hampshire attempted to take over Dartmouth College, which was a private institution. A lawsuit growing out of this effort ultimately resulted in the Supreme Court's first decision involving the legal rights of a private school. The Supreme Court decided that a private school's charter must be viewed as a contract and cannot be broken arbitrarily by a state. In other words, the Court decided that a private school could not be forced against its will to become a public school.

Subsequent court decisions have reconfirmed the rights of private education in a variety of ways. Generally speaking, for instance, courts have reconfirmed that private schools have a right to exist and in some cases even to share public funds as long as these funds are not used for religious purposes. Examples of such actions include the use of state funds to purchase secular textbooks and to provide transportation for students to and from private schools.

Not until after the Revolution, when there was a strong sense of nationalism, did certain educators advocate a strong public school system for the new nation. However, such recommendations were not acted on for many years.

In the meantime, some Protestant churches continued to expand their schools during the colonial period. For instance, the Congregational, Quaker, Episcopalian, Baptist, Methodist, Presbyterian, and Reform churches all, at various times and in varying degrees, established and operated schools for their youth. It was the Roman Catholics and Lutherans, however, who eventually developed elaborate parochial school systems.

Parochial Schools. As early as 1820 there were 240 Lutheran **parochial schools** in Pennsylvania. Although the number of Lutheran schools in that particular state eventually dwindled, Henry Muhlenberg and other Lutheran leaders continued to establish parochial schools until the public school system became well established. The Missouri Synod Lutheran Church has continued to maintain a well-developed parochial school system. Currently, there are approximately 1,700 Lutheran elementary and secondary schools, which enroll about 200,000 pupils, in the United States. Most of these schools are operated by the Missouri Synod Lutheran Church.

The Roman Catholic parochial school system grew rapidly after its beginnings in the 1800s. This growth continued into the twentieth century, and the Roman Catholic parochial school system in the United States is now the largest private school system in the world.

The Importance of Private Education. All of the early educational efforts undertaken in colonial America were private in nature. In fact, the concept of public education—that is, education paid for through public government—is a relatively new idea in the history of education. For many years, if parents or religious groups wanted to provide education for their children, they had to do so with their own resources. In this part of the book there have been many references to private schools and private education; at this juncture we simply wish to reiterate the tremendous importance of private education. In fact, were it not for private education as the predecessor, it is difficult to imagine that we would have evolved a public education system. Private education still plays an enormously important role at all levels of education in the United States.

It is interesting to note that in many ways the transformation from private to public education did not occur until the nineteenth century. For instance, in 1800 there was no such thing as a state system of public education anywhere in the United States—no elementary schools, secondary schools, or state colleges or universities. In fact, until the nineteenth century, all forms of education that were available were private in nature—from elementary school through graduate school. However, by the year 1900, nearly all states had developed a public system of education running from elementary school through graduate school.

Many historians suggest that the overriding motive for private education has always been religious in nature. Initially, parents wanted their children to be able to read so that they could read and understand the Bible and therefore gain salvation. Even the earliest colleges were designed primarily to prepare ministers. Harvard College, for instance, was created in 1636, for the express purpose of training ministers.

Likewise, Benjamin Franklin created his unique academy as a private institution to provide technical training to young men because there was no public institution yet created to do so. It was not until 1874 that the Michigan State Supreme Court established that it was legal for school districts to tax citizens for general support of public high schools. By that time, private schools had been providing secondary education for our nation's youth for a long time.

Summary and Implications

The history of American education is filled with many messages. Some tell of successes, some of failures, others of dedicated teachers, of humble beginnings, of individuals' thirst for knowledge—even of those who have been willing to die for the truth. A chronology of these highlights of the historical development of education in the United States is presented in Appendix 13.2 on page 362.

These historical events have implications for today's educator. Teachers can learn much from our educational history if they listen carefully to these messages from the past. In particular, they will come to realize how very important education is to the preservation and progress of our society—perhaps more important than any other human endeavor.

Discussion Questions

1. How did the development of public education differ in the northern, middle, and southern colonies?
2. Discuss the evolution of elementary schools.
3. What historical conditions led to that uniquely American institution, the comprehensive high school?
4. How has the concept of the nature of humankind changed in the past three hundred years? What effect has this change had on teacher education?
5. What are the highlights of the history of education of African Americans?
6. What are the highlights of the history of education of women in the United States?
7. Discuss the roles that private schools have played in American education.

Journal/Portfolio Development

1. Summarize the evolution of the goals of public schools in Colonial America and the United States. Develop a chart that creatively portrays this evolution.
2. Write an essay on the importance of education in the historical development of the United States.

School-Based Experiences

1. George Santayana said, "Those who forget the past are doomed to repeat it." Keeping that idea in mind as you read through this chapter, try to generate a list of practical suggestions that you can use as you work in the schools. Examples might include the practical idea of Pestalozzi for working effectively with children, some of the famous historical aims of American public education, and some of the moral wisdom espoused in early textbooks such as the *New England Primer* and McGuffey's *Reader*. During your clinical experiences in the schools, think about how applicable some of the historical ideas presented in this chapter are to today's teachers.

2. While you are in the schools, visit with older teachers and administrators to discuss the ways in which schools have changed over the years. Also ask how students have changed, how teaching methods have changed, and how parents have changed.

Notes

1. Paul Monroe, *Source Book of the History of Education.* New York: Macmillan, 1901.
2. Roe L. Johns and Edgar L. Morphet, *Financing the Public Schools.* Englewood Cliffs, NJ: Prentice-Hall, 1960, 378.
3. W. H. G. Armytage, "William Byngham: A Medieval Protagonist of the Training of Teachers," *History of Education Journal 2* (Summer 1951): 108.
4. Paul Monroe, 282.
5. Much of the material dealing with the history of African Americans up to the signing of the Emancipation Proclamation (1863) was taken from the doctoral dissertation of Samuel David, "Education, Law, and the Negro." Urbana: University of Illinois, 1970.
6. Emma Willard, "A Plan for Improving Female Education," *Women and the Higher Education.* New York: Harper & Brothers, 1893, 12–14.

Bibliography

Buetow, Harald A. *Of Singular Benefit: The Story of U.S. Catholic Education.* New York: Macmillan, 1970.

Button, H. Warren, and Provenzo, Eugene F., Jr. *History of Education and Culture in America.* 2nd ed. Englewood Cliffs, NJ: Prentice-Hall, 1989.

Butts, R. Freeman. *Public Education in the United States: From Revolution to Reform.* New York: Holt, Rinehart and Winston, 1978.

Church, Robert L., and Sedlak, Michael W. *Education in the United States: An Interpretive History.* New York: Macmillan, 1976.

Cohen, Sheldon S. *A History of Colonial Education 1607–1776.* New York: Wiley, 1974.

Cremin, Lawrence A. *American Education: The Colonial Experience 1607–1783.* New York: Harper & Row, 1970.

———— *The Transformation of the School: Progressivism in American Education, 1876–1957.* New York: Knopf, 1961.

Cuban, L. *How Teachers Taught: Consistency and Change in American Classrooms 1890–1980.* New York: Longman, 1984.

Franklin, John Hope. *From Slavery to Freedom: A History of Negro Americans.* 4th ed. New York: Knopf, 1974.

Gartner, Lloyd P., ed. *Jewish Education in the United States: A Documentary History.* New York: Teachers College Press, 1970.

Goodsell, W. *Pioneers of Women's Education in the United States.* New York: McGraw-Hill, 1931.

Perkinson, Henry J., ed. *Two Hundred Years of American Educational Thought.* New York: David McKay, 1976.

Pulliam, John D. *History of Education in America.* Columbus, OH: Merrill, 1991.

Smith, L. Glenn. *Lives in Education: People and Ideas in the Development of Teaching.* Ames, IA: Educational Studies Press, 1993.

Szasz, Margaret Connell. *Indian Education in the American Colonies 1607–1783.* Albuquerque: U. of New Mexico Press, 1988.

Tyack, David B. *The One Best System.* Cambridge, MA: Harvard University Press, 1974.

Washington, B. T., ed. *Tuskegee and Its People: Their Ideals and Achievements.* New York: Appleton, 1905.

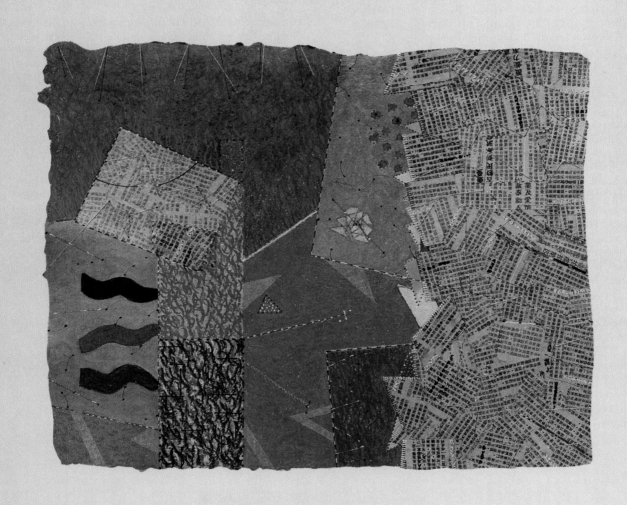

Chapter

13 Recent Developments in Education 1940–Present

Focus Questions

1. What important changes have taken place in education during your lifetime?
2. How did the special education program in our schools today come into being?
3. In what ways, if any, has the federal government contributed to education in recent history?
4. What is meant by *equal educational opportunity?*
5. What role have private schools played in the United States in recent history?
6. What trends have been evident in our school system over the past fifty years?

Key Terms and Concepts

Analysis of teaching: A contemporary trend to encourage teachers to critique their own performance in the classroom.

Behavioral theory: A theory that considers the outward behavior of students to be the main target for change.

Cognitive development: A learner's acquisition of facts, concepts, and principles through intellectualization.

Effective teaching: A movement to improve teaching performance based on the outcomes of educational research.

Equal educational opportunity: Providing every student the educational opportunity to develop fully whatever talents, interests, and abilities she or he may have without regard to race, color, national origin, sex, handicap, or economic status.

One-room school: A setting in which all grade levels are taught by a single teacher in a single-room school.

Population growth is just one of the huge differences between the schools of the twentieth century and those of early times.

More Students and Bigger Schools

There have been many changes in the American educational enterprise over the past half century. Space constraints will not allow a detailed discussion, but we will briefly examine three general topics that seem to characterize these changes since about 1940: the rapid growth of our educational system, the increasing complexity of the educational enterprise, and the recent trends in our schools.

The Rapid Growth of the Educational Enterprise

Since World War II, education has been characterized by a great deal of growth and change: growth in terms of school enrollment, educational budgets, complexity, and federal influence; change in terms of court decisions, proliferation of school laws, confusion about goals, school financial difficulties, struggle for control, and diversification of curricula. Perhaps the single most dramatic change that has occurred in education over the past half century is the growth of the educational enterprise, which took place in many ways.

Enrollment Growth. Table 13.1 shows that the total number of public school students in the United States nearly doubled from 1940 to 1990. While part of this rapid growth in school enrollment was due to overall population growth, a good part was due to the fact that greater percentages of people were going to school. Furthermore, people were staying in school much longer, as shown by the more than sixfold increased enrollment in higher education.

Need for More Teachers. Naturally, this dramatic increase in student enrollments required many additional teachers, and at times our colleges simply could not produce enough. In this situation, teacher certification requirements were lowered, sometimes to the point at which no professional education training was required at all. Over time, however, the nation seemed to meet the demand for more teachers.

As one would expect, the increased numbers of students and teachers cost a great deal more money. More schools had to be built, more buses purchased, more books and other instructional materials obtained, more school personnel hired—more of everything required to provide education was needed.

School District Consolidation

The consolidation of school districts was one development that inadvertently led to increased busing costs. Table 13.2 on page 346 shows that the number of separate school districts was reduced from 117,000 in 1940 to 16,000 in 1980. This table also shows the corresponding dramatic decline in the number of one-teacher schools over this same time period.

One-Room Schools. For many years, the **one-room school,** a single classroom taught by a single teacher and encompassing all grades, symbolized American education for millions of Americans. Although school consolidation undoubtedly

TABLE 13.1 Historical Summary of Public Elementary and Secondary School Statistics: 1949–1950 to 1989–1990

Population, Pupils and Instructional Staff	1939–1940	1949–1950	1959–1960	1969–1970	1979–1980	1989–1990
Total population, in thousands	130,880	149,199	177,080	201,385	224,567	248,239
Population aged 5–17 years, in thousands	30,151	30,223	42,634	52,386	48,041	45,330
Percent of total population 5–17	23.0	20.3	24.1	26.0	21.4	18.3
Total enrollment in elementary and secondary schools, in thousands	25,434	25,111	36,087	45,550	41,651	40,543
Kindergarten and grades 1–8, in thousands	18,832	19,387	27,602	32,513	28,034	29,152
Grades 9–12 and postgraduate, in thousands	6,601	5,725	8,485	13,037	13,616	11,390
Enrollment as a percent of total population	19.4	16.8	20.4	22.6	18.5	16.3
Enrollment as a percent of 5- to 17-year-olds	84.4	83.1	84.6	87.0	86.7	89.4
Percent of total enrollment in high schools (grades 9–12 and post-graduate)	26.0	22.8	23.5	28.6	32.7	28.1
High school graduates, in thousands	1,143	1,063	1,627	2,589	2,748	2,320
Average daily attendance, in thousands	22,042	22,284	32,477	41,934	38,289	37,779
Total number of days attended by pupils enrolled, in millions	3,858	3,964	5,782	7,501	[4]6,835	—
Percent of enrolled pupils attending daily	86.7	88.7	90.0	90.4	[4]90.1	—
Average lengths of school term, in days	175.0	177.9	178.0	178.9	[4]178.5	—
Average number of days attended per pupil	151.7	157.9	160.2	161.7	[4]160.8	—

Source: 120 Years of American Education: A Statistical Portrait, U.S. Government, Office of Educational Research and Improvement. Washington, DC: U.S. Department of Education. January 1993, 34.

had many educational advantages and saved even more school dollars in some ways, it did necessitate the busing of more students over greater distances.

Dr. Mark W. DeWalt, at Susquehanna University, recently completed a study that yielded surprising results: the one-room school has made a modest comeback over the past few decades. This phenomenon is shown in Figure 13.1 on page 346, which indicates that there has been considerable growth in the number of private one-room schools since about 1970. DeWalt attributes this growth, at least in part, to the U.S. Supreme Court's decision in *Wisconsin* v. *Yoder* (1972), which upheld Amish parents' rights to educate their own children. This decision opened up the opportunity for Amish parents, as well as other parents with similar views, to establish their own private elementary schools.

TABLE 13.2	Consolidation of Public School Districts, 1940–1990	
Year	School Districts	One-Teacher Schools
1940	117,108	113,600
1950	83,718	59,652
1960	40,520	20,213
1970	17,995	1,815
1980	15,912	921
1990	15,358	617

Source: 120 Years of American Education: A Statistical Portrait; U.S. Government Office of Educational Research and Improvement. Washington DC: U.S. Department of Education, January 1993, 56.

Of course, the number of one-room schools has diminished dramatically over a longer period of time. There were approximately 150,000 public one-room schools in existence in 1930, compared to just slightly over 500 today.

Growth of Busing. Both the number and percentage of students that were bused increased considerably from 1940 to 1980, as did the total cost and per-pupil cost. In addition to this general busing of students, efforts were later made to mix racial groups by busing students out of their neighborhood schools. This controversial practice is discussed elsewhere in this book.

Bigger School Budgets. The aspects of educational growth just discussed are only a few of the factors that have driven the nation's public education costs to

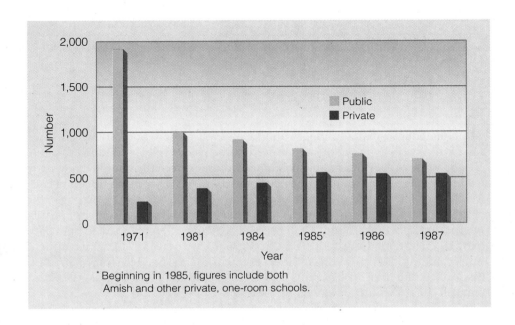

FIGURE 13.1

One-Room Schools

(*Source:* Education Week, *February 1, 1989, 3*)

* Beginning in 1985, figures include both Amish and other private, one-room schools.

record heights. This story of increasing public school budgets is vividly told by Table 13.3. Even if the figures are corrected for inflation, public education has become considerably more expensive. (The percentage of the gross national product spent on education rose from 3.5 percent in 1940 to 7 percent in 1980.[1])

Curricular Growth. The school curriculum has also experienced considerable growth during the past fifty years. This curricular growth, like most change, was the result of an accumulation of many smaller events. One such event was the publication in 1942 of the Eight-Year Study showing that students attending "progressive" schools achieved as well as students at traditional schools. This report helped to create a climate that was

Though rare, one-room school houses can still be found in contemporary education today.

more hospitable to experimentation with school curricula and teaching methodologies. The publication of a series of statements on the goals of American education (the 1938 "Purposes of Education in American Democracy," the 1944 "Education for All American Youth," and the 1952 "Imperative Needs of Youth") helped to broaden our schools' curricular offerings. (All of these goal statements were discussed more fully in the last chapter.)

Shortly after the Soviet Union launched *Sputnik*, the world's first artificial satellite, Congress passed the National Defense Education Act in 1958. This Act provided a massive infusion of federal dollars to improve our schools' science, mathematics, engineering, and foreign language programs. Eventually, innovative

---

TABLE 13.3   Public School Budgets, 1940–1990

| Year | Approximate Total Budget | Percentage Source | | |
		Federal	State	Local
1940	$2 billion	2	30	68
1950	$5 billion	3	40	57
1960	$15 billion	4	39	56
1970	$40 billion	8	40	52
1980	$97 billion	10	47	43
1990	$208 billion*	6*	47*	47*

Source: Bureau of the Census, *Digest of Educational Statistics 1982* (Washington, DC: U.S. Department of Commerce) 41.

*Estimates from: *120 Years of American Education: A Statistical Portrait*, U.S. Government Office of Educational Research and Improvement. Washington, DC: U.S. Department of Education, January 1993, 32, 34.

PROFESSIONAL DILEMMA

How Can a Teacher Better Understand the World?

Educators are admonished to "internationalize" their classrooms and their curriculum today. Most teachers really want to do so, but face the professional dilemma of developing their own understanding of the complex and richly diverse world in which we live. For one thing, while international study and travel are excellent learning opportunities for educators, it is expensive. Schools are not able to help teachers travel, and most international travel is no longer considered tax deductible by the Internal Revenue Service. Developing a better understanding of the world is difficult and expensive.

The United States played a key role in founding the United National Educational, Scientific and Cultural Organization (UNESCO) in the 1940s. Ironically, the United States withdrew its membership in UNESCO in 1983, for financial and political reasons. Teacher organizations such as the National Education Association continue to support UNESCO because of its potential to study and improve education around the globe. Understanding the world and working to improve global education is not only difficult for each teacher, but also difficult at the national level.

Still, understanding the world remains important for teachers, organizations, and nations. Accomplishing this task is a genuine professional dilemma for today's teachers. How will you cope with it? How will you internationalize your classroom and your curriculum? Will you, for instance, take international courses at a nearby college; find a way to travel outside the United States; subscribe to global publications; learn another language; take a foreign student into your home; encourage your school to offer in-service programs to help faculty better understand the world; or engage in some other activity that will help you internationalize your classroom and curriculum? We encourage you to start thinking about this professional dilemma right now—you and your future students will profit from your doing so.

curricula such as SMSG mathematics, BSCS biology, and PSCS physics grew out of these programs. Other school programs, such as guidance, were later funded through this Act. Note that in this case the federal government called on our schools to help solve what was perceived to be a "national defense" problem. Regardless of the motive, the NDEA represented another milestone that contributed significantly to the growth of our nation's educational enterprise.

If one were to compare today's school curriculum in nearly any subject with the curriculum in our schools fifty years ago, one would find impressive changes. The 1940 curriculum was very narrow and designed primarily for college-bound students, whereas today's curriculum is clearly broader and designed for students of all abilities. This fifty-year growth in our school curriculum has come about through the dedicated work of many people and represents one of the truly significant historical accomplishments in American education.

Growth of Special Education Programs. Perhaps curriculum growth is best illustrated in the area of special education. The public schools historically did not provide special education programs for handicapped children; rather they simply accommodated such children as best they could, usually by placing them in regular classrooms. Teachers had little or no training to help them understand and assist the special child. In fact, relatively little was known about common handicapping conditions.

TABLE 13.4			Children Served in Special Education Programs, by Type of Disability: 1939–1940 and 1989–1990 (in thousands)			
	1939–1940	**1952–1953**	**1962–1963**	**1969–1970**	**1979–1980**	**1989–1990**
Percent of Public School Enrollment	1.2	1.7	3.7	5.9	9.6	11.4
Learning Disabled	1.2	1.7	3.7	5.9	9.6	11.4
Speech Impaired	—	—	—	—	1,276	2,050
Mentally Retarded	98	114	432	830	869	548
Seriously Emotionally Disturbed	10	—	80	113	329	381
Hard-of-Hearing and Deaf	13	16	46	78	80	57
Orthopedically Handicapped	¹53	¹29	¹65	¹269	80	48
Other Health Impaired	—	—	—	—	106	52
Visually Handicapped	9	9	22	24	31	22
Multihandicapped	—	—	—	—	60	86
Deaf-Blind	—	—	—	—	2	2
Preschool Handicapped	—	—	—	—	(²)	422
Other Handicapped	—	—	22	126	—	—
Total	310	475	1,469	2,677	4,005	4,641

Source: U.S. Department of Education, National Center for Educational Statistics. *Biennial Survey of Education in the United States: Digest of Educational Statistics;* Office of Special Education and Rehabilitative Services. *Annual Report to Congress on the Implementation of the Education of the Handicapped Act;* and unpublished tabulations. (This table was prepared September 1992.)

Not until the federal government passed a series of laws during the mid-twentieth century—including Public Law 94–142, Education for the Handicapped Children Act—did schools begin to develop well-designed programs for handicapped students. These new special education programs required teachers who had been trained to work with visually handicapped students, hearing-impaired students, students with behavior disorders, and so forth. States and colleges then developed a wide variety of teacher-training programs for special educators (see Table 13.4).

Special education has developed very rapidly over a relatively short period of time in our recent history. It continues to evolve rapidly today and will likely do so in the future.

The Professionalization of Education

The field of education has taken giant strides toward becoming a profession during the past half century. In the following pages we will briefly explore the increasing complexities of our educational systems and look at some of the recent developments that have contributed to the professionalization of the field of education.

The Increasing Complexity of the Educational Enterprise

Our current educational system is much more complex than the school systems of the past, and this complexity is manifested in many different ways.

Increasing Federal Involvement. As we pointed out earlier, our federal government has played important roles in the development of national educational programs. This federal involvement in education has gradually increased over the years and it reached a crescendo during the past half century.

The 1940s saw the nation at war. The Vocational Education for National Defense Act was a crash program to prepare workers needed in industry to produce goods for national defense. The program operated through state educational agencies and trained over seven million workers. In 1941 the Lanham Act provided for building, maintaining, and operating community facilities in areas where local communities had unusual burdens because of defense and war initiatives.

GI Bill. The GI Bill of 1944 provided for the education of veterans of World War II. Later, similar bills assisted veterans of the Korean conflict. The federal government recognized a need to help young people whose careers had been interrupted by military service. These bills afforded education to over ten million veterans at a cost of almost $20 billion. Payments were made directly to veterans and to the colleges and schools the veterans attended. In 1966, another GI Bill was passed for veterans of the war in Southeast Asia.

National Science Foundation. The National Science Foundation, established in 1950, emphasized the need for continued support of basic scientific research. It was created to "promote the progress of science; to advance the national health, prosperity, and welfare; to secure the national defense; and for other purposes." The Cooperative Research Program of 1954 authorized the U.S. Commissioner of Education to enter into contracts with universities, colleges, and state education agencies to carry on educational research.

National Defense Education Act. Beginning in 1957, when the first Soviet space vehicle was launched, the federal government further increased its participation in education. The National Defense Education Act of 1958, the Vocational Education Act of 1963, the Manpower Development and Training Act of 1963, the Elementary and Secondary Education Act of 1965, and the International Education Act of 1966 are examples of recently increased federal participation in educational affairs. Federally supported educational programs such as Project Head Start, National Teacher Corps, and Upward Bound are further indications of such participation.

Appendix 13.1 on page 360 lists some of the most important federal laws and programs that have supported education. All these Acts have involved categorical federal aid to education—that is, aid for a specific use. Some individuals believe that federal influence on education has recently been greater than either state or local influence. There can be no denying that through federal legislation, U.S. Supreme Court decisions, and federal administrative influence, the total federal effect on education is indeed great. Indications are that this effect will be even more pronounced in the future. It will remain for future historians to determine whether or not this trend in American education is a wise one.

The Struggle for Equal Educational Opportunity. The past half century has also been characterized by an increasing struggle for **equal educational opportunity** for all children, regardless of race, creed, religion, or sex. This struggle was initiated by the African American activism movement, given additional momentum by the women's rights movement, and eventually joined by many other groups such as Hispanic Americans, Native Americans, and Asian Americans. The details of this relatively recent quest for equal educational opportunity are discussed in many other parts of this book. We mention it briefly at this point simply to emphasize that the struggle for equal educational opportunity represents an important but unrealized recent historical movement in education. Today, many observers are pointing out that with the accelerated growth of minority subcultures within our nation, our economic and political survival depends to a large degree on their educational opportunities and achievements.

The Professionalization of Teaching

As we pointed out in the preceding chapter, formal teacher training is a relatively recent phenomenon. Teacher training programs were developed during the first half of this century. By the midpoint of this century, each state had established requirements for a teaching certificate. Since then, teacher training and certification have been characterized by a "refinement" or "professionalization" movement. Teacher salaries have also improved considerably over this period.

In addition to teacher education, this professionalization movement touched just about all facets of education—curriculum, teaching methodology, training of school service personnel (administrators, counselors, librarians, media and other specialists), in-service teacher training, teacher organizations, and even school building construction. To clearly understand this professionalization movement, one need only compare pictures of an old one-room country school with a modern school building, read both a 1940 and a 1994 publication of the AFT or NEA, contrast a mid-twentieth century high school curriculum with one from today, or compile a list of the teaching materials found in a 1940 school and a similar list for a typical contemporary school.

Continued Importance of Private Schools

As was indicated in the preceding chapter, religion was the main purpose of education in colonial America. Children were taught to read primarily so that they could read the Bible and gain salvation. Most early colleges were established primarily to train ministers.

As the public school system developed, however, the religious nature of education gradually diminished to the point where relatively few American children attended religious schools. There have always been certain religious groups, however, that have struggled to create and maintain their own private schools so that religious instruction could permeate all areas of the curriculum. The most notable of these religious groups is the Roman Catholic Church. Over the past twenty-five

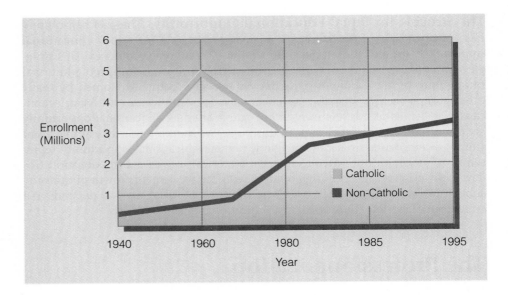

FIGURE 13.2

Estimated Private School Enrollments Since 1940

years, though, enrollment in non-Catholic religious schools has grown dramatically while the Catholic school enrollment has declined. These changes in enrollment are reflected in Figure 13.2.

Some Roman Catholic dioceses operate extremely large school systems, sometimes larger than the public school system in the same geographical area. The Chicago Diocese operates the largest Roman Catholic school system, enrolling approximately 150,000 students.

While space does not permit a thorough discussion of contemporary private school systems, we would like to emphasize that private schools provide elementary and secondary education for a very large number of American young people.

As the public school system developed, the relative prevalance of religious education diminished.

Teacher education students should become familiar with these private school systems so that they can decide whether they might be interested in pursuing teaching positions in such schools.

Recent Trends in Education[2]

Education experienced a major change following World War II when Dewey, Counts, Bagley, Charters, Terman, and other intellectuals who held sway during the first half of the twentieth century yielded to a somewhat less philosophically oriented breed of researchers represented by Harris, Maslow, Havighurst, Bloom, Guilford, Cronbach, Bruner, McLuhan, Chomsky, and Piaget. The Progressive Education Association closed its doors, and a series of White House conferences on children, youth, and education were inaugurated in an attempt to improve education.

No school system on earth has been scrutinized, analyzed, and dissected as profoundly and as mercilessly as the American one. During the late 1940s and middle 1950s, educational institutions at all levels were not only flooded with unprecedented numbers of students but also censored and flailed unmercifully by self-ordained critics (Rickover, Bestor, Mortimer, Smith, and Flesch). In retrospect, this frantic rush to simultaneously patronize and criticize the institution seems a curious contradiction. The public schools were characterized as "Godless, soft, undisciplined, uncultured, wasteful, and disorganized." Critics who remembered the high failure rates among World War II draftees were determined to raise the levels of physical fitness and literacy; others who detected a weakening of moral and spiritual values were eager to initiate citizenship and character-education programs. The enrollments in nonpublic schools doubled, correspondence schools of all kinds sprang into existence, and the popular press carried articles and programs designed to help parents augment the basic skills within the school program. In 1955 there were an estimated 450 correspondence schools serving 700,000 students throughout the country.

New Emphases in Education.   Fortunately, though some people were highly critical of our schools, not everybody panicked. There were physical fitness programs, character-education projects, a general tightening of educational standards, and much more. Guilford, Torrence, Getzels, and others explored the boundaries of creativity; A. S. Barr and Ryans carried out exhaustive studies of teacher characteristics; and just about everybody experimented with new patterns of organization. There were primary block programs; inter-age groupings; Joplin, Stoddard, and Trump plans; core programs; and a host of other patterns or combinations of plans structured around subject areas, broad groupings of subjects, or pupil characteristics. There were programs for the gifted and the not-so-gifted, and there was a new concern for foreign language instruction as well as the functional use of English. There was also a limited resurgence of Montessori Schools and several one-of-a-kind schools such as Amidon and Summerhill. While all this was taking place within the schools, the school systems themselves were consolidating, and by 1965 there were only half as many school districts as had existed twenty years earlier.

Automation was highly regarded during the 1950s, but the tools that gave education its biggest boost were more diverse. Social psychologists provided more advanced sociometric tools that offered new insights into the functioning of groups; reading specialists and psychologists developed highly refined diagnostic instruments for use in studying learning disabilities; and statisticians devised new formulas and designs for controlling and analyzing data by using modern computers. New research tools such as regression formulas and factoral analysis yielded data that had been unobtainable earlier. On a somewhat less sophisticated level more interesting and more flexible teaching tools were developed—audiovisual devices, learning games, more beautifully illustrated books, instructional television, machines for programmed instruction, and computers. Additional personnel such as teacher aides, counselors, social workers, and school psychologists were added as well.

Relevant Research

Classroom Analysis Systems

Some of the research studies that grew out of recent educational history deal with the analysis of the teaching/learning act. Hundreds of pieces of research contributed to this research movement, including the work of Flanders* who, along with many colleagues, developed the classroom verbal interaction analysis system, which helps a teacher better understand what takes place verbally in the classroom. This system uses an observation form developed just for the purpose of recording what is taking place, moment by moment, in a classroom for a given lesson. These observations are then placed on a grid that helps a teacher better analyze and understand what took place during the lesson. Often, teachers are surprised at the results, which may be quite different from what the teacher expected. For instance, often teachers spend more time talking than they realize.

There have been many other systems developed to help teachers better understand and control what takes place in their classrooms. We encourage you to become familiar with some of these classroom observation systems and to try them in your classroom. Ask your professors and cooperating teachers in the schools where you are doing clinical work, to help you get started on this task. What classroom analysis systems have you already become familiar with? Can you locate at least six such systems? Can you experiment with the three best systems you find?

*Flanders Verbal Classroom Interaction Analysis system

Analysis of Teaching. Another emphasis found expression in the **analysis of teaching.** For half a century, researchers had been attempting to identify the characteristics and teaching styles that were most closely associated with effective instruction. Hundreds of studies had been initiated, and correlations had been done among them. During the 1950s the focus began changing from what ought to occur in teaching to what actually does occur. Flanders and other researchers developed observational scales for use in assessing verbal communications between and among teachers and students. The scales permitted observers to categorize and summarize specific actions on the part of teachers and students. These studies were followed by studies of nonverbal classroom behaviors.

Another series of investigations involving the wider range of instructional protocols was patterned after the time-motion studies used earlier for industrial processes. Dwight Allen and several other educators attempted to use some of these findings in delineating the components of effective teaching. Specific formats were used to introduce teacher candidates to the elements judged most important to good teaching. The change in focus from studies of teacher characteristics to analyses of what actually occurs in classrooms has provided us with some of our best insights into teaching and learning and given us usable instruments for further investigations of classroom behavior. We can now assess the logical, verbal, nonverbal, affective, and several attitudinal dimensions of instruction as well as the intricate aspects of cognition and concept development.

Teacher Effectiveness. Recent research has focused even more closely on the instructional patterns of effective teachers. A recent review by Powers and Beard, *Teacher Effectiveness: An Annotated Bibliography,* catalogs over three thousand investigations into instructional competencies. Today's teachers, through **effective teaching,** are frequently viewed as having some important skills in common with the school teachers of sixty years ago. They are strong leaders who direct classroom activities, maximize the use of instructional time, and teach in a clear, businesslike manner.

Teachers now employ structured, carefully delineated lessons. They break larger topics into smaller, more easily grasped components, and focus on one thought, point, or direction at a time. They check prerequisite skills before introducing new skills or concepts. Step-by-step presentations are accompanied by a large number of probing questions. Teachers offer detailed explanations of difficult points, and test students on one point before moving on to the next. They provide corrective feedback where needed, and stay with the topic under study until students comprehend the major points or issues. Effective teachers use prompts and cues to assist students through the initial stages of acquisition.

This new emphasis on demonstration, prompting, and practice is a far cry from the relatively unstructured classroom activities of just ten years ago. We now emphasize carefully created learning goals and lesson sequences. It will be interesting to see whether the educational pendulum swings back to a new focus on student concerns and initiatives at some time in the future.

Sociological Studies.   A major breakthrough in education has resulted from a series of sociological studies relating to social class, social perceptions, and academic achievement. Coleman and Deutch were among the first to demonstrate that it is not the teaching equipment as much as children's social relationships that make the difference. Students' parents and peer groups at home and at school mold their perceptions and regulate their performances. These findings and those of Rosenthall and Jencks have given new direction to our efforts. Our concerns have changed, at least partially, from educational hardware to studies of pupil populations.

Study of the Learning Process.   In relatively recent years a number of leading American and European researchers have sought to analyze and describe how children learn. All of these investigators have stressed the importance of successful early learning patterns and the problems associated with serious learning deficits. They also believe that important elements within the environment may be changed or modified to promote learning.

Maria Montessori, an Italian physician, believed that children should be encouraged to teach themselves through the use of manipulative materials. She developed a wide range of educational resources, many of which could be matched or sequenced according to specific attributes (size, color, pitch, etc.). Montessori did much to promote the concept of pupil discovery and the use of tactile learning materials.

Global Perspectives: Jean Piaget.   Jean Piaget (1896–1980), a Swiss psychologist, was educated at the University of Paris. Through his work with Alfred Binet, who developed one of the first intelligence tests, Piaget became very interested in how children learn. He spent long hours observing different-aged children and eventually created a theory of mental or **cognitive development.** Piaget believed that children develop in four major stages. Up until about age two, a child is at the *sensorimotor stage* and learns mainly through the hands, mouth, and eyes. From about two to seven years of age, a child is at the *preoperational stage* and learns primarily through language and concepts. Between the ages seven and eleven, a child's learning is characterized by *concrete operations*, which involve the use of more complex concepts such as numbers. The final learning stage identified by Piaget is called the *formal operations* phase. This stage typically begins between ages eleven and fifteen and continues throughout adulthood. During this final stage the learner employs the most sophisticated and abstract learning processes. While children do not all fit neatly into these categories, Piaget's work has contributed much to our understanding of the learning process and has helped teachers to develop more appropriate teaching strategies for students at different developmental stages.

Robert Havighurst, a University of Chicago professor, has identified specific developmental tasks that he believes children must master if they are to develop normally. He even suggests that there may be periods during which certain tasks must be mastered if they are to become an integral part of children's repertoire of responses. There may also be "teachable moments" (periods of peak efficiency for the acquisition of specific experiences) during which receptivity is particularly high. Havighurst, like Piaget, has caused us to look carefully at the motivations and needs of children.

A contemporary of Havighurst, Jerome Bruner, of Harvard, has also postulated a series of developmental steps or stages that he believes children encounter as they mature. These involve action, imagery, and symbolism. Bruner's cognitive views have stressed student inquiry and the breaking down of larger tasks into components.

Benjamin Bloom, author of Bloom's Taxonomy of Educational Objectives and Distinguished Service Professor at the University of Chicago, has attempted to identify and weigh the factors that control learning. He believes that one can predict learning outcomes by assessing three factors: (1) the cognitive entry behaviors of a student (the extent to which the pupil has mastered prerequisite skills); (2) the affective entry characteristics (the student's interest in learning the material); and (3) the quality of instruction (the degree to which the instruction offered is appropriate for the learner). We can observe Bloom's research as reflected in models of direct instruction, particularly mastery learning, in which teachers carefully explain, illustrate, and demonstrate skills and provide practice, reinforcement, corrective feedback, and remediation.

B. F. Skinner. Burrhus Frederic (B. F.) Skinner (1904–1990) became one of the foremost early educational psychologists in American education. He developed a **behavioral theory** that suggested students could be successfully trained or conditioned to learn just about anything a teacher desired. This required the teacher to break down the learning into small sequential steps. Skinner even experimented with teaching machines that presented the learner with small sequential bits of information—an idea that has been revived today in computer-assisted instruction. Skinner published many works, including *The Technology of Teaching, Beyond Freedom and Dignity*, and *Walden Two*. He contributed much to our understanding of human learning and helped to advance the technology of teaching.

Educational Critics. Another development in education was triggered by a phalanx of critics, including Edgar Friedenberg (*Coming of Age in America*), Charles Silberman (*Crisis in the Classroom*), Jonathan Kozol (*Death at an Early Age*), Ivan

B. F. Skinner (1904–1990)

CASE STUDY   THE DISCOURAGED TEACHER

Your friend, Jim, is a third-year teacher who is somewhat discouraged about the teaching profession. When he graduated from his teacher preparation program he was full of enthusiasm; in fact, he accepted a teaching position in a school with a relatively high percentage of minority students because he thought he could make a difference. However, after three years, he is disillusioned about urban schools, which he claims are making pathetically little progress toward meeting the educational needs of most urban youth. He feels that students, for the most part, are apathetic, belligerent, and unconvinced that education is worthwhile. He further states that most urban parents do not support teachers or help their children with school work. Jim is also disappointed with his school's administration, which he claims does not adequately support the teachers.

Jim believes that little, if any, progress has been made over the past fifty years to improve equal educational opportunities for minority youth. He points out that minority students drop out of school much more frequently than do nonminorities, and they have more difficulty getting into college; in addition, our schools are still sexist institutions. In fact, Jim suggests that schools have very likely made these problems worse—not better—by perpetuating a value system that does not serve minorities and females well.

Jim then asks you, as a future educator, about your opinions regarding these problems. What is your response? Include answers to the following questions in your response.

1. What lessons can we learn, if any, from history, about the education of minorities and females?
2. To what extent and in what ways do you feel Jim's perception of urban schools is correct?
3. How well do you feel our schools are serving minorities and females at this time?
4. How might schools in general better serve minorities and females in the future?
5. Should schools make special efforts and spend extra funds to improve education for special groups, or should they serve all students alike? Why or why not?
6. What are some ways that you personally might be able to improve education for minorities and female students?

Illich (*Deschooling Society*), John Holt (*How Children Fail*), and a government report, *A Nation At Risk* (1983), which focused on low educational standards. Some, like Silberman, urge us to refurbish what we already have; others, including Illich, want to abandon the schools altogether. These critics have not gone unnoticed. Friedenberg's call for alternatives to traditional education, Silberman's endorsement of open education, and Kozol's plea for equal opportunity are all reflected to some degree in innovative programs from coast to coast.

Litigation's Influence on Education. In the years since 1970 we have seen an astonishingly large segment of our school patrons and students resorting to courts of law in confrontations with school officials and teachers. Considerable space is devoted to discussing many of these law cases elsewhere in this book. Suits have been filed challenging pupil placements, grades, the failure of the school to teach properly, disciplinary actions, dress codes, and numerous other previously accepted educational practices. The Buckley Amendment, which gives students and their parents the right to view official school records, added immeasurably to the demands of those seeking redress of grievances. In addition, the rights of due process have been extended to include students at all levels in an effort to protect their constitutional rights. Due process requires that rules and regulations facilitate the educational goals of the school and be clearly publicized. There must also be provision for a fair hearing when regulations are violated.

It is unfortunate that legal recourse has become a major modus operandi of recent years, for legal maneuvering is generally a substitute for good faith and mutual respect. However, individual abuses have probably diminished in the wake of threatened legal sanctions.

 Global Perspectives: Educators Share a World-Wide Responsibility. These last three chapters, which have briefly reviewed the history of education, point out that many, perhaps even most, of our educational concepts and practices were first developed long ago and in various parts of the world. We contemporary teachers in the United States owe a great debt of gratitude to our historical counterparts around the globe who pioneered and developed the profession we carry on.

History has shown that educators throughout the world have learned much from one another, and that education has improved and profited greatly from this sharing of educational ideas. This is even more true today than it has been in the past, and will increase as societies become ever more dependent on one another. Educators such as you will have to work even harder to share educational ideas in the future.

Summary and Implications

In this chapter we saw that the past half century has been characterized by tremendous growth, increased federal involvement, a struggle for equal educational opportunity, professionalization, litigation, and criticism. Many of the specific educational events that have taken place during this time period are listed in Appendix 13.2 on page 362.

It is difficult to draw meaningful inferences from recent events that have not yet stood the test of time. Implications of recent educational events will eventually be found in the answers to questions such as these:

- What should be the role of the federal government in education?
- How can we achieve equal educational opportunity in the United States?
- How professionalized do we want our school system to be?
- To what degree should educational policy and practice be influenced by itigation?

Discussion Questions

1. Other than those mentioned in this chapter, what additional recent educational developments seem particularly important to you? Why are they important?
2. Has the increased federal involvement in education been good or bad for our schools?
3. In your opinion, how much progress have we really made in providing equal educational opportunity in the United States? Defend your answer.

4. In what respect, if any, has education become professionalized, in your opinion?
5. What is happening in education at this very moment that is likely to be written about in future books about the history of education?

Journal/Portfolio Development

1. Interview a retired teacher about the educational changes she or he has observed over the past fifty years. Ask what advice this retired educator has for beginning teachers today.
2. Describe and evaluate a learning experience you remember from your own elementary school days.

What made it memorable, and what role did the teacher play in the learning process?

3. Create a list of the most useful outcomes of American education over the past fifty years. What can you as a beginning teacher learn, if anything, from your list?

School-Based Experiences

1. Most of the developments discussed in this chapter are so recent that they continue to influence contemporary American classrooms. As you work in the schools, look to see how our continuing struggle for equal educational opportunity is progressing. Also, analyze what you observe in order to determine the degree to which teaching has been professionalized—a movement that has gained impetus during the last fifty years. Finally, as you participate in classrooms, look for evidence that the work of educational pioneers discussed in this chapter (such as Bloom, Montessori, Skinner, and Piaget) has made an impact in our classrooms.

2. Discuss with experienced educators the changes they have observed during their careers. Visit with older educational administrators to discuss changes they have seen in their work over the years. Ask older people about their school experiences.

Notes

1. Bureau of the Census, *Digest of Education Statistics 1982.* Washington, DC: U.S. Department of Commerce, Government Printing Office, 1982, 23.

2. We thank Dr. Donald Barnes for many of the ideas presented in this section.

Bibliography

Avrich, Paul. *The Modern School Movement: Anarchism and Education in the United States.* Princeton, NJ: Princeton University Press, 1980.

Best, John Hardin, and Sidewell, Robert T., eds. *The American Legacy of Learning: Readings in the History of Education.* Philadelphia: Lippincott, 1967.

Church, Robert L. *Education in the United States: An Interpretive History.* New York: The Free Press, 1976.

Cremin, Lawrence A. *American Education: The Metropolitan Experience 1876–1980.* New York: Harper & Row, 1988.

_____. *The Transformation of the School: Progressivism in American Education, 1876–1957.* New York: Knopf, 1961.

French, William M. *American Educational Tradition: An Interpretive History.* Boston: Heath, 1964.

Gutek, Gerald L. *Education in the United States: An Historical Perspective.* Englewood Cliffs, NJ: Prentice-Hall, 1986.

Krug, Edward. *The Shaping of the American High School.* New York: Harper & Row, 1964.

Meyer, Adolphe E. *An Educational History of the American People.* New York: McGraw-Hill, 1967.

"The Negro and American Education." *Changing Education* (a journal of the American Federation of Teachers) (Fall 1966).

Perkinson, Henry J., ed. *Two Hundred Years of American Educational Thought.* New York: David McKay, 1976.

Ravitch, Diane. *The Troubled Crusade: American Education 1945–1980.* New York: Basic Books, 1983.

Spring, Joel. *The American School 1642–1990.* White Plains, NY: Longman, 1994.

Selected Federal Education Acts/Events

1787	Northwest Ordinance
1862	First Morrill Land Grant Act
1867	Department of Education Act
1887	Hatch Act
1890	Second Morrill Land Grant Act
1911	The State Marine School Act
1914	Smith-Lever Agriculture Extension Act
1917	Smith-Hughes Vocational Act
1918	Vocational Rehabilitation Act
1919	An act to provide for further educational facilities
1920	Smith-Bankhead Act
1935	Bankhead-Jones Act
1935	Agricultural Adjustment Act
1940	Vocational Education for National Defense Act
1941	Lanham Act
1943	Vocational Rehabilitation Act
1944	GI Bill of Rights
1944	Surplus Property Act
1946	National School Lunch Act
1946	George Barden Act
1948	United States Information and Educational Exchange Act
1949	Federal Property and Administrative Services Act
1950	National Science Foundation
1950	Financial assistance for local educational agencies affected by federal activities
1950	Housing Act
1954	Cooperative Research Act
1954	National Advisory Committee on Education Act
1954	School Milk Program Act
1956	Library Services Act
1958	National Defense Education Act
1958	Education of Mentally Retarded Children Act
1958	Captioned Films for the Deaf Act
1961	Area Redevelopment Act
1962	Manpower Development and Training Act
1962	Migration and Refugee Assistance Act
1963	Vocational Education Act
1963	Higher Education Facilities Act
1964	Civil Rights Act
1964	Economic Opportunity Act
1965	Elementary and Secondary Education Act
1965	Higher Education Act
1965	Health Professions Educational Assistance Amendments
1965	National Foundation on the Arts and the Humanities Act
1965	National Technical Institute for the Deaf Act
1965	National Vocational Student Loan Insurance Act
1966	International Education Act
1966	Adult Education Act
1966	Model Secondary School for the Deaf Act
1966	Elementary and Secondary Education Amendments
1967	Education Professions Development Act
1968	Elementary and Secondary Education Amendments
1968	Handicapped Children's Early Education Assistance Act
1968	Vocational Education Amendments
1968	Higher Education Amendments
1970	Elementary and Secondary Education Assistance Programs
1970	National Commission on Libraries and Information Science Act
1970	Office of Education Appropriation Act
1970	Environmental Education Act

1970   Drug Abuse Education Act

1971   Comprehensive Health Manpower Training Act

1972   Title IX Education Amendment

1972   Drug Abuse Office and Treatment Act

1972   Education Amendments

1972   Indian Education Act

1973   Older Americans Comprehensive Services Amendment

1973   Comprehensive Employment and Training Act

1974   Educational Amendments

1974   Juvenile Justice and Delinquency Prevention Act

1974   White House Conference on Library and Information Services Act

1975   Education for the Handicapped Act

1975   Indian Self-Determination and Education Assistance Act

1975   Indochina Migration and Refugee Assistance Act

1976   Education Amendments

1977   Youth Employment and Demonstration Projects Act

1978   Career Education Incentive Act

1978   Tribally Controlled Community College Assistance Act

1978   Education Amendments

1978   Middle Income Student Assistance Act

1979   Department of Education Organization Act

1980   Asbestos School Hazard Protection and Control Act

1980   Amendments to the Higher Education Act of 1965

1981   Education Consolidation and Improvement Act

1984   Education for Economic Security Act

1984   Perkins Vocational Education Act

1984   Talented Teachers Fellowship Program enacted

1986   U.S. Secretary of Education Report: *First Lessons, A Report on Elementary Education in America*

1989   Presidential Education Summit with Governors

1990   U.S. Supreme Court Decision to Allow Bible Clubs in Schools

1994   National Educational Goals: 2000 adopted by federal government

Important Dates in the History of Western Education

ca. 4000 B.C.	Written language developed
2000	First schools
1200	Trojan War
479–338	Period of Greek brilliance
469–399	Socrates
445–431	Greek Age of Pericles
427–346	Plato
404	Fall of Athens
384–322	Aristotle
336–323	Ascendancy of Alexander the Great
303	A few private Greek teachers set up schools in Rome
167	First Greek library in Rome
146	Fall of Corinth: Greece falls to Rome
A.D. 31–476	Empire of Rome
35–95	Quintilian
40–120	Plutarch
70	Destruction of Jerusalem
476	Fall of Rome in the West
734–804	Alcuin
800	Charlemagne crowned Emperor
980–1037	Avicenna
1100–1300	Crusades
1126–1198	Averroes
ca. 1150	Universities of Paris and Bologna
1209	Cambridge founded
1225–1274	St. Thomas Aquinas
1295	Voyage of Marco Polo
1384	Order of Brethren of the Common Life founded
ca. 1400	Thirty-eight universities; 108 by 1600
1423	Printing invented
1456	First book printed
1460–1536	Erasmus
1483–1546	Martin Luther
1487	Vasco de Gama discovered African route to India
1491–1556	Ignatius of Loyola
1492	Columbus lands in America
ca. 1492	Colonists begin exploiting Native Americans
ca. 1500	250 Latin grammar schools in England
1517	Luther nails theses to cathedral door; beginning of Reformation
1519–1521	Magellan first circumnavigates the globe
1534	Founding of Jesuits
1536	Sturm established his Gymnasium in Germany, the first classical secondary school
1568	Indian school established in Cuba by the Society of Jesus
1592–1600	Johann Comenius
1601	English Poor Law, established principle of tax-supported schools
1618	Holland had compulsory school law
1620	Plymouth Colony, Massachusetts, settled
1635	Boston Latin Grammar School founded
1636	Harvard founded

1642	Massachusetts law of 1642 encouraged education
1632–1704	John Locke
1647	Massachusetts law of 1647 compelled establishment of schools
1600s	Hornbooks evolved
1661	First newspaper in England
1672	First teacher-training class, Father Demia, France
1684	Brothers of the Christian Schools founded
1685	First normal school, de la Salle, Rheims, France
1697	First teacher training in Germany, Francke's Seminary, Halle
1700–1790	Benjamin Franklin
1712–1778	Jean Rousseau
1723	Indian student house opened by College of William and Mary
1746–1827	Johann Pestalozzi
1751	Franklin established first academy in the United States
1758–1843	Noah Webster
1762	Rousseau's *Émile* published
1775–1783	Revolution, United States
1776–1841	Johann Herbart
1782–1852	Friedrich Froebel
1778–1870	Emma Willard
1789	Adoption of Constitution, United States
1796–1859	Horace Mann
1798	Joseph Lancaster developed monitorial plan of education
1799–1815	Ascendancy of Napoleon, Waterloo
1804	Pestalozzi's Institute at Yverdon established
1806	First Lancastrian School in New York
1811–1900	Henry Barnard
1819	Dartmouth College Decision
1821	First American high school
1821	Troy Seminary for Women, Emma Willard, first higher education for women, United States
1823	First private normal school in the United States, Concord, Vermont, by Rev. Hall
1825	Labor unions come on the scene
1826	Froebel's *The Education of Man* published
1827	Massachusetts law compelled high schools
1837	Massachusetts had first state board, Horace Mann first secretary
1839	First public normal school, United States, Lexington, Massachusetts
1855	First kindergarten in United States—after German model, Mrs. Schurz
1856–1915	Booker T. Washington
1857–1952	John Dewey
1861–1865	Civil War
1861	Oswego (New York) Normal School (Edward Sheldon)
1862	Morrill Land Grant Act: college of engineering, military science, agriculture in each state
1868	Herbartian Society founded
1870–1952	Maria Montessori
1872	Kalamazoo Decision, made high schools legal
1875–1955	Mary Bethune
1888	Teachers College, Columbia University, founded
1892	Committee of Ten established
1896–1980	Jean Piaget
1904–1990	B. F. Skinner
1909–1910	The first junior high schools established at Berkeley, California, and Columbus, Ohio
ca. 1910	The first junior colleges established at Fresno, California, and Joliet, Illinois
1917	The Smith-Hughes Act, encouraged agriculture, industry, and home economics education in the United States
1932–1940	The Eight-Year Study of thirty high schools completed by the Progressive Education Association; reported favorably on the modern school
1941	Japanese bomb Pearl Harbor
1941	Lanham Act
1942	The Progressive Education Association published the findings of the Eight-Year Study

1944–1946	Legislation by 78th U.S. Congress provided subsistence allowance, tuition fees, and supplies for the education of veterans of World War II
1945	The United National Educational, Scientific, and Cultural Organization (UNESCO) initiated efforts to improve educational standards throughout the world
1946–1947	U.S. "baby boom," eventually causing huge increase in school enrollments
1948	*McCollum v. Board of Education;* U.S. Supreme Court ruled it illegal to release children for religious classes in public school buildings
1950	The National Science Foundation founded
1952	The GI Bill's educational benefits extended to Korean War veterans
1954	U.S. Supreme Court decision required eventual racial integration of public schools
1954	Cooperative Research Program
1957	The Soviet Union launched *Sputnik*
1958	Federal Congress passed the National Defense Education Act
1959	James B. Conant wrote *The American High School Today*
1961	Federal court ruled *de facto* racial segregation illegal
1961	Peace Corps established
1961	Approximately four million college students in the United States
1962	In *Engle v. Vitale,* U.S. Supreme Court ruled compulsory prayer in public school illegal
1963	Vocational Education Act
1963	Manpower Development and Training Act
1964	The Economic Opportunity Act provided federal funds for such programs as Head Start
1964	Civil Rights Act
1965	The Elementary and Secondary Education Act allowed more federal funds for public schools
1965	Higher Education Act

1966	The GI Bill's educational benefits extended to Southeast Asia war veterans
1966	One million Americans travel abroad
1948–1966	Fulbright programs in 136 nations involving 82,500 scholars
1966	U.S. International Education Act
1966	The Coleman Report suggested that racially balanced schools did not necessarily provide a better education
1967	Education Professions Development Act
1972	Indian Education Act passed, designed to help Native Americans help themselves
1972	Title IX Education Amendment outlawing discrimination on the basis of sex
1973	In *Rodriguez* v. *San Antonio Independent School,* the U.S. Supreme Court ruled that a state's system for financing schools did not violate the Constitution although there were large disparities in per-pupil expenditure.
1975	Indochina Migration and Refugee Assistance Act (Public Law 94-23)
1975	Public Law 94-142, requiring local districts to provide education for special and handicapped children
1979	Department of Education Act
1980	The U.S. Secretary of Education became a cabinet post
1983	*High School: A Report on Secondary Education in America* by the Carnegie Foundation
1983	*A Nation at Risk: The Imperative for Educational Reform,* report by the National Commission on Excellence in Education
1983	Task Force on Education for Economic Growth, Action for Excellence, Education Commission of the States Report
1983	Task Force on Federal Elementary and Secondary Education Policy,

Making the Grade, the Twentieth
Century Fund Report

1980–1984   Fundamentalist religious
movement advocating prayer in the
schools and teaching of Biblical
creation story

1984   Public Law 98-377 added new
science and mathematics
programs, magnet schools, and
equal access to public schools

1984   Perkins Vocational Education Act
to upgrade vocational programs in
schools

1984   Public Law 98-558 created new
teacher education scholarships and
continues Head Start and Follow
Through programs

1985   NCATE Redesign Standards
published

1986   Holmes Group report published

1986   Carnegie Report of the Task Force
on Teaching as a Profession

1989   Presidential Education Summit
with Governors

1990   U.S. Supreme Court Decision to
Allow Bible Clubs in Schools

1992   U.S. Supreme Court Decision finds
officially sanctioned prayers or
invocations unconstitutional

1994   National Educational Goals: 2000
adopted by federal government

Part

Philosophical Concepts, Educational Views, and Teaching Styles

CHAPTER 14

Philosophy: The Passion to Understand

CHAPTER 15

Educational Theory: Philosophy in Action in American Schools

CHAPTER 16

Building an Educational Philosophy

Dreamcatcher

AKBAR ALI New York City Surrounded by a world of turmoil, struggle, and poverty, Akbar Ali is an educator in the fullest sense of the word. He is a musician, a language and mathematics teacher, an administrator, a counselor, and a friend to thousands of students in New York City. Throughout his twenty years of teaching, Akbar has developed a complete philosophy, one that centers on an ethical concern and compassion for all children. His approaches to learning and knowledge, to testing and grading, and to discipline and responsibility are rooted in this axiological focus on respect for the innate dignity of all persons.

I have never studied education on a formal basis, so every classroom approach has truly been an experiment of experiential learning for me and my students. During my sophomore year ar Carnegie-Mellon University, I began teaching in a high school program that was housed on campus. I was stunned by the insights about math and physics that I gained by looking through the eyes of my students. I have been teaching (and therefore learning) ever since. As a musician and composer, I was struck again by the connection between mathematical problem solving and musical  problem solving in music composition and improvisation. The tensions and resolutions created through chords, rhythm, and melody reflected the same components as a logic puzzle. Connections became and remain for me a focus of understanding what learners need to experience.

Conceptually, I try to demonstrate the idea that I intend for them to grasp and then to quickly place them in a situation that will demand their use of that idea on a practical level.

I trust their ability to find their own way to the original idea and then to go beyond it. It is important to be able to recognize and support efforts of various types of intelligences and approaches. I view intelligences as mental, emotional, and physical—this is an ancient division of intelligences. I try to help students recognize which intelligence predominates in their own approach; then, after recognizing the limits of that single intelligence, I try to help them include a second intelligence. This is obviously the strength of integrated curriculum—the chance to include more than one intelligence.

I think my greatest realization about teaching is that within the content—concepts, skills, effort, and all else offered during the classroom experience—there is something else that can be transferred between teacher and student that is far more subtle and precious than skills and information. The process of sustained effort together reveals a deeper level of "education." When I can render it, my most selfless wish for what is best for them has a transforming effect on me and on my students. It is for this quality of interaction that I lovingly remember my best teachers, long after I have forgotten the literal content of their lessons. Their lessons made me a better person for living and further learning. These teachers "raised" me on many levels, like yeast in dough. It is this lesson I wish to convey within the heart of puzzles, computer programming, jazz improvisation, or any other subject that I now offer. It is to this lesson, the truest connection with my students, that I am committed.

Chapter

14 Philosophy: The Passion to Understand

Focus Questions

1 Are you able to identify your beliefs about knowledge, human nature, and values? How might your beliefs influence your teaching?

2 Do you believe authentic learning primarily occurs in real life experiences? How would you justify your answer?

3 Do you perceive students to be innately interested in learning for its own sake? How does your response influence your teaching and learning strategies?

4 Why is it valuable for prospective teachers to study philosophy?

5 Can you identify one way that students in your classroom might tackle an issue philosophically?

Key Terms and Concepts

Abstraction: A thought process of drawing away from experience to a conceptual plane.

Axiology: An area of philosophy that deals with the nature of values. It includes questions such as "What is good?" "What is value?"

Eastern thought: A varied set of philosophies from the Far, Middle, and Near East that stress inner peace, tranquility, attitudinal development, and mysticism.

Epistemology: An area of philosophy that deals with questions about how and what we know.

Existentialism: A school of philosophy that focuses on the importance of the individual rather than external standards.

Idealism: A school of philosophy that considers ideas to be the only true reality.

Metaphysics: An area of philosophy that deals with questions about the nature of ultimate reality.

Native North American thought: A varied set of beliefs, philosophical positions, and customs that span different tribes in North America

Pragmatism: A late nineteenth-century American school of philosophy that stresses becoming rather than being.

Realism: A school of philosophy that holds that reality, knowledge, and value exist independent of the human mind. In contrast to the idealist, the realist contends that physical entities exist in their own right.

Although there are many different ways of studying philosophy, it is best thought of as a passion to understand the underlying meaning of everything. Literally derived from the Greek *philos*, which means love, and *sophos*, which means wisdom, the word *philosophy* means "love of wisdom." Early philosophers were fond of pointing out that they did not claim to be wise—they were merely lovers of wisdom. To many philosophers, conveying information is not as important as helping others in their own search for wisdom.

Searching for wisdom is closely related to the essence of multiculturalism. Philosophy demands a habit of mind that is always searching to understand and incorporate different points of view, different voices. Philosophy compels us to consider the beauty and cohesion of seemingly diverse worlds of thought and existence.

This chapter explores ideas that were generated by different thinkers. It also describes the methods that philosophers use to answer abstract and complicated questions. Finally, the chapter clarifies how philosophy is related to education and how it provides a rich resource for educators who must guide themselves and others in the pursuit of knowledge and wisdom in a complex, global society.

Structure and Methodology of Philosophy

Education is inextricably intertwined with this passion to understand. Both philosophy and education are vitally concerned with a search for truth. By its very name education calls teachers "to lead from ignorance." Philosophy compels teachers to lead students in a direction that is meaningful and of most worth. Philosophy reminds teachers to continue the search for truth and not be satisfied with pat answers, even answers that are provided by so-called experts. To a philosopher, an expert is not one who professes truth or beauty; an expert is one who searches and questions.

Education presupposes ideas about human nature, the nature of reality, and the nature of knowledge. These questions are ultimately of a philosophical character. Teachers must constantly confront the underlying assumptions by which conduct is guided, by which value is determined, and by which the direction of all existence is influenced. Hence, the study of philosophy is at the heart of the study of education.

The Branches of Philosophy

Philosophy is not a collection of sterile, objective facts. Rather, it can be visualized as an internal desire that drives persons to search for better answers and better understandings. At its deepest level, philosophy consists of sets of profound and basic questions that remain constant because the basic dilemmas posed by these questions are yet to be answered adequately. At this basic level, philosophy does not provide answers; rather, it offers a range of possibilities or arguments that can be examined and used to guide decisions.

Because the questions of philosophy are so important, philosophy is structured around them. Philosophy includes branches that investigate large and difficult questions—questions about reality or being, about knowledge or knowing, about goodness and beauty and living a good life. Throughout the centuries, entire branches of philosophy have evolved that specialize and center around major

Classroom organization and priorities may reflect larger educational priorities.

questions. For example, questions concerning the nature of reality or existence are examined in metaphysics; questions concerning knowledge and truth are considered in epistemology; and questions about values and goodness are central to axiology.

Metaphysics.   **Metaphysics** is an area of philosophy that is concerned with questions about the nature of reality. Literally *metaphysics* means "beyond the physical." It deals with questions like: What is reality? What is existence? Is the universe rationally designed or ultimately meaningless? Metaphysics is a search for order and wholeness, applied not to particular items or experiences, but to all reality and to all existence.

In brief, metaphysics is the attempt to find coherence in the whole realm of thought and experience. Concerning the world, metaphysics includes the question of what causes events in the universe to happen, including the theories of creation and evolution. Metaphysics also involves questions concerning the nature of humans. Is human nature physical or spiritual (mind-body problem)? Does a person make free choices or do events and conditions force one into determined decisions?

The questions in metaphysics, especially those about humanity and the universe, are extremely relevant to teachers and students of education. Theories about how the universe came to be and about what causes events in the universe are crucial to interpret the physical sciences properly. George F. Kneller writes about the power of metaphysics in generating questions that lack scientific answers.[1]

Teachers often say, "If Johnnie kept his mind on his work, he would have no trouble in school." But what does the teacher mean here by "mind"? Is the mind different from the body? How are the two related? Is the mind the actual source of thoughts? Perhaps what we call "mind" is not an entity at all. Physiological and psychological studies of the brain have given us factual information and cyberneticians have compared the mind (or brain) to a computer. But such comparisons are crude; they do not satisfy our concern about the ultimate nature of the mind. Here again, knowing metaphysics and being able to think metaphysically helps the teacher when considering questions of ultimate meaning.

The answers to these questions are likely to be based on the teacher's metaphysical beliefs. If, for example, the teacher believes that very specific basic knowledge is crucial to the child's intellectual development, it is likely that this teacher will focus on the subject matter. If, on the other hand, the teacher holds that the child is more important than any specific subject matter, it is likely that this teacher will focus on the child and allow the child to provide clues as to how he or she should be instructed.

Epistemology. **Epistemology** is a branch of philosophy that examines questions about how and what we know. What knowledge is true and how does knowledge take place? The epistemologist attempts to discover what is involved in the process of knowing. Is knowing a special sort of mental act; is there a difference between knowledge and belief; can we know anything beyond the objects with which our senses acquaint us? Does knowing make any difference to the object that is known?

Because epistemological questions deal with the essence of knowledge, they are central to education. Teachers must be able to assess what is knowledge to determine if a particular piece of information should be included in the curriculum. How we know is of paramount importance to teachers because their beliefs about learning influence their classroom methods. Should teachers train students in the scientific methods, deductive reasoning, or both? Should students study logic and fallacies or follow intuition? Teachers' knowledge of how students learn influences how they will teach.

Axiology. **Axiology** is an area of philosophy that deals with the nature of values. It includes questions like "What is good?" "What is value?" Questions about what should be or what values we hold are highlighted in axiology. This study of values is divided into ethics (moral values and conduct) and aesthetics (values in the realm of beauty and art). Ethics deals with such questions as "What is the good life and how ought we to behave?" Aesthetics deals with the theory of beauty and examines such questions as, "Is art imaginative and representative or is it the product of private creative imagination?"[2] Good citizenship, honesty, and correct human relations are all learned in schools. They are not always a by-product. Often, students learn ethics from *who* the teacher is as well as from *what* the teacher says. One major question to be examined is: When does the end justify any means of achieving?

Both ethics and aesthetics are important issues in education. Should a system of ethics be taught in the public school? If so, which system of ethics should be taught? Aesthetics questions in education involve deciding which artistic works should or should not be included in the curriculum and what kind of subject matter should be allowed or encouraged in a writing, drawing, or painting class.

Should teachers compromise their own attitudes toward a piece of artwork if their opinion differs from that of a parent or a school board?

Thinking as a Philosopher

Philosophy provides us with the tools we need to think clearly. As with any discipline, philosophy has a style of thinking as well as a set of terms and methodologies that distinguish it from other disciplines. Philosophers spend much of their energy developing symbols or terms that are both abstract (apply to many individual cases) and precise (distinguish clearly). This tension between developing ideas that embrace more and more instances (abstraction) while maintaining a clear and accurate meaning (precision) is difficult, but is at the heart of the philosopher's task. The entire process is what is meant by understanding: uncovering the underlying, the foundational, and the essential principles of reality.

In the physical sciences, experimenters try to do the same thing when they devise a theory. The major difference between the scientist who empirically examines the material world and the philosopher who examines all reality is that the physical scientist mainly targets particular events or things in the material world and then tries to explain these events by some theory. The philosopher, on the other hand, strives to clarify the underlying principles for all events, material or immaterial, that are logically related. Philosophers tend to search for concepts that are larger than what the physical scientist is researching, and they also examine not only what seems to be, but what ought to be.

Abstraction. The notion of **abstraction** covers a multitude of meanings. The word *abstract* is derived from the Latin verb *abstrahere*, meaning to "draw away."

Contemporary philosophies of education support the notion that a classroom might just as likely be an art museum as a neat array of desks.

PROFESSIONAL DILEMMA

Should Ethics Be Taught in American Schools?

You may feel that this question demands an obvious affirmative answer. A problem arises, however, when you are asked to clarify the specific ethics that should be taught. How do you, as a teacher in a multicultural, public or private school setting, determine what values should be the focus of instruction? One school of thought, influenced largely by the work of Lawrence Kohlberg, endorses direct instruction in ethics. The educational theorists who endorse this position contend that there exists a body of professional ethics that spans all cultures. This body of ethics can be articulated at any point in time and should be taught directly to students in the public schools.

People—especially parents—may feel that children are faced with an increasingly complex and dangerous society, and that they cannot be expected simply to absorb the proper morals and values from the world around them. Because of this, the schools should step in.

This implies the drawing away from a concrete level of experience to a conceptual plane of principles or ideas. The process of abstraction can be thought of as a three-step process that moves thinking from singular concrete instances to more general, universal ideas. The three steps involve: (1) focusing attention on some feature within one's experience; (2) examining the precise characteristics of the feature; and (3) remembering the feature and its characteristics later so that it can be applied to other instances or combined with other ideas.

In general, philosophers distinguish between two basic types of abstraction: (1) parts, or abstractions of characteristics that could also be physically removed (features such as tabletops, legs, drawers, and the like) and (2) attributes or abstractions of characteristics that cannot be physically removed like shape, structure, or form. This second type of abstract thinking is the stuff of philosophers; they seek to understand the essential aspects of both material and immaterial things. These underlying, substantial aspects are sometimes referred to as qualities, relations, and functions.

Imagination and Generalization.   According to Alexander,[3] the second step of philosophic thinking is the use of imagination. Imagination can be thought of as the altering of abstractions. In philosophy, the use of imagination assists the process of abstraction by filling in the details of an idea, selecting details, and relating ideas to one another.

Imaginative explorations occur in many different ways. Usually, they occur by first focusing on some abstraction or idea. Ideas come from making observations, reflecting about some past experience, reading, viewing a dramatic work or piece of art, or conversing with others. Once ideas are selected, imaginative explorations can be made about them. Basic assumptions about things can be examined, arguments can be justified or clarified, and ideas can be distinguished from or related to other ideas. Experiential evidence, logical consistency, and a host of other criteria can be employed. The outcome of the whole imaginative process is the development of a system of ideas that has greater clarity and more interrelationships to other ideas or sets of propositions. This last step of the imaginative exploration

In contrast to this point of view, those influenced by the educational theories proposed by Syd Simon in his text, *Values Clarification,* reject the direct instruction of ethics because democracy demands that its citizens be free to clarify their own sets of values. This philosophy calls for public schools to refrain from the direct instruction of ethics and asks teachers to help students define their own sets of individually selected values. The approach requires teachers to remain neutral in their presentations of opposing value systems. The teacher's role is simply to assist students in the clarification of the consequences of selecting any one set of ethics or values.

This difficult problem of teaching ethics is especially problematic for a democracy. Who shall select the correct set of ethics to be taught?

- If the majority is given this right, then, what becomes of the individual rights of minorities?
- Yet, is it possible to teach a value-free curriculum?
- Does the very act of instruction imply a certain value system expressed and upheld by the individual teacher? What are your responses to these questions?

process is sometimes referred to as *generalization* because it ultimately results in the development of a comprehensive set of ideas.

Generalization sets ranges and limits to the abstractions that have been altered by imagination. As one's imagination relates more and more ideas to one another, the process of generalization determines which relationships should be emphasized and de-emphasized.

As an example of the philosophical thinking process, consider a simple chair that is located in a kitchen. First, the philosopher would abstract from the chair some idea on which to focus; for instance, the idea of support. Support is an underlying substantial characteristic of all chairs. Second, the philosopher might imagine how many physical parts of a chair could be removed without destroying the chair's ability to provide support. Are four legs always necessary for support? What must be supported to be a chair? As the philosopher ponders these questions (which are spurred by the imagination), precise generalizations can be made about the basic aspects of support. New questions or hypotheses can be developed. For example, how does the support provided by chairs relate to the support that a teacher should provide to students? What does teaching support really mean? To complete this inquiry, logic is required.

Logic. Philosophy deals with the nature of reasoning and has designated a set of principles called *logic.* Logic examines the principles that allow us to move from one argument to the next. There are many types of logic, but the two most commonly studied are deductive and inductive logic. Deduction is a type of reasoning that moves from a general statement to a specific instance. Induction is a type of reasoning that moves in the opposite direction from the particular instance to a general conclusion. Philosophy provides the tools that we need in order to think clearly. It is important for educators to have a philosophy as a means of developing their ability to think clearly about what they do on a day-to-day basis and of seeing how these things extend beyond the classroom to the whole of humanity and society. Studying philosophy enables you to recognize the underlying assumptions and principles of things so you can determine what is significant.

Schools of Philosophy and Their Influence on Education

As philosophers attempt to answer questions, they develop answers that are clustered into different schools of thought. These schools of philosophical thought are somewhat contrived since they are merely labels developed by others who attempt to show the similarities and differences among the many answers philosophers develop. Throughout the centuries, these schools of philosophic thought have been used to explain the diversity of responses from so many thinkers. As you examine the schools of thought developed in this section, keep in mind that the philosophers who represent these schools are individual thinkers, like yourself, who do not limit their thinking to the characteristics of any one label or school of thought. Four well-known schools of thought are idealism, realism, pragmatism, and existentialism. In addition to these, Eastern thought and Native North American thought are described. Technically, these two final clusters of thought are not termed "schools" because they encompass greater diversity and often extend beyond the limits of philosophy in beliefs, customs, and group values.

Idealism

The roots of idealism lie in the thinking of the Greek philosopher, Plato. Generally, idealists believe that ideas are the only true reality. It is not that idealists reject the material world, but rather, they hold that the material world is characterized by constant change and uncertainty, whereas ideas endure throughout time. Hence, **idealism** is a school of philosophy that holds that ideas or concepts are the essence of all that is worth knowing. The physical world we know through our senses is only a manifestation of the spiritual world. Idealists believe in the power of reasoning and they de-emphasize the scientific method and sense perception, which they hold suspect. They search for universal or absolute truths that will remain constant throughout the centuries.

The educational philosophy of the idealist is idea-centered rather than subject-centered or child-centered because the ideal, or the idea, is the foundation of all things. Knowledge is directed toward self-consciousness and

Relevant Research

Teaching Critical Thinking

Teaching critical thinking is an important educational outcome; it comes as no surprise that research studies about critical thinking abound. Many schools have adopted critical thinking as a specific district outcome. There is a great deal of controversy concerning the precise meaning of critical thinking, and this confusion makes instruction difficult.

A variety of thinking models have emerged, and schools have had to carefully reflect and select which critical thinking model to adopt. This selection is not simple, for cognitive scientists are not in agreement about the proper way to conceptualize critical thinking. For many years, two researchers have investigated how schools can effectively develop students' critical thinking skills. Robert Ennis, from the University of Illinois, has concentrated his research on the proper attainment of a set of skills, whereas Richard Paul, from Sonoma State University, has focused on students' attainment of a proper set of critical thinking dispositions or attitudes. Ennis has concluded that teachers who clarify a precise set of steps in the critical thinking process can more effectively teach students to be critical thinkers. Paul has concluded that critical thinking emerges when students are encouraged and taught to think from another's perspective. He calls this the dialog, dialectic thinking process (Paul, R., 1990). As a prospective teacher, you will need to determine your own answer to the question of how critical thinking should be taught.

Sources: Robert Ennis and S. Norris. *Evaluating Critical Thinking.* Pacific Grove, California: Midwest Publications, 1989. Richard Paul. *Critical Thinking: What Every Person Needs to Survive in a Rapidly Changing World.* Rohnert Park California Center for Critical Thinking and Moral Critique, 1990.

self-direction and is centered in the growth of rational processes about the big
ideas. Some idealists note that the individual who is created in God's image has
free will and this free will makes learning possible. The idealist believes that learning comes from within the individual rather than from without. Hence, real mental growth and spiritual growth do not occur until they are self-initiated.

Idealists' educational beliefs include an emphasis on the study of great leaders
as examples for us to imitate. For idealists, the teacher is the ideal model or example for the student. Teachers pass on the cultural heritage and the unchanging content of education, such as studying the great figures of the past, the humanities,
and a rigorous curriculum. Idealists emphasize the methods of lecture, discussion,
and imitation, and, finally, they believe in the importance of the doctrine of ideas.

No one philosopher is an idealist. Rather, philosophers answer questions and
some of their answers are similar. These similarities are what make up the different
schools of philosophy. To describe adequately any one school of philosophy, such
as idealism, one needs to go beyond these general characteristics and examine the
subtle differences posed by individual thinkers. Plato and Socrates, Immanuel
Kant, and Georg Wilhelm Frederick Hegel represent different aspects of the idealist tradition.

Plato and Socrates.   According to Plato, truth is the central reality; it is perfect,
and it cannot, therefore, be found in the world of matter since the material world
is both imperfect and constantly changing. Plato did not think that we create
knowledge; rather, we discover it. In one of his dialogues, he conjectures that
humanity once had true knowledge but lost it by being placed in a material body
that distorts and corrupts that knowledge. Thus, humans have the arduous task of
trying to remember what they once knew.

We only know the philosophy of Socrates through Plato, who wrote about
him in a series of texts called *Dialogues.* Socrates spoke of himself as a midwife
who found humans pregnant with knowledge, but knowledge that had not been
born or realized. This "Doctrine of Reminiscence" speaks directly to the role of the
educator. Teachers need to question students in such a way as to help them remember what they have forgotten. In the dialogue, *Meno,* Plato describes Socrates
meeting a slave boy and through skillful questions leading the boy to realize that
he knew the Pythagorean theorem, even though he does not know that he knows
it. This emphasis on bringing forth knowledge from students through artful questioning is sometimes called the Socratic Method.

The value of Socrates' and Plato's ideas is that they have stimulated a great
deal of thinking about the meaning and purpose of humankind, society, and education. Their ideas have influenced almost all philosophers who came after them
whether others supported or rejected their basic ideas. Alfred North Whitehead
even noted that modern philosophy is but a series of footnotes to Plato.

Writing in the *Republic,* Plato depicts his central ideas about knowledge in an
allegory about human beings living in a cave. He states:

> If I am right, certain professors of education must be wrong when they say
> that they can put knowledge into the soul which was not there before, like
> sight into a blind eyes. . . .Whereas, our argument shows that the power and
> capacity of learning exists in the soul already; and that just as the eye was
> unable to turn from darkness to light without the whole body, so too the

instrument of knowledge can only by the movement of the whole soul be turned from the world of becoming into that of being, and learn by degrees to endure the sight of being, and of the brightest and best of being, or in other words, of the good.[4]

Immanuel Kant.   The German philosopher Immanuel Kant (1724–1804), in the *Metaphysics of Morals* and the *Critique of Practical Reason*, spelled out his idealistic philosophy. Kant believed in freedom, the immortality of the soul, and the existence of God. He wrote extensively on human reason and noted that the only way humankind can know things is through the process of reason. Hence, reality is not a thing unto itself but the interaction of reason and external sensations. Reason fits perceived objects into classes or categories according to similarities and differences. It is only through reason that we acquire knowledge of the world. Once again, it is the idea or the way that the mind works that precedes the understanding of reality.

*Immanuel Kant
(1724–1804)*

Hegel and Marx.   Georg Wilhelm Friedrich Hegel (1770–1831), another German idealist, reasoned that the ultimate reality is composed of three stages or principles—*thesis*, the Idea; *antithesis*, Nature; and *synthesis*, Mind or Spirit. The thesis and antithesis as Hegel saw them are contradictory, and the synthesis unites the positive aspects of each. Karl Marx was greatly influenced by these ideas, although he transformed the Hegelian stages or principles into a materialistic philosophical base. Marx maintained that we become alienated from our own creations, such as society and the means of production. Rather than a dialectic occurring between ideas, Marx adopted the notion of a dialectic between economic conditions and human actions, or what has been called the materialist conception of history.

Realism

*Georg Wilhelm Friedrich
Hegel (1770–1831)*

Realism's roots lie in the thinking of Aristotle (384–322 B.C.). **Realism** is a school of philosophy that holds that reality, knowledge, and value exist independent of the human mind. In other words, realism rejects the idealist notion that only ideas are the ultimate reality. Refer to Figure 14.1, which illustrates the dualistic position of idealism and realism.

Realists place considerable importance on the role of the teacher in the educational process. The teacher should be a person who presents content in a systematic and organized way and should promote the idea that there are clearly defined criteria one can use in making judgments. Contemporary realists emphasize the importance of scientific research and development. Curriculum has reflected the impact of these realist thinkers through the appearance of standardized tests, serialized textbooks, and a specialized curriculum in which the disciplines are seen as separate areas of investigation.

Realists contend that the ultimate goal of education is advancement of human rationality. Schools can do this by requiring students to study organized bodies of knowledge, by teaching methods of arriving at this knowledge, and by assisting students to reason critically through observation and experimentation. Teachers must have specific knowledge about a subject so that they can order it in such a way as to teach it rationally. They must also have a broad background in order to show relationships that exist among all fields of knowledge.

IDEALISM	REALISM
a. Supernatural cause as creation of universe	a. Natural cause for evolution of universe
b. World of mental conceptions–ultimate reality in God	b. World of physical objects–ultimate reality in nature
c. Mind	c. Body

FIGURE 14.1

Dualistic Position of Idealism and Realism

Ed.

The realist curriculum would be a "subject-centered" curriculum and would include natural science, social science, humanities, and instrumental subjects like logic and inductive reasoning. Realists employ experimental and observational techniques. In the school setting they would promote testing and logical, clear content. In order to understand the complexity of the realist philosophy, we must once again turn to the ideas of individual thinkers: Aristotle, Locke, and Whitehead.

Aristotle. Aristotle (384–322 B.C.) thought that ideas (forms) are found by studying the world of matter. He believed that one could acquire knowledge of ideas or forms through an investigation of matter. He considered matter as an object of study to reach something further. In order to understand an object we must understand its absolute form, which is unchanging. To the realist, the trees of the forest exist whether or not there is a human mind to perceive them. This is an example of an independent reality. Although the ideas of a flower can exist without matter, matter cannot exist without form. Hence, each tulip shares universal properties with every other tulip and every other flower. However, the particular properties of a tulip differentiate it from all other flowers.

John Locke. John Locke (1632–1704) believed in the *tabula rasa*, blank tablet view of the mind. Locke stated that the mind of a person is blank at birth and that the person's sensory experiences make impressions on this blank tablet. John Locke distinguished between sense data and the objects they represent. The objects, or things we know, are independent of the mind or the knower insofar as thought refers to them and not merely to sense data. Ideas (round, square, tall) represent objects. Locke claimed that primary qualities (such as shapes) represent the world, while secondary qualities (such as colors) have a basis in the world but do not represent it.

The little or almost insensible, impressions on our tender infancies, have very important and lasting consequences: and there it is, as in the fountains of some rivers, where a gentle application of the hand turns the flexible waters

Aristotle (384–322 B.C.)

John Locke (1632–1704), left photo, and Alfred North Whitehead (1861–1947), right photo.

into channels, that make them at first, in the source, they received different tendencies, and arrive at last at very remote and distant places.

I imagine the minds of children as easily turned, this or that way, as water itself; and though this be the principal part and our main cure should be about the inside yet the clay cottage is not to be neglected. I shall therefore begin with the case and consider first the health of the body.[5]

Alfred North Whitehead.   Alfred North Whitehead (1861–1947), a philosopher and mathematician, attempted to reconcile some aspects of idealism and realism. He proposed "process" to be the central aspect of realism. Unlike Locke, Whitehead did not see objective reality and subjective mind as separate. He saw them as an organic unity that operates by its own principles. The universe is characterized by patterns and these patterns can be verified and analyzed through mathematics.

Culture is activity of thought and receptiveness to beauty and humane feelings. Scraps of information have nothing to do with it. . . . In training a child to activity of thought, above all things we must beware of what I will call "inert ideas"—that is to say, ideas that are merely received into the mind without being used, or tested, or thrown into fresh combinations.

In the history of education, the most striking phenomenon is the schools of learning, which at one epoch are alive with a ferment of genius, in a succeeding generation exhibit merely pedantry and routine. The reason is that they are overladen with inert ideas. Education with inert ideas is not only useless: it is, above all things, harmful—*Corruptio optimi, pessima.* Except at rare intervals of intellectual ferment, education in the past has been radically infected with inert ideas . . . Every intellectual revolution which has ever stirred humanity into greatness has been a passionate protest against inert ideas.[6]

Pragmatism

Pragmatism is a late nineteenth-century American philosophy that affected educational and social thought. It differs from most forms of idealism and realism by a belief in an open universe that is dynamic, evolving, and in a state of becoming. It is a process philosophy, which stresses becoming rather than being. Wedded as

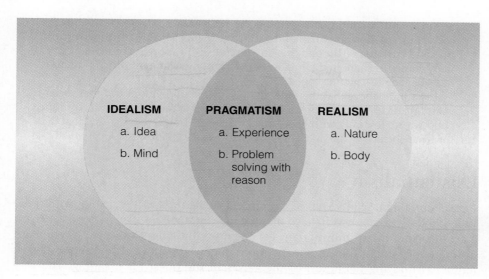

FIGURE 14.2

Relationship of Realism, Idealism, and Pragmatism

they are to change and adaptation, pragmatists do not believe in absolute and unchanging truth. For pragmatists, truth is what works. Truth is relative because what works for one person may not for another, just as what works at one time or in one place or in one society may not work in another.

Like the realist, the pragmatist believes that we learn best through experience, but pragmatists are more willing to put that belief into practice. While realists are concerned with passing organized bodies of knowledge from one generation to the next, pragmatists stress applying knowledge—using ideas as instruments for problem solving. Realists and idealists call for a curriculum centered on academic disciplines, but pragmatists prefer a curriculum that draws the disciplines together to solve problems—an interdisciplinary approach. Refer to Figure 14.2, which illustrates the relationships among realism, idealism, and pragmatism.

Charles Sanders Peirce. Charles Sanders Peirce (1839–1914) is considered the founder of pragmatism. He introduced the principle that belief is a habit of action undertaken to overcome indecisiveness. He believed that the purpose of thought is to produce action and that the meaning of a thought is the collection of results of actions. For example, to say that steel is "hard" is to mean that when the operation of scratch testing is performed on steel, it will not be scratched by most substances. The aim of Peirce's pragmatic method is to supply a procedure for constructing and clarifying meanings and to facilitate communication.

John Dewey. Early in his philosophical development, John Dewey (1859–1952) related pragmatism to evolution by showing how to view ourselves as creatures who have to adapt to each other and to our environments. Dewey viewed life as a series of overlapping and interpenetrating experiences and situations, each of which has its own complete identity. The primary unit of life is the individual experience.

Dewey wrote the following selection early in his career. In it he shows his zeal for education as a social force in human affairs.

I believe that all education proceeds by the participation of the individual in the social consciousness of the race. This process begins unconsciously almost

Charles S. Peirce (1839–1914)

at birth, and is continually shaping the individual's powers, saturating his consciousness, forming his habits, training his ideas, and arousing his feelings and emotions. Through this unconscious education the individual gradually comes to share in the intellectual and moral resources which humanity has succeeded in getting together. . . .

In sum, I believe that the individual is a social individual and that society is an organic union of individuals. If we eliminate the social factor from the child we are left only with an abstraction; if we eliminate the individual factor from society, we are left only with an inert and lifeless mass.[7]

Existentialism

In **existentialism,** reality is lived existence and the final reality resides within the individual. Existentialists believe that we live an alien, meaningless existence on a small planet in an unimportant galaxy in an indifferent universe. There is no ultimate meaning. Whereas some people might be paralyzed by this view, existentialists find the definition of their lives in the quest for meaning. The very meaninglessness of life compels them to instill life with meaning.

The only certainty for the existentialist is that we are free. However, this freedom is wrapped up in a search for meaning. We define ourselves, that is, we make meaning in our world, by the choices we make. In effect we are what we choose.

The existentialist believes that most schools, like other corporate symbols, deemphasize the individual and the relationship between the teacher and the student. Existentialists claim that when educators attempt to predict the behavior of students, they turn individuals into objects to be measured, quantified, and processed. Existentialists tend to feel that tracking, measurement, and standardization militate against creating opportunities for self-direction and personal choice. According to the existentialist, education is a process of developing a free, self-actualizing person centered on the feelings of the student. Therefore, education does not start with the nature of the world and with humankind, but with the human individual or self.

The existentialist educator would be a free personality engaged in projects that treat students as free personalities. The highest educational goal is to search for oneself. Teachers and students experience existential crises that involve an examination of oneself and one's life purposes. Education helps to fill in the gaps needed to fulfill those purposes; it is not a mold to which the student must be fitted. Students define themselves by their choices.

The existentialist student would have a questioning attitude and would be involved in a continuing search for self and reasons for existence. The existentialist teacher would help students become what they themselves want to become, not what outside forces such as society, other teachers, or parents want them to become.

Existentialist thinkers are as varied as the notion of individual thought and existence. There are atheistic existentialists as represented by Jean-Paul Sartre and theistic existentialists as exemplified by Sören Kierkegaard.

Jean-Paul Sartre.   Modern existentialism was born amidst the pain and disillusionment of World War II. Jean-Paul Sartre (1905–1980) broke with previous philosophers and asserted that existence (being) comes before essence (meaning).

Sartre saw no difference between being free and being human. This opens great possibilities; yet it also creates feelings of dread and nausea as one recognizes the reality of nonbeing and death as well as the great responsibilities that accompany such radical freedom to shape oneself out of one's choices. The process of answering the question "Who are we?" begins at a very crucial event in the lives of young people called the existential moment—that point somewhere toward the end of youth when we realize for the first time that we exist as an independent agent.

Sören Kierkegaard. Sören Kierkegaard (1813–1855), a Danish theologian and philosopher, criticized science, contending that its objectivity was an attempt to drive society away from the Christian faith. He described three stages to life: the aesthetic stage, in which humans live in sensuous enjoyment and emotions dominate; the ethical stage, in which humans achieve an understanding of their place and the function of life; and the religious state, for Kierkegaard the highest state, in which humans stand alone before God. It is only through faith that humans can bridge the gap between man and God. He believed that individuals must come to understand their souls, that they deny the reality of God through education. Kierkegaard maintained that individuals must accept responsibility for their choices, which they alone can make.

Eastern Thought

Most studies of Western philosophy typically begin with the Greek philosophers. Yet there is support that Platonic philosophy owed much of its development to Indian philosophy, which emphasizes the illusory quality of matter from Hinduism and Buddhism. There is much in the philosophies of the East that speaks to our concern for education. Although there are many different philosophical writings among the Far Eastern and Middle Eastern philosophers, there is one paramount idea. **Eastern thought,** unlike our Western, more empirical approach, stresses inner peace, tranquility, attitudinal development, and mysticism. Western philosophy has tended to emphasize logic and materialism while Eastern philosophy, in general, stresses the inner rather than the outer world; intuition rather than sense; and mysticism rather than scientific discoveries. This has differed from school to school, but overall Eastern thought begins with the inner world and then reaches to the outer world of phenomena.

Eastern philosophers have always concerned themselves with education, which they view as a way of achieving wisdom, maintaining the family structure, establishing the law, and providing for social and economic concerns. Instruction includes the things that one must do to achieve the good life, and education is viewed as necessary not only for this life but for achievement of the good life hereafter.

Eastern thought has not been as singular as has Western thought. One needs to study it system by system, culture by culture, and philosopher by philosopher. One good reason to study Eastern thought is that it represents a vantage point from which to examine Western thought. It encourages us to question seriously our most basic commitments to science, materialism, and nature. Eastern philosophy values order, regularity, and patience that is proportional to and in harmony with the law of nature.

Far Eastern Thought.   Far Eastern Indian philosophy is permeated by opposites. To the Western philosophers, these opposites need to be reconciled, but to the Eastern mind this need for consistency is unimportant. For example, great emphasis is placed on a search for wisdom, but this does not mean a rejection of worldly pleasures. Though speculation is emphasized, it has a very practical character. Far Eastern Indian philosophers insist that knowledge be used to improve both social and communal life and that people should live according to their ideals. There is a prevailing sense of universal moral justice in Far Eastern Indian philosophy by which individuals are responsible for what they are and what they become.

Hinduism, Buddhism, and Jain are three religions that provide different contexts for these philosophical principles. Hinduism does not generally encourage asceticism or a renunciation of the world, but believes that one should be able to control and regulate it. Fundamental truths include that there is an ultimate reality that is all-pervading and is the final cause of the universe. This reality is uncreated and eternal. Meditation on this ultimate reality leads to a life of virtue and righteousness. Buddhism stresses nonattachment to material things and concern for humanity; it emphasizes a sense of harmony with the universe where one is under no constraint to change forces within or without. Jain is a philosophy that rejects systems as absolutes and affirms them only as partial truths or "maybes." Jains believe that the universe has existed from all eternity, undergoing an infinite number of revolutions produced by the powers of nature. They have great respect for all life and take vows to avoid injury to any form of life.[8]

The emphasis of Far Eastern Chinese philosophy is on harmony: Correct thinking should help one achieve harmony with life. This harmony of government, business, and family should then lead toward a higher synthesis. Confucianism and Taoism provide two major contexts for Chinese thought.

Japanese thought is rooted in Shinto. This early religion of Japan encouraged nature worship. The Japanese perspective is one of acceptance and enjoyment of life and kinship with nature. Intuition is often prized over intellectualism, and there is a strong feeling for loyalty, purity, and nature. Japanese philosophy has successfully fused Confucian, Buddhist, and Taoist beliefs and practices in ways that permeate them with a distinct Japanese perspective. One example of this is the development of Zen Buddhism. Zen emphasizes a dependence on oneself rather than on an outside source for answers and wisdom; it depends more on intuition than on intellectual discovery.[9]

Middle Eastern Thought.   Many philosophies and religions (including Judaism, Christianity, and Islam) owe their origin to the Middle East. Historically, the Middle East has been a meeting ground between civilizations of the East and the West, and as such, Middle Eastern thought is more disjointed than that of the Far East. Judaism traces its origins beginning with the call of Abraham (around 1750 B.C.). Abraham believed in a God who had a special interest in humanity. Throughout the centuries Judaic thought has included a belief in one God who created the world and who cares for the world and all its creatures. In earlier conceptions of Judaism, God was viewed as possessing human qualities but later became more idealized, incorporeal. He is "I am who I am."

Christianity began as a Jewish sect, centered in Jerusalem. This sect proclaimed Jesus of Nazareth as the Messiah. The words and deeds of Jesus formed the basis of the New Testament, which was the fulfillment of Judaism. Christianity

| CASE STUDY | REQUIRED STUDENT SERVICE: A FORM OF SLAVERY? |

In April, 1990, Bethlehem Area School District in Eastern Pennsylvania adopted a community service graduation requirement. Under the program, every student in the district, except those in the special education program, has to perform sixty hours of community service between the start of ninth grade and the completion of twelfth grade. The school board decided to make the program mandatory based on the philosophy that education is not limited to the acquisition of knowledge. Rather, there was an underlying epistemology that knowledge included a societal component. The program was not adopted to provide benefit to the district in the form of free clerical and maintenance services. The board set the following goals for the program: (1) students will understand their responsibilities as citizens dealing with community issues, (2) they will know that their concern about people and events in the community can have positive effects, and (3) they will develop pride in assisting others.

The mandatory community service could be performed through an agency approved by the district, through an independent program selected by the district, or through an independent program selected by the student and approved by the district. Acceptable volunteer activities varied; examples included stuffing envelopes for the Lehigh Presbytery, playing with children at the Jewish Community Center, walking and grooming dogs for the Humane Society, and marching in the school band during the Halloween parade.

The parents of two Bethlehem students filed suit in federal court, claiming that the community service requirement violated their children's constitutional rights. Specifically, they alleged that the program violated the Thirteenth Amendment prohibition against involuntary servitude and the First Amendment guarantee of freedom of expression. They argued that although their children each engaged in various volunteer activities, the mandatory nature of the district's program constituted forced labor akin to slavery and compelled the students to declare, through their actions, that altruism is a desirable philosophy of life.

Although the federal lawsuit failed on the local level because the court found that the community service program was not sufficiently imbued with elements of communication to fit within the scope of constitutionally protected expression, the original parental concerns about forced labor and forced value acquisition are far from resolved. Parents who adhere to the political and religious right continue to mount challenges in various forms to the notion of mandatory community service in public schools. The original intent of the Bethlehem Area School District focused on a specific view of truth—knowledge is interconnected with society. Knowledge is not personal acquisition, but rather a shared reality.

1. Is such an epistemology legitimate in a contemporary, diverse society? Why?
2. Is knowledge value-free? Defend your answer.
3. What are the characteristics of an educated person?

---

incorporated many of the Judaic beliefs, but placed greater emphasis on the fatherhood of God and in God's concern for humanity.

Islam is the most prominent religion in the contemporary Middle East. Mohammed (A.D. 571–632) was born in Mecca. Through a revelation, Mohammed was called on to bring all people to worship Allah, the one true God. His mission was to restore to the Arabs the pure faith of their father, Abraham, and to free them from bondage and idolatry. Mohammed taught that Allah is a purposeful God who created things to reach certain desired goals. Those who follow the will of Allah will be eternally rewarded in paradise, an oasis of flowing waters. For those who do not follow the will of Allah, there is eternal suffering.

Global Perspectives: The Fabric of Eastern Thought. As you can see, Eastern thought is like a rich fabric of diverse ideas. It emphasizes sets of views that are quite different from the neat categorizations of Western thought. Eastern thought suggests that cohesive views can be achieved without the necessity of neat, hierarchically distinct categories. Although they are quite difficult to categorize, the philosophy and thought of both the Far East and the Middle East force us to reexamine our meanings and assumptions. As such, the study of Eastern thought is an important part of all future educators' preparation in an increasingly multicultural society.

Native North American Thought

Just as the rich past and diverse cultures make it difficult to summarize Eastern thought, Native North American thought is equally difficult to synthesize. **Native North American thought** includes a varied set of beliefs, philosophical positions, and customs that span different tribes in North America. These beliefs, positions, and customs center on the relationship of humans to all of nature including the earth, sun, sky, and beyond. Different tribes in different settings have developed varied approaches to this human-to-nature relationship.

The Navajo nation is the largest United States tribe. Its early history was nomadic and its thoughts and customs are known for their unique ability to assimilate with and adapt to the thought and customs of other tribes. As with most Native American cultures, the Navajo universe is an all-inclusive unity viewed as an orderly system of interrelated elements. At the basis of Navajo teachings and traditions is the value of a life lived in harmony with the natural world. Such a view enables one to "walk in beauty." In understanding the Navajo world view, one must note the teachings of the "inner forms" of things. These inner forms were set in place by First Man and First Woman. The concept of "inner form" is similar to the concept of a "spirit" or "soul" because without it, the Navajos say the outer forms would be dead.[10]

The Native American culture of the Great Plains, of which the Lakota form part, is based on mystical participation with the environment. Every aspect of this ecosystem, including Earth, Sky, Night and Day, Sun and Moon, are all elements of oneness within which life was undertaken. The Lakota celebrate the "sacred hoop of life" and observe seven sacred rites toward the goal of ultimate communion with Wakan-Tanka, the great Spirit.[11]

The Hopi follow the path of peace, which they believe is a pure and perfect pattern of mankind's evolutionary journey. The Road of Life of the Hopi is represented as a journey through seven universes created at the beginning. At death, the conduct of a person in accordance with the Creator's plan determines when and where the next step on the road will be taken. Each of the Hopi clans has a unique role to play, and each role is an essential part of the whole. Hopis must live in harmony with one another, with nature, and with the plan. Out of this complex interplay, then, the plan is both created and allowed to unfold.

Chief Sequojah, author of the Cherokee alphabet

We feel that the world is good. We are grateful to be alive. We are conscious that all men are brothers. We sense that we are related to other creatures. Life is to be valued and preserved. If you see a grain of corn on the ground, pick it up and take care of it, because it has life inside. When you go out of your house in the morning and see the sun rising pause a moment to think about it. When you take water from a spring, be aware that it is a gift of nature. (Albert Yava, Big Falling Snow, Hopi)[12]

Summary and Implications

The study of philosophy permeates every aspect of the teacher's role and provides the underpinning for every decision. This chapter described how philosophy is related to daily teaching decisions and actions, and it clarified some of the major ideas that different philosophers have developed in their private quest for wisdom.

Philosophy was shown to revolve around three major questions: those that deal with the nature of reality (metaphysics), those that deal with knowledge and truth (epistemology), and those that deal with values (axiology). Prospective teachers are encouraged to identify the personal philosophical positions that inform their own learning and teaching. The chapter further suggests three steps that help clarify such philosophical positions: abstraction, imagination, and logic. No implied best quality is ascribed to one philosophical position over another. Rather, the most successful teachers are those who are dedicated to and thoroughly understand their preferred beliefs. Decisions about the nature of the subject matter emphasized in the curriculum are metaphysical commitments to reality—What is real? Questions related to what is true and how we know are epistemological. Classroom methods are practices that aim to assist learners in acquiring knowledge and truth in the subject area. Classroom activities

that deal with ethics (what is good or bad), beauty, and character are in the realm of axiology (values). The task of the teacher is to identify a preferred style, understand that style as thoroughly as possible, and utilize that style with a unique group of learners seeking to accomplish reasonable educational outcomes under the leadership of the teacher. The classical philosophical concepts discussed are broad categories within the vast academic realm of philosophy.

Educational inferences with regard to curricular emphasis, preferred method, character education, and developing taste for each philosophical concept may be directly drawn. The metaphysical questions about reality in philosophy serve as the basis for the curricular emphases in current educational practices. Methodology in the classroom relates to the acquisition of knowledge, which is anchored in classic epistemological considerations. Character education (morals) and developing taste (aesthetics) are value determinants extended from the axiology branches of classical philosophies. Note that the relationships presented here are drawn from many elaborate schools and systems of philosophical thought, all of which provide the foundations for the six educational theories discussed in the following chapter.

Discussion Questions

1. How would you describe philosophy to a young child?
2. In your opinion, which is the most important aspect of a given philosophy (for the teacher)—the metaphysical view, the epistemological view, or the axiological view? State the rationale for your choice.

3. Early Greek philosophers suggest that all knowledge is based on experience. Discuss the implications of this statement for teaching methodology.
4. Describe the ways that Eastern and Native North American thought might influence what and how you teach.

Journal/Portfolio Development

1. Classroom activities that deal with what is good or bad are in the realm of axiology (values). Prepare lists of the "goods" and the "evils" of the American

educational system. Then pose solutions to counteract as many of the "evils" as possible.

2. In idealism, character education may be enhanced through imitating exemplars—heroes in the historical record. Identify an exemplar educator from history and describe the way in which you could teach character through the person's example.

School-Based Experiences

1. You are about halfway through your classroom experiences. In reflecting on those experiences, you feel that you need more knowledge about philosophical concepts and views to enable you to develop your own personal educational views. Some of your colleagues have similar feelings. You may wish to encourage them to establish a study group to discuss philosophical views. The group could develop questions to ask of your supervisor. Invite the supervisor to respond to your questions in one of your study group sessions.

2. As you visit schools and classrooms, be alert for indications of philosophical concepts and different philosophical views. You might wish to talk with teachers about their personal educational views. Many schools have written statements describing their philosophy of education. You could ask a number of schools to send you a copy of their philosophy of education. When you receive them, look for similarities and differences among the philosophical statements.

Notes

1. George F. Kneller, "The Relevance of Philosophy," in *Introduction to the Philosophy of Education.* Berrien Springs, MI: Andrews University Press, 1982, 7–8.

2. Ibid., 31.

3. Herbert G. Alexander, *The Language and Logic of Philosophy.* Lanham, MD: University Press of America, 107–108.

4. Selection from Plato, *The Republic,* trans. B. Jowett. New York: Dolphin Books, 1960, 208.

5. John Locke, "Some Thoughts Concerning Education," in *The Works of John Locke* Volume X. London: Printed for W. Otridge and Son et al., 1812, 6–7.

6. Alfred North Whitehead, *The Aims of Education.* New York: The Free Press, 1929, 1957, 1–2.

7. John Dewey, "My Pedagogic Creed," *The School Journal 54* (3) (16 January 1989): 77–80. Reprinted with the permission of the Center for Dewey Studies, Southern Illinois University at Carbondale.

8. Howard A. Osman and Samuel M. Craven, *Philosophical Foundations of Education.* Columbus, OH: Merrill Publishing, 1986, 66–85.

9. Ibid.

10. Terry P. Wilson, *Navajo: Walking in Beauty.* San Francisco, CA: Chronicle Books, 1994.

11. Terry P. Wilson, *Lakota: Seeking the Great Spirit.* San Francisco, CA: Chronicle Books, 1994.

12. Terry P. Wilson, *Hopi: Following the Path of Peace.* San Francisco, CA: Chronicle Books, 1994.

Bibliography

Abel, Donald C. *Theories of Human Nature.* New York: McGraw-Hill Press, 1992.

Adler, Mortimer. "A Revolution in Education." *American Educator 6*(4) (Winter 1982): 20–24.

_____ *Ten Philosophical Mistakes: Basic Errors in Modern Thought.* New York: Macmillan Press, 1985.

Bellanca, James. *Values and the Search for Self.* Washington, DC: National Education Association, 1975.

Coleman, James S. "International Comparisons of Cognitive Achievement." *Phi Delta Kappan* (February 1985): 403–406.

Dewey, John. *Democracy and Education.* New York: Macmillan, 1916.

Ennis, Robert and Norris, S. *Evaluating Critical Thinking.* Pacific Grove, CA: Midwest Publications, 1989.

Knight, George P. *Issues and Alternatives in Educational Philosophy.* Berrien Springs, MI: Andrews University Press, 1982.

Paul, Richard. *Critical Thinking: What Every Person Needs to Survive in a Rapidly Changing World.* Rohnert Park California Center for Critical Thinking and Moral Critique, 1990.

Scheffler, Israel. *Conditions of Knowledge: An Introduction to Epistemology and Education.* Chicago: University of Chicago Press, 1978.

Soltis, Jonas F. *An Introduction to the Analysis of Educational Concepts.* 2nd rev. ed. Reading, MA: Addison-Wesley, 1978.

Taylor, A. E. *Elements of Metaphysics.* 12th ed. London: Methuen, 1946.

Whitehead, Alfred North. *The Aims of Education.* New York: The Free Press, 1929, 1957, 1–2.

Wilson, Terry P. *Navajo: Walking in Beauty.* San Franciso, CA: Chronicle Books, 1994.

Wilson, Terry P. *Lakota: Seeking the Great Spirit.* San Franciso, CA: Chronicle Books, 1994.

Wilson, Terry P. *Hopi: Following the Path of Peace.* San Franciso, CA: Chronicle Books, 1994.

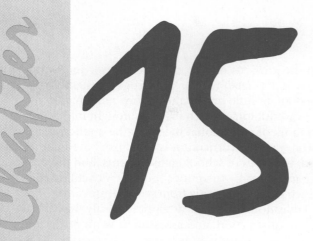

Educational Theory in American Schools: Philosophy in Action

Focus Questions

1　Perennialism is an educational theory that focuses on enduring ideas and principles that transcend time. Are there universal principles that seem to be taught in many different nations? If so, identify several; if not, why?

2　How does philosophy translate into action? Provide some examples.

3　Teaching methods that are nonauthoritarian regard the learner as active and interested in learning. What are some teaching methods that foster active learning?

4　Reconstructionism calls on schools to teach students to control institutions and be organized according to democratic principles. How can schools teach people to control institutions when schools themselves are institutions?

5　Do you agree with the notion that teachers teach the way that they were taught?

Key Terms and Concepts

Behaviorism: A psychological theory that asserts that behavior represents the essence of a person; behaviorists contend that all behavior can be explained as response to stimuli.

Constructivism: An educational theory that emphasizes hands-on, activity-based teaching and learning during which students develop their own frames of thought.

Essentialism: An educational theory that holds that there is a common core of information and skills that an educated person must have; school should be organized to transmit this core of essential material.

Humanism: An educational theory that contends that humans are innately good—born free but become enslaved by institutions.

Perennialism: An educational theory that focuses on principles of knowledge that are enduring; nature, human nature, and the underlying principles of existence are considered constant, undergoing little change.

Progressivism: An educational theory that emphasizes that ideas should be tested by experimentation and that learning is rooted in answering questions developed by the learner.

Reconstructionism: An educational theory that calls on schools to teach people to control institutions and to be organized according to basic democratic ideals.

*T*he philosophies presented in the previous chapter provide an overview of different ways that we can view the world: (metaphysics), knowledge (epistemology), and values (axiology). Such ideas are of little importance if they remain abstract; however, philosophic ideas are powerful forces when they are brought into action in educational theory. One can think of educational theory as the application of philosophy to the classroom. The way that curriculum is organized, the manner in which instruction is delivered, the types of school environments, and the processes of testing and grading are informed by the philosophic views held by educators, parents, and legislators. Such views vary greatly from school district to school district and from state to state. Educational theorists attempt to clarify how these different approaches to curriculum, instruction, and assessment work or do not work together. Table 15.1 describes the relationships between philosophic ideas and education.

Many teachers hold the view that the purpose of education is to train pupils' minds so that they can deal better with the intellectual concepts of life; they emphasize, in addition, the mastery of facts and information. The general notion that any child can learn any subject at any level if the subject matter is properly presented remains a strong challenge to teachers to arouse motivation for subject mastery among pupils. The concept of *mastery learning* suggests that, except for the few children who are mentally, emotionally, or physically impaired, every child can master the entire curriculum of the school when adequate time is provided. Continued attention to test scores, grade-level achievement, and other measures of subject matter competency reflect the importance that is still attached to the several views of education. School boards, parents, and the general public demand

TABLE 15.1   **Educational Implications of Philosophy**

Educational Aspect	Idealism	Realism	Pragmatism	Existentialism
Curricular emphasis	Subject matter of the mind: literature, intellectual history, philosophy, religion Education should be the same for everyone	Subject matter of the physical world: mathematics, science Initiative in education with the teacher	Subject matter of social experience Creation of a new social order	Subject matter of personal choice
Preferred teaching method	Teaching for the handling of ideas: lecture, discussion	Teaching for mastery of factual information and basic skills: demonstration, recitation	Problem solving: project method	Individual as entity within a social context
Character development	Imitating exemplars, heroes	Training in rules of conduct	Making group decisions in light of consequences	Individual responsibility for decisions and preferences
Art development	Studying the masterworks Values of the past heritage	Studying design in nature	Participating in art projects based on cross-cultural and universal values	Personal view of the world; self-initiated activities

Source: Adapted from Van Cleve Morris and Young Pai, *Philosophy and the American School*, p. 295. Copyright © 1976 Houghton Mifflin.

more and more often that teachers provide concrete evidence that their pupils have made progress in mastering subject matter. Teachers who identify with these views are considered to be more traditional regarding teaching strategies.

In contrast, many teachers uphold John Dewey's view that the mind is not just a muscle to be developed. They accept the notion that human beings are problem solvers who profit from experience. These educators also give credence to the existential position, which emphasizes the importance of the individual and of personal awareness. Since Dewey's philosophical views have prevailed in American teachers' colleges for the past half century, it is not surprising that American schools reflect this view more than do other schools throughout the world. When teaching techniques are focused on student interactions, teachers may find that some students appear to be aimless with regard to subject matter. In such instances the teacher is challenged to arouse student interest in inquiry leading to subject content, whereas the more traditional teacher is challenged to arouse student interest in subject matter directly.

Educational theorists explain how these two different sets of teaching and learning principles differ from each other. They clarify how each set forms a cohesive whole (theory), and describe the benefits and shortcomings of adhering to either set or theory. Six educational theories considered here are perennialism, essentialism, behaviorism, progressivism, reconstructionism, and humanism. To varying degrees, each of these educational views is drawn on by classroom teachers and applied to the way teachers organize their classroom, their instruction, and their assessments. As you study these different educational theories, you will find that one or more of them clearly represents your own views. Understanding your own position in terms of known theory will be an invaluable asset as you develop your personal philosophy of education.

Authoritarian Educational Theories

Perennialism, essentialism, and behaviorism are different educational theories that espouse an authoritarian approach to subject matter, classroom organization, teaching methods, and assessment. Although each theory forms a distinct cohesive whole, all three are rooted in an authoritarian principle, that is, that truth and goodness are entities that are best understood by the person with expertise who is in authority. The students' role is, then, to attempt to master and follow the directions of those in power who have experience and authority.

Each theory's focus on curriculum, teaching, and learning, is presented in this chapter. In addition, representative programs are described along with an illustrative class activity.

Perennialism

The basic educational view of **perennialism** is that the principles of knowledge are enduring. The term *perennial* may be defined as "everlasting," and the perennialist seeks everlasting truths. Although there are superficial differences from century to century, the perennialist views nature, human nature, and the underlying principles of existence as constant, undergoing little change.

Perennialists stress the importance of time-honored ideas, the great works of past and present thinkers, and the ability to reason. To know reality, perennialists maintain that we must examine individual things and objects around us to find their essence. To find the essence, one must discard the particulars and search for the underlying essentials. The essence of human beings lies in what they have in common—the ability to reason.

For the perennialist, the intellect does not develop merely by contact with relevant experiences. The intellect must be nourished by contact with ideas since truth ultimately resides in the nature of the things rather than in the sensory aspects of things. Perennialists contend that instead of focusing on current events or student interests, educators should teach disciplined knowledge with particular emphasis on the great ideas and works found in literature, the humanities, mathematics, science, and the arts. (See the Perennialist Class Activity box.)

Perennialist Focus of Learning.   The focus of learning in perennialism lies in activities designed to discipline the mind. Subject matter of a disciplinary and spiritual nature, like mathematics, language, logic, great books, and doctrines, must be studied. The learner is assumed to be a rational and spiritual person. Difficult mental calisthenics such as reading, writing, drill, rote memory, and computations are important in training the intellect. Perennialism holds that learning to reason is also very important—an ability attained by additional mental exercises in grammar, logic, and rhetoric, as well as through use of discussion methodologies. Reasoning about human matters and about moral principles that permeate the universe is the major focus of perennialism. Such learning activities are thought to contribute to the spiritual outreaching of idealism. As the individual mind develops, the learner becomes more like a spiritual being. The learner is closer to ultimate knowledge when he or she gradually assumes the mind qualities of God. Idealism also includes some of the recent findings that stress the psychology of learning; in this realm it is believed the mind can combine pieces of learning into whole concepts that have meaning.

Perennialist Curriculum.   Perennialists believe that early schooling is best directed toward preparing children for maturity, and they emphasize the three Rs in the elementary schools. In this view, perennialism and essentialism share some thoughts. Some lay and ecclesiastical perennialists consider character training, enhanced through Bible study, to be as important as the three Rs at the elementary level. A perennialist program for the secondary level is directed more toward educating the intellectually elite. Perennialism favors trade and skill training for students who are not engaged in the rigors of the general education program. Perennialists agree that the curriculum at the secondary level should provide a general educational program for the intellectually gifted and vocational training for the less gifted. However, not all perennialists agree on a curriculum design for general education.

The Great Books: A Perennialist Program.   Although the Great Books program, associated with Robert M. Hutchins and Mortimer Adler, has brought much attention to perennialism, other leaders in this movement do not support the program. Proponents of the Great Books program maintain that studying the works of the leading scholars of history is the best way to a general education. Perennialists who do not agree maintain that more modern sources can be used to obtain knowledge. The ecclesiastical perennialists insist that all programs give first importance to the study of theology.

PERENNIALIST CLASS ACTIVITY

Ms. Rosemont's literature class had been studying the works of Henry David Thoreau. Today's session focused on "Reading" from *Walden,* and discussion was based on the following questions:

- Do the classics embody truth? Why or why not?
- Have all our emotions and problems been written about by great authors?
- Are none of our experiences unique? Why or why not?
- What makes a book great?
- Does popular literature ever serve a noble purpose? Why or why not?
- With whom can one talk about the best book?
- Can only great poets read the works of great poets? Why or why not?
- Does dealing with truth help us become immortal? Why or why not?
- How can we get the most benefit from our reading?

This lesson follows the Great Books procedure for questioning and could, therefore, be considered a perennialist investigation of human nature.[1]

In this perennialist class activity the nature of the learner is *active,* the nature of the subject matter is *structured,* the use of the subject matter is *cognitive,* and the behavior trend is toward *convergent thinking.*

Essentialism

Essentialism holds that there is a common core of information and skills that an educated person must have. Schools should be organized to transmit this core of essential material as effectively as possible. There are three basic principles of essentialism: a core of information, hard work and mental discipline, and teacher-centered instruction. Essentialism seeks to educate by providing training in the fundamentals, developing sound habits of mind, and learning to respect authority. The back-to-the-basics movement is a truncated form of essentialism because it focuses primarily on the three Rs and discipline.

Although essentialism shares many of the same principles as perennialism, there are several important differences. Essentialists are not so intent on transmitting underlying, basic truths; rather, they advocate the teaching of a basic core of information that will help a person live a productive life today. Hence, this core of information can and will change. This is an important difference in emphasis from the notions of everlasting truth that characterize the perennialist. In addition, essentialism stresses the disciplined development of basic skills rather than the perennialist goals of uncovering essences or underlying principles. (See the Essentialist Class Activity box on page 396.)

Essentialist Focus of Learning. Essentialism's goals are to transmit the cultural heritage and develop good citizens. It seeks to do this by emphasizing a core of fundamental knowledge and skills, developing sound habits of mental discipline, and demanding a respect for authority. Sound study habits as well as discipline are stressed in a structured learning situation. The role of the student is that of a learner. School is a place where children come to learn what they need to know, and the teacher is the person who can best instruct students in essential matters.

Essentialist Curriculum. The essentialist curriculum focuses on subject matter that includes literature, history, foreign languages, and religion. Teaching methods require formal discipline through emphasis on required reading, lectures, memorization, repetition, and examinations. Essentialists differ in their views on curriculum, but they generally agree about including subject matter of the physical world. Mathematics and the natural sciences are examples of subjects that contribute to the learners' knowledge of natural law. Activities that require mastering facts and information about the physical world are significant aspects of essentialist methodology. With truth defined as observable fact, field trips, laboratories, audiovisual materials, and nature all furnish methods of instruction. Habits of intellectual discipline are considered ends in themselves. Essentialism advocates studying the laws of nature and the accompanying universal truths of the physical world.

Essentialism envisions subject matter as the core of education. Severe criticism has been leveled at American education by those who advocate an emphasis on basic education. Essentialism assigns to the schools the task of conserving the heritage and transmitting knowledge of the physical world. In a sense the school is a curator of knowledge.

With the burgeoning of new knowledge in contemporary society, essentialism may be contributing to the slowness of educational change. In this context, essentialism is criticized as obsolete in its authoritarian tendencies. Such criticism implies that essentialism does not satisfy the twentieth-century needs of our youth. Educators within the movement deny such criticism and claim to have incorporated modern influences in the system while maintaining academic standards.

Essential Schools Movement. The Essential Schools Movement is a contemporary school reform effort developed by Dr. Theodore Sizer. Sizer contends that there is a common core of information and skills that needs to be mastered by students, and he encourages schools to strip away the nonessentials and focus on having students "use their minds well." The Essential Schools Movement does not specify what specific content is essential. Rather, essential schools are required to analyze clearly what this core of information should be and change the curriculum to emphasize this core.

ESSENTIALIST CLASS ACTIVITY

Ms. Wright's second graders had just learned to count money. She decided to let them play several games of "musical envelopes." Although there was one envelope per student, each contained a different amount of paper "nickels," "dimes," "quarters," and "pennies." When the music stopped, students had to count the money in their envelopes. The one with the most money for each game got a special prize.[2]

In this essentialist class activity the nature of the learner is *passive*, the nature of the subject matter is *structured*, the use of the subject matter is *cognitive*, and the behavior trend is toward *convergent thinking*.

Behaviorism

B. F. Skinner, the Harvard experimental psychologist and philosopher, is the recognized leader of the movement known as **behaviorism.** Skinner verified Pavlov's stimulus-response theory with animals and, from his research, suggested that human behavior could also be explained as responses to external stimuli. (See the Behaviorist Class Activity box on page 398.) Other behaviorists' research expanded Skinner's work in illustrating the effect of the environment, particularly the interpersonal environment, in shaping individual behavior.

> Behaviorists share a common belief that a student's misbehavior can be changed and reshaped in a socially acceptable manner by directly changing the student's environment. The Behaviorist accepts the premise that students are motivated by the factor that all people will attempt to avoid experiences and stimuli that are not pleasing and will seek experiences that are pleasing and rewarding.[3]

Behaviorist Focus of Learning. Behaviorism is a psychological and educational theory that holds that one's behavior is determined by environment, not heredity. This suggests that education can contribute significantly to the shaping of the individual because the teacher can control the stimuli in a classroom and thereby influence student behavior. Behaviorists believe that the school environment must be highly organized and the curriculum based on behavioral objectives, and that knowledge is best described as behaviors that are observable. They contend that empirical evidence is essential if students are to learn and that the scientific method must be employed to arrive at knowledge. The task of education is to develop learning environments that lead to desired behaviors in students.

Reinforcement: A Behaviorist Practice. The concept of reinforcement is critical to teacher practices of behaviorism. Positive reinforcers (praise, special privileges, higher grades) are used to reward approved behavior with something desired by the student. Negative reinforcers (reprimands, extra homework, lower grades) are used to restrain behaviors that are not approved. Behaviorists generally believe that negative reinforcement is ineffective. Furthermore, they believe that learning takes place when approved behavior is observed and then positively reinforced.

When visually looking on, a teacher may provide positive reinforcement (smiling, nodding approval) or negative reinforcement (frowning, shaking the head in disapproval). Similarly, nondirective statements, questions, and directive statements may be positive or negative. Both children and adults respond to the models other people (peers, adults, heroes) represent to them by imitating the model behavior. Behaviorists contend that students tend to emulate behaviors that are rewarded.

The behaviorists have supplied a wealth of research that bears on the problems of attaining self-control, resisting temptation, and showing concern for others. Behaviorists do not attempt to learn about the causes of students' earlier problems. Rather, the teacher must ascertain what is happening in the classroom environment in order to perpetuate or extinguish the student's behavior.

BEHAVIORIST CLASS ACTIVITY

Students in Mr. Drucker's civics class were given merit tokens for coming into the room quietly, sitting at their desks, preparing notebooks and pencils for the day's lesson, and being ready to begin answering comprehension questions in their workbooks. On Fridays, students were allowed to use their tokens at an auction to buy items that Mr. Drucker knew they wanted. Sometimes, however, students had to save tokens for more than two weeks to buy what they liked best.

In this behaviorist class activity the nature of the learner is *passive,* the nature of the subject matter is *amorphous,* the use of the subject matter is *cognitive* or *affective,* and the behavior trend is toward *convergent thinking.*

Nonauthoritarian Educational Theories

Progressivism, reconstructionism, and humanism espouse a nonauthoritarian approach to subject matter, classroom organization, teaching methods, and assessment. Although each theory forms a distinct cohesive whole, all three are rooted in a nonauthoritarian principle, that is, that truth and goodness are entities that belong to all persons no matter what their station. Teachers are learners and learners are teachers, and education is the process in which individuals help one another to clarify personal meaning.

Each nonauthoritarian theory's focus or curriculum, teaching, and learning is presented in this chapter. In addition, representative programs are described along with an illustrative class activity.

Progressivism

With the rise of democracy in the late 1800s, the expansion of modern science and technology, and the need for people to be able to adjust to change, Americans had to have a new and different approach to getting knowledge to solve problems. An American philosopher, Charles S. Peirce (1839–1914), founded the philosophical system called *pragmatism.* This philosophy held that the meaning and value of ideas could be found only in their practical results. Later, William James (1842–1910) extended Peirce's theory of meaning into a theory of truth. James went further and asserted that the satisfactory working of an idea constitutes its whole truth. Pragmatism was carried much further by John Dewey (1859–1952), who was a widely known and influential philosopher and educator. Dewey insisted that ideas must always be tested by experiment. His experimental beliefs carried over into his educational philosophy, which became the basis for what was usually described as progressive education. **Progressivism** is an educational theory that emphasizes that ideas should be tested by experimentation and that learning is rooted in questions developed by the learners.[4]

Progressivism was a contemporary American educational theory. From its establishment in the mid-1920s through the mid-1950s, progressivism was the most influential educational view in America. Progressivists are basically opposed

John Dewey (1859–1952)

to authoritarianism and favor human experience as a basis for knowledge. Progressivism favors the scientific method of teaching and learning, allows for the beliefs of individuals, and stresses programs of student involvement that help students to learn how to think. Progressivists believe that the school should actively prepare its students for change. Progressive schools emphasize learning *how to think rather than what to think.* Flexibility is important in the curriculum design, and emphasis is on *experimentation*, with no single body of content stressed more than any other. Since life experience determines curriculum content, all types of content must be permitted. Certain subjects regarded as traditional are recognized as desirable for study as well. Progressivist educators would organize scientific method-oriented learning activities around the traditional subjects. Such a curriculum is called experience-centered or student-centered; the essentialism and perennialist curriculum is considered subject-centered. Experience-centered curricula stress the *process* of learning rather than the result.

Progressivism as a contemporary teaching style emphasizes the process of education in the classroom. It is more compatible with a core of problem areas across all academic disciplines than with a subject-centered approach to problem solving. It would be naive to suggest that memorization and rote practice should be ruled out. However, they are not stressed as primary learning techniques. The assertion is that interest in an intellectual activity will generate all the practice needed for learning. (See the Progressivist Class Activity box on page 400.)

Progressivism and Democracy. A tenet of progressivism is that the school, to become an important social institution, must be assigned the task of improving our way of life. To this end, experimentalism is deemed a working model of democracy. Freedom is explicit in a democracy, so it must be explicit in our schools. Certainly, freedom—rather than being a haphazard release of free will— must be organized to have meaning. Organized freedom permits each member of the school society to share in decisions, and experiences must be shared by all to ensure that the decisions are meaningful. Pupil-teacher planning is the key by which democracy in classrooms is realized and is the process that gives some freedom to students, as well as teachers, in deciding what is studied. For example, the teacher might ask students to watch a film about an issue of interest and have them list questions about the issue that were not answered by the film but that they would like to investigate. Student questions can then be analyzed by students and the teacher and refined for research. Such questions can become the basis for an inquiry and problem-solving unit of study. However, even if pupil-teacher planning is not highlighted as a specific activity, any experimentalist lesson allows students to give some of their own input in ways that influence the direction of the lesson. In that sense, progressivist lessons always involve pupil-teacher planning. For instance, asking students to make statements about life in 1908, using reprint pages from 1908 catalogues as their information source, allows students to focus on any items from the catalogues *they* choose—not items determined by the teacher.

The learner is seen as an experiencing, thinking, exploring individual. Progressivism exposes the learner to the subject matter of social experiences, social studies, projects, problems, and experiments that, when studied by the scientific method, will result in functional knowledge from all subjects. Books are regarded as tools to be used in learning rather than as sources of indisputable knowledge.

PROGRESSIVIST CLASS ACTIVITY

Ms. Long's second graders read "Recipe for a Hippopotamus Sandwich" from *Where the Sidewalk Ends: Poems and Drawings of Shel Silverstein* (New York: Harper and Row, 1974). Each student was asked to draw a picture of the hippopotamus sandwich. For homework, all class members were told to read the poem to someone, show the picture, and then tell about the person's reaction on the following day.[5]

In the progressivist class activity the nature of the learner is *active*, the nature of the subject matter is *structured*, the use of the subject matter is *cognitive*, and the behavior trend is toward *divergent thinking*.

Progressivism and Socialization.   Many people believe that the socialization aspect is the most valuable aspect of the movement. In this way, progressivism represents the leading edge of our culture and teaches us how to manage change. However, progressivism is criticized for placing so much stress on the processes of education that the ends are neglected. Its severest critics contend that it has little personal commitment to anything—producing many graduates who are uncommitted and who are content to drift through life. Progressivists counter by stating that their educational view is relatively young and therefore accepts criticism as an expected occurrence when trial-and-error methods are a part of the scientific method. The advent of progressivism as a counterview to the more traditional educational views provided exciting discussions that continue among thinkers in education.

Constructivism: A Progressivist Epistemology.   **Constructivism** is an educational theory that emphasizes hands-on, activity-based teaching and learning. Recently, the American Psychological Association (APA) has encouraged teachers to reconsider the manner in which they view teaching. The APA contends that students are active learners who should be given opportunities to develop their own frames of thought. Teaching techniques should include a variety of different learning activities during which students are free to infer and discover their own answers to important questions. Teachers need to spend time designing these learning situations rather than lecturing. Learning is considered the active framing of personal meaning (by the learner) rather than framing someone else's meaning (which belongs to the teacher).

Such a view of teaching is compatible with the tenets of progressivism and has profound ramifications for the school curriculum. If students are to be encouraged to answer their own questions and develop their own thinking frame, the curriculum needs to be reconceptualized. Constructivist theorists encourage the development of critical thinking and the understanding of big ideas rather than the mastery of factual information. They contend that students who have a sound understanding of important principles that were developed through their own critical thinking will be better prepared for the complex, technological world.

CASE STUDY	AUTHENTIC SCHOOL TESTING: VALUES ON THE LOOSE

*f*or the past decade California has tried to improve its public schools by revising textbooks, recruiting quality educators, lengthening the school day, and developing alternative paths to a high school degree. Other states have been dealing with similar issues, but California stands apart because it has consistently responded to problems with more authentic, person-centered solutions. Such an orientation has enabled California educators to generate a variety of creative educational products, some of which have been adopted and implemented in other states. In a very real sense, California has become a key player in the development of student-centered educational reform.

The most recent step in the reform effort was new testing. Under the old system, elementary and high school students simply checked off answers on multiple-choice tests; these are tests of memory and fact acquisition, but hardly of coherent thought. The new assessments, called CLAS (California Learning Assessments System) are essay tests. Students are given data and a fairly long problem, and are asked questions that require independent thinking. There is often a variety of valid solutions, and students are encouraged to use personal experience to clarify their responses. The new tests are meant to assess not only how individual students are doing, but also how each school and school district is performing.

The first CLAS tests were given last year to all public school pupils in the fourth, eighth, and tenth grades. The results from approximately one million pupils showed some strength in writing, but considerable weakness in comprehension and mathematical reasoning. One would think that such tests, like other reforms, would be widely praised as an improvement over multiple choice formats. Yet, such testing reform has been highly contentious. Some parents, including the Traditional Values Coalition, objected that the reading samples in the tests might corrupt their children's moral, ethnic, or cultural views. And the essays were an unwarranted intrusion into private thought; they might reveal the values of pupils or their families, and these were none of the state's business. Parents began demanding the right to keep their children out of the tests, and some districts went to court to plead for an exemption. On June 6, 1994, a Los Angeles superior court ruled that a school could not of its own volition decide to withdraw from tests imposed by state law. The tests stay and schools must administer them. But the state has retreated on several other fronts. In the future, questions such as "How do you feel about this situation?" will not be asked. And the state has already withdrawn extracts from the writings of Alice Walker and Annie Dillard. The governor's education advisor has publicly stated that too many of the extracts reflected inner city street life.

The CLAS controversy has caused California's governor to reconsider his original $33 million infusion into the continued development of such tests. It is unclear whether such an investment is warranted, and the obvious alternatives are not attractive.

1. Should California remove those test items that seem to authentically assess complex situations? Why or why not?
2. Or should the state retreat from this type of focus (at least in its testing materials) and use test items that are more abstract, that do not require a student to build a personal answer? Why or why not?

It may be that the underlying question is not *testing* but the focus of authenticity. Testing has simply clarified the implications of such an educational focus.

Constructionist philosophies emphasize the importance of developing in students a love of learning.

Reconstructionism

Reconstructionism emerged in the 1930s under the leadership of George S. Counts, Harold Rugg, and Theodore Brameld. Reconstructionism recognized that progressivism had made advances beyond essentialism in teacher-pupil relations and teaching methodology. However, progressivism fixated too heavily on the needs of the child and failed to develop long-range goals for society. Spurred by the Great Depression of the 1930s, reconstructionism called for a new social order that would fulfill basic democratic ideals. Advocates believe that people should control institutions and resources and that this could happen if there were an international democracy of world government.

Critical Pedagogy: A Reconstructionist Curriculum. An education for a reconstructed society would require that students be taught to critically analyze world events, explore controversial issues, and develop a vision for a new and better world. Teachers would critically examine cultural heritages, explore controversial issues, provide a vision for a new and better world, and enlist students' efforts to promote programs of cultural renewal. Although teachers would attempt to convince students of the validity of such democratic goals, they would employ democratic procedures in doing so. (See the Reconstructionist Class Activity box.)

A contemporary version of reconstructionism is rooted in the work of Henry Giroux, who views schools as vehicles for social change. He calls teachers to be transformative intellectuals and wants them to participate in creating a new society. Schools should practice **critical pedagogy**, which unites theory and practice as it provides students with the critical thinking tools to be change agents.[6]

Reconstructionism and World Reformation. A persistent theme of reconstructionism is that public education should be the direct instrument of world reformation. As a logical extension of experimentalism, reconstructionism accepts the concept that the essence of learning is the actual experience of learning. Reconstructionism espouses a theory of social welfare that can effectively prepare learners to deal with the great crises of our time—war, inflation, rapid technological changes, depression. From the experiences of World War I, the Great Depression, and World War II, reconstructionist educators believe that the total educational effort must be seen within a social context.

As was indicated earlier, John Dewey had an immense influence on progressivism. Dewey also made major contributions to reconstructionist philosophy with his efforts to define the individual as an entity within a social context. Reconstructionists go further in stressing that individuals as entities within a social context are urged to engage in specific reform activity. Classroom teachers tend to use affective emphases and moral dilemmas in directing attention toward social reform.

RECONSTRUCTIONIST CLASS ACTIVITY

Mr. Ragland asked his second graders to look at a cartoon that pictured a well-dressed man and woman in an automobile pulled by a team of two horses. The highway they were traveling along passed through rolling farmland with uncrowded meadows, trees, and clear skies in the background. He led a discussion based on the following questions:

1. What is happening in this picture?
2. Do you like what is happening in the picture? Why or why not?
3. What does it say about the way you may be living when you grow up?
4. Are you happy or unhappy about what you have described for your life as an adult?
5. How can we get people to use less gasoline now?
6. What if we could keep companies from making and selling cars that could not travel at least forty miles on one gallon of gasoline? How could we work to get a law passed to do this?[7]

In this reconstructionist class activity the nature of the learner is *active,* the nature of the subject matter is *structured,* the use of the subject matter is *affective,* and the behavior trend is toward *divergent thinking.*

Humanism

Humanism is an educational approach that is rooted in writings of Rousseau and the ideas of existentialism. Jean Jacques Rousseau (1712–1778), the father of

Relevant Research

The Use of Ill-Structured Problems

For decades there has been a great deal of research surrounding the use of problems as a teaching strategy. Recently, Howard Barrows began using case studies about patients to prepare medical students for their internships. The case studies were based on the actual medical records of patients and the studies were organized around a carefully designed problem statement called an *ill-structured problem*. Ill-structured problems are questions surrounding a series of situations that have multiple solution paths. During such a problem-solving experience, medical teachers focus on the reasoning that medical students employ more than the correct diagnosis. Dr. Barrows and other medical doctors contend that it is more important to instruct medical students in critical thinking than it is to have students memorize a lot of material.

Elementary and secondary teachers have begun to use ill-structured problems. To date, the research has shown that students tend to be more motivated, more involved in learning, and more focused on the implications that learning has for society. On the other hand, data on the long-term effects on student achievement are not available. In addition, allowing students to pursue ill-structured problems can be risky. Students may develop controversial answers to some of the real problems that they encounter. Community members may find it difficult to respond to these answers; they may even disagree with the answers students employ.

If problem-based learning is going to find a place in American schools, teachers must be willing to allow students to pursue their interests, even if it means taking students beyond the confines of the curriculum. How do teachers determine when it is worthwhile to test those curricular boundaries?

Sources: H. Barrows. *How to Design a Problem-Based Learning Curriculum in the Pre-Clinical Years.* New York: Springer-Verlag, 1985.
J. O'Neil. *Rx for better thinkers: problem-based learning.* ASCD Update, Alexandria, Virginia, 1992.
W. S. Stepien, S. Gallagher, and D. Workman. "Problem-Based Learning for Traditional and Interdisciplinary Classrooms." Aurora, IL: Illinois Mathematics and Science Academy.

Romanticism, believed that the child entered the world not as a blank slate but with certain innate qualities and tendencies. In the opening sentence of *Émile,* Rousseau's famous treatise on education, he states that "God makes all things good; man meddles with them and they become evil."[8] Thus Rousseau believed in basic goodness at birth. He also believed that humans are born free but become enslaved by institutions. Humanistic education mingles some of these ideas from Rousseau with the basic ideas of existentialism.

Humanism is an educational theory that is concerned with enhancing the innate goodness of the individual. It rejects a group-oriented educational system and seeks ways to enhance the individual development of the student. Humanism adopts many of these ideas from Rousseau and mingles the ideas of existentialism to form an educational theory. (See the Humanist Class Activity box.)

Humanists believe that most schools de-emphasize the individual and the relationship between the teacher and the student. Humanists claim that as educators attempt to predict behavior of students, they turn individuals into objects to be measured. According to the humanist, education should be a process of developing a free, self-actualizing person, centered on the feelings of the student. Therefore, education does not start with great ideas, the world, or with humankind, but with the individual self.

Humanistic Curriculum. Since the goal of humanism is a completely autonomous person, education should be without coercion or prescription. Students should be active and encouraged to make their own choices. The teacher who follows humanistic theory emphasizes learning situations in which each student makes choices. Instruction and assessment are based on student interest, abilities, and needs. Students determine the rules that will govern classroom life, and they make choices about the books to read or exercises to complete.

Humanists honor divergent thinking so completely that they delay giving their own personal opinions and do not attempt to persuade students to particular points of view. Even though they emphasize the affective and thereby may make students feel a certain urgency about issues, it is always left to the individual student to decide when to take a stand, what kind of stand to take, whether a cause merits actions, and if so, what kind of action.

Humanistic School Environments. From the 1960s to the present, the influence of humanism can be identified with various creative programs and written materials. A. S. Neill proposes a "radical approach to child rearing" in his book *Summerhill.*[9] Charles E. Silberman, in his *Crisis in the Classroom*, calls for remaking American education to provide for greater consideration of the individual. Various textbooks discuss issues like the open-access curriculum, nongraded instruction, and multiage grouping, each of which attends to the uniqueness of the learner. Educators are now making various attempts in their school programs to individualize education. Block scheduling permits flexibility for students to arrange classes of their choice. Free schools, storefront schools, schools without walls, and area vocational centers provide alternatives to traditional schools. Educational programs that treat the needs of the individual are usually more costly per pupil than the traditional group-centered programs. Consequently, as taxpayer demands for accountability mount, individualized programs are often brought under unit-cost scrutiny. Nonetheless, growing numbers of educators are willing to defend increased expenditures to meet the needs of the individual learner within the instructional programs of the schools.

HUMANIST CLASS ACTIVITY

Ms. Fenway wanted her ninth graders to think about the effectiveness of television and radio advertising. She asked students to write down any five slogans or "jingles" they could remember and the products advertised. Ms. Fenway selected from their items at random and tested the class. She read each slogan, and class members had to provide answers. The test was corrected in class by the students, who were very surprised that the grading scale was reversed. Those who had all correct answers received Fs, and those who had only one correct answer received As. When asked why she had reversed the grades, Ms. Fenway responded, "Why do you think advertising is so effective?" She asked whether students resented some companies' selling tactics. Then she told students to help her make a list of questions to ask themselves in order to avoid spending money in ways they might later regret. She also asked for specific examples of spending money for items they later wished they had not bought.[10]

In this humanist class activity the nature of the learner is *active*, the nature of the subject matter is *structured*, the use of the subject matter is *affective*, and the behavior trend is toward *divergent thinking*.

Global Perspectives: Looking beyond the Boundaries. Throughout this chapter, educational theories have been represented as consistent sets of

PROFESSIONAL DILEMMA

Should I Use Homogeneous or Heterogeneous Ability Grouping?

The issue of how to group students for instruction can be very controversial. Some propose homogeneous grouping and others argue for heterogeneous grouping. Homogeneous ability grouping is a practice that seems to have merit. Permitting students who require the same level of instruction to be clustered in a single setting makes planning and resource allocation much easier. Such grouping patterns permit students to receive instruction that is tied to their specific needs since they are with others who need the same information or skill development.

Those who oppose homogeneous ability grouping contend that labeling students and placing them in similar ability groups based on their academic skill sets up structures that often inhibit future growth and development. Both teachers and parents begin to view students according to these labels and, once tracked by ability, students seldom break out of the initial labels assigned at an early age. These individuals call for multi-ability or heterogeneous grouping. They believe that having students from a variety of backgrounds and ability levels work together is more in keeping with a democratic society. Furthermore, such multi-ability grouping permits students to more easily help one another, fostering cooperativeness and caring among those from different backgrounds. Indeed, opponents of tracking programs have pointed to the disproportionate number of minority and low-income students who seem to comprise the lower-level groups.

- List other pros and cons of homogeneous ability grouping that you can think of. List other pros and cons of heterogeneous ability grouping.

- Should one type of grouping be used in all instructional settings or circumstances, or should the types of grouping be varied according to task and context?

ideas linked logically together. The importance of such categorization is strongly related to the types of writings that were part and parcel of European thinkers from the eighteenth and nineteenth centuries. It is no surprise that current educational theories in the United States tend to display such clear sets of distinctions since, in large part, immigrants during these years came from Germany, Poland, Ireland, Scandinavia, England, France, Italy, and Switzerland. The last half of the twentieth century has expanded this European focus. Faster and better communication, the opening of once-closed societies, and increased interdependence has permitted differing thinking schemes to intermesh and at times conflict with one another.

Such clashes, although uncomfortable, assist in breaking or at least readjusting the limitations of categorical boundaries. The comfort of such categories can stagnate and imprison. Relying on neat sets of proven ideas provides a set of solutions. These solutions are limited by the original thinking schemes that generated them. Calling into question these categories of thought cannot be easily achieved without the infusion of other types of thinking. The influx of Asian, African, and other types of thinking are especially helpful in breaking down the rigidity of thought boundaries because many of the thinking schemes from these cultures do not require such rigid boundary sets. These flexible thinking schemes provide a different type of cohesion than that of strict logical distinctions.

Summary and Implications

This chapter provided an overview of six leading educational views utilized in part or entirely by teachers in the American schools. While one's ultimate teaching style might not be completely committed to perennialism, essentialism, behaviorism, progressivism, reconstructionism, or humanism, the basic descriptions of those views should be helpful in identifying several preferences. An individual's preferences are compatible with, if not formulated by, his or her personality. The extent to which one's teaching practices fit one's personality, and vice versa, is related to effective teaching.

Whether or not the teacher preparation program at your college or university contains formal coursework in classical or educational philosophy, we encourage you to expand your study in this area so that you may extract from the acquired knowledge meaningful beliefs to guide you in identifying preferences and methods for assisting your students.

Some classroom teachers continue to be skeptical about educational theory and proponents of theory as a basis for practice. Yet new theories about educating children continue to proliferate, while the older beliefs remain strong in today's schools. Chapter 14 presented digests of the structure and thoughts associated with selected classical philosophies. This chapter illustrated the relationship of current educational views to the classical philosophies, but described the educational views in terms of the learner, subject matter orientation, and authoritarian/nonauthoritarian tendencies. The next chapter will help you to understand how to utilize philosophy to become a better teacher.

Discussion Questions

1. What were the characteristics and behaviors of one of your favorite teachers who was authoritarian toward the students? Of a favorite teacher who was nonauthoritarian toward the students?

2. When might a teacher focus on personalized situations involving such things as death or injustice to stimulate student learning? How would such a strategy relate to the back-to-basics expectations of our schools?

3. The concept of reinforcement is very influential on the teacher practices of behaviorists. How would you use positive reinforcers and negative reinforcers while teaching your subject area concentration?

4. Experienced teachers often advise a beginning teacher: "Be firm with the students and let them know at the beginning how you intend to teach your classes." Is this advice good or bad? Discuss the pros and cons of such a procedure.

5. Humanism rules out some of the conventional notions about educating youth. Emphasis is given to the development of the individual rather than to the structure of a curriculum. What implications does humanism have for grouping students?

Journal/Portfolio Development

1. Schools are being challenged to develop students who can achieve in a complex business world. Interview business leaders from two different companies in order to determine the importance of ethics in the operations of the businesses. Determine the extent to which the business leaders' values were influenced by teachers. List recommendations for teachers made by the business leaders. Describe a teaching approach that responds to these recommendations.

2. Describe the teaching method and classroom environment that you believe is most effective for you as a learner. Identify the educational theory or theories that would encourage the teaching method and environment that you have selected. Create a graphic that visually represents your own theory of teaching and learning.

School-Based Experiences

1. This chapter contains a number of special features that give examples of classroom activities typically associated with various educational theories. As you work in the schools, take this book (or photocopies of the class activity features) with you and see whether you can determine which theory various teachers that you observe seem to be reflecting. Having done so, decide which educational theory you subscribe to and determine whether your own classroom activity is consistent with that typically associated with your personal educational philosophy.

2. Set up several interviews with teachers who organize their classrooms and teaching materials differently. Using probing questions, try to uncover the educational theory or theories that account for the differing teaching approaches.

Notes

1. Lloyd Duck, *Instructor's Manual for Teaching with Charisma.* Boston: Allyn and Bacon, 1981, Item 4, 53–54.
2. Lloyd Duck, Item A, 40.
3. Charles H. Wolfgang and Carl D. Glickman. *Solving Discipline Problems: Strategies for Classroom Teachers.* Boston: Allyn and Bacon, 1980, 121.
4. John Dewey, *Democracy and Education.* New York: Macmillan, 1916, 1–9.
5. Lloyd Duck, Item D, 41.
6. Henry A. Giroux, "Teachers as Transformative Intellectuals," *Social Education 49* (1985): 376–379.
7. Lloyd Duck, Item N, 47–48.
8. Jean Jacques Rousseau, *Émile,* trans. Alan Bloom. New York: Basic Books, 1979.
9. A. S. Neill, *Summerhill.* New York: Hart, 1960.
10. Lloyd Duck, Item C, 50–51.

Bibliography

Ackerly, Robert L. *The Reasonable Exercise of Authority.* Washington, DC: National Association of Secondary School Principals, 1969.

Bagley, William C. "An Essentialist's Platform for the Advancement of American Education." *Educational Administration and Supervision 24* (April 1938): 241–256.

Barrows, H. *How to Design a Problem-Based Learning Curriculum in the Pre-Clinical Years.* New York: Springer-Verlag, 1985.

Brameld, Theodore. *Patterns of Educational Philosophy.* New York: Holt, Rinehart and Winston, 1971.

Bricker, David C. *Classroom Life As Civic Education.* New York: Teachers College Press, 1989.

Lauderdale, William B. *Progressive Education: Lessons from Three Schools.* Phi Delta Kappa Fastback No. 166. Bloomington, IN: Phi Delta Kappa, 1981.

Morris, Van Cleve, and Pai, Young. *Philosophy and the American School.* 2nd ed. Boston: Houghton Mifflin, 1976.

O'Neil, J. *RX for Better Thinkers: Problem-Based Learning.* Alexandria, VA: ASCD Update, 1992.

Rich, John Martin. *Innovations in Education: Reformers and Their Critics.* Boston: Allyn and Bacon, 1985.

Rothman, Robert. "Standards Challenged in New Hampshire." *Education Week* (11 February 1987): 11.

Sizer, Theodore R. *Horace's Compromise: The Dilemma of the American High School.* Boston: Houghton-Mifflin, 1985.

Skinner, B. F. "Programmed Instruction Revisited." *Phi Delta Kappan* (October 1986): 103–110.

Stepien, W. S., Gallagher, S., and Workman, D. Problem-Based Learning for Traditional and Interdiscipli-nary Classrooms. Aurora, IL: Illinois Mathematics and Science Academy, 1992.

Strike, Kenneth A., and Soltis, Jonas F. *The Ethics of Teaching.* New York: Teachers College Press, 1985.

Wolfgang, Charles H., and Glickman, Carl D. *Solving Discipline Problems: Strategies for Classroom Teachers.* Boston: Allyn and Bacon, 1980.

Building an Educational Philosophy

Focus Questions

1. What does it mean to be an educational leader? In what ways could you be a leader during your first teaching assignment?

2. How do a teacher's instructional methods reflect an educational philosophy?

3. How does the organization of desks and tables in a classroom reflect an educational philosophy?

4. Why is it important for you to understand the philosophical reasoning behind your intended discipline practices?

5. During a job interview, what will you say when you are asked to state your philosophy of education?

Key Terms and Concepts

Adaptation: The promotion of a stable climate in schools so that students can attain an unbiased picture of the changes that occur in society.

Change agent: A role that emphasizes the responsibility for persons to actively participate in society.

Classroom organization: A multifaceted dimension of teaching that includes the content, method, and values that infuse the classroom environment, planning, and discipline practices.

Control theory: A theory of discipline that contends that we choose most of our behaviors to gain control of people or ourselves.

Dialectic: The conflict that occurs when opposing ideas are encountered; in change theory this conflict is the one between individual needs and societal needs.

Motivation: Internal emotion, desire, or impulse acting as an incitement to action.

Vision: A vision is a mental construction that synthesizes and clarifies what you value or consider to be of most worth.

*E*xtensive surveys of modern views of learning—as expressed in philosophy, psychology, and education journals and studies—reveal a seemingly endless and divergent range of views. Therefore, today's classroom teachers must identify their own beliefs about educating young people. Although labeling the classroom practice of any one teacher is not easy, we recommend that you, as a prospective teacher, carefully identify a personal set of operational principles with regard to classroom techniques. Whether your operational principles are drawn from the brief descriptions in this book or elsewhere, you should strive for consistent teaching behavior within the framework of sound principles—that is, behavior based on your personal philosophy of education. The previous two chapters introduced you to the philosophies from which modern educational theories have been derived. This chapter now helps you to identify your role as a teacher in society and to clarify meaningful practices for your classroom.

Educational trends, which are often identified by terms such as "the back-to-basics movement," are related to certain philosophies of education. The back-to-basics movement centers on subject matter and is clearly in the realms of essentialism and perennialism, whereas the concepts of "free schools" and "open education" are experience-based and focus on student activity as identified in progressivism and existentialism. Figure 16.1 illustrates the association of these primary educational theories with the authoritarian view, which stresses convergent thinking, and the nonauthoritarian view, which stresses divergent thinking. Note that the terms *authoritarian* and *nonauthoritarian* are meant to provide an overall view with regard to the student and subject matter and not to imply strict or permissive classroom management.

Using Philosophy to Examine Schools and Society

Schools play a role within the larger society. This role is determined by a number of factors: the expectations of society's leaders, economic conditions, the ideologies of powerful lobbying groups, and the philosophies of teachers. It is especially important for educators to examine the role of the school in terms of the larger society. If such reflection does not occur, schools will merely reflect the status quo or the needs and desires of a single powerful group.

Teachers as Change Agents

An age-old question regarding the role of schools in society concerns the proper role of the school and the teacher in relation to change. Should teachers be **change agents** or should they re-emphasize eternal truths and cultural positions? This question of change versus transmission of ongoing values has been articulated in a variety or ways.

Change as Adaptation. Isaac L. Kandel (1881–1965) was a leader in the essentialist movement who advocated change as a process of **adaptation**. This approach emphasized the importance of promoting stability and adapting the

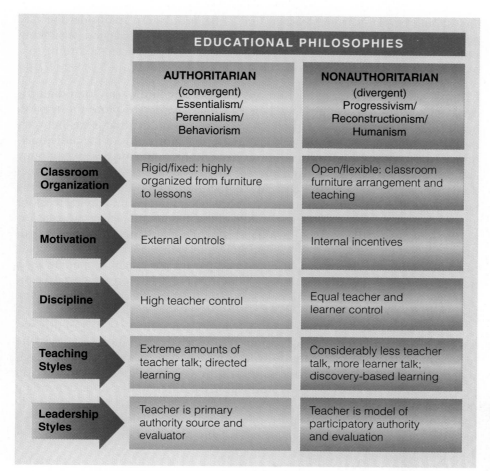

EDUCATIONAL PHILOSOPHIES

	AUTHORITARIAN (convergent) Essentialism/ Perennialism/ Behaviorism	NONAUTHORITARIAN (divergent) Progressivism/ Reconstructionism/ Humanism
Classroom Organization	Rigid/fixed: highly organized from furniture to lessons	Open/flexible: classroom furniture arrangement and teaching
Motivation	External controls	Internal incentives
Discipline	High teacher control	Equal teacher and learner control
Teaching Styles	Extreme amounts of teacher talk; directed learning	Considerably less teacher talk, more learner talk; discovery-based learning
Leadership Styles	Teacher is primary authority source and evaluator	Teacher is model of participatory authority and evaluation

FIGURE 16.1

Authoritarian versus Nonauthoritarian Views of the Classroom

individual to the environment. The school should be a place that provides students with an unbiased picture of the changes that occur in society. Hence, schools cannot educate for a new social order nor should teachers use the classroom to promote doctrine. Change occurs first in society. Schools follow the lead.[1]

Change as Rational Process. John Dewey believed school had a part in social change. He contended that change continually occurred, often without a clearly defined direction. Schools need to assume a leadership role in this change because educators have the time to study newer scientific and cultural forces, estimate the direction and outcome, and determine which changes were or were not beneficial. Schools need to provide an environment in which students can learn these analytic skills and participate in helping society determine a direction that is meaningful and of most worth.[2]

Change as Reconstruction. The reconstructionist Theodore Brameld contended that every educational system should help diagnose the causes of world problems. Schools need to do more than assess scientific and technological change;

they should be places where teachers and students alike can reconsider the very purpose of schooling and study new ways of formulating goals and organizing subject matter. Schools and society alike need to be reconstructed according to a set of human goals based on cross-cultural, universal values.[3]

Change as Dialectic. Samuel Bowles and Herbert Gintis[4] call for a **dialectical** humanism through which teachers can help students explore the tension between the individual and society. They identify a conflict that exists between the reproductive needs of society and the self-actualizing needs of the individual. Bowles and Gintis claim that institutions like schools and churches, peer groups and town meetings are places that attempt to mediate this tension between freedom of the individual and responsibility for the community. The problem schools face is that they are often unaware that they are mediating this underlying tension, and teachers are often caught in the middle of the dilemma. Teachers are asked to respond to the unique needs of the individual while simultaneously answering to the conflicting needs of society. Bowles and Gintis call teachers to develop a participatory democracy in which all interested parties are taught to pursue their interests and resolve conflicts rationally. Educators must develop a dialectical educational philosophy that seeks a new synthesis between the individual and the community.

As a teacher, you become part of the educational system. As part of this system, you will be asked to make decisions regarding student outcomes, discipline procedures, instructional methodologies, and assessment methods. Your decisions regarding these educational issues will be greatly influenced by how you perceive teachers as change agents. You will make different decisions depending on whether you determine that teachers need to help schools adapt, rationally change the social order, reconstruct, or participate in a dialectic. Your task is to carefully consider each of these change paradigms and select the one that matches your personal system of beliefs.

Teachers may find that their own philosophies of teaching do not match those of the school where they teach.

Teachers as Leaders

Whether teachers espouse this idea or not, they serve as leaders for their students. Evidence of this can be found in the testimonials that are offered by former students when they have become adults. Most students, whether they have achieved graduate degrees or have followed vocational pursuits immediately after high school, report remembering teachers who had a personal impact on their lives. These students will usually discuss the leadership and modeling behaviors of the teachers they remember.

The idea of teachers as leaders suggests that the new teacher should be aware of the need to develop a beginning repertoire that builds strong leadership qualities to which students may look for guidance during their developmental years. These leadership qualities—and the practice of them—are highly dependent on the classroom philosophy that the new teacher puts into practice. Some beginning concepts for teacher leadership are vision, modeling behaviors, and use of power.

Vision. Classroom leadership behaviors begin with a teacher having vision and the intent to actualize that vision for the students. How a teacher actually puts that vision into practice depends wholly on the teacher's philosophical practices. A **vision** is a mental construct that synthesizes and clarifies what you value or consider to be of most worth. The clearer the vision or mental picture, the easier it is for leaders to make decisions or persuade or influence others. Formulating a vision requires reflection concerning what you believe about truth, beauty, justice, and equality. It is important to consider these issues and formulate a vision about the way schools and classrooms should be organized and implemented.

Sheive and Schoenbeit offer five steps that leaders take to put their visions into actions:[5]

1. Value your vision.
2. Be reflective and plan a course of action.
3. Articulate the vision to colleagues.
4. Develop a planning and action stage.
5. Have students become partners in the vision.

Teachers serve as leaders for their students.

Cooperative learning situations provide an alternative method for promoting student learning.

If teachers reflect on their vision, they can plan the course of action they need to use with their learners. Articulation provides teachers with an opportunity to share their vision with colleagues. In-service or staff development sessions are excellent times to articulate a classroom vision. Visions require a planning stage and an action stage if they are to become a reality. Planning and action stages should involve the students who are intended to be the receivers of this vision. For example, if a teacher wishes students to be reflective in their learning environment, then the teacher needs to help the students see that vision and become partners in the planning. The teacher may engage the students in free and open discussions of the vision and its importance to the learning environment in the classroom.

Modeling. If teachers hold certain expectations of learner behaviors in the classroom, then it is imperative that they engage in modeling those behaviors with the students. If the classroom teacher is rigid and fixed in his or her classroom practices and presents an authoritarian atmosphere, then the students will probably respond in a similar fashion. On the other hand, if the teacher provides a more democratic classroom, the students will respond similarly in their classroom encounters. We would caution that a laissez-faire environment will probably produce a classroom with little or no direction on the part of the learner. Teachers should consider the modeling effect of leadership on the classroom environment and practice it on the basis of their accepted philosophy of the classroom.

Power. The concept of power in the classroom should not be considered good or bad. Power by itself has no value structure. The use of power, however, gives it a good, poor, or bad image. The nature of the teaching position entrusts a teacher with power. How a teacher uses power in the classroom or in the school building is wholly determined by the classroom philosophy the teacher wishes to project. All leaders have power that is associated with their position, but the successful leader is judicious in its use.

Teaching styles can be classified into two different uses of power: teacher dominant and learner supportive. Past and present practices in the school tend to lean heavily on the teacher-dominant style. Therefore, although many teachers in training study both categories of teaching styles, they tend to see only one major type in practice when they visit schools. We suggest that you continually study both major categories so that either can be applied as needed on the basis of classroom objectives for students and the teacher's classroom philosophy.

Teacher-dominant teaching styles are based on an authoritarian construct for the classroom. Learners are not expected to be active verbally in the learning process, but are generally expected to be receivers and practicing users of teacher-given information. Learning is very convergent. It is selected and given to the learner in the particular way in which the teacher wishes the student to acquire it.

CASE STUDY — HELPING THE FEMALES: A FORM OF SEGREGATION?

In 1994, the Illinois Mathematics and Science Academy (IMSA) completed an intensive examination of the research surrounding the success of females in higher mathematics and science. The results were astounding. Consistently, descriptive studies indicated that females dropped out or did not even attempt higher-level mathematics and science courses in high school and college. Although the research indicated that females could achieve in these courses, able female students generally refrained from the effort. The female students who did enroll in advanced science and mathematics classes tended to participate less and to drop out of these courses more often than males. Since IMSA is committed to increasing participation in science and mathematics, the faculty examined its own record. They discovered that considerably more of IMSA's female graduates majored in mathematics and science than from other high schools. This was a relief, but the faculty also discovered that while at IMSA, a significantly smaller number of females chose advanced physics electives compared to males.

Buoyed by a philosophy of equal access for all students, IMSA faculty and staff developed an exploratory research study. The physics teachers decided to conduct an all-female section of Calculus-based physics. The teachers contended that setting up such a segregated setting would assist them in clarifying what types of teaching strategies and classroom environmental characteristics were supportive of adolescent female learning. The exploratory study was designed, and twenty-one females volunteered to participate in the all-female section of Calculus-based physics for one semester.

The results of the study were generally positive. The results indicated that the all-female setting, in conjunction with a combination of hands-on teaching methods, open-ended questioning, and a cooperative learning environment, seemed to help the female students achieve and prompted them to sign up for another advanced physics course. Since the intention of this study was to implement the teaching, questioning, and environment findings in a coeducational classroom, the physics teachers used these teaching and environmental setting results in coeducational settings in subsequent semesters. However, the results have not been as powerful as they were in the coeducational setting.

Puzzled by this lack of transfer, the IMSA faculty is struggling to make sense of the entire effort. Since the original study did not completely control for a variety of factors, additional studies are being considered. It is possible, however, that these findings are only valid in an all-female setting. Such a finding is unacceptable within the context of an integrated society. Laws ban such segregation in public school settings.

1. What are the philosophical implications of this effort?
2. What is the meaning of educational equality for all?
3. How does diversity relate to equality?
4. Should one refrain from investigations that might uncover solutions that conflict with a philosophy?

Learner-supportive teaching styles view the learner as someone who is verbally active and who seeks divergence in learning. Learner-supportive teaching styles encourage the active participation of the learner in exploring learning and helping to determine the extent to which the learner will engage in alternatives. These teaching styles tend to recognize differences in learning, individual interests, and higher-order learning.

Using Philosophy in the Classroom

How you manage your classroom and the content, method, and values you stress will be based on your personal view of the proper role of the teacher in society. A classroom philosophy must incorporate this larger societal view into other views that relate to student learning and behavior in the classroom. A teacher's practices in the classroom reflect his or her personal philosophy. The best goal for beginning educators is to become comfortable with a variety of classroom practices that address the needs of learners. It is not a matter of selecting one methodology over another but rather of understanding these different approaches and using them responsibly. We believe that a sound preparation for teaching addresses the need to develop a workable classroom philosophy—one that incorporates the larger role of teaching in a complex society as well as the micro role of relating to students in the classroom setting.

Classroom Organization

All teachers must be able to organize the classroom in such a way that it is conducive to teaching and learning. In fact, many school principals are quick to assert that the easiest way to predict the success of a beginning teacher is to determine his or her ability to organize the classroom. A common misconception is that good classroom organization means maintaining a controlled atmosphere and refusing to allow any behavior that even looks like it is ungoverned or unplanned. Actually **classroom organization** is a multifaced dimension of teaching that includes the content, methods, and values that infuse the classroom environment. It is a dimension of teaching that requires analysis and selection similar to that used in the identification of a preferred teaching philosophy. Figure 16.1 on page 413 shows how closely one's teaching philosophy impacts the different components of classroom organization.

Lesson Planning.   Careful lesson planning is mandatory if effective teaching and learning are to follow. If the learners are considered to be passive, the lesson plan may emphasize absorbing the factual content of the subject matter. Adherents of teaching styles that consider the learners to be active participants (nonauthoritarian) would tend to emphasize processes and skills to be mastered and view the factual content of the subject matter as important but variable.

Regardless of the expectation for the learner, active or passive, the teacher needs to plan sound lessons. Every lesson should be built from a basic set of general objectives that correspond to the overall goals of the school district. This is not to suggest that every third-grade classroom in a school district should have the same daily learning objectives for the students. Daily lesson objectives can vary from classroom to classroom depending on the particular needs of the students being served. However, if those daily teaching objectives are closely related to the overall objectives of the school district, then cross-district learning will reflect the school district's overall goals.

Lessons should be tied to some form of teaching units. These units should be planned in detail to include suggestions for teaching the lessons, types of materials to be used, and specific plans for evaluation. Initially, these are all philosophic questions for the classroom teacher. How the teacher approaches these questions is very telling about his or her classroom philosophy.

The Physical Environment. The mere arrangement of classroom furniture and the use of classroom materials may be predicated on the teacher's perception of the learners as passive or active. Traditionally, the classroom has tended to be arranged in rows and columns at the elementary and secondary levels of schooling. This type of classroom arrangement has often been thought to be the best for classroom control and supervision. Often, however, the elementary teacher will rearrange the classroom into a series of small circles for special groupings in reading, mathematics, and other special subjects.

The nonauthoritarian philosophical view tends to support more open classrooms. The teacher intends learning for the students to be divergent in nature, and the student is expected to be more active in the learning process. This is not to suggest that one type of classroom arrangement is better than another or that one philosophy is superior to another, but we do suggest that the teacher in training examine classroom philosophy as it relates to the physical environment for learning.

Student Assessment. In assessing student progress and assigning grades, most teachers use a variety of techniques including examinations, term papers, project reports, group discussions, performance assessments, and various other tools. If the subject matter is treated as a bundle of information, teacher-made tests would tend to seek isolated facts and concepts as "right" answers, suggesting emphasis on convergent thinking. However, if the subject matter is treated as big ideas applicable to problem solving so as to emphasize processes and skills to arrive at several "right" answers, teacher-made tests would tend to allow for divergent thinking.

How you develop your classroom philosophy will also dictate the emphasis you place on a student's academic performance.

Relevant Research

Teaching Cooperation

Cooperative learning is an increasingly popular approach to instruction. In cooperative learning, students work in small groups to help one another master academic material. The approach encourages teachers and students to view learning as a community process; learning is innately social and teachers as well as students depend on each other in order to create personal meaning. Studies that investigate the pros and cons of using cooperative learning techniques in the classroom have begun to emerge. Small-scale laboratory research on cooperation has a longer history than cooperative learning. This research showed that when people cooperated on different projects, they began to like one another (Slavin, 1977). Research on specific educational applications in cooperative learning began in the 1970s and is now in full swing. Studies seem to indicate that there are positive achievement and social effects if cooperative learning includes both group goals and individual accountability (Slavin, 1983, 1990). That is, groups must be working to achieve some goal or to earn rewards or recognition, and the success of the group must depend on the individual learning of every group member.

As a prospective teacher, you will need to determine how you can structure learning activities that focus on goal achievement and individual learning. One question you will need to answer is: "How does cooperative learning fit in a competitive society?"

Sources: Robert E. Slavin. "Classroom Reward Structure: An Analytical and Practical Review," *Review of Educational Research 47*: 633–650.
Robert E. Slavin. "When Does Cooperative Learning Increase Student Achievement?" *Psychological Bulletin 94*: 429–445.
Robert E. Slavin. *Cooperative Learning: Theory, Research, and Practice.* Englewood Cliffs, New Jersey: Prentice Hall, 1990.

You must decide whether a student is to be compared with his or her peers or with a set of expectations based on individual needs and differences. Generally, teachers who tend to be nonauthoritarian and look for divergence in learning will tend to place less emphasis on group norms. Teachers who favor an authoritarian role for the classroom with a stress on convergence in learning will be more apt to favor student evaluation strategies based upon group norms.

Motivation

The meaning of **motivation** is derived from the word *motive*, which is an emotion, desire, or impulse acting as an incitement to action. This definition of motive has two parts: first it implies that motivation is internal because it relates to emotions, desires, or other internal drives and second, it implies that there is an accompanying external focus on action or behavior. Organizing a learning environment so that it relates to student needs and desires (internal) and also permits active participation in the learning process (external) is important to student motivation.

Many teachers seek to inspire their students to want to learn, rather than simply to memorize information.

Teachers want students to be motivated to do many things: complete homework, be responsible, be life long learners, be on time, have fun, care about others, and become independent. However, it is not always clear how one sets up a classroom environment that ultimately achieves these desired outcomes. For example, if an authoritarian orientation toward teaching is employed where control is primarily in the hands of the teacher, students' motivation may suffer because they recognize that the task of teaching and the responsibility for learning is primarily the teacher's. Even if the teacher tells students that they are responsible for their own learning, students will not be internally motivated. In an authoritarian setting, motivation tends to come in the form of rules and regulations. Students are given clear directions concerning their responsibilities and they are expected to follow these directions since the teacher is in charge. For some students, this clarity of expectations and rules is comfortable. Students achieve because they must; in such a setting the second half of motivation (action) is achieved but not the first (internal desire).

In a learner-dominant setting, the responsibility for learning is primarily borne by the students. The teacher attempts to produce a climate of warmth and mutual respect. Students are encouraged to achieve specific outcomes, but ultimately, they are free to select those that most interest them. In this type of setting, the internal aspect of motivation is achieved in that students select the learning outcomes and processes that interest them; however, the second aspect of motivation (action) is not as clearly achieved in that students act according to their personal desires and these desires do not always match those of the teacher.

As a teacher you should arrange the classroom environment so that it matches your personal philosophy. Your task here is to carefully consider the "sources of power" that best reflect your philosophy of education. As many as five different power sources that relate to five different levels of motivation have been identified.[6] Power can be coercive where the motivation is "to obey." Power can take the form of rewards where the motivation is "to get." Power can be seen as legitimate where motivation takes the form of "respect." Power can be in the form of reverence where motivation is "to cooperate." Finally, power can be knowledge where the motivation is "to understand." Your philosophy of learning could include all of these sources of power. All of them may be necessary at some time or another. On the other hand, it is important to assess how you set up your classroom rules and environment and make certain that they match your personal understanding of where power should lie in the teaching and learning process.

Discipline

The attention given by the national media to disruptive behavior in the classroom has rekindled conflicting views regarding discipline. Polls of parents and teachers alike list discipline among the top issues confronting the schools. The main source of dissatisfaction for nearly two-thirds of today's teachers is the inability to manage students effectively. Teachers also are concerned about the effect disruptive behavior has on learning. The discipline dilemma—stressing more teacher control in the classroom, yet adhering to a more open philosophy that advocates less teacher control—precludes the development of a school discipline policy that would satisfy both views. Depending on the school district's expectations, the teacher may be caught between conflicting demands. Despite the personal philosophy of the teacher, he or she

Teachers may improve disipline in the classroom by involving students in management programs.

must address the wishes of the district when establishing classroom management schemes. The division of views on classroom discipline has inspired numerous books to assist teachers with discipline problems, and many special courses and workshops have been developed to deal with classroom discipline strategies. Since very few beginning teachers are given extensive exposure to discipline strategies in teacher preparation programs, the vast range of alternatives makes it difficult to decide on strategies for teachers who have yet to develop their own styles.

Glickman and Wolfgang have identified three schools of thought along a teacher-student control continuum (Figure 16.2).[7] Noninterventionists hold the view that teachers should not impose their own rules, since students are inherently capable of solving their own problems. Interactionalists suggest that students must learn that the solution to misbehavior is a reciprocal relation between student and teacher. Interventionists believe that teachers must set classroom standards for conduct and give little attention to input from the students.

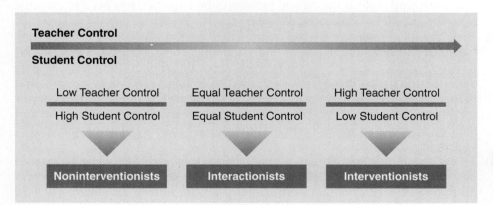

Teacher Control		
Student Control		
Low Teacher Control	Equal Teacher Control	High Teacher Control
High Student Control	Equal Student Control	Low Student Control
Noninterventionists	Interactionists	Interventionists

FIGURE 16.2

Teacher-Student Control Continuum

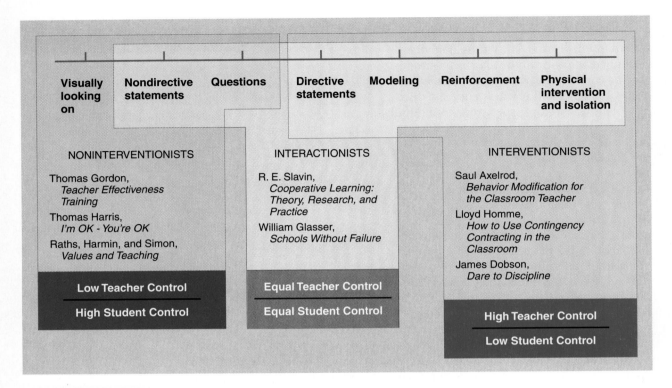

FIGURE 16.3   **Teacher Behavior Continuum**

Beginning teachers are challenged to identify their own beliefs regarding discipline in the classroom in order to keep disruptive behavior at a minimum, thus enhancing the potential for learning as well as for job satisfaction. Where maintenance of discipline is the primary concern, one might choose from among the entire range of possibilities along the Wolfgang-Glickman continuum regardless of one's teaching style preference. Figure 16.3 illustrates how the major theories of classroom management relate in terms of control issues along the teacher-student control continuum. It is the professional responsibility of each classroom teacher to understand how each behavior may be used to support his or her preferred teaching philosophy. As you prepare to be a teacher, you need to examine control principles of classroom discipline.

Control Theory.   The notion of understanding **control theory** as a requisite for classroom discipline practices has been advanced by William Glasser. He suggests that a person's total behavior is composed of feelings, physiology, actions, and thoughts. How a classroom teacher controls these aspects of his or her behavior makes up an operational definition of control theory. Glasser asserts, "Control theory contends that we choose most of our total behaviors to try to gain control of people or ourselves."[8]

As a beginning teacher thinking about classroom discipline, you should recall that it is somewhat natural and human for students not to take responsibility for disrupting class or deviating from some classroom norms. As a matter of fact, teachers also find it difficult to take responsibility for some of their own behavior

Should You Use Authentic Assessments to Grade Students?

There is a growing awareness that students should be assessed using a variety of methods that go beyond multiple-choice and essay examinations. Teachers are being asked to use students' journals, cooperative learning projects, interviews, portfolios, and other methods for assessing what a student can and cannot do. However, there is a debate concerning the appropriateness of using these more "authentic ways of assessing" for grading. The term *assess* comes from a Greek derivative that means to "sit beside oneself." When teachers grade a child, they are not only sitting beside the child, they are also making a value judgement. Is such a value judgement consistent with the notion of assessing one's strengths and weaknesses?

Some educators respond positively to this question of grading authentic assessments. They believe that society values some qualities more than others. Hence, it is appropriate to grade a student's portfolio. Other educators contend that such grading limits a child's creativity; it makes the assessments less authentic because there is an implicit standard that belongs to the teacher. Hence, teachers really are asking students to provide a certain type of portfolio; this makes the portfolio nothing more than a large essay-type test with portfolio entries as the correct answers.

You will need to determine your own answer to this complex dilemma. Should you rely on authentic assessments or merely use them as indicators of what a child knows or can do?

that deviates from the norm. It is usually being upset that causes some action and/or disruption by students and teachers. If you wish to be successful in meeting discipline challenges, you need to accept the totality of control theory. Accepting this means recognizing the elements of feelings, physiology, actions, and thoughts that make up the theory and working with students, counselors, and principals to attempt to adjust total behavior.

Discipline with Dignity.   Richard Curwin and Allen Mendler suggest that it is not enough to simply "control" students. Educators on all levels must help students learn to become decision makers and critical thinkers about their own actions. Their approach, called *Discipline with Dignity*, provides a method to teach students to take responsibility for their own behavior. The approach offers essential skills and strategies for dealing with angry, disruptive behavior while positively affecting the lives of students. The students learn to manage themselves as stress and pressures mount. The program emphasizes prevention by creating a positive classroom environment and sensitive communication. Students are viewed as partners in the process of ensuring positive, productive classroom environments.

Conflict Resolution.   Another approach to discipline, conflict resolution, focuses on the process of teaching students how to recognize problems and then productively solve them. Students are taught to be conflict managers and are trained to deal with difficulties on the playground, in the hallways, and in the classroom. They learn a specific set of skills to guide a discussion about the problem between two offenders. There are a variety of ways to train the student managers, but the underlying benefit is that the students solve their own problems with minimal assistance of adults. Advocates of conflict resolution contend that permitting students to share in the structure and even the enforcement of disci-

Many teachers are successful with personal teaching methods.

pline policies is another way to help them learn to contribute to the school and to the society as a whole.

Rules for Discipline. There is no cookbook formula for establishing discipline rules and procedures for maintaining disciplined classes. There are, however, some general guidelines that will help the beginning teacher to establish some operating rules that will be accepted by students and practiced in the classroom. These guidelines are:

1. Students and teachers need to learn the importance of behavior and communication.
2. Students need to be treated with dignity. Students who are treated with dignity develop strong self-esteem.
3. Teachers need to apply critical thinking skills when creating disciplinary rules or analyzing needed disciplinary action.
4. Teachers need to examine how their actions of a social or instructional nature may have caused misbehavior.

The way the teacher introduces and uses these general principles for establishing rules for discipline will set the tone for classroom interactions, creating an environment that is conducive to learning and that minimizes classroom interruptions.

Classroom discipline strongly reflects the teacher's operating classroom philosophy. As you examine the educational philosophy that wins your interest and support, search for its applications to discipline in your classroom.

Global Perspectives: The World as Classroom. Throughout this chapter, you have been encouraged to examine your beliefs and assumptions in an effort to develop a personal philosophy of education. It is important to consider the limitations that such a philosophy can impose. For example, to what degree does your philosophy incorporate the larger world of thinkers? Does your philosophy affirm or disaffirm varied thinking schemes, varied beliefs, and varied ways of arriving at answers? Relating to our global neighbors is no longer a matter of respecting differences. If we are to truly relate and work collaboratively, our thinking schemes need to intermingle as well. Yet, a personal philosophy implies the development of a cohesive set of views about knowledge and the nature of the world. Balancing this need to intermix with the importance of clarifying an individual point of view is the challenge given us by the world classroom.

Summary and Implications

While your classroom philosophy might not be completely committed to perennialism, essentialism, behaviorism, progressivism, reconstructionism, or humanism, you should be able to apply the characteristics of classroom philosophy discussed in this chapter to help you become comfortable with your own preferences for teaching. Prospective teachers, whether or not they have had educational philosophy coursework in their preparation programs, should find this practical classroom philosophy treatment a useful way to study teaching behaviors to identify trends and preferences related to a teaching style or philosophy. Perennialist, essentialist, and behaviorist teachers encourage students to view the subject matter only as experts in that field view the subject matter. Such teacher behaviors exhibit an authoritarian curriculum trend encouraging convergent thinking. Experimentalists, reconstructionists, and existentialists encourage students to use the subject matter as a means of determining more than one answer to the question at hand. This behavior can be viewed as a nonauthoritarian curriculum trend encouraging divergent thinking.

Remember that there are no perfect teaching styles or teaching methodologies. As a new teacher, you need to know how to minimize the negative effects and weaknesses associated with any particular teaching style. The styles that emphasize convergent thinking tend to reward students for giving an answer that is the exact phrase the teacher wants. Teachers using such methods must be very careful with their responses, or students will not risk participating in discussion unless they are absolutely certain that they have the exact answer. The divergent types of teaching styles may, in contrast, require students to participate in interesting activities but not make them fully aware of why they are participating or what they are learning. If students are not required to justify the generalizations they make and are not made to see that they are learning many facts and skills, they may end up feeling that all answers are so relative that problem-solving processes

are not worthwhile. Teachers who know enough about themselves and their teaching styles to show students how to succeed with both convergent thinking and divergent thinking are well on their way to reaching the ideal of being healthy eclectics.

In addition to understanding and practicing a teaching philosophy, all teachers must be prepared to integrate the several facets of classroom management in a way that is consistent with their teaching philosophy. Strategies for discipline maintenance, necessary to keep the number of problems at a minimum so that learning can occur, are very important for teaching success. Discipline is maintained when there is balancing interaction between teacher control and student participation. There are times, however, when a higher degree of teacher control is more effective.

The implications of this chapter are straightforward. Teachers who enter classrooms not understanding or knowing much about their intended teaching styles, as well as not knowing which classroom organization strategies best serve their philosophies, cannot be successful. We hope that from the material presented you will be able to begin to formulate your own classroom philosophy based on reality, knowledge, and value. Also, you should be able to envision how philosophical concepts carry over into and influence the educational views that are extant in our schools. These tasks are the theoretical, rational part of developing a personal philosophy of education.

Finally, to perceive a philosophy is one thing; to teach according to the philosophy is another. In teaching, one exhibits behavior that is compatible with a personal educational view. As long as this eclecticism serves the pedagogical purposes of the teacher and is a basis for consistent behavior by the teacher in the classroom, learning will take place. However, if eclecticism causes the teacher to change behavior frequently and with no apparent purpose, thus distracting pupils from learning, the teacher should reexamine her or his philosophy.

Discussion Questions

1. What is your vision of democracy in the classroom? To what degree should students be permitted to decide what they will study, when they will study, and how they will study? Why?

2. What characteristics or practices can you identify in a former teacher whom you would label your favorite?

3. Teachers must be able to manage the classroom in such a way that the environment created is con-ducive to teaching and learning. How do you plan to organize your classroom to set up such an environment?

4. Identify some significant beginning classroom practices that a new teacher should try to develop if he or she wants to be judged a successful teacher.

Journal/Portfolio Development

1. Think about the different student seating arrangements in various classrooms. Sketch each seating arrangement and describe the types of student interaction and the types of learning that each seating arrangement supports. Draw a seating arrangement that you prefer, and describe the types of student interaction and learning that it encourages.

2. Design a metaphor for each of the educational theories that you have studied. Then design a metaphor for your personal educational theory and clarify how it compares to the other educational theory metaphors.

School-Based Experiences

1. While you are visiting different classrooms as part of your practicum experiences, catalog the various classroom planning and disciplinary activities that you observe. Following these observations and your recording of practices in real classrooms, classify the various styles that you have observed and identify the classroom philosophy that you feel the teacher was employing. Seek out opportunities to discuss these findings with each of the teachers that you observe.

2. Select a teacher who has a classroom organization approach that matches your own. Set up an interview with the teacher and use probing questions to clarify the underlying reasons the teacher set up the classroom as he or she did.

Notes

1. Isaac L. Kandel, *Conflicting Theories of Education.* New York: Macmillan, 1938, 77–88.

2. John Dewey, "Education and Social Change," *The School Frontier III* (1937): 235–238.

3. Theodore Brameld, "Imperatives for a Reconstructed Philosophy of Education," *School and Society 87* (1959): 18–20.

4. Samuel Bowles and Herbert Gintis, *Schooling in Capitalistic America.* New York: Basic Books, 1975, 18–20.

5. Linda Tinelli Sheive and Marian Beauchamp Schoenbeit, "Vision and the Worklife of Educational Leaders," in *Leadership: Examining the Elusive.* Alexandria, VA: Association for Supervision and Curriculum Development, 1987, 99.

6. R. Schmuck, and P. A. Schmuck. *Group Processes in the Classroom.* William C. Brown, Dubuque, IA: 1983.

7. Carl D. Glickman and Charles H. Wolfgang, "Conflict in the Classroom: An Eclectic Model of Teacher-Child Interaction," *Elementary School Guidance and Counseling 13* (December 1978): 82–87.

8. William Glasser, *Control Theory in the Classroom.* New York: Harper and Row, 1986, 47.

Bibliography

Bloom, Benjamin. "The Search for Methods of Group Instruction," *Educational Leadership 42* (9), (1984): 5.

Cornett, Claudia E. *What You Should Know About Teaching and Learning Styles.* Phi Delta Kappa Fastback No. 191. Bloomington, IN: Phi Delta Kappa, 1983.

Curwin, Richard L., and Mendler, Allen N. *Discipline with Dignity.* Alexandria, VA: Association for Supervision and Curriculum Development, 1988.

Glasser, William. *Control Theory in the Classroom.* New York: Harper & Row, 1986.

Howe, Kenneth R. "A Conceptual Basis for Ethics in Teacher Education." *Journal of Teacher Education* (May–June 1986): 5–11.

Kierstead, Janet, "How Teachers Manage Individual and Small Group Work in Active Classrooms," *Educational Leadership* (October 1986): 22–25.

Schmuck, R. and Schmuck, P. A. *Group Processes in the Classroom.* William C. Brown, Dubuque, IA: 1983.

Slavin, Robert E. "When Does Cooperative Learning Increase Student Achievement?" *Psychological Bulletin 94* (1983): 429–445.

_____. *Cooperative Learning: Theory, Research and Practice.* Englewood Cliffs, NJ: Prentice Hall, 1990.

Part

6 School Programs and Practices

Dreamcatcher

SUSAN RAE BANKS is an Arapahoe Native American from Deer Park, Washington. She received her B.A. in Special Education from Eastern Washington University and her M.Ed. from Gonzaga University. She has been a teacher in regular, special education, and integrated classroom settings working with Native American and non-Native American children. She continues her work with culturally diverse children and their families. When she examined Section VI from the prospectus of the Dreamcatcher legend, she offered:

As an educator who has taught in a variety of settings with individuals from birth to fifty-eight years old, I have experienced the diversity among abilities and needs of students and their families. It is as this textbook tells it. One overarching challenge that I believe new teachers must embrace with our ever-changing society and schools is to take the time to develop and internalize the art of flexibility. The teacher who allows for individual patterns to emerge and develop will become a stronger facilitator of harmony and balance within the learner.

In order for the new teacher to feel confident in allowing for individual patterns to develop, a knowledge base encompassing teaching models, strategies, and practices must be established. In addition, skills in developing and modifying curriculum to fit an individual's learning path in culturally relevant ways is critical. This is especially true when one considers the movement of schools away from teacher-centered environments in favor of student-centered environments. This section of the text provides a solid framework from which a prospective teacher can begin to understand these practices as well as envision future educational changes and challenges.

Throughout this entire text, the issue of diversity among students has been highlighted. The teacher's role is to celebrate this diversity by guiding each student through the educational web, being sensitive to the potential good and bad effects of educational practices. This is as the ancients wished, with the "Dreamcatcher" that is sensitive, trapping dreams that are bad for the sleeper so only the good dreams are guided down the feather to the sleeping one below. Prospective teachers, follow the ways of the "Dreamcatcher" and learn the art of flexibility in gleaning the good practices for schools. In that way the learners you meet will be well served. Then, my grandmothers and their grandmothers will be happy!

School Programs

Focus Questions

1 Why do beginning teachers need to be knowledgeable about issues that affect the curriculum?
2 What key questions should the teacher address before determining the type of school program needed for learners?
3 Why should teachers be able to plan school programs that address differences among learners?
4 Why should daily lesson plans and unit plans reflect the goals and aims of a school district?
5 Why should teachers continue to stress general education throughout the K-12 school program?

Key Terms and Concepts

Activity curriculum: A student-centered organizational emphasis that begins with broad topic identification for learning and weaves the related academic components into that topic.

Carnegie Unit: A measure of clock time that is used to award high school credits toward graduation.

Constants: An offering of learning experiences that make up an academic or vocational track in the secondary school.

Core curriculum: A student-centered organizational emphasis that combines broad areas of academic disciplines into manageable instructional units such as social studies and language arts for integration in learning.

Education for career: A specialty educational offering that promotes and prepares learners for postsecondary educational efforts and/or career initiation.

Exploratory education: An educational offering that is broad in scope and is used to introduce learners to a variety of learning areas that may be pursued in depth as possible career interests.

Fused curriculum: A subject-centered organizational program created with some merger of the academic disciplines such as reading, writing, and speaking into language arts as a subject for teaching.

General education: An educational offering that is common and required of all students.

Single subject curriculum: A subject-centered organizational program in which the academic disciplines are taught in isolation from each other.

Variable: An offering of elective learning experiences for secondary school students.

There is no dominant design for the specific curriculum offerings in school districts across the nation. Although the fifty state departments of education have some common elements in what they require generically for inclusion in the curriculum, considerable variance is found in specific program offerings. This variance is due to the regional differences within American society. An examination of the differences in the types of school programs is necessary for preservice teachers if they are to appreciate why these differences exist.

A key issue is how the curriculum should be organized. Teachers need to understand the differences among the broad purposes and aims of education, subject- and student-centered emphases in curriculum, and program requirements. Why and how new experiences are incorporated into school programs are vital questions for teachers if they want to create excellent learning opportunities for their students. All teachers need to grasp the intricacies of curriculum development—to know how to recognize and discard what is not useful and to adopt beneficial methods so that learners may profit.

Aims of Education and the Curriculum

The traditional purpose of education, which can be traced to the ancient liberal arts, stresses a selected set of learning skills and a vast store of selected information for students. *Traditionalists* assume that students who acquire the necessary skills and facts are "educated" and thus will behave as intelligent adults. Students are not expected or directed to use their native intelligence creatively; they are to learn passively and store knowledge for future use. Learning is the same for all: Knowledge that was relevant yesterday remains so today.

A contrasting purpose of education, stressing active student involvement in learning, evolved from the work of John Dewey and his associates after 1900. This position, referred to as *progressivism*, has not been universally accepted in practice. It is, however, still examined and studied as a school of thought; and as a theory, it has enjoyed considerable acceptance. Ideally, progressivism, expressed as learners' living and practicing in the learning environment, stresses active participation and practice during the learning period. Students are encouraged to use experience as a means to new learning. This philosophy suggests that learning is relevant; learning is life; students learn best by participating in learning.

New National Goals for education were proposed and passed in 1990, and the current Administration bases its educational recommendations and funding on these goals. The goals are as follows:

By the year 2000,

1. All children in America will start school ready to learn;
2. The high school graduation rate will increase to at least 90 percent;
3. American students will leave grades 4, 8, and 12 having gained competency in challenging subject matter;
4. American students will be first in the world in science and mathematics achievement;
5. Every adult American will be literate and possess the knowledge and skills necessary to compete in a global economy and to exercise the rights and responsibilities of citizenship;

6. Every school in America will be free of drugs and violence and will offer a disciplined environment conducive to learning.

Education for the remainder of this century has a monumental task if these goals are to be achieved.

Roles for Education

In formulating what the school has to do, curriculum planners frequently find that planning is easy but actualizing that planning is not. National, regional, and state commissions have all expressed their thoughts about what education should be. The school may see its job as reproduction, readjustment, or reconstruction—or some combination of these. These tasks are examined here as they relate to the philosophical concepts that prescribe the school and curriculum.

Reproduction. If the school merely elects the role of *reproduction*, then its task is to transmit simply and unquestioningly our nation's cultural heritage to its youth. The subject matter that is selected should be what has survived through the ages. If the school is to fulfill only the reproductive function, the teacher must consider whether the subject matter has withstood the test of time and therefore should be included in the curriculum or whether irrelevant material may have survived along with the relevant. The teacher must also decide whether the relevant subject matter of yesterday is enough for today's youth. The problems associated with making this decision are increased by the vast and continually growing amount of knowledge that is available in our society. In addition to the old knowledge that must be passed on, there is new knowledge that continues to press for its rightful place in the curriculum.

Readjustment. Sole attention to *readjustment* calls for the school to gear its curriculum to social usefulness and efficiency. A curriculum for readjustment is concerned with preparing students for present-day adult life; it stresses civic training and social responsibility. Readjustment demands that the school retain parts of the past and also suggests that the school must do a certain amount of readjusting to meet current needs. Concentrating purely on this function may ignore some of the principles of child development and currently accepted psychology of learning. The child's need to understand and direct personal actions, the need to be able to adapt and organize in the light of prior experience, and the critical need for individual attention may be neglected when the theme of social utility is forced on the school. Readjustment, if it is the sole role of the schools, may tend to inhibit personal behavior changes that are necessary for adult life.

Reconstruction. The school that adopts the educational role of *reconstruction* establishes a curriculum that moves to the forefront of current thought and practice in society and strives to change the status quo. The school then undertakes not only to prepare young people for the future but also to prepare the future for young people. The school practicing this role is attempting to lead society; however, to date, schools in the United States have not accepted this role. In designing the curriculum the teacher must be aware of the pitfalls of this extreme approach and the hidden danger that past and current interests, traditions, and values may be sacrificed for the sake of change.

Combination of Roles. Overemphasizing any one of the three roles for schooling—reproduction, readjustment, or reconstruction—would produce a top-heavy operational and philosophical concept that is inconsistent with the eclecticism needed today. These three functions must be constantly blended so that students will have the best opportunity to become self-supporting, self-respecting, and self-directing participants in American and world society.

Students to Be Served

In meeting these roles for the school, the teacher must recognize at least five broad categories of students that attend school. The number and kinds of these students will vary from school district to school district, but every school district has some mix of these types of students. Although the categories appear to be distinctly different, students may fall into one—or more than one—of them. In tending to multicultural concerns, keep in mind that these different types of students are found in all cultural groups.

Terminal Students—At Risk. These students, for various reasons, drop out along the way and have to be absorbed by society. Currently, national high-school dropout rates are between 25 and 30 percent, with minority groups having considerably higher rates. In fact, the minority dropout rate may approach 60 percent in many of the large cities of this country.

College-Bound Students. These students are preparing for higher education. Nationally, approximately 50 percent of high school graduates pursue study beyond high school. This figure is misleading, however, because it does not account for students who have dropped out before graduating from high school. The preparatory programs for the 50 percent must be varied because of the range of post–high school educational desires and opportunities. These students may

Recent trends seem to reflect a healthy job market for high-school graduates from vocational technical education programs.

attend two-year community colleges leading to terminal associate degrees or four-year institutions leading to baccalaureate degrees. The drop in higher education enrollments in the 1990s is due in part to the changes in family size during the 1970s and early 1980s. The number will probably be reduced even further because of declining secondary enrollments and young people finding an increasingly lower correlation between college education and job placement.

Vocational-Technical Students. These students are primarily preparing for jobs while in a comprehensive or vocational-technical high school. Some of these students, however, may further their education later on, formally or informally. Although the percentage of students who fall into this category varies according to the criteria used, it appears to be on the increase. Data on job placement for college-trained students suggest a job shortage, whereas data for vocational-technical students suggest a healthy job market.

Destination Unknown. These are students who have native ability but do not realize an expected level of achievement during high school. They are often referred to as "late bloomers," and it is not uncommon to find, in follow-up studies of these students, that increasing numbers of them are pursuing some form of postsecondary educational programs. Because many of these students did not focus on career goals while in high school, they often lack the prerequisite preparation for further schooling and find that they must fill in the gaps before they can go on.

Special Students. These students are identified as emotionally, mentally, or physically handicapped. Court decisions of the 1970s ordered that many special students be included as regular school students and accommodated by the regular curriculum. As was explained earlier in the discussion of Public Law 94-142, this federal law now mandates a least restrictive environment for learning for exceptional children. Many such students are now being mainstreamed and infused into the regular curriculum.

Relevant Research

Improving Achievement of Hispanic Students

Citing many of the familiar problems associated with the achievement problems of Hispanic youth, Christopher Howe's case study research reports on two exploratory studies that offered suggestions for addressing the needs of Hispanic youth and thus improving their achievement. The two studies found that:

- Successful programs placed value on the students' language and culture.
- These programs set high expectations for language-minority students.
- These programs had effective staff development efforts for the teachers.
- The programs had special counselors available.
- Minority parents were involved in the programs.
- The staff encouraged minority student empowerment.

As the Hispanic population continues to grow nationally, teachers need to improve their efforts to meet the needs of these students.

Source: Christopher K. Howe, "Improving the Achievement of Hispanic Students," *Educational Leadership* 51 (8) (May, 1994): 42–44.

The best analysis of the current average school curriculum suggests that the needs of college-bound students continue to receive majority attention. If priorities were otherwise, the national dropout rate—especially for urban areas—would probably not be so alarmingly high. Some people feel the most slighted learner is the gifted child. Therefore, curriculum development should proceed from some special diagnostic attempts to identify the various kinds of students the curriculum is intended to serve.

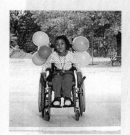

Can Teachers Adapt Their Classroom Philosophy to Meet the Diversity of Inclusion Students?

Except for the basic knowledge preparation you received about P. L. 94-142 in your teacher education program, you were probably never adequately prepared to accommodate and teach the full range of exceptional students. The school district where you have just begun your first year of teaching has moved to an inclusion program for exceptional learners. In your class are three students with exceptionalities of mildly learning disabled, emotionally disturbed, and cerebral palsy gifted. Prior to teaching you had assumed that these "special" learners would be accommodated for most of their learning in a separate learning area designated as special education, with their own teacher, and if mainstreamed with you, it would only be for social and emotional growth purposes. Now, you have these special students for all of their learning activities; an itinerant special education teacher will come to your class as you need him or her.

Your dilemma at this point is:

- How will you redirect your classroom philosophy to handle this type of classroom diversity?
- How will you prepare a separate curriculum for these students or modify the regular one so the special students can share with the regular students?
- Where will you go for help with this problem?
- How will you work with the nondisabled students in their development of positive attitudes and behaviors toward the special learners?

Keep in mind that the best teachers value all of their students and that this attitude is visible to those they teach.

Curriculum Structure

Any school system can choose its own pattern of curriculum organization. These patterns tend to range between the extremes of a *subject-centered* and a *student-centered* organization. Between the two extremes a continuum of curricular programs exists, and schools use various elements from either extreme or both. In general, curricular organization that tends to be subject-centered is content-oriented; if it uses a student-centered pattern, it is learner-oriented.

Subject-Centered Organization

By analyzing the curriculum continuum (see Figure 17.1), we can categorize patterns that offer separate courses for the various academic disciplines and those that fuse the disciplines under the broad heading "subject-centered patterns of curriculum organization." Correlated programs and activity programs are classified as student-centered organizations. You will recognize that the patterns of curricular organizations used by various schools often tend to be eclectic, borrowing from many sources. How a school district organizes its curriculum is related strongly to its philosophical position on the purposes of education.

Single Subject Curriculum. The **single subject curriculum** is the oldest and still most widely used in U.S. schools. In the modern, single subject curriculum, all the subjects for instruction are separated. In the extreme use of this approach,

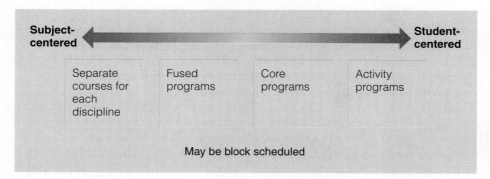

FIGURE 17.1

A Curriculum Continuum

the disciplines of knowledge are taught in isolation with no attempt at integration. The intent is to provide a discipline for students that alerts them to set classifications and to recognize arrangements of facts and ideas. An important criterion in selecting ideas for study is to choose those that have proved beneficial for solving problems of investigation in research. These facts and ideas are the ones that have lasted over time.

This curriculum calls for extensive explanation and oral discourse. The curriculum uses a formal, step-by-step study of ideas and facts; rarely are students expected or encouraged to explore or experiment on their own. The teaching methods include extensive verbal activities—lectures, discussions, questions, and answers—and written exercises such as term papers.

Supporters and defenders of the single subject curriculum argue that subjects that have withstood the test of time are the most worthy. They also contend that just because some children do not learn well in such a curriculum does not imply any inherent weakness in the curriculum organization. Supporters of this type of curriculum espouse an essentialistic philosophy of education, and advocates point out that not everything can be studied at once, nor can any study be all-inclusive. With the rapid increase in knowledge there simply has to be an ordered, segmented approach if one is to study a subject effectively. The separated subjects are a convenient way to clarify this knowledge so that it can be comprehended by students.

Fused Curriculum. The **fused curriculum** is an attempt to decrease the number of separate subjects that have gradually been brought into the single subject curriculum. In place of separate classes in reading, writing, spelling, grammar, speech, and literature, for example, the fused curriculum combines these subjects under English or language arts. The single subject curriculum remains almost intact, but students are introduced to the field as a whole rather than to bits and pieces. Subject matter goals are left whole, but the fused approach provides teachers and students more latitude within a broad subject area.

The fused curriculum has enjoyed its greatest success at the elementary level. Separate subjects, once taught for short periods during the day, are now more apt to be taught in a fused fashion over longer periods. Common fused studies in the elementary school center on language arts, social studies, general science, mathematics, art, music, and physical education and health.

In the past, junior high schools developed several variations of the fused program. Some schools combined language arts and social studies with block scheduling, thus providing a longer period for teaching these two groups of subjects. Block scheduling puts two fused programs such as language arts and social studies back-to-back in the daily school schedule. However, in recent years the movement of subject matter to lower grades has caused junior high schools to adopt the predominantly single subject pattern of the senior high school.

In the senior high school the fused curriculum has had relatively little success. Examples of the few high school courses that are so patterned are general science, problems of democracy in the social studies, and family living. The greatest effect the fused curriculum has had on the senior high school is probably the integration of unified areas into single subject courses. Many high school teachers of American history now try to interlace a certain amount of geography and political science into their history courses.

Student-Centered Organization

The concern for students' needs and interests has produced the *student-centered organization*. A student-centered organization describes either a core curriculum or an activity curriculum. In the past, and also today to some extent, these curricula have had both social and psychological interpretations. The current needs of youth are generally defined as what society expects of maturing young adults. While an extreme interpretation of the subject-centered organization stresses that learning is most effective if it is rigorous and difficult, the student-centered organization emphasizes encouraging students' interest in learning and their appreciation for it. When the interests and needs of learners are incorporated in the curriculum, motivation tends to become intrinsic rather than extrinsic. However, this description does not imply that the student-centered organization is directed by the whims of the learner; rather, it is based on the premise that learning is more successfully achieved if it is built on the interests the learner has developed before formal education begins. As you read about core and activity programs, compare and contrast the student-centered organization with the subject-centered organization.

Core Curriculum.   The core curriculum grew out of a general dissatisfaction with the piecemeal learning promoted by the subject-centered organization. In trying to offer students a more enriching education, proponents of the core curriculum believe that subjects should be unified and new methods should be adopted. Since society has become increasingly fragmented, with more emphasis on science and technology, proponents of the core curriculum feel that the only logical approach to developing social values and social vision is through a core organization. The core curriculum may have different degrees of organization and may cross broader subject lines, but it places even greater stress than the fused curriculum on the need to integrate subject matter.

The **core curriculum** emphasizes social values, and much time is given to studying the culture and its moral content. This curriculum promotes problem solving as a learning method; within this approach, facts, descriptive principles, socioeconomic conditions, and moral rules of conduct and behavior are stressed. In its purest form, the core is basically normative in its presentation; major focus is on topics such as the social needs of today.

CASE STUDY PERFORMANCE-BASED SCHOOL PROGRAMS

*I*ncreasing numbers of school districts are moving toward performance-based school programs. These programs are the natural outgrowths of competency-based education, but are not as controversial because the local districts have greater control over what performance-based expectations will be. Since you, as a new teacher, have recently studied the pros and cons of these types of programs, you could be asked to serve on school-district-wide committees that are contemplating these curriculum activities. You have learned that many veteran teachers do not look favorably on these programs because they deviate markedly from the typical school program with which these teachers have become comfortable.

As you prepare to take part in this type of school district activity, you know that you should do the following:

1. Talk with colleagues about their interests in individualizing instruction.
2. Prepare reading materials that discuss individualization activities with a variety of diverse learners.
3. Plan to keep communication channels open with your colleagues so they are informed on the status of the committee's activities.
4. Have your colleagues try and give you feedback on the sample materials that are investigated and developed by the committee.

Your task will not be easy because the majority of the instruction in your district is of the large group variety. Most teachers have the same set of expectations for all of their students, and little differentiation is made between students with greater and lesser abilities. What are your views on these ideas?

Activity Curriculum. At the extreme right of the curriculum organization continuum is the **activity curriculum** (see Figure 17.1 on page 437). In its purest form it operates with the child as the sole center of learning. Since education, like life, is ever-changing, the activity curriculum expects to change continually. Students' needs and interests are assessed, and the curriculum is built on that assessment. The psychology of learning in this approach is based on the emotional involvement of the learner. Thus, if a child develops an interest in something and becomes emotionally involved with it, learning is enhanced.

The activity curriculum encompasses all subject matter. Completely flexible, the activity for the early learner may center on topics such as play, pets, toys, boats, letter carriers, or police officers. Emphasis is placed on observation, play, stories, and handiwork. This curriculum has several characteristics that make it distinctive. First, the interests and purposes of children determine the educational program. Second, common learning (general education) comes about as a result of individual interest. Third, this curriculum is not planned in advance, but guidelines are established to help the students choose alternatives intelligently as they progress through the program. Activities are planned cooperatively by students and teachers, and what they plan and pursue may or may not have any deliberate social direction. In the pursuit of planned goals, solving problems becomes the principal teaching method. Little or no need for extracurricular activities develops because all interests are accommodated within the regular program.

Curriculum Contrasts

The subject-centered organization and the student-centered organization represent the two extremes of a curriculum continuum. These two organizational patterns can be contrasted in the following manner:

Subject-centered curriculum	*Student-centered curriculum*
Centered on subjects within the academic disciplines	Centered on learners and their diagnosed needs
Emphasis on subject matter to be learned	Emphasis on promoting all-around growth of learners
Subject matter selected and organized before it is taught	Subject matter selected and organized cooperatively by learners and teachers during the learning period
Controlled by the teacher or someone representing authority external to the learning situation	Controlled and directed cooperatively by learners (pupils, teachers, parents, supervisors, principals, and others) in the learning situation
Emphasis on facts, information, knowledge for its own sake or for possible future use; generally, lower-order learning	Emphasis on learning things to improve living and to solve day-to-day problems
Emphasis on specific habits and skills as separate aspects of learning	Emphasis on habits and skills as integral parts of larger experiences
Emphasis on improving methods of teaching specific subject matter	Emphasis on understanding and improving through the process of learning
Emphasis on uniformity of exposure to learning and uniformity of learning results	Emphasis on variability in exposure to learning and in results expected
Education conforming to set patterns	Education aiding each child to build a socially creative individuality
Education considered schooling	Education considered a continuous, intelligent process of growth

Global Perspectives: A Student-Centered Curriculum in New Zealand

New Zealand has the highest literacy rate in the world. The National Ministry of Education credits this achievement to the whole-language approach that is used in the schools and supported by teachers, parents, communities, teacher-training programs, and the national government. Although the system is legally controlled by the national government, there is a remarkable degree of autonomy encouraged and practiced by the local schools. In a sense, the local schools are like "charter" schools in England and those that are struggling to begin in the United States. The national government totally finances the schools, but local schools determine how the funds will be used. Nationally, the schools practice site-based management.

Children in New Zealand start school at the age of five. They come to school on their birthday, celebrate their birthday party, and move into the learning environment with the other children. The school environment includes: cooperative learning with an emphasis on small group and pair learning; multicultural immersion with special attention given to Maori, the indigenous people of New Zealand; use of journals in expression and evaluation; and total attention to readiness for learning and individual differences.

Teachers have a remarkable degree of autonomy in the schools of New Zealand. Although there is a printed national curriculum, the teachers are free to use it in any way they feel is appropriate for the special needs of their children. Teaching materials are not dictated nationally, but are developed at the local levels; however, the national government pays for the creation and support of these materials. Curriculum revision is led by the Ministry of Education, with considerable input from both professionals and the general public. Recent curriculum goal efforts for the country were begun using survey forms that were placed in and collected from McDonald's fast food chain outlets; customers responded to six questions about goals printed on the placemats. The data from this survey became the basis for further analysis and comment nationally.

Many of the current educational practices in New Zealand continue to be discussed as innovative practices in the United States. We have much to learn as we look at global efforts in education that seem to be successful at this time.

Program Requirements

Embedded in the operating program of the school are three broad academic components that constitute the function of the educational program: general education, exploratory education, and education for career. Their placement and emphasis depend wholly on the learner's needs as they relate to growth and development, the psychology of learning, instructional strategies, and various administrative arrangements.

General Education

General education is the broad area of the school program that is concerned primarily with developing common learning. Its central purpose is helping students to become participating citizens and well-adjusted individuals. Although general education is concentrated in the elementary school, some elements of it persist throughout the entire period of formal education. Although the other two broad areas of the school program, exploratory and personal education, include general education outcomes, they are not organized primarily for that purpose.

Basic Skills. The general education program concentrates on developing *basic skills* and introduces students to basic studies that include reading, composition, listening, speaking, and computing. Learners are expected to acquire creative and disciplined thinking skills that include different methods of inquiry and applying knowledge. General education also encompasses the humanities—an appreciation

The general education program concentrates on the basic skills of reading, composition, listening, speaking, and computing.

12

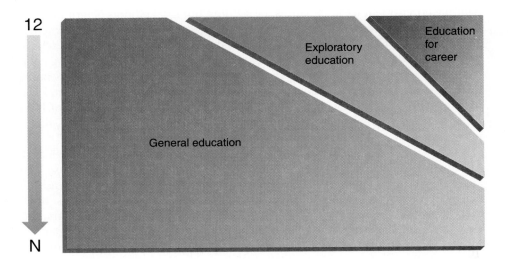

N

FIGURE 17.2

Educational Emphasis in the N-12 Program

for literature, music, and the visual arts—and the social and natural sciences. Within a general education program, learners are expected to acquire the essential, adult basic performance skills that are needed to function successfully in society. The way general education is accomplished varies among school districts. The identified components of common learning provide the core of general education in the elementary school and are improved and developed further throughout the total formal program of education. Figure 17.2 illustrates the general education emphasis for the formal N-12 structure.

One of the most perplexing problems facing general education planners is maintaining the placement sequence in the total scheme of education. As we have just seen, the number of years of schooling devoted to general education is determined by changing economic factors as well as by society's concern with efficiency and productivity. The people who demand accountability from today's schools have joined those who call for more general education. In the very recent past, the need for specialization caused a slackening of interest in general education and an increased emphasis on specialized studies and the applied fields. In contrast, the decades of the 1980s and the 1990s have shown more attention to the pressure for accountability in general education.

Career and Life Skills. During the 1960s and 1970s, increasing public pressure caused some subjects to be presented earlier in the curriculum. Advanced skills and some special training, previously reserved for the secondary school, were introduced into the elementary school. It is now a regular practice to introduce the formal teaching of career and life skills such as foreign language, principles of economics, chemical and sex education, advanced principles of mathematics, and introductory programs for vocational career choices in elementary school. Although there are justifiable reasons for this introduction, they do not change the nature and purpose of common learning in the elementary program. Because of this expanded common learning for younger students, educators must reassess the general education program and possibly redefine the concept of common learning.

As preschool and early-childhood education receive increased philosophical and financial support, the general education program, identified as common learning for all, should probably be redistributed over a broader continuum, from nursery school through grade 12.

Exploratory Education

The **exploratory education** program is designed primarily for an educational organization unique to the United States: the junior high school. Depending on school district organization, the junior high, intermediate, or middle school continues general education and introduces students, on a limited basis, to a variety of specialized subjects. It is expected that the students will take these exploratory experiences and utilize them in making career decisions that they will pursue in senior high school and beyond.

Junior High School. Following are five reasons for the existence of junior high school and for exploratory education programs:

1. The junior high school provides a transitional period, easing students' transfer from the elementary school to the high school. Junior high school is designed for students who are entering early adolescence, a trying period of growth and development. Since the transition period from childhood to adulthood is so critical, the junior high school is planned to accommodate the special physical, emotional, and social problems of this age group. In general, the students have come from an administrative unit that is child-centered, and they are preparing to enter one that is subject-centered. The junior high school has been planned to foster a gradual development of independence in learning and self-discipline. So that students have a "home base," block scheduling is sometimes used for the language arts-social studies program, and the teacher for this block has a better chance than others to know and help the students. Junior high school students also take several courses taught by specialists; in this way they are gradually introduced to the departmentalized, single subject senior high school.

2. The junior high school allows for the exploration of interests, aptitudes, and abilities, thus aiding the students in vocational and educational planning. The program introduces, in concentrated periods, such subjects as art, music, home economics, vocational education, and speech. The intention is that as the students progress toward senior high school, they will explore subjects in which they may specialize later. These exploratory programs may last nine weeks or one semester and are often offered on a rotating basis.

3. Junior high school students are introduced to an elaborate program of guidance and counseling that continues

The junior and senior high school programs should be designed to suit all students, regardless of their future plans for college or career.

through senior high school. This program is intended to help students plan intelligently for adult life. By using specially trained guidance personnel, the junior high school emphasizes development of wholesome attitudes for mental, emotional, and social growth among the student body.

4. Providing for variety in junior high helps to lower the school dropout rate. Variable programming considers the differing special abilities of youth, and its rationale stresses the important effects of the students' socioeconomic background on their interests, aptitudes, needs, and personality development.

5. Articulation of the total twelve-year school program may be stimulated by the junior high school. This administrative unit has the advantage of examining the elementary program and planning for articulation with the senior high school. Articulation is successful when all teachers within the school system work together to understand and appreciate the special tasks each must perform.

Like the elementary school, the junior high school has had to find ways to accommodate the continuing movement toward an earlier exposure for subjects. There is little doubt that the pressure of content requirements from the senior high school and the accompanying problems associated with Carnegie units of credits have caused the junior high school to become, as some say, "a senior high school in short pants."

The Middle School.   By way of returning to the initial philosophy that guided the junior high school, many school districts have put the ninth grade back in the senior high school and created a new administrative organization of 5–8, 6–8, or 7–8, labeled the intermediate or middle school. The new *middle school* is intended to provide for the exploratory learning that the junior high school never quite achieved. Many of the early intentions of the junior high school continue for the middle school, with the exception of the ninth grade. Because of societal changes, improvements in health and nutrition, and more accelerated rates of physical and social maturation, ninth graders are much more like senior high school students today than they were when the original junior high school idea was conceived.

Middle schools are enjoying phenomenal growth during the 1990s. Since their early growth during the 1960s when 1000 such schools were reported across the nation, estimates for numbers of these schools today are over 12,000.[1] These schools emphasize problem-solving skills, reflective thinking processes, and individualized learning programs. Curriculum content is easily integrated, and the emphasis in instruction is that the teacher is a personal guide and facilitator of learning as opposed to a dispenser of knowledge. These schools stress the use of interdisciplinary teaching teams, greater attention to advisory programs, and increased exploratory exposure to unified arts programs. There is a decreased emphasis on content and competition so commonly found in the junior and senior high school.

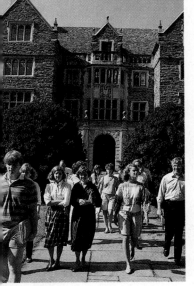

Because of the large number of high school students who go on to college, high schools have tended to emphasize college preparatory programs.

Education for Career

The senior high school assumes the special task of uniting the foundations of general education with the introductions to exploratory education, culminating in a rounded education that prepares one for an **education for career.** The senior high school will terminate formal education for many students, but it will prepare others for more advanced and specialized education in college or for special post–high school training. Because a large number of high school graduates go on to college, school systems are tempted to overemphasize the college preparatory program. However, the high school should offer programs designed to suit all students. Attention should be given to individual choice in establishing various programs. Although students can register in certain programs, they may take subjects in another curriculum. Presumably, each designation refers to special interest education.

Constants-Variable Program. The basic high school course requirements, more commonly referred to as **constants,** are required for all students; and many electives, the **variable** program offerings, become required coursework for a particular avenue of learning. Within the constants, however, additional provisions take into account the special needs, interests, and abilities of students. For example, a high school requiring three years of English may allow its students relative freedom in meeting this requirement. Other elective programs have, until recent years, provided this flexibility.

In continuing the program for general education (see Figure 17.2 on page 442), the high school has an established core of general courses required for all students. These requirements have traditionally accounted for seven to nine of the sixteen to twenty Carnegie units required for graduation. The national concern with the quality of education, as expressed in the many national commission reports, has led to an increase in the number of general education requirements for graduation. However, the requirements vary from state to state. Increasing numbers of states now require four units of English instead of three, two or three units of mathematics instead of one, and two or three units of science instead of one. The emphasis on mathematics and science is particularly heavy and comes at a time when there is a shortage of highly qualified teachers in these disciplines.

Relevant Research

Preventing Failure and Dropout among At-Risk High School Students

An action-research project was established in the Des Moines public schools to intervene against the failure and dropout rate of at-risk students in the middle and high schools. In this "school within a school" program, at-risk students were identified and assigned to smaller classes, with teachers giving greater personal attention to the students. The major goal of the program is to promote the social/emotional growth of the students. The program is also tied in to community programs and agencies for student referral activities. During the seven years that the program has been in operation, the dropout rate for the schools has decreased from 11 percent to 5 percent. Achievement and attendance rates for these students has reached the normal rate for the secondary schools.

This study suggests common-sense interventions for at-risk students. When given special services and modifications to the regular program, these students demonstrate success. It probably can be extrapolated from this study that the regular students would perform better if they also received benefits similar to those provided by this program.

Source: Randy Gordon, "The School within a School Program: Preventing Failure and Dropout among At-Risk High School Students." *ERS Spectrum* II (1) (Winter, 1993): 27–30.

Carnegie Units. One **Carnegie unit** of credit is awarded for each class that meets for two hundred minutes of formal education a week for thirty-six weeks in the school year. The remainder of the units required for graduation are satisfied

The senior high school will terminate formal education for many students, but it will prepare others for more advanced and specialized education.

by the elective programs for specialization and enrichment. The special programs vary in name, sequence, and scope, but the two most usual within the comprehensive senior high school are the tracking program and the constants-variable program. The main difficulty with the Carnegie unit system is that it does not take into account the research on student learning, which states that students do not all learn at the same rate, nor do they maintain a constant learning rate. Yet most American secondary schools continue to schedule students in established time modules that are consistent with the definition of a Carnegie unit given for time devoted to a particular experience. School systems simply do not apply sound reasoning supported by research when they conclude that all students need two hundred minutes a week of varied instruction for thirty-six weeks to accomplish one Carnegie unit successfully. If learning objectives are clearly specified, some students meet them in less time than others. The criterion for success should not be time or attendance; rather, it should be the successful attainment of the clearly specified learning objectives and minimum requirements. Many feel when students meet the objectives, they should be awarded the credit determined for the objectives.

Extended Programs

Schools may be directly or indirectly involved in one or several programs that extend beyond the regular K-12 structure. These programs provide differing emphases in school organization and instruction, educational opportunities for very young children, job opportunity training for older adolescents and adults, and outlets for avocational interests for community members who live in the school district. The extent of these programs depends upon the wealth and desires of the community.

Effective Schools

The plethora of national school studies that have focused on the characteristics of excellence in education has spawned the *effective schools* research studies that have identified the characteristics and practices that hallmark an effective school. These studies have been gleaned from school district data that show high student achievement and are marked by certain characteristics that contribute to this achievement.

Program Characteristics. The program characteristics of an effective school are as follows:

- The instructional program is goal oriented. Students know exactly what is expected of them as they pursue learning.

- There is constant and consistent assessment and monitoring of student progress. There is immediate feedback on student performance.
- Instruction is appropriate to the learner. Individual differences are given prime attention.
- The program gives emphasis to basic skills, including both academic and life skills.
- There is continuity of instruction across the grades. The staff works together to provide common types of learning experiences in all parts of the curriculum.
- There is effective grouping for instruction. Where grouping practices are used, they are flexible and correspond to the task at hand and the individual differences by task.
- Instructional time is organized to maximize the effectiveness of the "teachable moments." Students experience different time modules for learning.
- All lessons are adjusted to the students' needs. Teachers are concerned about the concept of "time on task" in learning.

Environment Characteristics. The environment characteristics are as follows:

- There is democratic administrative leadership. Fairness in leadership and fairness in decision making create a healthy environment that promotes sound mental health among teachers and learners.
- There is an orderly, safe environment. The social and academic environment is free from fear for safety for both learners and teachers.
- There is clear, firm, and consistent discipline. Learners know what is expected of them and practice that policy.
- There is a cooperative/family atmosphere. Students are encouraged to become part of an interactive family.
- There are few classroom interruptions. School announcements, visitors, and the like do not disturb the learning environment.
- There is parental involvement in student learning. Parents are encouraged and expected to be partners in their children's learning.
- The school exhibits positive community relations. The school invites community members to participate in the regular program and uses community resources.
- There are adequate facilities and learning materials. School district budgets provide teachers and learners with the type of materials and amount of equipment needed for each school's objectives.
- The school plant is well kept. Plant facilities are attractive and kept at a high degree of maintenance.

Expectations. School programs that encourage and enhance the professional sharing of ideas among teachers and provide inducements for those behaviors to occur become more effective for students. The "Pygmalion" effect is ever present in effective schools. When teachers hold realistic, yet high, expectations for their students, those students usually reach those expectations.

Vocational Education

The narrowness of the typical track program in senior high schools has undoubtedly contributed to the continuing shortage of high school graduates who are well prepared in the vocational-technical fields. All too often, students drift into the vocational track because they cannot meet certain academic standards. Sometimes, educators forget that this kind of training requires students who are capable of both academic and vocational-technical work. But the constants-variable program can include training for students that has meaning for new industry and the changing economy. Too often in the past, and even today, vocational-technical training has tended to be obsolescent. However, the constants-variable program can stress work experience and on-the-job training that relate to school experience. Although general enrollments in education dropped dramatically during the 1970s and into the 1980s, shifts in enrollments to vocational education were tremendous. During this period, enrollments in career education increased by over 200 percent.

School Criteria.   A well-conceived vocational-technical program meets the following twelve criteria:

1. The program is directly related to employment opportunities, as determined by school officials in cooperation with occupational experts and other competent individuals and groups.
2. The course content is confirmed or changed by periodic analysis of the occupations.
3. The courses for a specific occupation are set up and maintained with the advice and cooperation of the various occupational groups concerned.
4. The facilities and equipment used in instruction are comparable to what is found in the particular occupation.
5. The conditions for instruction duplicate, as nearly as possible, desirable conditions in the occupation itself and at the same time provide effective learning.
6. The length of teaching periods and total hours of instruction are determined by the requirements of the occupation and the needs of the students.
7. Training in a particular occupation develops marketable skills, abilities, attitudes, work habits, and appreciation to the point at which the trainee can obtain and hold a job in that occupation.
8. Day and evening classes are scheduled at hours and during seasons that are convenient to potential students.
9. Instruction is offered only to individuals who need and want it and who can profit from it occupationally.
10. The teachers are competent in the occupation and are professionally qualified for teaching.
11. Vocational guidance, including effective follow-up on all students who finish or drop out of a course, is an integral and continuing part of the program.
12. Continuous research is an integral part of the program.

Program Types.   Gene Bottoms and Patricia Copa[2] list five types of general vocational programs and four types of occupationally specific programs. The general programs are as follows:

1. Consumer/homemaking, focusing on family life.
2. Prevocational as introductory or exploratory.
3. Prevocational basic skills.
4. Related instruction in occupational service, mathematics, and communication skills needed for specific jobs.

5. Employability skills for cooperative work programs.

The occupationally specific programs include the following:

1. Occupational cluster programs of comprehensive high schools. These programs provide for a broader curricular approach, such as the study of the field of electronics.

2. Occupation-specific programs for one particular occupation. An example of this type of program is computer technology.

3. Job-specific programs for an individual job within a broader cluster of occupations.

4. Employer-specific programs as needed or requested by particular employers.

The latter three specific programs are usually found in community colleges and vocational-technical schools.

This type of vocational training has brought about significant changes in the comprehensive high school. Since it is extremely difficult and costly for a local school district to provide adequate vocational training in the regular high schools, area vocational schools have been developed for students from several participating school districts. The area vocational-technical school can provide a great variety of career clusters for vocational curricula. They can also provide a far more comprehensive program than a local high school that attempts by itself to serve the needs of all its vocational students. Federal funding has assisted in this type of vocational training but not to the degree needed.

Early-Childhood Education

Numerous research studies have emphasized the benefits of early learning for preschool learners, and, as a result, early-childhood educational programs have grown in number and kind. Originally, early-childhood programs were viewed primarily as child care programs for working families; but they have now assumed, in addition to providing for that continuing need, additional tasks in the formal education of young children. Although they are found in a variety of settings from sponsored day-care programs to private self-supporting schools, their aims tend to be similar in their offerings for young children.

Program Types. Current trends identify at least three types of early-childhood programs for young children. The first can be labeled traditional in nature, and it promotes a program that is not uncommon for most kindergarten programs in the United States. Depending on the age of the child, the program provides a readiness activity for the child as a preparatory stage for entering the public school structure. The philosophy of these pro-

Early childhood activities that develop children's curiosity and interest in learning contribute significantly to later success in school.

grams is similar to that practiced in the public schools and is basically essentialist.

A second type of program is associated with the behaviorist philosophy of education and, generally, is a behavior modification program. This program also provides day care for very young children and a preschool program for older early learners who are about to enter the public school system. The major difference between this program and a traditional one is its emphasis on a reward system for expected institutional performance of the learners. Reinforcement tactics predominate, and the young learner is schooled in the expected readiness competencies for the kindergarten.

The third major type of early-childhood program is referred to as the child development approach. Some of the current early-childhood theorists refer to it as a play curriculum. Its roots are embedded in the activity curriculum discussed earlier in this chapter, and it uses the play concept to help children get ready for the more formal learning atmosphere of the regular kindergarten. It, too, provides a day-care program for very young children, but it introduces more formal learning activities, via play activities, for the older preschool child.

Placement in the Curriculum. All of these programs remain outside the formal K-12 structure of the regular school, but program efforts have increasingly come to be seen as part of the educational continuum for learners. The promise of these programs is that they do promote individual growth in learners, and they undoubtedly have some important implications for the kindergarten and regular elementary program. That is, young children are entering the formal school structure with improved degrees of readiness. These individual differences among young learners are creating increasing demands on the elementary school to accommodate broader differences in readiness among learners who are beginning the kindergarten and first-grade programs.

Community Education

At the other end of the spectrum are adult learners who may or may not have completed their high school education. Increasing numbers of this group have also completed some form of post-high school education. As the U.S. population becomes older, the need for community education programs will grow. Pioneered by the Mott Foundation during the 1960s, community education programs have grown substantially since that time. Additionally, while the majority of early-education programs are not part of the regular school system's efforts, the community education programs are.

Adult Clientele. There are three types of adults whom community education programs must accommodate. The first is the returning adult student who seeks to complete his or her high school diploma. Growing numbers of these students are attending community education programs in order to increase their opportunities for worthwhile employment. The data that relate economic self-sufficiency with level of education are most compelling to individuals who have not completed a high school education. Many of these students seek the General Education Diploma (GED) offered by the community program, but some students are also returning to the regular classroom.

A second type of adult for whom community education programs attempt to provide is contemplating a career or job change. These programs may be offered in the evening at the regular high school or at a nearby vocational school or community college. The offerings may provide vocational training or a review of some of the basic skills that are needed to gain admission to some post–high school institution. The number of adult students returning to college and university campuses is on the increase, and colleges and universities are recruiting these students as the number of young applicants for admission declines.

The third type of adult to be accommodated by community education programs is seeking an avocational outlet for his or her leisure hours. As the adult population continues to increase, and as the percentage who complete high school and some form of occupational education increases, the need for community education programs that provide avocational offerings will also grow.

Future of Community Education. We see that the expression "education from birth to death" will take on new meaning as we move toward the turn of the century. Community education programs will surely be on the increase. However, the biggest deterrent to growth of these types of programs is finance. When recession periods and taxpayer unrest set in, the community education program is the first program whose viability in the school district will be challenged.

Summary and Implications

Issues for the curriculum are constantly changing as society acquires new expectations. The teacher working in program development must be knowledgeable about current issues and how those issues bear on the purposes and aims of the school program. Applications of this knowledge assist the teacher in designing a curriculum with student- or subject-centered emphases. Within this structure, student needs must be addressed through general education, exploratory education, and education for careers.

The implications for program development are associated with increasing demands on the education program. Schools must still provide for the individual differences of learners. Increasing state requirements for general education place greater stress on members of the student population who have had difficulty in meeting traditional academic standards. If increased requirements lead to increased standards of academic performance for all, the school may find that it has an increase in dropout rates. How teachers meet this challenge depends wholly on how well they accept special responsibility for curriculum development. Students may be expected to participate in more courses in general education—namely, mathematics, science, and English—but the reality and applicability of these subjects to the real world of the learner will have to be addressed.

Discussion Questions

1. Why should the general aims of education in the 1990s be different from those of the early 1900s?

2. How should the school curriculum be altered to address problems of basic literacy and development of survival skills?

3. Which type of curriculum, subject-centered or student-centered, do you prefer? Why?

4. How do the purposes of general education and exploratory education differ?

5. Why should every school be an effective school?

Journal/Portfolio Development

1. Research the National Goals for Education and assess how you can address these goals in your teaching area.
2. Examine promising educational practices in one or two of the global nations and assess the impact of those practices on those nations' educational programs.

School-Based Experiences

1. When making a visit to a school for one of your practicum experiences, plan to secure a copy of the school's curriculum guide. Make an analysis of the guide to determine whether the school has implemented a subject-centered or student-centered curriculum. Then, observe several teachers in classrooms to see whether the classroom practices support your analysis of the printed curriculum. Discuss your findings with the teachers you observed and record their perceptions of the guide and their efforts to practice what the guide prescribes.

2. When visiting a school as part of your practicum experiences, secure permission to visit and observe two classroom teachers. Before visiting the classes, meet with each of the teachers and discuss their school's curriculum with them. In particular, ask them how their program provides for the general education needs of their students. Have them identify two such provisions for you. Observe their classes to see if you can identify the general education provisions that they enumerated for you.

Notes

1. Sylvester Kohut, Jr., *The Middle School: A Bridge Between Elementary and High Schools*, 2nd ed. Washington, DC: National Education Association, 1988, 7.

2. Gene Bottoms and Patricia Copa, "A Perspective on Vocational Education Today," *Phi Delta Kappan 64* (5) (January, 1983): 349–350.

Bibliography

Brewer, Jo Ann. *Introduction to Early Childhood Education.* Boston: Allyn and Bacon, 1992.

Elmore, Richard F., and Fuhrman, Susan H. *The Governance of Curriculum.* 1994 Yearbook. Alexandria, VA: Association for Supervision and Curriculum Development, 1994.

Fullan, Michael, and Stiegelbauer, Steve. *The New Meaning of Educational Change.* New York: Teachers College Press, 1991.

George, Paul S.; Stevenson, Chris; Thomason, Julia; and Bean, James. *The Middle School and Beyond.* Alexandria, VA: Association for Supervision and Curriculum Development, 1992.

Glasser, William. *The Quality School: Managing Students without Coercion.* New York: Harper & Row, 1990.

Oliva, Peter F. *Developing the Curriculum.* 3rd ed. New York: HarperCollins Publishers, 1992.

Tanner, Daniel, and Tanner, Laurel. *History of the School Curriculum.* New York: Macmillan Publishing Company, 1990.

18

School Practices

Focus Questions

1 How do graded and nongraded schools differ?
2 How does the use of space affect the instructional program?
3 What are some of the important practices that teachers should look for when visiting schools?
4 What conclusions can be drawn about the grouping or nongrouping of students?
5 Why are testing and evaluating such difficult tasks for teachers?

Key Terms and Concepts

Articulation: The manner in which the various parts of the school program compliment each other in their relationship to a student's learning.

Authentic Assessment: An assessment of student learning that is based on real-world practice and attempts to measure learning in the same way it was acquired by the learner.

Continuity: Vertical articulation.

Graded schools: Schools that contain year-long levels such as first grade, second grade, tenth grade and the like.

Grouping: A practice whereby students are put into learning groups with others who have like abilities and interests.

Modules for learning: Time periods for learning that are in the daily schedule of the school.

Tracking: A method of placing students according to their ability levels in homogeneous classes or learning experiences where they all follow the same curriculum—that is, college preparatory or vocational.

*W*hen asked to describe an American school, one needs to create a picture that depicts the organization of space; the materials being used; the observed teacher, learner, and specialist behaviors; the grouping and learning patterns of students; the staffing arrangements of teachers; the pieces of written evidence that explain how things occur and what children learn; and so on. This brief list and many other pieces of observable, touchable, and experimental data constitute a patchwork portrait of the school. The interesting thing about this picture is that there will be as many different versions of it as there are people who are asked to describe the school. This chapter examines some of the easily identifiable school practices and discusses their impact on the teachers and learners.

Teachers and Space

The school building and the staff comprise the material and human resources of the school. How these resources are used determines the type of program that is offered to the student. It is important to remember that one of the most precious elements of the school is the professional staff. As a professional, you will want to take an active part in determining how your school organizes its staff and students for instruction and how the staff can get the maximum use of assigned space for instruction. Despite the fact that practices within an organizational structure and planned space vary from school building to school building, there are some commonalities among all American schools. We will discuss those in this section.

Organizational Arrangements

School organizations vary from school district to school district, and various degrees of emphasis on particular practices will be found in any description of the American school. There are, however, general categories of operation that are found in all schools. What is different is how these categories are emphasized. That difference can be attributed to the diversity of practices, size and wealth of the community, geographical location, and community expectations.

Another point to consider is the school plant itself. During periods of rapid pupil population growth, school districts experienced a constant and growing building program. Various building styles addressed intended programs of the time. As enrollment growth dipped and stabilized during the late 1970s and the 1980s, school space became fixed. Currently, only districts that are experiencing growth because of the "baby boomlet" are again building new schools. Some of the urban districts are also facing the need to replace extremely old buildings that have been condemned for some time by safety experts. However, in all of these cases the economic implications for the districts dictate how creative a district may be in its organizational arrangements.

The school building and staff comprise the material and human resources that determine what kinds of programs and practices can be used with students.

Graded Schools. The **graded school** is a borrowed European concept for organizing pupils in some orderly fashion by chronological age. Historically, children in the United States have usually begun formal schooling at the age of five or six. In almost every state of the nation that practice continues today. A few states mandate the age of seven as the starting age for compulsory education, but most use the age of five or six. It became only natural that children starting their first year of formal schooling should be called "first graders." When they returned for a second year of schooling, they were called "second graders." Gradually, requirements and standards were established for each of the formal years of schooling, and the twelve-year graded school emerged. Because of the graded requirements, however, not all students spend twelve years in graded schools. Students who fail to meet some of the graded requirements along the way must repeat a grade or several grades, and they may spend more than twelve years in school if they wish to receive a secondary school diploma. The diploma, however, typically indicates the equivalent of a minimum of twelve years of successful formal education.

Most schools in the United States are graded schools. They provide organization of pupils by ages and have established standards for each grade. Some of the problems with this type of school organization are:

1. Graded schools do not account for differences in learners with regard to either academic readiness or social, mental, and physical maturity. For example, it does not necessarily follow that thirteen-year-old girls and boys, who are vastly different physically, mentally, and emotionally, should be grouped together as seventh or eighth graders in an intermediate school. Girls are typically more mature at this age than are boys, yet they are grouped with boys for learning. Nor are all five- or six-year-olds similar in maturity.

2. Graded schools do not account positively for what a child actually has learned when the school decides that grade-level requirements have not been met and the child is forced to repeat the whole grade the following year. As a result, early failure rates among young learners help to contribute to school dropout rates later in the graded school. Individual differences in learning rates and achievement are seldom attended to, and learners suffer the greatest diversity differences in these types of schools. Although many elementary schools attempt to address this problem, few secondary schools do anything about it.

3. Since most graded schools tend to use group rather than individual expectations for test performance, and since so few of the tests that are used meet accepted criteria for good test making, learners who do not meet standards for grade levels may be unfairly penalized by these tests.

Nongraded Schools. The *nongraded school,* as now defined, involves a school organization that allows each child to progress through the system at an individual rate of development. The lockstep grade-level concept, with its set curriculum for each grade, is abandoned in favor of an individual, flexible, and continuous educational program. Sometimes referred to as "continuous progress education," this plan guides students through a series of stages of development geared to readiness for learning. Students are grouped flexibly according to age, ability, maturity, achievement, and other developmental factors. Within this grouping, students are encouraged to move ahead through each subject at their own speed; their grouping varies with the progress they make.

The nongraded curriculum makes the final move toward complete dissolution of the lockstep graded system. When an elementary school becomes nongraded, the kindergarten and early grades are often simply designated as the primary school. The upper elementary school—grades 5, 6, 7, and 8—becomes a new unit of organization labeled the intermediate or middle school, and the high school discards its strict traditional approach and graded pattern in favor of phases of learning and sequential development.

The nongraded school tries to minimize the shortcomings of the graded system, and the conventional grade designations of the typical American school are consequently discarded. With grade-level designations gone, able students can theoretically advance at a rate commensurate with ability. Whereas in the graded system it takes five years to teach the formal learning skills expected for grades K-4, children in nongraded schools might complete this learning in three, four, or five years. In addition, in the nongraded school, less able students may not have to experience psychological fear of failure or suffer the minimal learning associated with grade placement. They may take five or more years to master the necessary skills.

Most of the nongrading has appeared at the elementary level, although some high schools have attempted it. If nongrading were applied to all formal education, the curriculum could be divided into four parts: primary education, intermediate education, secondary education, and higher education. All these separate groups could be nongraded and could provide a continuous education organized around the individual progress of pupils. This type of organization more easily meets the needs of diverse students.

Instructional Organizational Elements

Teachers who are examining the operations of school organization should look for evidence of **articulation**, or interrelation, of the educational program. Too often, teachers tend to teach their own subject with little concern for what is taking place in other subjects in the same grade. Then teachers complain that there is little, if any, horizontal transfer of learning. However, a closer examination of this problem of poor articulation points to a lack of cooperative planning among teachers of the various academic disciplines. For instance, ninth-grade social studies teachers might feel little obligation to correct a student's careless English. In class the social sciences are emphasized, and teachers can easily ignore incorrect English usage.

Teachers can support students more effectively if they support one another.

Articulation Types. The same lack of horizontal articulation occurs between the mathematics teacher and the science teacher. The science teacher focuses on scientific inquiry and tends to slight mathematical exactness. Just as important as horizontal articulation among subjects is articulation within each subject. In many large schools where several teachers teach the same subject at the same level, they do not try to coordinate their presentations. Course guides and outlines, which theoretically could greatly improve the articulation within courses, do not even exist in many schools. Teachers tend to teach and emphasize what they want. With little or no supervision they go their own separate ways under the cloak of academic freedom. This lack of articulation also exists in large elementary schools among self-

Chronological Ages →	4 - 8				8 - 12			12 - 15			15 - 18			IDENTIFIED CURRICULUM CONCEPTS ↓
Grade Levels →	K.	1	2	3	4	5	6	7	8	9	10	11	12	
	I	I	I	E	E	Re	Re	E	DS	DS	DS	DS		Concept 1
		I	I	I	I	I	E	E	E	E	Re	Re		Concept 2
														Concept 3
	I	Re	I	I	Re	I	Re	I	I	DS	DS	DS	DS	Concept 4
														Concept K

Key: I = Introduction to concept   E = Exploratory work in the concept
       Re = Reinforcement   DS = Depth study of the concept

FIGURE 18.1

Vertical Articulation in the Curriculum

contained classrooms. Rarely do elementary teachers confer with one another to correlate the educational program. Any constructive move toward horizontal articulation should probably begin within the narrower confines of the subjects themselves before addressing the interdisciplinary aspects of the problem.

Continuity.   Within the school's curriculum, **continuity** refers to vertical articulation. In addition to considering horizontal articulation, the teacher must be concerned with the interrelatedness of all grade levels of the school program and how they provide students with continuous learning. Figure 18.1 suggests one way of examining the vertical articulation of the total curriculum. It applies whether the school district uses grade levels or nongraded organization. Every discipline comprises established concepts that can be identified. Because some concepts are easier to grasp than others, some can be studied at an early stage of a learner's development, while others must be introduced at a later date. The teaching staff determines what concepts will be taught and to whom, at what stage they should be introduced, and their rate of study.

Space for Learning

Since we work on the principle of mass education, the school manages and directs large numbers of staff and students at any given time during the school year. The way space is used within the learning environment has psychological implications. Humans—teachers and pupils—are very protective of their space, and teaching and learning have a better chance of being successful when space is allocated in a way that is sensitive to such personal needs. As humans, we do not like overcrowding, and we do not like to have our personal space violated. It is important to address this psychological need when we look at space and staffing for the school program.

Fixed Space. Most school buildings have been constructed along conventional lines with large corridors and self-contained classrooms on both sides of the corridors. Library, physical education, and other resource rooms are conveniently located for easy access to students. Use of *fixed space* in this way usually supports a grade-level type of school organization. Flexible space for instruction is often lacking, and there is often little or no cooperation among teachers regarding space utilization.

Open Space. Open-space facilities tend to be larger instructional areas with movable walls, flexible learning environments, and instructional organizations that are nongraded. However, this type of space does not automatically guarantee an instructional program that is developed around the philosophy of open education. It does provide the capacity for nongraded organization. Instead of having corridors faced by small classrooms, with about thirty students per room, a school plant has large instructional spaces that can be kept completely open for varieties of instruction or can be reduced to smaller areas through the use of movable walls and furniture. A school that is configured like this tends to be more conducive to diversified instructional and grouping patterns. Although its popularity has increased rapidly during the past fifteen years, the open-space facility is still found primarily at the elementary and middle school levels.

One of the biggest problems associated with the intended use of open-space facilities is the lack of adequate preparation of teachers. When school districts contemplate the use of open-space facilities, they should plan for adequate in-service staff development. If teachers learn how to be more comfortable in open space, they are more likely to use it as it was intended.

Staffing and Scheduling

School districts have complete flexibility in determining how to use their staffs. Except for the requirement that they must use appropriately certified teachers to teach the assigned offerings in the curriculum, the districts may arrange the teachers in any feasible configuration for instruction. Most schools are organized around a line and staff concept with teachers reporting to department heads or grade level chairpersons who in turn report to the administrator of the building. This has been common for schools for many years, but following are other ways to organize staff for instruction.

Team Teaching. The needs of students are more apt to be met when the students are exposed to varied learning experiences. In team teaching, learning can be most successful when large-group instruction (100 to 150 students), small-group instruction (eight to ten students), and independent study are combined. A teaching team, organized by subject or by a combination of subjects, can provide these three kinds of experiences. The distribution of time among the large groups, the small groups, and the independent study will vary according to the subject studied. Advocates of team teaching have suggested that, on the average, students should spend 40 percent of their time in large-group instruction, 30 percent in small-group discussion, and 30 percent in independent study.

Team teaching in both elementary and secondary schools may take different forms; the size and composition of the team may vary; and the teams may teach one subject or may cross subject lines. Some of the specific advantages offered by team teaching include the following:

1. The specialization of teaching, whereby the particular talents of a teacher are used to the fullest,
2. The improvement of supervisory arrangements, whereby team teachers critique one another's teaching performance,
3. The use of nonprofessional aides for routine duties, and
4. The expanded and multiple uses of many of the new teaching devices that aid the teacher.

The teaching team can be organized in two general ways. The first, a formal approach, is referred to as a *hierarchical* team organization. This approach is a line-staff organization in which a leader heads a team composed of regular teachers and teachers' aides. The second type of organization is referred to as a *collegial*, or equalitarian, team. There is no formal structure to this organization; leadership is shared or exchanged voluntarily, and all teachers receive the same pay and have equal responsibility and similar duties. Team organization is binding, however, in that although teachers enjoy a more informal organization, they must work together at a common task.

Differentiated Staffing.   *Differentiated* staffing has added a new dimension to the pattern for team teaching. However, it is merely a refinement of hierarchical teaching. Specifically, it establishes a career ladder that links the paraprofessional job with the superintendent's office. Different levels of instructional personnel are created, and each level requires certain kinds of training and experience. The director of curriculum and instruction becomes the school district program team leader. Each instructional and research staff assignment carries specific instructional responsibilities.

Modular and Flexible Scheduling.   The organizational terms *modular* and *flexible* refer to two different concepts in scheduling and should not be considered the same thing. *Modular scheduling* has existed for some time in both elementary and secondary schools. At the elementary level it has usually been associated with thirty-minute time blocks **(modules for learning)** and at the secondary level, with forty- to sixty-minute time blocks. The secondary school time blocks are tied to the instructional time allocation of the Carnegie unit. A modular schedule is just as rigid as the six- to eight-period schedule used for so many years in the secondary schools. In contrast, *flexible scheduling* uses smaller time blocks (mods), but the schedule changes regularly during the school year as students' needs and teaching objectives are altered for particular periods and types of instruction. Combining these two organizational concepts—modular and flexible scheduling—implies that the traditional organization for instruction can be changed to meet changing needs and concepts of learning as students pass through the school.

The regime of the six- or eight-period day of the typical high school does not allow enough flexibility for the best use of teacher and student resources and abilities. Classes tend to be the same size for everything, and the concern is maintaining an average teacher load. An increasing number of educators question the wisdom of devoting the same amount of time to each subject. Some subjects can be taught best in shorter blocks of time for fewer periods a week; others can best be taught in longer blocks. Some classes may be intentionally kept small; others may exceed the regular thirty-pupil classrooms. The size of the class is best determined by the intended objectives.

Modular and flexible schedules have unlimited possibilities regardless of how the curriculum is organized—that is, whether it is subject-centered or student-centered. However, as one introduces flexibility into the pattern for instruction, a theoretical shift begins to take place; the philosophical rationale adopted for flexibility tends to direct programs toward student-centered needs rather than subject-centered goals.

Student Placement and Evaluation

During the past thirty or so years a vast collection of research has accumulated that consistently suggests that children do not all learn at the same rate or in the same way. However, schools have tended to ignore that research and to group children in manageable-sized clusters of twenty-five to thirty students per teacher, without regard to learning progress. The practice is based on tradition. As a beginning teacher, you will want to address the individual differences among your students. As we discussed in Part Two of this text, the student body with which you will interact over the next thirty or so years will increase in its diversity. Your concern for that diversity will be reflected in your practices to recognize and attend to individual differences.

Class Size

Determining the optimal class size for elementary and secondary schools continues to be an uncertain exercise. There is little doubt that if all classes could have a one-to-one ratio with teacher and student, learning and teaching conditions would approach an ideal setting. However, there are valid arguments that can be offered for learning environments that are something other than a tutorial approach with a teacher. Significant numbers of studies on class size conducted over the past forty or so years have concluded little other than the notion that students can learn in a variety of class sizes. Valid arguments can be offered for group learning activities in which the student is expected and encouraged to interact with his or her peers. In addition, for some learning objectives the student is expected to receive significant amounts of information, and this can best be delivered in large groups. The problems associated with "inclusion" of special education learners creates a new question for classroom size research.

Instructional Management. Some guidelines that educational theorists have proposed for class size tend to be related to the intended objectives of the teacher. For example, if the learning objective is to have the student be a receiver of information, then class size may be any size that is manageable according to available space or attending personnel. But if the learning objective is to have students use information with other students in discussion, then the class size should be small enough that all members can participate with equal time. Classes for this type of learning environment probably should not exceed ten or twelve students. This size not only allows each student to become an active participant but also allows the teacher to observe critically each student's degree of participation as well as assess the quality of that participation.

Students often enjoy and benefit from interaction with other students.

Grouping.   The special problems of ability grouping are closely related to any examination of a school's curriculum practices. Ability **grouping** refers to the way in which student groups are created for instruction. Generally, ability grouping has been defended as a way in which the teacher can provide more adequately for individual differences. Elementary schools have tended to group pupils by subject area within the self-contained classroom, and secondary schools have tended to group students by subject, as learners develop and pursue special interests. The usual effects of grouping have caused special and separate classes to be established for the academically talented, the slow learners, and the average learners.

Philosophy of Grouping.   The position that school systems take on ability grouping depends largely on their conception of the individual child and of the general purpose of education. If the philosophical position of the school is focused on a predetermined curriculum, the school is more likely to support *homogeneous* ability grouping. In homogeneous grouping, the school uses some set of criteria (such as intelligence scores or achievement tests) to group like students. If, in contrast, the school is concerned about the personal and social development of students and believes in diversity as a technique of stimulating education, it is more likely to favor *heterogeneous* grouping. In heterogeneous grouping, the school intentionally puts students with a variety of abilities and interests together.

Despite the usual defense for ability grouping—that is, provision for individual differences—school programs still tend to be group-oriented, and individual differences are not given sufficient attention. Although ability grouping has been defended as a way to help increase learners' achievement levels, this defense is only weakly substantiated by research findings. Although many studies report positive achievement results for more able students, other studies report negative findings for less able students. One rather consistent type of research finding suggests more positive affective learning in heterogeneous grouping.

One of the chief difficulties in establishing truly homogeneous groups is the imprecise measurement instruments used to establish groups. Another constraint is the lack of flexible class and teaching assignments: It is almost impossible to select a completely homogeneous class when every class must have thirty students and when scheduling conflicts and student interests cause potentially valid diagnostic-testing data to be discarded. If the student population of a school district is a sample of the total population and if that sample is a mirror of some normal curve distribution, then class sizes cannot all be the same and still be classified as homogeneous for learning purposes.

Global Perspectives: Multi-Year Grouping in German Schools. German schools have not embraced behaviorism in learning to the extent that American schools have. Like many other European school systems, German schools emphasize studying the bigger ideas and theories, as opposed to learning the facts. Many German schools place students in heterogeneous classrooms and keep them with the same teacher for three or four years. This longer working relationship is potentially beneficial to both the teacher and the learner.

Since the teachers get to know the students better, they have a greater grasp of their students' learning patterns, interests, social skills, and emotional stability. This enriched knowledge of their students helps the teacher to prepare more meaningful learning activities and provide greater attention to individual differences. The multi-year grouping helps the students also. They get to know their peers better and are able to develop in a more socially safe environment where they can learn together and critique each other. All of this leads to greater understanding patterns on the part of the German students. This type of positive learning encourages thinking, risk taking, and personal involvement in the learning environment.

We know that grouping of this type exists in some schools in the United States, but it is far from the norm. As this country seeks to develop more heuristic approaches to be used in learning, the use of different grouping patterns may be considered. If students are to become better thinkers, perhaps they need environments where they can experience these behaviors in a safe, secure manner.

Grouping Problems. The potential for problems generated by ability grouping far outweighs the scant benefits to be gained by rigid grouping. Some of the serious problems associated with rigid homogeneous grouping are the following:

1. Teachers tend to favor teaching average or above-average groups rather than groups of low ability. Low-ability groups, however, are not always filled with low-ability students. These groups also become dumping grounds for learners with discipline problems, some of whom are not of low ability.

2. Students who are given labels of low ability usually perform poorly because of the teacher's low expectation of them.

3. Problems associated with social-class and minority group differences are usually increased with ability grouping.

4. Ability grouping tends to reinforce unfavorable self-concepts among children placed in low-ability groups.

5. Negative self-concepts are more severe among minority group learners who are assigned to low-ability groups.

6. For the learners, ability grouping does not enhance the value and acceptance of differences in society.

7. Although academically talented students achieve better in high-ability groups, low-ability students tend to perform poorly in low-ability groups.

Despite the many negative aspects of ability grouping, the advantage of using some limited and flexible grouping pattern is that it can contribute to teaching effectiveness. There is little doubt that the task of instruction—and the general intent to provide individualized programs—is made easier if the range of abilities and interests is reduced through grouping. If grouping remains flexible and is based on abilities, needs, interests, and social practices, and if students are not locked into fixed groups, the teacher can arrange instruction to achieve a set of appropriate objectives for a particular group.

Tracking. **Tracking** provides rigid, specified programs built on a system of prerequisite courses. A student who is identified with a particular high school program (such as college prep or business) stays "on the track" to complete the program and does not benefit from the flexibility associated with a constants-variable program. Rigid grouping practices are added, and the track becomes more specific. Although tracking programs were thought to provide for individual differences, they have introduced a rigid program of constants, with little elective participation by the student. For instance, one of the common tracks, the college preparatory program, has become a rigorous intellectual curriculum designed to prepare the student for more advanced learning. In so doing, it has tended to limit the student's development in aesthetics and appreciation of art and music.

The typical college preparatory program requires the student to satisfy requirements of four units in English, three in social studies, three to four in science, three to four in mathematics, three in foreign language, and at least two in physical education and health. These requirements total eighteen to twenty Carnegie units; therefore very little time is available for courses in art, music, drama, or practical skills such as computer science or driver education. These programs provide little other than instruction in the three Rs. The broader aspects of the basic, life-coping skills, aesthetic appreciations, the understanding of others, and any sense of the necessity for economic productivity are simply ignored in these rigid tracking programs. As state and local curriculum requirements continue to reflect tighter college-type programs for all learners, the nonacademic survival and appreciation skills may be placed in serious jeopardy.

Measurement and Evaluation

Teachers have a variety of techniques to appraise the curriculum and student achievement. Using classroom tests, they can evaluate whether or not specific objectives set forth for a certain subject have been achieved. Although test results are used primarily for teaching and for determining grades, they also aid teachers in adjusting methodology and course content. Additionally, they may be used to diagnose learners' readiness before beginning instruction. Standardized tests give the school system perspective about its relationship to the state, regional, or national picture. A few words of caution should be offered, however, about standardized tests: They should not be considered an effective method of evaluating students, and they should not be thought so important that they alone determine the curriculum. If tests were to determine the curriculum, the program would lose the depth of richness it can enjoy with a creative teacher.

The teacher can conditionally evaluate progress toward educational objectives—associated with students' social development, educational and social interest, and values—by checklists, rating scales, inventories, and questionnaires. Teachers and guidance counselors can also assess the effect of certain kinds of cur-

TABLE 18.1	Norm-Referenced and Criterion-Referenced Data Contrasts

Norm-Referenced Data	Criterion-Referenced Data
Are gathered from instruments established from local, state, or national norms	Gathered from instruments established from local instructional objectives
Indicate how a learner or a group of learners has performed in comparison with peers	Indicate the degree to which a learner has achieved a particular learning objective or set of objectives
Tend to be valid and reliable according to some national expectations or norms	Have a high degree of validity to a set of learner objectives; reliability of the data, by usual measurement standards, is questionable
Indicate a student's overall performance, aptitude, or attitude on some broad continuum or domain—usually used for ordering pupils	Indicate a specific level of competency or development as expected by previously stated objectives; usually used for individual diagnosis and prescription

ricular changes by observation, interview, anecdotal records, sociometrics, sociodrama, and student autobiographies. The school system can use opinion polls, interview community employers, and follow up on graduates to judge how effective the total school program is.

Normative Testing.   *Norm-referenced* (or normative) *data*—that is, data that are compared to local, state, or national norms—are easily obtained when teachers use standardized tests. In addition to the precautions mentioned earlier with regard to using them, an ever-present question is how effectively these tests measure a particular school program. They should be used with some degree of caution for student placement, and unless such caution is exercised in identifying and interpreting student progress, these tests may be detrimental in evaluating the curriculum.

Criterion Testing.   *Criterion-referenced* data are gathered from instruments that have been specially designed to measure expected learning changes. Whereas the learner performance in norm-referenced testing is compared to the performance of other learners, criterion-referenced testing shows performance of the student against himself or herself. Criterion-referenced measuring instruments involve stated operational learning objectives. They do not yield test scores that indicate a percentage of achievement based on some class standards or norms; they do indicate how well a particular student has met the stated learning objectives of the teacher. If these tests are planned specifically to show minimum levels of learner competence, they can be valuable to the teacher, the student, and the parents. For instance, criterion-referenced tests not only yield total scores but also indicate how well each objective was reached. If certain objectives have not been reached, the students repeat the learning activity for those objectives only and do not repeat the activities that have been completed successfully. Instead of assigning grades for achievement, the teacher assesses pupil progress on a pass/fail basis. When these measuring instruments are used along with norm-referenced instruments, the evaluation of a curriculum, especially pupil progress, becomes much more accurate. Table 18.1 shows the difference between norm-referenced and criterion-referenced data.

Authentic Assessment

The move toward the use of **authentic assessment** has come about because of the serious limitations associated with the exclusive use of standardized-type and criterion-type assessment techniques. These two types of assessment techniques are limited in at least two ways. First, they only give a measure of a point in time, and it is extremely difficult to obtain a more complete picture of what a child has actually learned or accomplished. They also suffer from problems associated with obtaining adequate sampling. Second, with changing national, state, and local goals for education, which include self-direction, collaboration, complex thinking, quality performance, and community contributions in learning, the traditional means of assessment fall short of providing data that can offer a more accurate picture of just what a student can or cannot do. Thus, the move to more authentic approaches to assessment has gained momentum in measuring learning.

In addition, there is a more apparent need to relate assessment practices to instruction and learning. As more cognitive approaches to teaching and learning replace behavioral theories, it has become more important to assess learning in a more holistic manner, rather than just gathering data on discrete bits of knowledge acquired by a learner. Conventional types of test formats (objective and subjective) serve an important purpose for some pictures of learning, but they just don't provide the whole picture.

Authentic assessment is considered authentic when it directly examines student performance on a learned task. A collection of these assessment techniques (sometimes called *performance assessment*) makes up the total authentic assessment approach. This is accomplished by using a context or situation that directly displays what the student has learned. This text has proposed (with an introduction in Chapter 1 and portfolio activities at the end of each chapter) that you engage in a beginning form of authentic assessment by developing your own professional portfolio that shows what you have learned and what kinds of performances you have exhibited. We encourage you to think about how these techniques can be used with your students when you begin teaching.

To be authentic, assessment activities must resemble actual classroom and life tasks. Characteristics of authentic assessment are:

- The assessment closely resembles the way the student will encounter the task or use the knowledge in real life.
- The teacher and the student constantly examine what has been learned, and they jointly determine the limits of that learning.
- The assessment has the learner display learning in a variety of contexts, not just one.

Relevant Research

The Road Ahead for Performance Assessment

Eva L. Baker has summarized some of the next steps to be taken with performance assessment. Citing a variety of studies that have been conducted with performance assessment, Baker's research lays out the issues for evaluating the forms and quality of the measures to be used in challenging the advocates of alternative assessments.

The first challenge is the promotion of equity in performance. Equity is discussed as it refers to the meaningfulness of measures that hold students' attention and have a specific purpose that makes sense. Other equity issues include linguistic appropriateness and the issue of sensitivity that the measurement has for instruction. The major concern of this research report is that performance measures be subjected to the strict tenets of validity.

Source: Eva L. Baker, "Making Performance Assessment Work: The Road Ahead," *Educational Leadership 51* (6) (March, 1994) pp. 58–62.

One significant change in contemporary school practices is the variety of methods by which students are allowed to demonstrate their learning.

- Assessment provides for active collaborative reflection by both teacher and student.

Methods Used for Authentic Assessment.   Traditional type test data can be used to provide part of the picture for authentic assessment. However, these types of data should be strongly supported by learning journals and logs that contain written descriptions, drawings, reminders, data, charts, conclusions, inferences, generalizations, and any other collection of notes and artifacts that have been developed and gathered by the learner during the learning process. Interviews and observations conducted by other students and the teacher can be recorded for immediate and later discussions. All of these activities need to be ongoing so that when examined collectively, real changes in learning behavior can be easily seen. Finally, this holistic set of authentic data should be collected and displayed in a portfolio. Teachers working with students in this type of authentic assessment approach will need to help learners acquire the skills necessary to gather and report these types of data. When successful, this measuring technique will replace the weekly student test approach and occur continuously.

Using a Portfolio.   Portfolios act as a compilation of a student's work based on a variety of criteria. They may contain beginning and ending performances on work or only the student's best work. They are collections of student performances that can be shared with parents, teachers, other students, and even employers. (The portfolio you are keeping with this text could be shared with a hiring school district.) The Northwest Evaluation Association offers this definition of a portfolio.

> A portfolio is a purposeful collection of student work that tells the story of the student's efforts, progress, or achievement in (a) given area(s). This collection must include student participation in selection of portfolio content; the guidelines for selection; the criteria for judging merit; and evidence of student self-reflection."[1]

PROFESSIONAL DILEMMA

Can You Prepare Authentic Assessment Tools?

As you start your first year of teaching, you are confronted with a very diverse class. In particular, the class has been heterogeneously grouped, and in addition to several Hispanic students who have a poor command of English, you have two inclusion students. Your principal has informed you that the district places a heavy emphasis on authentic assessment for students.

You have some initial breathing room because the supervisor is not requiring you to provide polished authentic assessment strategies for your first unit of instruction; however, she wants you to be more fully involved with this type of assessment as you start your second unit of instruction. You have about six weeks to get ready for your next unit, and the supervisor wants to see your assessment plans before you begin that unit.

Your dilemma is multifold.

- What will your second unit be?
- How will you determine what authentic assessments to use?
- Where can you turn for help as you prepare for the second unit?

Assess some of the techniques you can use with your class, and prepare some samples for the supervisor to evaluate. In particular, address the heterogeneous makeup of your class.

Some of the problems to be aware of when using portfolios are representativeness of materials, clear criteria for assessing, authentic work and extraneous response requirements, differences in interpretations, and conclusions reached by student and teacher. Portfolios should have purpose and be linked to instruction. They should be carefully managed and have *a priori* decisions made about storage and transfer, as well as ownership and access.

Authentic assessment is an attempt to make testing, both in and out of the classroom, more precise and less restricted. Its very name implies attempting to determine what students have really learned. When you are working with diverse groups of learners, this type of assessment yields superior data on what changes in learning behavior have occurred and to what level skills have been developed.

Grading. Evaluating student learning, or *grading,* is one of the most difficult tasks that teachers face. In a very real sense the teacher is labeling the student when an evaluation takes place. One of the major difficulties of grading students involves the evidence that the teacher has gathered on the student's performance. This evidence is usually obtained from paper-and-pencil test performance or some planned program of teacher observation of student performance. Two questions with which teachers must wrestle as they prepare to evaluate their students are the following:

1. Are the measuring instruments or other means of assessment that were used to evaluate student performance valid and reliable? In other words, do the classroom tests, or other procedures of authentic assessment that are used to determine grades, accurately and consistently measure what has or has not been learned?

2. Has the teacher sampled enough of the learning behavior to determine that whatever has been observed or measured truly reflects a student's performance?

Grading is not an easy task, and many experienced teachers continue to have difficulty with it. How a teacher determines the grades for his or her students tends to be wholly related to the teacher's personal philosophy. A school district may determine what constitutes an A or B or C in a course, but the teacher learns how to adjust a predetermined grading program to his or her personal philosophy. Good teachers constantly search for fair and consistent approaches to grading.

Planning for Instruction

The key to success for any planned curriculum is how the intended curriculum learning experiences are delivered to the learner. Instructional practices in the schools may vary considerably, depending on expectations for student performance and the teacher's repertoire of instructional skills. The expectations for student performance should be based on clusters of learning objectives by discipline, grade-level, or combinations of disciplines in a nongraded school organization. Well-planned objectives assist the teacher in planning for instruction.

Types of Learning

The broad aims that the many national committees and commissions have developed are valuable only if they have some relation to specific learning outcomes planned for the school. Teachers who are preparing to plan the curriculum, teach the subjects, and evaluate the intended outcomes should understand how planned objectives for learning are reached. Expected types of learning change as the world adjusts to change. Planning for different types of learning is never finished. The instructional planning activity is an active process.

Taxonomies. There have been several attempts to clarify and develop educational objectives. One is the comprehensive approach of Bloom and others—the taxonomy of educational objectives. These educators classified the objectives in three groups, or domains, according to the kind of learning to be produced: cognitive, affective, and psychomotor.

- *Cognitive* objectives are concerned with remembering, recognizing knowledge, and developing intellectual abilities and skills.
- *Affective* objectives are concerned with interests, attitudes, opinions, appreciations, values, and emotional sets.
- *Psychomotor* objectives are concerned with the development of muscular and motor skills. These three domains are presented in Appendix 18.1 on page 483.

Convergent Learning. Teachers work with learners to develop at least two types of learning practice and behavior: convergent and divergent. These behaviors are associated with the lower and higher levels of the taxonomies. The sole objective of *convergent* learning is that the learner experience the discovery and manipulation of new (for the learner) knowledge but then arrive at closure and acceptance of a single solution or generalization before moving on to new learning. This type of learning is anticipated when the teacher's intent is to work with the learner at the lower levels of the cognitive taxonomy.

Divergent Learning. *Divergent* learning encourages the learner to explore, develop hypotheses, gather information to test those hypotheses, and arrive at a defensible conclusion. The student does not have to search for the one "right" conclusion because there is not one. This type of learning practice prepares students to search for and accept answers that are different from one another. Objectives that focus on divergent learning are derived from the higher levels of the cognitive taxonomy.

Models of Learning

Students are different. They learn at different rates; they have differing abilities; some are more able and some are less able; some learn more easily through some mediums of instruction, and others learn more easily through other mediums of instruction. Teachers should consider using appropriate models of mastery learning, programmed learning, and individualized learning in order to meet the different needs of their students.

Mastery Learning Model. The *mastery learning model* attempts to address problems of learning rate and differences in ability. Although students of differing abilities and learning rates may work with the same or similar objectives, they are all still expected to acquire mastery or satisfactory achievement of the objective. Some students may be given more time than others, and some may be provided with opportunities at different levels of mastery in order to achieve the expectations. One of the keys to the success of a mastery learning model is the teacher's diagnostic and prescriptive work. Teachers must be realistic in their expectations for learners and be reasonably confident that what they desire in learning outcomes is achievable by the students with whom they interact. If mastery learning is planned to be sequential, then the student success rate is particularly important. Students need to experience success in learning.

Mastery learning models are difficult to employ if the school curriculum is rigidly fixed by grade level and all students are expected to master certain objectives every year. They are most effective in nongraded school programs in which time (by the year) is not as crucial. These programs are more flexible, and differences in learning rates can be attended to with fewer problems. Specific objectives for learners are still used, however, and clusters of students or individual students work with those objectives.

Programmed Models. *Programmed learning* can be traced to the early work of Sidney Pressy during the 1920s. Pressy was unable to promote his ideas to any extent during the 1930s, but B. F. Skinner presented them thirty years later. Since then, programmed instruction has gained significant acceptance. Although this model can be and has been used for application learning behaviors, it is perhaps best used for developing expected knowledge and comprehension.

Two approaches to programmed instruction are important for teaching. The first, linear programming, uses constructed-response frames for which the student must supply an answer. The student may receive immediate feedback to a single response or feedback only after a planned series of responses. In the second method, branch programming, the student proceeds to additional frames for learning only after correct responses are recorded; the learner is directed along an

Teaching practices now often favor interactive and hands-on learning experiences that engage students in learning.

alternative route for remedial or reinforcement activities. This branching technique is designed to help the student correct and understand his or her errors before moving on to an advanced series of frames.

Programmed instruction is considered to have the following advantages:

1. Students are free to learn at rates commensurate with their own abilities. Programmed instruction permits individual study. Fundamental subject matter can be presented through a program, providing the teacher additional time to work with pupils on an individual basis.
2. The confirmation-correction feature of the program provides reinforcement of learning and builds student interest.
3. Programs can be designed to instruct in affective as well as cognitive areas of learning.
4. Programming helps students to understand a sequence of complex material and has the potential for doing so in less time than formal classroom instruction.

One of the primary considerations to be made in using programmed materials is the student's reading level. Since programmed learning relies on the printed word, there may be damaging effects on the poor reader. Another consideration is that although programs can be designed for learning appreciation as well as for skills, not very much has been done for learning appreciation so far.

Individualized Models. Audiotutorial and *individually prescribed instruction (IPI)* models provide for individual pacing of learning activities. Direct student-teacher contact is at a minimum except when the teacher provides remedial, developmental, or enrichment services to the learner as a result of some diagnosis. One of the chief characteristics of these strategies is test-teach-test. From predetermined instructional objectives, curricular modules for individualized instruction are developed. For each module a diagnostic test is developed to measure, before instruction starts, how well the learner can reach the module objectives. After diagnosis, the learner proceeds through the instructional package and is retested at completion. If learners reach the expected criterion for the learning package, they go ahead at their own rate. The learning packages become individual tutors for the students. The task of the teacher is to monitor learner progress through diagnostic activities and testing.

The term *audiotutorial* refers to audiotape recorders for the instructional delivery system, whereas IPI may use a whole host of instructional delivery systems ranging from paper materials to computers. Teachers using IPI generally follow these steps:

Step 1: Administer a diagnostic test for the learning module, and establish entering behavior.

Step 2: Have the learner experience the elements of the learning module indicated by an entry-level test.

Step 3: Test the learner as he or she completes the module.

Step 4: If the expected criterion for the module has been attained, move the student to the next module and pretest.

Individually guided education (IGE) was developed by the Kettering Foundation's Institute for the Development of Educational Activities (IDEA) and the Sears Roebuck Foundation. The current activities of IGE are disseminated through two major

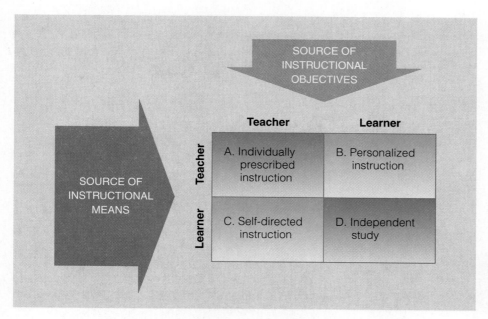

FIGURE 18.2

Individualized Learning Matrix

national groups. One is the IGE Teacher Education Project at the University of Wisconsin, and the other is the national IGE Project operating out of IDEA in Dayton, Ohio. Whereas IPI takes all learners through the same preplanned program with identical objectives, IGE promotes different specific objectives for individual learners and is heavily process-oriented. Objectives are planned by the teacher and student. IGE strongly emphasizes both individualized and group learning.

There are many types of instructional models that offer a variety of approaches to individualized learning. Cecil Trueblood[2] developed a model for categorizing these varieties (Figure 18.2). The model illuminates the sources of objectives and the sources of means of instruction as a classification matrix for individualized learning. Programs in which the teacher determines the objectives and means of instruction are described as category A. Programs in which the learner cooperates on either objectives or the means of instruction are described as categories B and C, respectively. The most sophisticated type of individualized learning is one in which the learner determines his or her own objectives and means of instruction, category D.

Thinking Skills Model. A *thinking skills model* has at last assumed its rightful place among the learning models for instruction. Because it has been regarded for countless years to be part of the language arts program of the elementary school, little has been done formally in the classroom; it has generally been assumed that thinking skills have been taught by the teacher and acquired by the learner during the normal process of teaching and learning. Teachers now know, as a continued emphasis on learning theory enriches the teacher preparation program, that if you want learners to know and practice how to think, that process must be taught. Students must become more responsible for their own learning if learning is to continue after the student leaves the teacher.

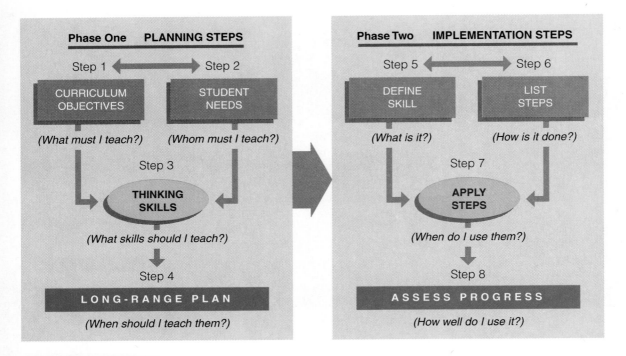

FIGURE 18.3

Thinking Skills Model

(Source: Antoinette Worsham, "A 'Grow As You Go' Thinking Skills Model," *Educational Leadership.* (April, 1988): 56–57.)

Antoinette Worsham[3] has developed a thinking skills model, which is shown in Figure 18.3. Her model presents an eight-step approach for teachers to use if they wish to develop thinking skills while delivering their instructional program. As the figure shows, the model has two phases, a planning phase and an implementation phase. As the teacher works with the students, he or she uses an inductive process to work on skills. Students are instructed in how to ask the questions that are appropriate to skill development and content acquisition. Interestingly enough, this type of learning model holds great promise for transfer from one academic class to another. The model can be used with the cognitive domain levels to help students move from lower-level learning to higher-level learning. If the teacher has objectives for learning that can be ascribed to the hierarchy of learning, then the thinking skills model can be used to increase the achievement of those objectives. Students are encouraged to be reflective in their learning and keep logs of what they learned and how they learned it. The greatest strength of this model is that the students, if they have acquired the requisite skills, see its applicability to all of their learning encounters and the relationships in learning among the many disciplines they study.

Use of Technology

The past and current decades have witnessed an explosion in the creation of technological aids for teachers. This technology, however, has been slow in gaining regular use in the schools. Cost of equipment has certainly played a significant role, but among other factors retarding the use of available technology are the lack of training on the part of teachers and the dearth of educational materials available for use with the technology. These two factors are beginning to disappear; increasing amounts of new materials are now ready for use, and teachers are receiving additional training through staff development programs.

Learning Resource Centers

Instructional materials centers are valuable for a variety of instructional strategies. This type of learning environment is established not to replace a school library but to enrich it. The typical verbal materials found in a library are supplemented with software and hardware instructional materials. In any teaching strategy used, students may be assigned, or be free to use, a center to pursue learning on an individual basis or through small-group activities. The learning resource centers are equipped with books, programmed materials, closed-circuit television, and audiotapes, videotapes, and computers. A variety of other materials provide auditory, visual, and audiovisual learning.

Although learning centers were used initially at the elementary level, they are found increasingly in the junior and senior high school. As school districts use more varied organization and instruction, the need for learning centers becomes more apparent. The learning center has become more than an administratively planned area; it has become an adjunct classroom on which the teacher can plan for instruction. The only limitation to the learning center is the teacher's imagination as he or she develops objectives for learning experiences for children.

Hardware and Software. Teachers must be alert to the importance of being informed about the new software and hardware media. The terms *software* and *hardware* acknowledge that this is an age of "systems" and "systems development,"

Computers in schools are becoming as basic as pencils and paper.

but in their application in education they refer to human resources and learning materials and their uses. Examples of software are books, filmstrips, audiotapes, and transparencies. Examples of hardware are projectors, television monitors, and computers.

Such products have greater significance today for learning than ever before. With the acceleration of the amount of knowledge, and the effect of this on the curriculum, the American educational system has to keep finding ways to incorporate this new knowledge systematically into planned programs. American inventive genius and advanced technology have produced a vast number of devices, programs, organizations for instruction, and materials to help the teacher do a better job. While the lay person, the educator, and the academician have recognized and clarified the disciplines of knowledge, technological genius has produced mechanical aids ranging from very simple recording equipment to complex computers. Many of the new instructional media have become part of the vast educational team that will continue to produce more advanced hardware and software materials to improve learning.

Television. *Instructional television* can be used as an open- or closed-circuit medium as an aid to instruction. With closed-circuit units, most often used within a school building or within a district, school districts can create their own instructional materials as local needs dictate while providing all learners with access to the best teachers in the school system. Open-circuit units usually receive television communication on a broader scale and not specific to a district. In both cases the television units use live or taped instructional packages for classroom use. The Communication Satellite System (COMSAT) has now opened new possibilities for mass education through television transmission anywhere in the United States. For formal class presentation, television has the capacity for reaching extraordinarily large groups of students. However, if instructional television is to be used successfully, it should fit into the general scheme of teaching. To allow it to become dominant in instruction is to misuse the medium, and if the misuse is allowed, the instructional value of television becomes as questionable as the single-textbook approach or overuse of the motion picture. Continuous evaluation of television instruction is all important, since as a medium of large-group instruction, its potential for misdirected learning or group indoctrination is ever present. Its primary emphasis should always be directed toward education—and not toward television for itself.

Microteaching. Another use of television is to help teachers improve in instructional practices. Although television is not an integral part of many staff development programs, those programs whose main objective is the improvement of instruction will find the use of videotape equipment very beneficial. An increasing number of teacher-training institutions have adopted television, or *microteaching,* techniques. If the early efforts of teacher training are to be successful, school districts should provide television equipment and help for teachers who are trying to improve teaching skills. Through videotapes, teachers can watch their classroom performance and thus identify and modify or eliminate teaching weaknesses. Television is a valuable tool for the in-service training of teachers. Through videotape, many outside consultants can be brought to the school district, where in-service training is most effective.

Dial-Access Systems. Dial-access audio and video systems provide more ways of individualizing instruction. *Dial-access systems* use a phone-type system to "dial up" preprepared learning packages that are used on an individual basis. These systems can be used either as the sole method of instruction for some parts of the curriculum or as a supplement to regular classroom instruction. Dial-access equipment was first used, on an experimental basis, in 1961 at the University of Michigan. Since then, it has been used primarily for language study. Use seems to be divided evenly between teacher-mediated instruction (instruction that is part of the teacher's planned lessons) and enrichment instruction (instruction that is provided for students who have completed all of the required work planned for all students). The dial-access carrels are conveniently placed in the school so that students can get direct help from a teacher if it is needed. The curriculum is built with instructional objectives, and students progress at individual rates based on diagnostic test batteries.

This particular use of technology creates time for small-group learning activities with teachers; students can pursue the required common learning through individualized dial-access systems. Another use of dial-access equipment is listening laboratories that accommodate small groups of students. These laboratories can utilize records or audiotapes. A more expanded use of existing language laboratories in many schools could provide similar instructional services that are being delivered by dial-access systems.

Videodiscs. *Videodiscs,* which resemble the old 78-rpm phonograph records, offer another significant advance in technology. These disks carry prerecorded video material or can be used to tape specific television programs for instructional use. Among the distinct features of this technology are the capacity for instant access to any part of a program and the high quality of still pictures.

Videodiscs, like videotapes, can be used for simulation programs and can help the teacher to move a step closer to the individualization of instruction. The combined use of these disks with microcomputers is currently being refined. The computer can be used to manage the individualizing of the instruction as the student proceeds through the videodisc frames.

Computers

Computer-assisted instruction has opened a new vista for individualized learning. When a computer is used, individual learning is limited only by what the programmer has put into the machine. The established techniques of linear and branch programming can accommodate individual or small-group learning sessions in a variety of ways. The computer now acts as a tutor in the learning environment. Through *computer-assisted instruction* a teacher can serve a large number of pupils and still have instantaneous

---

Relevant Research

Videodiscs Improve Student Outcomes

Optical Data Corporation, through its Educational Research Partnerships program, conducted a videodisc study in elementary science with their participating schools. The program is intended as a resource supplement to the regular program and features photographs, diagrams, movie clips, and animations. The videodisc program can be used for elementary, middle school, high school, and college level school programs. Optical Data provided staff development activities for the schools using the program.

Teachers using the program collected the data for Optical Data; it included both standardized type assessment and portfolio data. After one year of operation, the data indicated that students using the videodiscs had higher achievement levels than students not using the discs. Videodisc students had higher lab scores and better attitudes toward science. This study is continuing, but thus far, it suggests that students can do better in science when the regular program is augmented by videodiscs created for resource use.

Source: Heidi Marie Rock and Alysa Cummings, "Can Videodiscs Improve Student Outcomes?" *Educational Leadership* 51 (7) (April, 1994): 46–50.

CASE STUDY   SELECTING TECHNOLOGY

*S*chool use of technology continues to have a significant influence on the school program. As new generations of minicomputers continue to emerge and costs come down, the use and impact of this technology presents an increasing demand on the schools. Add to this the fact that increasing percentages (estimated at 30 to 40 percent currently) of children are beginning school with a sophisticated degree of computer literacy. This is due to the increased numbers of computers in homes. There is a caveat to this growth among school learners, however. There is a growing discrepancy between the learners who come from the middle class and above, and those children who are coming from lower class poverty families. Many of the children of this latter group are also diversity children, and this has had an impact on the direction the school takes with regard to computers for learners. Despite this difference in learners, schools are continuing to increase their use of computers in the classroom.

You have been asked to serve on a school committee to evaluate and determine the technology needs for your school building. Most of the technology now in use centers around overhead projectors, film projectors and the like, and some closed-circuit television receivers. You have become a strong computer advocate since your undergraduate teacher education program. However, many of the teachers in your building have not fully accepted computers and retain some phobias about this technology. Your student body is somewhat diverse and has a significant number of students who are coming from homes without computers.

1. As a committee member, what tactics will you employ to win support of your colleagues in giving considerable emphasis toward computer technology?
2. What assumptions can you explore about the financial feasibility of technology enhancement for your school?
3. What plans should your committee address about how the school should begin to use computers with the diverse student body described above?
4. Should you try and involve the parents of children attending the school? Why?

The principal has indicated that he wants a report from the committee in time for a superintendent's meeting in the near future.

---

evaluation of pupil progress readily at hand. Thus the role of the teacher takes on new dimensions. Instead of merely dispensing knowledge, the teacher can be, with increased precision, diagnostician, prescriber of learning materials, and devotee of increased teacher-learner interaction.

Simulation/Interactive Video. Simulation programs for the classroom computer can be developed by the teacher with minimal knowledge of computer operation. *Simulations* present the learner with lifelike situations and are very successful ways to reach the higher levels of the cognitive domain of learning while having an effect on the affective domain of learning. When combined with computers for interactive video programs, simulation techniques can be made as real as life. As a teacher in preparation for a full career, you should be preparing yourself not only to be computer literate, but also to use the computer to assist in your regularly planned classroom instruction. Computers are now found in almost every school district of the nation. In fact, as reported by Quality Education Data of Denver, Colorado, twenty-one of the states plus the District of Columbia now mandate computer instruction in the schools. Some of these mandates are built around competency tests for graduating seniors, and others call for at least a mandatory offering in computer literacy.

Record-Keeping and Management. Just as the computer can deliver instruction, it can also manage the whole instructional and record-keeping program of a school district. Records of student performance and accompanying reports, use of materials, management of scheduling, and records of learners' progress are but a few of the possibilities of computer-managed instruction. The computer management system operating in the Admiral Peary Vocational-Technical School in Ebensburg, Pennsylvania, for example, monitors learning progress for the teacher. As students complete prescribed tasks, modules, and units of learning, the students' progress is recorded and stored. On completion of a specified vocational program the student is given, in addition to a regular high school transcript, a printout that shows the level of competency development for the whole program—the sort of information that is most meaningful to prospective employers. With this technology now available for use, you might think that teaching has been greatly simplified. On the contrary, teachers must now face curricular issues that were previously reserved for administrators and supervisors.

Mainframes. Many early computer applications required an expensive mainframe computer with accompanying terminals for student use. As the technology developed, schools had to keep changing models with each new generation of mainframes—a costly exercise. For a considerable period of time, computer-assisted or computer-managed instruction was therefore severely limited by cost, but the introduction of microcomputers has reduced this problem.

Microcomputers

The microcomputers that are now increasingly being used in the schools cost considerably less than the huge mainframe computers of the recent past. The popular Apples, IBMs, and the like, with their floppy and hard disks, are being utilized to answer the need for computer literacy and individualized instruction. The newer microcomputers use less sophisticated and more easily learned program languages for curriculum development. In addition, the computer industry has developed a vast storehouse of academic programs for use with computers.

Boons and Banes. There are three significant difficulties associated with the use of microcomputers for instruction. First, technology is expanding so rapidly that the market is continually being flooded with new, more sophisticated hardware. The question of which computer to buy is tied not only to the original cost but also to the life cycle of the model. For instance, in the short span of five years the Apple computer evolved through five models, each more capable than its predecessor. The PC market has seen the same type of growth.

The second problem is that software tends to be developed for use with a specific type of microcomputer and is not always compatible with other types. As newer models are introduced, there is increased compatibility of available software; but the problem still remains. Third, and perhaps most important, instructional staffs are not trained to program or use microcomputers as they were intended. Teachers cannot willy-nilly buy software and inflict it on learners. They need to be retrained to evaluate software in light of both planned objectives for the curriculum and learner models.

Microcomputers can be used in many of the same activities that initially required mainframe computers. Teachers who have become computer literate and have microcomputers available to them can now manage instruction with their computers and maintain sophisticated records on students. As teachers develop test items for the programs they teach, these items can easily be programmed into a computer for random selection when testing students. Software houses have developed voluminous amounts of computer software to be used in the classroom in all of the content areas, and teachers need to know how to evaluate software. Instructional programs and games are now available for mathematics, science, social studies, foreign languages, and the language arts.

Microcomputers have become a popular delivery system for meeting the needs of special education learners. The special education teacher can prepare the required IEP with the computer and then provide programs for the learner to use. The common expression in the microcomputer field today is "user friendly," and the stress in development is to provide simple, uncomplicated software that encourages teacher and student use.

Kyle Peck and Denise Dorricott offer ten cogent reasons for schools to increase their use of computers.[4] They believe computers provide:

1. Greater attention to students' developing and learning at different rates;
2. Assistance in students' acquiring proficiency in accessing, evaluating, and communicating information;
3. Help in improving the quality and quantity of students' thinking and writing;
4. Assistance in students' learning problem-solving skills;
5. A nurturing of students' artistic expression;
6. Help in students' developing global awareness and the ability to use resources that exist outside the school;
7. Opportunities for students' doing meaningful work;
8. Access to high-level and high-interest courses;
9. A comfortable relationship with the tools of the information age; and
10. Increased productivity and efficiency for schools.

Computer Futures.   Computer literacy for the 1990s and beyond has become a new basic skill for all learners at all levels. Every daily encounter is somehow affected by computer technology. Current estimates suggest that by the year 2000, 98 percent of all households in the United States will have computers, which will be used for a wide variety of home activities. So why should you as a teacher prepare yourself to use the computer as a professional? Let us share with you at least five cogent reasons for you to become a computer user.

1. **Word processing.** As a teacher, you will constantly be producing reading materials for teaching—course outlines, handouts, tests, and so on. You will also be responsible for written student evaluations, communications with parents, and other paperwork. Word processing allows you instant creation and revision. If your written materials are kept on disk, you have the capability of easy revisions from semester to semester and year to year. As a side benefit, you will be modeling for your students a very practical use of the computer as they compose and write in the learning environment.
2. **Database information.** As a teacher, you constantly use data that you share with your students. The computer assists you in collecting and developing

databases that can be useful in your instruction in mathematics, social studies, business, language arts—with literary analyses and vocabulary building, science experiments, and many other areas. Additionally, the database information practice can be of assistance in the preparation of materials as well as determining how they were used and the outcomes of their use.

3. **Spreadsheet information.** As a teacher, you will also be a record keeper. The use of spreadsheets will free you from the traditional gradebook and help you to keep a considerably more accurate and up-to-date record of your students' performances. Routine activities at the end of a grading period, such as averaging grades, can be done automatically by pressing a few keys. Students who come and go during the year can easily be accommodated by your spreadsheet. The more literate you become in the use of the spreadsheet, the more you reduce your nonteaching load. As a professional, you want time to plan and teach, not to be a recordkeeper. Computers can help you to become a more effective professional.

4. **Use of CD-ROMS.** Many data-based programs are now available on a CD-ROM; they contain reading material, pictures, encyclopedia information, and stand-alone instructional lessons.

5. **Communication NETworks.** Through the use of Bitnet and Internet, teachers can now communicate with other teachers and programs around the country. The computer modem allows teachers to access libraries and their information storage facilities via telephone connection.

More than ever, teachers need to be computer literate. This textbook revision, for example, has been undertaken with the aid of computer technology. New word-processing programs now aid the authors in composing and editing text. Use of the typewriter has passed into oblivion. Thus the computer is more than just a tool for teachers to use in instruction. It is an instrument capable of mass communication and instantaneous decision making.

Summary and Implications

In examining the program of the school the teacher needs to consider several factors. Whether the school is graded or nongraded will affect the curriculum, the teacher, and the learner. Space, whether fixed or open, affects the type of operating school program. Scheduling practices affect both the teacher and the learner in the learning environment. How teachers test, the types of tests they use, and the way in which they evaluate students are all aspects of the picture of schooling. The instructional organization of the teachers' day yields further information about the operating philosophy of the school program. Technology holds the day in modern educational practice; how it is used depends on the teacher.

The implications of school practices are important for you as a beginning, and later a practicing, professional. You must have some knowledge of all of these areas in order to become an evaluator of school practices. Schools exist for learners; the learning atmosphere and the practices of the school reflect the attention given to the practice of quality learning environments. Finally, how the teacher uses technology will determine whether that technology is a sophisticated aid to the teacher or has become the teacher for the student.

Discussion Questions

1. How do different teacher scheduling arrangements affect student learning environments?

2. What are the pros and cons of ability grouping?

3. What do you think about authentic assessment practices?

4. How is the mastery learning model different from the thinking skills model?

5. Discuss the significance of the computer in individualizing instruction.

Journal/Portfolio Development

1. Develop a personal philosophy about your concepts and preferences in grouping students. In particular, base your philosophical tenets on your beliefs about students, their learning needs, their diversity, and their intellectual differences.

2. Select two pieces of software that can be used in your teaching field. Assess their appropriateness for a particular grade level of students; as well as their appropriateness as supplemental resource material or stand-alone instructional material.

School-Based Experiences

1. Visit a school and observe how teachers work differently with students as a result of homogeneous grouping. Discuss your observations with the teacher after you have had an opportunity to have the teacher explain his or her goals for different students.

2. Visit an elementary and a secondary school and observe the different uses of space. Write a paper that compares and contrasts the different uses of space in the two schools. Use organizational and instructional criteria for space as the basis for your comparisons. Verify your analysis with the administrators of the two schools.

Notes

1. Arter, Judith A., and Vicki Spandel, "Using Portfolios of Student Work in Instruction and Assessment," *Educational Measurement Issues and Practices* (Spring, 1992): 36–44.

2. Cecil R. Trueblood, "A Model for Using Diagnosis in Individualizing Mathematics Instruction in the Elementary Classroom," *The Arithmetic Teacher* (November, 1971): 507.

3. Antoinette Worsham, "A 'Grow As You Go' Thinking Skills Model," *Educational Leadership* 45 (7) (April, 1988): 56–58.

4. Peck, Kyle L., and Denise Dorricott, "Why Use Technology?" *Educational Leadership* 51 (7) (April, 1994): 11–14.

Bibliography

Educational Research Service. *Ability Grouping.* 2nd ed. Arlington, VA: Educational Research Service, 1990.

Joyce, Bruce, and Weil, Marsha, w/Showers, Beverly. *Models of Teaching.* 4th ed. Boston: Allyn and Bacon, 1992.

Marzano, Robert J., Pickering, Debra, and McTighe, Jay. *Assessing Student Outcomes.* Alexandria, VA: Association for Supervision and Curriculum Development, 1993.

Means, Barbara, and Olson, Kerry. *Technology and Education Reform: The Reality Behind the Promise.* San Francisco: Jossey-Bass, 1994.

Perleman, Lew. *School's Out: Hyper Learning, The New Technology, and The End of Education.* New York: William Morrow, 1992.

Sizer, Theodore. *Horace's School: Redesigning the American High School.* Boston: Houghton Mifflin, 1992.

U.S. Department of Education. *America 2000: An Education Strategy.* Washington, DC: U.S. Government Printing Office, 1991.

Wittrock, Merlin C, and Baker, Eva L. *Testing and Cognition.* Englewood Cliffs, NJ: Prentice Hall, 1991.

Appendix 18.1

Domains of Learning

The levels of cognitive learning are numerically ordered from the most superficial to the most advanced to establish a hierarchical arrangement for evaluating depth of learning.

Cognitive

1.00	Knowledge
1.10	Knowledge of specifics
1.20	Knowledge of ways and means of dealing with specifics
1.30	Knowledge of the universals and abstractions in a field
2.00	Comprehension
2.10	Translation
2.20	Interpolation
2.30	Extrapolation
3.00	Application
4.00	Analysis
4.10	Analysis of elements
4.20	Analysis of relationships
4.30	Analysis of organizational principles
5.00	Synthesis
5.10	Production of a unique communication
5.20	Production of a plan or proposed set of operations
5.30	Derivation of a set of abstract relations
6.00	Evaluation
6.10	Judgments in terms of internal evidence
6.20	Judgments in terms of external criteria

Source: Benjamin S. Bloom, ed., *Taxonomy of Educational Objectives* (New York: Longmans, Green, 1956), pp. 6–8.

Affective

1.00	Receiving (attending)
1.10	Awareness
1.20	Willingness to receive
1.30	Controlled or selected attention
2.00	Responding
2.10	Acquiescence in responding
2.20	Willingness to respond
2.30	Satisfaction in response
3.00	Valuing
3.10	Acceptance of a value
3.20	Preference for a value
3.30	Commitment
4.00	Organization
4.10	Conceptualization of a value
4.20	Organization of a value system
5.00	Characterization by a value or value complex
5.10	Generalized set
5.20	Characterization

Source: David R. Krathwohl, Benjamin S. Bloom, and Bertram B. Masia, *Taxonomy of Educational Objectives* (New York: McKay, 1964), pp. 176–193.

Psychomotor

1.00	Reflex movements
1.10	Segmental reflexes
1.20	Intersegmental reflexes
1.30	Suprasegmental reflexes
2.00	Basic-fundamental movements
2.10	Locomotor movements
2.20	Nonlocomotor movements
2.30	Manipulative movements
3.00	Perceptual abilities
3.10	Kinesthetic discrimination
3.20	Visual discrimination
3.30	Auditory discrimination
3.40	Tactile discrimination
3.50	Coordinated abilities
4.00	Physical abilities
4.10	Endurance
4.20	Strength
4.30	Flexibility
4.40	Agility
5.00	Skilled movements
5.10	Simple adaptive skills
5.20	Compound adaptive skills
5.30	Complex adaptive skills
6.00	Nondiscursive communication
6.10	Expressive movement
6.20	Interpretive movement

Source: Anita J. Harrow, *Taxonomy of the Psychomotor Domain* (New York: McKay, 1972), pp. 1–2.

19 Schools for the Next Century

Focus Questions

1 There are a few schools where major transformations are taking place. Describe the features of these schools.

2 What do you think society should do to address the social and emotional needs of children?

3 What kinds of changes in schools do you expect to see during your career as a teacher?

4 Leadership is an important part of school success. How do you think teacher leadership can make a difference?

5 In the past there were few career advancement opportunities for teachers that did not require them to leave the classroom. Do you know of career advancement possibilities today that allow you to continue being a teacher?

Key Terms and Concepts

Career ladder: A career path for teachers consisting of a number of rungs, or job roles, that carry with them increasing responsibility and performance of more complex professional tasks.

Core values: Statements of principles about teaching and learning that are fundamental to one's philosophy of schooling.

Metaphors: The use of words, images, and examples from one's experiences and background to explain and illustrate an idea.

Restructuring: An umbrella label for talking about a number of innovations and themes related to Site-Based Decision Making that are intended to improve school operations and, through these, student performance.

Second change facilitator/consigliere: A special leadership role in a school whereby a teacher offers facilitating assistance to other teachers during the unfolding of a school-based change process.

Transforming: Major restructuring, redesigning, or significantly changing the shape and function of schools.

In reading the first eighteen chapters of this book you have learned a lot about schooling. You have had the opportunity to learn about different philosophical bases and educational points of view, and you have explored the relationships between school and society. You have examined how schools are organized and governed, as well as their financial and legal structures. In the last two chapters, we have looked at contemporary school programs and practices. All of these chapters have summarized how American education has developed and evolved into the 1990s.

However, this cannot be the end of the story. In your career as a teacher, you will be participating in the continuing evolution and further development of American education. You will have the opportunity to test many exciting new approaches and technologies. In addition, as an American educator, you will have the opportunity to be creative and to employ innovative practices in your classroom. It will even be possible to share your experiences with many others across the land.

All types of exciting changes will take place for you in your career as a teacher. Changes around us are coming rapidly and have enormous impact on our lives. In the last several years we have witnessed the breakup of the Soviet Union, a number of multinational peace-keeping initiatives, the birth of a global economy, ever smaller and faster computers, new technologies for the home and the classroom, and exciting breakthroughs in medicine. This truly is a time of change and it is clear that, in your career as a teacher, you will be a key part of the dynamic and exciting world of change in education.

Change Is All around Us

One of the challenges you will face during your career will be to accept change and nurture the many innovations that will be introduced. Further, we hope you will be creative and contribute your own novel ideas for improving schools. Therefore, in this last chapter, we will introduce you to some of the innovative practices and resources that are being created for schools as they move into the twenty-first century. Everything that is described here is already in operation somewhere in America. However, as you will realize, most of the ideas have not touched the majority of classrooms and many educators are still unaware of these interesting, novel, and promising practices. We offer them here to *stretch* your thinking about schooling, teaching, and your role as a teacher in the next century.

Big Change or Little Change?

At this point in your life, you have spent many years in schools, and chances are they were rather typical schools in terms of how they were organized and the types of curriculum and teaching processes that were used. In many ways, the typical school has retained the worst features of the historical one-room schoolhouse; there is one teacher in a classroom with four walls, a chalkboard at the front, and twenty or more children are sitting in chairs arranged in rows. However, typical schools of today have lost such promising educational features of the one-room schoolhouse as children of a wide age range in the same classroom, children teaching children, flexible schedules, community involvement in the school, and teachers as leading members of the community. These very important educational features were lost early in the twentieth century as ideas from the industrial revolution were applied to the "business of schools." For example, the fifty-minute class period and ringing bells for class change are reflections of the efficient assembly line. In this image of schooling, students are "products," teachers are the "workers," and principals are "management." As you read the remainder of this chapter, keep in mind your images of the one-room schoolhouse. In many ways, the restructuring and transforming of schools that is taking place in the 1990s is a return to some of those "lost features."

One of the challenges students and teachers of the future will face is adapting to rapid changes in technology.

The Focus on Learning.   There is enormous pressure, from the changes that are taking place in society, to have schools respond in kind. The dynamics of the world are creating increasingly international and global perspectives. There are a number of trends in terms of work, the characteristics of the family, distribution of wealth, and the diversity of our students and population. All of these features are impacting what schools will become. Whether we are reading newsmagazines, listening to industrial leaders and politicians, or watching the evening news on television, it is impossible to escape the concern about the quality of American education and the demand for change. These demands are not for small tinkerings with schools; rather, there is an expectation for large-scale redesign. The wished-for changes have to do with the approaches to teaching, the design of the curriculum, the organization of schools, how states are organized to support schooling, changes in the roles of teachers and principals, and the redesign of teacher education programs.

There is also a major shift in the **metaphors** used to address schools. Metaphors are the images, examples, and models that are used to compare schools with other parts of society. For example, the metaphor of the school as a factory is undergoing a major change. Instead of our seeing the school as an assembly line, stamping out students as products, we now see students as the "workers," teachers and principals as "managers" of the instructional environment, and the "product" as a "student learning." This perspective change represents a dramatic shift in how one thinks about the role of teachers and students. Changing how one views the work of schools leads directly to changes in the roles and responsibilities of teachers and students, as well as the way schools are organized. Schools of the future will have different structures and role relationships. Such symbols as bells ringing every forty-eight minutes will be replaced by new symbols, such as students carrying lap-top computers instead of books and papers.

A Scale for Assessing the Size of Change.   Changes come in various forms and sizes. Just as in industry, change in schools can be vast and sweeping, or small and insignificant. Another aspect in considering change is that, in many instances, planned changes are not actually implemented: There is a great deal of talk, but the change itself is never really put into practice in classrooms. In other cases, there are very small changes that do not make a major difference in what students learn. Thus, a distinction can be made between talking about change and tinkering with relatively small changes. The critics of schools, as well as many educators, are asking for **transforming** types of changes—ones that would dramatically influence the shape, structure, and operations of schools and classrooms.

One way to view the different magnitudes of change is illustrated in Figure 19.1. In some recent research and writing, Hall has proposed a scale—similar to the Richter scale for grading the size of earthquakes—for grading the size of innovations. In this case, the sizes of different changes in schools are being compared. Referred to as the HIC scale, this ten-point scale goes from "Talking" to "Tinkering" to "Transforming." At the Talking end of the scale, there are speeches, press announcements, and published commission reports, but there is little if any change in classrooms. As one moves toward the middle levels of the scale, the Tinkering section, changes take place in schools and in classrooms; however, they are of modest impact. The categories of change at the Transforming end represent major, wide-ranging restructurings, redesigns, and alternative configurations of what schools and school practices can be like.

	LEVEL	NAME	EXAMPLES
Talking	0	Cruise Control	1950s Teacher in same classroom for many years
	1	Whisper	Pronouncements by officials Commission reports
	2	Tell	New rules and more regulations of old practices
	3	Yell	Prescriptive policy mandates
Tinkering	4	Shake	New texts Revised curriculum
	5	Rattle	Change principal Team teaching
	6	Roll	Change teacher's classroom Change grade configurations
	7	Redesign	Evening kindergarten Integrated curriculum
Transforming	8	Restructure	Site-based decision making Differentiated staffing
	9	Mutation	Teacher and principal belong to the same union Changing the role of school boards Coordinated services
	10	Reconstruction	Local constitutional convention Glasnost

FIGURE 19.1

Hall's Innovation Category Scale (HIC's)

(Source: G. E. Hall, "Examining the Relative Size of Innovations: A Scale and Implications." Greeley, CO: College of Education, University of Northern Colorado, 1993.)

Think about the changes in schools that you are aware of and the ones you have read about in this text. How many of the ideas for change that you know about have been put into practice? We suspect that you know of many good ideas that are not implemented in most schools. This is because change is difficult, and large-scale change is personally uncomfortable—as well as a lot of work. Also, the truly Transforming types of changes take many years to implement. Further, many of the Transforming changes tend to be seen as wild and crazy. Ideas such as placing schools in shopping centers, or having high school students teach elementary students, represent major shifts from schools as we know them. Truly Transforming ideas, such as having public schools begin with children at birth, or high school students taking two months to do an independent project away from the school, are hard to accept as "doable." Yet, an increasing number of Transforming innovations are being tried.

In the remainder of this chapter, various Transforming types of educational innovations are described. The purpose is to stretch your thinking and to increase your awareness of the vast variety of major changes that already exist in some American schools. As we move toward the twenty-first century, more of these Transforming types of innovations will be taking place, and in your career as a teacher, you will have the opportunity to participate in the implementation of many of them. At the very least, it is likely that you will experience working in a school district where one or more schools will be incorporating some of these types of practices. Perhaps, as your career unfolds, you will have the opportunity to create additional innovations in teaching, curriculum, and classroom and school operation.

Relevant Research

Moving to the Future with Our Schools

A futures researcher declares that critical mass changes are needed for the schools of the immediate future. Tying the concepts of childhood and schooling together, Dixon lays out a futures school that is learner based rather than adult based. Using examples of strong child influences on everything in their lives—influences from major industries, running households, creating and establishing social norms, and in the final analysis determining what they will or will not learn in school—he offers an empowerment to young learners in their educational development.

Some of the hallmarks of his futures school are: teachers who are leaders in defining education (rather than followers of corporate giants); students who govern in schools rather than "play" at governing; classrooms that are referred to as "living rooms"; and teachers who are human interactors, consultants, and tutors. This provides a challenge for the new teacher to explore. Are you getting ready professionally to become a practicing visionary?

Source: R. G. Des Dixon, "Future Schools and How to Get There from Here," *Phi Delta Kappan* 75 (5): 360–365.

Restructuring Schools

The current theme for bringing about major changes in schools is called **restructuring.** Restructuring is an umbrella label that encompasses a number of different innovations and themes. In the larger perspective, the restructuring movement addresses how to make schools more successful in relation to student learning. A number of the changes have been directed at student learning by introducing new tests, increasing the rigor of old tests, and using alternative assessment procedures such as portfolios. Other restructuring innovations have been directed at the design of the teaching-learning situation by changing the curriculum materials and introducing different teaching strategies, such as the 4MAT Program, TESA, and Madelyn Hunter's Essential Elements of Instruction.[1] Still other initiatives have been directed more toward organizational systems through emphasizing the instructional leader role of the principal and establishing interdisciplinary teacher teams. All three of these dimensions have extensive research bases to justify their use, and all have been directly associated with student success, teacher success, and schools that are more positive places for teaching and learning.

There are a number of concrete implications of the restructuring movement. One is that the role of the school principal changes dramatically. The principal can no longer be the authoritarian directive leader, but instead has to work in more collegial and collaborative ways—not only with the Site-Based Decision Making council, but also with the rest of the professionals and support staff in the building. A second implication in restructuring is related to the design of curriculum. For example, more academic courses are being required for high school graduation. Up to this time, high school students have been able to graduate with a relative minimum of courses in basic subject areas such as mathematics and science, and, in many instances, English as well. With the restructuring movement, increasing expectations for academic preparation for high school graduation are being put into place. Other innovations under the restructuring umbrella are described here.

Site-Based Decision Making (SBDM)

Parts of SBDM were covered in Chapter 8. The SBDM school council can include teachers, classified personnel, the principal, community representatives, business representatives, parents, and perhaps others. The premise is that all of the participants serving on the council will work together to make more informed decisions at the local site. A wide array of decision-making responsibilities is possible. Also, the composition of the site-based council can vary dramatically. One effort to summarize these components and variations of the innovation of Site-Based Decision Making is presented in Appendix 19.1 on page 515.

Another theme out of the restructuring movement is increased involvement of parents in schools. Through the SBDM process, parents have a more direct say in decisions affecting the school. Also, parents' increasing participation as aides in classrooms and in the development of projects and activities helps provide the school with more resources. This latter activity is becoming increasingly important with the serious cutbacks in funding that education is experiencing in the 1990s. Parent involvement in schools is happening not only in schools with children from well-to-do families. The increased concern about the failure to educate low-income and minority children has resulted in many educators, political leaders, and community groups advocating parent involvement in all schools. This trend toward a more shared responsibility between parents and schools is very promising.

Historically, there was a perceived separation by which schools dealt only with academic issues while parents and the community dealt with the social and emotional development of children. Now there is an understanding that the school, community, and the parents have to work together to address four domains: academic, social, physical, and emotional development of children. The situation has been driven by the demographics of our student population, which have been reported throughout this book. For example: 40 percent of today's school children will have lived with a single parent by the time they reach age eighteen. More than 20 percent live in poverty. Fifteen percent speak a native language other than

There are a number of ways in which parents can become involved in the education of their children.

PROFESSIONAL DILEMMA

Can You Successfully Involve Parents in Their Children's Education?

Throughout your professional training you learned about the importance of having parents involved with their children's learning. This text has strongly emphasized how important that involvement is for minority and single-parent children. You will be faced with this type of diversity in your classroom wherever you begin your professional teaching career. You will also encounter increasing school district demands that you take the time to reach out to parents and have them become partners with you in meeting the educational needs of their children. Successful accomplishment of this professional expectation takes considerable planning and time.

At the end of the first month of your initial teaching year, your principal approaches you and indicates that he wants you and your colleagues to begin this reach-out behavior with the community. The group of students that you teach are representative of the total student body: You interact regularly with able and less able students, you have nonminority and minority students who come from two-parent and single-parent families, and you even have two homeless students in one of your classes. The principal asks you to prepare a parent/school involvement program for your students, and he would like to discuss some of your plans with him in one month.

Your dilemma at this point is:

- Where do you begin? The principal suggests that you identify two or three students and prepare a case study approach to this task.
- What kinds of students will you select?
- How will you make preparations for this important venture?

English, and 15 percent have physical or mental disabilities. All of these data indicate that the complexion of the school classroom has changed dramatically. As a result, how we teach has to change in equally dramatic ways.

There are a number of ways that parents can become involved in schools. An example of direct involvement is parents being able to select the school their children will attend. Another is influencing the decision making that goes on in schools by participating on SBDM councils. A third way of involving parents in schools is through *parent training programs,* in which parents can develop new skills in such areas as communication, how to work effectively with children of different ages, how to help children develop self-discipline, and achievement orientation. Parents also learn guidance techniques for helping their children develop study habits and attend to homework. Parents can also be involved in the *development of resource and support programs.* These can range from the above-mentioned developing and soliciting financial and resource supports for the school to assisting in providing services to other parents in the school community. In addition, parents can be effective in working in counseling, training, advising in regard to substance abuse, and other types of *support and discussion group activities* that relate to the larger mission of today's schools.

Business Involvement in Schools

Another increasingly important set of school partnerships are those that are developing between businesses and schools. In the past, more of a one-way perspective existed in the relationships between businesses and schools. There were various types of "adopt-a-school" programs, where businesses would send often obsolete equipment and other types of resources to the schools. In many ways these programs treated schools as some sort of underprivileged client that businesses could assist; however, that simplistic one-way perspective has changed dramatically in the 1990s. Now there truly are reciprocal partnerships between businesses and schools. The business community is recognizing that not only do they have things to offer schools, but also schools have many types of resources to offer to the business community in return. One of the expanding steps in the ongoing dialogue between businesses and schools has been the number of chief executive officers, such as the former president of Xerox, David Kearns, former CEO of IBM John Akers, and the previous CEO of US West, Jack MacAllister, who have been advocates for schools. They have continued to express their interest in and support for schools, and they have invested in changing schools. These types of testimonies and initiatives by business leaders have kept public attention focused on the need to improve schools.

Transforming Schools

There are a small number of experimental efforts that are truly about transforming schools. In each instance, a local staff of teachers, principals, parents, and community representatives are struggling to implement a model of what all schools can become. Each of these schools has been through a two-to-four year process of developing images for what they want to be. In many instances they have had to confront school district and state policies that prohibit the types of transformations that they wish to implement. In response, some states are making major changes in their education policies and procedures to encourage more change. In all cases, transformed schools are being established that offer hints regarding what schools could be like for you in your career as a teacher. All of these transforming efforts have major implications for the preparation of teachers, such as yourself. It is important to note that at the same time schools are changing, there will be transforming efforts in relation to the design of teacher education programs. Further, as a teacher, you will be in a position to facilitate and lead change efforts. This section describes some current transforming activities.

In the late 1980s and early 1990s many of the efforts to transform schools were made under the label of "restructuring." As we summarized above, the so-called restructuring movement focused on a number of elements for making schools more responsive and effective, such as Site-Based Decision Making, cooperative learning, and the use of particular curriculum philosophies, such as whole language. A small number of the schools have gone far beyond those elements to entirely new school models. These transforming schools incorporate a number of different features and designs. The design of each school is based on a set of **core values** or beliefs. In each case the school has developed a statement and list of principles about teaching and learning that have guided the decision making for transforming the school. These statements include descriptions of what a particular community believes is important about children, the role of teachers, and expectations about the responsibilities of students. In nearly all instances, the key determinant for making changes has been judgments about what would most optimally affect student success. Note that success is not always determined in terms of narrow measures such as standardized achievement tests. In most of the

| CASE STUDY | CLASSROOM STRATEGIC PLANNING |

*S*trategic planning has become as commonplace for schools as it is for business and industry, government, and many growing church groups. In education, this can be a very strong professional growth activity or it can degenerate into a "busy-work" activity that meets some state mandate for filing a plan. However, most strategic activities are meaningful and give a school district a chance to stand back; take a fresh look at the whole school operation; and assess the needs of the students, the community, and the nation. With these types of baseline data for a school district, teachers and staff can plan for district-wide change, school building change, and classroom changes.

As a new teacher, you should constantly be involved in planning your classroom program. As you have seen, student needs change, the makeup of classroom diversity changes, and knowledge and needed basic skill requirements change. This requires you to be flexible in what you propose to do with your students in their learning environment. You will find that wherever you teach, your building administrator will have continuous expectations for you to keep your professional activities current with the changing times.

Prepare a plan of action to keep your classroom strategic planning up to date, using a teaching assignment perspective. Indicate how you will correlate your individual strategic planning efforts with those of your school building and the school district. How will you correlate your efforts with your classroom colleagues at a given grade level or discipline level? Where does all of this activity fit into what you believe about learning and student diversity? How will you seek evaluation of what you do, and will that evaluation alter your plans? How can you demonstrate leadership throughout this whole activity?

---

transforming schools, there is a broader, more robust perspective of what students need to accomplish and achieve. One example of a statement of principles is presented as Figure 19.2 on page 494. This set of principles was developed by a coalition of child advocacy groups that is collectively referred to as the National Coalition of Advocates for Students.

Education Family Style

One of the transformed schools that is implementing a wide array of features is the Laboratory School at the University of Northern Colorado. The basic theme for the restructuring of this school has been "Education Family Style." The emphasis on family is a direct reaction to the Laboratory School staff's concern that the lives of the typical student of the 1990s is filled with disruptions. In many ways, the typical school adds further disruption to the life of American students. For example, every fall students are placed with a new set of classmates and with a new teacher. From the students' point of view, instead of there being continuity from year to year, the school year begins with disruption. Then, nine months later, more disruption is introduced by breaking up the class; and the following fall the cycle begins anew.

In response to this, the staff at the UNC laboratory School has created families whereby 50–100 students of a two-to-three-year age span can stay together across a number of years. This "family" has two-to-three teachers who are also permanent across time. Thus, one source of disruption is minimized and a number

1. Children are entitled to have parents, advocates, and concerned educators included in all decisions affecting their education.

2. Children are entitled to learn in an integrated, heterogeneous setting responsive to different learning styles and abilities.

3. Children are entitled to comprehensible, culturally supportive, and developmentally appropriate curriculum and teaching strategies.

4. Children are entitled to access to a common body of knowledge and the opportunity to acquire higher-order skills.

5. Children are entitled to a broadly based assessment of their academic progress and grading structures that enhance individual strengths and potential.

6. Children are entitled to a broad range of support services that address individual needs.

7. Children are entitled to attend a school that is safe, attractive, and free from prejudice.

8. Children are entitled to attend school every day unless they pose a danger to other children or school staff.

9. Children are entitled to instruction by teachers who hold high expectations for all students and who are fully prepared to meet the challenges inherent in diverse classrooms.

10. Children are entitled to an equal education opportunity supported by provision of greater resources to schools serving low-income, minority, differently abled or immigrant students.

FIGURE 19.2

Ten Student Entitlements for Educational Success

(*Source: The National Coalition of Advocates for Students,* 1992.)

of new stabilizing elements are introduced. As you can see, the creation of families adds a number of new dimensions to the schooling context, one of the more salient factors being that children of multiple ages are together in the same class(es). Another difference is that, instead of working in isolation, teachers work together as an interdisciplinary team with their family of students. An overall picture of the design of the UNC Laboratory School is presented as Figure 19.3.

Vision 20-20. Another feature of the UNC Laboratory School is the absence of the typical grade-level structure. Instead of having kindergarten, first grade, second grade, freshman, and senior year, the Laboratory School has five levels. These levels cover the range from early childhood to young adult, conceivably from 20 days to 20 years. In other words, the staff in this school are exploring what the schooling environment can be like for children from very young ages to young adulthood; hence, the theme—Vision 20-20. In contrast to traditional grade levels, the five developmental levels reflect current research and theory about the age at which the typical transition points in learning style and perspective take place. The Lab School staff propose that a school be organized around these developmental levels, rather than the typical grade levels correlated directly with age and birth dates.

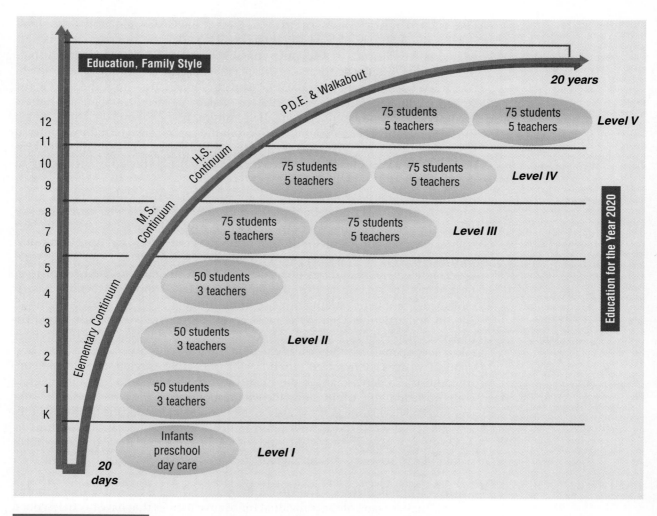

FIGURE 19.3

Organizing Framework for the University of Northern Colorado Laboratory School

Autonomous Learning. The UNC Laboratory School places a strong emphasis on students assuming major responsibility for their own learning. In addition, parents are directly drawn into the work of the school through the development of *Personal Learning Plans.* Each six weeks the parent and the teachers, along with the student, meet to review the student's accomplishments, to clarify objectives, and to set the list of tasks to be accomplished in the next interval. Heavy emphasis is placed on the expectation that the students will be self-directed, as well as individually guided by teachers, in their learning. Teachers have a responsibility to help students develop confidence and independence in order to become life-long learners. At the same time, it is assumed that students will increasingly assume more responsibility and initiative in relation to what they learn and how they learn it, especially if they have more of a role in managing the process.

Use of Authentic Assessment. The staff at the UNC Laboratory School, including the high school level, are interested in having the students demonstrate what they have learned in ways other than paper and pencil tests. Students display their learning through performances, displays, media productions, and other methods. It is envisioned, for example, that as part of graduation from the school, the students will have accomplished the equivalent of the Australian aborigine's "walkabout." At some point during their last year in the school, students take on the responsibility for developing a project in the community, or in the country at large, that is directly related to their learning objectives. Students move out on their own to accomplish this project, then they return to the school to report on the outcome.

Multi-Aging. Just think about it! The only time in your life when you were segregated by age was during your experience in the typical American school. In your college classes, your instructor did not begin the class by saying "All 21-year-olds sit over here. All 37-year-olds sit over here. All 42-year-olds. . . ." Yet this is what we do in elementary and secondary schools when students are grouped by their birth dates. In reaction to this, the staff of the UNC Laboratory School has established a number of mechanisms to bring children of all ages together around educational activities. One of the most novel is KAFE (Kids Alternative Food Experience). Rather than having a contracted food service, the staff and students have taken over operation of the school cafeteria. They are running it as a business! Students of all ages are involved in purchasing, preparing, serving, and cleaning up. In addition, students manage the finances of the business and have to grapple with profit and loss, while, along the way, responding to the tastes and food preferences of their customers. Obviously, in addition to addressing the theme of multi-aging, KAFE also offers students opportunities in cooperative learning, arithmetic, concepts of business, and many other types of skills that the critics of schools would like to see in high school graduates.

Many Other Features. The UNC Laboratory School is typical of transforming schools in that many of the individual innovative themes that have been described in earlier chapters have been brought together into one comprehensive plan. Some of the other themes at the UNC Laboratory School include: appropriate technology (there is a difference between being "high tech" and including "appropriate uses" of technology), business and community education, developmental grouping, early-childhood education, global and community awareness, interdisciplinary education, Site-Based Decision Making, and social responsibility and service. Schools of this type truly are at the higher ends of the HIC scale. They are engaged in transforming what schooling can be about, and they are responding to the unique needs of students in the 1990s.

Transforming High Schools

There is widespread agreement that it is more difficult to bring about change in high schools than in elementary or middle schools. There are a number of reasons for this, including the fact that many high schools are large, teachers tend to be more focused on their subject matter, and program offerings are more complex—because of the combination of basic disciplines, co-curricular activities, athletics, music, and drama that are offered in the comprehensive high school. Other factors that make change difficult include Carnegie units, fifty-minute time blocks, and the diversity of students and adults. However, transformations of high schools are happening too.

Essential Schools. One of the most promising efforts to bring about significant change in high schools is being lead by Ted Sizer and his colleagues in *The Coalition of Essential Schools.* This effort is based on an earlier study of high schools that was conducted by Sizer. The Coalition, which was a network of twelve high schools attempting to bring about significant change, joined with the Education Commission of the States, which is a national agency that brings together staffs of the governors' offices around major initiatives. The merged coalition is now called *Re-Learning.* In this nationwide effort, member high schools must address nine common principles, and school communities who wish to transform their high schools must agree to share in and work on achieving them. Through the Coalition it is possible for the schools to receive support from each other, learning more about the developmental work that needs to be done with the community and the staff, as well as with students, to bring about significant change. There are Re-Learning schools in most states. The leaders of this transforming effort have found that certain principles receive the most resistance and therefore have to be addressed most systematically.

Total Quality Management (TQM). The American business paradigm is being confronted with major challenges too. The challenge to the American way of doing business has many names, but in general it is referred to as Japanese management or Total Quality Management (TQM). Since World War II the Japanese have put together a very different way of thinking about doing business. TQM brings with it a different set of assumptions about business, and currently a number of educators are considering how TQM can be applied to schools. The TQM paradigm clearly confronts the current way American schools are run. To illustrate this comparison, think about the old impressions of Japanese products that were imported into the United States and contrast those with current impressions.

Early Japanese Products	*Japanese Products of Today*
Low tech	High tech
Cheap	High priced
Poor quality	High quality
Unreliable	Maintenance free

As you can see from these examples there has been a major metamorphosis in what we think of products made in Japan. The reason for this paradigm shift was the involvement of a number of American consultants in working with the Japanese to rebuild their economy following World War II. The most prominent of these consultants was W. Edwards Deming, who brought to Japan a very different set of assumptions about how to approach manufacturing. His whole thrust was to place the emphasis on building a quality product and to focus on *continuously improving* the quality of the product. Further, Dr. Deming emphasized collecting data about every aspect of the manufacturing process and using these data to make changes and to evaluate the success of efforts to improve quality.

This paradigm is very different from the way American business has been run. In American business, the assumptions, focus, and attitudes have been on producing products as cheaply as possible and in large quantities. The focus has been on making things at lower costs instead of on increasing the quality. In the American business paradigm, improvement has to do with how to make things more cheaply in order in order to increase profits. The TQM model assumes that increasing quality will result in decreased costs and therefore higher profits. Let us see what this would mean in terms of thinking about schools. Consider the following as attributes of regular schools and a paradigm TQM school:

Regular Schools	*TQM Schools*
Nine-month time module	Eighteen-year module (womb to graduation)
Self-contained classroom	Shopping mall school
Education only	Integrated services
Emphasis is on teaching	Emphasis is on learning
Each school year the same	Each year changes based on data about last year's teaching and learning
No systematic use of data, but students are graded	Data about students, teaching, and curriculum are constantly analyzed and used to change teaching and the curriculum
No feedback about how your students did after leaving class	Direct feedback on how your students do the next year
No feedback on student success in the next higher level of schooling	Direct feedback on how students do in subsequent schools
Teacher pay based on years of teaching	Teacher pay based on how successful your students are in subsequent years and adjusted by track record of the students once they leave school
Annual evaluation by the principal	No annual evaluation; instead, continuous feedback to individuals and staff as a whole about the effects of improvement efforts
Telling students what they need to know	Asking students, parents, and the community what future adults need to be able to do

As you can see, the emphases and assumptions of these two paradigms of schooling are quite different. They represent the kind of paradigm shift you will experience in your career. The emphasis on continuous improvement is especially important. The focus on learning, the multiyear perspective, and the idea that there needs to be cooperation among all members of the organization to improve quality are different from what goes on in the regular school paradigm. In the TQM model, three important questions that can be translated and applied to schools are:

1. Who are your customers?
2. What is your product?
3. How can the manufacturing processes be changed to improve the quality of the product?

As you explore these questions and develop your own answers, you will find that they represent a very different way of thinking. For example, who are your customers? You probably are giving the quick answer that they are your students, or the parents, or the community. In some cases this is true; however, have you thought about the fact that the teacher who receives your students next year is your customer? The product you deliver to that teacher is your student. Thus, in the TQM model, among the important customers you need to be interacting with and considering as consumers are the teachers at the next grade level.

Charter Schools.   In 1989, Minnesota was one of the first states to pass legislation in favor of parents choosing schools for their children. Ten years earlier, a strong national debate arose over the concept of school vouchers. During the 1990s school choice came into active existence as charter schools emerged in California, Texas, Wisconsin, and Arkansas in addition to Minnesota. The debates about this issue continue in many other states today.

Charter schools allow parents to choose what they perceive to be high quality education for their children—education they feel is not being given by the local public schools. They are different from the voucher concept in that the public school district financial vouchers are for parents to use in selecting educational experiences for their children. In Minnesota the law allows a charter school to operate with a contract with the local school board. This is an educational agreement between a charter school and the school board, with the board spelling out goals, objectives, and responsibilities of both parties, the board and the charter school.

With charter schools, there is a power shift in governance, funding, and accountability. The granting school board provides the funds for operation of the charter school, but the charter school has its own governing body (school board), teachers, and administrators. In situations in which charter schools house students from the regular school district, the local school district budget is reduced and shifted for use by the charter school. Charter schools must compete for students; thus, there is a high degree of accountability in their operation or they will not survive.

Global Perspectives: Charter Schools in England.   Charter schools began in England in 1989. Since the English system of public education is a national system, the Department of Education issues direct grants for the formation of charter schools. These charter schools move through a transitional period before being granted permanent status. Once the school has moved to a corporation basis it receives yearly grants of funds from the national education ministry for school operation and school plant services.

The charter schools of England are completely different from those described for Minnesota in that they, like their public school counterparts, are responsible to the state and not to the local school district where they are located. This appears to be more a function of a centralized system of schooling as opposed to the U.S. system, in which local autonomy has been granted by the state governments for operation of the schools. The charter schools of both countries, however, serve the same purpose—providing a quality educational alternative to learners.

Outcomes Based Education (OBE).   The philosophy of Outcomes Based Education is usually associated with William Spady. Outcomes Based Education differs from performance-type programs in that it is intended to address meaningful culminating experiences. The demonstrations of outcomes being achieved must occur in some contest or performance setting; they must be of high quality; and they are expected to occur at culminatng periods such as at fifth, eighth, and twelfth grade levels. The demonstrations of competence need to take place in an aura of what Spady calls the "Demonstration Mountain." This "mountain" contains the *traditional zone,* which is structured task performances with discrete content skills; the *transitional zone,* which is complex unstructured task performances with higher order competencies; and the *transformational zone,* which is life-role functioning with complex role performances.

Outcomes based education students are expected to be implementors and performers, problem finders and solvers, planners and designers, creators and producers, learners and thinkers, listeners and communicators, teachers and mentors, supporters and contributors, team members and partners, and listeners and organizers. In 1991 Pennsylvania moved to OBE and mandated all school districts to prepare their district strategic planning along OBE guidelines. The big issue with a movement of this type is determining what the desired outcomes will be. In Pennsylvania, "Moral Right" organizations and groups opposed the notion of affective outcomes that addressed values and morals leading to students' accepting homosexuality as a healthy lifestyle. Temporarily shelved because of the efforts of these critics, the Pennsylvania OBE program goes on, but it is muted in the affective areas of learning.

Schools as the Center for Delivery of Coordinated Services

Up to this point, we have looked at schools as if they were the single agency that deals with children. However, this is not the image of schools that will exist in the very near future. As a matter of fact, there are a number of very exciting initiatives under way at this time in which schools are serving as the center for coordination and delivery of a wide range of social, educational, and human service functions. Unlike the past, and for most of the schools in the present, schools in the future will be dramatically transformed from a single purpose to full service. Increasingly they will become the center for access to many services including emotional health, welfare, education, criminal justice, health, and dental services. Instead of attempting to address the educational needs of children in isolation of other needs and their families, some schools have already become holistic family resource centers.[2]

This is a dramatic move away from the array of individual agencies that have dealt with distinct parts of the child. Each of these agencies may have been performing well, but none dealt with the child as a whole person. In fact, it has not been uncommon to have on average five different social service agencies addressing the needs of one at-risk child. Typically, none of these agencies would communicate with the others concerning their knowledge of the child or the child's family, nor would they communicate about the interventions that were being made. In addition, the various levels of federal, state, and local human service agencies complicate the delivery of services. For example, in the California state government, there are 160 different programs and 35 state agencies that deal with services to children. The whole child is not seen by any one agency, as each is specialized in delivery of its service.

Obviously, when there are this many different agencies involved, with all of the associated professions and related policies, rules, and regulations, it is highly unlikely that any one child can be addressed as a whole, nor that all children will be receiving equal access to the available service resources. In fact, in many cases, agencies are required by law to withhold information from other agencies. There have been no means for developing linkages, communication, or coordination. Think about your own preparation to become a teacher. Has it been typical in your program for each of the human service professions to be aware of the work of the other professionals involved with other aspects of the child? For example, it is a typical pattern on college and university campuses for teacher education students to have no formal contact or training with social work, nursing, counseling, or criminal justice students. From the point of view of an at-risk student, all of these services and the related professional personnel are addressing the same child and his or her family. The need to address this compounding picture is obvious. The solution that is being tested across the country is coordinated or integrated services.

Services Problems. Many children are not receiving the needed services that are available. More and more children are at risk and so are an increasing number of families. Yet we have not made the transformation from the old way of doing business to new ways of addressing the increasingly prevalent and urgent needs. Melaville and Blank[3] have developed a report and analysis of this emerging effort to structure interagency partnerships so that children and families can receive these comprehensive services. In their report, they identify five reasons for the failures typical of our current system.

1. Most services are crisis oriented.
2. The current social welfare system divides the problems of children and families into rigid and distinct categories that fail to reflect interrelated causes and solutions.
3. The inability to adequately meet the needs of children and families reflects a lack of functional communication.
4. Specialized agencies are unable to easily craft comprehensive solutions for complex problems.
5. The existing services are insufficiently funded.

This set of indicators is obvious. The consequences of this condition are clear when one thinks about children and families and the experiences they can have in trying to seek help to resolve problems. Few if any of our systems are set up to be preventive. Instead, we focus on issues and problems once they reach crisis proportions. Also, in the past, as a problem was identified, a discrete agency or a set of professionals were trained and organized to deal with that specific problem area. Funding guidelines and accountability requirements, based upon the specific service area, would then follow. With time, each of these professions developed its own bureaucracy, vertical lines of communication, and professional standards. No mechanisms for communication *across* agencies with regard to functions and with regard to the needs and services offered to specific children and families were developed. In many ways, each of these professions is in *competition* with the others for funding, for policy support, and for coordination of interventions that its agency specializes in making. In general, there still are no mechanisms for these agencies to communicate and exchange ideas with each other. And of course, as the number of families and children in crisis has risen, funding support has not kept pace.

Given the enormity of the problem, it is clear that there needs to be a major transformation that will result in a comprehensive service delivery system. In their analysis, Melaville and Blank[4] offered the following features that should be part of a revised system.

1. There needs to be a wide array of prevention treatment and support services.
2. Comprehensive service delivery must include techniques to ensure that children and their families actually receive the services they need.
3. There must be a focus on the whole family.
4. High-quality services must empower children and families.
5. Effectiveness and high-quality prevention support of treatment services must be measured by the impact these interventions have on the lives of children and families they serve.

Promising Examples of Coordinated Services. The key to accomplishing the delivery of coordinated services must be partnerships and collaboration. No longer can we afford to have schools moving along with their own agenda without consultation with other social services, such as health care, mental health, social work and juvenile justice. Fortunately, there are a number of promising experimental efforts that are modeling how these new forms of interagency collaboratives can work. In most cases, the school is the central agency for the coordination and delivery of these services. The following are brief descriptions.

Schools attempt to help students understand how to address the challenges presented by a complex and changing society.

South Central School District #406, Tuckwila, Washington is working to coordinate services across the entire school district. In this community on the south central side of Seattle, an array of services is being centered around the school. A part of this work is built on defining what is meant by children at risk (those who experience an inability to participate successfully in the main institutions of society—family, home, school, community, and work force). In this school district, comprehensive services teachers and instructional assistants provide instruction to students both within and outside of the regular classroom. A case management system has been put into place for diagnosing student needs, designing interventions, monitoring, evaluating, and communicating about student success. Learning-support services are being funded through a combination of federal, state, and local dollars, which results in a more efficient and effective service approach. The program also includes a heavy component of involvement with hundreds of parents and other patrons who volunteer their time to be in schools and to serve on committees to assist teachers and to work one-on-one with students.

New Beginnings Integrated Services for Children and Family has been established in San

Diego. The goals of this project are to develop and test an integrated collaborative system of services for families and children. The types of services provided in the collaborative agency and the array of agencies working together to support this experimental effort is summarized in Figure 19.4 on page 504. In San Diego, Alexander Hamilton Elementary School is becoming a living model of the integration of school with social service agencies. In this one school setting, families are able to access health care, job training, welfare payments, English as a second language, adult classes, public housing referrals, and more. The ambitiousness of this experimental effort is reflected in some of the dramatic statistics about the needs of the Hamilton School community. For example, in 1987–88, about 28 percent of the children were at the school for less than 60 days. And only 40 percent were enrolled for the full year! These data clearly indicate the need for rethinking how educational and other services are delivered and the need for communication and coordination through integrated services. In a model such as Hamilton, it is possible for at-risk students and their families to gain much needed support. The core beliefs for the New Beginnings project in San Diego are listed here and are characteristic of other integrated service initiatives:

We believe that . . .

- Children and families in our community are a valuable resource and their healthy development is essential to the social and economic future of San Diego;
- The number of children and families that live in poverty and are at risk of not developing to their potential is growing in our community;
- The family is the primary care-giver and source of social learning, and must be supported and strengthened;
- Families cannot be assisted effectively and strengthened through fragmented services provided by public agencies in isolation from each other;
- The best hope for helping families and children comes through early intervention and continuing development services;
- Each public agency in the community, including the City of San Diego, County of San Diego, San Diego Community College District, San Diego Unified School District, and the San Diego Housing Commission, has a critical role in supporting children and families;
- Only an integrated service system involving all of these agencies and a full resource of professional staff can meet the complex needs of children and families in our community; and
- Such a system must not be dependent on short-term special funding, but must represent a fundamental restructure of existing resources.[5]

Intermediate School 218, Manhattan, New York opened in 1992 to 1,100 students, mothers, fathers, and other children in the neighborhood. Among the services offered are dental treatment, drug counseling, tutoring, after-school programs, eye and physical exams, and mental health and social work counseling. The school offers workshops on such topics as pregnancy prevention, racial awareness, parenting skills, and AIDS. This school is a joint project of both public and private agencies. It was launched as a partnership between the school district and the Children's Aid Society, a nonprofit organization based in Manhattan. Cooperative efforts of this type save each agency money in operating costs and facilities, and the professionals in the different social services are able to deliver in their area of expertise. This means, for example, that teachers can focus more on teaching and

NEW BEGINNINGS SERVICES

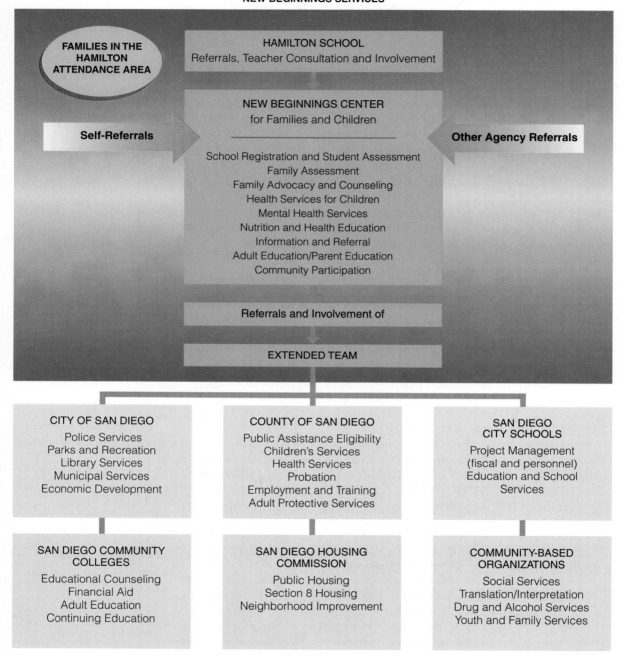

FIGURE 19.4

Organization of Collaborative Agencies to Deliver Coordinated Services to Hamilton School, San Diego, California

that the children will attend school both better prepared and better supported to learn. The schedule for Intermediate School 218 is interesting as well. The school is open six days a week, 52 weeks a year, and after 3:00 P.M. the school turns into a community center that offers courses, workshops, and tutors. On average, the school is open fifteen hours a day.

Teacher Education Is Changing

Clearly, if schools are going to be different, then teachers who will be working in those schools will need to be thinking differently and performing differently. This has direct implications for the initial preparation of teachers. A number of initiatives are under way at major universities, state universities, private universities, and small liberal arts colleges to redesign teacher education programs. As has been illustrated with many of the other initiatives for changing schools in changing times, the development of collaborative efforts, coalitions, and national networks is a pattern in the restructuring of teacher education. Three of the major national initiatives to reform teacher education are the Holmes Group, the Renaissance Group and the National Network for Educational Renewal.

The Holmes Group. The Holmes Group is a national consortium of schools of education dedicated to the reform of teacher education. This group has taken its name from Henry W. Holmes, who was Dean of Harvard University's Graduate School of Education, from 1920 to 1940. Holmes was a strong supporter of teacher education reform. The Holmes Group had its beginning in 1983, when a small number of deans of education in research-oriented institutions met to explore and debate their shared understandings and to develop a common agenda. Currently the Holmes Group consists of over ninety institutions from across the country. Membership is restricted to those institutions that place a heavy emphasis on research productivity, and the key member in the Holmes Group is the dean of each member institution. Out of their initial deliberations, the Holmes Group identified five goals for the reform of teacher education. These are:

1. To make education of teachers intellectually more solid.
2. To recognize differences in teachers' knowledge, skill, and commitment, in their education, certification, and work.
3. To create standards of entry to the profession—examinations and educational requirements—that are professionally relevant and intellectually defensible.
4. To connect our own institutions to schools.
5. To make schools better places for teachers to work, and to learn.[6]

One of the more controversial premises of the Holmes Group is that teacher education should be a post-baccalaureate program. In other words, those who wish to become teachers would first receive a bachelor's degree in a discipline, then move into a fifth year or post-baccalaureate teacher education program. The controversy is based on the fact that the expectation would add to the amount of time that it takes to become a teacher, as well as incurring the expense of another year of higher education, thus discouraging minorities and low-income students from the profession.

Another focus of the Holmes Group is the creation of Professional Development Schools—local schools where innovative practices and the best quality of teaching will be occurring. It is in these schools that the clinical experiences for future teachers, such as student teaching, would take place. In the development of the teacher, the Holmes Group places strong emphasis on a liberal education, which takes place through professional core studies. They also place heavy emphasis on the importance of clinical practice, guided opportunities, and focused practice in order to work toward the goal of high entry levels.

The Renaissance Group.   Another network of universities that is focusing on the reform of teacher education is the Renaissance Group. The membership of this group comes predominantly from those state universities that historically had been normal schools. As you remember, normal schools were the first formal teacher education colleges in America. In recent years, these institutions have become multipurpose universities, consisting of a number of professional schools and offering an array of master's degrees, and in many instances doctoral degrees. The primary participants in the Renaissance Group are the presidents, vice presidents for academic affairs, and the deans of schools/colleges of education; a unique difference from the Holmes Group is that presidents and vice presidents are expected to be ongoing active participants in the efforts to redesign teacher education. This triad of members is particularly important in addressing the first of the twelve principles of the Renaissance Group. Like many of the restructuring efforts in schools, the Renaissance Group has identified a set of core values or belief statements to guide the work. These principles are:

1. The education of teachers is an all-campus responsibility.
2. Programs for the preparation of teachers thrive in a university culture that values quality teaching.
3. Decisions concerning the education of teachers are the shared responsibility of the university faculty, practitioners, and other related professionals.
4. The initial preparation of teachers is integrated throughout a student's university experience and is not segmented or reserved to the student's final year.
5. The appropriate role of the state is to establish outcome expectations for teacher education graduates; the appropriate role of the university is to determine the curriculum, standards, and internal policies for teacher education programs.
6. Rigorous learning expectations and exit requirements characterize the program to educate teachers.
7. The academic preparation of teachers includes a rigorous general education program, in-depth subject matter preparation, and both general and content-specific preparation in teaching methodology.
8. Teacher education programs reflect American diversity and prepare graduates to teach in a pluralistic and multicultural society.
9. The education of teachers incorporates extensive and sequenced field and clinical experiences.
10. Quality teacher preparation programs have faculty who are active in scholarly and professional endeavors.
11. The continuing professional development of teachers and other education personnel is a shared responsibility of the university faculty and other education professionals.
12. Programs to educate teachers for the new world have sufficient support to implement these principles.[7]

One of the interesting principles of the Renaissance Group agenda for reform of teacher education is the theme that all university faculty are teacher educators— not just those in the school/college of education. An assumption of the Renaissance Group is that the faculty in the disciplines (e.g., chemistry, history, English) are models of the teaching of that discipline for future teachers. As a result, the Renaissance Group places heavy emphasis on teacher education as a campus-wide responsibility, as well as the need for all faculty to be aware of their being pedagogical as well as content models for future teachers.

National Network for Educational Renewal. The newest network of teacher education institutions has been assembled around the shared support for nineteen postulates that have been proposed by John Goodlad.[8] These postulates were based on extensive study of schools and teacher education institutions in twelve states. Institution members of this network are committed to redesigning their teacher education programs in ways that will address the nineteen postulates. Two examples of these postulates are:

Postulate eight. Programs for the education of educators must provide extensive opportunities for future teachers to move beyond being students of organized knowledge to become teachers who will inquire into both knowledge and teaching.

Postulate nine. Programs for the education of educators must be characterized by a socialization process through which candidates transcend their self-oriented student preoccupations to become much more other-oriented in identifying with a culture of teaching.

These and the other seventeen postulates then become the guiding assumptions for the design and organization of more relevant, effective, and rigorous teacher education programs. Again, there is a trend away from individual, isolated courses and experiences within particular institutions toward a more collaborative, interactive, and principled approach to education.

Teacher Leadership Is the Key

You are aware of the continuing concern about American schools and the education of children: The media run features about novel approaches to schooling and report the latest test results; politicians refer to themselves as the "education" president/governor/senator; leaders of business and industry continue to express concerns about the ability of American schools to produce skilled workers. You may not have thought about the reasons and assumptions underlying this persistent theme of concern and critiquing of American education. One of the key assumptions is Americans' basic faith that education and schooling can make a difference. While faith has been lost in many of our institutions, schools continue to be viewed as critical and essential to the opportunity for the individual, as well as society as a whole, to improve and advance.

The most important key to the success of the schools is teachers. The reason for the focus of so much attention on teachers is the understanding of parents, political leaders, industrialists, and the society at large that teachers do make a difference. And teachers make a difference beyond their own classrooms. How teachers work together within the school and provide leadership across the school district, the state, and the nation sets the themes and directions for schooling.

Without well-educated and dedicated teachers who are willing to provide leadership, the faith and hope that Americans place in schooling would be unfounded.

As a teacher you will have many opportunities—and the responsibility—to provide leadership in your classroom, across your school and your district, and for the profession at large. Do not enter the profession of teaching thinking that all you have to do is close the door to your classroom and teach "your" children. The leadership role of a teacher is a critical, exciting, and challenging part of the job.

Teacher Leadership in Schools

All too frequently teachers think only about what goes on in their classrooms and do not develop perspectives about the school as a whole. This is unfortunate, since teachers are an integral part of the larger organization, and only to the extent to which they are able to work together and to assist each other can they make a major difference in the success of students. From the students' point of view, they attend the total school, and teachers need to develop this school-wide perspective too. There are many ways that teachers can be involved in leadership activities. Obviously, they must first think about what leadership means in their classroom. In addition, there are many opportunities to be involved in leadership functions across the school, ranging from participating on various committees, to chairing committees, to serving in key roles in regard to particular change processes and school improvement efforts. Some examples of the different opportunities for teachers to be involved in leadership are described here.

Transformational Leadership. Of the many models of leadership, traditionally, the "top down" model was preferred. In this model the "boss" made the decisions and directed the "followers." More recently, the concept of "empowerment" has emerged. In professional organizations, such as schools, the principal cannot work as the "boss," and organizational norms must be developed across the school that facilitate teachers' work and allow them to learn and grow along with their students. Currently, the model of "transformational leadership" is being examined. In this perspective it is the responsibility of every member of the organization to help transform it and to see there is learning and growing. This, of course, requires that every member in the organization be a learner. Thus, teacher leadership entails not only thinking about how the students in your classroom learn and grow, but also thinking about how fellow teachers and the school as a whole are learning and growing. This growth must be in ways that empower the members of the organization to continually improve in job performance. As a teacher, you have not only the opportunity but also the responsibility to participate in leadership activities in your classroom, the school, and in larger arenas.

Advanced technologies notwithstanding, the teacher will continue to be the single most important element in the education of our children.

Leadership in the Classroom. You may not have thought about a teacher as the classroom leader; however, that is the case. Within the classroom, you have an amazing amount of leadership responsibility. You will have from twenty to thirty-five students for whom you are responsible. In high school you are responsible for groups of students for fifty minutes at a time, with well over one hundred students that you will be leading during a school day. In addition, other adults will be part of your classroom. You may have an aide, there may be student teachers, and there may be various "pull out" programs that identify selected students for special instruction. In all cases, you as the teacher will be the leader of the activities and the work of these people. How you provide direction and guidance and facilitate their work will make the difference in the success of their learning outcomes. This guidance of other people and their work is leadership. In other words, your job is not just to teach the children; it is also to be a manager of learning and a facilitator of the other managers who are there to assist in this important work.

School Committees. In your very first meetings in your school there will be opportunities to become involved in many of the working committees. At the beginning, you will probably serve as a member of one or more of these committees. Some are charged with addressing curriculum and instruction issues. There may be a social committee. There likely will be committees that work as liaisons with the community. In many committees it will be necessary to liaison with the district office and other schools. In all cases, as a member of the committee, you will be in a leadership role, because it is not just the chair of the committee who provides leadership. All members have a responsibility to carry out their part in making the committee effective. This includes setting a good example in terms of meeting attendance, being prepared, and participating. It also means being sensitive to the ideas and interests of the other members, and striving to facilitate the development of a consensus of all committee members about the directions that should be taken.

Relevant Research

Empowering Teachers to Reform Schools

Using a historical research base, Midgley and Wood offer a Site-Based Management (SBM) approach that can be used in the reform of schools.[10] The model is built around the notion of empowering teachers. Defining SBM as a "bottom up" as opposed to a "top down" management model, they set out the research needed to create such a management model. The tenets of their model include establishing a common vision for change, altering the school culture, collaborating, defining roles of leadership teams, having a task-focused environment, and finally, empowering staff.

As increasing numbers of schools are moving into SBM, teachers need to become better versed in their roles, relationships, and expectations. Change will come either in some organized and logical fashion or haphazardly. You must decide how you will prepare for and accept this change.

Source: Carol Midgley and Stewart Wood, "Beyond Site-Based Management: Empowering Teachers to Reform Schools," *Phi Delta Kappan 75* (3) (November, 1993): 245–252.

Site-Based Decision Making (SBDM) has been talked about at a number of points in this book. Earlier in this chapter we introduced a Configuration Component Checklist for Site-Based Decision Making (see Appendix 19.1). In this Component Checklist, note Components 1, 2, 3, 12, 13, and 16. In each of these components there is a direct expectation for teachers to provide leadership. There are other school-wide councils and committees that deal with the governance and operation of the school as well. For example, many schools and school districts have engaged in "school improvement" processes, which include a committee made up of teachers, their principal, and perhaps others. In each of these configurations of SBDM, there is the expectation of across-the-school leadership by teachers.

Second Change Facilitator/Consigliere. Another important role, which is less official but found in every school, is that of **second change facilitator**, or

consigliere. In extensive research on the change process, Shirley Hord, Gene Hall,[9] and their colleagues have observed that whenever a school is engaged in a substantial change effort, a special role exists for a teacher to provide day-to-day leadership for implementation of the change. Of course, the principal is most likely to serve as the *first* change facilitator. However, in most instances, a teacher will be identified to serve as a key resource to all teachers in the school. Hord and Hall have called this person the *consigliere* or *second change facilitator*. This person is most likely to have some released time to work as a facilitator and coach for other teachers and will tend to have more expertise and interest in the area of the change. For example, the teacher who is very interested in language arts could have the assignment of serving as the second change facilitator/consigliere for the implementation of whole language or a writing process curriculum. Perhaps a particular department chair with a great deal of interest in computers and educational technology takes on the role of consigliere to assist other teachers and chairs in the implementation of interactive video technology. Here, again, a role for teacher leadership has been identified that is important to school and student success.

Teacher Career Paths

In the "old days" teachers had one position, teacher. They were assigned as a regular teacher from the first day they entered the classroom, they were a teacher five years later, ten years later, twenty years later. . . . Unlike any other profession, there were no different levels of role and responsibility, and there was only one pay scale. Historically, teachers at the beginning of their career would have the same level of responsibility as those who had twenty-five to thirty years of experience. This is no longer the case. Today, there are exciting career advancement possibilities for teachers. The following brief descriptions are offered to encourage you to remember that your training—and learning about your profession—are not over with the completion of your initial teacher education program. There are many exciting avenues for professional growth, increased professional status, wider ranges of responsibility, and higher levels of salary through the career paths that are available to teachers today.

Levels of Certificates/Licenses.　Most states now differentiate between inexperienced and more experienced teachers by the type of license or credential that is issued. The increasingly common practice is that with the completion of your teacher education program and recommendation to the state you will receive a *provisional* certificate/license, which will allow you to begin your career as a regular teacher. States vary on the requirements for moving beyond the initial license. In most cases your provisional status will conclude following three years of successful experience as a beginning teacher and the completion of some amount of advanced training. More than likely you will be expected to do some study toward a master's degree, and perhaps even completion of a masters degree will be expected. The next level up the career path will be a *regular* certificate/ license. Typically this will be issued to teachers after the requisite three years of successful teaching experience and a recommendation from their principal or school district. Normally this license will be renewable every five years. There will be an expectation that you continue to study and to do advanced training, which can include study in higher education and/or training offered by your school district. In some states there is a third level of certificate that is referred to as a *master* teacher, mentor, or professional certificate/license. This advanced level of licensure will require more

This plan would provide a "career ladder" that could lead to salaries equivalent to mid-management pay ranges for teachers. The plan has a probationary period for teachers that stresses professional development. During the initial probationary period, teachers must complete in-service requirements equivalent to a master's degree and have satisfactory on-the-job performance evaluations. Changes made in the tenure system extend the probationary period to four to six years, but provide a flexible time frame for achieving tenure status.

PROBATIONARY STATUS:

First year	All teachers are probationary
Second year	Advance to career nominee status, continue as probationary teacher, or be terminated
Third year	Advance to career candidate, advance to career nominee, remain career nominee, or be terminated
Fourth year	Advance to career candidate status, remain as career nominee, or be terminated
Fifth year	Be awarded tenure, advance to career candidate, remain a career candidate, or be terminated
Sixth year	Be awarded tenure, remain a career candidate, or be terminated
Seventh year	Become tenured or be terminated

LEVELS FOR TENURED TEACHER:

Career Level I This first step for tenured teachers would provide an extra $2,000 per year. Teachers would be reevaluated every three years. Each evaluation that is satisfactory would provide another $2,000 increment. Teachers in this level would teach, evaluate curriculum materials, and work with probationary teachers.

Career Level II After three years' experience at the first level, teachers could move to Level II. The salary level would be approximately $2,000 above the Level I teachers. In addition to classroom teaching, these teachers would help with assigned projects, possibly assist in numerous schools, conduct research, or work on in-service projects.

Career Level III These teachers would work as curriculum specialists or on in-service projects. They would still serve as classroom teachers. They should be able to carry out research projects as needed by the district. The salary would be approximately $2,000 above the Level II teacher.

FIGURE 19.5 Charlotte-Mecklenburg Schools Career Development Plan

advanced study, a series of superior evaluations, and a track record of accomplishment in professional activities.

An expanded career plan for teachers, called a **career ladder,** has been proposed in a number of states, including Texas and Tennessee. In these models there are more steps and levels of advancement for teachers. With each level comes increased salary, increased roles and responsibilities, and more complex tasks. The best articulation of the career ladder perspective is by Schlecty and Crowell[10] (see Figure 19.5). In their model of the career ladder, each level represents a broader range of responsibilities and more complex professional tasks in relation to teaching and working with other teachers. From a professional point of view, this represents an idealized career path. Unfortunately, to date, very few school districts have experimented with implementation of this model.

There are other roles and career paths open to teachers. For example, becoming a team leader, where you work with two to six other teachers, offers an important opportunity for leadership. Teaming can be done for the purpose of exchanging lesson plans or co-teaching a discipline, and in a middle school an interdisciplinary team can be responsible for instruction in all areas for a set of students. Teachers also move to various roles in the district office. For example, in larger districts there will be positions for curriculum coordinators and specialists in gifted education, bilingual education, Chapter One, and compensatory education. In all of these examples, expert teachers have the opportunity to work with other teachers, principals, and children in different schools. In addition, all of these positions require leadership skills and place an emphasis on improving teaching and learning.

Will You Be Ready? Becoming a teacher is something special. Few people, even those in a teacher preparation program, really grasp the significance of this service profession. Despite the general public concerns about the overall quality of American education and the professional concerns about overburdened classrooms and learning environments and general financial support of education, teaching is a critical base for the maintenance of the American society. For that matter, it is a significant base for any society. A nation advances or declines on the basis of its educational development. A society's schools and teachers wield a tremendous impact on the future of the nation and the world.

The twenty-first century, close at hand, will mark over a two hundred-year history of this nation's growth from a small group of rebel people in the thirteen colonies to that of an international world leader in economic development; scientific achievement in medicine, agriculture, nutrition, knowledge creation, and cybernetics; and with one of the highest standards of living in the world. All of this can be linked to a nation committed to the importance of education for all people. In examining the foundations of American education, the authors of this text have provided you with all the boons, banes, and anodynes of American education. As we have indicated, the system has not been and is not a perfect one. However, the system has been somewhat elastic in nature and has successfully adjusted to the needs of the society it has served. The critical challenge for the third century of its history is how it will continue to adjust to the needs of a society growing closer in an interdependent world.

Our educational achievements tell us that there is little that we cannot learn or do. Teachers are better prepared than ever in our history, and our learners are more capable than ever before. Our educational history and societal development has led us to this point. We know that teachers will learn and teach differently than before, and that learners will acquire and use knowledge differently than before. The challenge to the new teachers of the twenty-first century is to move boldly into educational endeavors that we have read about and studied but never tried. That attitude, if put into practice, will stretch our efforts far beyond where we have been. The career of teaching will assume an added level of importance to the continued success and growth of this nation.

Summary and Implications

We live in a time of change. In this chapter we have highlighted some of the ways of thinking about change in schools. Unfortunately, too much of the time we just talk about change, and when we attempt to change we accomplish small tinkerings. Transforming is what we have to be about. Examples of transforming in schools have been presented. Probably the most important of these, for the 1990s, is the idea of the school serving as the center for the coordinated delivery of human services: the "full-service school." There are an increasing number of models of how this can work around the nation. It is an exciting and challenging opportunity to bring together professionals from education, social work, criminal justice, dental and health care, and in some cases the performing and visual arts, to focus on the growth and development of children and their families. There is a hint of movement toward the return of a sense of community and an interest in dealing with the wholeness of family life.

Schools will not continue to be as they were when you went through them. Our societies will continue to change. You will be a participant in the change process. Teachers are leaders, and teachers are a part of the leadership team for their schools. Your role begins in your classroom but extends beyond to the school, to the community, and to your profession at large. As your career unfolds, participate, share in leadership, and contribute your energies and creativity to continually improving what occurs in your classroom, your school, and your community. In other words, "Go for it!" "Do Something!" And good luck to you.

Discussion Questions

1. Some have referred to the coordinated services school as the "one-stop shopping" school. What other metaphors might describe a school of this type?
2. What do you think will happen to the role of the teacher in a school that is serving as the center for the delivery of coordinated services?
3. Develop answers to TQM questions: Who are the customers for teachers? What is the product of schools? What is the product of your classroom?
4. What are some of the basic principles about schooling and the role of teachers and students that you would advocate as the basis for transforming a school?
5. How do you feel about some of the school-transforming ideas that have been introduced in this chapter? Which of the ideas would you want to become involved with as a teacher?

Journal/Portfolio Development

1. Select one of the "transformation of schools" topics and assess its potential for becoming a regular part of the school operation. Contrast it with the current school operation.
2. Develop a career ladder for yourself and establish a personal management plan for achieving that goal. Indicate the importance of each step along the way.

School-Based Experiences

1. Visit a school that is doing innovative things. Develop a report of what is going on and use the HIC Scale to assess how different the school is.
2. Visit a school that is using Site-Based Decision Making. Complete the Checklist in Appendix 19.1. Do a comparison of what you have read about SBDM with what you find. What are implications you see for the leadership role of the teacher?

Notes

1. Madelyn Hunter, "Knowing, Teaching and Supervising," in *Using What We Know About Schools,* ed. P. L. Hosford. Alexandria, VA: Association for Supervisor and Curriculum Development, 1984, 169–192.
2. M. W. Kirst, "Improving Children's Services, Overcoming Barriers, Creating New Opportunities," *Phi Delta Kappan* (1991).
3. A. I. Melaville and M. J. Blank, *What It Takes: Structuring Interagency Partnerships to Connect Children and Families with Comprehensive Services.* Washington, DC: Education and Human Services Consortium c/o IEL, 1991.
4. Ibid.
5. "New Beginnings Statement of Philosophy." San Diego, CA: 1990.
6. "Tomorrow's Teachers: A Report of the Holmes Group." East Lansing, MI: 1986.
7. "The Twelve Principles Guiding Renaissance Group Activities." Cedar Falls, IA: The Renaissance Group, University of Northern Iowa, 1991.
8. J. I. Goodlad, *Teachers for Our Nations Schools.* San Francisco, CA: Jossey-Bass Publishers, 1990.
9. G. E. Hall and S. M. Hord, *Change in Schools: Facilitating the Process.* Albany, NY: State University of New York Press, 1989.
10. P. Schlecty and D. Crowell, *Staff Development and School Improvement: A School District Examines Its Potential for Excellence.* National Institute of Education, U.S. Department of Education (NIE Contract 400-79-0056).

Bibliography

Bechtol, William M. and Sorenson, Juanita S. *Restructuring Schooling for Individual Students.* Boston: Allyn and Bacon, 1993.

Kirst, M. W. "Improving Children's Services, Overcoming Barriers, Creating New Opportunities." *Phi Delta Kappan,* 1991.

Kuhn, T. S. *The Structure of Scientific Revolution.* 2nd ed. Chicago: The University of Chicago Press, 1970.

Melaville, A. I. and Blank, M. J. *What It Takes: Structuring Interagency Partnerships to Connect Children and Families with Comprehensive Services.* Washington, DC: Education and Human Services Consortium c/o IEL, 1991.

Sergiovanni, T. J. *Value Added Leadership: How to Get Extraordinary Performance in Schools.* San Diego, CA: Harcourt, Brace and Jovanovich, 1990.

Tripp, Robert L. *The Game of School.* Reston, VA: Extended Vision Press, 1993.

Weber, Robert J. *Forks, Photographs, and Hot Air Balloons.* Portsmouth, NH: Heinemann, 1993.

Ysselddyke, James E. and Thurlow, Martha L. *Self-Study Guide to the Development of Educational Outcomes and Indicators.* Minneapolis: University of Minnesota National Center on Educational Outcomes, 1993.

Configuration Component Checklist for Site-Based Decision Making

---

IMPLEMENTATION REQUIREMENTS

Staff Development

____ Initial training for principal ____ Initial training for council ____ On-going coaching

Context Support

____ Mechanisms to release site from traditional policies and procedures
____ Active accommodation by School Board
____ District office personnel role shifts to accommodate and support SBDM
____ Installation of new parallel systems for evaluation and accountability
____ Commitment of chairman level
____ Presumption in favor of granting waivers by reviewing party

---

SBDM OPERATIONAL COMPONENTS AND VARIATIONS

COUNCIL STRUCTURES AND PROCESSES

1. *Participant Representation of School Council* (indicate number of each)

____ Teachers ____ Custodians ____ Students ____ District administrators
____ Parents ____ Principal ____ Instructional aids ____ School board member
____ Business persons

2. *Strategies to Support Teacher Participation*

____ Team teaching ____ Part-time teachers ____ Volunteers
____ Instructional aids ____ After-school meetings ____ Early release day

3. *Decision-making Process*

(a) Consensus (b) Vote

4. *Participants Solicited in Decision-Making*

____ Other teachers   ____ Other parents   ____ Students
____ District office   ____ State   ____ Business persons

5. *Decision Sequence*

____ Prework by task force   ____ School decisions final
____ Council recommends to whole faculty ____ School decisions have to be confirmed by district office
____ Council decision final   ____ School board has final say
____ Council recommends to principal,   ____ State has final say
      has final decision

6. *Council Procedures*

____ Have minutes of previous meetings   ____ Provide members complete information
      available ahead of time
____ Publish agenda in advance   ____ Procedures are followed
____ Work load is shared by all members

7. *Council Meeting Process*

____ Steer discussions toward important agenda items
____ Chair sees that all have an opportunity to speak
____ Procedures are used to keep track of ideas, issues, and recommendations

8. *Waiver Process*

(a) Board   (b) Request goes   (c) District   (d) Committee   (e) A multi-   (f) Waivers
    receives   to one admin-   committee   reviews and   component   are not
    request and   istrator then   reviews then   recommends to   proposal and   permitted
    acts on   board   recommends   superintendent,   multiple review
    quickly   to board   who takes to   process is
                                                          board   required

9. *Types of Waivers Sought*

____ Testing   ____ District policies
____ Teacher load   ____ District rules and regulations
____ Class schedules   ____ State policies
____ School calendar   ____ State rules and regulations
____ Textbooks   ____ Federal policies
____ Staff development   ____ Federal rules and regulations
____ Teacher contract variations ____ Court rulings
____ Other contract variations

10. *Scope of Council Work*

____ Curriculum   ____ Coordination of social services
____ Staffing   ____ School improvement implementations
____ Budget   ____ Coordination of criminal justice system
____ Testing   ____ Coordination of community action
____ Teaching   ____ Legal and regulatory issues
____ School improvement planning

11. *Curriculum*   (Authority: ____ Set ____ Advise ____ No Role)

    (a) Selection of   (b) Selection of materials   (c) Selection of teacher   (d) Combination of
        goals only   including texts only   Delivery approaches   _____

12. *Budget Topics*   (Authority: ____ Set ____ Advise ____ No Role)

    ____ Principal salary   ____ Curriculum material purchases   ____ Teacher salaries
    ____ Lunchroom personnel   ____ Supplies   ____ Other _____

13. *Staff Evaluations*   (Authority: ____ Set ____ Advise ____ No Role)

    ____ of principal   ____ of teachers   ____ of aides   ____ of others _____

14. *Teacher Assignments/Scheduling*   (Authority: ___ Set ____ Advise ____ No Role)

    (a) Decide   (b) Advise   (c) No role

15. *Hirings*   (Authority: ____ Set ____ Advise ____ No Role)

    (a) All school   (b) Principal   (c) Teachers   (d) Classified   (e) No say
        employees   staff

16. *Teacher Work Hours/Work Week*   (Authority: ____ Set ____ Advise ____ No Role)

    (a) All   (b) Non-student contact   (c) Student contact   (d) No say

17. *Testing*

    (a) Site has full authority   (b) Site must receive   (c) Site must receive   (d) Combination
        to set testing   district approval   state approval   of (b) and (c)

Based on the earlier Innovation Configuration Component Checklist presented in:
G. E. Hall and G. R. Galluzzo, *Site-Based Decision Making: Changing Policy into Practice* (WV: Appalachia Educational Laboratory, 1991).

For more information on Innovation Configuration Component Checklists, see:
G. E. Hall and S. M. Hord, *Change in Schools, Facilitating the Process* (Albany, NY: State University of New York Press, 1987).

Glossary

Abstraction: A thought process of drawing away from experience to a conceptual plane.

Academic freedom: The opportunity for a teacher to teach without certain coercion, censorship, or other restrictive interference.

Accountability: Holding schools responsible for what students learn.

Acculturation: The process of learning the cultural patterns of a second culture.

Activity curriculum: A student-centered organizational emphasis that begins with broad topic identification for learning and weaves the related academic components into that topic.

Adaptation: The promotion of a stable climate in schools so that students can attain an unbiased picture of the changes that occur in society.

Affirmative action: A plan by which personnel policies and hiring practices do not discriminate against women and members of minority groups.

Age of Pericles (455–431 B.C.): A period of Greek history in which sufficiently great strides were made in human advancement to generate an organized concern for formal education.

Age of Reason: The beginning of the modern period of educational thought that emphasizes the importance of reason. The writings of Voltaire strongly influenced this movement and formed the basis for rationalism.

American Federation of Teachers: A national teachers' organization that is primarily concerned with improving educational conditions and protecting teachers' rights.

Analysis of teaching: A contemporary trend to encourage teachers to critique their own performance in the classroom.

Annual increments: Standard salary increases based on the number of years of teaching experience.

Articulation: The manner in which the various parts of the school program compliment each other in their relationship to a student's learning.

Assimilation: The process by which an immigrant group or culturally distinct group is incorporated into the dominant culture.

Authentic assessment: An assessment of student learning that is based on real-world practice and attempts to measure learning in the same way it was acquired by the learner.

Axiology: An area of philosophy that deals with the nature of values. It includes questions such as "What is good?" "What is value?"

Behavioral theory: A theory that considers the outward behavior of students to be the main target for change.

Behaviorism: A psychological theory that asserts that behavior represents the essence of a person; behaviorists contend that all behavior can be explained as response to stimuli.

Bias: A preference or inclination that inhibits impartial judgment, leading to prejudice or discrimination.

Block grants: Federal monies that are consolidated into a broader-purpose fund from categorical funds that had more focused purposes. Block grants give more discretion to the state and local agencies that receive them.

Career ladder: A career path for teachers consisting of a number of rungs, or job roles, that carry with them increasing responsibility and performance of more complex professional tasks.

Carnegie Unit: A measure of clock time that is used to award high school credits toward graduation.

Censorship: The condemnation of books, instructional materials, teaching content, or teaching methods because they are perceived as unsupportive of or in opposition to the values of an individual or group.

Change agent: A role that emphasizes the responsibility for persons to actively participate in society.

Chemical dependency: The habitual use, either for psychological or physical needs, of a substance such as drugs, alcohol, or tobacco.

Child benefit theory: A criterion used by the U.S. Supreme Court to determine whether services provided to public and nonpublic school students benefit children and not the school or religion. If they benefit only the children, the courts have ruled that the services may be funded by public funds.

Classroom analysis systems: Clearly defined sets of procedures and written materials that can be used to analyze the interaction between teachers and students.

Classroom organization: A multifaceted dimension of teaching that includes the content, method, and values that infuse the classroom environment, planning, and discipline practices.

Cognitive development: A learner's acquisition of facts, concepts, and principles through intellectualization.

Committee of Ten: An historic NEA committee that studied secondary education in 1893.

Common elementary schools: An early attempt to provide a basic elementary education for all children.

Compulsory education: School attendance that is required by law on the theory that it is to the benefit of the state or commonwealth to educate all the people.

Constants: An offering of learning experiences that make up an academic or vocational track in the secondary school.

Constructivism: An educational theory that emphasizes hands-on, activity-based teaching and learning during which students develop their own frames of thought.

Continuity: Vertical articulation.

Control theory: A theory of discipline that contends that we choose most of our behaviors to gain control of people or ourselves.

Core curriculum: A student-centered organizational emphasis that combines broad areas of academic disciplines into manageable instructional units such as social studies and language arts for integration in learning.

Core values: Statements of principles about teaching and learning that are fundamental to one's philosophy of schooling.

Cultural pluralism: A state that exists when different groups maintain their culture parallel and equal to the dominant one in a society.

Culture: The totality of socially transmitted ways of thinking, believing, feeling, and acting within a group of people that is passed from one generation to the next.

Current expenses: Expenditures necessary for daily operation and maintenance.

Dame school: A low-level primary school in the colonial and other early periods, usually conducted by an untrained woman in her own home.

De facto **segregation:** The segregation of students resulting from circumstances such as housing patterns rather than from school policy or law.

De jure **segregation:** The segregation of students on the basis of law, school policy, or a practice designed to accomplish such separation.

Delinquency: A term generally ascribed to the youth culture that denotes violation of rules and regulations of the society.

Desegregation: The process of correcting past practices of racial or any other form of illegal segregation.

Dialectic: The conflict that occurs when opposing ideas are encountered; in change theory this conflict is the one between individual needs and societal needs.

Differential pay: Extra pay or incentives (added to standard increments) awarded to teachers on the basis of merit.

Discrimination: Individual or institutional practices that exclude all members of a group from certain rights, opportunities, or benefits.

Diversity: The wide range of ways in which human groups and populations have observable and demonstrable physical and behavioral differences.

Dominant group: The cultural group that has the greatest power in society; in the United States it is composed primarily of persons from a European background who are Protestant, middle class, not disabled, heterosexual, and male. This term is sometimes used synonymously with mainstream culture or group.

Dropouts: Students who fail to complete a high school education.

Due process: The procedural requirements that must be followed to safeguard individuals from arbitrary, capricious, or unreasonable policies, practices, or actions.

Eastern thought: A varied set of philosophies from the Far, Middle, and Near East that stress inner peace, tranquility, attitudinal development, and mysticism.

Educated citizenry: A goal according to which all members of our society are capable of participating intelligently in its direction and development.

Education for career: A specialty educational offering that promotes and prepares learners for postsecondary educational efforts and/or career initiation.

Educational malpractice: Culpable neglect by a teacher in the performance of his or her duties as an educator.

Effective teaching: A movement to improve teaching performance based on the outcomes of educational research.

Emergence of Common Man: Coincides with the Age of Reason and emphasizes the rights of the common people for a better life, politically, economically, socially, and educationally. Rousseau was a leader in this movement.

Enculturation: The process of learning the characteristics of the culture of the group to which one belongs.

Epistemology: An area of philosophy that deals with questions about how and what we know.

Equal educational opportunity: A policy to ensure that all students, regardless of their cultural background or family circumstances, are provided access to a similar education.

Equality: The state of being neither inferior nor superior.

Essentialism: An educational theory that holds that there is a common core of information and skills that an educated person must have; school should be organized to transmit this core of essential material.

Ethnic group: Identification of membership in a group based on the national origin (that is, a specific country or area of the world) of one's ancestors, a shared culture, and sense of common destiny.

Ethnocentrism: The belief that members of one's group are superior to the members of other groups.

Exceptional learners: A classification identification used to describe handicapped and gifted learners.

Existentialism: A school of philosophy that focuses on the importance of the individual rather than external standards.

Exploratory education: An educational offering that is broad in scope and is used to introduce learners to a variety of learning areas that may be pursued in depth as possible career interests.

Fringe benefits: Job rewards in addition to salary that may include life, professional liability, health, and dental insurance; retirement programs; and tax-free investment opportunities.

Fused curriculum: A subject-centered organizational program created with some merger of the academic disciplines such as reading, writing, and speaking into language arts as a subject for teaching.

General education: An educational offering that is common and required of all students.

Graded schools: Schools that contain year-long levels such as first grade, second grade, tenth grade and the like.

Grouping: A practice whereby students are put into learning groups with others who have like abilities and interests.

Herbartian teaching method: An organized teaching method based on the principles of Pestalozzi that stresses learning by association and consists of five steps (preparation, presentation, association, generalization, and application).

Historical interpretation: Different ways to study and understand history, such as celebrationist, liberal, revisionist, and postmodernist historians would tend to do.

Hornbook: A single printed page containing the alphabet, syllables, a prayer, and other simple words, tacked to a wooden paddle and covered with a thin transparent layer of cow's horn, used in colonial times as the beginner's first book or preprimer.

Humanism: An educational theory that contends that humans are innately good—born free but become enslaved by institutions.

Hypothesis: A proposed relationship between two or more events or qualities.

Idealism: A school of philosophy that considers ideas to be the only true reality.

Inclusion: The federally mandated practice of placing all handicapped learners, except for profoundly handicapped, in regular classrooms where itinerant special education teachers assist the regular teacher.

Independent school: A nonpublic school that is unaffiliated with any religious institution or agency.

Informal curriculum: The norms and values that define expectations for student behavior and attitudes, and that undergird the curriculum and operations of schools.

Information age: A dynamic view of society that emphasizes the problems of dealing with vast amounts of changing information.

In loco parentis: A term used to describe the implied power of schools to function in place of a parent.

Integration: The process of mixing students of different races in school to overcome segregation.

Intermediate unit: A level of school organization between the state and the local district; a subdivision of the elementary school including grades 4, 5, and 6.

Latin grammar school: An early type of school that emphasized the study of Latin, literature, history, mathematics, music, and dialectics.

Liability: The failure to use a reasonable amount of care when such conduct results in injury to another.

Line: An organizational arrangement in which a subordinate is directly responsible to a supervisor.

Magnet schools: Specialized schools that are open to all students in a district, sometimes on a lottery basis or special needs basis.

Meritocracy: A system that is based on the belief that those who achieve at the highest levels deserve the greatest rewards.

Metaphors: The use of words, images, and examples from one's experiences and background to explain and illustrate an idea.

Metaphysics: An area of philosophy that deals with questions about the nature of ultimate reality.

Modules for learning: Time periods for learning that are in the daily schedule of the school.

Moonlighting: Holding a second job in addition to one's primary employment; it implies working in the evening, or "under the light of the moon."

Motivation: Internal emotion, desire, or impulse acting as an incitement to action.

Multicultural education: An educational strategy that incorporates the teaching of exceptional and culturally diverse students, human relations, and the study of ethnic and other cultural groups in a school environment that supports diversity and equal opportunity.

National Education Association: The largest organization of educators; the NEA is concerned with the overall improvement of education and of the condition of educators.

Native North American thought: A varied set of beliefs, philosophical positions, and customs that span different tribes in North America

Normal school: The first American institution that was devoted exclusively to teacher training.

Old Deluder Satan Act: The first colonial educational law (1647), which required colonial towns of at least 50 households to provide education for youth.

One-room school: A setting in which all grade levels are taught by a single teacher in a single-room school.

Parochial school: An educational institution operated and controlled by a religious denomination.

Perennialism: An educational theory that focuses on principles of knowledge that are enduring; nature, human nature, and the underlying principles of existence are considered constant, undergoing little change.

Political action committees in teacher education: Various organizations that engage in political activities in support of the organizations' purposes or causes.

Portfolio: A compilation for a specific purpose of the works, records, and accomplishments that a student prepares about his/her learnings, performances, and contributions.

Poverty: A relative standard of living defined by a number of complex and changing factors that may include hunger or lack of luxuries.

Poverty level: A level of family income judged by the United States Labor Department to be below the basic needs requirements of a family.

Pragmatism: A late nineteenth-century American school of philosophy that stresses becoming rather than being.

Prejudice: Preconceived negative attitudes toward the members of a group of people.

Professionalism and Unionism: A distinction that the NEA used in 1960 to claim that only an organization that stressed the professional aspects could represent teachers; hence a union would not be adequate, since it stressed organized labor.

Progressive tax: A tax scaled to the ability of the taxpayer to pay.

Progressivism: An educational theory that emphasizes that ideas should be tested by experimentation and that learning is rooted in answering questions developed by the learner.

Property tax: A tax based on the value of property, both real estate and personal.

Public confidence: The underlying trust that people have in their institutions.

Racism: The conscious or unconscious belief that racial differences make one group superior to another, leading to discriminatory actions that limit the opportunities for members of the perceived inferior group to share in the same benefits of society.

Realism: A school of philosophy that holds that reality, knowledge, and value exist independent of the human mind. In contrast to the idealist, the realist contends that physical entities exist in their own right.

Reconstructionism: An educational theory that calls on schools to teach people to control institutions and to be organized according to basic democratic ideals.

Regressive tax: A tax that affects low-income groups disproportionately.

Religious-affiliated school: A private school over which, in most cases, a parent church group exercises some control or to which it provides some form of subsidy.

Resegregation: A situation following desegregation in which segregation returns.

Restructuring: An umbrella label for talking about a number of innovations and themes related to Site-Based Decision Making that are intended to improve school operations and, through these, student performance.

Reverse discrimination: A situation in which a majority or an individual of a majority is denied certain rights because of preferential treatment provided to a minority or an individual of a minority.

Salary schedule: Salary chart organized by teaching experience and formal education.

Scholasticism: The logical and philosophical study of the beliefs of the church.

School-based clinics: Medical and advisory clinics in schools that are offered to provide personal help for students experiencing problems of sexuality.

Second change facilitator/consigliere: A special leadership role in a school whereby a teacher offers facilitating assistance to other teachers during the unfolding of a school-based change process.

Seven liberal arts: A curriculum that consisted of the trivium (grammar, rhetoric, logic) and the quadrivium (arithmetic, geometry, music, astronomy).

Sexism: The conscious or unconscious belief that men are superior to women, and subsequent behavior and action that maintain the superior, powerful position of males.

Single subject curriculum: A subject-centered organizational program in which the academic disciplines are taught in isolation from each other.

Socialization: Process of learning the social norms of one's culture.

Social justice: The desire for all individuals and families to share equally society's benefits.

Social stratification: Levels of social class ranking based on one's income, education, occupation, wealth, and power in society.

Socioeconomic status: Criteria to describe the economic condition of individuals based on their income, occupation, and educational attainment.

Socratic method: A way of teaching that centers on the use of questions by the teacher to lead students to certain conclusions.

Staff: An organizational arrangement in which one party is not under the direct control or authority of another.

Stereotyping: The application of common traits, characteristics, and behavior to a group of people without acknowledging individual differences within the group.

Structured observations: Those judgments or impressions that are conducted according to a predetermined plan.

Teacher certification: The process whereby each state determines the requirements for obtaining a license to teach, processes applications, and issues such licenses.

Teacher power: A term that stresses organized teacher groups that lobby for improvements in education; the group embodiment of individual teacher empowerment.

Teacher self-concept: How teachers view their participation in the profession of education.

Teacher stress: A condition that results from the many forces and pressures experienced through work as an educator.

Teacher supply and demand: A comparison of the projected number of school-age students with the projected number of available teachers.

Tenure: A system of school employment in which educators, after serving a probationary period, retain their positions indefinitely unless they are dismissed for legally specified reasons through clearly established procedures.

Tracking: A method of placing students according to their ability levels in homogeneous classes or learning experiences where they all follow the same curriculum—that is, college preparatory or vocational.

Transforming: Major restructuring, redesigning, or significantly changing the shape and function of schools.

Values: Principles, standards, or qualities considered worthwhile or desirable.

Variable: An offering of elective learning experiences for secondary school students.

Vision: A mental construction that synthesizes and clarifies what you value or consider to be of most worth.

Voice: The right and opportunity to speak and be heard as an equal.

World Confederation of Organizations of the Teaching Profession (WCOTP): Former name of the organization, now known as *Educational International*, that aims to foster international understanding and goodwill, stressing peace, freedom, and respect for human dignity. Members are from approximately one hundred nations and include the AFT and the NEA.

Name Index

Subject Index

Reader Feedback

We would sincerely appreciate your suggestions for improving *Introduction to the Foundations of American Education*, tenth edition. Please respond briefly to the following questions and return this form to Allyn & Bacon, 160 Gould St., Needham Heights, MA 02194-2310, or fax it to us care of Education Editor, 617/455–1294. Thank you.

1. What is the name of the course for which you used this book?

2. What is you general reaction to this book?

3. What were the most useful features of this book?

4. What were the least useful features?

5. Were all the chapters of the book assigned? If not, which ones were omitted?

6. Do you plan to keep this book after you finish this course? Why or why not?

7. Other comments or suggestions for improving this book.